323,329

ADULTHOOD AND AGING
an interdisciplinary, developmental view

ADULTHOOD AND AGING

an interdisciplinary, developmental view

second edition

DOUGLAS C. KIMMEL
Department of Psychology, City College
City University of New York

John Wiley & Sons
New York   Chichester   Brisbane   Toronto

Library of Congress Cataloging in Publication Data:

Kimmel, Douglas C
    Adulthood and aging.

    Bibliography: p.
    Includes indexes.
    1. Adulthood. 2. Aging. 3. Life cycle, Human.
I. Title.
HQ1061.K47   1980   301.43'5   79-24037
ISBN 0-471-05229-9

To Ron
and all who grow older

Adults control the political and economic power in society. They produce, reproduce, and usually reach the apex of their abilities in adulthood. They achieve success, they experience frustration, and they grow older. Yet these important years of the life span have only recently begun to receive the detailed attention that they deserve.

This second edition, similar to a second generation in the human life cycle, represents considerable change, but also resembles the first edition in many ways. Every chapter has been revised to be clear, relevant, current, and responsive to the recent changes in our society and to the new developments in the field of adulthood and aging. Recent studies on developmental transitions during early and middle adulthood, ethnic variations in families, homosexual life-styles, cohabitation, women in the occupational cycle, cultural variations in the process of aging, and issues related to dying have been interwoven with updated discussions of topics from the first edition. The Interludes—the six case examples presented between the chapters—have also been brought up to date by follow-up information on nearly all of the six people interviewed for the first edition. Murray, who was interviewed at the age of 48 in 1973, was interviewed again at the age of 54; this interview is included as a new Interlude in this edition.

As in the first edition, the book remains unique in the field of adulthood and aging in at least three ways. First, it applies the *developmental* approach as a systematic framework for viewing these adult years; thus, it focuses on issues of change and continuity throughout the years of the adult life cycle. Second, it approaches the study of adulthood from an *interdisciplinary perspective*, by emphasizing the interaction of psychological, sociocultural, and biological aspects of human development. The central theoretical framework is the interactionist perspective; this includes the interaction of these interdisciplinary aspects of development as well as the interaction between individuals and their environmental niche. Third, the Interludes provide a challenging opportunity to bridge the gap between theoretical concepts and the real world, by focusing on actual adults who are living rich and varied lives. The new Interlude, a follow-up interview, also calls attention to the developmental processes of change and continuity over time.

In writing this book, I have tried to create a personally-relevant text that will serve as a useful introduction to this emerging field and, in addition, will raise the level of awareness about this period of life and about the issues involved in growing old in a changing society. I have also attempted to contribute some new ideas, to encourage thinking, and to raise important questions. Since most readers of this book will be using it in college courses, I have included chapter outlines and summaries in this edition. Review questions, which may help organize students' study for exams, have also been included and are placed at the end of the book. An instructor's manual is also available.

The approach and much of the information I present reflects my study of human development at the University of Chicago. I am deeply indebted to Bernice L. Neugarten, whose course in adult development provided the initial outline for my conceptualization of the study of adulthood, and to the other faculty members of the Committee on Human Development. A considerable portion of the useful information in this book is a direct, or indirect, result of their research and insight. I also thank the other pioneers in the field, whose research and teaching have created the study of adult development and aging, and the new cohort of researchers in this field who are contributing many exciting ideas and research findings. And I am grateful to my students and colleagues at City College and the Graduate Center of City University who have read, criticized, discussed, challenged, and encouraged my ideas. Claire A. Selltiz, Mary Jo Meadow, and William Kessen were especially helpful in their reviews of this second edition while it was in preparation; Glenys Lobban, Eugenia Bain, and John Neulinger also made useful suggestions for various portions of the manuscript. Willis R. King III and Ronald W. Schwizer provided invaluable assistance with a variety of tasks involved in preparing this edition. I am especially grateful to the six persons who were so open to my questions in the interviews and shared part of their lives with us; Harry Charner requested to be mentioned by name.

I feel that adulthood and aging will continue to emerge as a significant field of study, and I hope that this book will be useful in a variety of contexts. For example, it might be a basic source book in undergraduate courses in psychology, sociology, and in interdisciplinary programs in human development. Graduate courses in fields such as geriatric social work, nursing, social gerontology, and life span or human development may also find this book helpful. I use it in conjunction with one of the growing number of books of readings in adulthood and aging and also encourage students to read some of the popular, fictional, or biographical books related to the field. In addition, I encourage students to work as volunteers in senior citizen centers, nursing homes, friendly visiting programs, and chronic disease hospitals, or simply to interview adults of varying ages.

Most of all, I hope that this book is good reading, and that it encourages continued growth of the knowledge about adulthood and aging.

Douglas Kimmel
New York, NY, 1979

CONTENTS

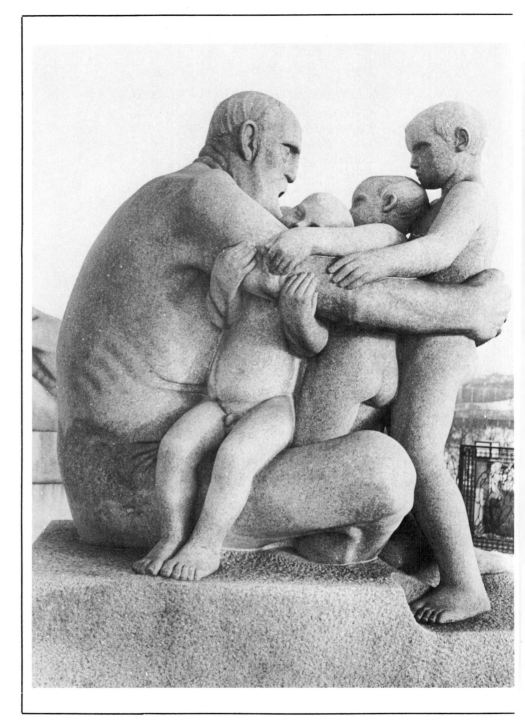

ADULTHOOD:
developmental theory and research

We are beginning a journey through the adult years of the human life cycle. Until recently, this was uncharted territory. Of course, many people have lived through these years over the centuries, but today we are seeking to understand the nature of the biological, psychological, and social changes and characteristics of these years. Like the early pioneers setting off for the uncharted wilderness of the western United States, we have a few maps and some good guides to rely on. But there is still much we do not know, even though the knowledge about adulthood and aging has been growing rapidly during the last several years. Today there seems to be a great interest in this newly discovered period of the life span. Sometimes it seems as if everyone is talking or writing about it—on television, in magazines, in newspapers, and in books. Perhaps this is because all of us have a personal interest in this topic since we certainly expect to grow older and to face the issues and challenges of the years that lie ahead. This new frontier of research is intellectually exciting because there are many unanswered questions and different points of view for us to think about. It is also relevant to personal or practical questions about growing older because it provides a greater understanding and appreciation of our own unfolding lives, the lives of the people we live with, and those we see from day to day. In addition, the study of adulthood and aging may provide a greater understanding of the changing world in which we all live.

As we begin our journey, we need to become familiar with the general concepts and basic information about this relatively new area. This first chapter provides an overview of the entire human life span, emphasizing the period of adulthood and aging. It introduces general themes that we will discuss in more detail in later chapters, and it focuses on the question of how we can best understand the patterns and characteristics of adult development. We will begin by introducing the concept of the life cycle and the way in which social and biological factors interact with age to mark developmental milestones and to "time" development. We will then consider some of the major theories of human development from birth to death that suggest the developmental changes that mark the adult part of the life span. Next, since an individual's life cycle is located in a particular historical time, we will examine the intersection of the individual's life with the historical period. Finally, we will discuss the ways in which developmental research is conducted, because it makes a considerable difference whether we are discussing age differences between different people (such as oneself and one's parents) or age changes in the same person at different times (such as oneself today and oneself in 30 years).

Throughout this chapter, the interdisciplinary and developmental themes of the book will be emphasized. The *interdisciplinary* perspective involves the ability to change "lenses" to get different views; sometimes we will use the lenses of a psychologist, sociologist, anthropologist, or biologist. Each of these disciplines has important information and a unique viewpoint on adulthood and aging. Frequently, we will note that psychological, social, cultural, and biological processes interact together to produce the phenomenon we are investigating. The *developmental* perspective integrates the viewpoints of these disciplines because it focuses on individuals as they grow and change as they become older. To understand development, we must focus on all of the factors that interact to cause the growth and change to take the forms and patterns we find. This developmental perspective tends to underemphasize individual variation and to stress general developmental trends that may be thought to apply to most people, but perhaps do not apply equally to everyone. However, it is not our goal to fit people into pigeonholes. Nonetheless, it seems useful to focus on these general developmental themes because, if we do not understand them, we may be overwhelmed by the many individual variations on these developmental themes. Once the developmental themes are recognized, individual variations may then be brought in to examine a specific individual, in a specific place, at a specific time in life.

CONCEPT OF THE LIFE CYCLE

Philosophers, writers, and social scientists have suggested a variety of views on the nature of the human life cycle. One of the most common views is the analogy between the seasons of the year and the stages of life: spring is the time of growth and coming into bloom; summer is the time of maturity and greatest productivity; autumn is the time of harvest and culmination, when the seeds are sown for new generations; and winter is the time of decline and death. Each season is beautiful in its own right—yet each is unique; there is a definite progression from one season to the next; and one complete cycle prepares the way for the next. Of course, this analogy is too simple to describe human development; but in a poetic way it captures much of the essence of the various developmental theories: development is progressive, sequential, and follows the same pattern generation after generation; it is also circular in the sense that as each generation matures, it nurtures the next generation.

Another poetic, but more satirical, view of human development as a series of seven stages was offered by Shakespeare.

> All the world's a stage,
> And all the men and women merely players.
> They have their exits and their entrances,
> And one man in his time plays many parts,
> His acts being seven ages. At first the infant,
> Mewling and puking in the nurse's arms.
> And then the whining schoolboy, with his satchel
> And shining morning face, creeping like snail
> Unwillingly to school. And then the lover,
> Sighing like furnace, with a woful ballad
> Made to his mistress' eyebrow. Then a soldier,
> Full of strange oaths, and bearded like the pard,
> Jealous in honor, sudden and quick in quarrel,
> Seeking the bubble reputation

Even in the cannon's mouth. And then the justice,
In fair round belly with good capon lin'd,
With eyes severe, and beard of formal cut,
Full of wise saws and modern instances;
And so he plays his part. The sixth age shifts
Into the lean and slipper'd pantaloon,
With spectacles on nose and pouch on side,
His youthful hose, well sav'd, a world too wide
For his shrunk shank; and his big manly voice,
Turning again toward childish treble, pipes
And whistles in his sound. Last scene of all,
That ends this strange eventful history,
Is second childishness and mere oblivion,
Sans teeth, sans eyes, sans taste, sans everything.

As You Like It, Act II, scene vii

Certainly Shakespeare paints a cynical and stereotyped view of human development (and speaks only of men, not women); but the seven stages are quite similar to the ones currently used: infancy, childhood, adolescence, young adulthood, middle age, old age, and senescence. Let us take a closer look at the life cycle in today's society.

Consider the lifeline in Figure 1.1 as a schematic representation of the human life cycle. It emphasizes the *progressive* and *sequential* nature of human development. That is, development progresses in only one direction (from birth to death) and it follows a regular sequence (age 18 always occurs before age 21, and childhood always occurs before adulthood). On this lifeline, certain ages are noted for special age-related events in our society. Obviously, the end points are set by biological and physiological variables. Biological growth plays an initially central but decreasingly important role as we scan the lifeline from conception to birth, from birth through puberty, and from puberty through middle age to old age. But what variables determine the significance of events on the lifeline that

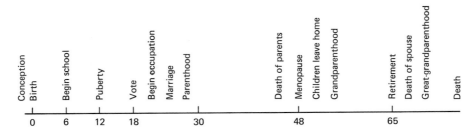

Figure 1.1
The human lifeline. Ages of important events are approximate since there are considerable individual and sex differences in the ages and the order of these milestones.

are not biological? What makes these events important markers along the life cycle?

One useful analogy is to think of the lifeline as a representation of a journey with a number of interesting places and crucial junctions along the way. Some years ago when travel was slower, roads were commonly marked with *milestones* or mileposts to mark off each mile traveled. These milestones were important because travelers were progressing toward a goal through time, and their progress was measured by the number of miles traveled in a unit of time (such as a day). Not surprisingly, humans tend to mark off their progress through their life cycle in a very similar way. We are consciously aware of our progress during the past year, and we have a sense of moving too slowly or very quickly along the path toward our goal based on a measure of time. So the notion of milestones in human development is an appropriate concept, because when we think of the life cycle we mark it off with developmental milestones and, in fact, often celebrate these milestones (such as graduation, marriage, or retirement). Let us define a *milestone* as an event that stands out in a person's memory or future plans as a significant, age-related turning point, or marker, or personal reference point.

The age of 5 or 6 is often significant, for example, because it is the milestone that marks the child's entrance into school and begins a long period of formal training in our culture. This event is, primarily, socially determined by the age at which a child is accepted into kindergarten or elementary school. The next major age-related event after the start of school is the beginnning of puberty, about age 12. Although our Western cultures ordinarily do not celebrate puberty as a *rite of passage*, anthropological reports of other cultures point out that initiation rites at puberty were very important in their societies, marking the end of childhood and the beginning of adulthood. In some Indian tribes, for example, the young male passed through a series of tests of his courage and endurance that culminated in a celebration of his new status as a warrior. Celebrations such as bar mitzvahs and confirmations in Western religions have some elements in common with these puberty rites; and fraternity or sorority initiations, although they may occur several years after puberty, also involve some of the components of this rite of passage. Perhaps, in our society, the award of a driver's license is emotionally similar to a rite of passage for some young people, because the child of the moment before has then received the keys to the symbol of adult technology and responsibility. However, the main event in our society signaled by puberty itself is the beginning of *adolescence* and the entry into what many consider to be a youth culture. Adolescence, in many ways, serves as an extended period of *moratorium* (a kind of pause or limbo) between childhood and adulthood in our society, so that adolescents are sometimes treated as children and sometimes treated as adults. As a result, there is no clear transition point between childhood and adulthood in our society. While this allows individuals to enter adulthood according to their own tempo of development, it does make the period of adolescence an in-between period.

Continuing up the lifeline, the next important age-related event in our society occurs at the age of 18. Many social and legal rights and privileges are awarded on the eighteenth birthday: the driver's license, voting rights, criminal trial as an adult, and the right to drink liquor. Some states distribute these rights over two or three ages (such as a driver's license at 16 and the right to drink at 21), but there is a growing emphasis on the age of 18 as a socially defined turning point in the life cycle that, in many ways, marks the beginning of adulthood in a social and legal sense. Of course, another major event that occurs at 18 for a growing number of young people is the completion of high school and, for a large number, the entrance into college. Frequently this involves leaving home for the first time and a sudden increase in self-reliance. For the young adults who begin work or marry at the end of high school, the age of 18 may signal the beginning of full participation in society as an adult, since one useful definition of the beginning of adulthood is the shift in roles brought about by entrance into the work and family cycles. For those persons who enter college, however, the period of moratorium is extended, often for 4 years and, frequently, for 6 to 10 years if graduate degrees are sought. For this group the moratorium between childhood and full participation in adult roles may last 15 years or even longer.

Although the twenty-first year has traditionally been a significant age in our society, the recent lowering of the age for voting and drinking has tended to decrease the age of 21 as a significant milestone and, as we just suggested, the entrance into adulthood is characterized more exactly by the shift in roles—from student to worker and from single person to husband or wife—than it is by a particular age. This observation foreshadows a difficulty in discussing the remainder of the lifeline, because what is the next significant age-related event after 18 or 21? We have noticed that somewhere during the late twenties, when we ask friends how old they are, they tend to have to calculate their age, subtracting in their mind the year of birth from the current year and correcting for the birthday that has not yet passed. In contrast, younger persons seem instantly aware of their age, perhaps because of the greater amount of social *age grading* during childhood and adolescence when so many events are linked to age.

Perhaps the age of 30 may be the next "significant" age—and each decade likewise often has greater significance than the birthdays in between. However, the age of 30 may be relatively inconsequential for some and an important milestone for others. Sometimes the age of 30 is suggested as the age that begins middle age and the "downhill slide." However, about 80 percent of a middle-aged sample (Neugarten, Moore, & Lowe, 1965) see "Middle age" as beginning at age 40 and lasting to age 50, while the decades of the thirties and forties are the ages when both men and women are seen by these respondents to have the most responsibilities and to accomplish the most; the "prime of life" for a man is generally seen to be between the age of 35 and 50 for these respondents. And, since physiological decline has been found to be highly dependent on the presence of mild disease instead of on age alone (Birren, Butler, Greenhouse, Sokoloff, & Yarrow, 1963), the "downhill slide" is likely to reflect the lack of exercise and sedentary life-style characteristic of middle age, rather than middle age itself.

There are, of course, many exciting things going on around the age of 30 and during the middle years of adulthood: marriage, parenthood, occupational advancement, child rearing, and launching the children from the home. In addition, the death of one's own parents may occur during this period. And, during this long age span, the individuals make much of their contribution to society and to the producing economy. It is, in fact, only this segment of the population (from the beginning of work to retirement) who are supporting the children, students, part of the elderly population, and the various levels of governmental service. Although these developmental milestones during the middle years are not rigidly related to age, they usually remain progressive and sequential and are partly governed by social expectations about the "proper time" to marry, to change occupations, or to become grandparents (and so on). In addition, adults seem to have an intuitive sense of a distinct middle-age period that is qualitatively different from other age periods (Neugarten, 1967).

Although the decades after adolescence are marked by few events that are precisely related to age in our society, there are two outstanding age-related events in middle adulthood: menopause and retirement. Menopause, the cessation of the menses and the decline in production of sex hormones, occurs in women between the ages of 45 and 55 (on the average); it is, of course, physiologically determined, but we do not yet know precisely what causes it to occur. Retirement, in contrast, is socially determined and is quite a recently established milestone that was set at age 65 as part of the Social Security legislation in 1935. Recently, it has been raised to age 70 for many workers in the United States.

The later years of life may be seen as initiated by this milestone of retirement, but they also involve grandparenthood and sometimes great-grandparenthood for many people, continuing involvement in a variety of activities, and, for a growing number of people who are described as the "young-old" (Neugarten, 1974), a period of good health, relative economic security, and freedom from traditional occupational and family responsibilities. For others, this period may involve declining physical health, economic hardship, and widowhood.

Death is the final point on an individual's lifeline. But there is a sense in which the finiteness of the life span helps to give it meaning. Part of the significance in life comes from appreciating the fact that today is one of a limited number of days in the lifeline. Life is not an endless repitition of days, but a progression of a limited number; and no one knows how many are left in one's own lifeline.

THEORIES OF THE LIFE CYCLE

Developmental theories of the human life cycle seek to explain the nature of growth and the patterns of change in individuals from birth to death. Clearly, they assume that adults continue to develop and change after adolescence. Since development is assumed to occur in a sequential progression, the goal of developmental theories is to understand the nature of that sequence and to explain why it progresses in the manner it does. In addition, many developmental theories seek to identify general themes within these patterns of growth, change, and development that may be thought to be valid for all people everywhere in the world. Often, developmental theories take the form of a series of stages that follow each other in sequence.

Because human development involves biological, psychological, and social influences, most theories focus on the interaction of these factors. However, the existing theories of human development describe the process of development in relatively general terms and tend to be particularly weak in explaining why development follows the patterns the theories describe. As a result, we do not have an adequate theory of *why* particular changes occur in the order they do, or how much of development results from social factors, biological factors, or psychological factors. Moreover, we are not certain whether these changes occur in individuals in *every* culture. At best, these theories have been able to describe only the interaction of culture, biology, and psychological development.

In this chapter we will discuss four differing theoretical models of life-span human development: the theories proposed by Bühler, Jung, Erikson, and Riegel. (In Chapter 3 we will focus on theories that limit themselves to the period of early and middle adulthood; in Chapter 7 we will discuss biological theories of aging. The life-span theories we will discuss here tend to be "armchair" theories; that is, they are based on inferences drawn from clinical or empirical observations, but have not been rigorously tested by empirical research. Yet they suggest significant dimensions of the life cycle and call attention to potentially important turning points during the adult years. Perhaps future research will indicate which theory or combination of theories is most useful for understanding human development, or at least the years of adulthood, and will indicate the ways in which variables such as social class and culture influence development.

Bühler's Theory of the Course of Human Life

Charlotte Bühler and her students studied the course of human life from biographies and autobiographies collected in the 1930s in Vienna; they developed a methodology for analyzing these biographies to reveal an orderly progression of phases on the basis of changes in events, attitudes, and accomplishments during the life cycle.

They were also interested in examining the parallel between the course of life revealed in the biographies and the biological course of life. They noted five biological phases: (1) progressive growth—up to age 15; (2) continued growth combined with the ability to reproduce sexually—age 15-25; (3) stability of growth—age 25-45; (4) loss of sexual reproductive ability—age 45-65; and (5) regressive growth and biological decline—age 65 on (Bühler, 1968).

Based on their studies of 400 biographies, they proposed five phases of life that correspond to these five biological phases (Box 1.1).

Box 1.1   Bühler's Five Phases of Life

Age	Phase
0–15	Child at home; prior to self-determination of goals.
15–25	Preparatory expansion and experimental self-determination of goals.
25–45	Culmination: definite and specific self-determination of goals.
45–65	Self-assessment of the results of striving for these goals.
65 up	Fulfillment of goals or experience of failure; previous activities continue, but in late life there may be a re-emergence of short-term goals focusing on satisfying immediate needs.

Source: Based on Horner (1968), p 65.

It may be assumed that the ages are intended to be approximate and in part reflect such social age-related events as retirement (at age 65). Frenkel, one of Bühler's students, describes the developmental progression as follows:

> The young person just passed through childhood—the first phase of life—makes the first plans about his life and his first decisions in adolescence or shortly afterwards. Here begins the second phase of experience. It is characterized first through the fact that the young person wishes to acquire contact with reality. He experiments with people and professions. An "expansion" of his person takes place. Also characteristic for him is the temporary nature of his attitudes as to what his life calling will be. . . .
>
> At the end of the second phase . . . the individuals have become clear as to their definite attitude toward life. . . . During the third phase, vitality is still at its high point, while direction and specification are now also present, so that very often this time is found to be the culmination period for subjective experiences.
>
> The transition to the fourth phase very often is introduced by a crisis, since at this point the unfolding of the individual powers has come to a standstill, and much has to be given up which depended upon physical aptitude or was connected with the biological needs. Contrary to the descent of the biological curve and the experiences which are connected with that, we find here an ascending scale by virtue of new interest in the results and productivity of life. . . .
>
> Finally, in the fifth phase we find more strongly mentioned age, premonitions of death, complaints of lonesomeness, and often those in this phase are occupied with religious questions. This last period contains experiences of a retrospective nature and considerations about the future, that is, about oncoming death and one's past life. The balance-sheet of life is drawn up, so to speak [Frenkel, 1936].[1]

[1]Reprinted with permission from *Character and Personality* (now *Journal of Personality*), copyright © 1936 by Duke University Press.

In general, this view emphasizes the parallel between the biological process of growth, stability, and decline and the psychosocial process of expansion, culmination, and contraction in activities and accomplishments. Often the biological curve is ahead of the individual's psychosocial curve; this is especially true when a reliance on mental abilities allows a person to continue a high degree of productivity for several years after physical strength has begun to decline. Also there is considerable individual variation, since one person may become highly productive rather late in life and reach the psychosocial culmination phase several years after reaching the biological culmination period.

More recent formulations of this theory (Bühler, 1968) emphasize the process of setting goals for one's life. Thus, this developmental sequence is also seen to reflect different perspectives in an individual's *goal setting* at different phases in the life cycle. For example, goals become gradually established during the first two decades of life that ideally lead to self-fulfillment during the culmination period; some zestful persons may reexamine these goals and strive for new goals during the fourth phase but, for most individuals, the goals probably shift to stability and retirement in the second half of life. A study by Kuhlen and Johnson (1952) illustrates the shift in goals during the middle years for a group of public school teachers (Figure 1.2). These data indicate marked sex differences as well as age differences—for example, in the goal "to get different job or promotion in education."

Kuhlen (1964) has elaborated on this growth, culmination, and contraction theory in a slightly different way. He proposed that the growth-expansion motives (such as achievement, power, creativity, and self-actualization) dominate an individual's behavior during the first half of life; however, these motives may change during a person's life because they have been relatively satisfied (for example, the need for success or for sex), and because the person moves into new social positions (such as becoming a mother or the president of a company). In addition, Kuhlen suggests that with advancing age there is "a shift from active direct gratifications of needs to gratifications obtained in more indirect and vicarious fashion" (ibid.). Thus, the human life cycle may be characterized by a "curve of expansion and contraction."

In the second half of life, anxiety and threat become more important sources of motivation in Kuhlen's model. This may begin in middle age when individuals sense that the process of expansion is coming to an end and they begin to be affected by irreversible losses (such as physical illness, death of friends, or loss of job opportunities). Kuhlen cites several studies that indicate that, with advancing age, people are less happy, see themselves more negatively, and experience a loss of self-confidence; there is also a marked increase in symptoms of anxiety among older persons. These data also indicate that aging has less marked (or slower) effects on women and persons in the higher socioeconomic classes compared with men and persons in the lower socioeconomic classes.

In sum, this view of adult development suggests that the life cycle may be seen in terms of two general tendencies—growth-expansion and contraction. Somewhere, during the middle of life, there would thus seem to be a major turning

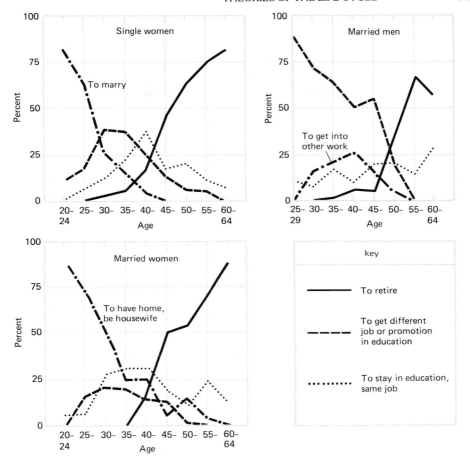

Figure 1.2

Changes in goals with increasing adult age of public school teachers to the question: "What would you most like to be doing ten years from now?" (*Source:* Kuhlen & Johnson, 1952. Reprinted with permission from the *Journal of Consulting Psychology*, copyright © 1952 by the American Psychological Association.)

point between these two contradictory tendencies. Bühler sees the turning point during the period of self-assessment following the culmination phase of midlife (about age 40–45). Kuhlen sees the turning point less clearly defined; it may result from a satisfaction of the earlier growth-expansion motives that allows the emergence of other motives; it may result from physical or social losses, from the sense of being "locked into" a situation, or even from the changing time perspective that results from having lived over half of one's life. Probably, it results from the interaction of social, biological, and psychological factors that may affect men and women differently and that may affect persons of different socioeconomic classes in different ways. However, as important as this shift in goal-setting (or in motivation) may be, Bühler concluded from her studies that a sense of not having fulfilled one's goals was more important than biological decline in triggering maladjustment in old age. So while avoiding or coping with anxiety and threat may be more important concerns during the second half of life (and growth-expansion motives may be more salient during the first half of life), one's own sense of having (or not having) realized one's goals and reached a sense of fulfillment may be the crucial final result of lifelong goal-setting and striving. It is also interesting to note that many aspects of the Bühler and Kuhlen models are very similar to the more contemporary research on development during young and middle adulthood and the "midlife crisis" that we will discuss in Chapter 3.

Jung's Concept of the Stages of LIfe

While Bühler's view of the life span grew out of a systematic study of biographies, and Kuhlen's concepts are based on considerable empirical research, Jung's view of the stages of life is based primarily on his clinical work and his theory of psychology. He begins his discussion of the stages of life with *youth*, the period extending from after puberty to the middle years (age 35-40). Jung was interested in problems of the psyche, and although it may seem strange that he does not include childhood, he argues that while the child may *be* a problem to parents, educators, and doctors, the normal child does not *have* problems of his own—only the adult "can have doubts about himself" (Jung, 1933).

The period of youth involves giving up the dreams of childhood, dealing with the sexual instinct and feelings of inferiority, and, in general, widening the horizon of life. The next important change begins between 35 and 40:

> At first it is not a conscious and striking change; it is rather a matter of in-direct signs of a change which seems to take its rise in the unconscious. Often it is something like a slow change in a person's character; in another case certain traits may come to light which had disappeared since childhood; or again, one's previous inclinations and interests begin to weaken and others take their place. Conversely—and this happens very frequently—one's cherished convictions and pricniples, especially the moral ones, begin to harden and to grow increasingly rigid until, somewhere around the age of fifty, a period of intolerance and fanaticism is reached. It is as if the existence of these principles were endangered and it were therefore necessary to emphasize them all the more [Jung, 1933, pp. 12-13].

He sees neurotic disturbances during the adult years as an indication that the person is attempting to carry the "psychology of the youthful phase" into these middle years—just as neurotic disturbances in youth reflect an inability to leave childhood behind. In old age Jung sees some "deep-seated and peculiar changes within the psyche" (p. 14). There is a tendency for persons to change into their opposites, especially in the psychic realm. For example, he suggests that older men become more "feminine" and older women become more "masculine"; and he points out "an inexorable inner process" that "enforces the contraction of life" (we will discuss these points in detail in Chapter 8). In general, he argues that "we cannot live the afternoon of life according to the programme of life's morning; for what was great in the morning will be little at evening, and what in the morning was true will at evening have become a lie" (p. 17).

There must be some purpose in human life continuing into the late years, such as the caring of children; but what is the purpose of life after this has been accomplished? Is the purpose to compete with the young, as so often happens in our society? Jung points out that in most primitive societies the old people are the sources of wisdom, the "guardians of the mysteries and the laws . . . [in which] the cultural heritage of the tribe is expressed" (p. 18). In contrast, we no longer have any clear sense of meaning or purpose in old age. Thus we try to hang on to the first half of life, clinging to youth instead of looking forward. Jung argues that many people reach old age with unsatisfied demands, but it is "fatal" for such persons to look back. It is essential for them to have a goal in the future. This suggests that the reason that all the great religions hold out the hope of an afterlife is to make it possible for man to live the second half of life with as much purpose as the first half. Jung recognizes that modern man has become accustomed to disbelieve in life after death, or at least to question it, and that we cannot know whether there is an afterlife. But he argues that "an old man who cannot bid farewell to life appears as feeble and sickly as a young man who is unable to embrace it" (p. 20). He feels it is psychologically positive "to discover in death a goal towards which one can strive, and that shrinking away from it is something unhealthy and abnormal which robs the second half of life of its purpose" (p. 20). He suggests that in the second half of life the individual's attention turns inward, and that this inner exploration may help individuals find a meaning and wholeness in life that makes it possible for them to accept death.

Erikson's Eight Ages of Life

Like Jung, Erikson's theory of human development is based primarily on his clinical impressions and on his theoretical (Freudian) view of psychology. However, his eight ages of life (Erikson, 1963, 1968, 1976) represent a series of crucial turning points stretching from birth to death and thus are somewhat more comprehensive than any of the views presented so far. Nonetheless, his stages emphasize childhood development, and the first five stages are largely expansions of Freud's stages of childhood development. Although we will focus only on the later stages that deal with youth and adulthood, the earlier stages, in his view, are the building blocks on which the later stages depend. Each stage presents a new challenge—we might say a new point of "turbulence" in the "stream of life" that must be negotiated successfully. Following our metaphor, if one's raft is severely damaged during one of the early turning points, the later turbulent points will be more difficult to negotiate. In this sense, Erikson's framework provides one view of the "river of life" and its major turning points and forks, so that we might have a sense of what the crucial challenges are for the individual at various points along the stream.

We use this river metaphor because it seems appropriate on two levels: first, it expresses the sequential, progressive course of an individual through the eight turning points; and, second, it suggests that this framework may be a simplified overview, from a great height as it were, of the general course of the life cycle. The theory is quite difficult to test empirically, and when it has been examined it has not borne up well (e.g., Gruen, 1964); yet it provides useful insights into the central issues of human development and, especially when expanded and refined (as we will indicate later), seems to provide a useful *descriptive* framework for understanding some general issues and changes during the adult years.

Each stage in Erikson's conception of the life cycle represents a dialectical struggle between two opposing tendencies, each of which are experienced by the individual (Box 1.2). Thus, each stage is represented by two opposite qualities, linked by the word *versus*.

"Versus" is an interesting little word. . . . Developmentally, it suggests a dialectic dynamics, in that the final strength postulated could not emerge without either of the contending qualities; yet, to assure growth, the syntonic, the one more intent on adaptation, must absorb the dystonic [Erikson, 1976, p. 23].

Each dialectical conflict between the two extremes is eventually resolved by a synthesis that represents one of the basic human strengths (these are: hope, will, purpose, competence, fidelity, love, care, and wisdom). The dialectical struggle is both conscious and unconscious within the individual. It involves both inner (psychological) processes and outer (social) processes. The psychosocial strengths that result are "an active adaptation rather than a passive adjustment" of the individual in a social environment, so that "they change the environment even as they make selective use of its opportunities" (ibid., p. 25).

Box 1.2   Erikson's Eight Ages of Human Life

Opposing Issues of Each Stage	Emerging Value	Period of Life
(1) Basic Trust versus Mistrust	Hope	Infancy
(2) Autonomy versus Shame and Doubt	Will	Early childhood
(3) Initiative versus Guilt	Purpose	Play age
(4) Industry versus Inferiority	Competence	School age
(5) Identity versus Identity (Role) Confusion	Fidelity	Adolescence
(6) Intimacy versus Isolation	Love	Young adulthood
(7) Generativity versus Stagnation (Self-Absorption)	Care	Maturity
(8) Integrity versus Despair (and Disgust)	Wisdom	Old age

Source: Based on Erikson (1963, 1976).

Each of the eight periods of the life cycle "has its stage of ascendence when physical, cognitive, emotional, and social developments permit its coming to a crisis" (ibid., p. 24). However, this sequential progression through the stages involves considerable overlap between them.

> Nobody . . . in life is neatly "located" in one stage; rather, all persons can be seen to oscillate between at least two stages and move more definitely into a higher one only when an even higher one begins to determine the interplay [ibid., pp. 24-25].

For the final stage, death itself functions as a kind of higher stage.

Since our concern is with adulthood, we will discuss only the later stages in Erikson's scheme, although each involves the issues, and builds on the strengths, of the earlier stages.

Identity versus Identity (Role) Confusion.   Erikson's fifth stage arises with the beginning of puberty and the increasing social need to find one's role in life as a sexual, productive, responsible adult with a reasonably consistent set of attitudes and values about oneself. It may also reflect the adolescent's newly acquired ability to think abstractly (the stage of "formal operations" in Piaget's scheme of cognitive development). The positive (or syntonic) side of the struggle is a sense of identity: a sense of continuity and consistency of the self over time. The negative (or dystonic) side is a sense of confusion about one's identity or role—a lack of certainty about who one is, or about the part one is playing in the scheme of life. The resolution of this stage involves experiencing each of these opposing tendencies within oneself and in relation to one's social environment. From that dialectical struggle emerges the psychosocial strength of *fidelity*—"the ability to sustain loyalties freely pledged in spite of the inevitable contradictions and confusions of value systems" (ibid., p. 25). The early period of this stage involves the overlap between Industry versus Inferiority (stage 4) and Identity versus Identity Confusion; the later period involves the overlap between Identity versus Identity Confusion and Intimacy versus Isolation (stage 6). The transition occurs when Intimacy versus Isolation begins to emerge as a significant issue.

Intimacy versus Isolation.   Although the capacity for sexual intimacy begins during adolescence, according to Erikson, the individual does not become capable of a fully intimate relationship until the identity crises is fairly well resolved. That is, one must have a sense of who one is before one can fuse that identity with another in full appreciation of the other's uniqueness and separateness; earlier attempts at intimacy are frequently attempts to try to define oneself through a romantic relationship with another.

> Sexual intimacy is only part of what I have in mind, for it is obvious that sexual intimacies often precede the capacity to develop a true and mutual psychosocial intimacy with another person, be it in friendship, in erotic en-

counters, or in joint inspiration. The youth who is not sure of his identity shies away from interpersonal intimacy or throws himself into acts of intimacy which are "promiscuous" without true fusion or real self-abandon.

Where a youth does not accomplish such intimate relationships with others—and, I would add, with his own inner resources—in late adolescence or early adulthood, he may settle for highly stereotyped interpersonal relations and come to retain a deep *sense of isolation* [Erikson, 1968, pp. 135-136].

The resolution of this stage involves the dialectical struggle between the opposing tendencies of intimacy and isolation. The psychosocial strength that emerges from this struggle is *love*. The early period of this stage involves the overlap between Identity versus Identity Confusion and Intimacy versus Isolation (as when one attempts to define one's sense of identity through relationships with others); the later period involves the overlap with Generativity versus Stagnation.

Generativity versus Stagnation (Self-Absorption). This seventh stage of life may be the longest, because it refers to producing something that will outlive oneself, usually through parenthood or in occupational achievements. The struggle is between a sense of generativity, or leaving one's mark in some way, and the sense of stagnation, or self-absorption. As in all of the stages, an individual may be involved in these issues as well as those of the previous stage, or in addition to those of the next stage. The outcome of this stage is *care*—"the widening concern for what has been generated by love, necessity, or accident" (Erikson, 1976, p. 24).

Integrity versus Despair (and Disgust). The final stage is brought on by a growing awareness of the finitude of life and of one's closeness to death. The crucial task during this stage is to evaluate one's life and accomplishments and to affirm that one's life has been a meaningful adventure in history; this would be the sense of integrity. The opposite is the sense of despair and disgust—an existential sense of total meaninglessness and a feeling that one's entire life was wasted or should have been different than it was. The dialectical struggle between these two opposing themes is the essence of this period and produces *wisdom*: "the detached and yet active concern with life itself in the face of death itself, and that it maintains and conveys the integrity of experience, in spite of the decline of bodily and mental functions" (ibid., p. 23).

Expansion and Refinement of Erikson's Theory. It may be noted that the last two of Erikson's stages include most of the middle and late years of the life cycle. In that sense they tend to be even more general in their focus than the earlier stages. Although they may be divided into early and late phases on the basis of their overlap with earlier or later stages, they remain quite general. For these reasons, Peck (1955) attempted to define the crucial issues of middle age and old age more precisely; he proposed seven central issues in these two periods. These challenges are: (1) *Valuing wisdom versus valuing phsyical powers.* That is, there is a transition point during the forties when persons who cling to physical powers become more and more depressed as these powers decline, but persons who shift to using their mental abilities as a primary resource seem to age more successfully. (2) *Socializing versus sexualizing in human relationships.* If men and women are redefined as individuals and companions with the sexual element playing a lessening role, then interpersonal relationships may take on a greater depth of understanding and enhance the marital relationship during the period when the children are leaving the home. (3) *Cathectic flexibility versus cathectic impoverishment.* A shift in emotional (cathectic) openness is suggested here, so that as parents die, old circles of friends are broken up, and children leave home, individuals are able to reach out and take advantage of their widening circle of possible friends (who may represent as large and as varied a group as they will ever know) and to take advantage of new emotional ties with their children's family. (4) *Mental flexibility versus mental rigidity.* Is one able to continue to be open to new experiences and new interpretations, or do past experiences dictate a set of inflexible rules that close off the person to the task of seeking new or different answers to current problems?

In old age, Peck sees the following three issues as central. (1) *Ego differentiation versus work-role preoccupation.* The task here is to establish a varied range of valued activities so that loss of one's occupation (at retirement) or one's accustomed roles (as when the children leave home) allows other meaningful activities that will provide a sense of satisfaction. (2) *Body transcendence versus body preoccupation.* Nearly all old people suffer illness and growing amounts of pain or discomfort; yet some persons remain able to enjoy life immensely, finding more comfort in human interaction or creative activities that allow them to transcend the frailty of their own aging bodies in a sense. (3) *Ego transcendence versus ego preoccupation.* Through children, through contributions to the culture, and through friendships, human beings can extend the significance of their actions beyond their lifetime; death is inevitable (and the full impact of this fact may be realized in old age for the first time), but some find a gratifying meaning for their lives in the future potential of their family, their ideas, or future generations of the human species.

Riegel's Dialectical Analysis of Development

A different perspective on the nature of human development is presented in the dialectical approach proposed by Klaus Riegel (1976). While the other theories we have discussed view development as a series of stages through which individuals progress, Riegel focused on the developmental processes of change. That is, instead of assuming that development can be understood by studying the periods of equilibrium and balance, he argued that it should also be studied by analyzing the periods of disequilibrium and change. Rejecting "the preference for stable traits, abilities, or competencies" and also rejecting "the preference for equilibrium, balance, or stability" often found in studies of development, Riegel argued that "at least equal emphasis should be devoted to the issue of how problems are created and questions are raised" (ibid., p. 689). Thus, he focused on the study of actions and changes instead of equilibrium and balance and saw developmental processes as being in "ceaseless flux" instead of as "static abstractions." He emphasized the view that humans are neither stable bundles of characteristics in equilibrium, nor are they passive reactors to conditioning mechanisms. Instead, "the human being is a changing being in a changing world" (ibid., p. 689). In this approach, the analysis of time and change over time is essential (Riegel, 1977).

He proposed that there are four major dimensions of development: inner-biological, individual-psychological, cultural-sociological, and outer-physical. Each of these is constantly interacting with the others and with other elements within the same dimension. Therefore, each may bring change, create problems, raise questions, or bring transitions in the life cycle. Since development involves progression through time, the individual simultaneously moves along these four major dimensions throughout the life cycle. The essence of the dialectical approach is to study the synchronization of these four dimensions as the individual grows older.

> Inner-biological progressions lead the individual away from home, to work, marriage, and parenthood. . . . Most of these events will be well synchronized with progressions along other dimensions. For example, many individuals marry when they are mature enough, when they have the appropriate psychological stature and intention, and when the social conditions are conducive and appropriate. In other instances such a synchronization is not achieved. Individuals marry without having reached a sufficient level of maturity; others may have attained the proper level but fail to find the right partner. Thus, the inner-biological and individual-psychological progressions are not always synchronized with the cultural-sociological or outer-physical conditions, for example, with the traditions and laws about marriage or the reduced availability of marriage partners after wars [Riegel, 1976, pp. 693–694].

Similarly, the synchronization of these four dimensions may be studied in the interaction of two or more persons, such as families, or in relations between individuals and social groups. Even natural catastrophies (outer-physical dimension) may produce disruption to the synchronization of these dimensions for individuals, groups, and societies—each of which may be seen as developing over time.

Because this fourfold progression is obviously complex and changes in one dimension are not always synchronized with changes in the other dimensions, there is usually some degree of conflict between the dimensions. In addition, major changes in any of the dimensions will bring a confrontation between that dimension and the other dimensions. If this confrontation brings a major re-organization of the other dimensions, then this may be seen as a period of developmental transition. Thus, a period of relative synchronization across the four dimensions may be followed by a significant change in one or more of the dimensions. This brings a period when they are relatively unsynchronized, leading to an attempt to reestablish synchronization. When this is possible, the transition is completed, and the stage is set for a new transition whenever the interacting dimensions again get out of step with each other.

> Critical changes occur whenever two sequences are in conflict, that is, when coordination fails and synchrony breaks down. These contradictory conditions are the basis for developmental progressions. Stable plateaus of balance, stability, and equilibrium occur when a developmental or historical task is completed. But developmental and historical tasks are never completed. At the very moment when completion seems to be achieved, new questions and doubts arise in the individual and in society. The organism, the individual, society, and even outer nature are never at rest, and in their restlessness they are rarely in perfect synchrony. Nevertheless, synchrony remains the goal. It can only be achieved through continuous human efforts. There is no preestablished harmony [Riegel, 1976, pp. 696-697].

Riegel died before he was able to carry these provocative ideas much beyond their initial formulation. Others have begun to explore this dialectical analysis of change and the synchronization of the various dimensions within development (cf. Datan & Reese, 1977), but it is too early to know whether this approach will prove to be a useful framework for analyzing human development. In any event, it provides a significant new perspective for the study of human development and suggests that the traditional view of development as a series of stages may not be adequate to understand the complex nature of development, especially during adulthood.

Conclusions

These theories of development during adulthood provide a number of useful outlines for understanding the sequential progression of the human life cycle. They indicate some of the ways in which persons in the second half of life might be expected to differ from persons in the early years of adulthood. And they sensitize us to some of the normative crisis points or central issues during the adult years. These concepts also suggest a possible midlife crisis when the growth and expansion trends of the earlier years gradually give way to a contraction of social participation and productivity in the later years. Thus, these theoretical perspectives help us to understand some of the broad outlines of the human life cycle and suggest a number of questions for further exploration.

However, the first three theories tend to be not only too general but also too idealistic. That is, they do not give very much indication of the ways in which cultural differences, sex differences, or social class differences interact with this general developmental progression; and they describe a process of development that leads toward the ideal of "human fulfillment" or "successful aging" as defined in the middle class in our society. For other persons, fulfillment or successful aging may mean physical survival and providing one's offspring with at least a reasonable chance for survival; for others, aging means illness, poverty, and isolation with little opportunity for fulfillment or success. Riegel's theory, while potentially providing a framework to analyze the effects of these biological, sociocultural, psychological, and environmental influences on development, is not well enough defined to do more than suggest the directions future research should take. Clearly, systematic research on the effects of social class, ethnic background, and male-female differences on adult development is greatly needed. Until these effects are better understood, we can only caution against accepting these rather speculative theories of the life cycle as applicable to *all* persons in *all* conditions of life.

This criticism of these theories leads us to raise two important questions that we will discuss in the remainder of this chapter. First, if we accept these developmental theories as useful general guidelines for understanding the human life cycle, does it not make an important difference whether that life cycle begins in 1860 or 1910 or 1960? That is, what is the effect of the intersection of an individual's life cycle with historical time?

Second, since theory is based on and tested by empirical research so that theory and research must go hand in hand, how does a developmental researcher study the course of human development? For example, would we learn the same things about adult development if we were to study young people and their parents as we would if we were to study the same group of young people when they were 20 and study them again when they were 40? Probably not—unless children grow up to be very much like their parents.

INDIVIDUAL LIFE CYCLES AND HISTORICAL TIME

An individual's developmental progression through the life cycle is only one source of age-related change. We have outlined some of the central biological and social age-related events that influence and serve to "time" the individual's progression through the life span; and we have discussed the changes that various theorists believe occur with age. But the historical time line that intersects with a person's lifeline is another age-related dimension that affects the individual's progression through the life cycle.

Recalling the lifeline described above (Figure 1.1), we will now intersect it with the historical time line at a moment in 1980 (Figure 1.3). Persons age 70 in 1980 were born in 1910 during a period in the United States of peace and isolation from world conflicts. They were at the forefront of the industrial expansion and westward migration. Obviously, a great deal has changed since then. Life expectancy has increased dramatically. Average length of education has increased by several years, and the tasks of living in society have become more

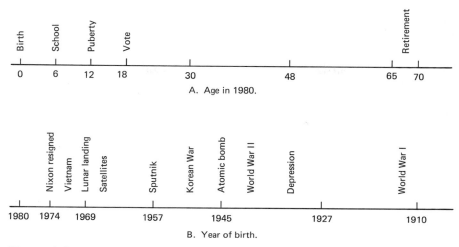

Figure 1.3

Intersection of individual lifeline (A) with historical time line in 1980 (B).

and more complex. For example, the elderly frequently have a difficult time understanding computer cards or forms required for Medicare.

If you are in college today, your parents were probably born between the end of World War I and the end of the Great Depression. They learned the interdependence of the nations of the world, but, most of all, they learned that economic security and material possessions may evaporate for reasons beyond their control. Your parents may have gone to school during the Depression and their early socialization experiences that influence later attitudes and values took place during this period of inadequate material resources. And they lived through World War II, perhaps fought in it, when the security of the United States was felt to be directly threatened, and the material products of the expanding economy continued to be in short supply.

With the atomic bomb came the end of the war and the beginning of the "atomic age." Everyone born after the mid-1940s has experienced not only the economic growth of the country and the increased abundance of the middle class but has also experienced the omnipresent threat of nuclear war. More recently, we have learned of other possible means of annihilation: overpopulation and pollution. We have lived through historical experiences unprecedented in their immediacy resulting from the development of television and news coverage via satellite. The post-Sputnik world not only has experienced an increase in technology and an amazing shrinkage in the effective size of the world but also has focused its attention beyond the earth. In addition, we have experienced a missile crisis, at least three major assassinations, the longest war in our history, and the resignation of a President.

There can be no doubt that there have been great historical changes during the course of the lives of individuals currently living, and that the pace of these changes is rapid and escalating. We can confidently predict that one important aspect of growing older in our society will continue to be an increasing complexity in the tasks and skills required of the adult. Speculate for a moment about the complexity involved in adjusting to a computer-based system of universal credit cards where money is no longer used; or about the possibility of spending the first year of your retirement vacationing on the moon!

Cohort Effects

A *cohort* is a group of people born at about the same time—for instance, in 1920, or between 1920 and 1929. Obviously, this group of people grows older together so that the cohort moves through the life span together. As members of the cohort die, the group shrinks in size until only a few survivors are left. Each cohort experiences somewhat similar historical influences. These shared experiences have an effect on the attitudes, values, and world view of those individuals living through them. For example, individuals born after World War II could not have been influenced by the Great Depression of the 1930s in the same way their parents were. Also, different cohorts of individuals are affected by historical experiences in different ways because each cohort of persons is a different age. Thus, the Vietnam War had a very different effect on young people than it did on children or older adults because it was the cohort of Americans between 18 and 25 during the 1960s and early 1970s whose lives were most directly affected by that war. Although the Vietnam war affected all young people to some extent, it clearly affected those who actually fought in the war to a much greater extent. Recently, attention has begun to be paid to the special problems and issues faced by the Vietnam veterans that are different from those faced by earlier cohorts of veterans. While soldiers from earlier wars came home as heroes, soldiers who fought in Vietnam often experienced mixed reactions because, by the time the war ended, many Americans had very ambivalent attitudes about it. As a result, the Vietnam veteran sometimes seemed to be almost a painful reminder of an embarassing national mistake. Thus, younger cohorts of veterans are quite different from older cohorts of veterans—not because they are younger, but because the war they fought in and the national reaction to that war was very different than was the case for older cohorts of veterans. In general, whether we are discussing cohorts of veterans or cohorts of Americans, such historical events help to establish attitudes, values, and a personal world view that are more enduring than the historical conditions that brought them about. In that sense, each cohort of people carries its own experience of history through the life span. Development, then, may be seen as a series of cohorts moving through the life span.

A visual example of these cohorts moving through the life cycle is shown in the population profile of the United States (Figure 1.4). This profile represents a "snapshot" of 18 different cohorts of men and women in 1977. If this "snapshot" were taken again in 1982, each cohort would have moved to the next higher age group (except for the 85 + group), and each group would be some-

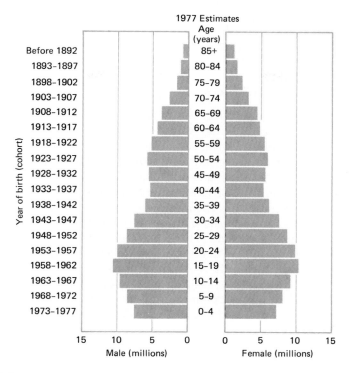

Figure 1.4
Distribution of the total population by age and sex: July 1, 1977. (Source: U.S. Bureau of the Census. Population Profile of the U.S., 1977. *Current Population Reports*, Series P-20, No. 303. Washington, D.C.: U.S. Government Printing Office, 1978, Figure 3.)

what smaller (especially the older cohorts) because some would have died. Note the "bulge" in the groups between age 15 and 34 (those born between 1943 and 1962). This is the so-called "baby boom" that followed the end of World War II. What occurred was that fathers came home from the war in 1945-1946 and began raising families at about the same time. In addition, few infants died in early childhood because of such medical advances as sulfa and penicillin. This bulge in the population is especially obvious today because the birth rate is declining as a result of birth control and family planning. However, the postwar population bulge will continue to move through the lifeline (the leading edge of this bulge would be about age 34 in 1980; refer back to the intersection of individual and historical time lines in Figure 1.3). It has brought a wide range of effects including overcrowded schools during the 1960s and empty elementary schools in the 1970s. It will have another profound effect while these young people are having their own children, although the trend toward smaller families will offset this increase somewhat. In addition, since they would be expected to live longer than in the past, these young people will eventually swell the ranks of the aged. Although only about 11 percent of the population is currently over 65, if the current drop in birth rate continues, the proportion of the population over 65 will be 15 percent by 2020—a "senior boom" resulting in part from the "baby boom" grown old.

Historical Period (Time) Effects

While many historical events affect one generation, or one age group (cohort), more than others, some historical events affect the entire society in relatively equal ways. For example, the invention of the automobile, electric light, transistors, and jet airplanes have affected the entire population. Similarly, improvements in medical care, nutrition, and sanitation have affected all people regardless of their age or cohort. To be sure, cohort differences still exist even in these large-scale changes, but life has changed so much since 1940 or 1900 that we must consider these changes in any study of development.

A dramatic example of this kind of historical effect is the increase in life expectancy (Figure 1.5). In 1900, the average baby would have been expected to live 32½ years if he was a black male; a black male born in 1976 would be expected to live an average of 64 years—essentially twice as long! The increase in the number of years the typical black female baby is expected to live has been even greater—from 35 to 73 years. Similar increases in life expectancy have occurred

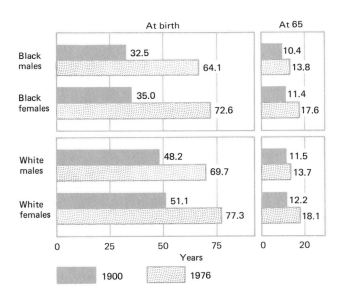

Figure 1.5
Life expectancy at birth and at age 65, by race and sex, in 1900 and 1976 in the United States. Most of the increase is the result of reduced childhood mortality; the increase for older persons is much less dramatic. (Source. U.S. Bureau of the Census. Prospective Trends in the Size and Structure of the Elderly Population. *Current Population Reports*, Series P-23, No. 78. Washington, D.C.: U.S. Government Printing Office, 1979, Table 5.)

for white babies. This extraordinary increase in life expectancy has resulted primarily from medical advances that have eliminated the major diseases that caused death in children—at one time, children were not given a name until they had survived smallpox because so many died as a result of it; today smallpox has been eliminated throughout the world. Other diseases require inoculations in order to prevent them, but children can now be readily protected. Similar medical advances have markedly reduced the effects of diseases that once killed young and middle-aged adults, such as pneumonia, tuberculosis, and influenza. As a result, while only 19 black male babies out of every 100 born in 1900-1902 survived to age 65, 53 black male babies out of every 100 born in 1974 are expected to survive to age 65; the change is even more dramatic for black females and also quite significant for white males and females (Figure 1.6).

However, the picture is somewhat different for those people who do survive to age 65. Clearly, they have always been the healthiest, strongest, and luckiest members of their cohort—otherwise, they would not have outlived so many of their contemporaries. Also, medical science has made less progress in preventing and curing the diseases of old age than it has against the major diseases of childhood. As a result, life expectancy has not increased nearly as dramatically for persons at age 65 as it has for persons at birth (see Figure 1.5; right side). While there has been an increase of about 2 years for white men and 3½ years for black men, the increase has been larger for black and white women—about 6 years. Interestingly, those black men who survive to age 65 actually have a very slight edge in life expectancy over white men of that age. This reflects the fact that older blacks and other minority persons are a more select group of survivors than white persons of the same age. That is, black men who were born in 1915 and are still alive in 1980 have outlived over three-quarters of their contemporaries, while a similar white man has outlived only about 55 percent of his contemporaries (see Figure 1.6).

Another way of making this same point is to note that 31 out of every 100 white men age 65 in 1900-1902 would survive to age 80; by 1974, only a few more—about 40 out of every 100—would live to age 80 according to Census Bureau statisticians. During this same period the proportion of black men at age 65 surviving from 65 to 80 also increased only a little—from 25 to 37 out of every 100. However, the proportion of women surviving from 65 to 80 increased greatly: from 35 to 61 out of every 100 at age 65 for white women and from 30 to 52 for every 100 black women at age 65 in 1900-1902 and 1974, respectively (U.S. Bureau of the Census, 1976, Table 5-1). Clearly, women have benefited more from the general improvement in health, nutrition, and living conditions than men have. The reasons for this are not clear, but we will discuss some of them in Chapter 4.

These general historical changes make the experience of adulthood and aging different today than it was in the past; and they will make the experience of aging different in the future than it is today (see Chapter 9). They reflect changes over time that affect all people living during the particular historical period. However, these changes in health, nutrition, technology, or level of education can af-

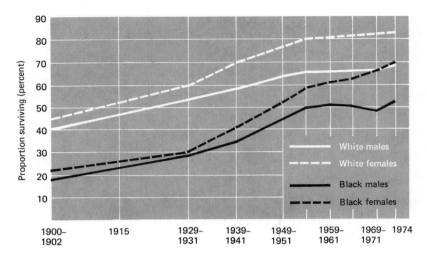

Figure 1.6
Proportion of every 100 newborn babies that are expected to survive to age 65 by race and sex, from 1900 to 1974, in the United States. (Source. U.S. Bureau of the Census, 1976, Table 5-1.)

fect some cohorts more dramatically than others while they generally affect all persons. That is, developmental (age) changes intereact with cohort (year of birth) effects, as well as with historical period (time) effects. To take a simple example, young adults are taller than children and are also taller than old people, on the average. The difference between the height of children and adults is obviously a result of development—children are not fully grown. However, better nutrition may produce children who will grow to be taller than their parents. Similarly, adults today are taller than adults in earlier historical periods. Thus, adults are taller than older people today since older people did not grow as tall when they were growing up earlier in this century because of less adequate nutrition.

This complex interaction of individual development and historical change can be illustrated most clearly in the phenomenon of the so-called generation gap.

Example: The Generation Gap

A great deal of attention has been focused on the "generation gap." This phenomenon, if it actually exists, is an interesting example of the interaction of individual life cycles with the historical time line.

Assuming that the "generation gap" consists of differing values, attitudes, and life styles between young people and persons in their parents' generation, there are two differing interpretations that are possible: developmental and historical.

From a developmental perspective, this difference results from the differing stages in the life cycle of young persons and their parents. Young persons are involved in resolving the identity issues of "Who am I," and "How do I link up with society?" In Erikson's (1968) view, this involves a period of questioning society's values and a partial rejection of parental values in order to develop one's own system of values and attitudes. Even Aristotle, writing 2300 years ago, noted this tendency of the young.

> The young are prone to desire and ready to carry any desire they may have formed into action. Of bodily desires it is the sexual to which they are the most disposed to give way, and in regard to sexual desire they exercise no self-restraint. They are changeful too, and fickle in their desires, which are as transitory as they are vehement. . . . They are passionate, irascible, and apt to be carried away by their impulses. . . . They have high aspirations; for they have never yet been humiliated by the experience of life, but are unacquainted with the limiting force of circumstances. . . . Again, in their actions they prefer honor to expediency. . . . If the young commit a fault, it is always on the side of excess and exaggeration. . . . They regard them-selves as omniscient and are positive in their assertions; this is, in fact, the reason of their carrying everything too far [cited in Conger, 1971, p. 1119].

In contrast, parents tend to be in a developmental period that is concerned primarily with transmitting the values of society, with providing economic and emotional stability, and with the concerns of leaving one's mark on the world (generativity versus stagnation in Erikson's model). Bengtson and Cutler (1976) described this by the term "generational stake"—each generation has a different stake in promoting or minimizing change. It seems evident that a conflict be-tween these generations is built into the human condition as Mannheim (1952) has argued. From this perspective, the generation gap is as old as human his-tory. And it is predicted that when these young people move into later devel-opmental periods and are faced with the tasks of raising children, producing in society, and earning a stable income, these responsibilites and their changed perspective on life (generational stake) will result in values that are more similar (but not identical) to their parents' values; they will then find a gap in values be-tween themselves and their children.

This process of conflict between generations may be one mechanism of social change through successive generations and may be particularly important during periods of rapid social change when the elders are not able to fully prepare the youth for the new and more complex society that is developing. The greater the speed of social change, the greater the importance of this readjustment between successive generations. Currently this period of youth has been stretched out so that it now extends into the mid-twenties for many young people. This provides more time to question and to evaluate society and social values from a position of (often) economic security, personal freedom, and intellectual inquiry. It also provides growing numbers of young people who are attending college (over 8 million today) with an *age-segregated environment*. This means that there is lit-tle contact with people of grandparental age, almost no contact with children, and only scheduled contact with people of parental age (such as teachers and professors—an atypical type of adult). One result of such an environment is to stimulate the growth of shared values and attitudes among college-age young people through mutual socialization by peers rather than the more traditional intergenerational socialization. The result is what may be termed a *de-facto* youth culture.

These historical factors that intersect with the period of youth—the prolonged moratorium between childhood and adulthood, the age-segregated communities where as many as 50,000 students may live in immediate proximity with one another, the affluence of many young people in comparison with the economic insecurity of their elders' youth, and the massive number of young people in the postwar population bulge—may all be seen as important historical factors that may have intensified this developmental period of generational conflict into a much more striking conflict that was picked up by popular media as the "generation gap." Thus we cannot fully understand the developmental phenomenon without also considering the intersection of the developmental period with the historical period. But also, in order to understand a phenomenon such as the conflict between generations, we need to be able to separate the developmental (age) factors from the historical factors.

An alternate explanation of the generation gap has been suggested by Margaret Mead (1970); this explanation emphasizes the historical changes instead of the developmental factors. Mead argues that young people are living in a radically different historical time brought about by the end of World War II and the atomic bomb that ushered in major changes resulting in a *cultural discontinuity*. Thus the values and attitudes of young people are different from those of their parents, because their parents grew up in a different world from the one in which young people are living (with the threat of nuclear annihilation, satellites, computers, threats of pollution and overpopulation, and a new sense of a worldwide community of humankind). She feels that this cultural discontinuity will move through the life cycle so that, in 1985, it will exist between persons who are 41 and those over 55, and so on. This prediction is in direct conflict with the developmental prediction that the "gap" will remain between young and middle-aged persons forever; it is only exaggerated now because of these historical factors.

The limited data available on the later development of student activists of the 1960s suggest that their experience in the civil rights movement was not a short-term developmental phenomenon, but that their lives 10 years later were generally consistent with their earlier political activism. For example, Fendrich (1974) compared college students who took part in marching and picketing to desegregate lunch counters, movie theaters, and restaurants with students who had been active in student government, but not in protest politics, and students at the university who took no part in any protest or student politics. On the basis of questionnaires that these respondents completed in 1971, Fendrich concluded that the activists of the 1960s continued to be politically active a decade later.

The results strongly suggest that college activists of the early 1960s retain their distinctiveness as a generational unit even today. . . . The former civil rights activists have not matured into moderate young adults, nor have they become disillusioned and dropped out. . . . Activists are concentrated in the knowledge and human service industries [e.g., universities and social service fields]; they participate in change-oriented voluntary organizations and have resisted the potential moderating influences of nuclear family commitments. Their political behavior reflects a radical commitment to political and economic changes in the United States and participation in both institutional and noninstitutional politics [Fendrich, 1974, p. 115].

These findings tend to refute the developmental hypothesis of the generation gap—that the difference between generations will remain associated primarily with the identity-formation period in adolescence and young adulthood so that individuals will pass through this period in successive generations and then adopt values and attitudes similar to their parents' attitudes and values. However, it may be that their parents were also politically liberal or radical. Flacks (1967) studied student political activists during the 1960s and concluded that activists tend to come from upper-status families; they are more "radical" than their parents, but their parents are much more liberal than others of their status; and activism is related to a complex set of values that are shared by both the students and their parents. For example, activist students were less likely to approve of the "bombing of North Vietnam" than their fathers; but both groups were less likely to approve than nonactivist students and their fathers. Thus, these former student activists may be following their parents' pattern, but are more radical in part because of the experiences they had in the civil rights movement and in part because of the general historical climate when they were in college. Similarly, most college students of that generation have moved into relatively conventional adult roles, as the developmental hypothesis would predict. At the same time, our entire society has been affected by the civil rights movement and by the war in Vietnam. Thus, there is evidence to support both the developmental prediction and the cultural discontinuity prediction.

As this example illustrates, the analysis of developmental change in individuals who are living in a changing world is very complex. In the next section we will discuss the ways in which developmental research deals with this issue.

DEVELOPMENTAL RESEARCH METHODOLOGY

The discussions of theoretical models of the life span and of the effect of historical changes on individual development call our attention to the importance of studying the process of development as it actually occurs in the real world. Our speculations may be interesting, but they do not increase our understanding of the human life cycle very much. However, the theoretical models, and the developmental approach in general, suggest research strategies for the study of adults that are far less obvious in nondevelopmental frameworks. That is, the central focus in developmental research is a systematic emphasis on age or change over time. Thus, the developmental approach might lead one to investigate the ways in which individuals of one age differ from individuals of another age, or the ways in which groups of individuals develop from one age to another. When this developmental perspective is combined with the interdisciplinary framework, the approach would lead one to investigate the ways in which biological, sociological, and psychological characteristics change with age during an individual's life span. Or this approach might lead one to investigate the interaction of biological, sociological, cultural, and psychological processes on an individual during a particular developmental phase—such as the effects of health, social participation, cultural attitudes about aging, and personality on the level of personal satisfaction of older people in a variety of different parts of the world.

In order to understand developmental research, we need to consider the meaning of age from a developmental perspective. Then, we will examine the kinds of research strategies that are used in developmental studies and point out the major problem posed by cohort effects and historical period (time) effects. We will conclude this chapter with an example of the strategies and problems of developmental research by looking at studies of changes in intelligence with age.

The Meaning of Age in Developmental Research

Developmental studies have one central concern: *age*. But age is merely a measure of the number of revolutions that the earth has made around the sun since a person's birth. Thus, chronological age by itself may not be a very meaningful indicator of development. At best, age provides a convenient index of the passage of *time*. Since some developmental processes are time-dependent (such as biological growth), these processes will correspond fairly well to the index of age. But other developmental processes may be time-independent (such as psychological well-being, or physical illness); while these processes may influence the nature and pattern of an individual's development, they are not related to the index of age. Thus, the goal of developmental research is to replace "age" with an understanding of the time-dependent and time-independent processes that bring about the changes that take place through the course of the human life cycle (Birren & Renner, 1977).

We might illustrate this idea by considering the different kinds of "age" that would be relevant to understanding development. *Biological age* would indicate the person's level of biological development and physical health. *Psychological age* could reflect the person's level of psychological maturity, or progression through a series of developmental stages such as the ones proposed by Erikson. *Social age* might indicate the person's passage through the socially defined milestones of development (such as working full-time, marriage, parenthood, and grandparenthood). *Perceived age* could measure the person's perception of themselves in terms of age ("young," "middle-aged," or "old"). Thus, one person who is chronologically 35 years old may be psychologically 45 (is responsible, has set goals to achieve before retirement, and has a sense of intimacy and generativity) but is socially 21 (still in training for a profession, unmarried, childless) and may be biologically 65 (has high blood pressure and greying hair). This person's perceived age may be "young adult." Thus, chronological age may not provide very much information about the individual. In many ways, perceived age may be more useful than chronological age because it would typically reflect the person's social, psychological, biological, and chronological age. One person might feel, act, and look like an adult (and others would respond to that person as an adult) at the age of 16; another person might not feel like a full adult until he or she finished graduate school at age 30. Similarly, one person of 70 may feel "old" and be in poor health unable to get around very much, while another 70-year-old may feel "middle-aged" and be as active and vigorous as a typical 45-year-old.

Thus, chronological age is most clearly seen as an *index* of a large number of factors that interact to produce development. It is an index of biological, psychological, social, and self-perceived changes that take place over time. Age alone does not cause these changes; it is merely an index of the speed with which the changes take place. For example, there are apparent age differences between 20-year-olds and 40-year-olds, including such factors as greater occupational achievement, greater family responsibility, and greater past experience for the 40-year-old group. These differences are not *caused* by age; instead, they are the result of social, biological, and psychological changes in addition to having lived longer and accumulated more experience. This does not mean that we should discard age as a variable—it may be the only one we have available at the present for describing changes that occur over time. But it does mean that we should look behind "age" to see the time-dependent and time-independent processes that cause development.

One attempt to get behind the index of age in order to isolate the actual causes of age-related changes has been suggested by Baltes and Goulet (1971). They propose that *age simulation* may be used systematically to manipulate the conditions under which age differences are found. For example, if we find that 65-year-old men perform less well in a dart-throwing experiment than 20-year-old men, we have no idea what may have caused this age difference. But if we manipulate the amount of light so that the 20-year-olds perform as poorly as the 65-year-olds when the light is very dim, but the 65-year-olds perform as well as the 20-year-olds when the lighting is increased, then we know that this age difference reflects differences in perceptual ability and indicates that the older men require more light to see as well as the younger men. Alternatively, it might be that lighting makes no difference, but when the older men are allowed to stand closer to the board, they score as well as the younger men, suggesting that physical strength is the important factor; thus we might simulate these age differences (i.e., experimentally cause the young men to perform like the old men, and vice versa) by varying the distance the dart must be thrown. Again, it might be that if the older men are allowed to practice for an hour they do as well as the young men, suggesting that the age difference really involves practice effects. This age-simulation methodology thus allows an investigator to experimentally manipulate the factors that might reasonably be thought to affect the performance and to identify the factors that are responsible for the age differences that may be found. However, Birren and Renner (1977) point out that this approach does not necessarily reveal the cause of the difference, since the variables that are manipulated may only simulate, but not reproduce, the actual age changes.

Cross-Sectional and Longitudinal Research Strategies

In order to investigate the factors that cause the age differences, it is obviously important to identify the changes that occur with age. The most apparent—and the easiest—way to find age differences is to gather a sample of persons of differing ages, give them questionnaires, tests, or interviews that are appropriate for the question being studied, and compare the results. Such studies are called *cross-sectional* studies, since they are based on a cross section of ages at one point in time. The differences that are found in this way are called *age differences*.

A second approach to studying the index of age is a *longitudinal* study. In this strategy, a group of subjects is selected, appropriate for the question being studied, and is given a series of questionnaires, tests, or interviews *periodically over several years* (an easy way to remember this is that *long*itudinal studies take a *long* time). For example, a group of persons would be studied when they were 20, again when they were 40, and again at age 60. These results would then be compared and any differences would be called *age changes*, since they represent changes within individuals over time; thus they allow the examination of individual differences and the ways in which different individuals change with age.

There are three central difficulties with longitudinal studies, however, that have limited their use in adult development (although there are several studies that have been carried out in child development, few have been continued into the adult years). One difficulty is that they obviously require a long time and are thus quite expensive; also, the study may outlive the investigators, and longitudinal studies typically involve a great amount of travel and effort to contact each subject at the next test interval. Nonetheless, longitudinal approaches are often superior to cross-sectional studies because they reflect individual differences and may include a large number of measures of other age-related, explanatory variables (such as medical history, past experiences, or family history) that are useful in determining the causes of the particular age changes that are being studied.

A second difficulty is that the measures that the researcher is using in a longitudinal study may be relevant at one age (in childhood or adolescence) but not at a later age (adulthood or old age), since the important issues for individuals' lives vary as they progress through their lifeline. In addition, as science progresses, new techniques become available to measure the variables of interest. As a result, a well-designed longitudinal study begun in 1930 may have focused on issues and relied on measures no longer relevant to either the subjects who are now 45 or to the social scientists who might prefer data on adjustment to menopause over data on the effect of early child-rearing practices. However, the longitudinal studies that were begun during the 1930s are beginning to provide some useful data on adulthood.

A third difficulty with longitudinal studies is that, because of the long time span involved, subjects may die or drop out of the sample before the study is completed. And these dropout rates may be relevant to the variables being investigated. For example, subjects with lower intelligence may drop out of longitudinal studies more frequently than those of higher intelligence; if one variable in the study is intelligence, this selective dropout rate would tend to increase the average intelligence in the sample over time and thus distort any age changes that might be found.

One solution to this dilemma is the use of *longitudinal sequences* (Baltes, 1968) in which a group of subjects is followed for a few years, possibly over a period of time that might represent a developmental turning point (such as marriage, parenthood, menopause, or retirement). In this way it is possible to assess longitudinal change (and individual differences) without committing the subjects and the investigator to a lifelong study.

Age, Cohort, and Time Effects

Since the bulk of data about adulthood and old age is based on cross-sectional studies, it is important to take a closer look at the implications of the differences between cross-sectional and longitudinal studies and to examine the difficulties implicit in cross-sectional studies.

A cross-sectional study is illustrated by any of the vertical columns in Figure 1.7; for example, C, G, K, N, and P. It is apparent that a study based on such a sample will provide information on age differences in 1980. And the problems encountered in a longitudinal study will be minimized by the collection of all the data for the study at one time-point. However, it is important to note that the difference between the groups of subjects is not only age but is also their *year of birth* (or cohort). That is, a 70-year-old in 1980 was born in 1910, but a 40-year was born in 1940.

Previously, we discussed the importance of social, historical, and cultural changes for the individual's development through the lifeline. Now it may be seen that a cross-sectional study does not separate the cultural-historical factors

Year Born	Year Measured			
	1960	*1970*	*1980*	*1990*
1910	(A) 50	(B) 60	(C) 70	(D) 80
1920	(E) 40	(F) 50	(G) 60	(H) 70
1930	(I) 30	(J) 40	(K) 50	(L) 60
1940		(M) 30	(N) 40	(O) 50
1950			(P) 30	(Q) 40
1960				(R) 30

Figure 1.7
Illustration of hypothetical cross-sectional and longitudinal studies, showing that chronological age reflects the interaction of year of birth and year of measurement.

from the age differences. That is, *age* and *year of birth* are confounded in a cross-sectional study, and the effects of one cannot be separated from the effects of the other. Thus, age differences may be partly or entirely due to cultural or social differences. For example, the combined effect of improvement in medical care and nutrition, increased education, and the effects of the Depression and World War II may explain any differences found among the five samples in the 1980 cross-sectional study (C, G, K, N, and P); hence the age differences may be associated primarily with the year of the individual's birth rather than with actual age-related factors. Recall that the effects of "year of birth" are called cohort effects, since a cohort is a group of individuals born at about the same time.

In contrast, longitudinal studies (such as A, B, C, and D) hold the year of birth constant so that whatever effects might be caused by cultural-historical changes are not a factor confounding the age changes in the study. However, these longitudinal studies also confound two variables: *age* and *year of measurement* (time). Thus, a change such as a sudden decrease in cigarette smoking in the population generally between 1960 and 1980 may counteract the age-related decrease in lung capacity expected with advancing age and would thus tend to conceal a possible relationship between lung capacity and age; there might also be effects on other related physiological measurements. One way to assess the influence of these confounding variables of year of birth and year of measurement is to compare persons of the same age (e.g., A, F, K, and O). While this does not provide any information on age, it does provide data on the effects of social-historical (time) factors; but it should be noted that these are confounded with cohort effects.

Perhaps ideal developmental studies would involve all three types of strategies. Schaie (1977) has proposed a sophisticated statistical procedure for separating the effects of time, cohort, and age. This methodology allows the samples to be followed longitudinally but, since a cross-sectional sample would also be available at each test point, it allows the speedy recovery of cross-sectional age differences and provides a means to compare each sample with others of the same age at different historical times. This type of study involves no more time than a longitudinal sequence study, described above, but does require a fairly large sample of subjects who are selected in a predetermined pattern, as well as sophisticated statistical analyses. Although this methodology has not yet been used widely, it probably represents the most powerful developmental research technique.

Example: Change in Intelligence with Age

An important illustration of the differences between longitudinal and cross-sectional studies, and of the influence of cultural-historical factors in contaminating the cross-sectional findings, is the change in performance on intelligence tests with age.

Botwinick (1977) reports that longitudinal studies on adult intelligence find that performance in IQ tests increases at least to age 50 or 60; during the seventies and eighties, the level of performance declines moderately. However, cross-sectional studies have shown that people in their twenties make the highest scores on intelligence tests, and each age group after 30 scores lower. These comparisons are shown in Figure 1.8. The longitudinal data were collected between 1931 and 1969 from 24 men and 24 women who were originally part of the sample of children that was used in the development of the 1937 Stanford-Binet intelligence test; since the Wechsler Adult Intelligence Scale (WAIS) was not developed until 1955, it was not used in this study until the subjects were 30 years old (Kangas & Bradway, 1971). The cross-sectional data are from the nationwide sample that was used to standardize the WAIS (Wechsler, 1955). Longitudinal data on older adults are not shown because they are based on different tests such as the "Army Alpha" used during World War I (Owens, 1966).

Clearly, there is a dramatic difference between the graph from the longitudinal study and the graph from the cross-sectional study. How do we explain this obvious discrepancy? Can we assume that either result is valid? What factors have to be considered? Suppose we consider the cohort effects first. Let us graph the average length of education completed for subjects in each group in the cross-sectional study and compare this graph with the intelligence test scores (Figure

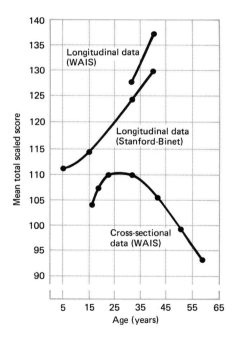

Figure 1.8

Comparison of longitudinal and cross-sectional data on changes in intelligence performance with age. Longitudinal data were based on the same sample from age 4 to age 42; two different intelligence tests were used in the last two testings. (Source: Longitudinal data from Kangas & Bradway, 1971, Table 3. Copyright © 1971 by the American Psychological Association. Cross-sectional data from Wechsler, 1955, Table 10. Copyright © 1955 by the Psychological Corporation. Adapted and reproduced with permission.

1.9). It appears that the differing amounts of education (a cohort effect) explain much of the difference between the age groups in test performance. Added factors may be the amount of time between the end of school and the test point (the longer the time, the lower the performance) or the decreasing relevance of intelligence test questions as individuals grow older. Thus, we may conclude that the cross-sectional result *underestimates* the level of intelligence in the later years under current social and educational conditions, and so it overestimates the amount of difference in intelligence with age.

But what about the longitudinal studies; are they more valid? There are several factors that indicate the longitudinal result *overestimates* the level of intelligence in later years: the selective dropout rate raises the average score, since the

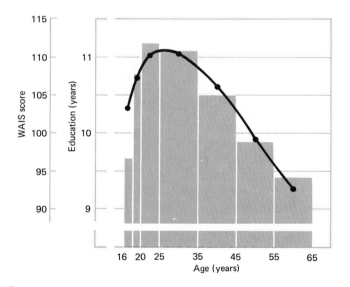

Figure 1.9
Comparison of cross-sectional measure of intellectual performance by age with the average education of the subjects. Vertical bar represents years of education for each panel of subjects; "X" represents average WAIS total score for that same panel. (Source: Based on Wechsler, 1955, Tables 5 and 10. Copyright © 1955 by The Psychological Corporation Adapted and reproduced with permission.)

more highly intelligent are less likely to drop out, the persons studied were generally of higher than average intelligence, and there is evidence of a general increase in IQ test performance between the 1930s and 1960s for people of the same age (Owens, 1966).

We may then conclude that the change in intelligence with age is neither the drastic difference indicated in cross-sectional data nor a continual increase shown for the highly intelligent subjects in longitudinal data. Instead, it is bounded by the cross-sectional data at the bottom and by the longitudinal data on the top and actually lies somewhere in between these two boundaries. In Chapter 7 we will discuss this topic in more detail, but this general overview clearly illustrates the importance of considering cohort factors in all cross-sectional research on adult development.

Implications

The developmental approach provides some unique perspectives on the adult years of the life span because it is concerned with changes that occur with age. It strives to understand age changes in persons of all social classes, cultures, and conditions of life. Yet it is apparent that these age changes interact with individual variation, social and cultural factors, and with historical change. We have discussed some of the age changes that theoretical frameworks have suggested and have pointed out the important interaction between historical changes and these developmental changes. In general, the task of developmental research is to attempt to disentangle the developmental processes from the historical changes.

However, since our task in the following chapters is to understand adulthood—primarily in our society in the 1980s—we will need to examine not only the developmental changes but also the interacting effects of historical changes. To take an obvious example, the women's liberation movement, the declining birth rate, and increasing longevity are modifying the timing of developmental milestones in the lives of many women who enter a second (occupational) career after raising a family, have a long postparental period of marriage, and not only have grandchildren but may have great-grandchildren while they are still strong and healthy. Because the effect of social factors is so thoroughly intertwined with developmental factors, we will turn to a discussion of the psychosocial processes of development in the next chapter.

CHAPTER SUMMARY

1. Many of the events that mark the individual's progression through the sequence of adult development are socially defined as being related to age—such as permission to vote, the "right age" to marry, or the age of retirement. Biological factors play a major role in childhood development, but social factors are more important for regulating the process of development during adulthood.

2. As people look back over their lives—or as they plan for the future—they see some events that stand out as especially important markers or turning points in their life cycle. We call these *milestones*. They help us to understand the development of a particular individual from his or her own perspective.

3. Several theories of the life cycle have included a focus on adulthood; however, there is no fully adequate theory of adult development. In all of these theories, it is important to consider the effects of socioeconomic status, historical conditions, ethnic factors, and sex differences before accepting any as applying to *all* people.

4. Bühler's theory emphasizes goal-related psychosocial expansion, culmination, and decline paralleling biological growth, stability and decline. Kuhlen's model is similar in emphasizing growth-expansion during the first part of life, followed by contraction during the second half of life.

5. Jung's perspective also sees a major change in life between the end of youth and the beginning of the second half of life—around the ages of 35 to 40. During the later part of life, an individual's attention turns inward, life tends to contract, and men become more "feminine" while women become more "masculine."

6. Erikson views human development as a series of eight stages, each involving a dialectical struggle between two opposing tendencies; the synthesis that results produces one of the eight enduring characteristics of human life.

7. Riegel's perspective focuses on the process of change instead of stages of equilibrium; development results from the dialectical interaction of four major dimensions of human life.

8. Since age reflects when individuals were born and the historical period through which they have lived, differences between people of different ages do not necessarily indicate developmental change; they could reflect historical effects.

9. A *cohort* is a group of people born at about the same time (e.g., 1950 or 1948-1953 or 1945-1955). People who directly experience a particular historical period may be affected by that period so that their characteristics differ from other cohorts of people who did not live through that historical period. Thus, people who lived through the Great Depression of the 1930s may be different from those born after World War II because they are older, because of cohort effects, or both.

10. Historical change may also produce effects that influence all persons living through a particular historical period. These *time*, or historical period, effects include improved nutrition and health care that have increased the length of time individuals are expected to live today, compared with 1900.

11. The so-called generation gap is an example of these developmental and historical effects, since both are involved in creating differences in attitudes and values between generations.

12. Chronological age is a convenient index of an individual's development. However, age in itself does not produce changes; social, biological, and psychological processes actually bring about the changes that occur with the passage of time.

13. Developmental research is usually cross-sectional (by age) or longitudinal—the first method uses groups of persons of various ages at one point in time; the second follows a group of persons over a long period of time. Cross-sectional studies need to be examined carefully for possible cohort effects; longitudinal studies often study only one cohort, so they may not be representative of persons born at other times.

14. The comparison of cross-sectional and longitudinal studies of changes in intelligence test performance during adulthood clearly show the importance of considering the potential significance of cohort effects in all studies of adult development.

REFERENCES

Baltes, Paul B. 1968. Longitudinal and Cross-Sectional Sequences in the Study of Age and Generation Effects. *Human Development, 11*(3), 145-171.

Baltes, Paul B., & Goulet, L. R. 1971. Exploration of Developmental Variables by Manipulation and Simulation of Age Differences in Behavior. *Human Development, 14*(3), 149-170.

Bengtson, Vern L., & Cutler, Neal E. 1976. Generations and Intergenerational Relations: Perspectives on Age Groups and Social Change. In Robert H. Binstock & Ethel Shanas (Eds.), *Handbook of Aging and the Social Sciences.* New York: Van Nostrand Reinhold.

Birren, James E.; Butler, Robert N.; Greenhouse, Samuel W.; Sokoloff, Louis; & Yarrow, Marian R. (Eds.). **1963.** *Human Aging: A Biological and Behavioral Study.* Publication No. (HSM) 71-9051. Washington, D.C.: U.S. Government Printing Office.

Birren, James E., & Renner, V. Jayne. 1977. Research on the Psychology of Aging: Principles and Experimentation. In James E. Birren & K. Warner Schaie (Eds.), *Handbook of the Psychology of Aging.* New York: Van Nostrand Reinhold.

Botwinick, Jack. 1977. Intellectual Abilities. In James E. Birren & K. Warner Schaie (Eds.), *Handbook of the Psychology of Aging.* New York: Van Nostrand Reinhold.

Bühler, Charlotte. 1968. The Developmental Structure of Goal Setting in Group and Individual Studies. In Charlotte Bühler & Fred Massarik (Eds.), *The Course of Human Life.* New York: Springer.

Conger, John Janeway. 1971. A World They Never Knew: The Family and Social Change. *Daedalus, 100*(4), 1105-1138.

Datan, Nancy, & Reese H. W. (Eds.). **1977.** *Life-Span Developmental Psychology: Dialectical Perspectives of Experimental Research.* New York: Academic Press.

Erikson, Erik H. 1963. *Childhood and Society* (2nd ed.). New York: W.W. Norton.

Erikson, Erik H. 1968. *Identity: Youth and Crisis.* New York: W. W. Norton.

Erikson, Erik H. 1976. Reflections on Dr. Borg's Life Cycle. *Daedalus, 105*(2), 1-28.

Fendrich, James M. 1974. Activists Ten Years Later: A Test of Generational Unit Continuity. *Journal of Social Issues, 30*(3), 95-118.

Flacks, Richard. 1967. The Liberated Generation: An Exploration of the Roots of Student Protest. *Journal of Social Issues, 23*(3), 52-75.

Frenkel, Else. 1936. Studies in Biographical Psychology. *Character and Personality, 5,* 1-34.

Gruen, Walter. 1964. A Study of Erikson's Theory of Ego Development. In Bernice L. Neugarten & Associates (Eds.), *Personality in Middle and Late Life.* New York: Atherton Press.

Horner, Althea J. 1968. The Evolution of Goals in the Life of Clarence Darrow. In Charlotte Bühler & Fred Massarik (Eds.). *The Course of Human Life.* New York: Springer.

Jung, Carl G. 1933. The Stages of Life. (Translated by R. F. C. Hull.) In Joseph Campbell (Ed.), *The Portable Jung.* New York: Viking, 1971.

Kangas, Jon, & Bradway, Katherine. 1971. Intelligence at Middle Age: A Thirty-Eight-Year Follow-Up. *Developmental Psychology, 5*(2), 333-337.

Kuhlen, Raymond G. 1964. Developmental Changes in Motivation During the Adult Years. In James E. Birren (Ed.), *Relations of Development and Aging.* Springfield, Ill.: Charles C Thomas.

Kuhlen, Raymond G., & Johnson, G. H. 1952. Changes in Goals with Increasing Adult Age. *Journal of Consulting Psychology, 16*(1), 1-4.

Mannheim, Karl. 1952. The Problem of Generations. In P. Kecskemeti (Ed.), *Essays on the Sociology of Knowledge.* New York: Oxford University Press.

Mead, Margaret. 1970. *Culture and Commitment: A Study of the Generation Gap.* New York: Doubleday.

Neugarten, Bernice L. 1967. The Awareness of Middle Age. In Bernice L. Neugarten (Ed.), *Middle Age and Aging.* Chicago: University of Chicago Press, 1968. (Originally published in: *Middle Age.* Roger Owen, Ed. London: British Broadcasting Corporation.)

Neugarten, Bernice L. 1974. Age Groups in American Society and the Rise of the Young-Old. *The Annals of the American Academy of Political and Social Science,* 1974 (Sept.), 187-198.

Neugarten, Bernice L.; Moore, Joan W.; & Lowe, John C. 1965. Age Norms, Age Constraints, and Adult Socialization. *American Journal of Sociology, 70*(6), 710-717.

Owens, W. A. 1966. Age and Mental Abilities: A Second Adult Follow-Up. *Journal of Educational Psychology, 57*(6), 311-325.

Peck, Robert C. 1955. Psychological Developments in the Second Half of Life. In Bernice L. Neugarten (Ed.), *Middle Age and Aging.* Chicago: University of Chicago Press, 1968. (Originally published in: *Psychological Aspects of Aging.* John E. Anderson, Ed. Proceedings of a Conference on Planning Research, Bethesda,

Maryland, April 24-27, 1955. Washington D.C.: American Psychological Association, 1956.)

Riegel, Klaus F. 1976. The Dialectics of Human Development. *American Psychologist, 31*(10), 689-700.

Riegel, Klaus F. 1977. The Dialectics of Time. In Nancy Datan & Hayne W. Reese (Eds.), *Life-Span Developmental Psychology: Dialectical Perspectives on Experimental Research.* New York: Academic Press.

Schaie, K. Warner. 1977. Quasi-Experimental Research Designs in the Psychology of Aging. In James E. Birren & K. Warner Schaie (Eds.), *Handbook of the Psychology of Aging.* New York: Van Nostrand Reinhold.

U.S. Bureau of the Census. 1976. Demographic Aspect of Aging and the Older Population in the United States. *Current Population Reports*, Series P-23, No. 59. Washington, D.C.: U.S. Government Printing Office.

Wechsler, David. 1955. *Manual for the Adult Intelligence Scale.* New York: The Psychological Corporation.

PSYCHOSOCIAL PROCESSES OF DEVELOPMENT:
stability and change over time

2

SYMBOLIC INTERACTION APPROACH TO ADULTHOOD

    The Self

    Development of the Self

    Taking the Attitude of the Other

    Self-Consciousness

    The Self and Mind

    The Self in Adulthood

    Conclusion

SOCIAL TIMING FACTORS: NORMS, STATUS, AND ROLES

    Age Norms

    Age-Status Systems

    Age-Sex Roles

    The Social Clock

SOCIALIZATION: LEARNING NORMS AND ROLES

    The Socialization Process

    Anticipatory Socialization and Resocialization

    Socialization in Adulthood

ADULT DEVELOPMENT: A SOCIAL INTERACTION PERSPECTIVE

    Timing in Adult Development

    The Meaning of Experience

    Change and Consistency in Adulthood

CHAPTER SUMMARY

REFERENCES

It is a common observation that individuals change in important ways during the adult years; yet at the same time they also remain relatively consistent as they pass through the milestones of adulthood. If we were to attend our high-school reunion in a few years, we would notice this simultaneous change and consistency. One old friend might have become a successful businessman and gained a sense of competence and power that contrasts with his happy-go-lucky attitude in high school; yet he would also be recognizably similar to the boy we knew years ago. Another old friend may have changed from the prom queen we remember to a brilliant research chemist; but she is still the outgoing, popular, and engaging person we remember. How does this happen? It is such a common phenomenon that we seldom examine it closely. However, it is puzzling. How do persons change, and how do they remain fairly consistent even if they have also changed considerably?

In the first chapter we presented an overview of the human life cycle and suggested some of the age-related changes that occur. This chapter will focus on the processes by which age changes occur in adulthood. We will pay particular attention to three central questions posed by the developmental study of adulthood: (1) What are the processes by which individuals change; and what processes are involved in the stability of individuals over long periods of time? (2) Is there any age-related sequence to these changes so that the adult years may be conceptualized as a sequential and progressive period of life; in addition, if there is a sequence, what serves as *timing* factors to order the developmental changes during adulthood? (3) What is the effect of *experience* on the individual—because it is this diffuse variable of "experience" that most clearly accumulates with age; moreover, what is the process by which experience affects the individual?

Our approach to these questions and to the processes of development in adulthood is a social-psychological one. That is, we see the adult as an individual in interaction with others in society, and we feel that this interaction process is central to an understanding of the processes by which age-related changes occur in adulthood. Thus, the processes of change, stability, timing of development, and the accumulation of experience seem to be best understood in terms of the individual interacting with others in social interaction.

At the same time, we expect that physiological changes (such as changes in hormonal production, blood chemistry or neural conductivity) also play an important role in producing developmental change and stability during adulthood. However, we currently know relatively little about the effects of age-related physiological changes on normal persons. Although we expect that eventual research will provide a great deal of information about these physiological processes of developmental change, we are currently able to draw only on the effects of such major physiological changes as menopause or disease (see Chapters 5 and 7, respectively), and we are left with the tentative conclusion that biological factors provide a great deal of latitude for the impact of social-psychological processes on development in adulthood. Thus it appears that, as individuals move through their lifeline, the biological factors that played an initially large part in determining the rate and order of change decline in relative importance after the early years of childhood; and after puberty social factors come to play an important role in the regulation of developmental change.

Our conceptual model of adulthood emphasizes the view that the *interaction* of the various factors is central (rather than any one factor alone); thus, even when physiological factors are more fully understood, they will probably be most profitably seen as one set of factors interacting with the social-psychological processes that we will discuss in this chapter. Our model also emphasizes the view that the individual is *active* in this complex pattern of interactions instead of a passive respondent to social, cultural, or biological changes. We view adults as actively selecting many aspects of their physical and social environment and being affected by their assimilation of that environmental experience. We also see adults as actively affecting their social and physical environment and being changed in that experience. Moreover, we view the human individual as a social being with a mind and a self that are brought about by the active interaction between the individual and society.

Our social-psychological framework for viewing the process of adult development is based on this interactive social process as analyzed by G. H. Mead (1934). In the following section we will introduce some of Mead's concepts and discuss their importance for understanding adulthood. The next two sections of the chapter will be devoted to more contemporary social-psychological concepts such as roles, norms, and the process of socialization as they apply to the adult years. The final section will focus on the three questions central to the study of adulthood: How do change and consistency occur simultaneously over time? What is the nature of "experience"? What regulates or "times" development in adulthood?

SYMBOLIC INTERACTION APPROACH TO ADULTHOOD

George Herbert Mead was a philosopher at the Universtiy of Chicago from 1894 until his death in 1931. He was especially interested in describing the process of social interaction, the nature of the self, and the relationship between mind, self, and society. He argued that humans evolved as social beings and that their ability to interact with one another through symbols (such as language or gestures) was particularly important for understanding the nature of the human self—thus, his approach became known as *symbolic interaction*.

One of Mead's teachers was William James, the influential early American psychologist, and he was a colleague of John Dewey and W. I. Thomas during the time that the Chicago School of Sociology was evolving among a star-studded faculty (Strauss, 1964). Mead's scholarly writing was devoted primarily to philosophical and psychological issues. He was 40 before his first major paper appeared and he had not published a single book when he died at the age of 68. However, graduate students in sociology at the University discovered his unique ideas a decade before his death and "flocked to his classes" (ibid.). After his death, these students published their collected notes as well as his own notes and unpublished writings in his posthumous book, *Mind, Self, and Society*, in

1934. These Chicago sociologists succeeded in carrying his ideas into the mainstream of sociology by 1939. Many of his concepts influenced modern sociology theory, and his ideas may also be found in the writings of psychologists (such as Carl Rogers) and psychiatrists (such as Harry Stack Sullivan). Symbolic interaction theory remains a current sociological framework, but its influence has not been a dominant one since the end of World War II. However, his approach is especially useful in describing the complex interpersonal and intrapersonal processes that characterize adulthood; we will use his framework extensively throughout this book.

Perhaps his approach may best be seen as a framework or perspective for understanding human interaction. It is not the kind of theory that allows us to predict behavior; but it helps us to understand it better. It is an approach that describes human functioning in society and provides useful concepts for conceptualizing the process of social interaction. Its main advantages for the study of adulthood are: the focus on the individual's inner experience, the emphasis on the continual capacity for change, and the significance given to social processes for the understanding of human functioning. We will discuss several of Mead's central concepts, emphasizing the importance of the self and self-consciousness for understanding adulthood.

The Self

The self is probably a uniquely human characteristic that humankind acquired as we evolved the capacity to interact with other persons in social settings through the use of communication and language. The self is different from the physiological organism. It is not present at birth; it develops through the process of social experience and social communication; and it continues developing and changing throughout one's life. Thus, the self is not a "thing" a person has, but is a *process* that requires human interaction to come into existence and is continually developing and changing.

Mead's concept of the self is that it consists of two aspects that are in continual interaction with each other. One aspect—called *I*—involves experiencing, awareness, and consciousness of oneself; *I* is "that-which-experiences" (James, 1892). Thus, thinking and feeling are *I* processes; thinking is the experience of a thought, and feeling is the experience of an emotion. The major characteristic of the *I* is that it exists only in the present moment; it is purely moment-by-moment experiencing. Once the experience or awareness can be put into words, or thought about, or told to another, it is no longer *I*. This is because *I* would then—at that moment—be experiencing and reacting to words or thinking about the previous experience. Thus, this component of the self is pure process—it is always changing, fleeting, existing only in the present moment. This provides a continuing source of creativity, surprise, and novelty to the self. This component of the self has often been left out by other writers who talk only about those aspects of the self that can be measured or counted or examined. *I* is not like an observable phenomenon; it is our *experiencing* of those "things" that others are counting, categorizing, and studying. While the term "*I*" is awkward and easily confused with other more common uses of "I" (perhaps it should be called "E" for experiencing), Mead probably chose *I* because it is the subjective term for the self; and *I* is purely subjective. It is private and cannot be examined because it is always changing as moment-to-moment experience occurs.

The other component of the self in Mead's scheme is the *me* (the objective word for the self). The *me* consists of all the characteristics of the person that can be seen, examined, touched, measured, or listened to: it is the body, the behavior, the gestures, clothing, words, personality characteristics, hair color—everything that can be seen.

Thus, the self consists of two components that are in continual interaction with each other. The *me* consists of all the objective characteristics of the self (tall, black, woman, mother, lawyer, etc.). The *I* consists of the person's experience *at that moment*. *I* experiences the *me* and is conscious of other people's reactions to the *me*; the *me* often shows the experiences of *I* through words, facial gestures, and so on. The self is *I*, the *me*, and their interaction (Figure 2.1).

Development of the Self

At birth, the infant cannot be said to possess a self, according to Mead. However, the origins of the experiencing, or *I*, aspect of the self would seem to be present: the infant experiences hunger, wetness, thirst, and pain as fleeting moment-by-moment experiences. The infant cannot conceptualize these experiences into thoughts, cannot express them in gestures or words, and cannot comprehend its own objective existence, so there is no *me* component of the self for the first few days or weeks of life. But soon the origins of the objective, or *me*, aspect of the self begin to appear. For example, the infant begins to understand that the thumb is part of itself, while the pacifier or blanket is not part of itself, by sucking the thumb and experiencing both the mouth sucking on an object and the thumb being sucked. Gradually, the objective aspect of the self begins to develop as the infant's mind develops the ability to perceive that the child is an object distinct from other objects.

The beginning of language greatly advances the development of the self because it provides the ability to communicate through the use of what Mead called *significant symbols*. These are words or gestures that have essentially the same meaning to everyone involved in the social interaction. Of course, some of the infant's cries and gestures may serve as significant symbols to those people who are caring for the infant—the "I'm hungry" cry, or the "I'm wet" cry—but the development of language brings a major advance in the development of the self. Children are able to talk to themselves, talk about themselves, and understand others when they talk about them. Thus, children become able to think about the objective (*me*) part of themselves and also become able to express their inner experiences (*I*) to others through the use of language.

During childhood, the self develops through social interaction with others and grows in complexity as the child's cognitive development allows greater under-

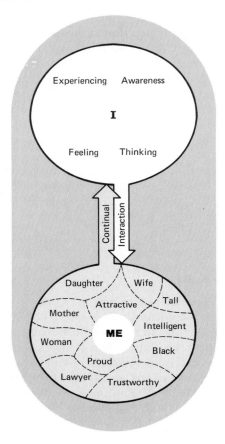

Figure 2.1
The self consists of *I* and *me* in continual interaction. *I* is entirely private or subjective; the many characteristics of *me* are seen by oneself or by others in social interaction.

standing of the subjective (*I*) and objective (*me*) aspects of the self. Mead noted that some of the people with whom the child interacts are *significant others* in the sense that they are particularly important for the child's developing sense of self. For children, significant others usually include parents and other important models. Adults also have significant others who are particularly influential in the continuing evolution of the self during adulthood.

By adolescence, the person has learned to respond to several others at the same time—as in the game of baseball where one's behavior must be affected by the other players on the field—and has developed the ability to think in terms of abstractions. This allows adolescents to consider the *generalized other*—that is, "others in general," or "society"—as one additional influence on their sense of self. Adults may also be very much aware of society's attitudes, so that the generalized other remains an important influence on the evolution of the self throughout the adult years.

Taking the Attitude of the Other

A central process in the development and evolution of the self involves what Mead termed "taking the attitude of the other"; in less technical terms, this means imagining oneself in the other person's shoes. It means understanding as fully as possible the other person's experiencing. In social interactions, one or more individuals are communicating with each other through significant symbols (language, gestures, etc.). One person's self—*I* and *me* in interaction—is communicating with the other person's self (Figure 2.2). Frank's *I* is experiencing his own *me* and Sally's *me*; and Sally's *I* is experiencing her own *me* and Frank's *me*. If Frank takes the attitude of Sally, Frank watches, listens, and senses Sally's *me* as a reflection of Sally's experiencing. Frank cannot see Sally's *I*, but Frank can see Sally's *me* and can guess what Sally is experiencing or feeling or thinking about Frank if Sally gives enough clues. Frank can then compare Sally's perception of Frank's self with Frank's own perception of himself.

Mead argued that the self develops through this process. As in a sensitivity or consciousness-raising group where one provides feedback to another on how each sees the other, so also one's self develops through the process of receiving information from others about oneself. This involves "taking the attitude of others toward oneself," or imagining how one looks through the eyes of another. Sometimes another person is actively involved in this process, as in feedback in a group. Or sometimes one simply looks in the mirror (in reality or imag-

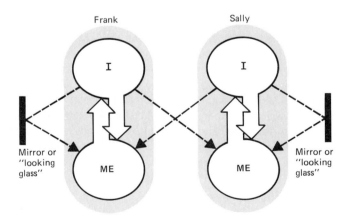

Figure 2.2

Taking the attitude of the other. Frank's *I* experiences his own *me* and Sally's *me*; Sally's *I* experiences her own *me* and Frank's *me*. If Frank takes the attitude of Sally toward himself, Frank tries to guess how Sally's *I* is experiencing Frank's *me* and compares this with the way his *me* appears to himself. Both see their own *me* as if they were looking at themselves in a mirror.

ination) and reacts to oneself as if one were another person (the concept of the "looking glass self"; Cooley, 1911). Sometimes one might "take the attitude of the generalized other toward oneself" in the sense of imagining how "society" would react to oneself. One example of a man who suddenly realized he was middle-aged illustrates the way in which taking the attitude of the other toward oneself may bring about a change in the way one sees oneself.

> "The realization suddenly struck me that I had become, perhaps not an old fogy but surely a middle-aged fogy. . . For the train was filled with college boys returning from vacation. . . They cruised up and down the aisles, pretending to be tipsy . . . boisterous, but not obnoxious; looking for fun, but not for trouble. . . Yet most of the adult passengers were annoyed with them, including myself. I sat there, feeling a little like Eliot's Prufrock, 'so meticulously composed, buttoned-up, bespectacled, mouth thinly set' . . . Squaresville" [Harris, 1965; cited in Neugarten, 1967].[1]

This middle-aged man is looking at himself from the point of view of another—perhaps a college student, perhaps an adult passenger, or possibly just imagined how he looked as if he were watching himself from across the aisle—and from that perspective realized that his *self* looked like a "middle-aged fogy."

Although taking the attitude of the other toward oneself is crucial for the development and change of the self, we probably do not use this process very often in ordinary social interaction. It is most useful when an individual is trying to understand or define or examine his or her *self*, or when the ordinary interaction process breaks down because the other people are not responding to the person the way he or she expects they should. For example, if a man is arguing with his wife and tries to see her perspective on the issue and imagines how she sees him and interprets his comments, he is taking the attitude of his wife in an effort to resolve the argument. Or if a professor is having difficulty explaining a concept to her class, she may try to take the attitude of the students toward the concept and ask them to describe what is confusing, or to imagine herself in their place and guess why they are having difficulty. Similarly, if she wishes to improve her teaching, she may ask for "feedback" from the students' perspective. This process of taking the attitude of the other is quite useful when one is trying to understand another (as in close freindships or in psychotherapy), and examples may be found in all kinds of social interactions. However, the vast majority of social interactions tend to be routine and proceed uneventfully without this kind of process being consciously used. Here are three examples of routine interaction:

> "Hi, how are you?" "Fine; and yourself?"
> "How much?" "Forty-nine cents plus tax."
> "A coffee and danish, please." "To go or to stay?"

[1] All quotations from Neugarten (1967) are reprinted with permission. Copyright © 1967 by Bernice L. Neugarten.

Nonetheless, even these very routine interactions assume that each person is implicitly taking the attitude of the other; this is clear when the interaction goes amiss or the expected response does not follow:

"Hi, how are you?" "Pretty bad, Kent left last night and took the kids."

Suddenly, one is drawn to take the attitude of the other and may take the time to find out what is going on from the point of view of the other person.

Self-Consciousness

Sometimes one takes the attitude of the other in social interactions to focus on the other person in an effort to understand that person more clearly. At other times, one uses this process to examine oneself from the perspective of the other person. The middle-aged man on the train in the earlier example was focusing on himself as he thought he appeared through the eyes of the college students. Similarly, the college professor asking for feedback from her students is focusing on herself. These are examples of Mead's concept of *self-consciousness*. It is the process by which an individual becomes aware of his or her *self* and focuses or reflects on it. Thus, when a man has just made a complete mess out of a social interaction, he may spend some time examining himself to try to understand what he did wrong and why his behavior or his words were so misinterpreted by the others. He may take the attitude of the others toward himself and try to see himself as they saw him. He may look at himself in the mirror as if he were another person and talk with himself in an introspective fashion about the interaction and the implications it may have for his *self*.

We may take the attitude of the other toward ourselves (that is, be self-conscious) when we are alone by imagining how we would look to ourselves if we could watch ourselves as if we were another person. We may take the attitude of a particular other toward ourselves when we are interacting with that person by imagining how we look to the person, or by receiving feedback about that person's perception of ourselves. Or we may take the attitude of others in general (the generalized other, or society) by imagining how others would see us if we were to get a divorce or if we were to leave our job and join a farming commune.

In each case, our *I* is experiencing something about our *me*. When we are alone, our *I* is experiencing our *me* as if it were reflected in a mirror. When we are interacting with another person, our *I* is experiencing the other person's *me* (in this case, largely words and gestures) as that person describes the way his or her *I* experiences our *me*. When we are considering what "society" might think about our behavior, we imagine the reaction of our image of the generalized other to our behavior.

Clearly, Mead is using the term self-consciousness in a slightly different way from ordinary usage. It does not necessarily imply any embarassment, although it might; it does not necessarily imply any insecurity or shyness, although it might. It is a process all persons experience when they wish to understand themselves. It is vital for the development of the self in childhood, and a central process in the continuing evolution of the self during adulthood. It is an important process for one to engage in when choosing a new job, or when seeking to maintain important relationships. In introspection, the process involves focusing on one's feelings (Gendlin, 1964). This involves attending to one's inner experiencing (*I*), turning those feelings or experiencings into *me*s by forming them into words or thoughts. Since *I* is moment-by-moment experiencing, all *I*s of the past moment may become *me*s of the present moment; each of these *me*s can then be reacted to by the *I* of the present, and so on in an ongoing chain of introspection. Sometimes this process is central to psychotherapy when clients or patients focus on and describe their feelings to the therapist and to themselves. It provides the person an opportunity to examine the *I-me* interaction within the self and to practice expressing the subjective *I*-experiencings in words (*me*s) that may be responded to by another person in social interaction as well as by oneself.

The Self and Mind

Mead's concept of the self does not include all of a person's inner functioning. It does not include rational thought, memory, or the kind of unconscious processes that psychoanalysts describe. However, Mead saw a close relationship between the functioning of the mind and the self. Our discussion has certainly assumed that the individual is a rational, thinking person who can reason, understand, and anticipate future consequences. Since an individual's self develops through the process of taking the attitude of the other toward oneself, the rational process of perceiving and understanding the meaning of the attitude of the other is clearly involved in the development of the self. Memory, foresight, the ability to understand language and to communicate, as well as thinking, planning, and creating, are all processes that are necessary for the self to function to its fullest extent.

We might also note that Mead's theory does not deal with unconscious processes. While much of the processes we have described here *might* be carried on without the individual's conscious awareness of them, in Mead's theory there is no reason that a person could not be aware of them. They are so basic to human interaction that they are similar to breathing—one is not ordinarily aware of breathing, but from time to time one can pay conscious attention to it, especially if it is important at that moment. Also, the psychoanalytic terms—id, ego, and superego—do not fit well in Mead's framework, so it is best not to confuse *I* and *me* with the id and ego; the two theories involve very different perspectives of human functioning and, on balance, are more different than they are similar.

The Self in Adulthood

Adults are characterized by a diverse range of *me*s that make up the social (or objective) self—the *me*. During the hours of a week, a typical adult may be a mother, daughter, student, politician, wife, and friend; she may attend concerts or the theater, express herself in writing, counsel a troubled friend, enjoy sex, become angry, feel joy, teach her children, and repair her car. All of these behaviors, feelings, and words that can be seen, thought about, or expressed are part of her *me*. Likewise, her physical and personal characteristics may be a part of her *me* if she or another reacts to them. Clearly, the social self (*me*) of adults can be highly complex and can change from hour to hour, or from interaction to interaction. Yet, all of these characteristics combine to make up the person's *me*.

Similarly, *I* provides adults with a rich and varied range of experiences. Human beings are equipped with the capacity to feel a wide range of emotions and to experience events and social interactions in a variety of ways. For Mead, these inner experiences are as important a part of the complex human self as are the parts of the self that can be observed. Every sunset, every interpersonal experience, every idea or musical sound or human word can bring an inner experience in *I*. All of these are part of the self. The essence of the self in adulthood is the interaction between the *I* aspects and the *me* aspects.

Adults also have a range of significant others who influence the person's self. These may include children, spouse, parents, employer, neighbors, close friends, and role models or mentors. Each of these relationships might involve a slightly different set of *mes*—that is, a different facet of oneself may be revealed to each person. Moreover, each significant other may evoke a different cluster of inner experiencings in one's *I*. All of these relationships, and the *Is* and *mes* associated with them, combine to provide the diversity and complexity of the self in adulthood.

Perhaps the hallmark of the self in adulthood is the person's highly developed ability to take the attitude of a diverse range of others—that is, to attempt to see the world through their eyes. Consider, for example, the young mother who is able to take the attitude of her husband, her children, her parents; but also to take the attitude of teachers toward her children, the attitude of the other parents (and the police and city council) toward the conditions of her neighborhood, and the attitude of federal and state politicians about schools, inflation, unemployment, and so on. She must be able to do this if she is going to participate in these complex social realities.

Likewise, most adults have a well-developed ability to be self-conscious (in the sense of being able to take the attitude of another toward oneself). For example, a successful lawyer self-consciously selects the impression he is conveying in the courtroom and attempts to influence the perceptions of his client held by others in the courtroom. In introspective moments of self-consciousness he may reflect on the morality or the political consequences of his behavior; and he may reflect on the future consequences or past experiences that pertain to the particular case. When he meets with his colleagues or has dinner with his wife, he is also engaging in social behavior that is characterized by the process of social interaction and may involve moments of self-consciousness. If his wife decides to divorce him, or if he enters psychotherapy or joins a consciousness-raising group, he will probably have many moments of self-consciousness when he focuses on himself as others see him and when he seeks to integrate these perceptions with his own experience of himself. These moments of self-consciousness are one of the main sources of change in the self. They involve the ability to take the attitude of the other, to communicate with oneself and with others using significant symbols, and to involve the interaction of the mind and the self. They may occur in moments of quiet introspection or in extended interactions in which one is attempting to understand a social interaction that has gone awry for some reason. An example from a middle-aged respondent illustrates this process clearly.

> "I used to think that all of us in the office were contemporaries, for we all had similar career interests. But one day we were talking about old movies and we realized that the younger ones had never seen a Shirley Temple film or an Our Gang comedy. . . Then it struck me with a blow that I was older than they. I had never been so conscious of it before" [Neugarten, 1967].

Conclusion

The symbolic interaction perspective calls attention to the interpersonal nature of human life. Since adults usually live in a complex network of social interactions, this perspective seems especially useful for understanding adulthood. At the end of this chapter we will use this perspective for an analysis of the central issues in the study of adulthood: the timing or regulation of adult development, the meaning of experience, and the nature of the processes of change and continuity in human development. In the next two sections we will focus on social norms, status, and roles, and on the process of socialization. These concepts have grown out of Mead's work, but have been modified by other sociologists in major ways. For example, Mead's concept of *I* has largely been lost in these modifications, and it is important for us to remember its central importance in human functioning.

Throughout this book, we must also keep in mind two other significant implications of Mead's approach. First, the self is not a "thing," but is a process. Only the *me* aspect of it exists in any objective sense; *I* is pure process, existing only from moment to moment, as a kind of stream of consciousness, or flow of experiencing (James, 1892). As soon as we can talk about *I*, it has become a *me*, and *I* of the present moment is reacting to that *me*. Thus, the *I-me* interaction is the essence of the self, and this prevents oneself from ever being fully defined, categorized, or measured. While this may be frustrating to some social scientists, Mead would have argued that this is the essence of humanness.

Second, the self, or the person, is always an active participant in social interactions. In this view, we are not passive creatures shaped by external forces; instead, we are constantly active in social interaction, creating and recreating ourself as the collection of *mes* and the flow of experiencing changes and evolves all the years of our lives.

SOCIAL TIMING FACTORS: NORMS, STATUS, AND ROLES

The discussion of Mead's approach to social interaction focused on the individual in the interaction. To expand this perspective, we shift our focus to the social side of the interaction. That is, we will examine the ways in which society affects individuals in age-related ways as they take the attitude of the generalized other (i.e., society or their social community or "others in general") toward themselves.

Age Norms

Norms are a set of expectations about behavior that people carry in their heads and use to regulate their own behavior and to respond to others' behavior. That is, norms are the attitudes of the generalized other and affect our behavior as we take the attitude of the generalized other toward ourselves in any social situation. Norms are linked to social *sanctions*; sanctions are the pressures brought to bear on an individual who violates the norms or expectations. Thus, norms exert some degree of *constraint* on behavior so that one chooses to do one thing and not do something else when the first choice is expected and the second is a violation of expectations. For example, social norms prescribe the expected behavior of persons in such socially defined positions as police officer, mother, student, and doctor; and there are informal as well as legal social sanctions that are used to maintain the expected behavior.

Similarly, individuals have expectations for what behavior is appropriate at different ages. We are all aware of these expectations, these *age norms*, and frequently our behavior and our responses to others are affected by them. We may note that we often respond differently to a young person than we do to a middle-aged person or an elderly individual. In addition, we are unlikely to see a 65-year-old woman wearing a two-piece bathing suit on the beach and, if we do see such a woman, we would think her behavior rather improper. On the other hand, if we see a 35-year-old woman dressed like an aged grandmother, we are just as likely to think that her behavior is inappropriate. Neugarten, Moore, and Lowe (1965) inquired about various age-related characteristics in a middle-class, middle-aged sample and found a high degree of consensus about the ages that the respondents associated with each characteristic (Table 2.1). For example, 80 percent of the men and 90 percent of the women felt that the 20–25 age range is the best time for a man to marry. The authors report that this consensus about age norms is not limited to persons residing in a particular part of the country, white persons, or middle-aged persons. The same set of questions was asked of other middle-class respondents aged 20–30 who lived in a midwestern city, a group of black men and women aged 40–60, and a group of persons aged 70–80 in a New England community. Essentially the same patterns of age norms were found for each group of respondents.

Since these age norms involve the individual's perceptions of what is appropriate and inappropriate behavior at different ages, it is also possible to measure

Table 2.1   Consensus in a Middle-Class, Middle-Aged Sample Regarding Various Age-Related Characteristics

	Age Range Designated as Appropriate or Expected	Percent Who Concur	
		Men (N = 50)	Women (N = 43)
Best age for a man to marry	20-25	80	90
Best age for a woman to marry	19-24	85	90
When most people should become grandparents	45-50	84	79
Best age for most people to finish school and go to work	20-22	86	82
When most men should be settled on a career	24-26	74	64
When most men hold their top jobs	45-50	71	58
When most people should be ready to retire	60-65	83	86
A young man	18-22	84	83
A middle-aged man	40-50	86	75
An old man	65-75	75	57
A young woman	18-24	89	88
A middle-aged woman	40-50	87	77
An old woman	60-75	83	87
When a man has the most responsibilities	35-50	79	75
When a man accomplishes most	40-50	82	71
The prime of life for a man	35-50	86	80
When a woman has the most responsibilities	25-40	93	91
When a woman accomplishes most	30-45	94	92
A good-looking woman	20-35	92	82

Source: Neugarten et al. (1965), Table 1. Reprinted with permission from the *American Journal of Sociology*, copyright © 1965 by the University of Chicago.

the amount of *constraint* that age norms exert. For example: Is it appropriate for a woman to wear a two-piece bathing suit on the beach (a) when she is 18? (b) when she is 30? (c) when she is 45? (Neugarten et al., 1965). If the answer is "yes" to all three ages, there is no age constraint reflected. If the answer is "yes" to only one, then the degree of constraint is fairly high. In this manner, age constraint can be measured for individuals of different ages and also for the individual's perception of "others' views" (that is, their perception of the generalized other).

Neugarten et al. (1965) found that age constraint was fairly low for young people's personal opinions but increased for older respondents (Figure 2.3). At the same time, the perceptions of other people's opinions in terms of age constraint were rather high for young respondents but were somewhat lower for older respondents. Personal opinions and others' opinions nearly converged for the sample aged 65 +. These findings indicate that while young people feel "others" think age is important, they do not feel much age constraint themselves; however, the older respondents (age 65 +) feel that age is moderately important in determining appropriate behavior, and that "others" place about the same amount of importance on it as they do themselves. Note, however,

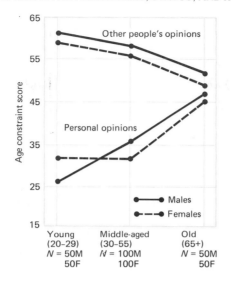

Figure 2.3
Perception of age constraints in adulthood, by age and sex. (Source: Neugarten et al., 1965, Figure 1. Reprinted with permission from the *American Journal of Sociology*, copyright © 1965 by the University of Chicago.)

that these data are from a cross-sectional study; thus, respondents born at the turn of the century may place more emphasis on age as an important variable for regulating behavior than respondents born in 1940, because of cultural changes rather than age-related factors. However, all age groups indicate that age determines to a considerable extent what behavior is appropriate, at least in the *eyes* of other people.

Age-Status Systems

In addition to socially defined age norms that indicate appropriate *behavior* on the basis of age, there is also an age-related status system in many cultures whereby one's social *position* and *status* is based at least partly on the person's age. That is, an age-status system in a society awards the rights, duties, and privileges to individuals differentially on the basis of age.

There is some degree of *age grading* in our social structure, so that status and power are awarded to individuals in part because of their age, but it is not nearly as tight a system as the age grading in elementary school where children pass from grade to grade as they age. However, some American Indian tribes, for example, placed their greatest status on the aged, especially the aged man, who was often their chief or medicine man. There is a certain logic to such a structure, since if a man were to live to an old age he had to be a successful warrior, strong and healthy, and adept at avoiding the various pitfalls that might have resulted in his earlier death. Other cultures, particularly Oriental societies, have fairly rigid age-status systems in which the aged are accorded high status. In our society, individuals seldom reach positions of power simply because they are aged. Even in the seniority system in Congress, both skill and age are required since there is the requirement not only for long service but also for continual re-election by the voters. However, skill alone does not automatically bring high status either, since "experience" is usually also required and, of course, accumulates with age. As a result, our age-status system tends to favor middle-aged persons.

Currently one of the serious problems in our society is the precarious economic and social position of many elderly, retired persons (see Chapter 9). Not only are they in positions of low social status, but also many are living in isolation and at subsistence levels of income. Thus, where there are age-status systems in the United States, they do not seem to reward advanced age after retirement. And, in general, age-status systems may be less important in our society than socioeconomic status that reflects the status of one's parents, one's education and occupation, and is manifested by one's style of life, power in the community, and geographic neighborhood in the city (cf. Coleman & Neugarten, 1971).

Age-Sex Roles

The concept of *role* is related to both the individual's social position and to the norms of the society. A role is the *behavior* that is expected from a person occupying a social position. The norms prescribe that expected role behavior. Since many social positions have role behaviors associated with them, the social position is often called a role. For example, the role of "mother" involves some very clear expectations and behaviors for the appropriate enactment of that role. It may be contrasted with the role of "wife" that she also plays or with the role of "business executive" that she may also play. In the symbolic interaction framework, the role is a *me* that the individual presents in a social interaction; it arises from taking the attitude of the other (or generalized other) toward one's own behavior. However, a *me* is not always a role; it may be any characteristic of the self that may be seen by others. A *me* may reveal a feeling such as "depressed" or "anxious," or it may be an attitude such as "honest" or "punctual"; but a role is always a *me*. One plays many roles during the day (that is, presents many *mes*), and it is the task of the *I* process to select and integrate these various *mes* into a sense of self.

Perhaps we play roles because it would be much too complicated to self-consciously work out moment-to-moment behavior without being able to rely on the partial scripts that accompany a role. Consider the chaos that would result if teachers, students, police officers, and doctors (and so on) forgot how to play their roles—how to teach, how to act in classes, and so on. Social interaction would become incredibly chaotic!

Individuals have a fair amount of latitude in how they ad-lib their roles, and we probably all play our roles in slightly idiosyncratic ways; but if one steps too far out of line, one feels some degree of social constraint. For example, a shopper in a large department store is playing the role of "customer"; he is greeted by a person playing the role of "salesclerk." As long as each of them plays his role, they can interact and complete the transaction quickly and easily. If the shopper changes his role, for example, by trying to sell a watch to the salesclerk, there is an abrupt shift and some interactional discomfort. Or if the shopper violates the expectations of his role, such as by offering to pay less for the item than the price marked, the salesclerk may give a response that means, "Get with it; that's not the way to play your role!" If the customer persists in playing his role incorrectly and, for example, pays the clerk $20 for a $30 pair of slacks and walks out of the store, he is likely to feel the social constraint of the store security guard.

Since roles involve norms, they also differ in their expectations at different ages; in addition, since roles are related to social position, they may begin, change, and end at certain ages. For example, at marriage there is a shift in role to that of husband or wife; at the birth of the first child there is a new role added, that of parent—mother or father. Such role change through the lifeline, in which new roles are added and old ones are dropped, makes it possible to view the life cycle in terms of the addition or change in roles. For example, when we discuss the family, we will examine the social timing for the adult as measured by role changes: unmarried, wife, mother, working mother, working grandmother, retired grandmother, and widow. Similarly, we may examine a man's life cycle in terms of his roles: student, married student, working father, working grandfather, retired grandfather, and widower. However, at the same time that individuals have one set of roles in the family they also have a number of other roles in their various activities and interactions. Thus, as roles shift they may change in a number of areas at once or change slowly over a longer period of time. Also, the range of roles may change with cultural changes such as the current phenomenon of women entering the work force today in much greater numbers than a century ago.

The Social Clock

The interaction of age norms, age constraints, age-status systems, and age-related roles produces a phenomenon that Neugarten (1968) called the *social clock*. This concept is sometimes mentioned by middle-aged people themselves as an internal sense of social timing that acts as a *prod* to speed up accomplishment of a goal, or as a *brake* to slow down one's progress through the social events of the lifeline. The sense of regulation comes from the self—from the internalized perception of social norms, expectations, and roles. These concepts act as timing cues that give individuals the idea that it is time to take that European trip before they are too old to enjoy it (or too old to think that they *should* take a long trip), or when it is time to go back to school to study painting "now that my children are on their own."

This internalized social clock is one of the major sources of timing in adulthood; that is, it regulates the sequential progression of an individual through the age-related milestones and events of the adult years. The norms and expectations of society (the generalized other) set off internal processes in the individual when he or she takes the attitude of the generalized other; these result in changes in behavior that are, then, age-related. Extending the analogy slightly, we say that there is a social "Big Ben" (the age norms), and we set our individual watches (internalized age norms) to Big Ben. Of course, some of our watches keep better time than others, so there is some variation in the timing of major milestones, but most of us have a reasonably good sense of "the right time" to marry, change jobs, or become a parent, and so on. One example of this social clock, here indicating that it is time to change jobs, is given by one of Neugarten's (1967) middle-aged respondents:

"I moved at age forty-five from a large corporation to a law firm. I got out at the last possible moment, because after forty-five it is too difficult to find the job you want. If you haven't made it by then, you had better make it fast, or you are stuck."

There is some evidence that the social clock is set slightly differently for persons from different social classes, for those of different ethnic and racial backgrounds, for persons who suffered economic deprivation during the Depression of the 1930s, and for men and women (Neugarten & Hagestad, 1976). For example, Olsen (1969) in a study of a representative sample of persons aged 50-70 in a midwestern city in the 1950s found that persons from higher socioeconomic classes experienced family-related events later than persons from lower social classes (Figure 2.4).

Neugarten and Hagestad (1976) also point out that *off-time* events—such as being widowed early in life, or a delay in occupational advancement—are particularly difficult, while *on-time* events are likely to be less stressful because one may anticipate and prepare for the event. Similarly, early marriages or being off-time in career advancement seem to have significant effects on many measures of satisfaction. However, there may also be events that are more satisfying if they are slightly off-time. For example, Nydegger (1973) found that "late" fathers were more comfortable and effective as fathers than either the "on-time" or "early" fathers. There may also be a kind of "idiosyncracy credit" given to persons who have performed according to the social clock in most areas of life. They are therefore allowed to vary from it in one or more areas, such as for middle-aged women who have raised a family and enroll in college or graduate programs (Neugarten & Hagestad, 1976).

The process by which these social norms, roles, expectations, and the social clock are learned and translated into behavior is the process of *socialization*, to which we turn our attention in the next section of this chapter.

SOCIALIZATION: LEARNING NORMS AND ROLES

Socialization is the process by which an individual learns to perform various social roles adequately; it is the process by which norms, values, and expectations are transmitted from one generation to the next. In the symbolic interaction framework, socialization involves the basic social process of taking the attitude of

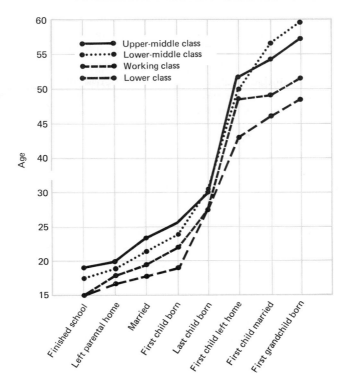

Figure 2.4

Median ages at which women of different socioeconomic classes reached successive events in the family cycle. Men showed similar socioeconomic class distinctions. (Source: Neugarten & Hagestad, 1976, Figure 1; from Olsen, 1969. Reprinted with permission.)

the other (or generalized other) toward oneself. In addition, it involves taking the attitude of the other toward the entire range of social objects. Much of this process, as well as the learning of the significant symbols required for the process to occur, undoubtedly occurs according to complex principles of learning theory such as the modification of behavior on the basis of the consequences of that behavior. However, because of the selective, innovative processes of the *I*, this socialization process is not a passive molding of an unformed, socially dangerous child but, instead, is a complementary fitting together of two active social processes—the individual and the social community—ideally maximizing the potential of both. That is, the socialization process is active and reciprocal so that both the *socializee* and the *socializing agent* are being socialized by each other in the process.

The Socialization Process

Until recently it was felt that socialization was primarily, if not exclusively, limited to childhood and early adolescence; so the idea that adults are also socialized by the persons with whom they interact is relatively new. However, the process of socialization does not differ much for children and for adults. It involves a relationship with a *significant other*. As these individuals interact, usually in an emotional relationship of some significance, they influence one another and provide feedback to one another through the symbolic interaction process. This feedback functions to build up a set of mutual expectations for each other's behavior. These mutual expectations contain the role prescriptions, the norms, and the values that the agent attempts to transmit. The agent, in turn, responds to the behavior and to the expectations of the socializee and may modify the expectations or provide corrective feedback to the socializee.

It may be that this interaction occurs whenever two people are interacting in a relationship with some emotional involvement; it is a broad, general view of the socialization process. However, it also pertains to such specific situations as those in which the socializing agent is informally conveying information or formally "teaching"; it pertains to the transmission of values and moral views, to ways of interacting with others, or to operating a piece of complicated machinery. That is, the degree of formality or informality varies and the content varies, but the relationship, the mutual influence, and the centrality of a significant relationship between the two interacting individuals does not vary.

However, as the individual develops from childhood into adulthood, certain parameters of the socialization process may change. For example, as children gain the cognitive capacity to think abstractly, to conceptualize situations that are not concretely present, and to take a more objective view of their own behavior, they also gain the cognitive ability to expand their set of significant others from people immediately present (parents, teachers, and peers) to people who are not now living or concretely present (historical figures, religious deities, or deceased parents and grandparents). This ability continues through adulthood so that individuals may base their central values and expectations for themselves on the remembered or imagined expectations of these not currently present significant others. Perhaps this ability plays a part, for example, in the often noted increase in religious fervor during adolescence.

In addition, the young adult has a wider range of social interactions than was true for the child, and this social world continues to broaden in adulthood. That is, the range of significant others who are physically present increases, and with it there is an increase in the range of individuals with whom one may choose to interact. Thus, there is greater freedom to select one's significant others—one's socializing agents—during adulthood than in childhood. However, allowing for the increased intellectual ability of adults and the different kinds of roles that adults are socializing themselves into, the process of socialization remains essentially unchanged from childhood.

Anticipatory Socialization and Resocialization

The general process of socialization may be subdivided into more specific types of socialization experience. Two of the most common types are anticipatory socialization and resocialization. *Anticipatory socialization* is the process of preparation for a change in role or status. It involves exploring the new norms and expectations that will be associated with the new role or status once the transition is made. It involves an element of practice and of trying out a new role before the actual shift takes place. Examples of this process include the college student choosing a career—imagining what it might be like, talking to persons in that career, and perhaps trying it out in a summer job—or a medical student in his first year who is given a "black bag," wears a white lab coat, and begins to play the role of "doctor" before he has his M.D. Later in life, a mother may return to school or begin preparing herself in other ways for returning to work several years before her children leave home, and she actually enters her field of special interest. Similarly, the father may begin exploring new interests and preparing for his retired status several years before it actually occurs. Or the family may begin reading different magazines and driving a different kind of car in preparation for the next promotion and a move to another neighborhood. In such cases there is a period of anticipation of the new roles or status and preliminary socialization into them before they are actually achieved.

Resocialization, in contrast, takes place when the role or status is actually begun. The amount of resocialization, or reorganization of one's expectations about oneself, depends on the amount of difference between the previous role and the new one. It may involve learning a new skill when one's job is replaced by a machine; or it may involve learning the role of grandparent when one's first grandchild is born. Adulthood involves a series of resocialization experiences, and many of the changes that occur during the adult years involve or reflect these experiences.

Socialization in Adulthood

Brim (1968) has suggested a number of situations in adulthood that typically lead to socialization experiences; we will discuss each of them.

Demands of Self or Others. From time to time individuals may feel that they are not living the kind of life they wish to live or not doing the kinds of things they wish to do; conversely, others may feel that about them. As a result they may change somewhat through informal socialization, or they may seek out a socialization experience to bring about the desired changes. For some people, this experience may be psychotherapy; for others, it may be a shift in reference group to bring about the desired change in roles and expectations (an example would be an executive who seeks out other people interested in new life styles and finally moves to a commune); for others, it may involve finding a new reference group (or spouse, perhaps) whose norms and expectations are compatible with their own so that they change relatively little. Insofar as there is change, however, socialization will be involved since there will be new norms, values, and expectations about oneself and about one's own behavior that one will learn. Even the changes that result from the individual's internal social clock (by which age norms exert constraint on a person to behave differently) lead one to learn the appropriate expectations for "people of that age." In general, individuals seek formal and informal socialization experiences when they feel that a change is in order.

Role or Status Change.   Social situations may change as a result of age-related changes, such as the shift in roles from "single" to "wife" to "mother." Or they may change from one's growing seniority on the job that brings shifts in role and status. In any case, there would be new expectations and norms to learn that would involve anticipatory socialization and resocialization; perhaps it would even involve a kind of radical resocialization if the shift is from, for example, "junkie" to "ex-addict" where there is a major shift in self-conception and a clear dichotomy between the previous role and the new role. One characteristic of role or status change is that the conflicts that result between the new role and previously held roles must be resolved; for example, the young husband may have some role conflict between his previous role of "swinging bachelor" and his present role of "husband" in his interactions with his unmarried friends. A second characteristic of such socialization is that the individuals will need some support in the new role, that is, someone (the socializing agents) to whom they can turn for encouragement and for help in working out their new role; for the young husband, these socializing agents would probably include his spouse, parents, and friends. Third, this process of socialization is likely to take place in informal ways; usually one's colleagues, neighbors, and relatives provide most of the socialization and do so subtly and informally. Only when there are distinct skills to be learned is the socialization formal, requiring education or reading.

Occupational Shift or Entry.   A frequent cause of resocialization is change in occupation or role in the occupation. A major change or even a promotion brings with it the necessity for developing new skills, for playing new roles, for forming new relationships, and for changing the level of aspiration. Thus, the man promoted from a machinist to a foreman has to develop some managerial skills, relate in different ways with the men in the shop and with the upper levels of management, and be more concerned with efficiency and productivity than with his skill on the machine (cf. Lieberman, 1956). Similarly, a woman who shifts from the role of housewife to novelist will find herself being socialized in many ways as she learns the role and norms that now apply for writing and publishing books; if she is very successful she may also have to learn the skills of appearing on TV interviews.

Changes in the Family.   During the course of the family cycle there are a number of role shifts that take place. In addition, there are mutual expectations that are set up by the husband and wife about each other's behavior; and the spouses function as very important socializing agents for one another. For example, the periods of courtship, engagement, and the first years of marriage involve a great deal of mutual socialization as the couple match their expectations with each other and reach working agreements on a great range of behaviors such as housework, sexual behavior, food preferences, entertainment, desire for children, brand of toothpaste, handling of finances, and so on. Then the birth of the first child brings a shift from previous roles of husband and wife to mother and father. This change not only brings about the socialization into their new roles as parents but also intensifies the mutual socialization for their ongoing relationship. The baby, of course, also has some "expectations"—in the form of the immediate and imperative needs—that influence the parents' expectations about their own behavior. As the children grow, they begin exerting an ever-increasing socializing influence on the parents. Although the parents may be the primary socializing agents for the children, the interaction is never only one way, and children's expectations ordinarily influence parents' expectations as well. Finally, as the children begin leaving home and the parents again resume a dyadic relationship, additional socialization may be needed to again match their expectations for one another. In addition, there may be some personality changes as well as biological changes that occur in the later years, so expected behaviors may change over time. Of course, divorce, wherever it may occur in the family cycle, brings with it a marked change in role and status. Again, there is socialization involved in learning to play the role of a divorcee; a new marriage brings another attempt at resocialization. Similarly, with the death of one's spouse there is a change of role and the need for some additional socialization to learn the norms and expectations for the role of widow or widower.

Geographic Mobility. Another socialization situation in adulthood may be brought about by physically moving from one community to another. This may result from a promotion and increase in status so that a new home is possible; or it may result from a promotion combined with a transfer. In the latter case, the shift in occupational role is combined with geographical transfer (often to preclude conflict with previous roles on the job). This brings the necessity for the wife and children to become resocialized into the new community; and it may be an abrupt shift in role and status for the wife if she is not also moving upward at about the same speed as her husband, and if she has not been able to anticipate the new role and status demands. A similar kind of situational change, but necessarily more intense, results from immigration. Frequently the socialization process resulting from this type of change continues up to the second or third generation, since the tendency is to decrease the disparity between the previous community and the present one by living in an ethnic community.

Downward Mobility. Finally, another change that brings about a need for adult socialization is a decline in status or in the number of roles. Although this is essentially the same process as upward mobility in terms of the demands for socialization, it is, unfortunately, a shift to a lower status. It is rather common for the aged to need to adjust to a lower standard of living after retirement (although this does not necessarily involve a loss of social status). Downward mobility may also occur in a period of national economic decline or as a result of an individual's emotional or social problems, such as alcoholism or mental illness. Accepting a lower status job because of overcompetition in one's field of training or because one was fired from a better job may also bring downward mobility. Similarly, divorce or widowhood may bring a decrease in income or in social status that leads to resocialization into the norms and expectations for the new position of widowhood or divorced adult. Again, the process of socialization is one aspect of the adjustment to such changed role and status demands.

ADULT DEVELOPMENT: A SOCIAL INTERACTION PERSPECTIVE

The study of adulthood and aging is relatively new and, as noted in the first chapter, there are few theoretical models of development during the adult years. Three of the central issues that need to be addressed in such a theoretical model are: the timing or regulation of adult development, the nature of experience as it influences adult development, and the process by which individuals change while they also remain relatively consistent over the many years of adulthood. While these issues do not encompass all of the theoretical issues that are important in the field of adult development, they are important issues that the social interaction perspective presented in this chapter can clarify.

Timing in Adult Development

Development during adulthood is not regulated primarily by time-dependent biological factors, as is early childhood development. Instead, it appears to be regulated by social processes so that the adult years follow a relatively regular developmental course for people in general. Three social processes are involved in regulating adult development and providing a marked degree of regularity and order to the sequence of adult life.

The first process is that in our society (and possibly in many others) we have an implicit notion that adult development should follow a *timetable* of events. This is a normative expectation that we use to organize our thinking about our own lives and about the lives of others. Age-norms, age-roles, and age-status systems as well as expectations about the order of life events all implicitly assume that most people follow a relatively orderly progression of events. Not only do we tend to share implicit timetables about family events (marriage, parenthood, grandparenthood, widowhood in that order) and occupational events (first job, second job, promotion, last chance to change jobs, reaching the peak, retirement), but we even have a timetable for death (the oldest die first). We, as members of society who share this expectation, tend to organize our own lives into these timetables. The timetables tend to be closely linked with age—in our own minds, and in social expectations. Thus, a self-made millionaire at age 30, a leader who dies in midlife, or a man in his seventies marrying and beginning a family all attract attention because they violate our shared sense of appropriate timetables. In this sense, adult development may be perceived as more regular and sequential for people in general than it actually is for an individual because we have the tendency to view it within the framework of socially defined timeta-bles. Other societies may have different timetables, or may view timetables in dif-fering ways, but our society views age as a very important timetable for human development.

The second process is the *social clock*. Not only do we tend to assume that timetables exist, but we pay attention to the social clock that chimes to remind us where we should be on our own timetable. Through the process of socialization we internalize the social clock and learn the "right time" to complete the events on the timetable. We know if we are "on time" or "off time," as Neugarten (1968) phrases it; if we are off-time, the social clock pushes us on faster, or slows us down, whichever is appropriate.

In addition to the general social expectation that development follows timeta-bles, and the social clock that links these timetables to individual lives, there is an individual sense of timing as well. We call this third social process individual *tim-ing events*. While adult development for people in general is regulated by the so-cial clock, an individual's development is timed by events that cause the person to modify the self in an age-related way. That is, age-related norms and roles as well as age-related events such as graduation, first job, parenthood, retirement, and death of one's spouse are significant timing factors for an individual only if they influence that individual's *self* in an age-related way.

Timing events may be triggered by the social clock, social norms, an age-re-lated shift in social roles, or by physical illness; but they may also occur in any moment of self-consciousness (in Mead's sense). The crucial characteristic of a timing event is that the individual's self is changed in an age-related way. It must be a self-conscious realization that one's *me* has changed in an age-related way. It may occur in a formal social event, such as retirement, or it may occur in an in-formal moment of self-conscious introspection, as in the example of one of Neu-garten's (1967) respondents who suddenly became aware that he was middle aged:

> "When I see a pretty girl on the stage or in the movies—we used to say 'a cute chick'—and when I realize, 'My God, she's about the age of my son', it's a real shock. It makes me realize that I'm middle-aged."

Similar timing events may be triggered by a son beating his father at tennis, by one's daughter entering medical school, by finding an old packet of "love letters" in the dusty attic, by a heart attack, by the death of a parent or co-worker, or by making the final payment on the mortgage. Each of these events—as well as shifts in roles and the social clock—may bring the self-conscious realization that one has changed in an age-related way.

Thus, development in adulthood is not timed in a uniform manner for all per-sons—as early childhood tends to be. Instead, adult development is timed by the interaction of external factors such as age norms and the social clock with inter-nal factors such as one's experience of oneself in a social environment in which age is a particularly salient characteristic. In this dynamic interaction, external factors such as retirement may jolt a person into a timing event; but also internal factors such as menopause or a man's sudden concern about occasional impotence may also bring on a timing event. In either case, the person's self is changed in an age-related way because the person has actively become self-conscious of the meaning of that event and related it to age.

It may also be noted that such events are not always timing events, because the individual may not interpret them in a self-conscious age-related way. A young man who is occasionally impotent does not suddenly think of himself as "growing old"; a young person who forgets to take a grocery list to the store does not seriously interpret this as a sign of "senility"; and a person who retires does not necessarily feel that this is a sign of being "old." Some of these events may be *milestones*, but not timing events—that is, they may be perceived by the person as an important turning point in their lives, but are not subjectively related to age or growing older. For example, moving from one house or one city to another may be a trivial event for some; it may be a milestone for others; and it may be a timing event for still others (such as an aged father who moves in with his children because he cannot care for himself any longer).

This discussion implies that we need to examine the individual's perception of the event or the change in self-perception in order to determine whether it represents a milestone, a timing event, or a nonevent. Although social age norms, age roles, and the social clock provide good clues to probable timing events in adulthood, the individual's perception of those events (the *I* experience of those events) is the crucial determinant of the meaning of an event for the person in this social interaction perspective.

The Meaning of Experience

It is obvious that as one grows older, one accumulates more and more "experience." The question for the study of adult development is what does this mean about the individual; furthermore, what is the nature of this "experience" that accumulates with age?

One of Neugarten's (1967) successful middle-aged business executives provided a vivid example of at least one kind of experience:

> "I know now exactly what I can do best, and how to make the best use of my time. . . . I know how to delegate authority, but also what decisions to make myself. . . . I know how to buffer myself from troublesome people . . . one well-placed telephone call will get me what I need. It takes time to learn how to cut through the red tape and how to get the organization to work for me. . . . All this is what makes the difference between me and a young man, and it's all this that gives me the advantage. . . ."

Certainly, this person has learned from past situations, has built up a network of contacts who can be helpful, and has kept track of whom to call and what to do for the ordinary kinds of problems that arise. But we wonder how relevant this "experience" is for this person outside the office—in family relationships, at a concert, or in dealing with close friends. Perhaps some of this "experience" generalizes to other situations; but it might also cause misperceptions, or ineptness, in other situations—such as intimate relationships.

The symbolic interaction perspective described earlier in this chapter suggests that there are at least three different kinds of experience. The first is *situation experience* where one gains a greater range of past situations from which one can draw possible responses for the present situation. In general, as individuals grow older they gain increased knowledge of what responses lead to which outcomes in a wide variety of situations. Much of this knowledge is reduced to automatic (nonself-conscious) habits, unless something unexpected arises. In that sense, experience consists of habituated reactions and memories of previous *I*s and previous *me*s; in most situations, one can call on such memories and habits to decide on the *me* to present in that situation. This kind of experience is learned through the process of socialization where one learns how to play the various roles in life and then learns to teach others. When something unexpected arises, one may become self-conscious or, in a more general way, take the attitude of the other in an attempt to straighten out the problem or interaction.

However, in situation experience it is important to distinguish between the *depth* of experience in a particular situation (such as running a business, relating to one's spouse, or skiing) and the *breadth* of experience across a variety of situations. Perhaps the business executive quoted above has considerable depth of experience in the business world, but relatively little breadth of experience in other areas of life. Or he may have equally deep experience in a broad range of situations or interests (such as tennis, art collecting, and love making). Thus, if we are to look at situation experience as a measure of development in adulthood, we need to focus on both the deepening and the broadening of experience over time.

A second kind of experience suggested by the symbolic interaction approach is *interaction experience*. As one interacts with a widening range of different persons over the years, one develops a greater amount of experience in interacting with a variety of other people. For example, a business executive may "know" that the best way for him to deal with subordinates is to be firm and distant, because in the past his employers were always firm and distant (the effect of socialization), and once when he was warm and friendly, he almost lost control of the office and was nearly fired (the effect of interaction experience). He may also "know" that the best *me* to present to his wife is the supportive, understanding, and not-too-dominant side of himself (because "she needs to feel important and loved"); he discovered this when she found out he was having an affair and since then he has been very careful to meet her needs because he does "need" her too. He also has habituated *me*s that he presents (for better or worse) to his children, his golf partners, his parents, and his in-laws. These roles (*me*s) have been built up over time and generally work fairly well. He knows what to expect from the others in the interaction and they know what to expect from him. If he finds that they do not work, he can draw on his interaction experience to find another role (*me*) to try, or to take the attitude of the other person to develop a more appropriate response. In turn, he will learn from this experience and will have this new style of responding to use in future interactions. Thus, in general, individuals become increasingly adept at taking the attitude of the other, at interpreting the significant symbols (words and gestures) in social interactions, and also in developing a repertoire of roles and styles of responding in interactions from which they can draw as they experience the wide variety of social interactions that characterize adulthood. In some cases, older adults may rely on styles of interacting that have proven to be effective in earlier years and thus may appear to be somewhat "set in their ways." However, this does not mean they cannot develop new styles of interacting when the situation calls for it, since they have had experience in creating new patterns of interacting in the past. Often, for all of us, familiar responses tend to be used first because they have worked in the past and because taking the attitude of other persons requires a considerable amount of effort. In addition, while interaction experience typically increases with age, it is obvious that some persons experience a more varied range of interactions than others. Thus, the response repertoires of some older persons will be much wider than others.

The third kind of experience suggested by this approach is *self experience*. That is, individuals become increasingly adept at seeing themselves from the point of view of the other and at integrating this awareness in the present moment with the memories of this awareness in past situations; thus, they develop greater self-conscious experience of themselves over time. They discover their inner reactions to a variety of persons and situations, so that self experience increases as situation experience expands. Likewise, their self experience grows as their interaction experience increases. They also engage in introspection (self-consciousness) from time to time so that this component of their self experience also becomes greater over time. This is not necessarily to imply that all older persons would have greater insight into themselves, or greater introspective abilites than a young person, but the older person would clearly have the potential to benefit from the greater range of experiences in a larger number of situations in comparison with a young person. In addition, there is some evidence that the middle years of adulthood involve an emphasis on self experience. For example, concluding her report on "The Awareness of Middle Age," Neugarten (1967) states:

> In pondering the data on these men and women, we have been impressed with the central importance of what might be called the executive processes of personality in middle age: self-awareness, selectivity, manipulation and control of the environment, mastery, competence, the wide array of cognitive strategies.
>
> We are impressed, too, with reflection as a striking characteristic of the mental life of middle-aged persons: the stock-taking, the heightened intro-

spection, and above all, the structuring and restructuring of experience—
that is, the conscious processing of new information in the light of what one
has already learned; and turning one's proficiency to the achievement of
desired ends.

In this description of the complex functioning of these economically successful
middle-aged men and women, we see the self—*I* and *me*—and self-consciousness very much involved in these "executive processes of personality" and in the
process of "reflection" as well. Certainly, the self's ability to profit from experience is also at work.

In summary, situation experience, interaction experience, and self experience
reflect three differing, but interrelated, components of experience during adulthood. The processes of socialization, changes in behavior as a result of age roles
and age norms, timing events, and the effects of the social clock, all these combine with personal interactions in a variety of situations to produce these differing
kinds of experience.

Change and Consistency in Adulthood

The issue of change and consistency in adulthood is a complex matter. On one
level, we recognize that an individual we have not seen for several years is somewhat different (in appearance, in the self and, perhaps, in personality) from
when we last saw him; yet he is also rather similar to our memories of him, and
we usually have little difficulty in resuming an old friendship and catching up on
the changes that have taken place. On another level, we note that some of the
changes we see in him may be the result of actual changes in him, but some of
them may be the result of changes in us. That is, we may have changed so that
our *I* notes and responds to different aspects of his *self* (as when we see something new in a painting or film or play we have not seen for years, but which has
remained unchanged). On yet another level, it may be that our friend is present-
ing a different set of *mes* to us than he did before—*mes* that were present in the
past but were never revealed to us.

Nonetheless, we recognize that our friend has had several years of *experience*,
and he has probably had some *timing events* since we last saw him. He may
have married, published several books, and become a highly respected judge in
the intervening years. Each of these events involves changes in roles, socialization, and changes in the self. Thus, not only will we see him differently than we
did years ago, but he will also see himself as different than he was when we last
knew him. However, even with all this change, we would also expect a reasonable amount of consistency as well. That is, we would recognize characteristics
about him that are quite similar to the memory we have of him years ago. How
do we explain these interrelated processes of change and consistency?

We might begin to explore that question by considering the three interacting
spheres in which change and consistency take place. One of these is the external
environment. A change in one's social or physical environment is likely to bring

some degree of change in oneself; and conversely, a relatively consistent environment is likely to promote consistency. For example, as long as one lives in the same neighborhood, goes to the same job each day, interacts with the same friends, and so on, one is not likely to feel much push toward change from that relatively consistent environment. In contrast, moving to a new city, developing a new set of friends, or coping with a natural disaster (such as a flood or tornado) that alters one's own physical environment is likely to push one to change—in large or small ways. Reacting to these changes in one's social and physical environment will involve the processes of socialization and resocialization. Thus, within a fairly consistent environment, socialization will tend to maintain the relative consistency of an individual over time; in a relatively new environment, socialization will bring some degree of change to an individual. Of course, there is always some degree of change within any environment, no matter how stable, and some degree of consistency, no matter how different the environment may be.

A second sphere in which change and consistency occurs is in interactions between oneself and others: roles change; the social clock brings new norms into play for individuals as they grow older; socialization, anticipatory socialization, and resocialization also bring change as individuals interact with different people over time, or as patterns of interactions evolve as one grows older and one's roles change. In the earlier example, the man changed as he became a husband, finished law school, and became a judge—in large or small ways. At the same time, however, not all roles change, many patterns of interaction do not change very much over time, and norms that are not age-related do not change as one grows older unless there is a change in society. Again, the pattern is one of both change and consistency, so that social interactions sometimes tend to push the individual to change and sometimes not to change; usually this involves some change and some consistency at the same time.

The third sphere of change and consistency is the self. Obviously, all three of these spheres interact so completely that it is a bit arbitrary to separate them here. Yet, changes in a person's experiencing (*I*) or in the social self (*me*) may also bring change to the individual, even when the external environment and pattern of social interactions is fairly consistent. For example, one might begin meditating or running that might lead to a new experience of oneself, or to a different view of oneself. For example, after running for several months on a regular basis, one might begin to experience greater self-condfidence, heightened energy, and a new contact with and appreciation of one's physical body. Similarly, a major change in weight or a physical illness may cause one to experience oneself differently (*I*) or to view oneself differently (*me*), or both. At the same time, however, one's experience of oneself is usually fairly consistent over time. One might have a new experience, but this usually affects only a small part of one's total experiencing; one's perception of an aspect of the self might change, but most of the rest of it remains fairly stable over time. Once again, the pattern is one of simultaneous change and consistency over time. One middle-aged woman in Neugarten's (1967) study described a change she found in middle age—but she also implies that she only came to recognize the abilities that were there all along:

"I discovered these last few years that I was old enough to admit to myself the things I could do well and to start doing them. I didn't think like this before. . . . It's a great new feeling. . . ."

Another man in the same study described his change in a way that emphasized the consistency even more:

"I know what will work in most situations, and what will not. I am well beyond the trial and error stage of youth. I now have a set of guidelines. . . . And I am practised. . . ."

In an important sense, these three spheres of change and consistency are integrated by the self processes. Just as *I* and *me* are simultaneous aspects of the self, so are change and consistency simultaneous processes of the self. Change in the self occurs when the situation prompts *I* to select a new *me* that is then integrated into the range of *me*s that make up the social self; or when *I* selects a new response in an old situation and that new *me* is integrated into the self; or when one self-consciously modifies the self as in the examples of timing events we discussed earlier. Situation experience, interaction experience, and self experience may also bring change to the self. Similarly, socialization and adaptation to changed environmental conditions bring change to the self. And *I* is a continual source of potential change, since one's experience is always somewhat unpredictable and a source of novelty within the self.

Consistency in the self results from one's memory of past experiences and past behaviors so that one's present *me*s are usually fairly consistent with past *me*s, for example, in one's behavior, vocabulary, and gestures. Some of these may be habitual patterns that work efficiently in social situations most of the time. Because social interactions frequently depend on people behaving fairly consistently over time, there is a tendency to perceive oneself as relatively consistent and to perceive others as relatively consistent, even when this may not be entirely the case. Also, there is a tendency for persons to select social situations that are relatively consistent with past situations, or to perceive the present situation as more consistent than it may actually be. In that sense, consistency of the self results partly from our tendency to expect consistency—in ourselves, in others, and in social situations. Only when change is fairly dramatic is it seen as important—otherwise it tends to be shrugged off much of the time. In a similar way, one's experience of oneself tends to emphasize consistency, both over time and across situations. For example, conflict between roles such as "lawyer" and "mother" may be uncomfortable and one would tend to integrate those two *me*s into one's conception or experience of oneself so that the conflict is minimized and the sense of consistency across those roles is maximized. While a major change in the self may bring a period of some distress, ususally the person finds some way to reinterpret the self so that the experience of conflict is reduced. In some cases, this simply involves time to reintegrate one's sense of self; in other cases, it may require outside help, as in psychotherapy, to regain a sense of oneself as a relatively coherent, although evolving, person within a relatively consistent social and physical environment.

In the next chapter we will focus on these processes of consistency and change during the early and middle years of adulthood. We will see that while consistency and change are always present, there are some periods of life that seem to involve greater change than others. Of course, traumatic events may bring change for a particular individual at any point in life. But, for all of us, the simultaneous processes of change and consistency within a social environment, which is also simultaneously changing and remaining consistent, is the essence of adulthood.

CHAPTER SUMMARY

1. Individuals change over time in many respects; yet they also remain relatively consistent in other respects. These simultaneous processes of change and consistency are brought about by the interaction of social, psychological, and biological factors.

2. George Herbert Mead conceptualized the *self* as consisting of two interacting aspects, *I* and *me*. *I* is the moment-by-moment awareness of one's experiences, feelings, and thoughts; it is completely subjective or private. The *me* is that aspect of the self others may see or experience when interacting with a person; in that sense it is objective and public. The *me* is also made up of all those characteristics one sees in oneself. Thus, the self is made up of the experiencing aspect (*I*), the aspect that can be described to or seen by others (*me*), and the continual interaction of *I* and *me*.

3. According to Mead, the self is not fully present at birth, but develops during childhood through social interaction, through the use of significant symbols (language and gestures that communicate the same meaning to both persons in the interaction), and by taking the attitude of the other toward oneself (seeing oneself from the point of view of the other person). In adulthood the self is very complex, possessing the ability to take the attitude of a diverse range of other people, as well as to be self-conscious (that is, to reflect on oneself) and to use one's mental powers for the varied patterns of social interactions in which adults engage.

4. Social norms, positions, roles, and statuses are frequently different for persons of differing ages. The "social clock" is the term Neugarten used to describe the influence of these social realities; it acts as a "prod" to speed up or as a "brake" to slow down an individual's development and thus acts to time or regulate development during adulthood.

5. Socialization is the process by which an individual learns to perform various social roles adequately; it involves learning the norms, values, and expectations of society. In the symbolic interaction framework, it is seen as an active process in which all participants influence each other—not as a kind of programming of a passive individual. Socialization and its two main forms in adulthood—anticipatory socialization and resocialization—continue throughout an individual's life. A variety of different situations are likely to bring about socialization during the adult years.

6. While the social clock times development for adults in general, individual lives are influenced by timing events that may be triggered by the social clock, may be personal age-related events, or may result from a self-conscious realization that one has changed in an age-related way.

7. Experience accumulates with age, but to understand the importance of experience it is useful to distinguish among experience with situations, interaction experience with other people, and self experience. An older person may have greater experience in any or all of these areas than younger persons.

8. Development consists of the simultaneous processes of change and consistency. Stable situations, memory, well-rehearsed habitual behavior, and consistent patterns of interaction tend to emphasize consistency over time. Changes in any of these areas, change in the self, and the *I* (a constant potential source of novelty in one's perception of oneself and others) may each bring change. The dynamic interplay between change and consistency is a central characteristic of development during adulthood.

REFERENCES

Brim, Orville G., Jr. 1968. Adult Socialization. In John A. Clausen (Ed.), *Socialization and Society*. Boston: Little, Brown.

Coleman, Richard P., & Neugarten, Bernice L. 1971. *Social Status in the City*. San Francisco: Jossey-Bass.

Cooley, Charles H. 1911. *Social Organization*. New York: Scribner's.

Gendlin, Eugene T. 1964. A Theory of Personality Change. In Phillip Worchel & Donn Byrne (Eds.), *Personality Change*. New York: Wiley.

Harris, Sidney J. 1965. Strictly Personal. *Chicago Daily News*, May 11, 1965.

James, William. 1892. *Psychology*. New York: Holt

Lieberman, Seymour. 1956. The Effects of Changes in Roles on the Attitudes of Role Occupants. *Human Relations*, 9(4), 385-402.

Mead, George Herbert. 1934. Mind, Self, and Society. In Anselm Strauss (Ed.), *George Herbert Mead: On Social Psychology*. Chicago: University of Chicago Press, 1964. (Originally published in: *Mind, Self, and Society*. Charles W. Morris, Ed.)

Neugarten, Bernice L. 1967.   The Awareness of Middle Age. In Bernice L. Neugarten (Ed.), *Middle Age and Aging*. Chicago: University of Chicago Press, 1968. (Originally published in: *Middle Age*. Roger Owen, Ed. London: British Broadcasting Corporation).

Neugarten, Bernice L. 1968.   Adult Personality: Toward a Psychology of the Life Cycle. In Bernice L. Neugarten (Ed.), *Middle Age and Aging*. Chicago: University of Chicago Press.

Neugarten, Bernice L., & Hagestad, Gunhild O. 1976.   Age and the Life Course. In Robert H. Binstock & Ethel Shanas (Eds.), *Handbook of Aging and the Social Sciences*. New York: Van Nostrand Reinhold.

Neugarten, Bernice L.; Moore, Joan W.; & Lowe, John C. 1965.   Age Norms, Age Constraints, and Adult Socialization. *American Journal of Sociology, 70*(6), 710-717.

Nydegger, Corinne N. 1973.   Late and Early Fathers. Paper presented at the meeting of the Gerontological Society, Miami Beach, November 1973.

Olsen, Kenneth M. 1969.   Social Class and Age-Group Differences in the Timing of Family Status Changes: A Study of Age-Norms in American Society. Unpublished doctoral dissertation, University of Chicago. (Cited in Neugarten & Hagestad, 1976.)

Strauss, Anselm (Ed.). **1964.**   *George Herbert Mead: On Social Psychology*. Chicago: University of Chicago Press.

TRANSITIONS IN ADULT DEVELOPMENT:
early to middle adulthood

Like the lobster or soft-shelled crab, humans seem sometimes to outgrow their "shells" and become somewhat more vulnerable as they move from one phase of life into another. This process may be as common as moving from childhood into adolescence and from adolescence into full adulthood, or it may be as traumatic as a divorce or coping with a serious illness. Marriage, parenthood, children leaving home, changing jobs, moving to a new city, restructuring one's lifestyle, or reordering one's goals in life may all involve this kind of transition. Some of these transitions may be positive changes, but others may involve negative changes; some may be joyous, while others are painful. And some may happen as naturally as graduating from high school, while others may tax one's ability to adapt to major unexpected changes.

In an important sense, the study of adult development involves the study of transitions from one pattern of life to another pattern. The difference between the two patterns may be major or relatively minor; and the transition may involve some degree of emotional crisis, but it does not necessarily involve emotional upset or distress. Essentially, the transition is from one life pattern that no longer "fits" into one that is new and different, in either large or small ways. Thus, the study of transitions focuses on the process of change in adult development. Of course, as discussed in the last chapter, there is always continuity along with the change, but the study of transitions calls our attention to the patterns of change during adulthood.

This chapter will focus first on the nature of these transitions in adult development and then will discuss the recent research on the transitions during early and middle adulthood. This chapter is an overview of the first third of adult development; the remaining two-thirds—from midlife to retirement, and the retirement years—will be discussed in detail in later chapters.

TRANSITIONS IN THE LIFE CYCLE

An exciting new area of research in human development is the study of transitions throughout the life cycle. In the first two chapters we noted that human development consists of the simultaneous processes of change and continuity—from birth through childhood, adolescence, young and middle adulthood, the later years, and old age. Now we will examine this process of change and continuity by focusing on the nature of the transitions from one period of development into the next. Some of these transitions appear to follow a sequential pattern, so that they provide a kind of developmental timetable through the adult years. Other transitions may represent major milestones or turning points in an individual's life. Thus, the study of transitions is providing a great deal of new information about the nature and pattern of adult development. While this research has only begun to reveal the diversity of transitions during adulthood, this focus on periods of change from one life pattern to another offers an important perspective on the nature of change and continuity in adulthood.

Normative and Idiosyncratic Transitions

Two differing types of transitions may be distinguished from one another. The first are *normative* transitions—those changes that are expected according to the social norms for individuals at particular times of their lives (Lowenthal, Thurnher, & Chiriboga, 1975). They include such events as graduation from high school, marriage, grandparenthood, and retirement. Most people in our society expect these events to occur and, as described in Chapter 2, have clear expectations about the age at which they should occur based on their internalized sense of the social clock. The second type of transitions may be termed *idiosyncratic* transitions. In contrast to normative transitions, idiosyncratic transitions are those changes in life patterns that are unique to a particular individual. They are not affected by age norms because there are no social expectations about when these idiosyncratic transitions should occur; in addition, it is not expected that most people will experience any particular idiosyncratic transition. For example, divorce, death of a child, major illness, economic setback, or winning a lottery may bring a major transition to those individuals who are affected, but they may occur at any age and are not expected to occur to everyone, as is the case for normative transitions.

Since normative expectations are usually anticipated, it may be that the idiosyncratic transitions have more impact on individuals because they are unexpected and somewhat unique (Fiske, 1978). Chiriboga (1978) has been studying divorce as an idiosyncratic transition and has found that it brings a major period of upset and reorganization to individuals during the period between the time the divorce papers are filed and the time the divorce becomes final. In contrast, Fiske's study of normative transitions—such as the last child leaving the parents' home or retirement—has found that these transitions are so clearly anticipated by the respondent that they appear to have relatively little impact (Fiske, 1978).

Of course, some major transitions may lie between these two extremes—such as early retirement or remarriage after divorce; these are neither wholly idiosyncratic, nor fully normative. It might be expected that they would be less unsettling than idiosyncratic transitions, but somewhat less aided by social support than normative transitions. In general, however, the study of transitions, or milestones, in an individual's life may prove to be a powerful approach to discovering the patterns of continuity and change in a person's life. We would speculate that those major transitions that are more idiosyncratic than normative would be especially influential in an individual's life; and that those transitions that are normative would be most useful for revealing the general pattern of development for groups of individuals, but less useful for understanding the pattern of a particular individual's life.

Since normative transitions are part of the social timetable for human development and are internalized by individuals through the social clock (Neugarten, 1968; Neugarten & Hagestad, 1976), they serve as one of the primary timing mechanisms of adult development, as we discussed in Chapter 2. In a paper first published in 1970, Neugarten (1977) summarizes the role of these events:

> The normal expectable life events do not themselves constitute crises, nor are they trauma producing. The end of formal schooling, leaving the parents' home, marriage, parenthood, occupational achievement, one's own children growing up and leaving, menopause, grandparenthood, retirement—in our society, these are the normal turning points, the markers or the punctuation marks along the life cycle. They call forth changes in self-concept and in sense of identity, they mark the incorporation of new social roles, and accordingly they are the precipitants of new adaptations. But in themselves they are not, for the vast group of normal persons, traumatic events or crises that trigger mental illness or destroy the continuity of the self [p. 40].

Neugarten also points out that it is not only these major life events that serve as normative transitions. For example, she found that middle-aged people pay greater attention to their development within their various involvements and concerns—especially physical health, family, and career changes—than they do to chronological age for "clocking" themselves. Thus, chronological age itself tends to be replaced by cues from the social clock as the major determinant of one's developmental issues and concerns during the middle years. We can observe this in Neugarten's studies; respondents often would have to stop and think before they could state their exact age: "Let's see . . . 51? No, 52. Yes, 52 is right" (ibid., p. 39). This suggests that transitions in the various life contexts are a major source of developmental timing in adulthood. In addition, her studies found that the respondents also tended to estimate how much time they had left, at least covertly, as they examined their position in their various life contexts: "Now I keep thinking, will I have time enough to finish off some of the things I want to do?" (ibid.). Implicit in this shift in time perspective to the amount of time left is a growing acknowledgment that death is, at least, a real possibility for oneself—if not yet accepted as a personal certainty from which one cannot escape. She finds that a "rehearsal for widowhood" begins among women and that men tend to emphasize "sponsoring" relationships with their children and younger associates during this midlife period, with an eye toward "the creation of social heirs."

From this perspective it seems that not only the major transitions but also the more subtle ones—such as changes in physical health, promotions and other signs of progression in the career, and minor family events, for example, a daughter's first date—combine to provide a constant series of cues about where one is along the socially defined timetable of normative transitions. Later in this chapter we will discuss the recent research on the stages of adult development. There we will see how precisely these age-related normative transitions seem to regulate development. Not only do people who share a common social environment tend to share similar patterns of transitions and development during adulthood, but also they tend to enter and leave those transitional periods at about the same chronological age. Thus, the "ages and stages" of adulthood tend to confirm the importance of normative transitions for regulating adult development; they also emphasize the sensitivity and precision with which the social clock appears to function.

Internal and External Causes of Transitions

A second dimension along which transitions differ is whether the changes are brought about primarily by external events—such as the birth of grandchildren or a promotion on the job—or whether they are caused primarily by internal forces—such as puberty, menopause, or a growing dissatisfaction with one's career or life-style. Most transitions are probably a mixture of these two types, but theories about the nature of transitions tend to emphasize either one or the other. For example, the theories of Erikson and Jung described in Chapter 1 focus on changes in adult development that primarily result from internal factors. Thus, the shift from the issue of Identity versus Identity Confusion to the issue of Intimacy versus Isolation in the Erikson scheme is essentially an internally motivated change. In contrast, Neugarten's concept of the social clock as a major factor timing adult development emphasizes external social norms as the primary cause of transitions. However, even social norms are internalized, and Erikson's eight ages of life involve social interactions. Nonetheless, the distinction is based on the relative importance given to some kind of inner scheme of development in contrast to the significance of external factors for determining an individual's developmental progression.

The internally determined pattern of adult development may be represented by Levinson's (1978) study of development in early and middle adulthood, which we will discuss in detail later in this chapter. He sees adult development as consisting of a series of stable periods lasting six to eight years alternating with transitional periods lasting four or five years. During the transitional period, the person reappraises the life structure that had been built up during the preceding stable period and prepares for the next stable period. Although the transition may be set off by an external event, Levinson's perspective emphasizes the internal factors in completing the transition; that is, it does not end "when a particular event occurs or when a sequence is completed in one aspect of life. It ends when the tasks of questioning and exploring have lost their urgency, when a man makes his crucial commitments and is ready to start on the tasks of building, living within and enhancing a new life structure" (Levinson, 1978, p. 52). Similarly, transitions may both begin and end because of internal factors. "A period begins when its major tasks become predominant in a man's life. A period ends when its tasks lose their primacy and new tasks emerge to initiate a new period" (ibid., p. 53). In his concluding chapter, he speculates about the universal nature of this developmental progression:

> This sequence of eras and periods exists in all societies, throughout the human species, at the present stage in human evolution. The eras and periods are grounded in the nature of man as a biological, psychological and social organism, and in the nature of society as a complex enterprise extending over many generations. They represent the life cycle of the species. Individuals go through the periods in infinitely varied ways, but the periods themselves are universal. These eras and periods have governed human development for the past five or ten thousand years—since the beginning of more complex, stable societies [ibid., p. 322].

Thus, his assumptions about the nature of development clearly emphasize internal factors and parallel in many ways the perspective of development proposed by Erikson (cf. Levinson, 1978, p. 323).

In contrast, Neugarten's view of adult development emphasizes the individual's internalization of social norms and the adaptation to external social processes (Neugarten & Hagestad, 1976). While she does not see the individual as a passive responder to external events, she does not see any inner developmental scheme that has regulated human development for thousands of years. Her perspective is an interactive one, similar to our discussion in Chapter 2, in which the interaction between the individual and social processes regulates development.

> Because individuals live in contact with persons of all ages, they learn what to anticipate. There is a never-ending process of socialization by which the child learns what facets of his childhood behavior he must shed as he moves into adolescence; the adolescent learns what is expected of him as he moves from school to job to marriage to parenthood; and the middle-aged learn approved ways of growing old. Thus the social ordering of age-statuses and age-appropriate behavior will continue to provide a large measure of predictability.
>
> There are certain other regularities of the life cycle which may be said to arise more from within the individual than from without. To draw a dichotomy between "inner" and "outer" is, of course, merely a heuristic device, given a transactional view of personality. As the result of accumulative adaptations to both biological and social events, there is a continuously changing basis within the individual for perceiving and responding to new events in the outer world. It is in this sense that orderly and predictable changes occur within the personality as well as in the social environment [Neugarten, 1977, p. 37].

While we currently lack adequate data to determine which of these perspectives on adult development is more accurate—or whether neither is wholly adequate—I find both approaches to be very attractive. The emphasis on internal factors is fascinating because it implies that there is a regular pattern of human development that may be found for the adult years as has been discovered for the childhood years. However, before we can accept the evidence for this view, it needs to be examined in widely differing cultures, and Levinson's data are based only on middle-aged American men. In Chapter 8, we will discuss cross-cultural evidence of a personality change that does seem to occur between middle and late life among men and women in widely differing cultures (Gutmann, 1977); however, this personality change occurs later in life and is much less specific than the eras and periods that Levinson describes.

Yet, I would reject the extreme view that adult development has no structure other than the one imposed by external events and social norms, because there are, at least, biological factors in adult development that set limits to the range of variation that is possible; also there may well be psychological and endocrinological factors that influence adult development. However, Neugarten's interactive view seems to be the most reasonable perspective at the present time. Not only does it allow the possibility that there may be some inner factors that are involved in spite of its emphasis on the effects of socially normative influences, but also it emphasizes the interaction of the individual with the social environment—a perspective that is central to my own thinking. Thus, on balance, I tend to view the transitions of early and middle adulthood as normative transitions that are caused primarily by external factors. And I will argue that the very fact that they occur in such a close age-stage sequence is validation of the subtle and important influence of age norms and the social clock for persons from similar social environments.

Transitions and Crises

At the beginning of this chapter we noted that transitions need not involve emotional upset or crisis. However, Levinson's study and the reports of adult development by popular writers have emphasized the extent of emotional crisis involved in the various transitions. For example, Levinson noted that 62 percent of his respondents experienced a "moderate or severe crisis" during the period he called the "Age Thirty Transition," while only 18 percent had a smooth transition during that period (Levinson, 1978, p. 87). Similarly, about 80 percent of his respondents experienced "tumultuous struggles within the self and with the external world" during the period he called the "Mid-life Transition" (ibid., p. 199). Sheehy (1976) also called attention to the crises of adult development in her book.

In contrast, Neugarten's (1977) report on her studies indicates that normative transitions that are expected to occur do not bring emotional crises for most people. In her view it is the unexpected change that is more likely to cause a crisis. Based on her concept of the social clock, she notes that those events that occur *off-time*—either too early or too late according to social norms—are those that bring a crisis. Events or transitions that occur *on-time* according to the social age norms are much less likely to involve emotional upset.

> In summary, then, there are two distinctions worth making: first, that it is the unanticipated life event, not the anticipated—divorce, not widowhood in old age; death of a child, not death of a parent—which is likely to represent the traumatic event. Moreover, major stresses are caused by events that upset the sequence and rhythm of the life cycle—as when death of a parent comes in childhood rather than in middle age; when marriage does not come at its desired or appropriate time; when the birth of a child is too early or too late; when occupational achievement is delayed; when the empty nest, grandparenthood, retirement, major illness, or widowhood occur *off-time*. In this sense, then, a psychology of the life cycle is not a psychology of crisis behavior so much as it is a psychology of timing [Neugarten, 1977, p. 45].

These two perspectives are clearly in conflict with each other. To some degree it appears that the assumption of internal causes for transitions has led to a greater emphasis on transitions as crises, while the assumption about externally caused transitions has led to the finding that they may be upsetting if they are idiosyncratic (such as divorce, leaving a job, or a major change in life-style), or if they are off-time; but if they are normative transitions and occur on-time, they are not likely to produce marked crises. Part of the explanation for this difference is that the perspective that sees internal causes for transitions tends to include the idiosyncratic transitions (that are clearly likely to produce crises) as frequent manifestations of normal developmental turmoil during each transitional period. This suggests that these idiosyncratic transitions tend to occur during periods of internally caused developmental transitions—that divorce, for example, would tend to occur during the Age 30 Transition or the Midlife Transition and thereby add to the amount of crisis during the transition. From the perspective of transitions caused by external factors, there would be no link between normative and idiosyncratic transitions unless there were norms about the "right age" to get divorced or to have a midlife crisis.

Clearly it is not possible to draw any firm conclusions about the link between transitions and crises until more research has been completed on the nature and causes of crises during the life span. Such research will need to examine developmental patterns of men and women in various social and ethnic groups in our society as well as in other cultures. We may recall that early research on adolescence viewed this time as a period of "storm and stress"; many believed this to be universal until Margaret Mead (1928) reported on the smooth transition from childhood to adulthood among the Samoans in the South Sea Islands. More recent research has found that only a minority of adolescents in the United States actually experience a period of crisis, and when it occurs it reflects the adolescent's personality rather than a period of crisis that is inherent in the human life cycle (Conger, 1977; Offer & Offer, 1975). It seems likely that similar conclusions will eventually be drawn about the crises during early and middle adulthood. As we will discuss in Chapter 6, retirement—often thought to be a major crisis in life—does not bring emotional upset and inner turmoil for the vast majority of persons. Similarly, the research noted earlier by Fiske and her colleagues indicated that blue-collar men and women who were interviewed when they were about to undergo a normative transition—high school seniors, newlyweds, middle-aged parents whose children were nearing the age to leave home, and preretirees—and interviewed again five years later when most had completed the transition had not experienced emotional crises as a result of these events. In many cases, the transitions were not even discussed until the interviewer asked about them. Instead, changes that were unexpected and those that were idiosyncratic were more likely to bring an emotional crisis (Fiske, 1978; cf. Lowenthal, et al., 1975).

Let us take a closer look at the research on these transitions during early and middle adulthood. In the concluding section of this chapter, we will return to this question of the link between transitions and crises.

DEVELOPMENTAL PERIODS OF EARLY ADULTHOOD

Until recently, development from young adulthood to middle age had been an uncharted area of the life span. Although considerable research had been reported on development in childhood, adolescence, and old age, the period from early adulthood to middle age had been essentially neglected by social science researchers. This was a little curious, since most researchers were, themselves, in that period of the life cycle. Then suddenly, between 1976 and 1978 at least four books were published reporting studies of this newly discovered period! Not surprisingly, at least one of these books was extremely popular since many people are curious about the two major questions the book discussed: What lies ahead for me in my development? and Is what's happening to me normal? While, of course, no book can answer the first question precisely for any individual, these studies have provided a great deal of new understanding about the transitions, issues, and challenges that many men and women seem to be living through, at least during this period of history in the United States.

One of the four studies was longitudinal: George Vaillant (1977) reported on the developmental progression of a group of 94 male graduates from an elite eastern university in the United States. Each man began the study during college (in 1942-1944) and was studied periodically over the years; the average age of the men was 47 at the latest round of interviews. The other three studies were cross-sectional: Roger Gould (1972, 1978) based his reports on three samples: 524 men and women between the ages of 16 and 50 who were not in psychotherapy; approximately 125 psychiatric patients in therapy, with residents under his supervision; and 14 groups of psychiatric outpatients that were organized by age. Daniel Levinson (1978) studied four groups of men who were between the ages of 35 and 45 in 1969—hourly workers in industry, business executives, novelists, and biologists working in universities. Gail Sheehy (1976) based her report on 115 interviews with men and women between the ages of 18 and 55 and on her discussions with researchers, including Gould, Levinson, and Vaillant. The sampling and methodological details of these four studies are shown in Box 3.1

It is important to note that these studies have set out to explore a topic that was highly personal for each of the investigators, since the respondents they studied were essentially similar to themselves and the experiences they described had personal relevance for the researchers—as each made clear. Thus, these studies may be somewhat less "objective" than similar studies of childhood or old age and, in the same way, less "objective" than a study of adulthood in another culture. Even more significant, however, is the fact that the respondents in all of these studies have grown to adulthood during the same historical period in essentially the same social-cultural environment. With only few exceptions, the respondents are white, middle-class, college-educated persons; and in the Levinson and Vaillant studies, all of the respondents are males. This suggests that we should be very cautious about generalizing from these data to all persons. Put

Box 3.1   Samples and Research Methods Used in Studies of Adult Development during Early and Middle Adulthood

GOULD (1972), STUDY 1

Sample: Fourteen outpatient therapy groups, organized by age (16–18, 18–22, 22–28, 29–34, 35–43, 43–50, and 50–60 +).

Design: Cross-sectional by age group. Groups observed for several months.

Method: Observation of groups and rating by observers of the characteristics for each age group.

Comments: Age groups, not individual respondents, were studied. Initial age groupings may have determined age differences in concerns expressed by group members. All felt a need for therapy.

GOULD (1972), STUDY 2

Sample: Five hundred twenty-four white, middle-class persons not in psychotherapy. Selected through friendship networks of eight medical students and hospital staff. About half were men and half women. Age range: 16–60.

Design: Cross-sectional by age. Questionnaire administered only once.

Box 3.1 Continued

Method:	Questionnaire based on characteristic statements from the previous "phase of life" groups. It consisted of 160 questions on 10 different areas of life.
Comments:	Average scores on each questionnaire statement were used to graph characteristics that were then visually examined to determine "unstable periods." No statistical tests were reported. Age periods identified correspond closely to the original predetermined groups in Study 1.

GOULD (1978)

Comments: Same data used as in the 1972 studies; no information given in this report about sample, design, or methods. The age periods differed somewhat from the 1972 report, however.

LEVINSON (1978)[a]

Sample: Forty men between 35 and 45 years old in 1968–70; all were from the northeastern United States. Respondents were recruited in each of four groups: 10 hourly workers from two companies (3 were black); 10 executives from two companies; 10 Ph.D. biologists from two universities; 10 novelists who had published at least two books (2 were black). Fifty percent Protestant; 70 percent completed college; all had married at least once; 80 percent had children; 20 percent were divorced; 42 percent were from "stable working-class or lower-middle-class families"; 32 percent were from "comfortable middle-class origins" (p. 12). A secondary sample of famous persons about which biographical or other literary information was available was also mentioned.

Design: Cross-sectional and retrospective, with 2-year follow-up interview with many of the respondents.

Method: Tape-recorded interviews of 1–2 hours at weekly intervals for 5–10 weeks (total 10–20 hours) over a 2–3 month period. It covered the entire life from childhood to the present. There was a follow-up interview 2 years later "in most cases." Only one interviewer saw each respondent. TAT pictures were used to bring up personal experiences. Most wives were interviewed once. The interviewer visited the

[a]Also reported in *Counseling Psychologist*, 1976, *6*(1), 21–25.

Box 3.1   Continued

---

man's office and home and read some of each novelist's books and reviews of their writing. An informal organizational analysis of the two companies and two universities from which the respondents were recruited was done.

Comments: All male sample. No empirical data or statistical tests reported. Rich biographical information was used to make interpretations that, in the absence of supporting empirical data, are difficult to evaluate.

SHEEHY (1976)

Sample: One hundred fifteen educated, middle-class men and women between 18 and 55 in the mid-1970s. They were described as a "pacesetter group" and included "lawyers, doctors, chief executives, middle managers, ministers, professors, politicians, and students, as well as men in the arts, the media, the sciences, and those who run their own small businesses. I sought out top-achieving women as well and also followed the steps of many traditionally nurturing women" (p. 17). Most lived in urban centers across the United States. Over half were divorced and some had no children.

Design: Cross-sectional by age. Opportunistic sample.

Method: Collected "life stories" in interviews. Saw couples first separately and then together.

Comments: Impressionistic data reported by a professional writer; no empirical data or usual social science methodology used. Sought to find "inner changes" within individual's development, to compare "developmental rhythms" of women and men, and to study "predictable crises" among couples. Considerable reliance on the studies of Gould and Levinson. High divorce rate indicates respondents may have been unusually prone to crisis.

VAILLANT (1978)

Sample: Ninety-four male graduates attending one or more of the elite northeastern U. S. colleges between 1942 and 1944. They were part of the original sample of 268 carefully selected college sophomores in the Grant Study begun in 1938; random selection from the 1942–44 graduates led to 102 respondents, but 2 had dropped out of the study and 6

Box 3.1   Continued

had died. Initial selection involved likelihood of graduating, sound physical and psychological health, and motivation to continue in the study. Forty-one percent were the oldest child in their families; nearly all served in World War II, often with distinction. At the time of the study (about 1969), average age was 47; average income was $30,000; 71 percent viewed themselves as "liberal"; 95 percent had been married and 15 percent were divorced; 25 percent were lawyers and doctors. Most were "extremely satisfied" with their occupation; their health and mental health was much better than average, although 40 percent had seen psychiatrists (pp. 36–37).

Design: Longitudinal. Multiple methods were used, including physical, physiological, and psychological assessments, repeated questionnaires, and periodic interviews by different interviewers. Data were also gathered from the parents.

Method: A "social history" of the respondent's childhood was collected during college from the parents in their home; extensive physical, physiological, and psychological examinations were conducted during the college years. After graduation, each was sent a questionnaire every year until 1955, and every two years after that. All respondents were interviewed in their homes by a social anthropologist during 1950–52. In 1969 Vaillant interviewed each of his 94 respondents, usually in their home, and reviewed all previous data. The interview questionnaire was identical for each man (Appendix B); it took a minimum of 2 hours and often much more time was spent, sometimes including an informal meal and conversation. Raters developed empirical data from selected study records, while kept "blind" to other ratings for Adult Adjustment, Childhood Environment, Objective Physical Health, Marital Happiness, Maturity of Psychological Defenses, and Overall Outcome of the Respondent's Children (over age 15).

Comments: Only men from elite educational backgrounds were studied. The focus was on mechanisms of adaptation, especially psychological defenses, and on the patterns of development. Especially rich data because of the longitudinal nature of the study. Report is unusually interesting because it contains Vaillant's personal reactions as well as the respondents' critiques of the study.

another way, cohort factors (especially the cultural pressures and social experiences of this generation of adults) may have created many of the characteristics of this period of development in our society.

Several of these studies have emphasized chronological age as if to imply that the developmental processes during this period of adulthood are caused by becoming a particular age—such as the "Age 30 Transition" in Levinson's study. While it is clear that all of these ages are averages and may vary by as much as two or three years in either direction, this emphasis on chronological age needs to be examined. On the one hand, we pointed out in Chapter 1 that chronological age is only an index of development and that it does not regulate adult development in the same rigid manner that it controls child development, because social factors are more important than age-linked biological factors in adulthood. On the other hand, in Chapter 2, we discussed the importance of age norms and the social clock for regulating behavior in adulthood. Since all of the respondents in these studies grew up and are living in relatively similar social-historical-cultural environments, it would seem that age norms and the social clock would affect these respondents in similar ways. Thus, as discussed earlier in this chapter, the regularity of the developmental progression in terms of chronological age appears to result from the internalized social clock, at least to a large extent. Only when cross-cultural studies of this period of adulthood are available will it be possible to determine whether there are internal developmental processes operating within individuals to provide some of the predictability to these sequences of challenges, crises, and transitions.

Levinson (1978) identifies the period from about age 17 to 40 as Early Adulthood; in his scheme, this includes "Early Adult Transition," "Entering the Adult World," the "Age 30 Transition," and "Settling Down." (Figure 3.1). For Gould (1978), this period ranges from age 16 to 34; it includes "Leaving Our Parents' World" (age 16–22), "I'm Nobody's Baby Now" (age 22–28), and "Opening Up to What's Inside" (age 28–34). Sheehy (1976) describes the stages of this period as "Pulling Up Roots," "The Trying Twenties," and "Passage to the Thirties." Vaillant describes the entire period between adolescence and age 40 as one of "Intimacy and Career Consolidation." Since Levinson's study was the only one to include a range of occupational groups—some respondents who were not college graduates (30 percent of his sample) and some black persons (12 percent)—we will use his scheme to organize this discussion and will integrate the other studies into his framework. However, we should keep in mind that his study dealt only with men.

Early Adult Transition

The task of the "Early Adult Transition" (age 17–22) in Levinson's scheme is "leaving the pre-adult world," which includes separating from one's parents and becoming more independent, financially and psychologically. He noted that only 18 percent of his respondents maintained close personal relationships with parents or lived geographically near their parents during their twenties; in addi-

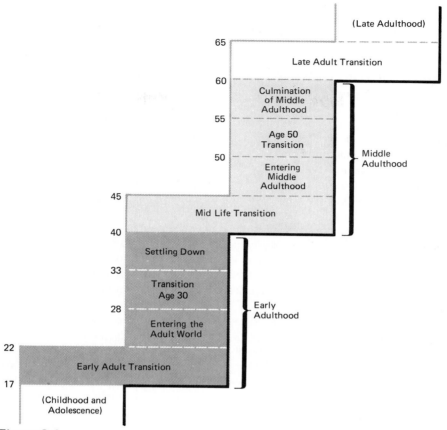

Figure 3.1

Developmental periods in early and middle adulthood from the study by Levinson (*Source:* Levinson, 1978, p. 57. Copyright © 1978 by Daniel J. Levinson. Reprinted with permission of Alfred A. Knopf.)

tion, 20 percent experienced a serious conflict with their parents that often went on for several years. The majority, however, moved away from parents—either geographically or socially—without a major conflict, or to avoid one. Other pre-adult aspects of the self are also given up during this period, including important relationships with adolescent groups, teachers, and a range of significant others; other relationships are modified because the young person is becoming a social adult and the person's self-perceptions are also changing. All of these changes may bring a sense of loss and some feelings of fear or insecurity about the future. Sixty-five percent of his respodnents were in military service during this period, and 70 percent completed college; thus, much of the "Early Adult Transition" was spent in these settings. During this period, nearly all of the men established a life pattern that was very different from their parents: some moved to a higher social status, others moved into artistic or academic fields that differed from the business world of their parents. Fifty percent of the men married during this period.

According to Levinson, for many of the men this is the period in which "The Dream" is formed. The Dream is the inner sense one has of how one wants life to work out; it is used in the sense of Martin Luther King's famous speech, "I have a dream. . . ." The Dream begins as an undefined sense of what one wants to accomplish or move toward; it may include a fantasy such as winning a Nobel Prize or making a million dollars, or it may be simply to pursue a particular career or interest. One-half of the biologists and seven of the ten novelists in his sample entered their field as a realization of their Dream; few of the executives and only one of the hourly wage workers had an occupation-related Dream or were able to realize it. For example, several of the executives had a Dream that involved family and community life rather than their occupation; thus they continued living near where they grew up or restricted advancement at work in favor of a stable family life. The hourly workers generally did not form a Dream in Levinson's sense, although some had a general vision of what a good life would be; however, one did realize his Dream of becoming a master plumber, and another gave up his Dream of being a major-league athlete at 30 and devoted himself to family life instead.

Gould (1978), in his analysis, focused on the false assumptions that need to be challenged during each phase of development. During this young adult phase, the major assumption to be challenged is "I'll always belong to my parents and believe in their world." Other assumptions that need to be discarded follow from this one: "If I get any more independent, it will be a disaster"; "I can see the world only through my parents' assumptions"; "Only my parents can guarantee my safety"; "My parents must be my only family"; and "I don't own my own body." Gould sees marriage during this period as an expression of the need for a partner to help the person break away from the parents and gain greater independence; however, he feels that such marriages are likely to fail since they provide greater dependence, not greater independence.

In the longitudinal study by Vaillant (1977), one of the most interesting findings about this period of development was that the research staff was unable to predict later psychological adjustment from personality traits observed while the men were still in college. That is, the characteristics the staff thought would predict midlife success—such as friendliness and humanism—were later found to be, in fact, unrelated to successful adaptation in middle age. In addition, traits that were thought to predict later emotional problems—shyness, introspection, inhibition, lack of purpose and values—also did not predict male midlife adjustment; instead, they appeared to have been one manifestation of the stress of adolescence for those men. However, looking back from the vantage point of the men at middle age, he did find that adolescents who had been seen as "well-integrated" and "practical and organized" in college were found to be the "Best Outcomes" in midlife; conversely, those men who were seen as "asocial" in young adulthood were the least likely of the group to be the "Best Outcomes" in middle age.[1]

A couple Sheehy (1976) interviewed expressed many of the themes of this period—the Dream, separation from parents, and a practical, well-organized stance toward life. At the time of the interview the man was 48, the woman was 46:

> *Of his dream at 21:* I was taught as a small boy to strive for financial success. To be a good provider for my family. Stand on your own two feet and make good. This was drummed into me at an early age, and this was the goal I had in mind—to have children, support my wife, have a nice house, send my kids to Yale like my father did, and be a success in business.
>
> What made me want to get married? When we met, we were both very young and immature. My father thought she was the greatest ever. My family was of more modest means.
>
> *Her point of view:* I was very lonely growing up. One of the reasons I wanted to marry him was to have a big family. I was very attracted to the closeness I saw between his parents and the four children in his family.
>
> *On how she saw his dream:* I had great hopes for him. I believed he would rise to the top of any business he was in. He was so dynamic. He came across with the idea that he could do anything. . . .
>
> *Her aspirations:* I had a year of college, majored in television and radio. Then I gave up all ideas of a job to do with that field. I went to work just to make some money. Nothing jobs. I wasn't dedicated to what I was doing. I wanted to get married and have a big family [Sheehy, 1976, p. 24].

Entering the Adult World

This period in Levinson's scheme lasts from about age 22 to 28. It is a relatively tranquil period—a pattern he finds repeated each decade: a time of transition, followed by a more stable period. During this time, a man tests the life structure he has formed during the early adult transition. It is a period of exploration, of making tentative commitments that, the man believes, can always be changed; it is a time of adventure and wonder. However, there is also a need to make choices, to "grow up" in terms of establishing an occupation or marriage, and to define goals. By this time three-quarters of his sample had married, and usually

---

[1]"Best Outcomes" were thirty men who in middle age were rated highly in career adjustment, social adjustment, psychological adjustment, and self-reported physical health by raters who did not have access to other ratings made on the respondents by Vaillant, staff physicians, or the social workers who interviewed the parents about the respondent's childhood history. Another thirty men were rated very low in adjustment in these areas; they were termed the "Worst Outcomes." Thirty-four men were in between these two extremes (Vaillant, 1977, pp. 261-262, Appendix C).

the man had made an initial, but serious, occupational choice. The tension between these two contradictory demands—to explore and to commit—is the essence of this period, in his view. Some men, especially the novelists, had made a commitment to their occupation, but had difficult intense relationships with women; half of the hourly workers felt this time was a "rock bottom" period for them and doubted they would be able to afford marriage. Other men committed themselves to a spouse, but did not settle on an occupation. Still others did make firm commitments in both areas, but wondered if perhaps they had committed themselves prematurely.

Levinson noted that two unique relationships seemed especially important during this phase: the "Mentor" and the "Special Woman." The *mentor* is typically a person who is older, more experienced, and a kind of "guru" who leads the man into the field he is entering. One of the most important functions of the mentor is to support the man's efforts to realize his Dream. In his sample, the mentor was often a boss, editor, senior colleague, or teacher; it was also sometimes a neighbor or a friend. Initially, the mentor is superior to the younger man, but gradually they become more equal and the relationship may be relatively intense. Sometimes the younger man surpasses the mentor or threatens his image of superiority; at other times the young man may feel inept or inadequate; frequently the relationship becomes stormy. Eventually the younger man will give up his mentor—as he had to separate from his parents—and perhaps will be a mentor, in his turn, to another young person. One example of a stormy mentor relationship was given by a novelist:

> Randall gave me tremendous support and encouragement. I was very close to this man—enormously, deeply committed to him in fact. He had a wonderful quality, but I later realized that this quality was good only if you were very young, and once you became a man yourself it almost became a matter of competition. I had to break, and it was too bad because there was a lack of insight on his part, I think [Levinson, 1978, p. 148].

The second unique relationship that Levinson stresses during this period is the *special woman*. She not only brings out the man's affectionate, romantic, and sexual feelings, but also facilitates his Dream in a manner parallel to the mentor. In part, she encourages the development of the man's sense of self in the direction of his Dream by believing in him; and she is a critic, guide, and sponsor as he works toward his goal. She helps to shape his Dream, shares it with him, and nourishes his aspirations and hopes. Just as in the mentor relationship, the special woman is a transitional figure helping the man to grow from dependency on his father and mother toward autonomous independence. Thus, if the special woman is the man's wife, their relationship will continue most strongly if each spouse has been able to nourish and support the other's Dream. Otherwise, one partner is likely to feel cheated when only the spouse's Dream was nurtured and when the spouse no longer needs this type of support and encouragement. In the Age 30 Transition, or the later Midlife Transition, marriages that did not mutually nourish the Dreams of the partners may be strained or may break up.

Although Levinson studied only men, he assumes that both the mentor and the special woman (special man) relationships apply equally in the developmental processes of this period of life for both men and woman. He notes that one of the problems for women is that in many professions there are few female mentors available, so that the mentor is often a man—for both men and women. However, he does not indicate the proportion of his respondents who actually had mentors or special women during this period. It would seem that many persons may not have these intense relationships, or may have only one or the other of these important supports for their Dream. Of course, as noted earlier, some persons do not have a Dream in Levinson's sense, or are not able to realize it. Also, some married couples may have individual Dreams that are not compatible, so that either one Dream will have to be abandoned, or the couple will experience conflict, or both.

While not explicitly discussing the "special woman," Vaillant (1977) pointed out that nearly all of the men in his longitudinal study who were seen as "Best Outcomes" at age 47 had married before age 30 and remained married to the same woman; conversely, three-quarters of the "Worst Outcomes" either married after age 30 or were separated before age 50. Moreover, the majority of "best marriages" were formed between the ages of 23 and 29.

Sheehy (1976) paid particular attention to the complexities of marriage during this period:

> These are the seesaw years for the couple. The ups are breathtaking, rapturous, triumphant breakthroughs of "We can!" The downs are surprise thuds. We try to deny and dismiss them because the last thing we want to accept at the summit of our illusions is that there are some things we can't. Optimism rides as high now as expectations. This *will* be a happy time. We never know until we leave the twenties whether or not it was.
>
> Ignorant of our own and our mate's inner life, we are ruled largely by external forces at this stage. And because the adult world is not in the mental health business, it rarely presents the young couple with opportunities that serve equally each one's readiness to individuate and need to feel secure. Occasionally there will be the perfect compromise. Much more often, the growth spurts will be uneven. When he is moving up, she is likely to feel herself slipping; and just when she feels ready to soar, he may descend into the sloughs of despond. Trying to stabilize—that is what the twenties are all about [p. 90].

Vaillant (1977) sees this period as one that emphasized "career consolidation." Adolescent idealism was often given up for "making the grade." Instead of questioning their choice of mate or career, these graduates from prestigious universities were mainly concerned about competition with other men in their field. As a result, "Men who at nineteen had radiated charm now seemed colorless, hard-working, bland young men in 'gray flannel suits'" (p. 217). Many of these men indicated they had mentors; although the role models they discussed at age 19 frequently had been forgotten by the age of 47, they acknowledged the importance of a mentor—often one who served as a kind of "father figure." While 95 percent of the men felt their actual father either had no influence or a negative influence, the presence of a mentor appeared to facilitate their career consolidation. That is, men who had "relatively unsuccessful careers" had no mentors between adolescence and age 40. Many of the more successful men had mentors who were given up by the age of 40, and later they themselves were serving as mentors for their young apprentices.

Gould (1978) describes this period with the phrase, "I'm Nobody's Baby Now." Its major false assumption—the misconception that needs to be discarded for successful development—is: "Doing things my parents' way, with willpower and perseverance, will bring results. But if I become too frustrated, confused or tired or am simply unable to cope, they will step in and show me the right way" (p. 71). He expands this major theme into four misconceptions that are often carried from childhood, but need to be discarded in adulthood: (1) "Rewards will come automatically if we do what we're supposed to do"; (2) "There is only one right way to do things"; (3) "My loved ones can do for me what I haven't been able to do for myself"; and (4)"Rationality, commitment and effort will always prevail over all other forces." Thus, the young person (between approximately 22 and 28) learns that "trying" is not enough—as in childhood when the statement "At least I tried" was often accepted by the parents, even if the attempt did not succeed. Similarly, working hard does not always bring success. And expecting one's spouse or children to provide one's own fulfillment or sense of success is unrealistic if one cannot do it oneself. Gould describes how this unchallenged assumption can turn into a destructive situation:

> When our temporary dependence on others to reassure us becomes a fixed requirement—that is, when we *expect* others to take *responsibility* for us—we form a *conspiracy* to avoid confronting our disguised childhood demons. In this conspiracy, we don't have to do anything; they, our loved ones, will do all that we can't do for ourself. . . .
>
> In this conspiracy, we no longer feel inadequate. Our disguised demonic badness is magically covered up and controlled by our loved one. The problem is that a relationship built on conspiracy must eventually become hostile because of dependency.
>
> Although we no longer feel inadequate, we still feel inferior to our partner because he or she is able to do for us what we can't do for ourself.
>
> On the other hand, when our partner does a "bad job," when he or she doesn't reassure us and we still feel inadequate, we feel let down. This person we love so much has such superior powers (like parents) that he or she could have helped us but chose not to. Therefore we feel very hostile.

The conspiracy is a no-win situation. Eventually we feel either hostile or dependent and often both. In any case, our simple pact with our loved one becomes a destructive conspiracy that prevents our developing a fuller, more independent adult consciousness [Gould, 1978, pp. 110-111].

Age 30 Transition

Between the ages of about 28 and 33, Levinson found a period of transition in which the person could rework parts of the "life structure" that were tentatively constructed during the period of entering the adult world and to create a second life structure that would form the basis of the next period. For some of his men, this period was one of relatively smooth change—the modification and enrichment of an essentially satisfying life pattern. For others, there was a "crisis" or painful transition with fears of a chaotic disruption, or an inability to achieve a satisfactory future life structure. He reported that 62 percent of the men experienced a moderate or severe crisis during this time. The novelists and hourly workers were more likely to experience a crisis than were the biologists or executives.

For example, one novelist, a black writer, experienced a crisis that was similar to many, but was made even more extreme by the effects of all that is involved in being a black man in our society. He and his wife divorced when he was 28 because his aspirations were not compatible with hers. This was followed by a long period of guilt about "the corrosive theme of the Black father abandoning his wife and children." The years from 28 to 30 were spent "moving around, often living from hand to mouth, working at transient jobs, hitting 'rock bottom,' nearly succeeding in killing himself, getting psychotherapy, starting a serious love relationship—and through it all finding time to write his novels" (Levinson, 1978, p. 88). By age 34 he had established the beginning of a new life structure—an occupation that brought an adequate income and also allowed him time to write, as well as permitting him an enduring relationship with another woman; however, it took several more years to establish his writing at the core of his life structure.

In contrast, another man had a much smoother transition; nonetheless, he had moved from a secure job in an accounting firm to a middle-management job in a major corporation, left his lower-middle-class, religious-ethnic community and his extended family when he moved to an upwardly mobile, diverse suburban community, and became much more ambitious in his career. Thus, his new life structure was considerably different after the transitional period, but there had been relatively little emotional distress or break in continuity with his previous life structure.

The essence of the Age 30 Transition in Levinson's scheme is the growing sense that change must be made soon; otherwise, one will become locked into—and out of—commitments that will become more and more difficult to change. Sheehy (1976) points out that many people are terrified by all the choices they must make in their twenties, but seldom realize that change is not only possible, but often is inevitable during this period, which she terms "Catch-30." One of her respondents, a 29-year-old lawyer, displays some of the tendencies commonly seen at the beginning of this transitional period:

> "I'm considering leaving the firm. I've been there four years now; I'm get-ting good feedback, but I have no clients of my own. I feel weak. If I wait much longer, it will be too late, too close to that fateful time of decision on whether or not to become a partner. I'm success-oriented. But the concept of being 55 years old and stuck in a monotonous job drives me wild. It drives me crazy now, just a little bit. I'd say that 85 percent of the time I thoroughly enjoy my work. But when I get a screwball case, I come away from court saying, 'What am I doing here?' It's a *visceral* reaction that I'm wasting my time. I'm trying to find some way to make a social contribution or a slot in city government. I keep saying, 'There's something more' " [Sheehy, 1976, p. 29].

He is also examining his family life: he enjoys his son more than he ever thought he would and now wants more children; however, his wife wants to go to law school. He wants to place more emphasis on family life, but she feels he is more concerned with his convenience than with her development. The struggle sug-gested by this couple will likely continue for several years—and it is not possible to predict what the outcome of this transition will be for them.

Gould (1978) focuses on a new central misconception for this phase of devel-opment "Life is simple and controllable. There are no significant coexisting con-tradictory forces within me." It includes the following assumptions: "What I know intellectually, I know emotionally"; "I am not like my parents in ways I don't want to be"; "I can see the reality of those close to me quite clearly"; and "Threats to my security aren't real." He terms this period from 28 to 34 one of "Opening Up to What's Inside," since it involves discovering (or rediscovering) aspects, feelings, goals, interests, and talents that were ignored or hidden during the earlier period. Sometimes these were pushed aside because they interfered with the beliefs or goals of the earlier period; sometimes they caused inner con-flict and were suppressed; other times they simply required time that was not available earlier because so much effort was involved in establishing indepen-dence and securing a niche for oneself in the social and occupational world. This stage may begin with a period of depression, but it is followed by a different per-spective on the world. It may involve a deeper sense of beauty or the develop-ment of a personal philosophy of life. It may also lead to a more realistic under-standing of one's strengths and abilities. This period also involves recognizing the contradictory and competing feelings inside oneself and the contradictory and competing pressures outside in the social world.

Settling Down

Following the transitional period of the late twenties and early thirties, Levinson found a calmer period from age 33 to 40 that he called "Settling Down" into a second stable life structure. Sheehy terms this period "Rooting and Extending," since her respondents tended to focus on buying a home and climbing career ladders. Among her respondents, the focus on child-rearing often brought a decline in social contacts outside the family and a decline in marital satisfaction as the overly romantic ideals of the couple's twenties lost their glamour.

Not only did Levinson's respondents settle down emotionally from the sometimes turbulant Age 30 Transition, but also they "settled for" a few of their major goals and began building their life structure around those central choices. It tended to be a period of "getting serious," a period in which to decide what is really important in one's life. It is the period of growing beyond the mentor relationship and becoming a full adult instead of an apprentice. Levinson terms this process "Becoming One's Own Man." He found two major tasks of this phase of adulthood: establishing one's niche, and working at advancement. Since sometimes advancement involves challenging more senior, established persons, these tasks may be contradictory; the message is often to play it safe by not challenging one's superiors, but one cannot advance that way very quickly. Similarly, the man not only seeks affirmation of his worth and advancement up the career ladder, which he now sees clearly ahead of him, but also he becomes vulnerable to the social pressures of superiors who determine his advancement. As Levinson phrases it:

> A man is likely to be rather sensitive, even touchy, about anything in the environment or in himself that interferes with [becoming more senior and expert, and getting affirmed by society]. Since the successful outcome of this period is not assured, he often feels that he has not accomplished enough and that he is not sufficiently his own man. He may have a sense of being held back—of being oppressed by others and restrained by his own conflicts and inhibitions [Levinson, 1978, p. 145].

Neither Gould nor Vaillant found this settling down phase a distinct period in their studies. In fact, Vaillant described the entire period from 20 to 40 as one of "Intimacy and Career Consolidation." Gould, on the other hand, included the period of the late thirties in the midlife transition, to which we now turn.

THE MIDLIFE TRANSITION

Many years before the "midlife crisis" became so widely discussed, Carl Jung (1933) described the important psychological changes that he felt begin between the ages of 35 and 40. As discussed in Chapter 1, Jung saw the period of "youth" extending from puberty to the middle years. During these middle years he noted a gradual change as some characteristics of the personality reemerge after being dormant for several years while other characteristics become less important and may be replaced by different or opposite personality traits. This period of change ushers in the second half of life that ideally reflects different psychic characteristics than the first half of life. These differences include greater emphasis on inner exploration and a search for meaning and wholeness in life that makes eventual acceptance of death more possible.

Elliott Jaques (1965) appears to have coined the term "midlife crisis" based on his study of the lives of 310 artists, including biographies of composers, painters, poets, sculptors, and writers. He noted that the incidence of death for these creative artists was higher than expected between the ages of 35 and 39, and lower than expected between 40 and 44. He also observed that after age 40 there was often a major change in the person's artistic works that resulted in less "hot-from-the-fire creativity" and more "sculpted" works. In addition, he detected a progression from "lyrical and descriptive" works in young adulthood, through a period of "tragic and philosophical content" during the midlife period, to greater "serenity" later in life; he cited the works of Shakespeare and Dickens as classic examples of this progression. He felt that the middle-aged person's growing awareness of mortality was the main theme of the midlife crisis, and his analysis of the issues of this period relied heavily on the psychoanalytic perspective of Freud and others.

However, until recently there has been little empirical research on this midlife period, except for a few studies of menopause in women. Brim (1977) suggests that this lack of research may reflect the assumption that middle-aged people—at least men—are stable, reliable, stalwart pillars of society and the family; thus, there would be very little change in their lives to study. As we will see, the research presently available suggests that this assumption is not valid; there appears to be a great deal of interesting change taking place in the midlife period of many men and women.

Each of the four studies of developmental periods in adulthood we have been discussing focuses on the midlife transition, but each views it in differing ways. For example, Gould places it between age 35 and 45, similar to both Jung and Jaques; however, Levinson found it to occur between 40 and 45, while Vaillant placed it at age 40, "give or take as much as a decade." Levinson and Sheehy reported it to be a time of marked crisis, but Vaillant found that the "high drama" often associated with a midlife crisis was relatively rare in his sample. We are also able to include data from a small longitudinal study of women and men that focused on those persons who changed markedly during midlife and those that remained relatively stable (Livson, 1975, 1976). We will also examine the family and the midlife transition, exploring the intergenerational nature of this transition, and will briefly discuss menopause and the sexual aspects of this transition. To conclude the chapter, we will focus on the various historical and social factors that are related to the issues that seem to be characteristic of this midlife transition in our society.

Developmental Changes and Issues at Midlife

In Levinson's scheme, the midlife transition begins around age 40 and serves as a link between early and middle adulthood. It has three major tasks: (1) review and reappraise the early adult era; (2) modify the unsatisfying aspects of the previous life structure and begin testing elements of a new structure; and (3) resolve the major psychological issues introduced by entering the final half of life— these involve forming a new and more realistic picture of oneself and one's world and exploring the meaning of significant themes such as "young" versus "old" and "masculinity" versus "femininity." He found that 80 percent of his respondents had experienced "tumultuous struggles within the self and with the external world" during this period. They questioned every aspect of their lives and were "horrified" by what they found; they were angry and resentful about themselves and toward others. He noted that the men often were "somewhat irrational," but concluded that this was a normal part of the developmental challenge at this point in their lives; much of the difficulty, he felt, was caused by the anxiety, dependency, guilt, and vanity the men had built up over the earlier years that kept them locked into an oppressive life structure. Thus, in his view, the intense reexamination of this period often brings emotional upset, especially since one is challenging the status quo—the established way one's life structure has been. For example, those aspects of the self that were pushed aside during the earlier Settling Down period may reemerge as if to demand attention once again.

Gould (1978) focused on the entire decade from 35 to 45 in his description of the midlife transition. The major misconception that he felt should be challenged during this period is: "There is no evil or death in the world. The sinister has been destroyed." This misconception has five components: "The illusion of safety can last forever"; "Death can't happen to me or my loved ones"; "It is impossible to live without a protector" (for women); "There is no life beyond this family"; and "I am an innocent." Each of these is, to some degree, an expansion of the misconceptions that are troublesome during the earlier period in his sequence. The first three deal with coming to terms with one's own mortality and the fact that the death of one's parents or friends is a clear reminder that one also will eventually die. The issue of a "protector" he found to be especially important for women—in contrast to the shock of acknowledging one's own mortality that seemed to hit men harder. Thus, while men are often badly shaken by the realization that death will come for them, and it may already have come for their parents or co-workers during this midlife period, women often feel a greater drive to strike out on their own, to overcome the notion that they need to be protected, and to expand their lives in new directions. This may include returning to work, striving to realize their own dreams, or simply feeling more independence. Gould notes that earlier in life many women tend to rely on men for protection and to feel that they can exercise their power only through men; but during the middle years, women challenge this assumption as a part of their own increased realization of mortality. While men struggle to recognize that success, hard work, and their family cannot protect them from eventually dying, women must confront their own separateness as well as their mortality.

From the perspective of his longitudinal study, Vaillant (1977) focused on the emerging importance of the search for a sense of Generativity versus Stagnation, Erikson's seventh period of life (discussed in Chapter 1). The men he studied tended to shift away from their earlier emphasis on career achievement and mundane responsibilities at work toward more inner exploration and reassessment of their earlier life. He found several parallels between this period and the earlier developmental transition of adolescence. It is a time of feeling somewhat "gangly and uncertain"; it is a time for reassessing the experiences and relationships of the previous period—childhood and parental relations for the adolescent; career consolidation and intimacy strivings for the man in his forties. It is often a time of breaking out from the restrictions of the earlier period. He disagreed with Jaques' emphasis on the central importance of the fear of death in determining the midlife crisis, but stressed instead the renewed vigor and excitement of this period that seems to result from a sense of liberation after the overconstraint of the thirties. Of course, many of the men had greater contact with the death of persons close to them than they had previously, and this often brought increased feelings of vulnerability; but many also experienced a kind of rebirth. For example, half of the men who had been seen as "unusually bland and colorless" during adolescence became "vibrant and interesting" by age 45.

> Thus, if men in their forties are depressed, it is because they are confronted by instinctual reawakening and because they are more honestly able to acknowledge their own pain. It is not because they fear death. If they are no longer satisfied with their careers, it may be because they wish to be of more service to those around them. If their marriages are sometimes in disarray and their groping toward love seems adolescent, it may be because they are less inhibited than they were in their thirties. . . .
>
> But always, such transitional periods in life provide a means of seizing one more chance and finding a new solution to old instinctual or interpersonal needs [Vaillant, 1977, p. 222].

Unlike Levinson, Vaillant found that radical changes during the midlife period were relatively rare. However, one respondent took up deep-sea diving and underwater archaeology in the Mediterranean; another built a "dramatic, shamelessly exhibitionistic" home; and a third had an exciting love affair that surprised the researchers because he had kept his inner life so well controlled when he was younger. The more common, less dramatic changes were also significant. One man who had a secret ambition to travel extensively never did, but he became editor of a travel magazine. Another respondent in an unsatisfactory nonsexual marriage had several discreet affairs and, at the same time, became more satisfied with his marriage which remained stable. These midlife changes often brought some upset and anxiety, but Vaillant felt they were no more troubling than the similar range of changes during adolescence (which was also not typically a period of crisis for his respondents). Usually these changes involved a sense of vigor and challenge instead of crisis; one 47-year-old stated:

"I am onto a whole new life, a personal renaissance, which has got me excited most of the time. If I can make it pay adequate to my family responsibility, I will 'really be livin', man' " (ibid., p. 221).

Vaillant also called attention to the intergenerational nature of this transition. The interaction between middle-aged parents and adolescent children is especially important since each is going through somewhat similar processes; the parents play an important part in the adolescent's transition just as the adolescent plays a part in the parents' transition. In addition, an adolescent son or daughter may rekindle feelings in the parent that had been ignored for years. One striking example of this was a father who disapproved of his son's antiwar activities; however, the father had forgotten that (as the study records showed) he had been strongly opposed to United States participation in World War II until Pearl Harbor was bombed and he was drafted. Similarly, the changes taking place in the lives of the parents' own parents may be an important influence on these intergenerational midlife issues. We will discuss this theme in more detail later in this chapter.

Vaillant's research also pointed out two findings that contradict some popular views of the midlife period. First, for those men who were seen as "Best Outcomes" at age 47, he found that the period from 35 to the present was reported to have been the happiest of their lives, while the period from 21 to 35 was the unhappiest. Only those who were less well-adapted at 47 preferred the younger period of adulthood to their more recent years. Second, those businessmen who had the best marriages and richest friendship patterns were the ones who became presidents of their company. This finding was confirmed in a later study of the men who head the 100 largest companies in the United States; 95 percent were still married to their first wife (King, 1978).

Because most of the respondents in these studies were men, we have been focusing primarily on the male midlife transition up to this point. However, a small longitudinal study by Florine Livson (1976) provides some information about this midlife transition for women. She examined a group of 24 women who were part of the original sample of adolescent girls in the longitudinal Oakland Growth Study begun in 1934. When the women were 50 years old, Livson selected those who were in the higher half of the sample on a measure of psychological health. Looking back over the data collected during earlier years of the study, she determined that 7 of the women had also been high on the measure of psychological health at age 40, while 17 had markedly improved in psychological health between age 40 and 50. She called the stable group "traditional," because their personalities appeared well-suited to the traditional female roles of wife and mother. "The stable group at fifty are gregarious, nurturant women, pleased with their appearance, and conventional in their outlook. They place high value on closeness with others. They are seen as 'feminine'" (Livson, 1976, p. 110). The second group appeared different from the stable group not only because their psychological health had improved, but also because they were more "independent": they were "ambitious, skeptical, and unconventional in their way of looking at things. They rely on their intellect to cope with the world. . . . They are more autonomous than traditionals and more in touch with their inner life" (ibid.).

Examining the two groups when they were adolescents, Livson noted that the *traditionals* had been popular, socially successful, feminine young women who appeared to be establishing a sense of Identity, in Erikson's sense. The *independents* were also establishing a sense of Identity in their own style during that period, but they appeared somewhat more intellectual than the traditional women.

At the age of 40 when the women were contacted again after a lapse in the study, the *traditional* women were resolving the issue of Intimacy in Erikson's scheme very well—they formed close, trusting relationships, were well liked, and were quite successfully sociable. By age 50, they showed evidence of Erikson's stage of Generativity—they seemed especially nurturant and protective, in addition to remaining gregarious and sociable. Thus, their pattern was essentially stable and consistently feminine from adolescence through midlife, leading to high psychological health within a traditionally feminine life-style.

In contrast, the *independent* women showed much more evidence of a midlife crisis. Their life pattern at the age of 40 was dramatically different from the traditional women, and different also from what it would be 10 years later. They were relatively low in psychological health, depressed, irritable, and their earlier intellectual strength seemed to have decreased or turned to fantasy and daydreaming. They did not seem to be resolving the Intimacy stage, in contrast to the traditional group. It appeared that this group had been in the midst of a midlife crisis, since there was some evidence that their morale had declined from the child-rearing years (although they were not studied directly between adolescence and age 40). By age 50, however, these women showed a dramatic rebound—intellectually and emotionally. They were close and trusting with others, sympathetic and open with feelings. They appeared to be achieving the Intimacy stage as positively as the traditional group of women did 10 years earlier; however, they did not seem to be achieving the sense of Generativity exhibited in the traditional women.

These data suggest that the independent group experienced a midlife crisis that delayed psychological development, but did not hamper their psychological health in the long run, since they were among the most well-adjusted women at the age of 50. Livson suggested that the fit between the woman's personality and life-style may be the key factor in this midlife crisis:

> Traditional personalities fit conventional feminine roles. As wives and mothers, they are able to live out valued aspects of themselves. They continue to find satisfaction in relationships with others, even as their children grow older and leave home. They are not motivated to change themselves or their situations at middle age. . . .

Independents do not so easily fit conventional definitions of femininity. By age forty, when children are moving into adolescence, they seem to be confronted with an identity crisis. Having suppressed their intellectual competence and grown away from child-care skills, they seem unable for a time to connect with a workable identity. I would suggest that it is disengagement from the mothering role by fifty that stimulates these women to revive their more assertive, goal-oriented skills [Livson, 1976, p. 112-113].

Examining men in the Oakland Growth study in a parallel fashion, she found strikingly similar results (Livson, 1975). That is, of the 21 men who were in the upper half of the sample on psychological health at age 50, 7 had been relatively stable while 14 had shown a marked improvement between age 40 and 50. The stable men were also "traditional" and had followed a consistent life pattern of conventional masculinity—valuing intellectual control and rationality instead of feeling; they were also ambitious, productive, and self-controlled. In contrast, the 14 men whose psychological health had improved from age 40 to age 50 were seen as "non-traditionals." They had been emotionally expressive during adolescence and seemed unable to integrate their assertiveness and their emotionality. By age 40 they appeared to have suppressed their feelings under a power-oriented, exploitative kind of "masculine protest." She noted, "Their defenses are brittle, easily punctured. They are hostile and generally anxious. I suggest that their stress results from suppressing their emotionality to fulfill sex-role expectations for high-achieving men" (Livson, 1975, p. 3). However, perhaps as a result of the midlife transition, these nontraditional men had given up this masculine protest by age 50. They were more nurturant and sensual, less anxious, and seemed to have integrated the emotional aspects with their sense of masculinity into a much more comfortable life pattern. The psychological health of both groups was equally high by age 50.

These data suggest that many, but not all, psychologically healthy adults at age 50 may experience a distinct reorganization of their life patterns during the decade of their forties; in contrast, about one-third of both the women and men retained consistent traditionally feminine or masculine patterns from adolescence to age 50, with little evidence of a period of emotional crisis during the middle years. However, these studies do not examine the fate of well-adjusted women and men at age 40. Nonetheless, these data suggest an interesting hypothesis about the midlife transition. Perhaps the transition is more disruptive to persons of otherwise high psychological health if the individual's personality characteristics are not readily integrated into the demands of the life pattern they are leading during their thirties and forties. If, let us say, they have played the social roles and followed the age and sex norms that supposedly lead to success and "happiness," but have had to sacrifice a signficant portion of their individual uniqueness for the sake of social expectations, the midlife decade may bring an acute awareness that their lives are moving rapidly away from that part of themselves they valued, but had tried to suppress. At the same time, their growing awareness of their own mortality may lead them to question the meaning of the social expectations of "success" and "happiness" for their own lives. Erich Fromm (1941) observed this phenomenon, although he did not link it specifically with a midlife transition:

> All our energy is spent for the purpose of getting what we want, and most people never question the premise of this activity: that they know their true wants. They do not stop to think whether the aims they are pursuing are something they themselves want. In school they want to have good marks, as adults they want to be more and more successful, to make more money, to have more prestige, to buy a better car, to go places, and so on. Yet when they do stop to think in the midst of all this frantic activity, this question may come to their minds: "If I do get this new job, if I get this better car, if I can take this trip—what then? What is the use of it all? Is it really I who wants all this? Am I not running after some goal which is supposed to make me happy and which eludes me as soon as I have reached it?" These questions, when they arise, are frightening, for they question the very basis on which man's whole activity is built, his knowledge of what he wants [pp. 277-278].

Perhaps this is the essence of the midlife crisis. Levinson found a set of questions characteristic of the midlife transition: "What have I done with my life?" What do I really get from, and give to my wife, children, friends, work, community—and self? What are my central values and how are they reflected in my life?" (Levinson, 1978, p. 89). Thus, it may be that the emotional crisis of the midlife transition often results from a growing awareness that one's life, or style of living one's life, has become more and more out of step with one's inner characteristics, wishes, desires, goals, needs, and feelings. It is as if, early in adulthood, one followed the well-worn footpath through the dense forest in pursuit of a distant mountain and for the next 10 or 15 miles (years) the climb was so difficult that one never looked back or paid attention to all that was being ignored along the way. Perhaps not until the summit is reached does one realize that the path led to the wrong mountain. Or perhaps it is the first cool day of autumn that reminds one to smell the flowers because soon they will be gone.

The Family and the Midlife Transition

Intergenerational relationships between the person in midlife and younger persons (usually one's children) and older persons (especially one's parents) play an important role in this transitional period. In a sense, as Neugarten (1967b) has noted, middle-aged persons see the reflection of who they were in their children, and see the reflection of who they will become in their parents. Thus, the dynamic relationship between parents and adolescents and between parents and the adolescents' grandparents may be crucial for triggering the midlife transition.

For example, the fresh sexuality of the adolescent may pose sexual issues for middle-aged parents. Gould (1978) describes this very candidly:

> As mothers, we are attracted to our sons and their friends. After reading a magazine article about older women with younger men, we may wonder what it would be like. We find that our husbands are slightly aware of what's going on and are reacting competitively with the boys. One of the young girls comes into the room in tight shirt and without a bra, and we feel a flash of hatred and envy of her firm breasts as the young boys turn to her.
>
> As fathers, we do what we can to avoid staring at our daughters' curves or their friends who make a game out of seducing us; we do what we can to keep our wives from knowing. Our sons' girls are awfully appealing, and sometimes we daydream about being in their place during this sexual revolution. It was never like this in our day. From time to time we wonder whether our anger at our sons is really jealousy [pp. 269-270].

As the children become more sexually informed and aware, conversations about sex may become more frequent in the family. At the same time, as the parents begin having more time alone (when the children are out on dates, away for the weekend, or off at college), opportunities for relaxed sex between the parents become more frequent than during the child-rearing years.

All of these factors are likely to increase the importance of sexuality in the lives of middle-aged persons. In addition, the "second adolescence" that Vaillant (1977) described as occurring during the forties—which brings a reawakening of instinctual urges or, at least, the inner exploration and reevaluation of one's life pattern—may focus renewed attention on matters related to sexuality. At the same time, marital satisfaction tends to be at a low point (c.f., Rollins & Feldman, 1970); and intact marriages may be 20 years old at midlife. Thus, the relationship with one's spouse is likely to be very much involved in the midlife transition.

Sheehy (1976) described still another thread in the midlife couple's relationship by the catchy title, "the sexual diamond." She argued that men and women are much more similar at age 18 and at age 60 than they are during the middle years of adulthood; between these years they gradually diverge, so that at age 40 they are as dissimilar as they will be. Thus, a diagram of this pattern would take the shape of a diamond: together at age 18, far apart at age 40, back together at age 60. In sexual terms, she suggests that young men and women are equally sexually responsive at 18, but the woman's sexual responsiveness increases while the man's sexual responsiveness decreases between 18 and 40. After age 40, she writes, "The sexually educated and experienced middle-aged man can be a most satisfying lover. Once he overcomes the anxiety of no longer being a boy, he can begin to appreciate his matured powers to give tenderness and receive love, and to prolong his own state of excitement by withholding ejaculation while he brings his partner to ecstasy again and again" (p. 312). At this stage, the two lines of development again converge, closing the diamond.

Sheehy includes more than just sexuality in this model, however. The man and woman grow apart from 18 to 40 in many ways because of their differing experiences in the home, caring for children, at work, and in relationships with others. At the same time, they may have little time to spend communicating with each other at a deep level because of the demands of children, work, and other responsibilities. Therefore, it may not be until the children are leaving home that the couple recognizes how each has grown and changed; they can then begin to get to know each other and draw together again through sharing experiences and mutual involvement in similar projects. Again, the lines of development diverge, then come together later in life to form a diamond. While this analysis may require a few grains of the proverbial salt to be acceptable, especially regarding the ages Sheehy uses in the model, it succinctly describes a frequently important theme in the midlife transition for a couple. It may also be further complicated by both persons experiencing their own midlife transitions simultaneously, when the sentiment is often, "Don't bring me your crisis, I'm busy with my own!"

Menopause, the ending of the menstrual cycle in women, typically occurs during the latter part of this period—between 45 and 55. We will examine the role of hormones in the female sex cycle and discuss male hormones in Chapter 4; in Chapter 5 we will review studies of the psychological effects of menopause in detail. Briefly however, it is important to note that these biological processes seem to be relatively insignificant in comparison with the social, interpersonal, and psychological factors during the midlife transition. Only a few women, 4 percent in a study by Neugarten (1967a), felt that the worst thing about menopause was not having any more children; in contrast, 30 percent felt that the best thing was not having to worry about getting pregnant. In general, about half of the women in another study (Neugarten, Wood, Kraines, & Loomis, 1963) felt that menopause was an unpleasant experience, and half disagreed. Many also felt there were positive changes but, overall, most women felt that menopause does not change a woman in any important way. Similarly, only a few women (4 percent) listed menopause as the worst thing about middle age (Neugarten, 1967a).

Since men do not menstruate, they do not have a menopause. However, they do have sex hormones that may affect their sexual and psychological moods or functioning. Very little is known about the role of these hormones, and it is not yet known whether men experience any important change in these hormones in midlife other than a gradual decline that is related to a similar decline in sexual interest. Of course, men in their seventies and eighties may retain their ability to engage in satisfying sexual relationships and often are able to father children (see Chapter 5). Thus, the pattern of changes in male sex hormones, while not well understood, appears to have little relation to the midlife transition. Although impotence, the inability to have an erection when desired, is usually caused by nonphysiological factors (such as overindulgence in food or drink, stress, or boredom with partner), periodic episodes of impotence might be misinterpreted by the man as a sign of declining biological potency and advancing age and thus increase the stress of his midlife period. But such a connection, based on the man's own misinterpretation, is not a direct link between biological changes and his midlife transition. The connection between other biological factors—such as a doctor's warning about high blood pressure, overweight, or an actual heart attack—and a midlife crisis is much more direct than the link between sex hormones and midlife concerns for men.

In addition to the middle-aged person's relationships with the children and with the spouse, the third family element that is often involved in the midlife transition is the relationship with one's own parents. For example, concern over the elder parents' greater health problems, or possibly the death of one or both of the elders may bring the middle-aged person's growing awareness of aging into sharp focus. Not only is the relationship pattern shifting toward greater dependence of one's parents on oneself, but also the parent is likely to be caught "in between" the generations, feeling the conflict between independence and dependence on the part of both the children and the elder parents. Sometimes it may seem that everyone is depending on the person in the middle, who, in turn, has no one on whom to depend, having lost the illusion of always being able to rely on Mom and Pop. Illness of an aged parent may drain a person in midlife financially and emotionally and may require a large expenditure of time and effort; simultaneously, the costs of a college education, emotional concerns about the children, and making time for visits with them can also be stressful. Combined with pressures at work, self-examination, and relations with the spouse, the midlife period can be a difficult thicket indeed. Add the increased awareness of one's own mortality, brought on in part by the aging of one's parents, plus concerns about one's own health and we see many of the threads that can combine to create this midlife transition.

Themes and Variations in Middle Age

The midlife transition demonstrates a number of the important themes we have discussed in the first two chapters, so perhaps it will be useful to cast a critical eye on the problems and shortcomings of the research and theoretical assumptions that underlie the idea of a midlife transition. Let us begin with some of the central theoretical assumptions.

As noted in Chapter 1, it is very important to be aware of the interaction between historical (cohort) forces, psychosocial age-related influences, and maturational effects. Clearly, each influence is of a different kind, yet they combine to produce "development" in the general sense of that term; in the more specific sense, development might be equated with maturation. What, then, is the nature of the midlife transition? Are there historical forces playing a part? How important are the psychosocial influences? And is there a maturational component in it as well?

Looking first at historical forces, clearly the growing affluence, changing work and family patterns, increased education, greater emphasis on self-realization, and the women's (and men's) liberation movements are some of the historical factors that may have combined to influence the midlife transition. For example, greater affluence among the middle class in our society has allowed many persons more freedom to explore experiences that once were reserved only for the very wealthy, such as European vacations, second homes, camping trailers, and, in general, the experience of free time made possible by the multitude of "labor-saving devices." No longer do these people feel that fulfillment in life can come only through hard work, sacrifice, child-rearing, and a few community activities. Instead, our society now encourages the pursuit of individual happiness and self-fulfillment.

This change has been especially dramatic for those persons who are now middle-aged, since they were raised during the Great Depression and World War II when the opportunities that are now available for many were quite foreign to the vast majority. While the greatest personal fulfillment for many of their parents was to keep body and soul together and to raise their children to achieve the goals that were impossible for the parents, today's middle-aged men and women are frequently achieving those dreams and are wondering what else there is, since many of those dreams do not automatically provide fulfillment. Similarly, shorter working hours, smaller families, more women entering the work force, and greater education are encouraging these trends as all of these increase family income and free time that may be used at one's discretion. Smaller families also mean that the last child leaves home during the midlife period, while this was not the case 50 years ago. In addition, the increased life expectancy of middle-aged people has meant that more and more of them are actually nearer the midpoint of their lives than they would have been 50 years ago. As will be discussed in Chapter 5, at the turn of the twentieth century, because of larger families and shorter life expectancy, the average father barely lived long enough to see his last child leave home; this is clearly not the case today. Thus, historical factors may have played an important part in creating the meaning and intensity of the midlife transition in our society in the latter part of the twentieth century. Many other sociocultural factors could also be listed, including television, the possibility of nuclear destruction, and the various liberation movements.

The central question raised by this perspective is whether *all* persons experience this midlife transition, or whether it is limited primarily to those who have been most affected by these historical changes—white, middle-class, married persons. We do not know whether midlife crises are also experienced by poor persons who are struggling to raise families and keep food on the table. We do not know how racism and discrimination may affect the midlife transition for members of racial minority groups, or how their cultural background and experience may affect it. And we do not know about the midlife experience of heterosexual persons who are not married or not raising a family, or of those who are lesbians or gay men who may or may not be raising families. We also do not know about the midlife experience of persons in cultures different from our own. Obviously, all of these groups of people may experience the midlife crisis in ways that are different from white, middle-class, married parents in the United States—if they experience one at all. Thus, much further research with more diverse samples, including cohorts other than those studied so far, will be required before we can discount the hypothesis that the midlife transition is largely a historical phenomenon confined to a particular group of persons in the United States. Interestingly, those persons studied generally tend to be highly similar to the researchers themselves (and similar also to the group of people who are most likely to buy a book about midlife development).

Turning next to the psychosocial factors that may cause the midlife transition, we recall from Chapter 2 the discussion of age norms, age roles, and the social clock. As suggested earlier, the relatively rigid age-related pattern Gould, Levinson, and Sheehy found in these recent studies of adult development may result primarily from the age-related social norms in our society about the "right" time to accomplish the various expected tasks of adulthood. Since the respondents in these studies generally are drawn from a single historical cohort and from similar social backgrounds, the uniformity of their social clock is not at all surprising. Thus, the age at which they finish college, get married, have children, buy houses, receive promotions, and have a midlife transition all tend to be fairly similar. This would be especially likely for "successful" or "well-adjusted" persons whose very success and adjustment may reflect the fact that the timing of their adult tasks is in step with social expectations. This suggests that the midlife transition begins at age 35 or 40 not because the person becomes that age, but because the person has internalized the social expectations that lead to a period of transition around age 40. Recall the study of age norms shown in Table 2.1 (Neugarten, Moore & Lowe, 1965). The essence of the "deadline decade," Sheehy's name for this midlife period, can be described with characteristic responses: between age 40 and 50 one is "middle-aged"; one is no longer "a good-looking woman"; a woman no longer "has the most responsibilities." It is the time "when a man accomplishes most," and "when most men hold their top jobs"; it is also the time "when most people should become grandparents"; it is the "prime of life for a man."

These data suggest that middle-aged people in the 1960s had a set of age-related social expectations that included a decade or so of considerable transition during the middle years. Since the midlife transition has now received so much public attention, it is likely that a new social expectation about "the right time for a midlife crisis" is emerging, which in turn will reinforce its occurrence. This argument implies that the midlife transition is not necessarily inherent in the process of human development, but that it occurs in our society because of the social expectations about the tasks middle-aged persons should face. This view does not diminish the importance of the midlife transition, but it does argue that it is socially timed in a manner similar to the socially timed transition at retirement. That is, it is a normative transition, at least in part. Therefore, it would not necessarily occur in all cultures, since social expectations are not the same in all societies. Even in our society, some persons may lessen its impact by anticipating it and preparing for it, while still others may be somewhat exempt from it because their life pattern is to some degree outside the social mainstream—such as members of tight-knit ethnic groups, persons living in poverty, or never-married persons. Moreover, the studies by Livson suggested that personality factors—or the fit between the individual and social expectations—may play a major role in causing the midlife crisis.

In spite of the cultural-historical and the psychosocial influences, the authors of the four studies we have been examining assume there is an intrinsic pattern and order to this development. They imply an internal process of change in midlife that brings about this introspective period and a shift in values and orientation toward life. Vaillant (1977) finds the Erikson scheme of development particularly useful and sees the midlife shift as caused by the issue of Generativity versus Stagnation. That is, he found that his male respondents became more caring and more helpful toward those around them and sought to avoid continuing on in the same old pattern. Levinson and Sheehy both found Jung's (1933) perspective of a psychological shift during the middle years very compatible, since he emphasized the importance of a significant change toward greater inner freedom, self-knowledge, and devotion to others during the middle years. Although Jung's theory is not a dominant one in developmental psychology, his clinical intuition about the midlife changes do find some support in these studies of adult development, and his conception of other changes during the second half of life are also supported by research; we will discuss these changes in Chapter 8.

Gould's approach, as we have noted, focused on examining and casting aside various misconceptions about life that individuals carry over from their childhood. Although he does not propose a "stage" theory as in the Erikson-Vaillant approach, or a single major turning point as in Jung's approach, his view is similar to Levinson's in that the middle years consist of a series of developmental tasks to be accomplished at particular ages.

While these developmental-maturational assumptions are appealing, this approach is not wholly convincing either. Brim (1977) reviewed the research on the male midlife crisis and concluded:

> A "male mid-life crisis" will occur for some men if there are multiple, simultaneous demands for personality change; if, for instance, during the same month or year the man throws off his last illusions about great success; accepts his children for what they are; buries his father and his mother and yields to the truth of his mortality; recognizes that his sexual vigor and, indeed, interest, are declining, and even finds relief in the fact.
>
> These challenges may be stretched out over ten or twenty years. Some men are obsessed about their achievements, but not yet confronting the fact of death; other men are sharply disappointed in their children's personalities but not yet concerned about sexual potency. The events come early for some men, much later for others. There is no evidence that they are related to chronological age in any but the most general sense, e.g., "sometime during the forties."

There is as yet no evidence either for developmental periods or "stages" in the mid-life period, in which one event must come after another, or one personality change brings another in its wake. The existence of "stages," if proved true, would be a powerful concept in studying mid-life; meanwhile there is a danger of our using this facile scheme as a cover for loose thinking about human development, without carrying forward the necessary hard-headed analyses of the evidence.

The "growing pains" of mid-life, like those of youth and of old age, are transitions from one comparatively steady state to another, and these changes, even when they occur in crisis dimensions, bring for many men more happiness than they had found in younger days [p. 16].

Finally, since the only answer to the many questions raised by the studies we have discussed lies in much greater research, with more diverse samples, let us conclude with a brief critique of the research, drawing again from the discussion in Chapter 1.

The longitudinal studies (Vaillant, 1977; Livson, 1975, 1976) were especially helpful in pointing out the continuity of life over several decades of adulthood. Both, but especially Livson, suggested the characteristics of those persons who did undergo a major change in midlife, compared with those who did not. These studies suggest that a midlife transition occurs for many, but not all, respondents. In addition, a dramatic midlife crisis was rare in the Vaillant study. This long-term perspective is obviously not possible in a short-term study, since the latter is limited to data gathered within a relatively brief period of time and relies on the respondents' retrospective report of their earlier years. Therefore, it is impossible to determine the actual characteristics of the respondents in the Levinson study before the midlife period began. Thus, we cannot tell, for example, whether the 80 percent of respondents who had major midlife crises might also have been "crisis prone" all of their lives. Similarly, retrospective studies are more likely to find evidence of change, while longitudinal studies are more likely to find evidence of continuity. Not only is this inherent in the methodology, since retrospective studies combine developmental and cohort changes while longitudinal studies tend to lose those respondents over time who change the most, but also persons typically perceive that they have changed more than they actually have (cf. Woodruff & Birren, 1972). Thus, as in the example of cross-sectional and longitudinal changes in intelligence discussed in Chapter 1, the "truth" probably lies somewhere in between the relative stability found in longitudinal studies and the considerable change found in the retrospective studies.

An additional problem is that all of these studies have focused on essentially the same cohort of men, so that these data—both short-term and longitudinal— are based on only one segment of the male population in the United States in the 1970s. Thus, future studies on the midlife transition should ideally follow a more complex approach, following each of the several different cohorts over the period of early and middle adulthood (Schaie, 1977). Of course, they should also select respondents from a much wider variety of social and ethnic backgrounds and life patterns, or compare respondents from markedly different cultures. As is also obvious, they should include women as well as men in the studies. This approach is likely to provide a picture of the midlife transition that uncovers much more diversity than the present data suggest. Within the theme of a midlife transition, we would expect considerable variation.

Some of the diversity in the patterns of development during early adulthood is displayed in the first case example, or Interlude, that follows this chapter. It illustrates a number of the issues we have considered in these first three chapters, and more. However, we will not attempt to integrate these Interludes with the chapters either here or in the later chapters. Instead, this is the task and challenge that we will share because it seems that an important part of the learning process is being able to bridge the gap between theoretical concepts and real persons living their complex lives. If these chapters have done their work, the Interludes will be illuminated and will challenge you to apply the concepts we have discussed to them, and, in turn, the concepts may be illuminated. Following the Interlude, the next chapter will discuss the complex similarities and differences between men and women.

CHAPTER SUMMARY

1. Throughout the life cycle, changes or transitions are made from one pattern of life to another. These transitions may be minor, as an advancement in one's career, or major, as a divorce or the sudden death of a loved one. Transitions may be caused by internal factors, such as biological changes, or by external influences, such as social expectations. They may be changes that cause little notice, or they may bring on a crisis.

2. There are two major types of transitions—normative and idiosyncratic. Normative transitions are changes that are expected by social norms, such as graduation from high school, marriage, and retirement. Idiosyncratic transitions are changes that are unexpected, that do not occur in everyone's life, and that cannot be predicted by social norms. Examples would include divorce, serious illness, or death of one's child. Idiosyncratic transitions often have more of an impact on the individual than normative transitions and may involve an emotional crisis. Normative transitions that occur "off-time" (compared with "on-time") may also produce emotional upset.

3. Recent studies have begun to explore development during the periods of early and middle adulthood. In this chapter, Levinson's study is used as a format in describing these periods because his sample was reasonably diverse; however, he did not study women. Studies by Gould, Sheehy, and Vaillant are also important because they provide different perspectives on this period of adulthood. Vaillant's study is

especially important because his respondents were followed from college to age 47 in a longitudinal study.

4. During early adulthood (about age 17 to 40), Levinson described four phases of development, alternating between relatively stressful periods of transition and relatively stable periods: Early Adult Transition, Entering the Adult World, Age 30 Transition, and Settling Down. During these periods, the "Dream" is often important; this is an inner hope about how life will work out. A "mentor" and a "special woman" can play important roles in facilitating the young man's Dream.

5. Vaillant viewed this period as a time of striving for intimacy and career consolidation. Stable marriages and a mentor who served as a kind of "father figure" seemed to contribute to the successful resolution of these tasks in middle age. He did not find as much emotional crisis during this period as Levinson reported.

6. Gould emphasized the misconceptions that individuals need to discard as they progress through a series of stages similar to the ones Levinson described. He stressed the importance of examining the meaning of interpersonal relationships and beliefs about oneself, shifting away from those that are appropriate in childhood to ones that are more appropriate during adulthood.

7. Sheehy focused on "pacesetters" who appeared to be experiencing the stages Levinson described. She reported on women as well as men. Her respondents often provided dramatic examples of emotional crises during periods of transition.

8. A "midlife transition" was observed among many of the respondents in all of these studies around the age of 40. It often involved the issue of one's own mortality, the search for meaning and wholeness in life, and an inner search and examination of one's goals for the future.

9. Livson, in a longitudinal study of men and women, found that traditionally masculine men and traditionally feminine women earlier in life showed less evidence of a difficult midlife transition than nontraditional men and women. This suggests that the congruence between one's personality and one's life-style may affect whether the transition is quiet or stormy.

10. The influence of intergenerational family relationships appears to be central to many of the issues of the midlife period. Relationships with one's parents and one's children, reevaluation of the importance of sexuality, inner exploration, and menopause (for women) combine to provide some of the major themes of the midlife period.

11. Historical changes, the influence of social age norms and the social clock, inner psychological changes—such as those proposed by Erikson and Jung—each may contribute to the developmental changes during midlife. The close relationship between chronological age and the developmental changes during early and middle adulthood prob-

ably result, to a large degree, from the direct and indirect influence of social age norms.

12. Several factors must be considered in evaluating these studies. For example, they have focused almost exclusively on a single cohort of predominately white, middle-class men in the United States. More representative samples of middle-aged men and women are needed to determine if these themes apply to all people in our society. Data obtained form other cultures would indicate whether these developmental changes occur in other societies, or whether they are limited to our society.

REFERENCES

Brim, Orville G., Jr. 1977. Theories of the Male Mid-Life Crisis. In Nancy K. Schlossberg & Alan D. Entine (Eds.), *Counseling Adults*. Monterey, Calif.: Brooks/Cole. (Reprinted from *Counseling Psychologist*, 1976, *6*(1), 2-9.)

Chiriboga, David. 1978. The Divorce Experience in Later Life. Paper presented at the meeting of the American Orthopsychiatric Association, San Francisco, March 31, 1978.

Conger, John Janeway. 1977. *Adolescence and Youth: Psychological Development in a Changing World* (2nd ed.). New York: Harper & Row.

Fiske, Marjorie. 1978. Adult Transitions: Theory and Research from a Longitudinal Perspective. Paper presented at the meetings of the Gerontological Society, Dallas, November 18, 1978.

Fromm, Erich. 1941. *Escape from Freedom.* New York: Avon.

Gould, Roger L. 1972. The Phases of Adult Life: A Study in Developmental Psychology. *The American Journal of Psychiatry, 129*(5), 521-531.

Gould, Roger L. 1978. *Transformations: Growth and Change in Adult Life.* New York: Simon and Schuster.

Gutmann, David. 1977. The Cross-Cultural Perspective: Notes Toward a Comparative Psychology of Aging. In James E. Birren & K. Warner Schaie (Eds.), *Handbook of the Psychology of Aging.* New York: Van Nostrand Reinhold.

Jaques, Elliott. 1965. Death and the Mid-Life Crisis. *International Journal of Psychoanalysis, 46,* 502-514.

Jung, Carl G. 1933. The Stages of Life. (Translated by R.F.C. Hull.) In Joseph Campbell (Ed.), *The Portable Jung.* New York: Viking, 1971.

King, Barbara. 1978. Marriage at the Top. *Town & Country, 132*(4978), 75-77.

Levinson, Daniel J. 1978. *The Seasons of a Man's Life.* (With Charlotte N. Darrow, Edward B. Klein, Maria H. Levinson, & Braxton McKee.) New York: Knopf.

Livson, Florine B. 1975. Sex Differences in Personality Development in the Middle Adult Years: A Longitudinal Study. Paper presented at the meeting of the Gerontological Society, Louisville, October 29, 1975. (To appear in: Dorothy Eichorn, John Clausen, Norma Haan, Marjorie Honzik, & Paul Mussen (Eds.), *Present and Past in Midlife.*)

Livson, Florine B. 1976. Patterns of Personality Development in Middle-Aged Women: A Longitudinal Study. *International Journal of Aging and Human Development*, 7(2), 107-115.

Lowenthal, Marjorie Fiske; Thurnher, Majda; Chiriboga, David; & Associates. 1975. *Four Stages of Life: A Comparative Study of Women and Men Facing Transitions*. San Francisco: Jossey-Bass.

Mead, Margaret. 1928. *Coming of Age in Samoa*. New York: Dell (Laurel).

Neugarten, Bernice L. 1967a. A New Look at Menopause. *Psychology Today*, 1(7), 42-45, 67-69, 71.

Neugarten, Bernice L. 1967b. The Awareness of Middle Age. In Bernice L. Neugarten (Ed.), *Middle Age and Aging*. Chicago: University of Chicago Press, 1968. (Originally published in: *Middle Age*. Roger Owen, Ed. London: British Broadcasting Corporation.)

Neugarten, Bernice L. 1968. Adult Personality: Toward A Psychology of the Life Cycle. In Bernice L. Neugarten (Ed.), *Middle Age and Aging*. Chicago: University of Chicago Press.

Neugarten, Bernice L. 1977. Adaptation and the Life Cycle. In Nancy K. Schlossberg & Alan D. Entine (Eds.), *Counseling Adults*. Monterey, Calif.: Brooks/Cole. (Reprinted from *Counseling Psychologist*, 1976, 6(1), 16-20; originally titled "Dynamics of Transition of Middle Age to Old Age," in *Journal of Geriatric Psychiatry*, 1970, 4, 71-87.)

Neugarten, Bernice L., & Hagestad, Gunhild O. 1976. Age and the Life Course. In Robert H. Binstock & Ethel Shanas (Eds.), *Handbook of Aging and the Social Sciences*. New York: Van Nostrand Reinhold.

Neugarten, Bernice L.; Moore, Joan W.; & Lowe, John C. 1965. Age Norms, Age Constraints, and Adult Socialization. *American Journal of Sociology*, 70(6), 710-717.

Neugarten, Bernice L.; Wood, Vivian; Kraines, Ruth J.; & Loomis, Barbara. 1963. Women's Attitudes Toward the Menopause. *Vita Humana*, 6(3), 140-151.

Offer, Daniel, & Offer, Judith B. 1975. *From Teenage to Young Manhood*. New York: Basic Books.

Rollins, Boyd C., & Feldman, Harold. 1970. Marital Satisfaction Over the Family Life Cycle. *Journal of Marriage and the Family*, 32(1), 20-28.

Schaie, K. Warner. 1977. Quasi-Experimental Research Designs in the Psychology of Aging. In James E. Birren & K. Warner Schaie (Eds.), *Handbook of the Psychology of Aging*. New York: Van Nostrand Reinhold.

Sheehy, Gail. 1976. *Passages: Predictable Crises of Adult Life*. New York: Dutton.

Vaillant, George E. 1977. *Adaptation to Life*. Boston: Little, Brown.

Woodruff, Diana S., & Birren, James E. 1972. Age Changes and Cohort Differences in Personality. *Developmental Psychology*, 6(2), 252-300.

Interlude
George, Age 27

George is the first of six case examples to be presented in this book; taken together, these examples represent a series of views of the life span from early adulthood to old age. Each is an edited transcript of an interview that lasted one to two hours. Six interviews were conducted by the author during the spring of 1973: George, age 27; Theresa, age 34; Murray, age 48; Joan, age 67; Henry, age 75; and Mrs. K., age 89; Murray was interviewed again in 1979 at age 54, and follow-up information is available for all except one of the respondents. These individuals do not represent "typical" adults —whatever that might mean; instead, they were selected to represent a range of adults—in age, social class, and life-style. One respondent lives in a nursing home; another lives in Harlem and has five grandchildren; one man is a successful modern dancer; another is a successful executive; and another is a waiter looking forward to retirement; the sixth respondent is a young working mother.

The interview was designed to explore the major milestones and crisis points during the respondent's adult life. Questions about the family, the occupation, thoughts about the future, and reflections about the past were central issues that were explored. The questions are indicated by italics in the text; the respondent's own words are used throughout with a minimum of editing or grammatical correction. All of the names have been changed, and basic identifying names and places have been changed in order to ensure anonymity.

One important characterisitc of these interviews is that the respondents knew how they were to be used. Thus, the information is censored by the respondent to the extent that each tended to present his or her life in a relatively positive light under these conditions. To be sure, negative aspects and crises are discussed also but, in general, these interviews are revealing the more integrated, better understood, and socially acceptable aspects of their lives. Of course, this is a characteristic of well-functioning persons who have a reasonably good understanding of their strengths and shortcomings and who do not dwell on their failures or weaknesses. However, one should read these cases with a healthy mixture of skepticism and openness. While there is probably much under the surface that is less positive, the strengths and ability to cope with mistakes, conflicts, and flaws are as important for understanding human functioning as any "deeper" conflicts and frustrations may be. In short, these are *developmental* interviews that are exploring the contours and milestones of human life; they are not clinical interviews attempting to uncover neurotic or unconscious psychodynamic conflicts.

At the time of this interview, George was a 27-year-old man who had moved to New York to join a dance company after graduating from college. He makes no secret of his gay life-style and has been living with his lover (Rick) for several years. By almost any standards he is successful and has a promising career ahead; he is comfortable with his life-style and, as he puts it, they live very well. His parents have accepted his homosexuality and his lover and take considerable pride in his accomplishments. Yet he feels un-fulfilled in an important way that seems to be puzzling and disturbing to him.

This case raises a number of questions. What does it mean to be a "nor-mal" adult? Why did the milestones and crisis points he selected to discuss stand out in his memory? In what ways has his gay life-style affected the de-velopmental milestones of young adulthood? Was his decision to become a dancer a usual example of vocational choice? How has he changed in the last few years; that is, what effect has "experience" had on him? Is there any evidence of the developmental themes of early adulthood in his life? What do you think the future might hold for him?

As you look back over your life, what are some of the milestones that stand out? In terms of just profession, in terms of personal life? Do you want specifics? Yes. What made me choose my profession? *Was that a milestone?* It certainly was, I became a dancer out of the blue, literally—overnight. It wasn't my first dance class as such that made me become a dancer, because, although I en-joyed it very much, I knew I loved to dance. I've known that all my life. I had never seen dancers performing to even know there was such a thing as dance, other than ballet. I remember seeing [a famous dancer] on stage, watching him perform. I can even picture one thing that he did that just so struck me, abso-lutely hit me, and was such a fabulous thing to be able to do. I said "I want to do that." *Do you remember the time that you saw him do that?* I remember the exact moment. I can see it right now, I can picture it happening again— the ex-act moment in a particular dance—it was one particular solo that I remember as breathtaking. *And that was the turning point for you?* I look back and that's what I remember, so that's a milestone for me, what one would have to call a milestone. . . .

Other milestones. I don't know, they just flow in. . . . Probably teachers I con-sider milestones in shaping my personality. My speech teacher in high school was very elemental in how I think today. He was a superb teacher, ultra-conser-vative. His political views just turn my stomach, but he was such a fabulous teacher that as a teacher he could overcome some of these . . . well, almost fas-cistic views. He was just a great teacher. He developed many things that I didn't know existed as such. The drama department was nothing in high school. He was a vital force, a vital person. And an English teacher . . . as I struggled to find my own identity as a homosexual, besides my identity as a person, as George. Just this little thing she did that made me realize that homosexuals as a class can be accepted by respected people. She called me in quite late in the se-mester just for a little talk. She was having some terrible times of her own, in terms of her lover of some 40 years, who I assume was her lover, a woman who lived with her for 40 years, who was dying of cancer. This was a very trau-matic period for her. And she called me in and she said, "George, I just want you to know that I understand." She didn't say understand what. "And as far as your English grade, don't worry about it. I understand you're having problems and you'll have many more. This is some way I can help you. But you don't have to worry about your English grade." And that was it. She never said what or anything else, but of course I understood and she understood. I'm a sentimental slob and, of course, tears and all of that, but it was just a beautiful moment to know that there was. . . . It was the first time I was confronted, outside of a doctor situation. I did have psychiatric care in school. Here was someone who was not . . . I was not talking to in a medical way which is ugh, dry . . . even when you're probing inner problems, and because, I guess the way I think—I become so clinical as a person probing these problems and so far outside of them that I never feel a sense of satisfaction or of real searching, as I did with this teacher.

Anyway, other milestones. Oh, I'm sure I have some. Oh! Telling my folks I was gay was a milestone. Partly because of the way they responded (laughs). *When did that happen?* I was a junior in college. It was at the breakfast table, where in our family "great events" occur. 'Cause that's where most of the talking happens. And I finally just said, "Mom, Dad, I have something I just have to say, have to tell you." I told them I was gay. They both sighed, the two biggest sighs of relief you ever heard. And I was perplexed until they explained that they'd known for years. They never said how they'd known, I've never asked. And they just knew some day that I would tell them, and they just hoped that I would express my trust that they felt I had in them—which I do—could express it enough to say, "Folks, I am different than what we consider a norm," and that was about the way I said it. What could they say besides "Whew! Golly, you finally trusted us enough to tell us," and they were so pleased. That began a great chapter in our parent-child relationship. I still am their child. I love being their son, not a child, well yes, child, meaning offspring, not meaning adolescent.

Okay. More milestones. Can you think of some other areas maybe that would interest you? Or that would be relevant? Or that would help me remember? *What about more recent milestones? Like coming to New York?* Well, coming to New York wasn't really a milestone for me because that was so planned, so matter-of-fact that I was going to do it, that it wasn't really a milestone. Let me see. My life has been going so according to schedule lately, and so very planned. My working life I mean. *You planned everything out at some point back?* It seems to have evolved that way, you know. Because I'm going in the direction with goals, specific goals in mind and I'm going that way and nothing has really detoured me off. My traveling has been very exciting. I wouldn't call any of it a milestone because I think of a milestone as changing, as a point where I can say from here on there is a real change. Richard, in a way maybe, I could call a milestone, meeting him and settling down with him; that's something I always wanted; even though maybe other people wouldn't interpret it that way, I've always been a very settled down kind of person. And we've just integrated our lives together, so it didn't really change my life or his, I don't believe. Other than it fulfilled for each of us something we needed and wanted. But again not a milestone. *It sounds like in a very real sense, once you made the decision to become a dancer, then somehow the rest of it is kind of an unfolding and fairly continuous.* Oh, yes; very much, very much a kind of an unfolding kind of thing. I went ahead and graduated from college, came to New York, studied, moved into the dance company, and have been working ever since as a dancer. Now I have started for the past year and a half getting jobs of my own, teaching dance last summer; and I have two offers to do teaching this coming summer, both for one-month periods. That would be two months of very well-paid teaching I might add, and do very well for myself in terms of building my own career. It's still all part of an unfolding. I live well now, very well.

As you look back over your life, have you changed much do you think, or has it been pretty similar all the way through? I was going to say I haven't changed. That's silly, of course I've changed. I've changed a lot. But to me, I'm still just me. And that me has always been here and present. Just different facets of it are more evident now as opposed to other facets which were more evident then, which I'm sure are still part of me, and could in the future be shown again. I have not changed as a person. Because people are such complex beings, like great crystal, the different sides are shown at different times, and at different angles, and because of different presences and outside influences, different things are seen. If nothing but green lights are shining on something, it's going to appear green, now matter what color it is. It's going to be changed. And yet it itself is not changed. It is still whatever it is. Take away the green lights and it's still there. So, I have not changed. I may appear different and seem to show different things.

We've been talking about milestones. What about crisis points? Have there been any crisis points that stand out? Yes, I've had a lot of crises. Do you want some of them? *Yes.* Well, younger crises, the natural crises of growing up, going through puberty, adolescence. I was a very nervous child. I'm still highly strung, but I just express it in very different ways. *Adolescence was a difficult time for you?* Oh, terrible. But, it is for everyone. I just probably expressed it more obviously than most children do. Through eighth, ninth, tenth, eleventh, twelfth [grades] and the first year of college I had my annual spring nervous breakdown, for which I had to be shuttled off for a time. Because it might have built to the point where I couldn't, in the course of my everyday things, I could not handle myself. *What do you mean by "shuttled off"?* Well, sometimes it just meant going home for a few days, staying away from everyone. The last couple of years of high school and the first year of college it meant running off to the hospital. I just became that bad. So, just getting out of my mainstream, away from my peer group, which is for me where the real pressures are. The people I work with now is where the real pressures are. *Was that partly because of your homosexuality?* I thought so at the time. I look back now and I say maybe it is, or was; maybe it was because I was gay; but it was because I felt so extraordinarily different, and was treated as someone very very different, and because I had some very sick high school and junior high counselors. I know now; then I didn't know. I trusted them and they simply could not cope with it. I'm an open person. I tell people how I feel. In eighth grade I said, "I'm in love with that boy" and my counselor simply could not cope with it. He didn't know what to do, so it turned out he did all the wrong things. He said, "No, you're not," and such other stupid things, or "That's wrong." So my feelings of being different were constantly being reinforced by the very people who should have been helping me. *You say "different." What do you mean "different"?* How was I different? How do I consider myself different? *I gather that was more than just being gay.* Well, we don't know what being gay means as an adolescent, I don't think. We're all growing up and we're all changing. I didn't seem to be changing the way I saw the people around me changing. I always felt, especially from my male peers, that I was not like them. I didn't know why. And I was angry because I wasn't like them. Sometimes this anger was in terms of fighting and I would fight. Sometimes it was in terms of crying. I was extremely high strung, emotional; I'm still emotional. I'll cry. I did just Monday night, after talking to Mom. Just knowing what pain she was in talking to her on the phone [in the hospital]—she could hardly communicate—it just killed me. Tears just streamed down my face. I couldn't control it. Other boys were not so emotional. And so, I was ridiculed. And ridicule at 15 is tough, very tough.

Any other crises? Any other crises. Ah, I should go back to my building of my personality, because of my strong Christian background, I think I have a double set of morals inside of me that is constantly having trouble. I do not even understand them both. One comes from life as I lived it so far, and one comes from the morals that I've been taught. Maybe we all have these, probably. *Somehow these Christian values are in conflict with the values that you live with day by day?* Right. And to add on to that, the ideas and values that I live with day by day I consider correct. How can they both be correct? I don't know. This is my problem. And I admit this, because I have said to myself many times, if I did not truly believe what I was doing was correct, I wouldn't be doing it. And yet, at the same time, I will acknowledge to myself that I believe this, whatever it is, is wrong or not right, and yet I'm doing it. I don't know how to justify that and I don't know if I can. These are the kinds of philosophical questions one justifies, maybe never. *Is a lot of the content of this conflict sexual?* Part of it is. Like, just today I read something in the [New York] *Post* that deeply disturbed me—a Catholic priest saying that one cannot be a Christian and be a homosexual. That's intellectually sick, but inside me, I say maybe he's right. Yet, I know he's not right, and yet I can still believe he could be right. You know, there's an example of what I mean. *Can you think of another kind of example that is not sexual?* Yeah . . . abortion. I do not believe in abortion, and yet there are arguments that I have to agree with *for* abortion. How can this be resolved, because I can argue both sides and believe both sides? Absolutely believe them. And that is not compartmental thinking. *You really believe both and are caught in between.* Right, I truly believe both sides are correct.

Have there been any crisis points in your relationship with your family? Not really. Some childish things. Nothing really recently. I've never run away from my family or anything like that as a child. *You said at one point when we didn't have the recorder on that your mother was in the hospital.* Yeah, she is. *Is this a serious matter?* It's not, now, as it's turned out, thank goodness. Oh, I see what you mean, a crisis in those terms. No, there's not even been any in those terms, no. Were my Mom and Dad, and they're not young, to die, that could be critical to me, I believe. Not permanently hurt, or upset by it, but I would be truly hurt because I love them as human beings, I want them to be around, to enjoy them. It's such a very selfish thing to be saying, but it would be such a personal loss; the reason I can say that is because I know how fully they've both lived, and that in terms of them, there's no loss. They could both have died tomorrow, and they have lived very full lives. I think their lives may have been fulfilled a long time ago, and this is just all the frosting on the cake. I know a few young people who are such good people that their lives are fulfilled and that everything they do, the goals they reach, their quests and so forth are just growing beyond them. A tree can be a tree at two foot high, and can be a whole tree, and there it is—but if it grows to be 50 feet high it's just all grand and fabulous. *Is that somehow the way it is for you? Do you feel that way about yourself?* I'd like to think it were true, but it's not, no I'm not.

Before you changed [the topic] I was going to say that I have a romantic ideal in my psychic sexual fulfillment that I do not have. And I have had about three maybe four boys, and I knew that they were my desired sexual outlet, who, in my eyes could have been the fulfillment of that psychic sexual need. And, as yet, it still goes unfulfilled. And whether it even can be fulfilled, I don't know. And whether any of these boys could have fulfilled it I've no way of knowing. I just know that there are people who I have said to myself or even to them, "I love you," and it has not gone beyond. It has not been a fulfillment of that "I love you." *It never turned into a relationship?* Right. *So then your relationship with Rick is not one of these?* No, it's not, because my relationship with Rick is very fulfilled. I wouldn't give it up for anything. I have questioned it before. But I've only questioned it because I think it's healthy to question. I would not give it up for any of these ["ideal" boys] because this is something I truly need, want, have found, and am not going to let go of. So, I truly love Rick. But this thing, whatever it is in my head that I call a need; right now I call it a need for Bill or before him it was another Bill. Whatever that is in me, I don't know. I guess I'll have to find out, if I ever do. Don't people as they all grow older have unanswered questions, about themselves, about their living? It is almost accepted there will be unanswered questions in my life. I won't know everyhting. I'll see through the glass darkly and it gets clearer, but will never be gone.

How long have you and Rick been together? Five years last November, and this is February . . . a long time. *Have there been any crisis points in that relationship?* Oh, yes, several (laughter). *Do you regard it as a marriage?* I suppose so. I look on it as very similar to the relationship that my parents have. Because we're two people who want to live together and are greater because we're together; and that's perhaps, what a marriage is. *Have there been some crisis points?* Yes, there have been crises. For example, when we first got together we were still discovering each other, and I'm sure you know that one doesn't understand someone else immediately. We must all make concessions. That's a good word, it doesn't have to be a bad word. All have to make concessions if we are going to live with someone else. None of us can perfectly fit into someone else's life; such a thing doesn't exist. It takes you a while to find out how you must act or react to someone else before you can be together. Now, considering this I was talking about earlier—I don't know if I'll ever find [that "need"] fulfilled, like for example [with] Bill. Richard has had some real troubles because he feels that maybe somehow he's to blame for not "fulfilling" me. I, of course, say that's silly, because I don't even know if I can be fulfilled; how could you blame yourself for not fulfilling me? Then maybe I am fulfilled, and this other is a manifestation of some other problem. It has nothing to do with *fulfillment* as such. These are all possibilities that a person must face in their own lives. So, this has been a crisis a couple times—where he has felt outrageous jealousy, what I consider outrageous jealousy, and then self-pity after thinking about it because he felt that he was inadequate. So, this has been a crisis. But, there have been no others as such. We hardly even argue anymore. We do get mad at one another and it's usually silly; but we forgive so quickly anymore, so easily. I'm glad, and I think he's glad that we both know that we can get mad at one another and just get outraged and throw things, and be furious, and even shout and it doesn't matter. That's very important to both of us because we're both volatile people; and to know that we don't have to be anything else or anybody else when we come into this house. When we come home we can be ourselves; we can be angry, we can literally take out our day's frustrations on each other, which we do do, both of us. The night before last, both of us had horrible, frustrating, interminably long days. And we both came home at different times, outraged, and we both took it out on the other one (laughter). But that really didn't matter, you know; we were cuddling and having a good time.

How long did you know him before you decided to move in with him? The whole thing was so gradual that it's really hard to tell. There's no date I can list of having moved in because I had two apartments; I lived here sort of and still had my other apartment. Some nights I slept there; eventually I slept here more than there, and then eventually I sublet that one out and eventually got rid of that one completely and then only lived here; but this was all so gradual that there's no way to say. I knew when I met him that I was interested. Here's a point that I think is very interesting. He is more like my best friends that I went to college with than any of my previous lovers ever were. He is more like the people I wanted to spend time with than the people I spent [time] in bed with, which is an interesting point. I knew he was bright and that probably attracted me to him more than anything else, because he's just so exceptionally bright. That's very important to me.

I gather that neither of you have any children. No. *Do you resent that?* No, I don't. That's interesting timing on that question, because just a couple days ago I was reading about adoption. And also, someone else had been talking about a way man is immortal is by having children. And I tried to think about that; what that meant to me. I said maybe I should worry about that. I'm a good worrier. Maybe I should think about that too. Would I some day worry about my own immortality and would not having a son make that hard for me. Well, I thought and I said, "What about the people who do not have children and who adopt?" I know from experience that they consider them their children every bit as much. And yet, if they were to think about it intellectually, I'm sure they would have to say, "No, I'm not passing myself on." And so I say this doesn't really interest me—having children—I don't particularly want children. I know that I will probably do a great deal of teaching in my life and I can be a grander father to more people that way. Already, the list of people, young men in general, even young ladies who have written to me after I've been somewhere teaching and said, "You have changed my life." And that, you know . . . how much greater father can I ever be than to have people tell you that you've changed their lives. Just a couple days ago I got a letter from a boy in Iowa who, after seeing me and talking with me in class—this was his first dance class ever—he's changed his whole life. He's come out, told his family. I was the first homosexual he met who was proud; not proud to be gay, that's so dumb—who was *proud* and who was a homosexual. Because I must make a distinction between saying I am not ashamed of being gay, and I am proud of being gay. I'm not proud of being gay any more than a heterosexual is proud of being heterosexual. But I am not ashamed of being gay any more than a heterosexual is ashamed of being heterosexual. There is a big, big difference there that I think is very important, [in contrast] to the idea currently in vogue that I'm gay and I'm proud that I'm gay. I think that's silly. They're making the wrong thing important in their lives. So, this young man has dropped out of school, applied to another school which has a big dance department; it's in the West; he'll be going to study dance. He's been accepted there already. It really changed his life. [I've received] several page letters. This has happened to me several times. And I couldn't feel more of a father than that. I wouldn't want to be. I'm not interested in bringing more children into the world; we've got enough and therefore I can, as a father, in terms of a father, in the old Biblical sense of a father, I can father people. I'll be doing more than most people do.

In terms of your occupaton as a dancer, have there been any milestones or crisis points? Oh, I've almost quit several times, if that's what you mean. I almost quit the company I'm currently in. But that's, that's still in grappling with knowing the situation I am in is not perfect, and I must be continually aware that I have to be there—this may sound crass and I don't mean it to sound crass—to get out of it what I can get out of it. Now I'm *giving* a hell of a lot too. So, that's why it's not crass to be getting out of it what I can get out of it, because I'm also giving every bit as much as I'm getting out of it. But I am there to get out of it what I can. And so, sometimes a really bad situation will arise; some personal thing with the director, some impossible tour situation—because touring can be impossible. And I'll say, "What am I doing? Why am I doing this? I'm not enjoying this. I've got to get out," and then I say, "No; my greater goals are more important and are satisfied better and can be reached better by staying." So I stay, although that's how I get over these kinds of crises. One of the most exciting personal things that happened to me arose out of my being a dancer besides the applause—which is the greatest thing in the world for me—was meeting Mr. and Mrs. Shah, the Shah of Iran, which was so exciting. I am excited by great people and I really felt I was in the presence of two great people when I met them. I am middle class, bourgeois, mid-America . . . I shouldn't . . . forget that. That is my background. I think it's important I remember that this is from where I came. I've been lucky. I just this morning made a list of countries I've been to— twenty-five of them. That's pretty impressive. And, it's unusual for someone from my circumstances and background. And in that way I can appreciate it even more because I can say, "This is unusual. I have gone beyond myself in some way." In some ways I am a better person for it. How could a son of a multimillionaire be proud at my age of having traveled all over the world when he can do it at will?

Thinking back to when you first came to New York and started dancing with the company, how was that? Was that a crisis point in some way? Well, it was planned. It was all planned. I just did it. It was exciting. I loved it all. I was thrilled by everything. Golly, eager? Was I eager!

How did you come to the point of deciding that you were going to come to New York and be a dancer? I was always going to come to New York as long as I can remember. Someday I was going to go to New York. For many years I said that I was going to come to New York and be an actor. Practically, I never said that. I said things like, in ninth grade, you know, it's time to make a report on what you're going to be when you grow up, and I said I was going to be an accountant; and another time I was going to be something else, because I always thought of myself as a very practical person. But I always said to myself, "Someday I'm going to go to New York and be an actor." So that's how I got to college, thinking in those terms. Then I discovered dance. For me this somehow seemed even better, and even greater; I could see more fulfillment, and as it turned out that's where it looks like I belonged. And so I did come to New York, not as an actor; I came as a dancer.

How does your future look in terms of your career as a dancer? How do you see it developing? Well, if we only knew what lies ahead. I know what I want, I know what my goals are, and I know that's what I'm striving for. I value myself as an artist and a dancer, they are two very different things, which gets back to some basic philosophy of what a performer is. Is the performer an artist or is the performer a craftsman? Just to make things simple, I'll say the performer is a craftsman for me and I value myself as an artist. And therefore, I have to do my art; my art is theater. And so I'm working toward that goal. I'm a dancer; I work all the time to get better, to become continually a better technician and a better performer or craftsman, and I'm also learning the art of dance. I practice it as a craftsman with increasing craft·ability, knowing that I also have artistic abilities. How good they are? All I can say is that what I have done so far artistically has been successful. I just hope that by continuing that I'll be more successful. That's what I'm working toward—which may mean my own company or maybe being part of another company. Maybe it will eventually lead its way from dance as such. *What are your career goals?* I don't know what it is specifically. I know that it will be in the theater. It may not even be as a performer. I don't know. I'll find out what peaks I can reach as a performer. And there's the age variable. One gets better as they get older. It's through sheer doing that one gets better. So, for my age I will be able to judge my peak as an artist. But, I don't know if it will even be in dance; it might be in some other form of theater. I don't know.

Has the way people reacted to you changed over the years? I'm still different. I still feel very different, and think I am treated as such. People are not ready for candid observation and conversation. People are not ready to be touched. If I want to touch someone I do; I get in trouble with it sometimes—male or female.

Or, to say, "I love you" or to say, "I want to go to bed with you," or to say any everyday little thing, they're not ready for that kind of candidness, and I am. I am that way and I don't think it's wrong. If I thought it was wrong, I would have stopped it. So I will continue doing it, even though it offends people. I will say, "Okay, I'll watch myself under certain circumstances." If I think there will be long-range problems by my being candid or being open, or being too emotional, then I say, "Okay, George, don't. This is the time to say no. . . ." I am still different, and I'm treated differently; but now I kind of like being different because I have met enough people to whom that differentness was not bad, it was exciting, and I found out that the people to whom it seemed exciting were more the people I liked, were more the kind of people I was interested in. And the people who found it offensive were the people I didn't care about anyway. *So it's not so much that the people respond to you differently in general, but that you've found more people who respond to you the way you want them to respond.* Yeah, it's one of the reasons I probably love New York City. It's a huge city and I love big cities. I'm excited by them. I'm excited by many people. For me maybe it takes many people to find the few I want to call my peers, that I want to be my associates.

Would you say that you've got a pretty firm sense of who you are right now? Do you know who you are? Oh, that's a hard one. Let me think. . . . I know *exactly* who I am. *Who are you?* I'm George and my friends all know. That's all I can say. I am complex. I am simple. I'm emotional. I'm volatile. Creative. I'm an S.O.B. I have a nasty temper at times. I love sex. I love giving; I love receiving. I love beautiful things, and I even like some ugly things. I think I'm open. I don't have a closed mind, and yet I know that at times I will absolutely shut everyone and everything off because I think they're wrong, which is a closed mind, as closed as you can be. So I know that's part of me too. I'm opinionated. I'm educated. All those opinions mean things to me. Do I think I'm right? Darn right I think I'm right! If I didn't think I was right I would do different things and say different things. Am I always right? Oh, no! I'm not always right. That's been obvious through my life. But when I did it I thought I was right, or I wouldn't have done it, whatever it is at the time. *Have you always felt that way about yourself, that you really knew who you were? Or was there some time when you began to get more of a sense of really knowing who you were?* Probably always thought I knew who I was, but I can look back and say I hadn't the foggiest idea who I was when I was 15, 16, 17, 18, . . .19, . . . 20, . . . 21. And I'm sure at 35 I'll say, "George you had no idea really what you were at 27." Now I think I do. That's what I hope maturing is; that's what I hope wisdom is—all of which I want. I'm not mature. God knows I'm not mature (laughter), but it's not bad to be immature because when I'm mature I'll probably be dead (laughter). Because maturing means "full," "the end," maturing is the top, and I hope I don't reach the peak until I'm gone. I want to reach the peak on my death bed.

Do you sometimes think about death? I guess. Death's death. Someday, maybe soon, maybe not. It doesn't matter. It really doesn't. I have wanted to die, so I guess then it mattered. I have enjoyed myself so much that I don't think I want to die right now, because it's so fabulous; but, at the same time I've said, "May-be this would be a good time." But, I'm going to die; I hope it's not painful for someone else. Or I hope it's as painless as it can be. Death always seems to cause pain to the living. I assume mine will, because I know there are people who care. I know Rick cares. If I were to die tomorrow he would be very very hurt. My family would be very hurt. But, this is why, even though I thought about suicide because I was suffering a pain which I don't understand, I said, "Well, when I die I want to hurt as few people as possible. And if I die now by killing myself it would probably hurt as many people as possible, so I don't want to die." But . . . I'm not dead yet. So, that's about it. *Do you sometimes look over your life and review where you've been, what you've done?* I love memo-ries, if that's what you mean? I value memories greatly. I have such fabulous memories! They are very important to me. . . . I love to go over them, I love to reexperience. My life has been exciting! And sometimes exciting-bad. And even then it was exciting. I wouldn't trade it. That doesn't mean it couldn't have been different or couldn't have been better, and even maybe wished it had been bet-ter, but the whole thing I wouldn't trade. I value my past.

Is sex as important to you now as it used to be? Yes. *More, about the same?* About the same. I don't have as much, yet it's still very, very important. Seri-ously important, not frivolously. I love sex. I love to talk about it. I love to do it, even though I don't do it much, because it is so much a part of *every* person. It is a great expression of giving and taking between two or more people. And sometimes, just one—giving yourself—because I enjoy masturbation, too. . . . I enjoy fantasizing. Oh, my fantasies when I masturbate are extraordinary, they're beautiful. If you wanted to find a fault you could probably say I fantasize too much in my life. That's probably my greatest fault, as I see it. One of the things I would change is, perhaps, I would be more real—fantasize less. Although I en-joy my fantasies, so I doubt that I will. *Why are you having sex less now than you used to?* Partly because I know I can get it when I want it. So, the urge to be constantly in there fighting for it—it's hard work—sex can be hard work too. You go in there and prove yourself, which all of us, I think, tend to do, espe-cially in more frivolous circumstances. I know that if I see a boy I want sexually, I can probably have him 99 times out of 100, straight or gay. I don't have to prove that anymore. So, I'll see a pretty boy and say, "Oooh, I'll have to go to bed with him," and I just don't put out the effort that it might take, because I have lots of things to do, and the rewards of just having conquered someone are not always equal to the effort involved. I know I could probably do it, and I have lots of other things to do, and I do the other things. *How about your rela-tionship with Rick in terms of sex; are you having less sex now than you once did?* Oh, yes. We don't have sex very often. *Why is that?* Well, I'm not really sure. I know it's probably a good thing, but once again, we don't have to per-form for one another. We both work extraordinary hours, we're tired, so when we have it it's because we want it, and for no other reason. Oh, there are some times when one of us wants it and I know we just do it for the other one, just to please the other one. I've been too tired and Rick has really wanted sex, and I say "Oh, okay." I hope he doesn't . . . well, intellectually we both know we do that, but I hope he doesn't know when it has happened, because I want to please him and I know it wouldn't please him if he thought I were doing it out of obligation. And, the same for him. I know he's done it for me. I don't know when . . . I have no particular times in mind. I have sometimes known afterwards when he's told me, like the next day . . . "Oh, I really didn't want to . . . I was so tired last night. I hope it wasn't too bad."

In general, in your life, do you have a sense of being particularly productive, of leaving or having left your mark? Yes, I think it's obvious by the things I've said. *I guess you've also said this before, but has life been a meaningful adventure for you?* Very. Yes, I've also said that, yeah. *You are pleased with how it's been?* Pleased, not satisfied, pleased. *What are some of the things you'd like to change?* About my life? I would like to understand why I think I love Bill. I'd like to understand that . . . or why I think I need him, and need him to love me, because I don't understand that. I would like to learn a better way of being candid without insulting and hurting, which sometimes I do. But it is usually of more value for me to be honest than not to hurt. So sometimes I'll say things and other people will say, "You shouldn't have said that," and I'll say, "It needed to be done. Somebody had to say it." *Finally, would you say that your life is different now than it was a year or two ago? Have you changed? Are you different now than you were a year or two ago?* No, I'm not different at all. I know more. I have a greater understanding of some things; not as great as it will be next year. I hope it's better next year. I hope I understand more. I have to grow in wisdom. I want to be wise, truly wise; what I consider wise. I want to be generous. I can be more generous. *What would you like to be doing in five years?* Exactly what I'm doing right now . . . getting ready for another New York season . . . whatever that may mean. That could mean a hundred things.

It was not possible to interview George again in 1979 because of his busy schedule; however, I did talk with him long-distance by telephone for a few minutes. At the age of 33, he had been in the dance company for ten years and had just returned from one of his many extended foreign tours with the company. He and Rick have now been together for 12 years. He finds that the long periods of separation while he is away on tour are more difficult now than they used to be, since the relationship seems to be even more important in his life than it was six years ago; he recently traveled several thousand miles to be at home when Rick had an operation, but then had to return to the company. When asked about milestones and crisis points, he reported that they had bought a house 5½ years ago; this brought a period of strain in their relationship because of the financial difficulties that were involved. Another difficult period was when they no longer had sex, partly because Rick was drinking alcohol while using prescribed tranquilizers. Rick eventually stopped drinking, no longer takes the tranquilizers, and has lost 40 pounds; their sex life has also been reestablished.

I asked George about his feeling of being unfulfilled and his fantasy about Bill that he discussed in the interview six years earlier. He responded that Bill is still important in his fantasy life, but he now understands its significance better than he did earlier, at least at an intellectual level. Part of this feeling involves the "romantic fantasy" that he feels occurs in heterosexual relationships as well as in homosexual relationships. Another part of it is a kind of identification with someone who is not gay; Bill is predominately heterosexual. At least intellectually, he now understands that the values and attitudes of his upbringing made him feel that being gay was wrong, or unfulfilling. Thus, Bill represents being liked and accepted by a heterosexual man; and the feeling of being unfulfilled has something to do with the stigma of being homosexual. Although he understands these feelings, he still recognizes that they are not fully resolved emotionally.

He reported no particular change or transition when he turned 30, but does feel a great deal of relief at having "grown up" and being further away from the many problems he had when he was younger. The problems he felt even 10 years ago took a great deal of his energy, but now he feels that he is able to use that energy for work and living, since it is being drained less by emotional problems. He has just completed choreographing a new work that was performed by a group of dancers and is looking forward to his eleventh season with the company.

$$4$$

MALE AND FEMALE
IN ADULTHOOD

Few areas of psychosocial inquiry are currently as controversial as the study of sex differences; and perhaps one's bias is least easy to detect in this field because sex differences are so familiar and so well-recognized (both physically and stereotypically). Also, it is impossible (in our view) to discuss sex differences without confronting the essentially political issue of sex discrimination, whereby the differences between the sexes are not only facts but have political and economic consequences as well. Equally controversial, however, is the origin of these differences; that is, it is impossible to discuss sex differences without dealing in some way with the controversy of "nature" versus "nurture" or "heredity" versus "environment." And as if all of this did not present enough difficulty for one chapter, we must also point out that the research on sex differences (and on the "psychology of women") as well as the women's, men's, and gay liberation movements are focusing attention, challenging old assumptions, and rapidly producing new data and new theories on the nature, origin, and meaning of sex differences. At the same time, our society is evolving toward increased flexibility of sex roles and greater equality of economic participation (at least on the surface and in legislation). Thus, our discussion of sex differences in adulthood may best be seen as a description of how things appear at the moment in a field of seeming constant motion. Nonetheless, as difficult as it may be to describe this field-in-motion, it is probably many times more difficult to work out one's individual sense of what it means, personally, to be a man or a woman when everyone is writing, studying, and debating about it. Perhaps our discussion may add some light, if not many final answers, to this current and important topic (both personally and intellectually).

This chapter, then, explores the complex question of what difference it makes whether one is a man or a woman during the adult years from a perspective of interacting physiological, social, and psychological factors. To be sure, our understanding of this complex area is only beginning to develop, and new data are constantly being discovered. Nonetheless, it is apparent that an individual's gender (male or female) is an important characteristic—physiologically, socially, and psychologically—and it influences the individual in countless ways. For example, an individual's gender is apparent from a wide variety of cues, and it plays an important role in most social interactions; that is, one's gender implies that certain roles and behaviors are appropriate while others are not, depending on the gender of the other actors and on the nature of the social situation. Thus, in our society, two women or a man and a woman may embrace and kiss in greeting, but two men typically do not; women are allowed to cry, but men are expected not to; men may be physically aggressive with one another, but not with women; and women are typically not physically aggressive with one another; and so on. In many ways sex functions as a similar kind of social cue as age, and these two social cues operate in combination so that the kind of age-sex roles or age-sex statuses we discussed in Chapter 2 typically function as important social frameworks for behavior. Also, individuals usually react differently to men and women and also tend to expect different behavior from men and women. This leads, of course, to smooth social interaction (since appropriate expectations facilitate the interactions). But it may also lead to the kind of discrimination pointed out by the various liberation groups—that is, those situations where men and women are constrained to play roles that do not meet the individual's needs, or where women are expected to perform less rewarding roles than men, or are expected to perform the same roles with less reward. Certainly, social-cultural factors are involved in these manifestations of sex differences; however, physiological factors and psychological characteristics undoubtedly interact with social-cultural norms and expectations as well.

In our view, sex differences at any given time and in any particular society may best be seen as the result of the interaction of physiological and social factors; and each factor is influenced to some degree by the other. Were there no physiological differences between men and women, and were there no social distinctions made between the behavior expected of men and women, then sex differences would be essentially individual differences. However, in our society there are pervasive and subtle sex-related norms and expectations; also there are considerable physiological differences between men and women that we will discuss in some detail. As a result of the interaction of these factors, men and women differ in their internal experience, in their external experience, and in their psychological makeup. At the same time, men and women are probably at least as similar as they are different and there is considerable individual variation. In a sense our society has tended to stress and perhaps amplify the differences between men and women; another society might stress and amplify the similarities. In either case, men and women need not be assumed to be opposites: active versus passive, rational versus emotional, independent versus dependent, and so on. Instead of this commonly assumed oppositeness, we would stress both the similarities and the differences. For example, a well-adjusted man or woman may be high on both "masculine" and "feminine" qualities if both sets of characteristics consist of similar and different personality traits and are not assumed to be opposite to one another. Similarly, one woman may be less "feminine" than another, but need not be any more "masculine"; and a man may be highly "masculine" while also relatively high (or low) on "feminine" qualities. As long as it is clear that "masculine" is not necessarily the opposite of "feminine," both sets of personality characteristics may involve positive, adaptive, and different qualities.

In sum, we feel that less confusion results if it is kept in mind that men and women are probably as similar as they are different; they share many of the basic human characteristics of individuals in our society, and they share many of the same social values and attitudes. The two differences we will discuss in this chapter are physiological differences and differences that result from the interaction of physiological, social, and psychological factors. The goal of our discussion is to examine these differences—and the similarities—and to explore the effects they have on the progression of the adult life cycle for men and women. We will begin with the discussion of physiological similarities and differences.

PHYSIOLOGICAL DIFFERENCES BETWEEN MEN AND WOMEN

Perhaps one of the reasons male and female characteristics are generally assumed to be opposite and mutually exclusive is that most persons are indeed *either* a male or a female. Few persons have physiological characteristics of both sexes; usually the internal and external genital organs, the hormones, and the chromosomes are in agreement with one another as well as with the sex the child was assigned by society. However, one or two infants out of every 1000 live births have abnormal sex chromosomes (McKusick, 1969); in some cases these genetic characteristics affect physical or hormonal characteristics. Hampson and Hampson (1961) studied a group of hermaphrodites (persons with one or more characteristics of both sexes) and found that *assigned sex* (by parents and society in general) before the age of 2½ years was nearly always the gender role (or psychological sex) adopted by the child. Many of these children were characterized by underdeveloped male genitalia and female chromosomal or hormonal reversals, but were raised as males, and chose at puberty to remain males; surgical and hormonal treatment during adolescence helped reduce the contradiction between the various aspects of sex characteristics. This study suggests that physiological sex differences, while usually either all male or all female, are considerably more complex than the obvious anatomical differences. Thus, to understand the nature and origin of physiological sex differences we must begin at the beginning.

Prenatal Differentiation and Sex-Role Behavior

When a sperm fertilizes an egg, the chromosomes that determine the sex of the offspring usually form either an XY pair (producing a male) or an XX pair (producing a female); the ratio of XY to XX is estimated to be as high as 150:100. There is also a slight excess of live male births—the ratio is about 106:100 and 103:100 for American white and black populations, respectively (Harrison, Weiner, Tanner, & Barnicot, 1964). The rate of prenatal and childhood survival gives an edge to girls, so that the excess of male births leads to an approximately equal number of men and women during the childbearing years; thereafter women outnumber men of the same age (Figure 4.1). The Y chromosome seems to be so powerful in producing a male that even when there is an extra chromosome and the configuration is XXY, the offspring is a nearly normal male, often with small testes and an inability to produce sperm.

There is a sense in which the female form is the basic one and the male form is a differentiation of the female form that would develop in the absence of an androgenic hormone (similar in chemical composition to the male hormone testosterone). About the seventh week after conception, the genes on the Y chromosome (in males) cause the gonads in the developing embryo to become recognizably testes; about the twelfth week they begin to produce this androgenic hormone. This hormone causes the genitalia to form a penis and scrotum out of the same organs that would otherwise become the clitoris, labia minor, and

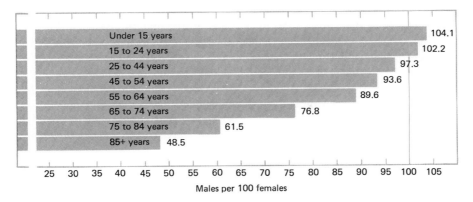

Figure 4.1
Sex ratio by age in the United States, 1975 (males per 100 females). (Source: U.S. Bureau of the Census. Demographic Aspects of Aging and the Older Population in the United States. *Current Population Reports*, Series P-23, No. 59. Washington, D.C.: U.S. Government Printing Office, 1976, Table 3-1.)

labia major; one set of internal ducts (Wolffian) develops into a system of sperm ducts in the male while another set of ducts (Müllerian) develops into the vagina, uterus, and oviducts in females (Harrison et al., 1964; Money & Tucker, 1975). Thus, the male becomes differentiated by the action of a self-produced androgenic hormone during this critical period of prenatal development; in the absence of this hormone, the female form develops.

The presence or absence of androgen appears to have other effects on the developing embryo in addition to producing the male or female genital structures. Harris (1964) argued that the *hypothalamus*, the part of the brain that plays an important role in regulating the female sex cycle, and perhaps other aspects of the central nervous system, including the brain, are also differentiated into male and female forms before birth by the effects of prenatal hormones. Several studies have found characteristic male and female behaviors in young rhesus monkeys and have also found that the behavior of females becomes more like the behavior of males when androgens were injected into their mothers when the young monkey was an embryo (cf. Young, Goy, & Phoenix, 1964). Studies with human hermaphrodites have also found that the *predisposition* toward various sex-typed behaviors may be affected by prenatal hormonal factors. In this research, Money and his associates studied individuals who were genetic females but had been accidentally exposed to androgens during prenatal development when certain drugs used in the 1950s were given to their mothers to prevent miscarriages. Although reared as girls, their behavior appeared to be "tomboyish" in the sense that they were athletic, competitive with boys for dominance, showed little interest in self-adornment or doll-play, and emphasized achievement in a career over romance and marriage (Money, 1977; Money &

Ehrhardt, 1972). Studies with genetic males who were hermaphrodites because their body did not respond fully to prenatal androgens are less clear because these boys often appeared to be female at birth and were reared as girls. Those underandrogenized boys who were reared as boys, however, appeared to be quieter and less interested in competitve sports than most boys (Money & Tucker, 1975). Nonetheless, for either the overandrogenized girls or the under-androgenized boys, their behavior was within the range of normal variation for girls and boys in their culture, and there is no evidence that they are less likely to be heterosexual than other adolescents (ibid.). Based on this research, Money and Tucker (1975) conclude:

> The prenatal sex hormone mix apparently does not create any new brain pathways or eliminate any that would otherwise be there. The wiring for all the affected behavior is present in both sexes. What your prenatal mix did was to lower the threshold so that it takes less of a push to switch you on to some behavior and to raise the threshold so that it takes more of a push to switch you on to other kinds. . . . If you had the higher percentage of an-drogen in that prenatal mix that males normally have, the potential for strenuous physical activity and dominance behavior was later apt to be more sensitive, would respond to weaker stimuli, than if you had less an-drogen. And if you did not have that higher percentage of androgen in your prenatal mix, your potential for parental behavior, which all of us have, tended to remain somewhat more sensitive to the stimuli that evoke it than if you had had more androgen prenatally. After you were born, environ-mental influences increased or decreased your sensitivity to stimuli that elicit behavior of various kinds, so that the sex differences created by the prenatal sex hormone mix were either maximized, equalized, or minimized, de-pending on your environment. In the United States, the main cultural effect is to reinforce and maximize sexual differences. What the prenatal sex hor-mone mix did *not* do was to preordain sexual differences in you in an im-mutable formula that would either equip or bar you from strenuous physical activity, dominance behavior, or parental behavior [pp. 78, 80-81].

Thus, it appears that the *predisposition* to respond or be influenced in differing ways by various social stimuli may be biochemically affected by factors such as prenatal and hormonal influences. Although knowledge of the interaction be-tween physiological (e.g., hormonal) factors and human behavior is only begin-ning to develop, it seems clear that the internal (physiological) environment and the external (psychosocial) environment interact, and neither is "all important." Instead, it is likely that each may affect the other in complex ways that are not yet fully understood.

Two additional dimensions of physiological differences between men and women—manifested in adulthood but defined in this prenatal period—are the female sex cycle and differences in sexual anatomy. We will discuss each one, keeping in mind possible psychosocial implications of these biological and physiological sex differences.

Sex Cycles, Mood Shifts, and Menopause

Until recently it was thought that one basic difference between men and women is that women have a monthly menstrual cycle that involves periodic shifts in hormonal levels, periodic times of fertility, and monthly menstruation, while men are constantly able to produce sperm and were thought to produce hormones at constant rates. To be sure, the menstrual cycle is a uniquely female characteristic; but recent evidence has suggested that men may also experience cyclic fluctuations in hormone production. For example, Exley and Corker (1966), in a study of four men over a period of 47 days, found an 8-to-10-day cycle in the fluctuating level of chemicals in male urine that results from testosterone production (probably from the testes). Recently developed techniques of measuring testosterone levels in the blood were used in a study of 20 men over a period of 60 days (Doering, Kraemer, Brodie, & Hamburg, 1975). Twelve of the men were found to have cycles in testosterone level that ranged from 3 to 30 days; no cycles were evident for the other men. If further studies over longer time periods confirm the presence of male cycles, they may shed considerable light on the similarities and differences of the hypothalamus (up to this point thought to function cyclically in women but not in men) and hormonal funcions in men and women.

In women, the sex cycle is a complex process involving the interaction of the hypothalamus, pituitary, ovaries, and uterus. One complete cycle lasts about 28 days and is repeated fairly continuously from puberty until menopause. Two major hormones—*estrogen* and *progesterone*—play a central role and fluctuate cyclically during the 28 days. Two gonadotropic hormones, follicle-stimulating hormone (FSH) and luteinizing hormone (LH), are produced by the pituitary gland and interact with the level of estrogen and progesterone in a complex feedback process to regulate the cycle. Estrogen is at a low level during and immediately following menstruation; it rises before ovulation and appears to trigger the surge in LH that leads to ovulation 16 to 24 hours later (Villee, 1975). Estrogen rises again after ovulation and declines a few days before menstruation begins (Figure 4.2). Progesterone rises after ovulation and peaks about the twenty-second day; it declines along with estrogen before menstruation.

Several studies have found a shift in various psychological measures, reflecting the woman's mood and sense of well-being during the menstrual cycle. Frank (1931) termed these mood changes that occur after the twenty-second day "premenstrual tension." Benedek (1959) reported a nearly total absence of anxiety-related themes during the ovulation phase but found a high degree of feelings of anxiety and depression, fears of mutilation and death, and sexual fantasies during the premenstrual phase. In a study of 465 women, Coppen and Kessel (1963) found that depression and irritability were typically more severe

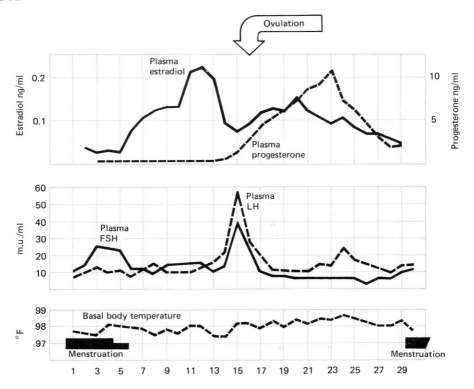

Figure 4.2

Diagram illustrating the concentrations of gonadotropins, estrogens, and progestins in the plasma during a single human menstrual cycle. The changes in basal body temperature are also shown. (Source: Villee, Claude. *Biology*. Philadephia: W.B. Saunders Company, 1972, p. 517. Copyright©1972. Adapted and reprinted with permission.)

before menstruation (when both estrogen and progesterone levels are declining rapidly) than during menstruation. Gottschalk, Kaplan, Gleser, and Winget (1962) and Ivey and Bardwick (1968) found a decrease in levels of anxiety and hostility, and high levels of self-esteem at ovulation and a significant increase in anxiety, hostility, and depression during the premenstrual period (when estrogen and progesterone are declining).

In the Ivey and Bardwick (1968) study, 26 "normal female college students" were asked to tell of an experience they had had. The level of anxiety (based on scores of the reported experience on the Gottschalk Verbal Anxiety Scale) was found to be significantly higher just before menstruation than at ovulation. However, there was no difference in anxiety scores between two successive ovulation phases, nor between two premenstrual phases—this indicates a clear pattern of fluctuation. One theme of the stories that typically characterized the ovulation phase were feelings of self-satisfaction either about success, or about being able to cope successfully: ". . . so I was elected chairman. I had to establish with them the fact that I knew what I was doing. I remember one particularly problematic meeting, and afterwards, L. came up to me and said, 'you really handled the meeting well.' In the end it came out the sort of thing that really bolstered my confidence in myself" (Bardwick, 1971, p. 31).[1]

The same girl, premenstrually, expressed strikingly different feelings: "They had to teach me how to water ski. I was so clumsy it was really embarrassing 'cause it was kind of like saying to yourself you can't do it and the people were about to lose patience with me" (ibid.). Another example at premenstruation expresses anxiety about death: "I'll tell you about the death of my poor dog M. . . . Oh, another memorable event, my grandparents died in a plane crash. That was my first contact with death and it was very traumatic for me. . . . Then my grandfather died" (ibid., p. 32). In contrast, at ovulation, the same girl said, "Well, we just went to Jamaica and it was fantastic, the island is so lush and green and the water is so blue . . . the place is so fertile and the natives are just so friendly" (ibid.).

One striking confirmation of their findings was that one respondent told of an experience that was scored quite high on anxiety, although it was told at the time that ovulation would be expected; she began to menstruate the next day, two weeks early. More systematic confirmation was provided in a later study by Paige (1971) that compared women on two different types of contraceptive pill. One type, the combination pill, prevents ovulation by providing constantly high levels of both estrogen and progesterone so that there is no cyclic fluctuation. For these women, there was no significant change in levels of anxiety or hostility during what would otherwise be their monthly cycle. The second group of women were taking a sequential pill that consisted of 15 days of estrogen pills, followed by 5 days of estrogen and progesterone pills, and 7 days off (essentially duplicating the ordinary cyclic fluctuations). The group on the sequential pill was found to differ from the group on the combination (noncyclic) pill. They showed the same signs of anxiety when both estrogen and progesterone were low as women in a third group who were not taking any pill. This evidence suggests a causal link between fluctuations of the female sex hormones and shifts in mood.

In sum, these data lead to the tentative conclusion that declining or low levels of estrogen and progesterone are associated with negative emotions such as anxiety and hostility, while high levels of estrogen are associated with positive moods such as high self-esteem and feelings of well-being. Although these data are not sufficient to infer a causal relationship or even to pinpoint the specific hormonal changes involved or the ways in which the moods are affected, these initial data are highly suggestive. Bardwick concludes:

> As psychologists we would expect to find strong individual differences in reactions during the menstrual cycle. Instead, in almost all of our subjects

[1]All quotations from Bardwick (1971) are reprinted with permission of Harper & Row, Inc., from *Psychology of Women*, copyright © 1971 by Judith M. Bardwick.

we found the consistent and significant mood swings characteristic of a particular menstrual phase. These physical changes, probably endocrine changes, so influence psychological behavior that in spite of individual personality differences, even in normal subjects, psychological behavior seems predictable on the basis of menstrual cycle phase alone. Women may cope or not cope, become anxious, hostile, or depressive, appear healthy or neurotic, due as much to menstrual cycle phase as to core psychological characteristics [Bardwick, 1971, pp. 32-33].

To be sure, not all women report such mood shifts during their monthly cycle. Moos (1968) found that between 30 and 50 percent of 839 "normal young married women" reported cyclic symptoms of mood swings in irritability, tension, and depression. This suggests that many women, perhaps most, either do not experience marked mood changes, are not aware of them as cyclic changes, or successfully cope with them so that they are of minor importance. Certainly, we would expect that personality factors, satisfaction with one's various roles, and general coping ability would be as important in determining the effect of these shifts in hormone levels as the physiological changes themselves. Indeed, we again argue that the effects of physiological sex differences are most usefully seen as an interaction of biological, psychological, and social factors. One woman may feel little change in mood—or little negative effect of the mood shift—because she is involved in ego-satisfying projects. Another may automatically anticipate or adjust to the changes by scheduling her activities to minimize the effects of negative moods and to maximize the effects of positive moods. Most probably continue functioning without major change, just as all of us do on days when we "get up on the wrong side of the bed" or are dealing with other factors that decrease or enhance our feelings of competence and well-being.

The recent findings of male hormone cycles may indicate some cyclical variations in men's moods also. Ramey (1972) reports that a private transport company in Japan has adjusted bus routes and schedules to maximize efficiency and to minimize accidents among its male drivers on the basis of "the time of month for each worker." She also reports that a study made over 40 years ago of male factory workers found that their emotions varied on a near-monthly cycle. "Low periods were characterized by apathy, indifference, or a tendency to magnify minor problems out of all proportion. High periods were often marked by a feeling of well-being, energy, a lower body weight, and a decreased need for sleep" (Ramey, 1972, p. 11). More recently, Parlee (1978) reported finding mood cycles that ranged from 6 to 90 days in a sample of 15 men; she also found that their ratings of mood fluctuated on a larger number of mood scales than was the case for a comparison group of 7 women.

Menopause typically occurs between the ages of 48 and 51 in a wide variety of populations (Talbert, 1977). For example, the age of menopause in Japanese, Caucasian, Chinese, and Hawaiian women in Hawaii was between 49 and 50 and was unrelated to the age at which the women began menstruating

(Goodman, Grove, & Gilbert, 1978). Although it is not clear why menopause occurs, it appears that the ovaries stop responding to the FSH produced by the pituitary; they do not respond by bringing an egg to maturity and do not produce estrogen. Thus the cycle stops. The onset may not be sudden, but may be preceded by a period of irregular cycles and menses. Once it has stopped, however, it does not begin again and a renewed "menstrual" flow should be checked by a physician to determine the cause (Comfort, 1976). A surgical removal of the uterus and ovaries (hysterectomy) would have similar effects, but often the ovaries are not removed so that estrogen and progesterone are still produced even if the uterus has been removed and there is no menstruation.

Technically, the term *menopause* refers to the cessation of the menses; the term *climacterium* refers to the loss of reproductive ability. In women they are two sides of the same coin since, when the menstrual cycle ends, reproductive ability also comes to an end. In men there is no menopause (since there are no menses), but there probably is a climacterium late in life when fertile sperm are no longer produced. A related change with advancing age is a change in hormone production. Unlike the marked drop in estrogen and progesterone in women after menopause, in men the level of testosterone declines gradually with age, eventually reaching a very low level. However, fertility and the production of testosterone are separate phenomena in men and some rather old men have fathered children. In addition, for both men and women, the ability to engage in satisfying sexual relations is unrelated to either hormone levels or to fertility. Thus, men and women are typically capable of continued sexual intercourse following female menopause; and indeed, since there is no longer a need to worry about conception, sexuality may be enhanced. We will discuss menopause as a developmental event in the sexual and family lives of women in Chapter 5.

In sum, it seems clear that much more research needs to be done on the nature and the implications of these male and female sex cycles and on the interaction of the differing male and female sex hormones with psychosocial factors. While men and women differ in the levels of various hormones, and perhaps in other biochemical ways as well, there may be important similarities in sex cycles that are only beginning to be understood. However, these data are more suggestive than conclusive at this point; current large-scale research on male cycles, as well as greater research on the interaction of sex hormones, behavior, emotional moods, and psychosocial differences between men and women, may shed considerable light on these issues in the next few years.

Similarities and Differences in Sexual Response

Perhaps genital anatomy is the most apparent physiological difference between men and women. Certainly, the complementarity of sexual organs and the insertion of the penis into the vagina until quite recently has been necessary for producing children. Surprisingly, however, until a few years ago little was known about the precise similarities and differences in the functioning of male and female genitalia. Of course, the physical structure of the gentials and the physiology of the male's ejaculation has been known for some time; but the physiology of the female's orgasm—what causes it, how it is similar to and different from the male's orgasm, and what the connection is between the vaginal and the clitoral aspects of the orgasm—has been little understood. However, the recent research by Masters and Johnson (1966, 1970) produced a marked improvement in our knowledge about sexual physiology.

They report that male and female orgasms are physiologically similar, disregarding (of course) the anatomic differences. That is, the orgasm is initiated by similar muscles and involves a similar reflex mechanism in the responding muscles; the muscle contractions produce the expulsion of blood from the erectile chambers in men *and* in women (men have three chambers in the shaft of the penis that fill with blood to produce the erection; women have five such "erectile bodies") and indirectly also produce the ejaculation of semen in men and contractions of the lower vagina in women (Sherfey, 1972, p. 94). In addition, the female's orgasm results from congestion of blood in these erectile tissues in a manner akin to the male's erection, and the "actual orgasmic experiences are initiated in both sexes by similar muscle components" (Masters & Johnson, 1963, p. 90).

In both men and women the sexual response cycle may be divided into four stages (somewhat less well-defined in men than in women). *Phase I* (excitation) occurs more rapidly in men than women and is characterized by the erection in men and by the rapid production of lubricating fluid in the vagina, increased diameter of the clitoris, and increased blood congestion in the labia major and labia minor in women; nipple erection occurred in all women and in about one-third of the men studied. *Phase II* (plateau) is marked by a high degree of blood congestion and sexual tension in the entire pelvic area for both men and women; there is a sexual flush of the chest, neck, and forehead in either sex and, in women, it frequently includes the lower abdomen, thighs, and lower back; it was noted in about 75 percent of the women and 25 percent of the men studied. The orgasm, *Phase III*, occurs in two stages for men—the first part involves slight contractions of all the involved organs and is experienced as a sign of imminent ejaculation; the second part is the actual ejaculation produced by the same contracting muscles as are involved in the female's orgasm; the initial contractions occur at intervals of 8/10 of a second (the same as in women) for two or three expulsive efforts and then slow in spacing and in expulsive force. The female orgasm occurs in one longer stage. It is characterized by contractions of the uterus, vagina, and labia minor providing the sensation of pelvic visceral contractions associated with the orgasm. In both sexes there are contractions of the rectal sphincter muscles (intervals of 8/10 of a second), contractions of other body (skeletal) muscles, rapid and shallow breathing (hyperventilation), and rapid heart rates (100 to 160 beats per minute); a "sweating reaction" develops in 30 to 40 percent of either sex—usually on the soles of the feet and palms of the hands for men, but more widely distributed over the back, thighs, and chest for women. *Phase IV* (resolution) is a lengthy process of decreasing congestion of the many blood vessels involved in the sexual response cycle; this usually proceeds more slowly in women than in men.

Despite the many similarities in the sexual response cycle of men and women, there are marked differences as well. Most notable are the "refractory period" characteristic of the male's cycle and the ability of the woman to have repeated orgasms. That is, after completing the orgasm, the male requires a period of return to the plateau stage before another orgasm can be achieved (Figure 4.3). This period is relatively short in young men (the highest frequency was three orgasms in a 10-minute period) but typically requires complete resolution and a new response cycle in men over the age of 30. Women, however, are usually able to experience successive (or multiple) orgasms without loss of sexual tension below the plateau level; more than 50 percent of the female sample was capable of immediate return to the orgasmic experience.

If a female who is capable of having regular orgasms is properly stimulated within a short period after her first climax, she will in most instances be capable of having a second, third, fourth, and even a fifth and sixth orgasm before she is fully satiated. As contrasted with the male's usual inability to have more than one orgasm in a short period, many females, especially when clitorally stimulated, can regularly have five or six full orgasms within a matter of minutes [Masters & Johnson, 1961, p. 792].

Masters and Johnson (1966) found that there are three general patterns of female sexual response (Figure 4.4). Type A is the multiple-orgasm pattern where the woman reaches one or more physiological orgasms, returning to the plateau stage after each. Type B involves reaching the plateau level of arousal, but is sexually frustrating because it does not reach the level of a full orgasm. Type C

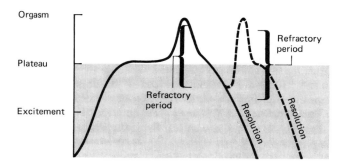

Figure 4.3
The male sexual response cycle. (Source: Masters & Johnson, 1966, Figure 1-1. Copyright©1966 by William H. Masters and Virginia E. Johnson. Reprinted with permission.)

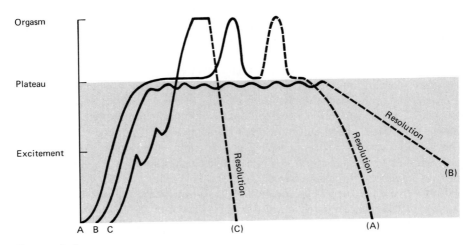

Figure 4.4
The female sexual response cycle. (Source: Masters & Johnson, 1966, Figure 1-2. Copyright © 1966 by William H. Masters and Virginia E. Johnson. Reprinted with permission.)

involves a maximal orgasm, lasting longer than in the Type A pattern; it is often preceded by the beginning and withdrawal of effective stimulation ("teasing technique") and is followed by a refractory period similar to the male pattern. According to Bardwick (1971), the latter type may also be preceded by several smaller (Type A) orgasms.

Other notable differences include, first, the male's ability to continue the orgasmic response, once begun, even in the event of distracting external stimuli or the cessation of stimulation; but the female's orgasmic response ceases when the stimulation ceases and is ended by external distractions. Second, there is a greater response time in the female pattern during intercourse so that the excitement phase, which may last only seconds in men, may last several minutes in women (since the vasocongestive process is more generalized and takes longer to develop). Also, the speed with which women reach orgasm seems to depend on whether the stimulation is direct to the clitoral area or indirect through vaginal intercourse; the latter may produce slower arousal and orgasm than more direct clitoral stimulation. Third, orgasmic responses are experienced by essentially all young men (peaking in frequency between puberty and age 20 according to the Kinsey data), but become most frequent among women during the adult years (ages 26-40). One part of the reason for this is that childbirth involves a "flooding" of the body with hormones (estrogen and progesterone) that Sherfey (1972) argues produces a "sudden and enormous growth and vascularization of the pelvic structures as great as or greater, I believe, than the pubertal transformation" (p. 127). She argues that this *pregnancy effect* combined with increased sexual experience is "much more" responsible for the increased capacity for regular and multiple orgasms (at the time the husband's sexual capacity may be declining) than any "recovery from neurotic fears or inhibitions" (p. 134). That is, after the birth of the second or third child and several years of sexual experience, the woman's capacity for orgasm is likely to increase to its peak, while the man's capacity peaks much earlier; yet, advancing age does not set any limits to sexual orgasm as long as there is continued sexual experience. Fourth, there is variation in intensity of orgasm between individuals (both men and women) and between orgasms for the same individual, but there is apparently little difference in intensity of orgasm between men and women. However, sexual arousal tends to occur more readily during the premenstrual phase of the woman's sex cycle. Kinsey, Pomeroy, Martin, Gebhard, and Associates (1953) noted that about 90 percent of American women prefer sexual relations during this luteal period (or last 14 days). Sherfey (1972) reports that

> during the luteal phase, the majority of women have a greater spontaneous interest in sexual matters, experience a greater desire to initiate love-making, find an increased ease in reaching the plateau phase of arousal, have a more copious transudate of a different, slightly "slippery" consistency, and achieve multiple orgasms with greater ease. This facilitation of sexual responsivity is due primarily to the higher base line of pelvic congestion and edema [accumulation of fluid] characteristic of the premenstrual phase and, in part, to the increased influences in support of a possible pregnancy at this time [pp. 96-97].

One of the most important findings of the Masters and Johnson research is that there is no difference, physiologically, between an orgasm reached through vaginal or clitoral stimulation and that, indeed, some clitoral stimulation is always achieved during intercourse. That is, there is no vaginal orgasm without a clitoral orgasm since the orgasmic reaction includes all of the pelvic sex organs and is identical regardless of the mode or area of stimulation. While they found that the lower third of the vagina is an erotic zone during intercourse, its sensitivity is about equal to that of the clitoral shaft, but the clitoral glans is much more sensitive. During vaginal intercourse, the vaginal passageway narrows because of the increased accumulation of blood in the many veins; this leads to greater stimulation of the penis; the penile thrusts increase the stimulation on the tighter vaginal walls and also create simultaneous stimulation of the labia minor, the clitoral shaft, and glans as an integrated unit. However, the clitoral glans seems to be the most important source of stimulation. Thus, some women may need more direct stimulation of the clitoral area than is provided by vaginal intercourse if they are to reach highly satisfying levels of orgasm.

The implications of these findings about the sexual functioning of men and women are currently having important theoretical and practical influences— such as the recent proliferation of clinics dealing with practical techniques of therapy with persons experienceing some kind of sexual dysfunction. For our purposes, however, the important implication is that men and women are at once physiologically similar and different in terms of sexual functioning. Certainly, an understanding of the differences may enhance sexual relations, but the striking data on the similarities clearly suggest that adult men and women have a great deal in common that may aid in understanding and communicating with one's partner; neither men nor women can ever really know what the experience of the other is like, but they can discuss it, if they will, so that the sexual relationship is a fully integrated aspect of their total relationship.

INTERACTION OF PHYSIOLOGICAL, PSYCHOLOGICAL, AND SOCIAL SEX DIFFERENCES

Although basic physiological differences are little affected by cultural or psychological factors, it is clear that sex differences (and similarities) are very much affected by society (through differential socialization of boys and girls) and by individual developmental progression. That is, all women experience relatively similar internal environments (such as fluctuations in levels of estrogen and progesterone), menstruation, pregnancy, and menopause; but the psychological meaning of these sex-related experiences differs from individual to individual; and the culture interprets and defines these experiences—and indeed, the entire meaning of being male or female—in differing ways. For example, Margaret Mead (1949), in her classic study, *Male and Female*, describes the great impact of culture:

> In every known society, mankind has elaborated the biological division of labour into forms often very remotely related to the original biological differences that provided the original clues. Upon the contrast in bodily form and function, men have built analogies between sun and moon, night and day, goodness and evil, strength and tenderness, steadfastness and fickleness, endurance and vulnerability. Sometimes one quality has been assigned to one sex, sometimes to the other. Now it is boys who are thought of as infinitely vulnerable and in need of special cherishing care, now it is girls. In some societies it is girls for whom parents must collect a dowry or make husband-catching magic, in others the parental worry is over the difficulty of marrying off the boys. Some peoples think of women as too weak to work out of doors, others regard women as the appropriate bearers of heavy burdens, "because their heads are stronger than men's." The periodicities of female reproductive functions have appealed to some peoples as making women the natural sources of magical or religious power, to others as directly antithetical to those powers; some religions, including our European traditional religions, have assigned women an inferior role in the religious hierarchy, others have built their whole symbolic relationship with the supernatural world upon male imitations of the natural functions of women. In some cultures women are regarded as sieves through which the best-

guarded secrets will sift; in others it is the men who are the gossips. Whether we deal with small matters or with large, with the frivolities of ornament and cosmetics or the sanctities of man's place in the universe, we find this great variety of ways, often flatly contradictory one to the other, in which the roles of the two sexes have been patterned [pp. 7-8].

In our view, what it means to be a woman or a man is a product of the interaction of at least three interrelated processes: one's inner physiological environment, one's social-cultural environment, and one's psychological development from birth on. That is, in our view, sex differences in adulthood are not the result of socialization alone, nor of physiological factors alone, nor of psychological factors alone (although each is certainly important). Instead, sex differences result from the interaction of the inner and outer experience of being a male or a female in a social network (family and society) from birth until death. All individuals forge their own sense of maleness or femaleness out of this interaction of experiences as they progress through the differing developmental experiences of boys and girls.[2]

Important manifestations of the interaction of these factors are differences in the self, differences and similarities in personality patterns, and the impact of these sex differences during adult years for men and women in our society. Let us first discuss the differences in the self.

The Social Self: Male and Female

In many ways, one's gender functions as a label that is applied to oneself; thus one's gender is a salient aspect of the self and may be seen as one of the most important *me*s in a person's collection of *me*s. For example, beginning in adolescence, the sexual *me* is one of the major components of an individual's identity, and the change brought about in that aspect of the self at puberty is a crucial part of the identity conflict: "Who am I as a sexual person?" "What does it mean to be male or female?" "How do I integrate the little boy/girl I was with the man/woman I have become and the adult/parent/spouse I will become?"

Such questions are at the core of the identity issue in adolescence and young adulthood and, in the symbolic interaction framework, one works through such issues by taking the role of others toward oneself (as a man or a woman), by reflexively looking at oneself as if one were someone else viewing oneself, and by integrating the various *me*s that one sees in such moments of self-consciousness into a coherent concept of the self. Simultaneously, one's *I* is experiencing one's bodily feelings of being a male/female, feelings of being a sexual person, feelings of guilt, anxiety, and pleasure associated with sexual experiences, feelings one has as a man or woman in social interactions with other men and women,

[2]This topic of differing developmental processes in childhood is too complex and beyond the scope of this chapter for discussion here; see Bardwick (1971), Chapter 1, Block (1973), and Hoffman (1977) for an introduction to the area.

and such inner experiences as mood shifts and other feelings that may result from hormonal sex differences. From such *I-me* interactions, one evolves a concept of oneself over a long period of time, beginning in early childhood and continuing into adulthood.

In general, an individual's gender affects the self in two ways. First, part of our collection of *mes* includes a *me* that is a man or a woman; we clearly perceive and experience this *me*, and others also perceive it and respond to us accordingly. Second, many of our other *mes* are also permeated by those qualities that are typically called "masculine" or "feminine." Thus, an individual's *mes* are affected by the social sex roles in the society; one's *mes* as a student, as a teacher, as a lover, and as a parent (and so on) are expected to be consistent with one's gender and, when they are not, social pressure may be brought to bear to encourage conformity of all of one's *mes* to the *me* specified by one's gender. This is one example of *role conflict* in which one's roles (*mes*) do not mesh well with one another; that is, when one takes the attitude of the other toward oneself, there is an inconsistency felt by *I* and the offending *me* may be altered or this felt inconsistency may be managed internally by several coping or defensive mechanisms. For example, if one's *I* experiences a conflict between a *me* as a lover and the *me* as a man, serious questions of consistency may be experienced; or, if one experiences a conflict between the *me* as a lawyer and the *me* as a woman, the inconsistency (or role conflict) will be felt. However, such perceived inconsistencies (from the point of view of the other) may be outweighed by the feeling of consistency—for example between one's *me* as a man and one's *me* as a father who takes a paternity leave from work to care for his newborn infant; one's feeling of consistency between the *me* as a woman and the *me* as a business executive; or one's *me* as a man and as a homosexual lover. In such cases the self is consistent (as one's *I* experiences it), and the inconsistency is between this sense of consistency and the perception of significant or generalized others who perceive an inconsistency. To resolve such conflict, one may attempt to change one's significant others to find persons whose perceptions concur with one's own perceptions of consistency; or one may (perhaps simultaneously) attempt to change the perceptions of these others to convince them that, indeed, these various *mes* are essentially consistent; or one may modify his or her set of *mes* to conform more closely to the perception of these others. Probably all of these processes occur in varying degrees at the same time. And it is of such processes that the evolution of an individual's self is made; it is from such unique combinations of *mes* that individualized selves and individual differences arise. And it is in the midst of such perceptions of inconsistency that the creative characteristic of one's *I* may be most important, since new *mes* and new combinations of *mes* may always be produced to promote a sense of unity and coherence to the self.

In general, the content of the male or female *me* and the connotations of "masculine" and "feminine" are primarily produced by the continuing socialization processes begun at birth. As we discussed in Chapter 2, this process of socialization is the main mechanism by which cultural transmission of roles and norms takes place. It includes the subtle impact of "pink or blue" clothes (and so on) for the baby, encouragement of sex-typed behaviors, discouragement of sex-inappropriate behaviors ("girls don't fight; boys don't cry"), and standards of acceptable sexual behavior in adolescence. Typically, boys are responded to differently by significant others than girls; and as the self develops, the attitude of the generalized other is taken toward oneself, and the child learns that his or her gender *me* is linked to a range of sex-appropriate behaviors in society generally. To be sure, the content of this socialization differs from one culture to another. And it does not operate in a vacuum since the physiological differences undoubtedly interact with the socialization process; for example, it is likely that socialization not only modifies physiological predispositions (perhaps greater aggressiveness and activity in males) but also reflects these differences (by allowing greater physical aggression and activity for boys).

By adolescence, the content of culturally prescribed sex roles is clearly understood, and the task becomes one of establishing a firm individual sense of one's sex and sexual role. Adult parental and occupational role behaviors also involve socialization, of course, and typically confirm and strengthen one's gender identity (or possibly put it to the test). However, with advancing age and completion of the tasks of child-rearing, the meaning and importance of one's gender may change so that, on one hand, sex roles become less salient in the perception of one's *me* and, on the other hand, greater tolerance is allowed for both men and women in the range of acceptable sex-role behavior—for example, retired men and women may play a number of roles that are more similar than different, such as "grandparent." At the same time, with greater social and personal experience, one's set of *mes* would be likely to have evolved in such a way as to have resolved the feelings of inconsistency between the gender *me* and one's other *mes*. In addition, social expectations about role behavior change during the life span so that, for example, an old man would no longer be expected (or expect himself) to have an athletic *me* and could feel quite "male" sitting and watching younger persons playing football; and an old woman might not feel at all inconsistent in her set of *mes* if she took over the family business when her husband became too sick to manage it; but similar behavior at younger ages would tend to "raise the generalized other's eyebrow," so to speak.

Thus, one important way in which an individual's gender influences the person in adulthood is in terms of the self, role behaviors, social expectations, and one's experience of oneself as a sexual being. Through a complex interaction of physiological and social influences, children develop into male or female adults; and they develop along somewhat different paths because they are boys or girls. They develop a sense of self (and, later, an identity) that is "male" or "female," and they experience adulthood in differing ways. Of course, the meaning of these differences, and the extent that the differences are emphasized or differentially rewarded, is largely a matter of the society (culture). But, in our society, these interacting differences seem clearly to produce some general sex differences—for example, in personality—that we now discuss.

Personality Differences

The study of differences in personality between men and women is one of the most controversial and inconclusive areas in social science research. Many studies have attempted to determine whether there are sex differences in personality characteristics such as aggression, compliance, curiosity, dominance, emotional expressiveness, self-esteem, and verbal ability. However, the results are nearly always contradictory and there are almost no differences in personality between males and females that are always found in all studies. In addition, the vast majority of studies have focused on children, so any sex differences that do not become evident until adolescence or adulthood may not be noted (Block, 1976a).

Maccoby and Jacklin (1974) reviewed about 1600 studies of sex differences and concluded that there were only four "fairly well established" differences between males and females. A closer examination of the studies they reviewed, however, found that other differences seem to be as well-established as the ones they listed (Block, 1976a, 1976b). The four "fairly well established" differences cited by Maccoby and Jacklin and those they concluded were "equivocal" or "unfounded," as well as other characteristics that show comparable sex differences based on Block's examination, are shown in Table 4.1. On the basis of these data Block (1976a) concluded:

> I would agree with Maccoby and Jacklin that these data suggest that boys and men are higher with respect to spatial and quantitative abilities and are also more aggressive. But the data also impress me as indicating that males are better on insight problems requiring restructuring, are more dominant and have a stronger, more potent self-concept, are more curious and exploring, more active, and more impulsive (when impulsivity is not narrowly construed). I would agree with Maccoby and Jacklin that girls and women score higher on tests of verbal ability. In addition, however, the available data suggest to me that females express more fear, are more susceptible to anxiety, are more lacking in task confidence, seek more help and reassurance, maintain greater proximity to friends, score higher on social desirability, and, at the younger ages at which compliance has been studied, are more compliant with adults [pp. 304, 307].

Examination of these data, however, indicates that, with regard to most of the characteristics studied, a large proportion of the studies found no difference between males and females. In addition, many of the studies used a relatively small number of subjects, and the measures used to assess the various characteristics frequently differed. Moreover, most of the studies were conducted with white,

Table 4.1 Personality Differences between Males and Females and the Percentage of Studies Reporting "Males Scored Higher," "Females Scored Higher," and "No Difference" between Males and Females

Personality Characteristic	Number of Studies	Percentage of Studies Reporting		
		Males Higher	Females Higher	No Difference
"Fairly Well Established"[a]				
Verbal ability	131	9	28	63
Spatial abilities	64	39	5	56
Quantitative abilities	35	40	17	43
Aggressiveness	94	55	5	40
"Equivocal Evidence"[a]				
Fear and timidity	25	00	40	60
General anxiety	24	00	58	42
Test anxiety	8	00	62	38
Activity level	59	41	5	54
Dominance	47	42	4	54
Strength of self-concept	8	88	00	12
Compliance	24	4	54	42
"Unfounded Beliefs"[a]				
Proximity to friends	23	9	52	39
Confidence in task performance	18	78	00	22
Impulsivity	43	33	7	60
Insight problems	14	86	00	14
Other Areas				
Help-seeking	13	00	100	00
Curiosity	29	48	14	38
Social desirability	9	00	78	22

Source: Block (1976a), Table 1. Copyright © 1976. Adapted and reprinted with permission.
[a]Based on the report by Maccoby and Jacklin (1974).
Note: Only those characteristics indicating sex differences are shown; other data from the original table have also been omitted for simplicity.

middle-class Americans, and relatively little attention has been given to cultural variation even within the United States (Stewart, 1976). Thus, the issue of which sex differences are well-established remains an open question, subject to debate and controversy.

At the individual level, it is important to note that even where significant differences are found between groups of males and females, it is possible for a man to be more "feminine" on some characteristics than some women, and vice versa, because there is considerable overlap of scores between men and women even when there is a statistically significant difference on a particular characteristic (Stewart, 1976).

While it would be impossible to review all of the data that have been collected on sex differences in personality, even omitting the much larger number of studies that deal with children, there are three themes that stand out and that seem important for understanding adult men and women. One of these themes is the set of *stereotypes* about characteristics of men and women. A second dimension is *self-esteem*, and the different sources of esteem that seem to be meaningful for men and women. A third theme is the differing types of *motivation* that seem to be important for men and women. All of these are complexly interwoven in their effect on personality and it is difficult to attempt to separate them, but it is even more difficult to discuss them all at once; thus, let us attempt to maintain a sense of their interaction as we explore each theme.

Sex-Role Stereotypes.   Regardless of actual sex differences, there clearly are stereotyped differences that are generally thought to characterize the personality of men and women. These stereotypes usually portray men and women as *opposite* (we will examine this assumption of oppositeness in detail shortly). For example, Rosenkrantz and his colleagues (Rosenkrantz, Vogel, Bee, Broverman, & Broverman, 1968) found that 41 items were agreed on by at least 75 percent of a college sample as either "masculine" or "feminine" (Table 4.2). In a later report of these data the authors conclude:

> Our research demonstrates the contemporary existence of clearly defined sex-role stereotypes for men and women. . . . Women are perceived as relatively less competent, less independent, less objective, and less logical than men; men are perceived as lacking interpersonal sensitivity, warmth, and expressiveness in comparison to women. Moreover, stereotypically masculine traits are more often perceived to be desirable than are stereotypically feminine characteristics.
>
> The stereotypic differences between men and women described above appear to be accepted by a large segment of our society. Thus college students portray the ideal woman as less competent than the ideal man, and mental health professionals tend to see mature healthy women as more submissive, less independent, etc., than either mature healthy men, or adults, sex unspecified. To the extent that these results reflect societal standards of sex- role behavior, women are clearly put in a double bind by the fact that different standards exist for women than for adults. If women adopt the behaviors specified as desirable for adults, they risk censure for their failure to be appropriately feminine; but if they adopt the behaviors that are designated as feminine, they are necessarily deficient with respect to the general standards for adult behavior [Broverman, Vogel, Broverman, Clarkson, & Rosenkrantz, 1972, p. 75].

Such stereotypes are very difficult to separate from more "real" sex differences between the personalities of men and women, precisely because the

Table 4.2   Stereotypic Sex-Role Items (Responses from 74 College Men and 80 College Women)

Competency Cluster: Masculine pole is more desirable	
Feminine	*Masculine*
Not at all aggressive	Very aggressive
Not at all independent	Very independent
Very emotional	Not at all emotional
Does not hide emotions at all	Almost always hides emotions
Very subjective	Very objective
Very easily influenced	Not at all easily influenced
Very submissive	Very dominant
Dislikes math and science very much	Likes math and science very much
Very excitable in a minor crisis	Not at all excitable in a minor crisis
Very passive	Very active
Not at all competitive	Very competitive
Very illogical	Very logical
Very home oriented	Very worldly
Not at all skilled in business	Very skilled in business
Very sneaky	Very direct
Does not know the way of the world	Knows the way of the world
Feelings easily hurt	Feelings not easily hurt
Not at all adventurous	Very adventurous
Has difficulty making decisions	Can make decisions easily
Cries very easily	Never cries
Almost never acts as a leader	Almost always acts as a leader
Not at all self-confident	Very self-confident
Very uncomfortable about being aggressive	Not at all uncomfortable about being aggressive
Not at all ambitious	Very ambitious
Unable to separate feelings from ideas	Easily able to separate feelings from ideas
Very dependent	Not at all dependent
Very conceited about appearance	Never conceited about appearance
Thinks women are always superior to men	Thinks men are always superior to women
Does not talk freely about sex with men	Talks freely about sex with men

Warmth-Expressiveness Cluster: Feminine pole is more desirable	
Feminine	*Masculine*
Doesn't use harsh language at all	Uses very harsh language
Very talkative	Not at all talkative
Very tactful	Very blunt
Very gentle	Very rough
Very aware of feelings of others	Not at all aware of feelings of others
Very religious	Not at all religious
Very interested in own appearance	Not at all interested in own appearance
Very neat in habits	Very sloppy in habits
Very quiet	Very loud
Very strong need for security	Very little need for security
Enjoys art and literature	Does not enjoy art and literature at all
Easily expresses tender feelings	Does not express tender feelings at all easily

Source: Broverman et al. (1972), p. 63. Copyright©1972. Reprinted with permission

stereotypes tend to be internalized by the individual as guides for one's behavior and feelings. As Broverman et al. phrase it:

> Most importantly, both men and women incorporate both the positive and negative traits of the appropriate stereotype into their self-concepts. Since more feminine traits are negatively valued than are masculine traits, women tend to have more negative self-concepts than do men. The tendency for women to denigrate themselves in this manner can be seen as evidence of the powerful social pressures to conform to the sex-role standards of the society [ibid.].

Thus, these stereotypes are not only internalized to some degree through the socialization processes, but also influence levels of self-esteem for men and women. One side of this self-esteem coin is: "Am I really feminine/masculine?" The other side is: "Is a woman (or women's activities and characteristics) valued as much by the social-economic system as a man?" Obviously, self-esteem is likely to be a personality characteristic differing between men and women, and we will discuss it in more detail in a moment.

Sex stereotypes also affect one's personality characteristics since, as a result of socialization, men and women tend to develop differing degrees of aggressiveness, dependency, social sensitivity, and so on, as well as differing patterns of social rewards (such as achievement or being highly popular). But we would also expect that physiological and developmental factors are involved in addition to these socialization pressures. That is, while social stereotypes and even the level and sources of self-esteem may be largely socially determined, personality characteristics also result from differing childhood development (such as patterns of identification with the same- and cross-sex parent) and physiological factors.

Self-Esteem.   Several years ago Simone de Beauvoir (1953) described the "problem" of women from an existential framework. She analyzed the role of woman as an *object*, by which she meant more than a "sex object" (although it is only quite recently that men have been used as sex objects in magazine pictures designed for women). She argued that men function as a *subject*—active, manipulating, controlling, and generally taking an active stance toward the world of objects that includes women. Women, however, are looked at, manipulated, controlled, and generally passive—like objects. Certainly this view is partly a stereotype but, when we examine the sources of self-esteem for women and men, women tend to be prized for how they appear to others (i.e., as "objects") while men are prized for what they accomplish (i.e., as "subjects"). For example, Bardwick (1971), based on her review of the psychological literature, asserts that

> Women . . . tend to esteem themselves only insofar as they are esteemed by those they love and respect. Unlike the man, who is considered success-

ful when he has achieved within his occupation, the woman who achieves is generally not considered successful unless she also has a husband and children [p. 158].

In addition, there appears to be a greater importance placed on external or inter-personal sources of esteem among typical women and, consequently, less emphasis placed on internal standards of success. This difference need not be inherently negative toward women's self-esteem, except that in our society accomplishment tends to be valued as a source of esteem. That is, male-type, objective accomplishment is prized (and rewarded monetarily) while interpersonal success is less rewarded, and the woman's apparently major source of esteem turns out to be "second rate." Furthermore, stereotypes about the lesser value of women decrease the value of being a woman in one's own eyes and in the eyes of others. One study (Pheterson, Kiesler, & Goldberg, 1971) found that 120 women rated a series of abstract paintings higher if they were told that the artist's name was male (such as *David* Smith) than when told it was female (*Jane* Jones); another study (MacBrayer, 1960) found that females perceive males significantly more favorably than males perceive females. In sum, it appears that women tend to have different sources of esteem, and maler sources of esteem and males generally are more highly valued. However, this pattern may be changing for at least some women today. For example, Baruch (1972) found that daughters of employed mothers did not downgrade written articles attributed to women compared with those attributed to men, while daughters of full-time housewives did. Thus, having a mother who provides a model of a competent woman outside the home seems to affect the daughter's perception of the competence of women in general.

Achievement and Affiliation Motivations. McClelland, Atkinson, Clark, and Lowell (1953) defined a concept that they called *achievement motivation* as a propensity to compete in situations where there are standards of excellence. It is generally assumed that this motive is internalized so that a high degree of achievement motivation may be characteristic of a particular individual. Also it is assumed that this motive to achieve is independent of (i.e., not related to) another motive, *affiliation motivation*. In brief, a person high on achievement motivation would strive because of the internal standard of excellence and would gain satisfaction from producing successful accomplishment; a person high on affiliation motivation would strive for esteem from others. Certainly, any person would respond to either type of motivation, but it is typically found that women are characteristically higher on affiliation motives than men (Oetzel, 1966; Walberg, 1969). This appears to be consistent with the importance of interpersonal sources of self-esteem for women. For example, Hoffman (1972) concludes her review of research on achievement motivation in childhood by pointing out that "the data suggest that they [females] have higher affiliative needs and that achievement behavior is motivated by a desire to please. If their achievement behavior comes into conflict with affiliation, achievement is likely to be sacrificed or anxiety may result" (p. 149). In contrast, men are more readily motivated by internal standards of excellence and competition that are reinforced by the social role for men and by our highly achievement-oriented society. This suggests that "achievement" may mean different types of accomplishment for men and women. Veroff (1969) has suggested that, in girls, external support is of critical importance for achievement while, for boys, achievement is stimulated by internal standards of excellence. And Bardwick (1971) has hypothesized that although the motives for achievement and affiliation are independent of each other in men, they are combined for women so that women strive for "affiliative-achievement" and are motivated to achieve success in interpersonal relationships and in the affiliative role with husband and children. However, there are some interesting data that suggest that (at least among college-educated women) "male-type" achievement motivation (measured from stories told after looking at Thematic Apperception Test cards) increases among women who have been out of college for 15 years (Baruch, 1966); while longitudinal data are crucial to confirm this hypothesis, it may be that the success in family roles and changes in one's self-concept allow women to respond to achievement needs without conflict with their feminine self-concept and needs for affiliation. To be sure, this difference in motivation between men and women (as well as achievement motivation in general) may be primarily a cultural characteristic. A study comparing American and Danish adolescents found a much higher emphasis on affiliative concerns for the Danish adolescent than for the American, and that achievement was emphasized much more by adolescents in the United States than in Denmark (Kandel & Lesser, 1972).

Personality Similarities: Androgyny

Stereotypes about men and women and many research studies on sex differences assume that masculinity and femininity are opposite one another; that is, the more masculine one is, the less feminine one is. But are men and women really opposite each other in personality characteristics? Several theoretical analyses of human development have argued that both men and women have differing degrees of similar characteristics, not different sets of characteristics, and that maturity involves establishing a blend of both masculine and feminine attributes (Jung, 1933; Bakan, 1966). Recently this approach has begun to gain a great deal of attention in research on sex differences.

If we assume that masculinity and femininity are not opposite characteristics (a bipolar model), but that they are parallel sets of characteristics (a duality model), then an individual may be higher on one than on the other, or equally high or low on both. In this approach, a masculine person would be high on characteristics associated with masculinity and low on characteristics associated with femininity; a feminine person would be high on femininity and low on masculinity; and an *androgynous* person would be high on both masculinity and femininity, or at least equal in the degree of masculinity and femininity. Thus, *androgyny* may be defined as a mixture or blending of both masculine and feminine characteristics. It implies that an individual may be both assertive and compassionate, for example, depending on the situation, or that a person may be able to act decisively while at the same time being sensitive to the impact of the decision on other individuals. This approach implies that many important human characteristics are not, and should not be, confined to either one sex or the other and that a man may be no less masculine, but possibly more human, if he is androgynous or that a woman may be no less feminine, but perhaps more completely human, if she is androgynous. Obvious examples include fathers caring for and reacting sensitively to their children and wife, or mothers who are able to achieve success in a "masculine" career.

Androgynous persons have been found to have greater maturity in moral judgment (Block, 1973), greater self-esteem (Spence, Helmreich, & Stapp, 1975), higher levels of both independence and nurturance when appropriate (Bem, 1975), and are able to perform cross-sex behavior with little reluctance or discomfort (Bem & Lenney, 1976). In general, it is assumed that androgynous individuals are less confined by sex roles and thus have greater freedom to respond to a wide variety of situations with an appropriate blend of masculine and feminine abilities.

Two slightly different methods have been used to measure androgyny. In both, an inventory of sex-role characteristics, such as the list of stereotypes presented earlier (Table 4.2), is given to a group of men and women. The most widely used are the Bem Sex Role Inventory (Bem, 1974; 1977) and the Personal Attributes Questionnaire (Spence & Helmreich, 1978; Spence, Helmreich, & Stapp, 1975). Scores on a scale of masculinity and on a separate scale of femininity are then analyzed. One method of classifying the respondents is to compare the difference beween and individual's scores on the two scales (Bem, 1974). This results in five groups: feminine (much higher on femininity than on masculinity), near-feminine (slightly more feminine than masculine), masculine (much higher on masculinity than on femity), near-masculine (slightly more masculine than feminine), and androgynous (equal on both masculinity and femininity). In a study of 723 college students, Bem (1975) found that about one-third of the males and one-quarter of the females were androgynous; 36 percent of the males were distinctly masculine with almost no feminine characteristics, and 34 percent of the women were distinctly feminine with almost no masculine characteristics. Very few of the respondents described themselves primarily by characteristics of the other sex (Table 4.3).

The second method of analyzing the scores divides the sample into those who are above and below the average score on the separate masculinity and femininity scales (Spence et al., 1975). This produces four groups: masculine (high on masculinity, low on femininity), feminine (low on masculinity, high on femininity), androgynous (high on both), and undifferentiated (low on both). In a study of 715 college students, Spence and Helmreich (1978) found that the propor-

Table 4.3   Percentage of College Student Respondents in Each of the Five Sex-Role Categories

Sex role	Females (N = 444)	Males (N = 279)
Feminine	34	6
Near-feminine	20	5
Androgynous	27	34
Near-masculine	12	19
Masculine	8	36

Source: Bem (1975), Table 1. Copyright©1975 by the American Psychological Association. Adapted and reprinted with permission.

tion in the androgynous, feminine, and masculine categories were quite similar to Bem's findings. That is, 27 percent of the women and 32 percent of the men were androgynous; one-third of the women were feminine; one-third of the men were masculine; and about one-quarter of the respondents were in the undifferentiated category (low on both masculinity and femininity).

Thus, regardless of which method is used to measure androgyny, it seems clear that there are substantial proportions of androgynous men and women, at least in college populations. However, an equally substantial proportion describe themselves according to traditional masculine and feminine roles that involve a rejection of the characteristics of the so-called opposite sex. It is unclear whether similar findings would be obtained in studies of middle-aged or older people, but it would be one interesting direction for future research on androgyny. As we will discuss in Chapter 8, there is some evidence from a number of different cultures that men and women become more androgynous as they grow older.

One of the most significant advantages of this approach to the study of sex differences is that it allows sex role (masculine, feminine, or androgynous) to be separated from biological maleness or femaleness. Thus, it makes it possible to examine the effects of sex roles in addition to examining differences between men and women. For example, in studies of self-esteem, both Bem (1977) and Spence et al. (1975) found self-esteem to be related to sex-role classification among college students. Specifically, androgynous and masculine respondents were higher in self-esteem than feminine or undifferentiated respondents among both men and women (Table 4.4). Thus, sex role may be more important than biological sex in understanding sex differences in self-esteem. However, this perspective allows the analysis to be carried a significant step further—it also allows an analysis of the interaction between sex and sex role. That is, using the respondents' actual scores on masculinity and femininity, Bem (1977) found different patterns for men and women on self-esteem. In men, self-esteem was related to masculinity, but unrelated to femininity. In women, self-esteem was associated with both masculinity and femity. This suggests, first, that self-esteem is associated with masculine characteristics for both men and women. However, men were high on self-esteem if they were high on masculinity, regardless of

Table 4.4 Self-Esteem Scores as a Function of Sex-Role Classification

Sex role	Bem Study		Spence et al. Study	
	Females (N = 71)	Males (N = 93)	Females (N = 270)	Males (N = 234)
Androgynous	126.0	117.1	98.7	93.7
Masculine	115.6	119.8	92.2	87.0
Feminine	107.6	100.6	75.4	74.6
Undifferentiated	99.5	103.5	69.7	66.8

Source: Bem (1977), Table 2; Spence et al. (1975), Table 4. Copyright©1977, 1975 by the American Psychological Association. Adapted and reprinted with permission.
Note: In these two studies, self-esteem was measured by using different versions of the Texas Social Behavior Inventory.

whether they were high or low on femininity, while women were highest on self-esteem if they were high on both masculinity and femininity and lowest if they were low on both. This suggests a second point—that men appear to have multiple paths to high self-esteem, including conventional masculinity and androgyny; but women are most likely to have high self-esteem only if they combine masculinity and femininity in an androgynous sex role; conventionally feminine women are likely to have lower self-esteem. However, we must be cautious in generalizing this finding to men and women who are not college students. Recalling the Livson (1976) study discussed in Chapter 3, the "traditional" women appeared to experience less turmoil during middle age than the "independent" women; it is this latter group who might be termed androgynous, but their self-esteem and psychological health were relatively low during their forties—not until age 50 did their self-esteem match the higher level of the traditionally feminine women.

In sum, this new research on androgyny provides a unique approach to the study of sex differences and promises to be an interesting area of research in the future. Since there is considerable evidence that men and women are similar in many ways, there is little reason to assume that their personalities are made up of opposite characteristics. Instead, the differences may be more a matter of degree than we had previously realized, and many young people appear to merge masculine and feminine characteristics into an apparently adaptive personality style. Thus, this research is especially important now that men and women are individually exploring the meaning of masculinity and femininity and the mixture of the two for their own self-realization through the life cycle.

SEX DIFFERENCES THROUGH THE LIFE CYCLE

While much attention has been focused on the personality characteristics of men and women, perhaps an even more important consideration is the differing developmental progression for men and women through the adult years in our present society. Although there are differences in childhood and in early development, we will begin our summary of some of these differences in adolescence, when sexuality becomes explicitly important. In this section, we will focus primarily on issues that are important from a woman's perspective.[3] In the next section, we will examine the male role in our society. And in the final section of this chapter, we will discuss some of the recent changes in our society that have had important effects on both male and female roles through the life cycle.

Adult Development: A Female Perspective

Adolescent boys typically value men, want to become a man, and feel no conflict between their sexuality and being a man; girls, however, may feel ambivalent about their sexuality as the physical changes are linked with blood and pain and may bring fears of being entered by a man and being pregnant while, at the same time, these changes mark the beginning of womanhood. For girls, the conflicts between achievement and affiliation, between doing well and being attractive, and between being feminine and being a sex object come to the fore. Certainly boys have conflicts about whether they are adequately masculine; but being popular, masculine, and successful do not contradict each other. In late adolescence (and young adulthood), young men come to grips with their identity and, again, the links between masculinity and vocational and academic success do not conflict but together form a major part of the man's sex identity. For young women, it is usually assumed that their identity involves being a wife and mother, regardless of whatever else they may do. Somehow this conflict between being "traditionally feminine" and also productively involved in a vocation or a profession needs to be resolved, and even today this seems not to be an easy task. Fear of success, fear of losing affiliative satisfactions, and fear of failure, as well as anxiety seem to be some of the responses to this conflict. However, Gump (1972) found that most women believe it is possible to be a wife and mother while also being involved in extrafamilial interests, and respondents high on a measure of "ego strength" (purposiveness, resourcefulness, and self-direction) were actively pursuing both goals rather than "traditional" goals of only wife and mother roles. Also, Hoffman (1977) notes that adolescent daughters are more likely to plan to work when they are mothers if their own mother works.

While marriage is an important milestone for a man, it is typically merged with an enduring vocational commitment and is an additional manifestation, but not a definition, of his masculinity. For a woman, marriage may mark the resolution of her identity crisis (perhaps symbolized by her change of name).

> Because of their investment in the relationship, because of their history of assessing themselves by others' responses, and because they really do perceive reality in interpersonal terms, they overwhelmingly define and eval-

[3]This discussion is based on Judith Bardwick's (1971, pp. 207-216) excellent summary.

uate identity and femininity within the context of this relationship [Bard-wick, 1971, p. 211].

We will discuss the family and occupation during the middle years in Chapters 5 and 6; however, a brief overview of the sex differences is appropriate here. Bardwick suggests that the birth of the first child is the greatest developmental task for a woman. While the father takes pride and is psychologically invested in his child, the mother may feel that her femininity is fulfilled—she has produced a "real achievement"—and her needs for affiliative satisfaction shift to encompass the child in addition to her husband. "Pregnancy and early maternity may be 'peak' experiences, the emotion felt toward the child, largely joy" (ibid., pp. 211–212). However, maternity is an ambivalent and difficult role. Not only is child-rearing difficult and complex, but the energy required by this task leaves little for occupational investment, and there are a host of normative behaviors (such as participation in the PTA) that are expected of mothers. Educated women may fear that they are losing their intellectual abilities while doing routine repetitive household tasks. And many women may feel isolated in the home and frustrated by the routine demands of child care. Several studies, including nationwide samples, have found that full-time housewives with school-age children have low self-esteem and a relatively high rate of psychological symptoms of emotional distress (Hoffman, 1977). While the mother who is also working may have higher self-esteem, she also may feel anxious about depriving her children, husband, and herself of rightful "feminine" attention. Seldom do these issues pose conflicts with a man's occupational role or his sense of masculinity.

If the marriage breaks up, although divorce is usually a devastating experience for both partners, it may be particularly traumatic for the woman. It is a personal crisis for both persons, but it is also a failure of "affiliation achievement" for the woman and is likely to bring up questions of identity that may have been passed over as she shifted her identity (and dependency?) from daughter to wife. She must cope with a double or triple crisis, often with the added burden of children; in contrast, the man can rely on his occupational identity and may find dating and remarriage easier, in part because he is less likely to retain custody of the children.

If the marriage is a good one, it is probably 10 to 15 years old during the partners' thirties, and the woman's level of sexual satisfaction has probably developed fully while the man's sexual desire may be declining, partly because he is highly involved in his occupation. The wife-mother may feel "trapped" at home while the husband-father is exposed to a potentially more "exciting" world, and he may continue growing at a faster rate than his wife.

The forties brings the launching of the children from the home, menopause, and the awareness of middle age. These changes may involve redefinitions of the self, awareness of one's own mortality, and a kind of mourning process for the women when the children leave home. Neugarten (1967) found that middle-aged women tend to associate "middle age" with the launching of their children. Even unmarried women often time the beginning of middle age by the family they might have had. Men, in contrast, are more likely to time the beginning of middle age by cues from the occupation or from physical decline and the illness or death of friends. Neugarten reports that women become concerned over the health of their husbands at this time and, while men are feeling increased physical vulnerability, women tend to engage in what she terms "rehearsal for widowhood." At the same time, women are likely to feel a sense of increased freedom and may gain a new degree of self-understanding. Women who are widowed or divorced during this period and are forced to become self-supporting often experience a particularly dramatic change as a result of centering their interest on their work. Maas and Kuypers (1974) reported on a subgroup of women in their longitudinal study who followed this pattern and experienced a significant improvement in self-esteem and general adjustment. Similarly, Livson's (1976) study, discussed earlier, found a marked improvement in psychological well-being between 40 and 50 for the nontraditional women in her longitudinal study.

Aging also differs between men and women. Death rates and suicide rates are higher for men than women at all ages. Thus women can almost always expect to live longer and healthier lives (from childhood on) than men and to live out the late years of their lives with other women far exceeding men in their circle of friends.

Popular writers such as Sontag (1972) and Beauvoir (1972) have called attention to the "double standard of aging"—which may have far more impact than simply living longer. For example, insofar as women receive considerable esteem for their physical appearance, when advancing age reduces their attractiveness (in our "youth-oriented" society), their self-concept and self-esteem are diminished in ways that do not occur for men (especially "successful" men). Similarly, while older men receive social approval for marrying or dating younger women, older women are seldom likely to date younger men because of social norms (despite that fact that women generally outlive men and this social convention exaggerates the difference in life expectancy). Thus, older women who divorce or are widowed are usually less able to find suitable marriage partners than is the case for older men.

Many of these patterns are currently changing, but the evolution of well-established social expectations is a slow process. We will discuss some of these changes in the last section of this chapter. But first, let us briefly examine the traditional male role in our society.

The Male Role in Adulthood

Recently a greater amount of attention has been given to the characteristics and limitations of the male role during adulthood. For example, Pleck and Sawyer (1974) noted that "getting ahead" is an important theme for boys and men. Whether it is through grades in school, prowess in sports, or success at work, men's performance is tested in competition with other men. Winning once is not enough, for men often feel they have to keep winning, continue evaluating themselves in relation to other men and, as a result, never really win once and for all. This may leave many men dissatsified with their lives. Another major theme is "staying cool, no matter what." That is, men do not cry, they show excitement only in particular settings such as sports events, and they tend to repress their emotions even to the extent of not showing tenderness or fear, and muting or controlling their joy and anger. As a result, men may not fully experience their emotions, may ignore signs of physical or emotional distress, and tend to place greater stress on their body through the denial of feelings.

It has been suggested that there are links between these demands of the male role and greater physical vulnerability, as well as shorter life expectancy, for men as compared with women. Jourard (1971) found that men typically disclose less information about themselves than women do, so that men have more intrapersonal "secrets" than women do. He argues that men are therefore more tense than women and that being masculine requires wearing "neuromuscular armor" as a defense against the threat that his "secrets" will be exposed in a moment of weakness. This characteristic lack of personal self-disclosure may make men feel vulnerable and cause them to be constantly alert. He concludes that all this makes being manly a continual effort that causes chronic stress and requires emotional energy, possibly leading to the characteristically shorter male life span. In addition, women may be more aware of and may reveal physical or emotional discomfort at much earlier or more subtle stages, thereby seeking aid before the problem becomes so serious as to be untreatable. Harrison (1978) analyzed data on causes of death and concluded that the male role is a major contributor to the greater mortality rate of men in more obvious ways. He noted that the so-called "Type A" behavior that has been linked with heart attacks is highly consistent with the male role: speaking, walking, and eating rapidly, hostility, aggression, impatience, difficulty relaxing, sense of urgency about time, acquisitiveness, preoccupation with work and advancement, and concern about the evaluation of peers and supervisors (Friedman & Rosenman, 1974). Also, risking accidental injury, drinking alcohol, and smoking, as well as aggressive and violent behavior, are traditional elements of the male role that are related to leading causes of death among men. Waldron (1976) estimated that the male role contributes about 75 percent of the difference in life expectancy between men and women; smoking alone contributes between one-third and one-half of the difference (Waldron, 1976; Retherford, 1972).

Other elements of the male role have been suggested by David and Brannon (1976):

1. No Sissy Stuff: The stigma of all stereotyped feminine characteristics and qualities, including openness and vulnerability.
2. The Big Wheel: Success, status, and the need to be looked up to.
3. The Sturdy Oak: A manly air of toughness, confidence, and self-reliance.
4. Give 'Em Hell!: The aura of aggression, violence, and daring [p. 12].

These components of stereotyped male-role behavior suggest that the man's social role is something that is achieved by continual effort, in contrast to other social roles that one receives automatically as a result of social position or status. In that sense, masculinity may be threatened at any point by "sissy stuff" or by not being sufficiently independent, self-reliant, and powerful. This implies an element of chronic insecurity and vulnerability that may affect a wide range of behaviors and interpersonal relationships. For example, Jourard (1971) suggests that, because men are not adept at giving or receiving self-disclosure information, they may be awkward or crude in dealing with others and that even their friends or spouse may not know their inner feelings; as a result, they may be difficult to love and may also lack insight into themselves. Similarly, most men are not emotionally close to other men, and many men have never had a close male friend (Lewis, 1978); of course, the male role in our society strongly discourages displays of nonsexual affection between men, unlike other societies. Competition between men, fears of homosexuality, distrust of openness and vulnerability, and a lack of models for affection between men are major factors in this lack of male closeness, according to Lewis. Pleck and Sawyer (1974) also note the effects of the male role on men's relations with women and children: "getting ahead" interferes with commitment and involvement, while "staying cool" blocks emotional expression and warmth. These factors also prevent close relationships with one's children and, at the same time, preclude the father as a role model for emotional expressiveness and involvement for his sons and as a model of a tender, loving man for his daughters. Fein (1978) called attention to the changing patterns of fathering and the possibility of "equal parenting" as a satisfying style for both fathers and mothers; we will examine this in more detail in Chapter 5.

Sexual relations with women may also be hindered by the various components of the male role. For example, the "sturdy oak" image does not suggest a very human, open, and warm relationship. The man may feel that he must take total responsibility for the relationship (as "the big wheel") and thus prevents the equality of involvement and responsibility that is necessary for relationships. His avoidance of "sissy stuff" may lead him to be less tender, vulnerable, and emotional than he might desire. And his need to be powerful ("give 'em hell") may place him in the role as the initiator of sexual activity and, at worst, lead him to be a dominating, sometimes brutal, sex partner.

In these and other ways, the male role in our society seems limited, and some men are seeking ways to uncover the manifestations of their own conception of this masculine role and the ways it interferes with their individual needs and emotional expression. While the white male role may promise greater status and power than the white female role, the voices of men's liberation have noted that it also involves significant sacrifices. Perhaps, since male and female roles are essentially interdependent, liberation will necessarily involve both men and women.

The situation is more complex for black men and women in our society, however, because of the effects of racial discrimination and the different pattern of sex-role equality that has evolved in the black American culture (Staples, 1978). For example, the black male may be caught between the demands of the male role in our society, with its promise of high status and power, and economic and social oppression as a result of his race. Therefore, liberation from sex-role restrictions may be much less important for black persons than liberation from the significant stigma of race in our society.

As we will discuss in Chapter 8, sex differences seem to decrease in salience with advancing age; for instance, it is likely that a grandfather will be around the house and will be willing to play with young children as readily as will the grandmother. Thus, while aging may affect women more severely and earlier than men, and men are likely to live shorter lives than women, there is also a sense in which sex differences and sex-role stereotypes become less important among older persons. In that sense, liberation from sex-role stereotypes may, to some degree, be built into the normal course of human development.

Men and Women in a Changing World

As we noted at the beginning of this chapter, the study of sex differences involves examining an area that is seemingly in constant motion. Not only has there been considerable public and scientific debate and attention given to the nature and meaning of differences between men and women in recent years, but also there have been major social changes in our society during the last few years. Federal legislation has prohibited many traditional forms of sex discrimination—in employment, in granting credit, and in the schools. For example, women must now be allowed to participate in the same kind of athletic sports that have traditionally trained men to be aggressive competitors on the playing field, and in business; the long-term effect of this change will be interesting to observe—will women adopt these qualities of the male role that many men are now criticizing? Other important examples of recent social changes include the rapidly growing numbers of women who are working, especially including mothers with school-age children. Also, because of the "baby boom" following World War II and other factors, a growing proportion of women are postponing marriage—in part because the older men they are expected to marry are outnumbered by the women who are in the forefront of the baby boom. Similarly, the growing number of divorced or separated women and men are bringing a significant increase in single parents (usually single mothers) who are self-supporting. But perhaps the most significant change has been in the woman's ability to control when and whether she becomes pregnant through the general adoption of effective contraceptive techniques and, to a lesser extent, the availability of legal abortions.

If we trace the history of women, until very recently a woman was frequently and unpredictably pregnant. As a result, in most cultures her role was limited to activities that were located close to the home; she may have farmed, or engaged in craft work, but it was the men who were the hunters and warriors (Hoffman,

1977). Earlier in this century, unless she was unmarried, her employment was typically interrupted by childbearing and, as a result, women were employed in jobs where they could be replaced easily and were forced to accept low wages and jobs that were defined as low status "women's work." Similarly, these jobs did not require extensive on-the-job training, but typically relied on the assumed skills of women, such as handwork or child care (Van Dusen & Sheldon, 1976). In contrast, today, women are limiting their number of children to two or three instead of five or six, as was typical for earlier generations of women; and they are planning their pregnancies to allow greater education and occupational advancement. The current trend is to postpone the first pregnancy, and the age of marriage, to have fewer children, and to spend more years working outside the home than is spent in mothering. Without effective contraceptive techniques, this pattern would be impossible but, with them, women are able to organize the "dual careers" of motherhood and employment so that each interferes to a minimal degree with the other.

These changes are really quite recent. At the turn of the century, women also married late (because they were expected to wait until their prospective husbands could support them), but they had large families and spent nearly all of their adult lives rearing children. By the mid-1950s, age of marriage was much earlier, but families were still large and family planning had not gained widespread acceptance. However, since then the birth control pill and other contraceptive techniques have revolutionized the life cycle for women in our society. By 1973, one-half of married couples of childbearing age were using birth control (Hoffman, 1977). At the same time, women have also dramatically increased their level of education. Between 1966-67 and 1976-77, the number of women earning bachelor's degrees from college increased by 90 percent (from 236,000 to 448,000), while the number of male college graduates of that "baby boom" generation increased by a much smaller 65 percent (from 323,000 to 532,000); as a result, women have rapidly narrowed the educational gap between themselves and men (National Center for Education Statistics, 1978). Thus, to a large extent, women are now becoming educated and are seeking meaningful employment during the years they would have been raising children three decades ago.

The impact of these changes on men and on the family is also significant. For example, husbands of working women tend to help with household tasks, including child-rearing, and also tend to have less-traditional attitudes about sex roles. While this may reflect characteristics of husbands that encourage women to work, it may also increase the husband's understanding of sex discrimination (Hoffman, 1977). That is, he may be very aware that his wife is earning less than a man would in a similar job, is not advancing as rapidly as a man would, and also has to manage both the household and the job. Moreover, these changes may also have a long-term effect on male and female children who are likely to see women as more competent and effective if their mother is working outside the home. Similarly, both sons and daughters may see their father as more nurturant and emotional if he is directly involved in child care; this would affect their attitudes about the male role in society (ibid.). Thus, these effects of maternal employment could lead to reduced sex differences among the children of working mothers—and over half of all mothers are working today. Clearly, these effects could alter the meaning of sex differences for the next generation and will be an important area for future research.

Of course, social attitudes about women and men are also changing, so these children will grow up in a world that may have different attitudes and expectations about the roles of men and women and the differences and similarities between them. We will discuss some of these changes in the next two chapters. Specifically, we will examine women's changing roles in the labor market and the discrimination they experience in employment and salary in Chapter 6. Chapter 5 will explore the family in our society and the varied life-styles of "single" women and men. But, first, let us pause for another interlude—a case example of a young working mother who is dealing with a number of the issues we have discussed.

CHAPTER SUMMARY

1. Differences between men and women reflect the interaction of biological and physiological differences, social and cultural influences, and psychological and developmental processes. No single factor alone produces sex differences; they result from all of these factors as they interact with and affect each other.

2. Physiological differences between males and females begin at conception and involve genetic and hormonal differences that may affect later behavior by influencing the predisposition (or threshold) to respond to social stimuli. However, these factors do not determine behavior. Sex differences result from the interaction of this "internal environment" and the external (social) environment.

3. Women's monthly menstrual cycles appear to be related to changes in moods, although these changes may have little effect on the woman. The cycle stops at menopause and there is a drop in estrogen and progesterone. Men may also have hormonal cycles, but the data are not clear; their sex hormone, testosterone, declines gradually with age, but old men may still be able to father children.

4. Many more similarities have been found in male and female sexual response patterns than had been recognized in the past. Disregarding the obvious differences in genital anatomy, men and women have a great deal of shared sexual reactions that can provide a basis for improved communication between heterosexual partners.

5. Through the process of socialization, each individual becomes aware of his or her gender and the social expectations related to maleness or

femaleness. The formation of the self-concept involves integrating the attitudes of others toward oneself as well as reflexively looking at oneself and combining these *me*s into a coherent sense of self. Then, as one's *I* experiences one's feelings, moods, and sexuality, and integrates these experiences with one's roles, a concept of one's self is formed. This self-concept can continue to change throughout the life span as role expectations change.

6. Studies of personality differences between men and women have established only a few gender-related personality characteristics. However, stereotypes of differences between men and women are clearly defined. These stereotypes usually define men and women as opposite to each other (e.g., men are independent, women are dependent).

7. Women and men appear to have differing sources of self-esteem and motivation. Interpersonal rewards and affiliation motivation (the desire for esteem from others) have been found to be more important for women; in contrast, men tend to base their self-esteem on their accomplishments or achievements and tend to be motivated by achievement motivation (the desire for reaching internal standards of excellence).

8. The study of androgyny has focused on the relation between gender and sex role. This view does not see masculinity and femininity as opposite. Androgynous men and women combine "masculine" and "feminine" characteristics in their self-description. Thus, they are less confined to stereotyped sex roles; this gives them greater freedom to respond to a wide variety of situations with an appropriate blend of "male" and "female" reactions and skills.

9. Differences between men and women during adulthood are affected by social norms and conventions, psychological differences (such as greater affiliation motivation among women), and biological and physiological differences (menopause, and the longer life expectancy of women).

10. The male role in our society has been criticized as limiting men's ability to express emotions and to relate to women and men; it is also thought to be one cause of the shorter life expectancy of men as compared with that of women.

11. Many of the differences between men and women are being affected by a number of significant changes in our society. Federal legislation, greater attention to sex discrimination, and the growing number of young men and women in the "baby boom" generation have each had an impact. But the most significant change has been in the use of birth control techniques that have allowed women to plan whether, and when, they will become pregnant. Also, the rapid increase in working mothers has had a major impact, and its effects may alter social attitudes about the roles of women and men in the future.

REFERENCES

Bakan, David. 1966. *The Duality of Human Existence.* Chicago: Rand-McNally.

Bardwick, Judith M. 1971. *Psychology of Women.* New York: Harper & Row.

Baruch, Grace K. 1972. Maternal Influences Upon College Women's Attitudes Toward Women and Work. *Developmental Psychology, 6*(1), 32-37.

Baruch, Rhoda. 1966. *The Interruption and Resumption of Women's Careers.* Cambridge, Mass.: Harvard Studies in Career Development, No. 50.

Beauvoir, Simone de. 1953. *The Second Sex.* (Translated by H. M. Parshley.) New York: Knopf.

Beauvoir, Simone de. 1972. *The Coming of Age.* (Translated by Patrick O'Brian.) New York: G. P. Putnam's & Sons.

Bem, Sandra L. 1974. The Measurement of Psychological Androgyny. *Journal of Consulting and Clinical Psychology, 42*(2), 155-162.

Bem, Sandra L. 1975. Sex Role Adaptability: One Consequence of Psychological Androgyny. *Journal of Personality and Social Psychology, 31*(4), 634-643.

Bem, Sandra L. 1977. On the Utility of Alternative Procedures for Assessing Psychological Androgyny. *Journal of Consulting and Clinical Psychology, 45*(2), 196-205.

Bem, Sandra L., & Lenney, Ellen. 1976. Sex Typing and the Avoidance of Cross-Sex Behavior. *Journal of Personality and Social Psychology, 33*(1), 48-54.

Benedek, Therese F. 1959. Sexual Functions in Women and Their Disturbance. In S. Arieti (Ed.), *American Handbook of Psychiatry.* New York: Basic Books.

Block, Jeanne H. 1973. Conceptions of Sex Role: Some Cross-Cultural and Longitudinal Perspectives. *American Psychologist, 28*(6), 512-526.

Block, Jeanne H. 1976a. Issues, Problems, and Pitfalls in Assessing Sex Differences: A Critical Review of *The Psychology of Sex Differences. Merrill-Palmer Quarterly, 22*(4), 283-308.

Block, Jeanne H. 1976b. Debatable Conclusions About Sex Differences. *Contemporary Psychology, 21*(8), 517-522.

Broverman, Inge K.; Vogel, Susan Raymond; Broverman, Donald M.; Clarkson, Frank E.; & Rosenkrantz, Paul S. 1972. Sex Role Stereotypes: A Current Appraisal. *Journal of Social Issues, 28*(2), 59-78.

Comfort, Alex. 1976. *A Good Age.* New York: Crown.

Coppen, Alec, & Kessel, Neil. 1963. Menstruation and Personality. *British Journal of Psychiatry, 109*(463), 711-721.

David, Deborah S., & Brannon, Robert (Eds.). **1976.** *The Forty-Nine Percent Majority: Male Sex Role.* Reading, Mass.: Addison-Wesley.

Doering, Charles H.; Kraemer, Helena C.; Brodie, H. Keith; & Hamburg, David A. 1975. A Cycle of Plasma Testosterone in the Human Male. *Journal of Clinical Endocrinology and Metabolism, 40*(3), 492-500.

Exley, D., & Corker, C. S. 1966. The Human Male Cycle of Urinary Oestrone and 17-Oxosteroids. *Journal of Endocrinology, 35*(1), 83-99.

Fein, Robert A. 1978. Research on Fathering: Social Policy and an Emergent Perspective. *Journal of Social Issues, 34*(1), 122-135.

Frank, R. T. 1931. The Hormonal Causes of Premenstrual Tension. *Archives of Neurology and Psychiatry, 26*, 1053.

Friedman, Meyer, & Rosenman, Ray H. 1974. *Type A Behavior and Your Heart.* New York: Knopf.

Goodman, Madeleine J.; Grove, John S. & Gilbert, Fred, Jr. 1978. Age at Menopause in Relation to Reproductive History in Japanese, Caucasian, Chinese and Hawaiian Women Living in Hawaii. *Journal of Gerontology, 33*(5), 688-694.

Gottschalk, L. A.; Kaplan, S.; Gleser, G. D.; & Winget, C. M. 1962. Variations in Magnitude of Emotion: A Method Applied to Anxiety and Hostility During Phases of the Menstrual Cycle. *Psychosomatic Medicine, 24*(3), 300-311.

Gump, Janice Porter. 1972. Sex-Role Attitudes and Psychological Well-Being. *Journal of Social Issues, 28*(2), 79-92.

Hampson, J. S., & Hampson, J. G. 1961. The Ontogenesis of Sexual Behavior in Man. In W. C. Young (Ed.), *Sex and Internal Secretions.* Vol. 2. Baltimore: Williams & Wilkins.

Harris, Geoffrey W. 1964. Sex Hormones, Brain Development and Brain Function. *Endocrinology, 75*(4), 627-648.

Harrison, G. A.; Weiner, J. S.; Tanner, J. M.; & Barnicot, N. A. 1964. *Human Biology.* New York: Oxford University Press.

Harrison, James. 1978. Warning: The Male Sex Role May Be Dangerous to Your Health. *Journal of Social Issues, 34*(1), 65-86.

Hoffman, Lois Wladis. 1972. Early Childhood Experiences and Women's Achievement Motives. *Journal of Social Issues, 28*(2), 129-155.

Hoffman, Lois W. 1977. Changes in Family Roles, Socialization, and Sex Differences. *American Psychologist, 32*(8), 644-657.

Ivey, Melville E., & Bardwick, Judith M. 1968. Patterns of Affective Fluctuation in the Menstrual Cycle. *Psychosomatic Medicine, 30*(3), 336-345.

Jourard, Sidney M. 1971. *The Transparent Self: Self Disclosure and Well-Being.* New York: Van Nostrand Reinhold.

Jung, Carl G. 1933. The Stages of Life (Translated by R. F. C. Hull.) In Joseph Campbell (Ed.), *The Portable Jung.* New York: Viking, 1971.

Kandel, Denise B., & Lesser, Gerald S. 1972. *Youth in Two Worlds.* San Francisco: Jossey-Bass.

Kinsey, Alfred C.; Pomeroy, Wardell B.; Martin, Clyde E.; Gebhard, Paul H.; & Associates. 1953. *Sexual Behavior in the Human Female.* Philadelphia: Saunders.

Lewis, Robert A. 1978. Emotional Intimacy Among Men. *Journal of Social Issues, 34*(1), 108-121.

Livson, Florine B. 1976. Patterns of Personality Development in Middle-Aged Women: A Longitudinal Study. *International Journal of Aging and Human Development, 7*(2), 107-115.

Maas, Henry S., & Kuypers, Joseph A. 1974. *From Thirty to Seventy: A Forty-Year Longitudinal Study of Adult Life Styles and Personality.* San Francisco: Jossey-Bass.

MacBrayer, Caroline T. 1960. Differences in Perception of the Opposite Sex by Males and Females. *Journal of Social Psychology, 52*, 309-314.

Maccoby, Eleanor E., & Jacklin, Carol N. 1974. *The Psychology of Sex Differences.* Stanford, Calif.: Stanford University Press.

Masters, William H., & Johnson, Virginia E. 1961. Orgasm, Anatomy of the Female. In Albert Ellis & Albert A. Abarbanel (Eds.), *Encyclopedia of Sexual Behavior.* Vol. 2. New York: Hawthorn.

Masters, William H., & Johnson, Virginia E. 1963. The Sexual Response Cycle of the Human Male. I. Gross Anatomic Considerations. *Western Journal of Surgery, Obstetrics, and Gynecology, 71*, 85-95.

Masters, William H., & Johnson, Virginia E. 1966. *Human Sexual Response*. Boston: Little, Brown.

Masters, William H., & Johnson, Virginia E. 1970. *Human Sexual Inadequacy*. Boston: Little, Brown.

McClelland, D.C.; Atkinson, J.W.; Clark, R.A.; & Lowell, E.L. 1953. *The Achievement Motive*. New York: Appleton.

McKusick, Victor A. 1969. *Human Genetics*. Englewood Cliffs, N.J.: Prentice-Hall.

Mead, Margaret. 1949. *Male and Female*. New York: William Morrow (Apollo ed., 1967).

Money, John. 1977. Human Hermaphroditism. In Frank A. Beach (Ed.), *Human Sexuality in Four Perspectives*. Baltimore: Johns Hopkins University Press.

Money, John, & Ehrhardt, Anke A. 1972. *Man and Woman, Boy and Girl: Differentiation and Dimorphism of Gender Identity from Conception to Maturity*. Baltimore: Johns Hopkins University Press.

Money, John, & Tucker, Patricia. 1975. *Sexual Signatures: On Being a Man or a Woman*. Boston: Little, Brown.

Moos, Rudolf H. 1968. The Development of a Menstrual Distress Questionnaire. *Psychosomatic Medicine, 30*(6), 853-867.

National Center for Education Statistics. 1978. *Projections of Education Statistics to 1986-87*. Washington, D.C.: U.S. Government Printing Office (Stock No. 017-080-01918-3).

Neugarten, Bernice L. 1967b. The Awareness of Middle Age. In Bernice L. Neugarten (Ed.), *Middle Age and Aging*. Chicago: University of Chicago Press, 1968. (Originally published in: *Middle Age*. Roger Owen, Ed. London: British Broadcasting Corporation.)

Oetzel, R. 1966. Annotated Bibliography. In Eleanor E. Maccoby (Ed.), *Development of Sex-Differences*. Stanford, Calif.: Stanford University Press.

Paige, Karen E. 1971. The Effects of Oral Contraceptives on Affective Fluctuations Associated with the Menstrual Cycle. *Psychosomatic Medicine, 33*,515-537.

Parlee, Mary Brown. 1978. The Rhythms in Men's Lives. *Psychology Today, 11*(11: April), 82-91.

Pheterson, Gail L.; Kiesler, Sara B.; & Goldberg, Philip A. 1971. Evaluation of the Performance of Women as a Function of Their Sex, Achievement, and Personal History. *Journal of Personality and Social Psychology, 19*(1), 114-118.

Pleck, Joseph H., & Sawyer, Jack (Eds.). **1974.** *Men and Masculinity*. Englewood Cliffs, N.J.: Prentice-Hall (Spectrum).

Ramey, Estelle. 1972. Men's Cycles. *Ms.*, Spring, 1972, 8ff.

Retherford, Robert D. 1972. Tobacco Smoking and the Sex Mortality Differential. *Demography, 9*(2), 203-216.

Rosenkrantz, Paul S.; Vogel, Susan Raymond; Bee, Helen; Broverman, Inge K.; & Broverman, Donald M. 1968. Sex-Role Stereotypes and Self-Concepts in College Students. *Journal of Consulting and Clinical Psychology, 32*(3), 287-295.

Sherfey, Mary Jane. 1972. *The Nature and Evolution of Female Sexuality*. New York: Random House.

Sontag, Susan. 1972.   The Double Standard of Aging. *Saturday Review of the Society*, September 23, 1972, 29-38.

Spence, Janet T., & Helmreich, Robert L. 1978.   *Masculinity & Femininity: Their Psychological Dimensions, Correlates, and Antecedents.* Austin: University of Texas Press.

Spence, Janet T.; Helmreich, Robert; & Stapp, Joy. 1975.   Ratings of Self and Peers on Sex-Role Attributes and Their Relations to Self-Esteem and Conceptions of Masculinity and Femininity. *Journal of Personality and Social Psychology, 32*(1), 29-39.

Staples, Robert. 1978.   Masculinity and Race: The Dual Dilemma of Black Men. *Journal of Social Issues, 34*(1), 169-183.

Stewart, Vivien. 1976.   Social Influences on Sex Differences in Behavior. In Michael S. Teitelbaum (Ed.), *Sex Differences: Social and Biological Perspectives.* Garden City, N.Y.: Anchor.

Talbert, George B. 1977.   Aging of the Reproductive System. In Caleb E. Finch & Leonard Hayflick (Eds.), *Handbook of the Biology of Aging.* New York: Van Nostrand Reinhold.

Van Dusen, Roxann A., & Sheldon, Eleanor B. 1976.   The Changing Status of American Women: A Life Cycle Perspective. *American Psychologist, 31*(2), 106-116.

Veroff, J. 1969.   Social Comparison and the Development of Achievement Motivation. In Charles Smith (Ed.), *Achievement Related Motives in Children.* New York: Russell Sage Foundation.

Villee, Dorothy B. 1975.   Human Endocrinology: A Developmental Approach. Philadelphia: Saunders.

Walberg, H. J. 1969.   Physics, Femininity and Creativity. *Developmental Psychology, 1*(1), 47-54.

Waldron, I. 1976.   Why Do Women Live Longer Than Men? *Journal of Human Stress, 2*, 1-13.

Young, W. C.; Goy, R. W.; & Phoenix, C. H. 1964. Hormones and Sexual Behavior. *Science, 143*(3603), 212-218.

Interlude
Theresa, Age 34

Theresa is a 34-year-old woman who moved to New York to pursue a career as a laboratory technician. She worked for nine years until her first son was born; when he was five she returned to work and is doing what seems to be important research. However, she returned to her career almost accidentally and is now thinking of eventually having a second child and working for her husband (Al) in his free-lance business. She seemed rather unsatisfied staying home when her son (Jan) was young, but even now does not seem entirely clear about how to be a mother, a wife, and also to have a satisfying career.

Several questions are raised in this case example. How important is her career to her? What are the important satisfactions in her life? In what ways does it make a difference that she is a woman in terms of her milestones, satisfactions, and goals in life? What would her life have been if she had not returned to work? Is she different from other women in that way? In what ways has she changed in the last few years? Is there evidence of an "Age 30 Transition" and a "Settling Down" period in her life?

What are some of the milestones that stand out in your memory as you look back over your life? Well, the first thing that I think of . . . when I was in fourth grade we were asked to write a theme on my ambition. I had no idea what I wanted to be. And my mother first brought up the subject of what I eventually ended up doing—medical technology. And she told me when she was young she wanted to work in a laboratory and work with animals and work in a health field. And so I wrote my theme about being a laboratory technician and from that time on every time somebody asked me what I was going to be, this was it. And I did, I just went right on.

Another milestone was . . . well, I guess that's not really a milestone . . . my mother has a blood disease, and because of her connections with a blood specialist I eventually got into the field of hematology and that's something I enjoy doing. When I returned to work this time I didn't go into hematology, though; I went into cancer research. It's also very interesting. In a way it's allied to hematology, blood diseases like leukemia are cancer. *Were there any particular reasons you changed?* Only because there was an availability. In fact, I wasn't even going to go back to work. A friend of mine heard about an opening—some doctors needed a technician very badly, so she called me up and asked me if I wanted to come in. And, Jan is getting on three-and-a-half and he's going to start nursery school and I've a pretty easy routine around here; I thought it might be stimulating; and I'm glad it worked out. I was getting pretty bored, I think—addicted to the afternoon movies, the soap operas, you know, that rut that I didn't want to be in. *How long ago was it that you went back?* Last October [five months ago].

Are there any other milestones that stand out to you? I guess another milestone was moving to New York, because I met my husband. *You met him in New York?*

Right. A mutual friend, who was our best man, came to New York and visited me and asked if I'd like to come with him. He had to visit a friend of his, and then I met Al. We didn't start dating right away. We eventually had our first date back in Hartford when we were both home for Thanksgiving. *Another milestone?* It's hard, you know, when you think back for milestones you can't think. *Anything more recently?* More recently. Not really. I guess my husband's business probably is a milestone. I'm getting . . . I feel like I'm getting out of the sciences and into the arts, because I do work with him. I help him with some editing, and practically every aspect of his business we consult together, and I find that very interesting. *Are there any milestones in terms of your career? Your occupation?* I guess so. I went from an $80-a-week technician when I started out in my home town to a research assistant for my mother's blood specialist and then I came to New York and became supervisor of hematology at _____. And when I got married and we moved to _____, I started to work at _____ because it was more convenient, and I did some pediatric hematology, and now I'm back in the research field. It's been a progressive rise up the ladder, so to speak.

Would you say that being married or the birth of your child was a milestone? Oh, yes. It was. Getting married for me was especially a milestone. We have a mixed marriage [religions], and, you know, we had so many hurdles to overcome before we actually got to say "I do," so to speak; that was a big accomplishment. And our son was a big thing too. He was a planned child, and we looked forward with great anticipation. My husband took some courses [in natural childbirth] with me. We went through the Lamaze Method. He was present when Jan was delivered, and he was present in the labor room and everything. At first he didn't want any part of it. He didn't want to look at blood or anything and can't stand hospitals. But he rallied and really came through very nicely and I think he was glad to have been there. This was something very big. It's a long wait, you know, to have a child. You build up to a certain point. We were delighted with him. He's shaping up.

What about crisis points? Have there been any crises? Oh, yeah, There have been crises. Well, I guess we had a crisis over our marriage. When I moved to New York there was a crisis. When I left home [in a nearby suburb] and moved to Hartford there was another crisis with my family. As far as personal crises—I like to think of myself as a fairly stable, fairly calm, fairly relaxed, easy-going individual, so I usually don't get too upset about things. My parents are both alive, so there have been no crises over death. I did lose my grandmother when I was living in Hartford, and although this didn't really wreak havoc with my life, you know, it left a fairly marked scar, 'cause I was very close to her. She's the only grandparent I knew. All the others died before I knew them. I got through college pretty easily, there was no problem there. I guess there weren't too many crises.

No real crisis points in your marriage? No, no, we have a pretty good life. Of course, occasionally, we have a little blow-up, but we get along well, I think.

What about in terms of your job? Any crisis points there? There was a crisis with Jan. When I first returned to work; actually I started working on a part-time basis before October—Saturdays and Sundays from four to midnight. I was getting a little bit bored around the house and I thought maybe I'll try working part-time and see what happens, because I didn't know if I could handle everything. At first, Jan didn't really understand what was happening, Mommy was going to work. But when he got to realize that on certain nights I wasn't putting him to bed, he got very upset about this, and the days that I had to go to work would reach an absolute tantrum on his part. And especially if my husband was working on the same night. So, eventually, I got to bribing Jan with certain things. "When mommy goes to work I'll bring you something back." Sometimes it would be a candy bar, a package of M & Ms, or something. And he got to associate my going to work with something nice that would come to him the next day, so that's a pacifier. And then, when I found out about the full-time job, we enrolled him in nursery school and he was ecstatic. He was going to go to school like the big kids. It was just wonderful, until the first week. The second week of putting him on the bus was such an emotional thing. I'd put him on the bus and he'd cry, cry, cry. So I talked to the teachers at school and they said that's very strange because when he gets to school, he's very happy; he's a very well-adjusted child; he mixes with the other children; he loves being there; he loves to do things; he does whatever they tell him. So we had another period the second week of school where he went from this real enthusiasm about going to this reluctance to go; finally in the third week he got on the bus with a smile and a wave again. There were times when he did not want me to go to work, he wanted me to come to school with him, or he did not want to go to school, he wanted to stay home with me, and I'd explain that mommy wasn't going to be home, "Mommy's going to work." And "Why do you have to work? Why can't you stay with me?" Finally now he's pretty well over this. Saturdays and Sundays come and he says, "Why can't I go to school today?" Occasionally he'll ask me if I can be home to meet his bus. My husband usually meets his bus about four-thirty and then they come and pick me up. I try to get out once in a while early so that I can be there. It seems to please him. And, another thing that makes him happy is that my husband or I will go to school at four o'clock and pick him up instead of letting him take the bus home. *What were your feelings about leaving him like that?* It tore the heart out of me when he started to cry. It was very important that he did have some contact with other children because right now he is our only child and there are no other children in the building his age. There's one little boy but he doesn't really enjoy playing with him. Most of his contact has been with older children. Now he does have children of his own age and he refers to his friends at school as "my friends."

How do you feel about working? Very good. For sanity reasons I wanted to go back. I think I was getting in a terrible rut. I feel I'm now being stimulated again. We talk about someday having another child. I just have this feeling, you know, how soon after we have this second child can I go back to work again? Because I just don't want to get into the same rut, but I have a feeling that I probably won't go back to work again, that I'll do work at home with my husband, which is all right, as long as I'm not with that boob tube [TV] on all the day. That gets very bad. I guess I have always looked forward to the day I'd be married and home with a child and I didn't have to do anything. Well, I had three years of this and, you know, it was just too much. You don't need that. *You couldn't stand that any longer.* Right. I think that I could probably have filled my days more efficiently, but, you know, you grow up in the middle American society thinking the epitome of life is to get married, have a family and stay home, and take care of your family. But that's just not it. You've got to have other things to fill your days. Before I went to work I started to do some paintings and some crewel. I do sew, so I've always done a bit of that, but I find now working with my husband, working, and helping my son, I'm doing more things now than I ever did and I seem to have just as much free time. You know, just on the go, I don't watch television as much; I don't get to read much either. I'm out every day. I get out early in the morning. When you're home you . . . well, maybe I'll get the house picked up and get dressed, then you find that it's eleven o'clock before you're dressed. You know, we have another cup of coffee, and then you get a phone call, and don't get dressed until one, and if it's summertime you don't get out to the park until two, then the baby has to have a nap, and you're in until four. It's really bad.

How did you happen to take the career route rather than just be the mother that middle American entices you to be? I don't know. I guess . . . well, probably it was financial. We had just started a business, and my husband's brother is a Ph.D. in finances and he came over from Chicago on his way to Hartford last summer and Al says please look at the books and tell me what's happening here; and he said, "Believe it or not, your trouble isn't financial." It was just that we're having growing pains. So he said the best thing you could do is send Theresa out to work. So I said, "I don't want to go out to work. Are you kidding? I've got things to do here." And, finally, I started to think about it and I said, well, maybe that wouldn't be such a bad idea. So, all things considered, the best thing is to find something suitable. And a friend of mine had heard about this opening. So I guess if the need had not been financial, I probably would still be sitting home. *So in a sense it's almost accidental.* It's accidental, but it's probably the best thing that ever happened. *Yet you had a career before Jan was born.* Right. Well, I had worked. I graduated in 1960 and Jan was born in '69, so I had been working for nine years already. You know, I felt that this is almost a decade of work and that's enough. I had also worked while I was in college because I lived right near a hospital and I was doing weekend technology work, which was good because it pointed out to me that I was on the right track. I was getting into something that I would enjoy doing later. This was something my mother encouraged me to do, because I guess she knew a lot of people that graduated, and then they found when they went into their field they finally hated it. So, she said . . . even in high school: "If you think you're going to want to work in a hospital you should go down and see if you can get a job there to try the atmosphere." So I did. I started in my senior year and kept the job all through college. *Did you do graduate work in this?* No, I didn't. I didn't feel it was necessary because you know, that middle America bit, I said some day I'm going to be home—I didn't want to make a full-time career for the rest of my life. *How does it look to you now? Do you think that you will?* No. I think I'll be working, but . . . I think there's more of a need here. I do his [Al's] book-keeping, I write out all the checks for the employees. I do all his typing. You know, I never meant to be a secretary or bookkeeper, but I think it's better. He really can't afford to hire anybody right now and we're in at the beginning of it together so that as it grows I can grow with it. And I think in a way I like this. I don't want to feel too much apart from my husband; I don't want to feel that I don't really know what he's talking about. I just want to be able to communicate with him. I was in the sciences and he's in the arts; you know, I just don't want there to be a distance there. The other nice thing about working for him is that I guess it is not quite as regimented as being some place at nine o'clock and being there 'til five. You know, if my husband is my boss, then he's not really. I don't have to impress him.

I guess it's almost obvious in the way you've answered the questions so far, about how he feels about your working. He was negative also. He didn't want me to have to go to work. In fact, just the other day he said, "I wish you didn't have to go to work." I guess he's seeing that I'm enjoying it. He always felt that, you know, it was his place to support the family, and by the fact of my working, he gets a little feeling that he is not quite able to do it, which isn't right at all, because he's always been able to do it, and it's just been that, you know, he started a business and he's got to work very hard to have it grow. If I can help out, well, I'm glad to.

I'm curious what your feelings are about women's liberation. Well, I've been liberated, I guess. I've never run into any discrimination problems, so I can't feel very sympathetic towards women's liberation. I feel, however, that they're doing something very good and that's equality in wages. . . . I believe that this should be—equal money for equal work. However, I feel some of their, well, getting into a men's bar, is absolutely ridiculous! I believe that there should be places where men can go and women can go. Why does it always have to be integrated? I don't really approve of that. I think the work they're trying to do for the overpopulation is very good. I think the work they're trying to do for day care is very good. They've got some very good things. I think that if women want to work, they should be able to have good care for their children. A lot can go out and do what they want to do, but I can't agree with everything. *I get the feeling from you that you don't feel that either motherhood or having a career is the necessary way of life for a woman.* Well, some people are just not meant to be mothers. Some people are getting married today, and just not having children, which is very fine, if they don't feel cut out to have children. I think they should do what's best for them. *The two can merge and being a career person doesn't necessarily mean being full time in some occupation completely separate from the husband, it can be almost like a partner.* Right. Another thing about work too, when I first started to go back my feeling was that I didn't want anything that was going to take too much time away from me at home. I didn't want to have to come home and think about the work that I was doing. I felt that I don't want to have anything that is going to infringe on my time with my family. And so, that's why I took this weekend evening job, because it was purely routine—absolutely nothing to think about when I got home. And yet, now that I'm in research, I do come home and, you know, there'll probably be a time during the evening when I'll think I know a way to do something and I'll go in the next day and try it out. So, I do think about it . . . it's not really infringing as much as I thought it would be. I think the thing that I had feared was when I was supervisor at _____, I used to have to often come home with paperwork that I couldn't get to; and absolutely none of that I wanted here. Now whatever I take home is up here [gesturing toward head].

If I would ask you who you are, how would you answer? Who I am? I don't like to think of myself as a woman, because a woman has always been to me an older person and I like to think of myself as young. I'm 34 and somebody asked me the other day how old I was and I said "[19]38 from [19]72. . . ." I don't think in terms of age. I feel young and I like to think of myself as young. I don't think numbers are significant. Who I am. I guess primarily I'm a mother because I can feel so much emotion for my son. I also feel emotion for other parents, you know when you see something on television in the news about some trage-dy—I never used to feel this way before—I feel emotional. I'm a wife. I care about my home and care about my family. I want to do things for my husband and child. And I guess, naturally, I'm in a career which I care very much about also. It's something that means a lot to me also—cancer research. I feel that I can probably make a signficant contribution. Cancer means—to me—something that will probably strike in our family, because it's been coming from all angles in our family. My grandfather died of it. My husband's mother had a form of can-cer. My mother's blood disease was a benign type of cancer. I just feel that, you know, it's doomed that it's going to happen to us; if I can help by working now, maybe help science discover more about, not how to cure it, but how to prevent it and treat it, maybe I can be doing something for my family, which makes it all worthwhile. *It sounds like very exciting work for you. Very meaningful.* I'm hap-py doing this. I find it stimulating, challenging, rewarding.

Do you feel you have a firmer sense of identity now than you had before? Oh, yes, much so. *How has that changed? How has that firmer sense come about?* Well, it's come about by my life being full again. By being very active, getting me out of the house, getting me to do more things. I guess I'm stronger emotionally; stronger about wanting to get things done. Before I might have said well, I have this and this to do, I'm home ad infinitum and so I'll get it done, some day, but now I say I have these things to do and I assign a day to them in order to get them done. I make up a little schedule. I really live by a schedule. It's the only way you can fit everything in when you're so busy. We're working now to move out of an apartment into a house, because one little room for my husband's business is not adequate, so we're considering getting a two-family house where we can have some help on some income coming in, to help pay off the mortgage, where he can have an entire basement to set up as his studio. We have goals.

Would you say that you've changed very much over the past few years? I don't know if I've changed *very* much. I've probably become more mature. I probably worry a lot more. I think mothers do. *What do you mean, "more ma-ture"?* I always used to think of myself as—not really silly, but I used to take things lightly. I was probably more daring. You know, now I worry about going too fast in a car. Before, I would speed to get there faster. I think I take the business of running a house a lot more seriously, more maturely. Certainly, when you have a child you have to become more mature. I think one thing is I can probably handle situations better now. My husband would sometimes say, "I guess I'm not a good father. I don't know the proper things to do." But this is something you learn, you know; I've learned. When my son doesn't want to do something that I feel he has to do, what is the best way of getting him to do it? And so I've learned these little tricks to get him to do what I want him to do. My husband hasn't learned them because, you know, he hasn't had to deal with him as much. And so, I've been passing these little tricks along to him. I guess that's maturity too.

What other ways have you changed? I think in my relationship with my husband too, I've become more mature. I know that in our early courtship and marriage, if he were away from me, it really bothered me a lot. It's just growing used to each other a little bit. If I have to go to Hartford for a weekend, you know, I don't feel falling apart as we leave one another. I can take it easier. *Any other ways that you've changed in the last few years?* Not really; I guess the biggest change in our lives in the last few years is having a child, and trying to do what's best for our son. Seeing that he gets a liberal enough upbringing. You know, just enough discipline.

Was giving birth to him a big event for you? Oh, yes. It really was. I don't know how old I was—I must have been a teenager probably—sixteen or seventeen. I had seen a movie and I believe it was called "The Case of Dr. Laurent." And for some reason the interpretation from the French, the word "strange" was put before "case . . ." "The Strange Case of Dr. Laurent." And a couple of girlfriends and I had gone to see this movie. We knew nothing about it, and we got there and found out that it was a movie on natural childbirth. It was playing at the local cinema, so it wasn't anything educational at all. This girl had, through breathing, delivered her child without pain, and I'd never forgotten this. I guess it must have made some impression on me. And when I did become pregnant, I had since been hearing more things about what they call the Lamaze Method and I started to investigate. We got involved in a course on breathing. And the big thing was that I had heard from so many people that childbirth is the most terrifying of all pains, and that what you go through—you curse your husband, you say that you're not going to have any more children, and then, you know, a couple years later you have another child. So, it can't be all that bad, but everybody says "Well, you forget pain. You don't remember pain." Well, I just did not want to be in this position of coming to pain. I wanted to be in control, so we took this course, and were very pleased with the outcome of it. You know, I felt on top of everything. We had a very good experience. Now, everybody that I find out is pregnant I recommend the Lamaze Method to. It worked for us. We were both there and we saw our son being born and it was a very rich experience.

Has your outlook on life in general changed in the last few years? Yes, it has. Again, I think because of our child. I have this overwhelming drive to preserve myself. Before, I didn't care if . . . I didn't care when death came. I never thought about it, you know . . . death, it has to be part of life, so when it comes it comes. Now . . . I think part of it may be the violence that is so prevalent. You hear about it constantly. I worry more about living. I'm very happy; I don't want to die and I want to protect myself.

Has your marriage changed in any way? Your relation with your husband in the last few years? We've been married five years. I think the only way it possibly has changed is for the better. I think that it's nurturing. I think we're helping each other a lot. We had been dating for over three years before we got married and so we didn't enter a marriage as strangers. We knew each other very well. And, in spite of it, the first year was a big adjustment. Some friends of ours had said that the first year of marriage the word "divorce" flies around so much because there is such an adjustment. You have two virtual strangers coming together—you know, he puts his dirty socks by the bed, she hangs her stockings in the bath tub—all these things that you have to work out and adjust to. It's a big thing. *So the first year was pretty difficult.* The first year, I don't think was as difficult for us as it was for some of our friends. We'd lived together for a while before we were married. We sort of got some of the wrinkles ironed out. We also knew each other for three years. I knew his hangups and he knew mine before we got married. Knowing them we went into marriage not wanting to change one another, but willing to accept each other's idiosyncracies. You know, you cope—you just have to understand. Somebody wise made the best statement I ever heard: "If you are willing to each give into your marriage, feel that you're giving more; if you can always go through your marriage giving the most of yourself; if each one does that, you're always giving and you're not wanting to take all the time, you'll have a good marriage," and I think we give a lot.

Has sex become more important, less important, or about the same in your marriage? I think it's less important. I think that probably in the beginning it's something new; it's probably the thing that brings you closer together. As your marriage gets older, it becomes less important because there's other things that you do together. Unfortunately we don't get to do too many social things because we're too busy. But whenever we do it [sex], it seems to be enough. It's not that driving need that there used to be in our early marriage. I guess it's still fairly important, but I guess it's not quite as imperative, so to speak.

Have your relations with your parents changed in the last few years? Yeah, I guess. I feel that I'm not quite as close to my father as I used to be and would like to be. It's probably that we don't get to see each other too often. You know, when you think about going home once a month for a weekend after I've spent a lifetime with people, you only see them for . . . twenty-four days a year. I find that I don't know what to say to him any more, outside of his work. . . . What do you talk about? I think that I'm in a different world now. I feel that they're not really into our world. It's just, you know, we have this gap. I can talk to them about Jan. They can talk to me about the other grandchildren. My mother and I talk about what's going on in the family—who's doing what. It's not that I have trouble talking. I just feel that I don't have as much to say as I would like to. I'd like to be able to talk more to him [father]. *Is your relationship now different from, say, when you were a teenager?* Oh, yes. Heavens! There's a great deal of difference. My mother was very strict and my father tended to be more liberal. As a teenager growing up I hated to ask my mother for permission to do anything. I'd much rather ask my father. I resented very much that lack of freedom that I grew up with. A lot of my friends had a lot more freedom, and this was, you know, [a source of] . . . good arguments; [I was] really rebellious. *I take it that there was a fair amount of tension between you and at least your mother then?* Yes, terrific tension when I was a teenager. As I grew older, when I left home to go to Hartford—I don't know how I got away. I really don't know how I got away. I must have been very strong. I'm sure there must have been arguments, but I must have mentally blocked them out. When I moved to New York I came home and announced . . . I think this is what I said, "They need me in New York!" (laughter). You know, I don't know how they ever fell for this stuff. "There's a job and they need a hematology supervisor and I must go." I drove off in my Volkswagen into the sunset; my mother's standing at the door saying, "This is terrible! This is a terrible way to go!" But I went and I got there. It was always my mother I had to work the hardest to get to do what I wanted to do, but we're very good friends now. And once we got married, once all the hurdles were over, you know, and I finally settled down—after she came to New York and saw where we were living and saw our furniture and saw that we did have substantial material things—she stopped pressuring me. We're very close now.

Has the way other people think of you changed over the years? The way other people think of me? I guess I care about what people think of me. Some people can just go on in life. It bothers me. It bothers me if I'm not well-accepted. That doesn't bother me as much now, where as a child in grammar school . . . I was part of a popular group, but I never felt that I was completely accepted. But today I am more accepted for myself. I still worry what the neighbors think—that sort of thing. I try to keep up appearances.

Would you say that you married at about the right time? Or early or late? No, we married about the right time. I was 29, I think, I'm not sure any more. I had traveled what I thought was fairly extensively. Probably not as extensively as some people, but I had gone to Europe once. I've gone cross-country. I went to a couple of islands. And, you know, I enjoyed being single. I worked what I thought was sufficiently. There was nothing left that I wanted to do. Like a lot of kids get married at 17 and 18 and that's it. They get nowhere. I think I got married at the right age. Maybe a year or two years earlier would have been okay, too. But I don't feel that it was too late. Certainly not too early. *Did you feel much pressure to get married earlier?* Oh, yes. My mother was always urging a little bit. She didn't like the fact that I was single and living in an apartment. That's not the way she was brought up. She probably would have been happy if I had stayed at home and gotten married a couple of years after I got out of college, but I enjoyed it very much.

Would you say that you have a pretty firm sense of who you are? Yes. I'm not confused about my personality. I don't try to fool myself in being something

I'm not. The only thing that I hope is that I can "grow up" to be as gracious as some of the more mature women I see today. You know, you learn things as you go through life. You learn things like tact; you learn things about being kind to people, which, I think, as a teenager . . . you just don't consider. I think about them more now. You know, I feel it's important to be charitable. I think if every woman could learn to be gracious, if every person could be gracious, if every man. . . . Graciousness is a composite of everything I'd like to be. *How long have you felt that you had a firm sense of who you were?* I guess most of my life. Maybe not most of my life; well, at least since probably the middle of college. I guess in high school you don't think about that too much. Maybe it's become more important that I was aware of who I was since maybe the last five years or so. So much of your youth is finding out where you're going, what you're going to do and getting there. I think once you get there—like, I probably got there after I got married—the rest of your life becomes pretty much a straight course. You find your mate and start your family and you go in one direction. I guess, getting married [was the point] now that I think about it.

Do you sometimes look back over your life and review what's happened? Yes. I think about things I would have done differently . . . ways I would have handled situations differently. I think if my mother had been different, probably things would have been a lot different too. Maybe not, maybe I don't resent the strictness as much now as I did then. You know . . . when you want to do something and you can't do it you're very upset about it. It's probably very good for you.

Do you sometimes think about death? I think I mentioned that I think about it with great trepidation. I didn't mind it before, but I mind it now. I don't want my husband to die, I don't want my son to die, I don't want me to die. As far as my parents now, I love them very much; I know they are getting older, you know; I'm more willing to accept the fact that maybe in this decade, maybe in the next decade, they'll go. This is a fact that I can accept, whereas—this is something too when I was not married and I didn't have a child—I just couldn't conceive of my parents dying. I didn't want them to die. I knew that I'd get very, very upset if they died. Now, I feel that I could accept it. So, I guess I've got my own family too—it's not as important.

How does the future look to you in terms of your life? It's good. We have dreams. We have dreams about a home in the country and a prosperous business. I think the business is getting good. As far as a dream house in the country, I don't know. We obviously dream too hard. But if you don't have something to aim for, what are you going to work for?

I gather that you'd say that you have a very intimate relationship. Yeah, we do. We have a good understanding of one another. It's good. If lovers can be friends, that's important; and I think we're friends. Anybody can be a relation, but to be a friend is to know somebody, and we know each other. It's nice. *Do you feel pretty productive in your life now?* Yeah, I do. And again, it's all since I returned to work. I'm doing a lot; I'm doing a lot more and I enjoy it. I enjoy being busy. I thought I was going to enjoy just having lots of leisure time, but I don't. I'm not cut from that mold, and the busier I can be, it seems, the better I function.

Do you have any sense of leaving your mark? I guess I'm leaving my mark. I'm not a radical. I don't feel that I've got to go around and change everything, leave my mark in that way, but I guess, you know, in very quiet, subtle ways I do leave my mark. *Is that important to you?* No, no. Not especially. I just get along and get things done. I know that . . . maybe it sounds vain but once I've been somewhere, like once I've worked somewhere, I must have left some impressions there. One thing my boss said to me a couple of weeks ago: "Whenever you take your vacation, I'm going to take mine," because . . . you know, I'm getting so much work done that if he stays and I'm away, that he's going to have all the work to do and he'll never get it done. I just feel that after I'm gone I think he's going to have a difficult time finding someone as efficient, as vain as it may sound. You know, I think this is how I leave my mark, but it's not important.

What kind of things are important for right now? I guess they're all material things. Getting a flourishing business, getting a house, having one more child. I think those would have to be the three important things. Getting my son into a good school is really important, too. That's just about it. As far as material possessions, the house is the only real thing.

Would you say that your life has been a meaningful adventure? Yes. I think so. I feel sorry that it didn't start becoming more meaningful earlier. But, I guess . . . you just can't have a more meaningful life too early. I'd say that my life has probably become more meaningful again in the last five years. It seems to me, since I've been married that things have had a definite purpose. Before that, you know, you're just running from here to there; you're unsettled. Now I feel this is home, because for many years I would always refer to home as my parents' house, and now I refer to my own home as home. And like, thoughts are channeled here.

Are you looking toward the future mostly, or thinking about the past, or just concerned with the present? I'm more concerned with the future. Well, I guess I'm concerned with the present in order to get to the future. Yeah, I don't really think about what's gone past. I never cry over spilt milk, but I care about the present—whether we're going to survive in the jungle long enough to get to the future. *But the future is important for you now.* Yes, it's important. I guess it's important that I get my home in the country and I get my children, well, raised without getting them hung up on drugs and, you know, without having them travel with some wild crowd—protecting them in this world is important.

In 1979, Theresa had moved and was no longer working at the medical center. I was unable to locate her through the personnel office or to contact her husband's business. Thus, we do not know what happened in her life during the six years following this interview.

NATHAN HAWLEY, and FAMILY, Novr 3.^d 1801.

5
FAMILIES AND SINGLES

Adults are highly complex human beings, and in twentieth century America they live in a highly complex society that offers a range of possible life-styles and institutional involvements. Yet, nearly all adults invest a great deal of time and emotional energy in one of these social institutions—the family. Sometimes families provide deeply meaningful intimate relationships and signficant opportunities for personal growth and fulfillment. Occasionally they provide some of the greatest emotional upsets and potentials for violence. For example, homicide rates indicate that most people are killed by family members, the problem of "battered" wives and children is receiving increasing attention, and police approach all family disputes with great caution. Still other families provide little more than comfortable bedrooms and dining facilities. But, by and large, adults marry, have children, launch them into their own families, and grow old along with their mate.

However, some adults do not marry, and others do not remain married. We are curious about the characteristics, life-styles, and developmental milestones of the single adults in our society. We are also curious about some of the emerging family styles since there seems to be a great variety of family life-styles that are possible in our complex, pluralistic society.

Still, regardless of the style these intimate personal relationships may take, they obviously are only part of the significant involvements during the middle years. That is, they interact with the satisfactions, challenges, and frustrations involved in the occupation (which we will discuss in the next chapter). These are the issues that Erikson described by the terms Intimacy versus Isolation—where the task is to achieve a truly intimate relationship—and Generativity versus Stagnation—where the task is to gain a sense of productive accomplishment through one's occupation or as a parent so that there will be something one has done that will outlive oneself. These are philosophic ideals, of course, and many people may be too busy caring for the family and earning a living to consider these issues very seriously. Yet, there is a sense in which they describe the challenge and potential satisfactions of these middle years fairly clearly.

In this chapter, we examine three aspects of the family. First, we will explore the kinds of families that currently exist in our society and describe some of the characteristics of minority families, focusing especially on black families. Second, we will focus on the developmental perspective of the family and summarize the major events in the family cycle. And, third, we will discuss unmarried adults since we are curious about the ways in which their lives and life-styles are similar and different in comparison with the married majority. Throughout the discussion of the family, we will also note the continuing importance of sexuality through the adult years, because sexual desire and capability do not end with the birth of the last child, at menopause, nor necessarily at widowhood; we may assume that sexuality has a similarly long life for single adults as well.

THE AMERICAN FAMILY

There is much controversy about the American family. Some feel that the growing divorce rate indicates a decline in the stability of family life. However, Glick

(1977) pointed out that 84 percent of all families in 1975 consisted of husband-wife families and that seven out of every eight husbands were in their first marriage. For those who do divorce, about three out of four women and five out of six men marry again, usually within three years, and over half of these remarriages last as long as the partners live. Although it seems likely that the divorce rate may eventually reach the point where one-third of all first marriages are ended by divorce, two out of three couples will still have intact marriages for as long as they live. Since more and more adults are living into old age today than in the past, marriages are also lasting longer today. For those married in the first decade of the 1900s, the average marriage lasted 35.6 years; for those married in the 1970s, the average marriage is expected to last 44 years if it is not cut short by divorce (ibid.). Thus, a person could spend more time in a second marriage today than his or her grandparents spent in their single marriage.

It has also been argued that the contemporary family is losing its function because society is becoming so complex, family members are living apart from each other, and bureaucratic institutions are performing many of the functions once left to the family, such as caring for aged family members. However, Shanas (1979) suggests that the family is gaining greater importance as the place where one can relax, be appreciated as a unique person, and find support and interpersonal warmth as society becomes more technological and impersonal. In her 25 years of research on the family, Shanas finds no evidence that the family is becoming irrelevant.

It is still the family, that group of individuals related by blood or marriage, that is the first resource of both its older and younger members for emotional and social support, crisis intervention, and bureaucratic linkages [Shanas, 1979, p. 5].

We will discuss her findings in detail when we focus on the aging family, but now we will take a closer look at the structure and diversity of American families.

Extended, Nuclear, and Modified Extended Families

Most of the families in our society seem to be *nuclear families*, since they are made up of a mother, a father, and their children sharing a household. However, these nuclear family units have a variety of ties with other members of their family—that is, with their *extended family*. An extended family is made up of those individuals one is related to through blood or marriage, as well as "fictive kin" who are treated as family members even though they are not actual relatives. Although the young couple typically establishes a home separate from the parents, family ties generally remain intact. Even if the family units are separated by a considerable distance, they keep in contact by telephone, airplane, and automobile. Sussman and Burchinal (1962) and Shanas (1979) report that, in general, nuclear family units retain close ties with other family units in a kin network and that mutual aid and social interaction are frequent. Financial help, as well as help by providing services (house cleaning, baby sitting, and shopping, for example), frequently occur between generations of the family, so that parents help the newly married couple, and later the younger couple help their parents after retirement or during illness. Sussman and Burchinal (1962) term this family structure a *modified extended family* (after Litwak, 1960). It differs from the isolated nuclear family since the family units maintain interrelations across generations and among siblings while also maintaining much autonomy and mobility; it differs also from the extended family household in which three or more generations live together (Kerckhoff, 1965).

While it has been thought that multigenerational households were very common during earlier periods, especially before the industrial revolution, recent research has challenged the notion that this family form was a prevalent family pattern in Western society, except during periods of economic adversity or family disruption. For example, Back (1974) examined census records in England from 1574 to 1821. He found that only 6 percent of households contained three or more generations of family members, and these nearly always appeared to result from a family calamity such as widowhood or a broken household. He concluded that there is no evidence that three-generation households were the preferred family pattern before the industrial revolution, or that industrialization led to a decline of multigenerational households. Similarly, van de Walle (1976) examined census records for a small community in Belgium for the period 1847–1866. He found that, at any given time, about two-thirds of the households were nuclear families, compared with about 10 percent extended households and 11 percent multiple households (consisting of more than one nuclear family living together). The nuclear families were also more lasting than the other forms, suggesting that multiple and extended households were transitional patterns that resulted from family disruption. Thus, there is no evidence in these studies that multigenerational households were prevalent in rural areas or before the industrial revolution in Western society.

However, other cultures have emphasized extended family households. For example, Rogers and Gallion (1978) found that about two-thirds of older Pueblo Indians living in New Mexico were in extended households. Similarly, Murdock and Schwartz (1978) found that over half of the older Sioux Indians living on a reservation in North and South Dakota were living in a multigenerational household. Also, Staples (1976) pointed out the importance of the extended family in the African culture that is carried on today in many black families. One illustration of this is that 48 percent of black families headed by elderly women have relatives under 18 in the household, compared with only 10 percent among white families (ibid.). And Palmore (1975) found that among persons over age 65, nearly four out of five couples, and slightly higher proportions of single persons, were living with their children in Japan. The proportions are much lower in Great Britain, still lower in the United States, and less than one out of five in Denmark (Table 5.1). This does not imply that the aged move in with their children in Japan, since they typically grow old living in the family of the oldest son. Nor does this imply that the aged in Denmark, for instance, are isolated and abandoned. Independence and a close friendship network are as important in

Table 5.1   Composition of Households of Persons Over Age 65 in Four Countries (Percentages)

Composition	Japan M	Japan F	Great Britain M	Great Britain F	USA M	USA F	Denmark M	Denmark F
Couples:								
Alone	16	15	67	68	77	82	80	84
With child	79	79	29	28	18	15	17	14
With relatives	4	5	3	5	3	2	1	—
With nonrelatives	1	1	1	2	2	1	2	2
Total	100	100	100	100	100	100	100	100
Single:								
Alone	10	8	37	45	52	46	58	63
With child	82	84	41	37	38	37	20	21
With relatives	6	6	14	13	11	22	6	7
With nonrelatives	2	2	8	5	8	5	10	9
Total	100	100	100	100	100	100	100	100

Source: Palmore (1975), Table 1. Reprinted with permission. Data from Shanas et al., (1968); Nasu, S. *The Aged and the Development of Nuclear Families.* Metropolitan Institute of Gerontology, Tokyo, 1973.

Danish society as respect and loyalty to the elders are in Japanese society. Thus, family structure reflects cultural values and cannot be understood apart from its larger cultural context.

Within the modified extended family structure that is prevalent in the United States today, there are a wide variety of family structures. For example, some families have only one parent living with the children—because they were divorced, widowed, deserted, or never married. Other families have "extra" people in the family—an aged parent, a housekeeper, or an unmarried relative, and so on. And some families may be incredibly complex since they reflect the effects of divorce and remarriage. Thus, one "nuclear" family may consist of parts of two previous families living together during the week as a single family; but on weekends the members may shift as the children visit their parents as if they were part of a different nuclear family. If relationships with the various sets of grandparents are included, the family structure becomes very complex indeed.

Sussman (1976) analyzed the census data on family structure and estimated the proportion of the adult population that is living in various family structures, recognizing that the census data do not always accurately reflect those persons who are living in nontraditional family patterns. Thus, his figures are educated guesses that are based on census data for 1976. Interestingly, he suggests that only about 18 percent of adults are living in the traditional American family (intact, nuclear family with children living in the same household, and only one parent working); the "dual career" family where both husband and wife work is about equally common (Table 5.2). Single, widowed, separated, or divorced adults are also about equally prevalent, according to his estimates. Couples who have no children, or whose children have grown up and left home, remarried

Table 5.2   Family Type by Estimated Percent Distribution in the United States, 1976.

Family Type	Estimated Percent Distribution
1. Nuclear family—husband, wife, and offspring living in a common household ("intact").	37
a. Single career	18
b. Dual career	19
1. Wife's career continuous	No estimate
2. Wife's career interrupted	No estimate
2. Nuclear dyad—husband and wife alone: childless, or no children living at home.	11
a. Single career	4
b. Dual career	7
1. Wife's career continuous	No estimate
2. Wife's career interrupted	No estimate
3. Nuclear family—husband, wife, and offspring living in a common household (*remarried*). No estimate of career patterns.	11
4. Single-parent family—one head, as a consequence of divorce, abandonment, or separation (with financial aid rarely coming from the second parent), and usually including preschool and/or school-age children.	12
a. Career	8
b. Noncareer	4
5. Kin network—three generation households or extended families where members live in close geographical proximity and operate within a reciprocal system of exchange of goods and services.	4
6. Other single, widowed, separated, or divorced adults.	19
Emerging experimental forms	6
1. Commune family	
a. Household of more than one monogamous couple with children, sharing common facilities, resources and experiences; socialization of the child is a group activity.	
b. Household of adults and offspring—a "group marriage" known as one family—where all individuals are "married" to each other and all are "parents" to the children. Usually develops a status system with leaders believed to have charisma.	
2. Unmarried parent and child family—usually mother and child, where marriage is not desired or possible.	
3. Unmarried couple and child family—usually a common-law type of marriage with the child their biological issue or informally adopted.	
	100

Source: Sussman (1976), Table 2. Copyright©1976 by Litton Educational Publishing, Inc. Reprinted with permission of Van Nostrand Reinhold Company.

nuclear families, and single-parent families each represent about 11 to 12 percent of all adults. Although his estimates differ from the census statistics presented earlier in this chapter, it may be noted that he is describing all adults; when we look only at those 59 percent who are living as husband-wife couples, we see that 82 percent are intact marriages while 18 percent have been remarried.

Perhaps the growing acceptance of a diversity of life-styles in our society will lead to an increased prevalence and stability of a variety of family structures. Thus there may be, as Sussman (1976) suggests, a need for a twofold definition of the family: the conjugal family, established by contract with legal rights and responsibilities, and the "everyday family" that is not based on kinship, but is "composed of individuals in a cohabitating domestic relationship, one which provides love and emotional bonding and is sexually consequential. It, therefore, includes sanctioned and unsanctioned variant forms such as group marriage, communal, lesbian, and homosexual" (Sussman, 1976, p. 140). For example, he notes that while experimental family forms have not been particularly common among the elderly, there are some older persons living in communal homes such as "Share-a-Home" in Florida, and that one-fifth of all men over 65 who were living with nonrelatives in 1970 were living with a woman. At the same time, however, the basic family pattern that has existed for centuries will undoubtedly continue to evolve and survive since there is considerable evidence that the conjugal family continues to be the most important social network and source of aid for the vast majority of persons.

Ethnic Diversity among Families in America

Frequently it is assumed that all families are, or should be, basically similar. This overlooks the considerable variations within families, especially among the diverse ethnic groups that make up American family life. While it is not possible for us to explore the vast range of similarities and variations among ethnic families here, we need to be aware of the heterogeneity of family life in the United States. One recent book discussed the historical background and contemporary characteristics of families in fifteen different ethnic groups: Amish, Arab, Black, Chinese, French, Greek, North American Indian, Irish, Italian, Japanese, Jewish, Mexican, Mormon, Polish, and Puerto Rican (Mindel & Habenstein, 1976). Each of these groups has established family patterns based on their unique cultural heritage. Gradually through the mutual process of retaining their heritage and traditions while being assimilated into American life—often with the burden of social stereotypes and oppression—these families have evolved in differing ways. In attempting to understand families, we need to avoid stereotyped descriptions of the rich variation between ethnic groups and to be especially careful about the tendency to see ethnic variations as abnormal or deviant family forms. Instead, they should be seen as cultural variations that exist in different cultural and social environments (Allen, 1978).

Woehrer (1978) summarized the research on ethnic families with a particular focus on the elderly, pointing out a number of interesting observations that may provide us with a flavor of the rich diversity among ethnic families in America. For example, a nationwide study of American families found striking ethnic differences in the proportion of persons who visited their parents weekly: 79 percent for Italian Americans, 65 percent for Polish Americans, 61 percent for French Americans, and 39 percent for English and Scandinavian Americans

(Greeley, 1971). Moreover, Italian and Polish Americans tend to emphasize family ties and to have fewer nonfamily friends, to value friends less than kin, and to belong to fewer organizations than other ethnic groups. Scandinavian Americans, in contrast, are likely to belong to organizations. Black and Irish Americans are likely to have close ties with siblings and also to value friendships very highly; for black Americans, friends who are very close often have a kinshiplike bond in which they are regarded as family members. Thus, in some ethnic groups—such as Italian, Mexican, Polish, and Jewish Americans—the family is the major source of emotional and financial support; others—such as Irish and black Americans—rely on friendship to a higher degree than other ethnic groups; and still others—such as Scandinavians—count on social organizations for an important part of their daily life (Woehrer, 1978). These differences are important to understand, since the pattern of behavior or social environment that is meaningful for one group may be different for another group.

> The Scandinavian senior in the high rise who sees her children only occasionally and the Polish grandfather who has no close friends outside the family and belongs to no organizations may both be socially integrated within the context of their own cultural values and expectations. Likewise, the German grandmother who sits alone at her sewing machine stitching together doll clothes for her granddaughters and patch quilts for the missions and the Irish grandmother employed at the information booth when the state legislature is in session may both find meaning and happiness in their work. Make them switch roles, however, and you may have two unhappy and alienated seniors [Woehrer, 1978, p. 335].

Clearly, the family and individuals can be seen only within the cultural framework of their ethnic background. In addition, socioeconomic differences, including educational level, the particular family background, rural or urban heritage, and individual uniqueness as a family, all combine into the mosaic of American families. Just as it is a misconception to think of all white families as similar, so also it is inaccurate to think of all Chicano or black or Greek American families as similar. In the next section, we will take a closer look at black families as one example of the diversity among American families.

Black Families in America

A number of misconceptions about black families continue to exist, despite recent research on the variations, strengths, and historical background of black families in the United States. For example, it is often not recognized that there are important differences among black families—just as there are among white or Hispanic families. Whether the parents have a college education or finished only eighth grade, immigrated from the West Indies or were born in a Northern urban center, live in the rural South or in a small midwestern community may make considerable differences in family patterns and characteristics—just as similar differences would affect any other ethnic group of families. At the same time, however, black families share a cultural and historical background and often retain close ties with the black community, maintaining a cultural tradition within a predominantly white society in the United States. In that sense, black families tend to be bicultural, embodying characteristics of both the black and white culture, and to raise children to function in both black and white society (Peters, 1978). Thus, black families reflect not only the diversity of family life in the United States, but also their own unique cultural and historical background, as well as the effects of racism and minority status in American society.

Frequently black families have been studied from a perspective in which white family structures and patterns were considered to be the norm, and black families, insofar as they differed from this norm, were considered to be maladapted, pathological, or deviant (Nobles, 1978). Since that perspective views black families as if they were inherently different from white families, the analyses and interpretations of data about black families have often focused on the characteristics and origins of these supposedly alien or deviant family patterns. One of the most prevalent misconceptions about black families that has resulted from this perspective is the notion that black families are dominated by women. This interpretation has grown out of the fact that about 39 percent of all black families are headed by women, compared with about 12 percent of all white families (U.S. Bureau of the Census, 1979, Table 8). Also, many studies have found a more equal division of status and authority between mothers and fathers in black families compared with white families (Staples, 1976). However, the proportion of black families headed by women is strongly related to income; about 53 percent of female-headed black families were below the officially defined poverty income level in 1974 (U.S. Bureau of the Census, 1976a). At higher income levels, the proportion of male-headed families is similar for black and white households (Staples, 1976). Bronfenbrenner (1975) found that 71 percent of parents under age 25 with low income (below $4000) were single parents, so that "regardless of color, families in similar circumstances are affected in the same way for better or for worse" (p. 18). Similarly, an equal division of power and status between husband and wife does not imply female dominance, except from the perspective of traditional white families in which the wife is expected to be less powerful than the husband. Finally, the important question is not whether black families are dominated by women but, instead, what is the structure and function of contemporary black families in the United States?

Staples (1978) pointed out that research on decision making between husbands and wives has revealed that black couples are as egalitarian—or nonegalitarian—as white couples. Differences among black couples are very clear in this research, calling attention to the diversity among black families (Willie & Greenblatt, 1978). For example, Mack (1978) studied decision making among 80 couples, 20 from each of four groups: black middle class, white middle class, black working class, and white working class. She found that social class differences were greater than racial differences on the dimension of which marital partner was more dominant in a number of experimental bargaining tasks and on responses to questionnaires. In addition, for both black and white couples, she found that marital dominance was not a characteristic of the relationship in all situations, but depended on the specific context of the decision within the larger context of the marital relationship. In another study comparing self-reported dominance in various family decisions among an inner-city sample of Anglo, black, and Chicano husbands and wives, Cromwell and Cromwell (1978) found that both spouses had approximately equal power within the family in all three ethnic groups. Thus they caution that "categorical labeling of family structure based on ethnic group membership is unwarranted and inappropriate" (p. 757).

As is the case for all ethnic families, the black family cannot be understood apart from the cultural history of black persons. The experience of slavery is a dominant theme in the cultural history of a vast majority of black persons in the United States, although about 500,000 were free and formed the black middle class during the period of slavery (Staples, 1976). An equally important influence is the cultural heritage from the African homeland; this was preserved and passed down from generation to generation (Gutman, 1976; Haley, 1976). According to Staples (1976), these cultural values emphasized the unity of the African family and the importance of the marital bond; these values were stressed even when slavery made unity of the family difficult or impossible to maintain. After slavery was ended, marriage rates soared since black persons were free to marry, and the typical black household was a nuclear family headed by a male. It was not until the late 1800s that women were encouraged to seek work because of the enormous racial discrimination of that period; although women working was considered a carry-over from slavery, it was accepted only because black men could not find employment. By 1900, about 40 percent of black women were in the labor force (ibid.). Nonetheless, black families remained stable as men and women shared in child-rearing and economic support of the family. Then, the migration from the rural South to the industrial North added strains to the black family. Staples argued that the twentieth-century urban ghettos and the pressures of survival in an industrial society were primarily responsible for the dramatic increase in female-headed households among low-income black families. However, the emphasis on the unity of the family persists through an extensive and cohesive kinship network. While this may result in part from the need for mutual aid in a hostile environment, it also clearly reflects the African heritage within black social organization. That is, there is a signficiant link between the individual's identity and the family or group identity. The kinship network is broad, including not only uncles, aunts, and cousins as well as parents, grandparents, and siblings, but also there are special friendship patterns in which persons "go for" brothers or sisters and become part of the kinship structure (ibid.).

Many studies have called attention to this cohesive kinship network among blacks. While some white ethnic families also maintain similar kinship networks, Hayes and Mindel's (1973) study of kinship relations found 7 out of 25 black families, compared with 2 out of 25 matched white families, had relatives living with them—a total of 16 besides their own children in the black families and only

2 in white families. Siblings, grandchildren, nieces, and nephews were frequently living in these black families. Similarly, Stack (1972) found that children become part of the personal kinship network of the family when they are born and, if the mother is unable to care for the child, the grandmother, older sister, or aunt becomes the child's "mama" who serves as a parent throughout the child's lifetime. Moreover, the extended kin network often provides support to the single-parent family, providing not only child care and financial aid, but also providing a variety of male role models in long-term relationships with the children (Stack, 1974). McAdoo (1978) found that these extensive patterns of kin involvement were maintained among three generations of upwardly mobile black families; respondents born in the middle class, as well as those born in the working class, and those living in urban or surburban areas each maintained close kin ties. The older black person also often has a kinship network for support and, in addition, has a friendship network to call upon for aid, since "that's what friends are for" (Woehrer, 1978, p. 335).

Conclusion

The family remains very important in the lives of a vast majority of Americans, and there is no evidence that the family is losing its function as the most flexible and most significant source of support. In addition, the modified extended family pattern prevalent in America today seems to have been the preferred family form in Western society for at least several generations.

Although the American family has often been viewed as if it were a single phenomenon, in reality there are many variations among American families. Black families are one important example of the need to examine the rich patterns of variations among families within their own cultural perspective. While in the past black families have been seen as deviant or inadequate when viewed from a white perspective, they are now beginning to be studied from the perspective of cultural variation and their own unique cultural heritage. However, we know very little about the developmental progression of black families and the timing and sequence of their milestones, since this has so far been studied only among white families. Similarly, we have very little data available about Hispanic families in America, despite their emergence as a numerically significant minority group. Also, very little research has been done on the diverstiy of family patterns in other racial and ethnic groups in the United States. But we hope to continue to discover the many facets of diversity within the mosaic of American family life in the 1980s.

In the next section, we will take a closer look inside the family by using the developmental perspective.

THE FAMILY CYCLE

Just as each individual goes through a life cycle with developmental stages marked by milestones, so *families* go through a *cycle* with milestones that mark stages in the development of the family. The major milestones in the life of the family are: marriage, birth of the first child, birth of the last child, the last child leaving home (the "empty nest"), and widowhood. These milestones suggest a framework for examining the differing demands and possibilities that are present for the adult at various times in the cycle of the family.

However, the events that make up this family cycle reflect cultural factors and social change. This is another important example of the effect of cultural-historical factors on the developmental progression through the life span (which we discussed in Chapter 1). That is, the average length of time between the family events of marriage and the last child leaving home has decreased since 1880, while the average age at widowhood has increased. Thus, the parental years of the family cycle have speeded up as a result of the combined effects of smaller families and the earlier departure of the children from the family. However, the length of time between the departure of the last child and widowhood has increased so that the *postparental* years of the family cycle have been steadily lengthening and are expected to continue growing longer (Figure 5.1). These

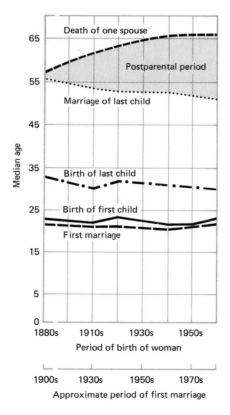

Figure 5.1

Median age of mothers at selected milestones in the family life cycle. (Source: Glick, 1977, Figure 1.) Copyright © 1977 by the National Council on Family Relations. Reprinted with permission.

historical changes have affected the family cycle considerably. They have brought about "middle-aged grandparents " and an increase in four-generation families (that is, great-grandparents). A cross-national study of older persons found that, in 1962, 40 percent of persons over 65 in the United States had great-grandchildren; 23 percent in Denmark and 22 percent in Britain were also at the top of four-generation families (Shanas, Townsend, Wedderburn, Friis, Milhøj, & Stehouwer, 1968). In Britain, the average woman became a grand-mother at 54 and a great-grandmother at 72; men averaged three years later (Townsend, 1966). This change has a wide range of effects on the structure of the extended family. That is, the grandparents may have to divide their time and energy between caring for their aged parents and providing attention to their adult children and grandchildren. And one person may have 20 to 30 grandchil-dren and great-grandchildren spread across the country in a complex extended family network.

These events of the family cycle also call our attention to the social and psy-chological effects of these family cycle events on the individual. For example, the birth of the first child not only brings a shift in role from "spouse" to "parent" (with the consequent shift in norms and expectations), but may also bring a shift in self-conception and motivation as well as a possible reawakening of unre-solved childhood conflicts in the parents.

Thus, the milestones of the family cycle suggest a progressive development of the family through a series of sequential phases. The division of these phases within the general guidelines of the family cycle is somewhat arbitrary, so we will discuss the family in each of the following phases: establishment, new parents, child-rearing family, and postparental family.

Establishment

This phase begins at marriage (or when the partners begin living together as a couple) and continues through the initial period of settling into the relationship; it is characterized by the couple functioning as a dyad and may last until the first child is born. The process of mutual socialization is undoubtedly of great impor-tance during this phase as the partners seek to fulfill their new roles with one an-other, with parents, and with society in general. To aid in this respect, the event of marriage serves as a kind of rite of passage between past roles and future roles so that at least the entrance into these new roles is clearly defined. Of course, couples who live together before marriage do not have as clear a shift in roles as couples who follow a more traditional pattern, but the event of marriage may mark a subtle transition for those couples as well.

One of the early tasks in this phase is to develop mutually satisfying patterns of sexual interaction and patterns of living intimately with another person. Carl Rogers (1972) studied several couples who had been together from 3 to 15 years, in order to understand those relationships that appeared to be satisfying, growth-oriented, and possibly enduring; he also included his own 47-year mar-riage in the analysis—he and Helen were in their seventies at the time. Four themes stood out for him in his analysis of these couples. The first was dedication or commitment to the relationship and to working together on the relationship as it changed and evolved over time. A second theme was communication of persisting feelings and understanding the response of the partner whether the feelings or responses are positive, negative, critical, or self-revealing. The third theme was the dissolution of roles in the sense that one does not perform specific roles, or expect the partner to perform specific roles, simply because they are prescribed by one's parents, culture, or religion; as the relationship grows and becomes more uniquely suited to the couple, new roles evolve that fit the partners more fully than those externally prescribed roles. The fourth theme was becoming a separate self and finding greater acceptance of oneself as a unique person while one's partner also grows to greater self-awareness and acceptance. During the early months of marriage or a committed relationship, many of these themes are likely to involve the resolution of specific conflicts between the couple (such as whether to squeeze or roll the toothpaste tube, as well as more serious conflicts); the development of styles of conflict resolution, decision making, and social interaction; the development of role patterns within the family; and the division of responsibilities. As the relationship grows and matures, the four themes Rogers noted are likely to be important as ideal goals toward which enduring and satisfying relationships strive.

New Parents

This phase begins with pregnancy and the birth of the first child. It involves a major shift in roles from wife and husband to mother and father. In addition to the resocialization involved in that role shift (or addition of a new role to one's set of roles), the couple needs to adjust to the presence of a third family member. Up to this point the couple has probably established a fairly stable relationship. The addition of a third person, who is also a demanding, dependent infant, may bring some upset to the couple's relationship and may involve some jealousy or anger at the disruption. For example, the father may feel that his wife cares more about their child than about him; and in some sense this might be realistic and accurate, and he will have to deal with it. Or the mother may feel "tied down" to the child and the home while her husband is outside in the "exciting" world. If the mother is working, arrangements for the care of the child are likely to complicate family life. Financial pressures may put additional strain on the parents. Couples who did not get married earlier are likely to feel pressure for a formal marriage; and couples that have been married for a period of time may feel an increased commitment and responsibility with the birth of the first child. And the infant does not wait patiently to be fed or cared for—even if the parents are in the midst of sexual intercourse.

Clearly this period is a time of transition for the parents and, for some couples, it may involve considerable readjustment and be seen as a time of crisis. An exploratory study by LeMasters (1957) found that the birth of a first child had been a "severe" or "extensive" crisis for 83 percent of the 48 couples he interviewed. However, these parents were not drawn from a representative sample of new parents: all were middle class, the husbands were college graduates, none was divorced, and the wife did not work after the child was born. The couple was interviewed together, and the degree of crisis was determined jointly by the parents and the interviewer. Although all of the parents had their first child within five years of the interview, many were looking back on this time from the perspective of having resolved whatever degree of crisis may have occurred. He found that those couples who experienced a major crisis had "romanticized" parenthood and had little preparation for their new role as parents—little anticipatory socialization. Their expectations about parenthood were disconfirmed when the child turned out to be demanding and to upset their routine. In addition, all eight mothers with professional training and with extensive work experience suffered "extensive" or "severe" crises with the birth of their first child. Since they had all given up their work, this probably intensified the role shift and brought about an even greater change in self-concept that added to the severity of the transition.

However, other studies of new parents have found much lower levels of crisis. For example, Hobbs and his colleagues found that over 75 percent reported no crisis or only a slight crisis in two studies of white parents randomly selected from public birth records a decade apart and one study of black parents randomly selected from family planning and prenatal clinics (Hobbs, 1965; Hobbs & Cole, 1976; Hobbs & Wimbish, 1977). These studies differed from the LeMasters study not only because their samples were much more representative of all new parents, but also because the respondents reported their degree of crisis by checking the extent to which each of 23 items on a standard questionnaire was felt to have been bothersome. Typical items included "Worry about wife's loss of figure," "Physical tiredness or fatigue," and "Decreased contact with friends." By adding the scores on all of the items, each rated from 0 to 2 (where 2 was "Bothered Very Much"; 1 was "Bothered Somewhat"; and 0 was "Bothered Not At All"), it was possible to calculate the average difficulty score for men and women and to determine the proportion in each of the three samples reporting various degrees of crisis (Table 5.3). Using this scheme, practically no respondents reported an "extensive" or "severe" crisis (scores greater than 23). In all three studies, women reported significantly more crisis than men did, and black parents reported somewhat more crisis than white parents. No set of variables was found that predicted the extent of difficulty for all three samples, and it was concluded that those factors that cause some couples to have greater difficulty than others during this period are not yet known. Nonetheless, the data suggest that romanticizing parenthood may be at least partly responsible, since in all three groups the most bothersome aspect was "Interruption of routine habits of sleeping, going places, etc." On the basis of these studies Hobbs and Cole (1976) conclude, "It is more accurate to think of beginning parenthood as a transition, accompanied by some difficulty, than a crisis of severe proportions" (p. 730).

These conflicting studies raise a number of questions that we cannot yet answer. Perhaps the respondents in the studies by Hobbs tended to hide, even

Table 5.3 Mean Scores on a Measure of Difficulty Adjusting to Parenthood and Percentage Distribution of Couples by Difficulty Category for Two Studies of White Couples and One Study of Black Couples after the Birth of Their First Child

	Hobbs (1965)	Hobbs & Cole (1976)	Hobbs & Wimbish (1977)
	White Couples (N = 53)	White Couples (N = 65)	Black Couples (N = 38)
Mean difficulty score			
Men	6.3	5.9	8.1
Women	9.1	9.7	11.6
Difficulty category[a]			
None	0.0	6.9%	0.0
Slight	86.8%	68.4%	78.9%
Moderate	13.2%	22.3%	21.0%
Extensive	0.0	2.3%	0.0
Severe	0.0	0.0	0.0

Source: Hobbs and Wimbish (1977), Tables 1 and 4. Copyright©1977 by the National Council on Family Relations. Adapted and reprinted with permission.
[a]Category of difficulty was based on the average score for the couple. The range of scores for each category were: None = 0; Slight = 1-11.5; Moderate = 12-22.5; Extensive = 23-33.5; Severe = 34-46.

from themselves, the extent of the crisis they were experiencing because parenthood is expected to be a uniquely rewarding achievement. In contrast, the respondents in the LeMasters study may have been more willing to describe, and perhaps exaggerate, their extent of crisis, since many of them were looking back on a period of transition that they had successfully completed. It might be that interviewing couples together produced more reports of crisis than the questionnaire technique used by Hobbs. Also, the unrepresentative sample used by LeMasters may have accounted for most of the difference between these studies. In any case, it seems that prospective parents might benefit from greater education about the potential difficulties and realistic changes they may expect with the birth of their first child; new parents also should not be surprised if they experience some degree of crisis during this transitional period.

Child-Rearing Family

Some of the central tasks of this family phase include maintaining an intimate relationship with one's spouse, providing space and financial resources for the expanding family, and raising the children. The task of child-rearing may receive quite a lot of attention because it involves nurturing, socialization, and providing opportunities for the child's maximum emotional and psychological growth. According to psychoanalytic theory, the child is developing rapidly and progressing through a series of psychosexual stages. Benedek (1952) suggests that the child's development may also cause the parents to re-work their resolution of these psychosexual stages at the same time. In addition, the parents need to develop effective and comfortable styles of parenting that allow them to interact with their children as fully human beings and to allow for themselves to change at the same time their children are growing and changing. For example, the process of socialization—by which the parents teach their children the norms, values, and expectations of society—is a mutual process that also allows the parents to be socialized by their children. This mutual socialization process is especially clear when the children become adolescents. But through this complex process of learning how to be a parent for this particular child, and fitting that *me* as a parent together with one's other *mes* into a coherent sense of self, both the children and the parents ideally grow in their own ways. Sometimes parents become anxious about how to raise their children "correctly." Of course, this a realistic concern and there probably are some ways that are "better" in some sense than others. But, in general, children are rather hardy creatures and manage to grow and develop surprisingly well, even in relatively difficult circumstances. After all, if children had to have perfect parents, few of us would be functioning today! Perhaps the best guide is for parents to develop a style of parenting that is comfortable for them and comfortable and realistic for the child; yet the more one knows about children, the more comfortable and realistic one can be.

The child-rearing period of the family cycle includes the overlapping phases of the family with preschool children, the family with school-age children, and the family with adolescents; it begins with the birth of the first child and ends when the children begin leaving home. Obviously, entire books have been witten on child-rearing and parenting (cf. Group for the Advancement of Psychiatry, 1973), so we can focus only on a few of the important issues involved in this period. Three topics that seem especially relevant are the growing awareness of the father's role in child development, stepparenting, and single parents. The important topic of maternal employment will be discussed in Chapter 6.

Fathers and Children. Child-rearing and housekeeping have traditionally been seen as the mother's responsibility, while the father was the breadwinner for the family. He was seen as a stern but kind figure, somewhat distant from the children, both respected and somewhat feared; his primary contribution to the family was through his efforts outside the home (Fein, 1978). Except for unusual cases, studies of child development focused on the mother–child relationship and typically ignored the effect of the father; only when the father was absent from the family did he receive research attention, and then only in the backhanded way of noting the effects of his absence. Within the last decade, however, the effects of the father's presence in the family have begun to receive attention. At the same time, there has been an emergence of interest among fathers in taking a more integrated part in raising their children alongside the mother, often as a way of sharing household responsibilities when the mother is employed outside the home, and as a way of achieving their own fulfillment as fathers. Fein (1978) suggests that this new perspective on fathering assumes that men are capable of performing the full range of responsibilities, that paternal involvement is beneficial to the child, and that fathering may provide an important source of well-being for adult men. The only functions men cannot perform are gestation and lactation. Also, a growing number of fathers are raising children on their own as a result of divorce, widowhood, or even as unwed fathers.

Studies of the father's role in intact families and of the effects of the father's absence on the development of both sons and daughters have suggested that the father is much more important within the family system than has often been thought. For example, Hetherington (1972) found that father absence has a clear effect on the daughter's comfort and style of relating with men. Lynn (1976) reviewed the studies of the father's role in children's sex-role development and concluded that fathers are more concerned than mothers with the sex-role behavior of their children, especially their sons, but that they appear to be more influential in enhancing their daughter's femininity than they are in influencing their son's masculinity. And Lynn (1974) noted that the limited research on father–child relationships indicated that fathers affect their son's scholastic achievement, occupational choice, delinquency, competence, and dependency. In general, it seems that children are affected by both parents, that the pattern of relationships differs between child–mother and child–father, and that fathers, as well as mothers, are capable of having a significant and unique effect on the psychosocial development of their children from infancy on (Lamb & Lamb, 1976). This is consistent with the concept of the family as a system of interacting personalities in which each person has an impact on the others and the total impact reflects the interaction of all family members with each other. Thus, it is likely that the fathering role also affects adult men.

> We believe that if the self-esteem of fathers was reinforced by the assurance that they, like their wives, had important roles to play in the socialization of their children from infancy onwards, this would significantly reduce the incidence of marital conflict engendered by a baby's birth. In addition to this, one might predict that an enthusiastic commitment to fatherhood would both expand the amount and improve the quality of father–infant interaction[Lamb & Lamb, 1976, p. 383].

Stepparents: Reconstituted Families.   Although most children grow up with their mother and father, in 1977, an estimated 8 percent of all children under 18, about 5 million children, were living with a stepparent (Glick, 1979). These reconstituted families may also include siblings, stepsiblings, stepgrandparents, and many of the participants may retain emotional ties to their previous family as well. Thus, these families are often very complex and can involve a variety of conflicting loyalties and relationships. For example, "turf" problems are common since there is some ambiguity about whose family or whose house it really is; for this reason, it may be useful for the newly reconstituted family to move into a different home so they can begin on neutral turf (Chavez, 1979).

These problems are intensified if the parents have hostile feelings about their previous spouse (the child's other parent), or if the parent died and has become so idealized that the stepparent can never compare favorably; also children may feel guilty if they like the stepparent better than their parent by birth (Group for the Advancement of Psychiatry, 1973). If the children are older and dealing with their own sexuality, their parent's remarriage may make them aware that their parents also have sexual needs; also sexual feelings sometimes develop between children and stepparents, especially if the stepparent is much younger than the child's parent (ibid.). Rice (1978) pointed out that younger children are often easier to cope with than teenagers for the stepparent, that there are many different kinds of reactions to stepparents, and that there are many different styles of stepparenting. At the same time, he noted that the remarried couple may find that the demands of parenting leave little time and emotional energy for the important task of building their own relationship.

Several studies have found that children raised by stepparents are as well-adjusted as children raised by their parents of birth. For example, Bohannan and Erickson (1978) compared 106 stepchildren (who had not been legally adopted by their stepfather) with 84 children raised by their natural parents. They found that the stepchildren were as happy, social, academically successful as the other children, and that they got along as well with their stepfather as the other children did with their natural father. However, the stepfathers saw themselves as less effective and felt their children were less happy than was the case for the natural fathers. Since these views were not shared by the mother or the children, the stepfather's less positive evaluation of his role in the family may reflect the added difficulties of being a stepparent and the stepfather's lack of confidence in his role.

Another study using a more representative sample drawn from two national surveys also found no substantial difference between children who were raised in stepparent families and those who were raised by their natural parents (Wilson, Zurcher, McAdams, & Curtis, 1975). They concluded that a reconstituted family appears to be, at least, not inevitably detrimental and that the stereotype of the "evil stepparent" is not evident in their data. It is probable that these reconstituted families, like intact families, are sometimes positive, sometimes negative, and sometimes mixed, depending on a number of other factors. However, much more research needs to be done to examine the effects of factors such as contact with the natural parent, presence of stepsiblings, and whether the original family was broken by death or by divorce (Rallings, 1976).

Single Parents.   In 1978, about 13 percent of white children under 18 (6.6 million) were living with their mother as the only parent and another 1½ percent (0.8 million) were living with their father only; 42 percent of black children (4 million) were living with their mother as the only parent and 2 percent (0.2 million) were living with their father as their single parent. It has been estimated that about one-half of all children will experience a single-parent family for a significant portion of their childhood; however, this may be only a transitional period between the parent's divorce and remarriage. Of the 8 million single parent households headed by women in 1978, 34 percent were divorced, 29 percent were widowed, and 15 percent had never married; these households have increased by 44 percent from 5.6 million in 1970 (U.S. Bureau of the Census, 1979).

Among the issues faced by the single parent are loneliness, a sense of being trapped by the demands of parenting and finding an income, lack of time for oneself and one's personal or sexual life, fatigue from the heavy responsibilities of supporting and raising children essentially alone. While extended family support is often very significant, the sense of responsibility for the child's success or failure often cannot be shared. Also, anger and resentment about the broken marriage, or a sense of failure and low self-esteem, because it ended in divorce or separation, may contribute to the difficulty of being a single parent. If the spouse died, there is the added burden of grief and mourning, as well as a tendency to idealize the spouse and to feel especially alone and inadequate. The child may attempt fo find answers to why the missing parent is no longer there, and these may bring up unresolved feelings for the single parent; the child may also create an elaborate fantasy about the absent parent, especially if it is a subject that cannot be discussed. There is also some degree of social stigma about being a single parent that may involve a kind of "second-class-citizenship" in settings where two parents are the norm or where single persons without children are more easily accepted. Organizations such as Parents Without Partners can provide an important support group for some single parents (Group for the Advancement of Psychiatry, 1973). Also, some divorced couples are now experimenting with a co-parenting arrangement where the children are shared more equally between their two parents when this is feasible.

For single mothers, the greatest difficulty is often obtaining adequate income either through employment, child-support payments, or public assistance. Working is often difficult unless child-care facilities are available and, often, they cost more than the mother can afford. Income problems are especially difficult for working mothers since women typically earn less than men (see Chapter 6). Child-support payments involve remaining in contact with the previous spouse and may be a source of continuing resentments. Public assistance requires the family to survive on only basic necessities and is a dehumanizing, bureaucratic experience under the best of conditions. For single fathers, care for the children is usually a major problem. Mendes (1976), in an exploratory study of 32 single fathers, found that most preferred child-care centers and other out-of-home facilities, although most had tried having a caretaker come into the home. Most of the men knew how to cook before they became widowed, divorced, or separated, and nearly all of them managed the household without any feeling of lack of masculinity; the regularity of cooking, cleaning, and shopping did bother them, however. The fathers with daughters were concerned about the lack of female role models for their daughters, especially in regard to sexual issues such as menstruation. Another study noted the importance of dating for single fathers. While their social-sexual life was a concern for them, they were not in a hurry to marry again, but the majority felt that "living together" was not an acceptable life-style for them because of their children (Orthner, Brown, & Ferguson, 1976). Similarly, Rosenthal and Keshet (1978) in a study of 127 divorced fathers found that only 16 were living with a woman and, while most would allow a woman to sleep over, most were uncomfortable about being open with their children about their sexual life. It would seem that women face similar concerns about sexuality and dating.

Postparental Family

As the children reach midadolescence, they begin departing from the family into other living arrangements or their own nuclear families. This phase of the family cycle has been described as the *launching center*, but it is seldom as clear-cut as the term implies since ties between the parents and children often remain very close, with frequent visits, financial support, and other forms of assistance from the parents to the children. However, this period—often extending over a period of several years—involves the gradual progression of the child from a position of dependency on the parents to one of more equal status as an independent, self-supporting adult. Although the effect on the parents of launching their children would seem to involve some degree of upset and conflict, especially for the mother, it seems to depend on cultural and ethnic factors related to the meaning of motherhood. For example, Bart (1971) conducted an extensive study of depression in middle-aged women and found that, in general, it was related to a lack of important roles and a recent loss of maternal roles. However, in cultures where women's status increased with age, depression in middle age was rare compared with societies such as ours where, in the traditional view, women's status declines with age. Those women in her study who were most likely to be hospitalized for depression during the middle years were those who were "overprotective or overinvolved" with their children; also housewives were more likely than working mothers to suffer depression when their children left home. Ethnic differences were also important.

When ethnic groups are compared, Jews have the highest rate of depression, Anglos an intermediate rate, and blacks the lowest rate. Since in the traditional Jewish family the most important tie is between the mother and the child and the mother identifies very closely with her children, the higher rate of depression among Jewish women in middle age when their children leave is not surprising. . . . Black women had a lower rate of depression than white women. The pattern of black female role behavior rarely results in depression in middle age. Often, the "granny" or "aunty" lives with the family and cares for the children while the children's mother works; thus, the older woman suffers no maternal role loss. Second, since black women traditionally work, they are less likely to develop the extreme identification, the vicarious living through their children, that is characteristic of Jewish mothers [Bart, 1971, pp. 110-112].

Thus, for some women, the launching of their children may involve a considerable role shift that occasionally may bring on an emotional crisis. For other women, it may bring a sense of freedom from the career of child-rearing and, possibly, the opportunity for a "second career" of their own choosing. Deutscher (1964) interviewed 49 men and women between 40 and 65 whose children were no longer living at home. Nearly half felt this postparental period was better than any earlier period of the family cycle, and wives were almost twice as likely as husbands to feel this way. A typical response from a mother was:

> There's not as much physical labor. There's not as much cooking and there's not as much mending, and, well, I remarked not long ago that for the first time since I can remember my evenings are free. And we had to be very economical to get the three children through college. We're over the hurdle now; we've completed it. Last fall was the first time in 27 years that I haven't gotten a child ready to go to school. That was very relaxing [Deutscher, 1964, p. 265].

Because the last child leaves home earlier today than 80 years ago, and because more people are living into old age nowadays, the postparental period of the family cycle is growing longer. Today it begins at about the time the woman experiences menopause. This period typically involves becoming grandparents, and the kin family network continues to be an important resource for older persons. In addition, both men and women remain capable of satisfying sexual relations.

Menopause.   The physiological aspects of menopause were discussed in Chapter 4. This section will examine the effect of menopause on middle-aged women. In general, the frequency of menopausal symptoms appears to be much lower than may be thought. Goodman, Stewart, and Gilbert (1977) examined the medical records of 332 Caucasian and 346 Japanese women who came to a clinic for health screening and were found to be representative of their ethnic groups in terms of biomedical profiles and health problems. Comparing women who had not menstruated within the past 12 months with those who had menstruated within 2 months, they found that 28 percent of the Caucasian women and 24 percent of the Japanese women who were menopausal reported traditional symptoms of menopause such as hot flashes, irritability, insomnia, sweats, nervousness, depression, and crying spells. Thus, three out of four menopausal women reported none of the symptoms usually associated with menopause. In addition, 16 percent of the Caucasian women and 10 percent of the Japanese women who were not menopausal reported these symptoms. This suggests that the extreme physical symptoms of menopause often reported in popular books are biased by the fact that women who are experiencing severe problems would be the ones most likely to come to a physician's attention, while the majority of women may not report any problems at all.

Another study found that about one-half of the middle-class women who were interviewed felt that menopause was a disagreeable event; and one-half disagreed (Neugarten, Wood, Kraines, & Loomis, 1963). However, those women over age 45 were more likely than younger women to see positive changes after menopause had passed. They were also more likely than younger women to feel that menopause creates no major change in life, that women have a relative degree of control over the symptoms, and that they need not inevitably experience a crisis. The women between 45 and 55 also indicated that, of all the changes and fears of middle age, menopause does not rank very high (Table 5.4)—the greatest concern was widowhood. The most common complaints about being middle-aged were "getting older," "lack of energy," and "poor health or illness"; only a few women related these changes to menopause. Three-fourths of the women reported the "best thing" about menopause was either not worrying about pregnancy or not having to bother with menstruation; the worst things were not knowing what to expect, the pain and discomfort, and the indication of getting older. Most felt menopause has no effect on sexual relations or on physical and mental health; however, one-half felt that it has a negative effect on a woman's appearance. Individual differences in coping ability were also evident, since some respondents indicated great discomfort but discounted the importance of menopause, while others did the opposite. In general, the respondents were eager to discuss menopause since there are apparently few social supports for menopausal women (as compared with the many such supports for pregnant women); and they frequently indicated an interest in more information about this seemingly taboo topic. These respondents also indicated that there is a social expectation for a crisis at menopause, since they generally felt that "other women" see it more negatively than they see it themselves (Neugarten, 1967a).

Currently there is considerable debate about the prescription of estrogen replacement to relieve menopausal symptoms. There is evidence that estrogen may promote the development of cancer, but there are also arguments that there may be no causal connection between estrogen and cancer (Greenblatt & Stoddard, 1978). At present, it seems wise to be cautious and to discuss this issue candidly with the physician who is being consulted.

Grandparenthood.   Two of the major changes during this postparental period involve the oldest and the youngest generations in the extended family. On one hand, sometime during these middle years the couple is likely to be faced with providing some form of care for one or more of their aging parents. And eventually they will have to deal with the grief and mourning upon the death of their parents. Certainly the death of one's parents and of one's siblings would

Table 5.4   Attitudes toward Menopause among White Mothers 45-55   *(N = 100)*

	Percent
The worst thing about middle age	
Losing your husband	52
Getting older	18
Cancer	16
Children leaving home	9
Menopause	4
Change in sexual feelings and behavior	1
What I dislike most about being middle-aged	
Getting older	35
Lack of energy	21
Poor health or illness	15
Feeling useless	2
None of these	27
The best thing about the menopause	
Not having to worry about getting pregnant	30
Not having to bother with menstruation	44
Better relationship with husband	11
Greater enjoyment of sex life	3
None of these	12
The worst thing about the menopause	
Not knowing what to expect	26
The discomfort and pain	19
Sign of getting older	17
Loss of enjoyment in sexual relations	4
Not being able to have more children	4
None of these	30
How menopause affects a woman's appearance	
Negative changes	50
No effect	43
Positive changes	1
No response	6
How menopause affects a woman's physical and emotional health	
Negative changes	32
No effect	58
Positive change or improvement	10
How menopause affects a woman's sexual relations	
Sexual relations become more important	18
No effect	65
Sexual relations become less important	17

Source: Neugarten (1967a), p. 44. Reprinted with permission from *Psychology Today*, copyright © 1967 by Ziff-Davis Publishing Company.

seem to be events of importance during middle and late adulthood; however, we do not know of any studies on it. Perhaps this topic may be too threatening for middle-aged social scientists to investigate. On the other hand, at the opposite end of the generational continuum, the parents probably will become grandparents. Thus, the progression and continuity of the family cycle may seem especially clear from the perspective of these middle-aged "children-parents-grandparents."

Neugarten and Weinstein (1964) explored the satisfactions and the styles of grandparenthood among middle-class respondents in their fifties and sixties. They found that the majority of grandparents felt comfort, satisfaction, and plea-sure in the role; but about one-third felt some discomfort or disappointment in the role of grandparent (Table 5.5). The meaning of the role varied considerably among the respondents. Some felt it provided a sense of biological renewal ("It's through my grandchildren that I feel young again") or biological continuity ("It's carrying on the family line"). Others felt it provided a source of emotional self-fulfillment ("I can do for my grandchildren things I could never do for my own kids. I was too busy with my business to enjoy my kids, but my grandchildren are different. Now I have the time to be with them"). Others felt they served as a re-source person to their grandchildren, and still others felt they were able to achieve something through their grandchildren that they (and their children)

Table 5.5   Ease of Role Performance, Significance of Role, and Style of Grandparenting

	Grandmothers (N = 70) N	Grandfathers (N = 70) N
A. Ease of role performance:		
(1) Comfortable-pleasant	41	43
(2) Difficulty-discomfort	25	20
(Insufficient data)	4	7
Total	70	70
B. Significance of the grandparent role:		
(1) Biological renewal and/or continuity	29	16
(2) Emotional self-fulfillment	13	19
(3) Resource person to child	3	8
(4) Vicarious achievement through child	3	3
(5) Remote: little effect on the self	19	20
(Insufficient data)	3	4
Total	70	70
C. Style of grandparenting:		
(1) The formal	22	23
(2) The fun-seeking	20	17
(3) The parent surrogate	10	0
(4) The reservoir of family wisdom	1	4
(5) The distant figure	13	20
(Insufficient data)	4	6
Total	70	70

Source: Neugarten and Weinstein (1964), Table 1. Copyright©1964 by the National Council on Family Relations. Reprinted with permission.

were not able to achieve. A substantial number felt remote from their grandchildren ("It's great to be a grandmother, of course—but I don't have much time"). They also identified five different styles of grandparenting. Three are fairly traditional grandparent roles: the "formal," who leave parenting to the parent but like to offer special favors to the grandchild; the "surrogate parent," usually the grandmother, who assumes parental responsibility for the child at the invitation of the parent; and the "reservoir of family wisdom," who maintains his authority and sees himself as the dispenser of special wisdom or skills (it was usually the grandfather, but this type was not very frequent). The two other styles of grandparenting seem to be emerging in our society as new roles for grandparents: the "fun seeker," who joins the child in activities to have fun and to enjoy leisure and tends to ignore authority issues; and the "distant figure," who is present only on special occasions and has only fleeting contact with the grandchild. Neugarten and Weinstein found that these two new roles were significantly more common among younger grandparents (under 65), while the most traditional role ("formal") was more frequent among older grandparents.

Ethnic background may also influence styles of grandparenting. Wood and Robertson (1976) studied a representative sample of 257 grandparents in a working-class area of Madison, Wisconsin; they were predominantly of Germanic and Scandinavian backgrounds. For this sample, a good grandparent was nearly always described as "someone who loves and enjoys their grandchildren and helps them out when they can" (p. 301). Although the grandparents felt their role was significant, there was very little they actually did as grandparents —some baby-sitting, trips to the zoo, movies, giving gifts, and remembering birthdays—and these happened only a few times a year. "Less than half the grandparents reported that they had told their grandchildren about family and customs, or had taught them a special skill such as sewing, cooking, fishing, or a craft" (pp. 301-302). Interestingly, there was no significant relationship between the grandparents' life satisfaction and their grandparenting activities; their life satisfaction depended on friendships and activities in organizations. They seemed content to boast about their grandchildren when they achieved success and to ignore them when they did not; they expected nothing tangible from them and were satisfied if their grandchildren showed some interest and concern. Although we might conclude from this study that the grandparent role is not very significant, instead, it is likely that these grandparents were displaying the influence of ethnic differences discussed earlier in this chapter. We may recall that Scandinavian Americans have the lowest frequency of kin visiting and the highest rate of membership in organizations (Woehrer, 1978); thus, the importance of organizational activities and friendships for these grandparents is not surprising.

Mutual sharing and exhange of help and resources takes place within a family context with culturally defined expectations. Whereas a German or Scandinavian American may perceive carefully defined boundaries around the nuclear families of her children, those boundaries may be much more vague for a black grandmother. Thus, while the German grandmother may not view it as in her place to give advice or rear her grandchildren, the black grandmother may very well perceive it as her responsibility to rear a grandchild, or a niece or nephew, or to give advice and assistance in rearing the children of her kin. The ways in which people of different ethnic backgrounds perceive family boundaries, responsibilities, and expectations varies greatly and affects the patterns of help and social and emotional support across generations and between kin [Woehrer, 1978, p. 333].

Clearly, more studies need to be done on the significance and characteristics of the grandparent role among various ethnic groups in our society; the interview with Joan, age 67, in the Interlude between Chapters 7 and 8, provides a brief look at one black grandmother who differs very much from the white grandparents described in these two studies. In addition, there has been no research attention given to the meaning or significance of great-grandparenthood in different ethnic groups.

Kinship Ties.   Contrary to the myth that older persons in the United States are isolated and neglected by their family, there are close ties within the kinship network between older people and their children. Using data from three national surveys of noninstitutionalized persons over age 65 in 1957, 1962, and 1975, Shanas (1979) concluded:

> In contemporary American society, old people are not rejected by their families nor are they alienated from their children. Further, where old people have no children, a principle of family substitution seems to operate and brothers, sisters, nephews and nieces often fulfill the roles and assume the obligations of children. The truly isolated old person, despite his or her prominence in the media, is a rarity in the United States [pp. 3-4].

She found that about 80 percent of persons over 65 have living children. Of these, slightly over one-half have a child within 10 minutes of their home; three-quarters live within one-half hour of their children. Although the proportion of older persons living in the same household as their child declined from 36 percent in 1957 to 18 percent in 1975, the proportion of older persons either living with a child or who had a child within 10 minutes remained fairly constant: 59 percent in 1957 and 52 percent in 1975. Apparently both older people and their children typically prefer separate households that provide both generations with independence and privacy; as economic conditions improved from 1957 to 1975, greater numbers of older people were able to live in separate households, but did not lose close contact with their children. In fact, there was frequent contact. About 80 percent saw one of their children during the week before the interview, and over half had a visit the day of the interview or the day before. Only one out of ten older persons with living children had not seen at least one of their children for a month or more. These figures had not changed from 1957 to 1975.

Brothers and sisters are also important kin for older people. One-third of the respondents with living siblings had seen at least one during the week before the interview, and one-half had seen one during the month before the interview. Contact with siblings was especially important for widowed persons and older persons who had never married. In addition, 30 percent of the older persons in 1975 had seen some relative other than a brother, sister, child, or grandchild during the week before the interview; for older persons without children, this relative was often a niece or nephew.

There is also no evidence to support the myth that families refuse to care for their older relatives. Shanas (1979) noted that in both 1962 and 1975 about twice as many older persons were homebound and cared for by relatives as were living in nursing homes and other institutions (10% and 5% in 1975, respectively). Those persons in nursing homes are three times as likely to have never married than those older person who live in the community (ibid.). Older persons in nursing homes tend to be those who have outlived their families and are the sole survivor of the kinship network, those never-married persons who have no younger family members to care for them, or those in such need for care that the family had no other alternative. Brody (1977) reported that:

> Studies of the paths leading to institutional care have shown that placing an elderly relative is the last, rather than the first, resort of families. In general, they have exhausted all other alternatives, endured severe personal, social and economic stress in the process, and made the final decision with the utmost reluctance.

Sexuality and Aging.   The capacity for satisfying sexual relations continues into the decades of (at least) the seventies and eighties for healthy persons. Masters and Johnson (1966) report:

> The most important factor in the maintenance of effective sexuality for the aging male is consistency of active sexual expression. When the male is stimulated to high sexual output during his formative years and a similar tenor of activity is established for the 31–40-year age range, his middle-aged and involutional years usually are marked by constantly recurring physiologic evidence of maintained sexuality. Certainly it is true for the male geriatric sample that those men currently interested in relatively high levels of sexual expression report similar activity levels from their formative years. It does not appear to matter what manner of sexual expression has been employed, as long as high levels of activity were maintained [pp. 262–263].

They report a similar indefinite ability for sexual expression among women.

> In brief, significant sexual capacity and effective sexual performance are not confined to the human female's premenopausal years. Generally, the intensity of physiologic reaction and duration of anatomic response to effective sexual stimulation are reduced . . . with the advancing years. . . . Regardless of involutional changes in the reproductive organs, the aging human female is fully capable of sexual performance at orgasmic response levels, particularly if she is exposed to regularity of effective sexual stimulation [p. 238].

> In short, there is no time limit drawn by the advancing years to female sexuality [p. 247].

During the early years of the postparental period, many women report an increase in sexual interest, perhaps because they no longer have to worry about pregnancy after menopause and because the children are out of the home so the couple can spend much more time alone in privacy. However, their husbands may feel less interest in sexual intimacy at this time due to their preoccupation with vocational goals as they begin to deal with the emerging threat of younger competitors and see retirement on the horizon. They may seek extramarital affairs and may experience impotence (the inability to have an erection) with their date or with their wives; unfortunately, this is often interpreted (incorrectly) as a sign of aging. Masters and Johnson (1970) point out that the incidence of sexual inadequacy increases sharply after age 50 for men. They cite six reasons for this increase: (1) monotony of a repetitious sexual relationship; (2) preoccupation with the career or economic pursuits; (3) mental or physical fatigue; (4) overindulgence in food or drink; (5) physical and mental infirmities of either the individual or his spouse; and (6) fear of performance associated with, or resulting from, any of the other categories. None of these are physical changes related to aging, and impotence caused by any of these factors is often successfully treated by a qualified sex therapist. Although the aging man may note some physiological changes such as slower erections, less quantity and power of the ejaculation, less hard erections, less awareness of an impending ejaculation, the need for more stimulation for an ejaculation, and a longer delay between successive erections, these changes do not alter his ability to have highly satisfying sexual relations; in fact, they may allow him to delay ejaculation and to enhance both his own and his partner's enjoyment (Butler & Lewis, 1976). It is possible that even these changes do not reflect age as much as one of the manifestations of other factors such as arteriosclerosis (hardening of the arteries). In addition, contrary to popular myth, sexual activity is not likely to cause heart attacks.

> The incidence of death during intercourse is estimated at less than one percent of sudden coronary deaths. (In one major study the rate was less

than 0.3 percent!) Of this small percentage, seven out of ten deaths occur in extramarital relations, suggesting that the stressful aspects associated with such affairs, such as hurry, guilt and anxiety, are a factor [Butler & Lewis, 1976, p. 29].

Men who have suffered heart attacks are usually able to resume sexual activities (ibid.); and masturbation can resume as soon as one is able to walk around the room (Comfort, 1976). The greatest risk to a male's sexuality in the later years is abstinence; thus, if one's partner is hospitalized or unavailable for several weeks, masturbation or some other sexual activity is important to retain sexual ability.

Women's sexual capacity is even less affected by age, although maintaining one's accustomed level of sexual activity can be important for maintaining the capability for satisfying sexual relations in women as well as in men. The decline in estrogen and progesterone in women after menopause typically causes some thinning of the lining of the vagina that may make it more easily irritated during intercourse; the bladder and urethra may also be more easily irritated during sex and it may be helpful to urinate before sex. The vaginal secretions become less acid so vaginal infections are more likely; sometimes infections also occur in the bladder and urethra and need medical attention. Vaginal itching and discharge should not be assumed to be caused by age, but suggest the need for a medical examination, including a Pap test to be certain of the cause. The clitoris remains the source of sexual arousal, and women who are healthy and had experienced orgasms earlier in life can continue high levels of sexual satisfaction well into the eighties (Butler & Lewis, 1976).

> Women who have had patterns of regular sexual intercourse once or twice a week over the years seem to experience fewer symptoms of sexual dysfunction than women with patterns of irregular and infrequent intercourse. Even though older women with regular patterns may show physical signs of steroid insufficiency [decline in estrogen and progesterone], their lubricating capacity continues unimpaired, while regular contractions during intercourse and orgasm maintain vaginal muscle tone. Contact with a penis also helps preserve the shape and size of the vaginal space. . . .
>
> Self-stimulation (masturbation) can be effective in preserving lubricating ability and the muscle tone which maintains the size and the shape of the vagina. In addition, it can release tensions, stimulate sexual appetite and contribute to general well-being [ibid., pp. 14-15].

A water-soluble lubricant (such as K-Y) can reduce irritation of the vagina that may result from decreased vaginal secretions; however, lubricants that do not dissolve in water (e.g., Vaseline) may increase the risk of infection. Of course, sexuality need not involve intercourse; touching, caressing, and just being intimately close can be very satisfying, so if health, physical problems, or personal preference rules out intercourse, sexuality need not be ended in all of its forms.

Probably the main factors involved in limiting sexual activity for aging persons are the shorter life expectancy for men than women (combined with women's tendency to marry men who are a few years older), which leaves women without a sexual partner when their husband dies and with little chance of finding another male partner (Newman & Nichols, 1960), the possiblity that the man may lose his ability to have an erection because of sexual abstinence in his later years (e.g., when he or his wife is hospitalized), and social norms that imply that sexuality is only for "dirty" old men and women.

Two studies of sexuality among a randomly selected sample of white men and women between age 45 and 69 who were members of a medical group insurance plan found that sexuality remained important for the vast majority of the respondents (Table 5.6). Only 6 percent of the men said they were no longer interested in sex, and only 12 percent reported they no longer had sexual relations; one-third of the women said they were no longer interested, and 44 percent said they no longer had sexual relations (Pfeiffer, Verwoerdt, & Davis, 1974). Surprisingly, the oldest age group reported greater sexual involvement than the next oldest age group, possibly because they were a somewhat elite group of survivors—perhaps their above-average sexuality reflected a number of factors that led to their survival, such as good health. Nearly all of the respondents admitted a decline in their sexual interest and activity. Women typically attributed the ending of sexual relations to their husbands (because of death, divorce, illness, or inability to perform sexually); men who felt they were responsible for ending sexual relations attributed it to inability to perform sexually, illness, or loss of interest in sex. The second study (Pfeiffer & Davis, 1974) found that

Table 5.6 Frequency of Sexual Intercourse Reported by White Participants in a Medical Group Insurance Plan

		Percent Reporting Intercourse				
Group	Number	Not at all	Once a month	Once a week	2-3 times a week	More than 3 times a week
Men, age						
46-50	43	0	5	62	26	7
51-55	41	5	29	49	17	0
56-60	61	7	38	44	11	0
61-65	54	20	43	30	7	0
66-70	62	24	48	26	2	0
Total	261	12	34	41	12	1
Women, age						
46-50	43	14	26	39	21	0
51-55	41	20	41	32	5	2
56-60	48	42	27	25	4	2
61-65	44	61	29	5	5	0
66-70	55	73	16	11	0	0
Total	231	44	27	22	6	1

Source: Pfeiffer et al. (1974), Table 7-9. Copyright©1974 by Duke University Press. Reprinted with permission.

past enjoyment of sex was the most significant factor in the level of present sexual activity. In addition, the person's assessment of his or her health was important for the men's level of sexual enjoyment and interest, but an objective health rating was the significant health measure related to frequency of intercourse for men; both health ratings were less important in relation to the women's sexuality. Both studies supported the important conclusion that "an aging woman's sexual activity and interest depends heavily upon the availability to her of a societally sanctioned, sexually capable partner" (ibid., p. 261). Also, these studies point out the inaccuracy of the perceptions many young people have about sexuality during adulthood. A study of 646 college students revealed that over half thought their parents had sex only once a month or less; one-quarter of them thought their parents no longer had intercourse, or had it less than once a year (Pocs, Godow, Tolone, & Walsh, 1977). In contrast, the data in Table 5.6 show that most of the men and a plurality of the women in the 46–50 age group said they had intercourse once a week. Perhaps, as Comfort (1974) noted, "Freudian anxieties about parental intercourse" are involved in the myth that older persons are no longer sexual, but the reality is that "Most people can and should expect to have sex long after they no longer wish to ride bicycles" (ibid., p. 442).

Conclusion

We have presented an overview of the family cycle in rather generalized terms. Our intent has been to view the family developmentally, while also calling attention to a variety of issues that affect the family and the overwhelming majority of adults who live in families. We see the social clock at work in the family, timing the "right" time to get married, to have the last child, to enter the work force (for the mother), to launch the children, and to move out of the family home. The process of adult socialization is also clearly involved in the many role shifts that occur during the family cycle. Of course, each individual progresses through the family cycle in slightly different ways, and these individual differences, as well as ethnic differences between families, provide a great deal of diversity within the general family cycle among families in America.

In the final section of this chapter, we will focus on single adults to gain a greater understanding of the diversity of experience in adulthood.

SINGLES: THE UNMARRIED AND THE PREVIOUSLY MARRIED

Although marriage is typical in our society, there are a numerically sizable minority of the population who are not married at any census point. For example, in 1978 about 4.8 million men and 7.7 million women in the United States (over 14) were listed as separated or divorced; this does not include those who were divorced and remarried by the census date. Another 1.9 million men and 10.1 million women were recorded as widowed. And 3.6 million men and 3.2 million women over the age of 30 were single (U.S. Bureau of the Census, 1979, Table 1).

We would expect that there is at least as much diversity among these single and previously married adults as there is among their married counterparts. That is, their life-styles may be found to consist of distinct qualities that differentiate them from married life-styles in more important ways than the simple lack of marriage. Ethnic differences and the reason for remaining single would be expected to affect the nature and meaning of their life-style. For example, a homosexual's life-style may differ from the life-style of a heterosexual more because of a difference in sexual orientation than because of the absence of marriage. Similarly, widowed persons differ from divorced persons, and both differ from single persons, in many ways, despite the fact that they are all unmarried. Thus, we are interested in single adults since we expect that knowing more about their life-styles will increase our understanding of adulthood. One central developmental question in this regard is: What are the milestones that mark the developmental progression through the adult years for single people? We currently lack the data to answer this; but perhaps the milestones primarily involve only the occupation, or perhaps they are based on the person's love affairs, or possibly they reflect the family cycle that singles would be going through if they were married even though it does not fit their own lives very well. Certainly, such events as divorce or widowhood would be plausible milestones in the lives of previously married adults; the death of one's parents would be expected to be important for all single adults; and the beginning and development of long-term homosexual or heterosexual relationships would probably be a source of important milestones for some single adults (who are "single" only in a legal sense). We would also expect that there are important differences between social classes and ethnic groups in both the life-styles and characteristics of unmarried, divorced, separated, and widowed persons; however, almost nothing is known of these differences. In addition, since social norms are less well-defined for unmarried persons, it is unlikely that any particular group of single persons will be as similar as a parallel group of married persons. Nonetheless, let us investigate some of the characteristics of single adults, recognizing that each group is undoubtedly much more varied than our present knowledge allows us to describe.

Divorced and Separated Persons

Termination of a marriage, either by divorce or by separation, results from a variety of causes both personal and social. On one hand, divorce is more common among persons poorly prepared for marriage, among those who married to escape their parents, and among couples who cannot tolerate differences; it is more common among children of divorced or unhappy parents, among childless marriages, and among pregnant brides (Duvall, 1971). It is also much more common among couples who married early. According to the 1970 census, men and women who married before the age of 20 had the highest rate of divorce; they were over two times more likely to divorce than men and women who married between the ages of 25 and 29, and were nearly three times more likely to divorce than men and women who married after age 30 (U.S. Bureau of the Census, 1973, Table 4). Divorce is also more likely during the early years of marriage. Thus, about two-thirds of all women whose first marriage ended in divorce in the United States by 1975 had divorced before age 30 (U.S. Bureau of the Census, 1977). In addition, divorce rates reflect a range of social factors. For example, college graduates, couples with high income, and persons born earlier in this century are least likely to have been divorced (ibid.). In addition, the percentage of persons who are separated or divorced (and not remarried) is higher for black than for white persons, and higher for women than for men (Figure 5.2). The percentage of Hispanic men who are separated or divorced is slightly below the rates for white men up to age 40; the percentage is then somewhat higher, but not as high as the rates for black men; the percentage of divorced or separated Hispanic women are in between the rates for black and white women at all ages, reaching a peak of 17.9 percent at ages 45-54. These proportions reflect not only differences between these groups in the divorce rate, but also differences in remarriage rates, since white men are the persons most likely to remarry and black women are least likely to do so. In 1978, there were 3.9 million persons who were separated and 8.6 million who were divorced (U.S. Bureau of the Census, 1979). Income data indicate that separation often

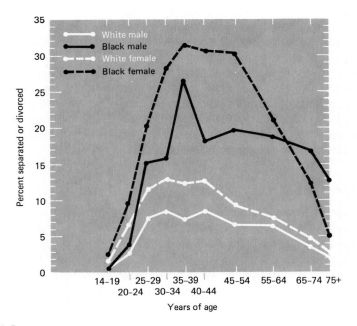

Figure 5.2
Percent of persons separated or divorced, by age, sex, and race in the United States, 1978. (Source: U.S. Bureau of the Census, 1979, Table 1.)

functions as a poor person's divorce, since it is much more common among low-income persons (Carter & Glick, 1970, p. 320).

Census data provide a few clues about the life-style of divorced persons. Since divorced women are more likely to have children living with them, they are more likely to be heads of households and heads of families; moreover, fewer divorced women than divorced men live alone. "Going home to mother" appears more common among young divorced men than young divorced women (Bernard, 1975). Living with a nonrelative—either a roomate or cohabiting—is more common for divorced men than women. In 1978, almost 10 percent of divorced men were living with a nonrelative; this person was more likely to be a woman than a man but, at most, only 9.4 percent of divorced men were living with a nonrelated woman (and these men were between the ages of 30 and 34; the percentage for all divorced men was only 4.4 percent). Overall, about half of divorced women lived with their children, and almost one-third lived alone or with a nonrelative in 1978; about half of all divorced men lived alone or with nonrelatives, and one-third lived in someone else's household, usually a relative's (U.S. Bureau of the Census, 1979).

These clues from census data provide useful basic information, but do not provide an adequate sense of what it means to be a divorced person. For an individual, divorce often involves a period of moderately severe emotional crisis and a process of resocialization that typically leads to rediscovering the art of dating and, in most cases, eventually leads to remarriage.

Change in Status and Resocialization. Just as marriage involves a change in social role and status from "single" to "married," so does the process of divorce—which is often a lengthy one—also involve a marked change in role and status. This change is not only shifting to a single life again, but also involves reformulating the whole range of social ties—to one's ex-spouse, to one's children, to one's relatives, and to one's friends. Unlike marriage, divorce is not an institutionalized status passage in which the new roles are prescribed by social norms. Instead, one has to reformulate all these roles with little outside support and with almost no normative guidelines. Often there is a feeling of failure involved in terminating a marriage, and one's married friends are apt to feel somewhat divided and threatened in their loyalties to the divorced couple. Legal aspects of the process are often difficult and may provide more chance for expressing anger than for smoothly meeting responsibilities and dividing up joint possessions. The long-term family upset that frequently precedes divorce increases the difficulty of reformulating new role relationships and of explaining the new relationships to the children. The process often involves a complex tangle of emotions and adjustments to new situations; feelings of love and hate, of mourning and relief, of failure and a new beginning, all alternate while one attempts to adjust to sleeping alone, eating in restaurants (especially for men), and dividing up treasured joint possessions. Loneliness is frequently a major reaction. If children are involved, they frequently also experience a period of upset and provide an added dimension of complexity to the resocialization process for the parents, as well as one stable focus for the parent who retains custody. In many cases, the children experience more stress during the predivorce phase than during the divorce, or postdivorce phase. Luepnitz (1979) found that half of her sample of 24 undergraduate respondents who had experienced divorce as children reported that the predivorce phase was the worst, while one-quarter felt the postdivorce period was the worst.

Chiriboga (1978) focused on the period of transition during divorce, viewing it as an idiosyncratic transition in contrast to a normative transition that has a clearly defined shift in social roles (see Chapter 3). He studied 310 randomly selected men and women who had filed for divorce in two counties in California; they had separated from their spouse, but the divorce was not final. He found that women were more likely than men to report emotional turmoil, such as feeling angry, uneasy, and "unable to get going." But men were twice as likely as women to report lower overall happiness; and in comparison with national surveys that have found no difference between men and women in reported happiness, these divorcing men were much more likely to report that they were "not too happy" (Chiriboga, Roberts, & Stein, 1978). In addition, the women reported more emotional trauma during the period before the decision to divorce than the men, but the actual fact of the separation seemed to have affected the men more; however, a sizable proportion of the men and women reported that they were "feeling better than they had in a long time" when they were interviewed (Chiriboga & Cutler, 1977).

> The whole process of separation is highly traumatic, generally more so than is the stress associated with the marriage from which our respondents were seeking to escape. Judging from the interview transcripts, the troubles associated with the marriage represented old, familiar problems that had been faced for a considerable period of time. Shifting gears from the state of couplehood to the state of singlehood was exceedingly difficult, and created a demand for much new learning, and relearning, of appropriate behaviors. . . .

> Men, however, appeared to be more vulnerable than women to the stresses of separation, particularly in dealing with the emotional issues at stake: It was in the emotional rather than in the behavioral indices of trauma that men differed most from women. Their emotional vulnerability may stem from the tendency for men in American society to deny or suppress the existence within themselves of emotional problems [ibid., p. 104].

The morale of older men and women was significantly lower than for the younger respondents in the divorce study. Compared with nondivorcing men and women in a related study of normative transitions, divorce seemed to be especially difficult for the men over age 50. For example, they were much less willing to predict what their future would be—fully 77 percent refused to predict, compared with only 11 percent of the nondivorcing men of similar ages. Although older divorcing women reported lower morale than the nondivorcing comparison group, there was evidence that the most distressed group were those divorcing women in their twenties; for example, they were much less happy, showed more emotional tension, and had more contact with doctors than nondivorcing women of similar ages, and this difference was greater than for any of the other age groups (Chiriboga, 1978). Thus, it appears that the "betwixt and between" state of the divorcing person is traumatic, especially for older persons and particularly for men. In comparison with the stresses of normative transitions, the idiosyncratic transition of divorce seems much more traumatic and to be especially pronounced for older men and for younger women.

Remarriage. Most divorced persons eventually remarry, according to the census bureau study of the marital history of men and women in the United States; three out of four women and five out of six men who are divorced eventually remarry—within three years, on the average (U.S. Bureau of the Census, 1976b). Remarriage was much more likely if the woman was under 30 when she divorced (as was the case for two-thirds of all divorced women); three out of four of these women remarried. Age of the woman at the time of her divorce was more important than the number of children in terms of her remarriage; in fact, young divorcees who had large families and remarried did so quickly—81 percent of women divorced before age 30 who had three to five children remarried within two years. At the same time, nearly all women without children who are divorced eventually remarry (U.S. Bureau of the Census, 1977).

It is estimated that between one-half and two-thirds of remarriages will last until one of the partners dies (U.S. Bureau of the Census, 1976b). However, these second marriages appear to be less homogamous (i.e., similar in age, education, and religion) than marriages of persons who have not divorced at all and, in fact, less homogamous than the first marriages of those persons now remarried (Dean & Gurak, 1978). If we assume that similarity between the marital partners is important for marital stability in both first and second marriages, then the choice of the second marital partner as reflected in these data would not appear to predict success in the second marriage. However, since these persons are older than when they first married, and since they may be more similar in personal characteristics than in the more general age-education-religion characteristics, it is unclear whether the second marriage will be more likely to survive or not. Clearly, more research on this question is needed. In any event, second marriages that do not quickly end in divorce appear to be as satisfying as first marriages that do not end in divorce. Based on three national samples from 1973 to 1975, Glenn and Weaver (1977) found no significant difference between the reported marital satisfaction of never-divorced and ever-divorced couples.

Those who do remarry may follow the pattern of persons in their first marriage, especially if they did not have children in the marriage that ended in divorce; others become stepparents or marry a spouse who becomes a stepparent.

However, not all divorced persons choose to remarry or have the opportunity to remarry. Those who do not remarry may be single parents or may visit their children on weekends, or less frequently. And some, whether they have children or not, may move into life-styles that are more similar to unmarried persons, where "unmarried" is used in the legal sense only. For example, some may be homosexual and live in a long-term relationship with another person of the same sex, perhaps raising their children as a lesbian mother or gay father. Others, especially those who are not raising children, may closely resemble either heterosexual or homosexual "unmarried" adults. In the next section, we will focus on some of these life-styles.

Unmarried Persons

Although an overwhelming proportion of all adults eventually marry, there has been an increase in the percent of single persons under the age of 35 since 1960; this change has been most dramatic during the 1970s, especially for those persons between 22 and 24 in 1977 (Table 5.7). Apparently, a growing number of young persons are waiting a few years to marry. This may reflect the greater than threefold increase in women who were enrolled in college and the doubling of the number of men in college during this period (National Center for Educational Statistics, 1978, Table 5). In addition, the sharp rise in employment among women and the women's movement may have contributed to—and also benefited from—the increase in singleness (Glick, 1975). There may also be greater social acceptance of the various alternatives to marriage today than in the past, so that young people may feel more freedom to experiment with, or commit themselves to, a nonmarital life-style.

In 1978, there were 2.4 million single men and 1.6 million single women between the ages of 25 and 29. Of course, the number of single persons declines dramatically with age. In general, persons with little education (less than 5 years) and women with more than four years of college are the groups most likely to be single—at least among that highly married group of persons between 35 and 54 in 1975 (U.S. Bureau of the Census, 1977, Table C). It is likely that those persons with very little education may have a range of problems that make them less likely to marry (such as low income and possibly physical or mental handicaps). The highly educated women might not have been seen as suitable partners in traditional male-dominated marriages, or they may have attained this education (and the income it implies) in order to be self-supporting. However, it is probable that the growing acceptance of egalitarian marriages will reduce the disproportionate number of single highly educated women; some reduction did ccur between 1970 and 1975.

As with divorced persons, census data provide some clues about the life-styles of single men and women in general terms. Overall, the absence of children and the greater freedom to choose living arrangements distinguishes unmarried persons from divorced or separated individuals; those who have children probably resemble either married persons if they have a committed nonmarital relation-

Table 5.7   Percent of U.S. Population Never Married, by Age and Sex, 1977 and 1970

	Male			Female		
Age	1977	1970	Change, 1970 to 1977	1977	1970	Change, 1970 to 1977
Total, 14 and over	30.2	28.1	2.1	23.4	22.1	1.3
Under 35	56.4	54.8	1.6	45.9	44.4	1.5
35 and over	6.1	7.3	− 1.2	5.1	6.1	− 1.0
14 to 17	99.4	99.4	—	97.5	97.3	0.2
18	97.5	95.1	2.4	84.8	82.0	2.8
19	90.2	89.9	0.3	73.8	68.8	5.0
20 to 24	63.7	54.7	9.0	45.3	35.8	9.5
20	82.6	78.3	4.3	63.3	56.9	6.4
21	71.8	66.2	5.6	53.1	43.9	9.2
22	64.5	52.3	12.2	45.6	33.5	12.1
23	54.1	42.1	12.0	34.5	22.4	12.1
24	44.0	33.2	10.8	27.6	17.9	9.7
25 to 29	26.1	19.1	7.0	16.1	10.5	5.6
25	35.9	26.6	9.3	23.1	14.0	9.1
26	29.2	20.9	8.3	20.8	12.2	8.6
27	25.8	16.5	9.3	15.4	9.1	6.3
28	18.4	17.0	1.4	12.4	8.9	3.5
29	19.9	13.8	6.1	9.0	8.0	1.0
30 to 34	12.2	9.4	2.8	7.0	6.2	0.8
35 to 39	7.3	7.2	0.1	5.4	5.4	—
40 to 44	6.9	6.3	0.6	4.7	4.9	− 0.2
45 to 54	5.6	7.5	− 1.9	4.2	4.9	− 0.7
55 to 64	5.8	7.8	− 2.0	4.6	6.8	− 2.2
65 and over	5.9	7.5	− 1.6	6.4	7.7	− 1.3

Source: U.S. Bureau of the Census. Marital Status and Living Arrangements: March 1977. *Current Population Reports,* Series P-20, No. 338. Washington, D.C.: U.S. Government Printing Office, 1968, Table A.

ship, or divorced and separated persons if they do not (Bernard, 1975). The similarities in living arrangements between single men and women is striking. Most live with relatives—probably with parents during the early years, and with parents, siblings, or other relatives in the later years. In 1978, 11 percent lived alone (although this proportion increased with age to over one-half late in life); even fewer lived with nonrelatives and, at most, only 5.4 percent were living with a nonrelative of the opposite sex—for men between age 25 and 29 (U.S. Bureau of the Census, 1979). A surprising proportion of single persons seem to acquire a family one way or another—over 11 percent of men and about 25 percent of women (ibid.). Are these families made up of their children, someone else's children, parents, siblings, nieces, or nephews? In any event, a substantial proportion of single women are supporting a household (Bernard, 1975).

Behind these data are a diversity of life-styles, probably differing by ethnic group, social class, sex, age (cohort), and sexual orientation. Only two of these life-styles have received very much research attention so far—the gay life-style and heterosexual cohabitation. We will take a brief look at each.

Gay Persons.   The diversity of gay male and lesbian life-styles is clearly demonstrated in a recent study of black and white, male and female homosexuals (Bell & Weinberg, 1978). They interviewed 979 gay persons who were as representative of the invisible homosexual population as could be managed and 477 heterosexuals who were similar to the homosexuals in age, education, and religion. The study was conducted in San Francisco in 1969, before the gay liberation movement had gained much public attention, but in a city that was selected in part because its less repressive attitudes toward homosexuals were thought to be a precursor of more liberal attitudes toward homosexuality nationwide. The central finding of the study was that there are many different kinds of homosexualities, so that knowing a person is homosexual tells one nothing more than knowing a person is heterosexual. For example, about 20 percent of the gay men had been married heterosexually, and over half of them had children (this was the case for 71 percent of the black gay men who had been married); over one-third of the white lesbians and almost half of the black lesbians had been married, and over half who had been married had children. Attempting to describe some of the major types of gay life-styles, they used a statistical analysis to identify styles of gay persons; five styles emerged that seemed to fit about three-quarters of the respondents. (1) The "close-coupled" style described the life of those who had partners to whom they were committed emotionally and sexually; while they were not necessarily monogamous (more women were than men), they found more sexual and interpersonal satisfactions from their partner than from others. They had few sexual problems, little regret about being homosexual, tended to spend evenings at home, enjoyed a wide variety of sexual techniques (there was very little evidence of "masculine/feminine" role playing for the respondents in general), and seemed to have little problem communicating with their partner. They differed very little from the heterosexual sample in psychological adjustment and were higher on two of the measures of happiness. (2) The "open-coupled" style described the life of those respondents who frequently sought social and sexual satisfaction outside the relationships; the males in this group were not much different from the typical gay man in the study in adjustment—neither high nor low; however, the lesbians in this style were less self-accepting than the other gay women. (3) The "functionals" were those who were not coupled and were sexually active; they were unlikely to regret being gay, were most interested in sex, most involved with friends, and frequently were highly involved in the gay world; they were not looking for a partner and felt they were sexually attractive. (4) The "dysfunctionals" were those who regretted being homosexual, found little gratification in life, were worried about their sexual adequacy (for men this included impotence and premature ejaculation), and were generally lonely, depressed, tense, and unhappy; while the sample cannot be considered to be representative of all homosexuals, only 12 percent of the men and 5 percent of the women were in this category. (5) The "asexuals" were lowest of all the groups in sexual activity and also were very likely to be isolated from others; they were least likely to report that they were exclusively homosexual and were least likely among the men to be open about their homosexuality. Although these five styles shed much light on the characteristics and diversity among gay persons, they represent only a beginning of an understanding of homosexuality. Bell and Weinberg (1978) conclude their report by noting:

> While the present study has taken a step forward in its delineation of types of homosexuals, it too fails to capture the full diversity that must be understood if society is ever fully to respect, and ever to appreciate, the way in which individual homosexual men and women live their lives [p. 231].

Very little has been known about older gay men and women until recently. Kelly (1977) interviewed 30 gay men over age 65 in Los Angeles; most had many gay friends, had a "moderate" to "high" degree of social contact with other gays, reported that their sexual life was satisfactory (83 percent said they were sexually satisfied), and often preferred relations with men in their own age cohort. Although about six out of ten middle-aged men he also studied were in gay partnerships, this was less common for the older gay men, in some cases because of the death of the lover. Special problems faced by older gays included discriminatory visiting regulations in hospitals where only the family may be allowed in intenseive care units, in nursing homes where the family may prohibit visitation by gay friends, problems in inheritance, property ownership, malpractice suits that can be filed only by surviving spouses, and the general lack of openness about the relationship with family, "in-laws," physicians, hospital or nursing home staff, and funeral directors. As a result, the bereaved partner may have very little support during bereavement and very little chance to openly grieve, except when no one is looking. Thus, Kelly concludes that homosexuality does not cause special problems for older gays; it is the social stigma about homosexuality that causes problems for them.

A small study by the author (Kimmel, 1979) in which 14 gay men over 55 were interviewed supported these conclusions and also pointed out the diversity in the life histories of these gay men. Some had been in relationships for as long as forty years; two had experienced the death of a lover and had since established a new long-term relationship. Others were lifelong loners and continued living alone in old age; however, half of those living alone had been married heterosexually, and two were grandfathers; a third had adopted a heterosexual son many years earlier and was also a grandfather. A preliminary report on a large study of older gay women suggested that older lesbians face many problems similar to gay men, but typically older gay women have several long-term close friends, often including former lovers, with whom birthdays and holidays are celebrated and who are seen as significant supports for whatever may happen as the women grow older (Wolf, 1978).

Masters and Johnson (1979) recently reported on the sexual differences and similarities between heterosexual and homosexual men and women. Not surprisingly, they found no physiological difference in sexual response patterns between the two groups of men, or between the two groups of women. However, they did find striking differences in the degree of verbal and nonverbal communication between the partners during sex, and between the extent to which the partners focused on providing pleasure to the partner, or simply focused on achieving orgasm. Interestingly, it was the homosexual couples who communicated better; they shared information about sexual wishes, level of excitement, preferences, and dislikes freely and openly. In contrast, married heterosexual couples seldom exchanged this kind of information; frequently the man acted as the "sex expert" who seldom indicated any curiosity about what might please or displease his wife, and she rarely told him or asked his preferences. Also, it was the homosexual couples who were more relaxed about sex, while the heterosexual couples focused on achieving orgasm.

The homosexual couples tended to move slowly through excitement and to linger at plateau stages of stimulative response, making each step in tension increment something to be appreciated. Stimulative approaches were usually free-flowing rather than forceful or directive in character, and rarely was there overt evidence of goal orientation. The exchange of pleasure at all levels of sexual excitation appeared to be of greatest importance, with the orgasmic experience merely one more step in the pleasure sequence.

In contrast, the sexual behavior of the married couples was far more performance-oriented. An apparent pressure to "get the job done" was usually evident during partner manipulation and fellatio/cunnilingus and was consistently present during coition [Masters & Johnson, 1979, p. 65].

They concluded that although homosexual couples were more likely to understand their partner's sexual feelings because they were of the same sex, they enhanced this inherent empathy by relaxed, free-flowing sexual communication; thus, heterosexuals, lacking this intragender empathy should strive to communicate their sexual needs and "attempt to educate each other in the intricacies of intergender interpretation" (ibid., p. 218).

Homosexuality was officially removed from the American Psychiatric Association list of mental disorders in 1973 and, in 1975, the governing body of the American Psychological Association urged "all mental health professionals to take the lead in removing the stigma that has long been associated with homosexual orientations" (Conger, 1975, p. 633). However, antihomosexual attitudes and stereotypes continue to force many gay people to keep their sexual orientation secret or to feel ashamed about their affectional feelings. A recent study of lesbian and gay members of the American Psychological Association suggests that the development of a positive gay identity seems to take longer than the development of a positive heterosexual identity (Riddle & Morin,

1977). That is, the average age at which the respondent was aware of homosexual feelings was usually early in adolescence; however, there was a significant gap between this awareness and the average age of the first homosexual relationship (Table 5.8). It was not until their late twenties that these respondents achieved a positive gay identity, and they did not reveal their sexual orientation to significant others until their late twenties or early thirties—much later than heterosexuals reveal their sexual preference to their family and friends. Apparently, the social stigma of homosexuality slowed, but did not prevent, the development of a positive identity and did not prevent these respondents from achieving the professional credentials of a psychologist.

Much more research is needed on the developmental prerequisites for healthy functioning as a gay person, or as a heterosexual person, throughout the life span. We currently know very little about ethnic differences among gay persons. Lesbians, like all women, have tended to be overlooked in most research studies. And much research on homosexuality has seemed to approach the topic with a bias toward heterosexuality as superior to, or more natural than, homosexuality (Morin, 1977). Clearly, just as studies of ethnic diversity or differences between women and men are important to a complete understanding of adult development, so also the study of gay men and lesbians may enhance our understanding of the patterns and variations in adulthood.

Unmarried Heterosexuals. Libby (1978) discussed the range of singlehood—those who have chosen to remain single ("creative singlehood"), those for whom singlehood is a stage before marriage or remarriage, and those for

Table 5.8 Average Age of Events Related to "Coming Out" as a Homosexual among Lesbian and Gay Male Psychologists

Event	Lesbians	Gay Males
Aware of homosexual feelings	13.8	12.8
Had first same-sex sexual experience	19.9	14.9
Understood what "homosexual" was	15.6	17.2
Had first homosexual relationship	22.8	21.9
Considered self "homosexual"	23.2	21.1
Acquired positive "gay" identity	29.7	28.5
Disclosed identity to spouse[a]	26.7	33.3
Disclosed identity to friend(s)	28.2	28.0
Disclosed identity to parent	30.2	28.0
Disclosed identity professionally	32.1	31.2

Source: Riddle and Morin (1977), p. 16. Copyright©1977 by the American Psychological Association. Reprinted with permission.

[a]Forty-one percent of the lesbians and 18 percent of the gay men had been or were currently heterosexually married.

Note: Average ages are based only on those respondents who had experienced the event. The total sample consisted of 63 lesbians and 138 gay males who identified themselves as gay/lesbian/homosexual and as members of the American Psychological Association who responded to an anonymous questionnaire in the APA *Monitor*.

whom it is a stage leading to *cohabitation* (e.g., living with a person of the opposite sex in a sexually intimate relationship) that may lead to a monogamous relationship and/or legal marriage. Although Libby does not assume that one progresses from one stage to the next, some do while others may skip one or more of the life-styles along the way, and others remain in one for a long period. He notes that, "even though creative singlehood cannot be viewed as a life-long choice for most, it appears to offer an attraction for an increasing proportion of people who are dissatisfied with other more traditional choices involving sexual exclusivity and other restrictions often in conflict with the need to be free" (p. 190). However, there has been very little research on singlehood, and most of it has been limited to upper-middle-class persons. For example, Starr and Carns (1972) studied Chicago's singles community, interviewing only college graduates in their early to midtwenties. They report that, unlike some cities and even some suburbs, Chicago has no "singles only" buildings, and even one complex that is called "swingle's city" near the singles bars has only a minority of single residents under 25. They found that there is relatively little socializing with other residents of the apartment building and, contrary to media impressions, their "typical" graduates (who often moved to the city without expectations about the city's social life) frequent singles bars one or two nights a week (or less) and go less often the longer they have lived in the city; by the age of 25 the "typical" female has little use for the single bars—males tend to frequent them for a longer time. Many of the more popular bars are noisy and crowded especially on weekends, and many are arranged to discourage sitting and to allow for nonverbal and (later) verbal contact. One of my students (Kaplan, 1974) studied men in singles bars in New York. He reported that the bartender often functions to introduce patrons and works hard to learn the names of regular patrons for that purpose and to talk with them when they come in to socialize. At least three types of male patrons are common: the neighborhood type who comes in to see friends and to have a drink or two; the out-of-town businessman who wants to meet a potential date; and the weekend single who hopes to meet a date, often with marriage as only a vague possibility. Thus, singles bars function as social centers, with the bartender an important participant, and as places for meeting potential dates or sexual partners; in addition, they may offer a re-creation of college-type environments for casual evenings and for meeting friends and dates. Most singles, however, probably only go to such bars infrequently. Starr and Carns (1972) report that most of their sample of singles do not establish dating relationships in bars, in the apartment building, in organizations, or in "singles only" dances. Instead, most dates arise from contacts at work—usually co-workers are not dated, but they arrange dates in a friend-of-a-friend pattern. In fact, they conclude, the popular image of "swinging singles" is a misnomer, for these singles are persons coping with the same kinds of problems everyone else is and are not living lives of "wild abandon." Of course, not all singles are young, social, and interested in dating. One study of older single persons (between 60 and 94) found that, in fact, they tend to see nothing special about being unmarried—it's "just another way of life" (Gubrium, 1976, p. 190). They valued being independent, tended to be relatively isolated but not lonely, and were generally satisfied with their solitary activities. They felt a continuity to their lives and found nothing particularly different about being old—unlike married persons, they did not have to face widowhood or divorce and tended to take their life-style for granted. Thus, they conveyed a sense of being unique persons—not misfits, but persons who tended to see things differently than the majority of others do.

One aspect of single life-styles that has received considerable research attention is *cohabitation*. Macklin (1978) reviewed these studies, noting that in many states nonmarital cohabitation is considered to be a crime; at the same time, if the partners present themselves as a married couple, they may find their relationship eventually becomes regarded legally as a common-law marriage in some states; also, if they break up, one partner may be able to force the other to pay a financial settlement similar to alimony under some conditions. This confusion about the social and legal definition of these relationships is also reflected in the term used to describe one's partner; most seem to say "the person with whom I am living," according to Macklin. Many studies have found that about one-quarter of undergraduate college students have had a cohabitation experience at some point (ibid.). Although most of the research has focused on these relationships, it is clearly not limited to college students. One nationwide study interviewed a random sample of men between 20 and 30 in 1974–75 who had registered with the Selective Service. Eighteen percent reported that they had lived with a woman for six months or more. Those who were most likely to have cohabited were formerly married men, black men, and those who had dropped out of high school (Clayton & Voss, 1977). The dramatic increase in persons who report they are living as an unmarried couple is shown in census reports for 1970 and 1978 (Table 5.9). The greatest change has been in those unmarried couples without children; 865,000—over twice as many as in 1970—reported living as an unmarried couple. Most of the couples had a "householder" (self-reported head of the household) who was under age 35, but 105,000 of these couples had a householder who was over age 65—34,000 men and 71,000 women. It is impossible to know if some of these unrelated persons were "fictive kin" or not, but it is clear that cohabitation is a life-style that is not limited to young people. These older persons may choose not to remarry late in life for several reasons, including the loss of the deceased spouse's pension, the wish to preserve the rights of one's children to their inheritance, and pressure from children not to remarry. Among the younger couples who have been the focus of the research on cohabitation, it appears that most do not see it as an alternative to marriage, but a relevent step toward marriage (Bower & Christopherson, 1977). The relationships tend to emphasize commitment less than marriages do, especially for men, are not necessarily more egalitarian than marriages (and less egalitarian than gay cohabiting couples; Stevens, 1975), tend to emphasize voluntary restriction of sexual activity to the partner, and seem to be as satisfying as marriages; in general, married and cohabiting couples tend to more similar than

Table 5.9 Unmarried Couples by Sex and Age of Person Reported as Householder and Presence of Children under 14 Years Old, 1978 and 1970

Subject	1978		1970		Ratio, 1978 to 1970
	Number	Percent	Number	Percent	
All unmarried couples	1137	100.0	523	100.0	2.17
Householder:					
Man	741	65.2	266	50.9	2.79
Woman	396	34.8	257	49.1	1.54
No children present	865	76.1	327	62.5	2.65
Householder:					
Man	567	49.9	174	33.3	3.26
Woman	298	26.2	153	29.3	1.95
Age of householder:					
Under 45 years	620	54.5	89	17.0	6.97
Under 25 years	236	20.8	29	5.5	8.14
25 to 34 years	325	28.6	60	11.5	6.40
35 to 44 years	59	5.2			
45 years and over	246	21.6	238	45.5	1.03
45 to 54 years	63	5.5	123	23.5	1.15
55 to 64 years	78	6.9			
65 years and over	105	9.2	115	22.0	−0.09
With children present	272	23.9	196	37.5	1.39
Householder:					
Man	174	15.3	92	17.6	1.89
Woman	98	8.6	104	19.9	−0.06

Source: U.S. Bureau of the Census (1979), Table D.
Note: Numbers in thousands. Noninstitutional population of the United States.

different (Macklin, 1978). The vast majority report that their cohabiting experience was successful, pleasurable, and helped them to mature. Macklin concludes that research now needs to focus on the internal aspects of these relationships.

The ability to initiate and sustain meaningful and mutually satisfying relationships seem central if one is to find happiness in any intimate relationship—traditional or innovative—and it is these inner qualities and skills rather than the outward form on which we must now focus. To know simply that a couple is cohabiting tells us very little about that couple—either about the individuals involved or the relationship itself [ibid., pp. 235-236].

In addition, we need to learn more about ethnic diversity and the nature and development of relationships throughout the life span.

Widowed Persons

Marriages inevitably end in either divorce or widowhood for one spouse or the other (unless both spouses die simultaneously in an accident, for example). Because of the lengthening of the life span, women are likely to be widowed later in life and to spend a greater number of years in widowhood if they do not remarry than a person widowed earlier in this century. For widows under 30 when their husband died, the chances of remarriage are better than for divorced women of the same age; however, older women are not as likely to remarry as divorced women, and the likelihood of remarriage declines with age (U.S. Bureau of the Census, 1977). In general, widowed women who remarry typically do so a year later than divorced women, although there is little difference for women who were under 30 at the time of widowhood or divorce.

In 1978, there were 1.9 million widowed men and 10.1 million widowed women in the United States; most of these persons (1.3 million men and 6.9 million women) were over the age of 65, and there is, not surprisingly, a dramatic increase with age in the percentage of persons widowed. Widowed women outnumber widowed men by more than five to one because of the longer average length of life for women, the tendency of women to marry older men, and the higher remarriage rate of widowed men. Because of higher mortality rates and lower remarriage rates, widowed persons constituted a larger proportion of black adults than white adults.

Over 80 percent of all widowed persons in 1978 were living independently as heads of households. Four out of nine men and two out of three women who were widowed and under age 55 were heads of families, probably with dependent children. Among the larger group of widowed persons over 65, over 60 percent lived alone and 31 percent lived in families; of those living in families, slightly over half lived in someone else's family (perhaps their adult children's home), and the rest had some dependent family member living with them (children? grandchildren? sibling?). A few were living with nonrelatives, including about 1 percent (28,000 men and 97,000 women) who were living with an unrelated person of the opposite sex; for at least some of these women, this person might be an adolescent child they acquired from "fictive kin" and are raising, but we do not know. There were relatively small differences between men and women in any of these living arrangements, although the older women were more likely than older men to be living as a dependent member of a relative's family (U.S. Bureau of the Census, 1979).

We will discuss bereavement in detail in Chapter 10; now we will only point out some of the more important aspects of the widowed life-style. In some respects, particularly for younger widowed persons, many of the characteristics of the "formerly married" life-style discussed in the preceding section are applicable. However, we would expect that the process of resocialization into the role of widowed would be an important transition—perhaps, more structured than for the divorced; but more direct grief and mourning would be involved, and the emotion reactions of failure and love-hate ambivalence would probably be less prominent. Loneliness would be a central experience for most and, for some (especially younger persons), the resocialization process would involve new friends, some dating, and some participation in social activities with other widows.

Lopata (1973) interviewed a random sample of 301 widows in Chicago over age 50 who had not remarried; they had been widowed an average of 11½ years. Most were between 45 and 65 when they were widowed, and many had cared for their husband at home for over a year during his last illness. Thus, many had some opportunity to "rehearse" for widowhood—a process that is frequently reported by middle-aged women (Neugarten, 1967b); but they also had the ordeal of caring for a terminally ill spouse. Four out of five women reported that their grief lasted longer than one year, and 20 percent felt one never gets over it. Lopata found three general patterns of adaptation to widowhood among these women. One pattern was the "self-initiating woman"; although she experienced much disorganization in her life when her husband died, she modified her social relations with friends and children in realistic ways, built a new life-style that was relatively flexible to accommodate future changes, and did not try to hang on to unrealistic aspects of her previous life-style that were impossible to maintain. She continued relationships with her children, developed relationships that provided personal intimacy, created a life-style that suited her needs and potential and, in general, attempted to match the resources available to her own needs and goals. A second pattern was the widow living in an ethnic community that paralleled a traditional village life-style. She did not experience much change, was involved in relationships with relatives, friends, and neighbors, and generally lived out her life as her earlier socialization had taught her. A third group were "social isolates"; these women had generally never been highly involved in social relationships and were unable to maintain their few previous relationships because the friends had died or moved away and were not replaced. Often, poor finances increased their difficulty in maintaining contact with old friends or making new ones. Thus, as in all of the single life-styles, there are differing life patterns among widowed persons.

For many reasons, older widows (most are women) tend to live alone, some in relative isolation. There seems to be little opportunity for older widowed persons to form sexual and social relationships as younger formerly married persons do. Furthermore, remarriage after age 65 is not widely encouraged; in some cases, widowed persons may lose payments from the deceased spouse's pension if they remarry, and some fear losing control over their finances or plans for their inheritance if they remarry. Loneliness, health problems, and maintaining an adequate income are major burdens for many widowed persons, especially for older widows. Inadequate income seems to be a particularly important cause of lowered morale among widows. Morgan (1976) compared over 500 widowed and married women between the ages of 45 and 74; black, Mexican American, and white women were selected in representative samples from Los

Angeles County. She found that poor health had a greater impact on morale among the widowed women than it did among the married women, and greater family interaction had positive effects on morale among all the women. In general, the widowed women were lower in morale than the married women. However, this difference in morale was not found when the level of income was considered. That is, across all three ethnic groups, the lower morale of widows appeared to result from their social situation (lower income) than from bereavement and grief, or from the loss of social roles associated with widowhood. Thus, Morgan suggests that the problems of widows, not widowhood as a problem, should be the focus of future research on widowhood.

Conclusion

We have examined unmarried life-styles during adulthood to sketch at least broad outlines of the diversity among single persons in contemporary American society. Clearly, our society is becoming more aware of a variety of nontraditional patterns of life. Also, this diversity of life-styles appears to be growing as, for example, substantial proportions of young persons are adding cohabitation to the sequence of steps between dating and marriage. While there is some evidence that these emerging life-styles are not limited to young people, there is no evidence that large numbers of older persons are likely to adopt communal living or some other alternate life-style. Cohort-related attitudes about acceptable life-styles, sexual behavior, and the nature of intimacy are likely to restrict an older person's willingness to experiment with these life-styles—even if younger people believe they bring happiness. Indeed, "old-fashioned" intimacy and human contact that is nonsexual and genuine may bring more happiness to an older person than encouragement and instruction in masturbation, or communal living.

In sum, it is apparent that adults currently live out their lives in a wide variety of styles. Although nearly all people seem to try their hand at beginning a family, most people, if given the chance, would join in the continuing debate about whether the family is a valuable institution and whether it is vital, changing, or dying. Certainly, families are very complex social systems that provide some of the most deeply satisfying rewards, frustrations, and challenges during the adult years. Yet they are probably not suited to all individuals, and birth control combined with an apparently greater tolerance and interest in alternative life-styles may lead to a decrease in the proportion of adults who live in nuclear families. The divorce rate might also decrease if there were less social pressure for everyone to marry, regardless of whether they are suited for marriage or not. But, whatever their life-style, most adults have important intimate relationships for longer or shorter periods of time. These relationships are typically significant for understanding and timing the developmental progression through the middle and late years of life. Much more research is needed on the developmental course within each of these diverse life-styles among various ethnic groups and across the entire life span.

We will now turn to a case example of a successful middle-aged executive and father of a teenaged son. This Interlude touches on many of the issues we have discussed about the family and sets the stage for our next chapter's discussion of the occupation in adulthood; it demonstrates the complex ways the family and occupation interact to produce the challenges, satisfactions, and disappointments during the middle years of adult life.

CHAPTER SUMMARY

1. Contrary to popular belief, most American families still consist of a husband and wife in their first marriage and their children if any. Of those who do divorce, five out of six remarry, and over half of these remarriages last as long as the partners live.

2. In the United States, the modified extended family is prevalent; it consists of nuclear family units that maintain close ties with other family units in a kin network. This appears to have been the dominant family pattern in Western society for centuries; multigenerational households were common only during periods of economic adversity or family disruption. In some other cultures, multigenerational extended families are the dominant pattern.

3. Ethnic groups influence family patterns because of their unique cultural heritage. These cultural differences play an important role in how the family network interacts, in the value placed on friends and outside organizations, in family support, and in social integration. For example, the cultural history of black people explains much of their family structure and cohesive kinship network.

4. Just as each individual goes through a life cycle, so families have a cycle with milestones that mark stages in the development of the family.

5. During the *establishment* phase of the family cycle, the partners function as a dyad and develop styles of interaction through the process of mutual socialization; these include patterns of decision making, division of household responsibilities and roles, styles of sexual interaction, and planning for children if they are desired.

6. The birth of a child begins the *new parents* phase of the family cycle. Adjustments have to be made to the presence of a third, dependent, and demanding family member. Although some studies find less emotional upset during this period than others, this transition into parenthood may be a time of crisis as well as joy.

7. Three aspects of the *child-rearing* family are gaining attention today. The role of the father is becoming recognized as more significant to the child and to the father than in the past. Special issues of stepparents are being acknowledged, although children raised by stepparents appear to be as well-adjusted as children raised by their parents by

birth. And there is a growing number of single-parent families, and many children are expected to experience this type of family, often for only a few years between their parent's divorce and remarriage.

8. After the children leave home, the *postparental* phase begins. It typically involves menopause for the wife, grandparenthood, and continued close relationships with one's children and siblings. Older men and women continue to engage in sexual relations, and there is no significant loss of capacity for satisfying sexual relations into the decade of the seventies or eighties for healthy persons.

9. Divorced persons experience a major transition that has few social expectations or norms to ease its impact. It involves resocialization, care of children (especially for women), and dating.

10. Growing numbers of young persons are remaining unmarried longer, so there is an increase in single women and men. The life-styles of single adults are as diverse as their reasons for not marrying.

11. Homosexual men and women are leading a variety of life-styles; only recently has attention been given to their diversity, their patterns of aging, and their sexual interaction. The social stigma of homosexuality has caused many problems for gay men and lesbians.

12. Unmarried heterosexuals also differ among themselves. Some remain single into old age and see singleness as just another way of life. Others are exploring cohabitation, sometimes as a prelude to marriage; there has been a dramatic increase in the number of persons who report living with an unrelated person of the opposite sex.

13. Widowed persons are likely to be older women who are living independently with few marriage partners available. Some widows reorganize their lives, others find support in a close-knit ethnic community, and some are socially isolated. Level of income seems more important than bereavement, or the other problems of widowhood, for determining the morale of widows.

REFERENCES

Allen, Walter R. 1978. The Search for Applicable Theories of Black Family Life. *Journal of Marriage and the Family,* 40(1), 117–129.

Back, Kurt W. 1974. The Three-Generation Household in Pre-Industrial Society: Norm or Expedient. Paper presented at the meeting of the Gerontological Society, Portland, October, 1974.

Bart, Pauline. 1971. Depression in Middle-Aged Women. In V. Gornick & B. K. Moran (Eds.), *Women in Sexist Society.* New York: Basic Books.

Bell, Alan P., & Weinberg, Martin S. 1978. *Homosexualities: A Study of Diversity Among Men and Women.* New York: Simon & Schuster.

Benedek, Therese. 1952. *Psychosexual Functions in Women.* New York: Ronald Press.

Bernard, Jessie. 1975. Notes on Changing Life Styles, 1970-1974. *Journal of Marriage and the Family, 37*(3), 582-593.

Bohannan, Paul, & Erickson, Rosemary. 1978. Stepping In. *Psychology Today, 11*(8: January), 53-54, 59.

Bower, Donald W., & Christopherson, Victor A. 1977. University Student Cohabitation: A Regional Comparison of Selected Attitudes and Behavior. *Journal of Marriage and the Family, 39*(3), 447-452.

Brody, Elaine. 1977. *Long-Term Care of Older People.* New York: Human Sciences Press.

Bronfenbrenner, Urie. 1975. The Challenge of Social Change to Public Policy and Developmental Research. Paper presented at the meeting of the Society for Research in Child Development, Denver, April 2, 1975.

Butler, Robert N., & Lewis, Myrna I. 1976. *Sex After Sixty: A Guide for Men and Women for Their Later Years.* New York: Harper & Row.

Carter, Hugh, & Glick, Paul C. 1970. *Marriage and Divorce: A Social and Economic Study.* Cambridge, Mass.: Harvard University Press.

Chavez, Linda. 1979. Second Marriages: No Time for Bliss. *New York Times,* April 6, 1979 (Long Island Supplement), 6.

Chiriboga, David A. 1978. The Divorce Experience in Later Life. Paper presented at the meeting of the American Orthopsychiatric Association, San Francisco, March 31, 1978.

Chiriboga, David A., & Cutler, Loraine. 1977. Stress Responses Among Divorcing Men and Women. *Journal of Divorce, 1*(2), 95-106.

Chiriboga, David A.; Roberts, John; & Stein, Judith A. 1978. Psychological Well-Being During Marital Separation. *Journal of Divorce, 2*(1), 21-36.

Clayton, Richard R., & Voss, Harwin L. 1977. Shacking Up: Cohabitation in the 1970's. *Journal of Marriage and the Family, 39*(2), 273-283.

Comfort, Alex. 1974. Sexuality in Old Age. *Journal of the American Geriatrics Society, 22*(10), 440-442.

Comfort, Alex. 1976. *A Good Age.* New York: Crown.

Conger, John Janeway. 1975. Proceedings of the American Psychological Association, Incorporated, for the Year 1974: Minutes of the Annual Meeting of the Council of Representatives. *American Psychologist, 30*(6), 620-651.

Cromwell, Vicky L., & Cromwell, Ronald E. 1978. Peceived Dominance in Decision-Making and Conflict Resolution Among Anglo, Black and Chicano Couples. *Journal of Marriage and the Family, 40*(4), 749-759.

Dean, Gillian, & Gurak, Douglas T. 1978. Marital Homogamy the Second Time Around. *Journal of Marriage and the Family, 40*(3), 559-574.

Deutscher, Irwin. 1964. The Quality of Post Parental Life. *Journal of Marriage and the Family, 26*(1), 263-268.

Duvall, Evelyn Millis. 1971. *Family Development* (4th ed.). Philadelphia: Lippincott.

Fein, Robert A. 1978. Research on Fathering: Social Policy and an Emergent Perspective. *Journal of Social Issues, 34*(1), 122-135.

Glenn, Norval D., & Weaver, Charles N. 1977. The Marital Happiness of Remarried Divorced Persons. *Journal of Marriage and the Family, 39*(2), 331-337.

Glick, Paul C. 1975. A Demographer Looks at American Families. *Journal of Marriage and the Family, 37*(1), 15-26.

Glick, Paul C. 1977. Updating the Life Cycle of the Family. *Journal of Marriage and the Family, 39*(1), 5-13.

Glick, Paul C. 1979. The Future of the American Family. *Current Population Reports*, Series P-23, No. 78. Washington, D.C.: U.S. Government Printing Office.

Goodman, Madeleine J.; Stewart, Cynthia J.; & Gilbert, Fred, Jr. 1977. A Study of Certain Medical and Physiological Variables Among Caucasian and Japanese Women Living in Hawaii. *Journal of Gerontology, 32*(3), 291-298.

Greeley, Andrew M. 1971. *Why Can't They Be Like Us.* New York: Dutton.

Greenblatt, Robert B., & Stoddard, Leland D. 1978. The Estrogen-Cancer Controversy. *Journal of the American Geriatrics Society, 26*(1), 1-8.

Group for the Advancement of Psychiatry. 1973. *The Joys and Sorrows of Parenthood.* New York: Scribner's.

Gubrium, Jaber F. 1976. Being Single in Old Age. In Jaber F. Gubrium (Ed.), *Time, Roles and Self in Old Age.* New York: Human Sciences Press.

Gutman, Herbert G. 1976. *The Black Family in Slavery and Freedom, 1750-1925.* New York: Pantheon.

Haley, Alex. 1976. *Roots: The Saga of an American Family.* Garden City, N.Y.: Doubleday.

Hayes, William C., & Mindel, Charles H. 1973. Extended Kinship Relations in Black and White Families. *Journal of Marriage and the Family, 35*(1), 51-57.

Hetherington, E. Mavis. 1972. Effects of Father Absence on Personality Development in Adolescent Daughters. *Developmental Psychology, 7*(3), 313-326.

Hobbs, Daniel F., Jr. 1965. Parenthood As Crisis: A Third Study. *Journal of Marriage and the Family, 27*(3), 367-372.

Hobbs, Daniel F. Jr., & Cole, Sue P. 1976. Transition to Parenthood: A Decade Repplication. *Journal of Marriage and the Family, 38*(4), 723-731.

Hobbs, Daniel F. Jr., & Wimbish, Jane Maynard. 1977. Transition to Parenthood by Black Couples. *Journal of Marriage and the Family, 39*(4), 677-689.

Kaplan, Philip. 1974. Single's Bars and Single Men. Unpublished honors thesis, City College of C.U.N.Y.

Kelly, Jim. 1977. The Aging Male Homosexual: Myth and Reality. *The Gerontologist, 17*(4), 328-332.

Kerckhoff, A. C. 1965. Nuclear and Extended Family Relationships: Normative and Behavioral Analysis. In Ethel Shanas & Gordon F. Streib (Eds.), *Social Structure and Family Generational Relations.* Englewood Cliffs, N.J.: Prentice-Hall.

Kimmel, Douglas C. 1979. Gay People Grow Old Too: Life History Interviews of Aging Gay Men. *The International Journal of Aging and Human Development, 10*(3), 239-248.

Lamb, Michael E., & Lamb, Jamie E. 1976. The Nature and Importance of the Father-Infant Relationship. *Family Coordinator, 25*(4), 379-385.

LeMasters, E. E. 1957. Parenthood as Crisis. *Marriage and Family Living, 19*(4), 352-355.

Libby, Roger W. 1978. Creative Singlehood as a Sexual Life Style: Beyond Marriage as a Rite of Passage. In Bernard I. Murstein (Ed.), *Exploring Intimate Life Styles.* New York: Springer.

Litwak, Eugene, 1960. Geographic Mobility and Extended Family Cohesion. *American Sociological Review, 25*(3), 385–394.

Lopata, Helena Znaniecki. 1973. *Widowhood in an American City.* Cambridge, Mass.: Schenkman.

Luepnitz, Deborah A. 1979. Which Aspects of Divorce Affect Children? *Family Co-ordinator, 28*(1), 79–85.

Lynn, David B. 1974. *The Father: His Role in Child Development.* Monterey, Calif.: Brooks/Cole.

Lynn, David B. 1976. Fathers and Sex-Role Development. *Family Coordinator, 25*(4), 403–409.

Mack, Delores. 1978. The Power Relationship in Black Families and White Families. In Robert Staples (Ed.), *The Black Family: Essays and Studies.* Belmont, Calif.: Wadsworth.

Macklin, Eleanor D. 1978. Review of Research on Nonmarital Cohabitation in the United States. In Bernard I. Murstein (Ed.), *Exploring Intimate Life Styles.* New York: Springer.

Masters, William H., & Johnson, Virginia E. 1966. *Human Sexual Response.* Boston: Little, Brown.

Masters, William H., & Johnson, Virginia E. 1970. *Human Sexual Inadequacy.* Boston: Little, Brown.

Masters, William H., & Johnson, Virginia E. 1979. *Homosexuality in Perspective.* Boston: Little, Brown.

McAdoo, Harriette Pipes. 1978. Factors Related to Stability in Upwardly Mobile Black Families. *Journal of Marriage and the Family, 40*(4), 761–776.

Mendes, Helen A. 1976. Single Fathers. *Family Coordinator, 25*(4), 439–444.

Mindel, Charles H., & Habenstein, Robert W. 1976. *Ethnic Families in America: Patterns and Variations.* New York: Elsevier.

Morgan, Leslie A. 1976. A Re-Examination of Widowhood and Morale. *Journal of Gerontology, 31*(6), 687–695.

Morin, Stephen F. 1977. Heterosexual Bias in Psychological Research on Lesbianism and Male Homosexuality. *American Psychologist, 32*(8), 629–637.

Murdock, Steve H., & Schwartz, Donald F. 1978. Family Structure and the Use of Agency Services: An Examination of Patterns Among Elderly Native Americans. *The Gerontologist, 18*(5), 475–481.

National Center for Educational Statistics. 1978. *Projections of Education Statistics to 1986–87.* Washington, D.C.: U.S. Government Printing Office.

Neugarten, Bernice L. 1967a. A New Look at Menopause. *Psychology Today, 1*(7), 42–45, 67–69, 71.

Neugarten, Bernice L. 1967b. The Awareness of Middle Age. In Bernice L. Neugarten (Ed.), *Middle Age and Aging.* Chicago: University of Chicago Press, 1968. (Originally published in : *Middle Age.* Roger Owen, Ed. London: British Broadcasting Corporation.)

Neugarten, Bernice L., & Weinstein, Karol K. 1964. The Changing American Grandparent. *Journal of Marriage and the Family, 26*(2), 199–204.

Neugarten, Bernice L; Wood, Vivian; Kraines, Ruth J.; & Loomis, Bar-

bara. 1963.   Women's Attitudes Toward the Menopause. *Vita Humana, 6*(3), 140-151.

Newman, Gustave, & Nichols, Claude R. 1960.   Sexual Activities and Attitudes in Older Persons. *Journal of the American Medical Association, 173*(1), 33-35.

Nobles, Wade W. 1978.   Toward an Empirical and Theoretical Framework for Defining Black Families. *Journal of Marriage and the Family, 40*(4), 679-688.

Orthner, Dennis K.; Brown, Terry; & Ferguson, Dennis. 1976.   Single-Parent Fatherhood: An Emerging Life Style. *Family Coordinator, 25*(4), 429-437.

Palmore, Erdman. 1975.   The Status and Integration of the Aged in Japanese Society. *Journal of Gerontology, 30*(2), 199-208.

Peters, Marie F. 1978.   Notes From the Guest Editor. *Journal of Marriage and the Family, 40*(4), 655-658.

Pfeiffer, Eric, & Davis, Glenn C. 1974.   Determinants of Sexual Behavior in Middle and Old Age. In Erdman Palmore (Ed.), *Normal Aging II: Reports from the Duke Longitudinal Studies, 1970-1973.* Durham, N.C.: Duke University Press.

Pfeiffer, Eric; Verwoerdt, Adriaan; & Davis, Glenn C. 1974.   Sexual Behavior in Middle Life. In Erdman Palmore (Ed.), *Normal Aging II: Reports from the Duke Longitudinal Studies, 1970-1973.* Durham, N.C.: Duke University Press.

Pocs, Ollie; Godow, Annette; Tolone, William L.; & Walsh, Robert H. 1977.   Is There Sex After 40? *Psychology Today, 11*(1:June), 54-56, 87.

Rallings, E. M. 1976.   The Special Role of Stepfather. *Family Coordinator, 25*(4), 445-449.

Rice, F. Philip. 1978.   *Step-Parenting.* New York: Condor.

Riddle, Dorothy, & Morin, Stephen. 1977.   Removing the Stigma from Individuals. *American Psychological Association Monitor* (November), 16, 28.

Rogers, C. Jean, & Gallion, Teresa E. 1978.   Characteristics of Elderly Pueblo Indians in New Mexico. *The Gerontologist, 18*(5), 482-487.

Rogers, Carl R. 1972.   *Becoming Partners: Marriage and Its Alternatives.* New York: Dell (Delta).

Rosenthal, Kristine M., & Keshet, Harry F. 1978.   The Not-Quite Stepmother. *Psychology Today, 12*(2:July), 82-86, 100-101.

Shanas, Ethel. 1979.   Social Myth as Hypothesis: The Case of the Family Relations of Old People. *The Gerontologist, 19*(1), 3-9.

Shanas, Ethel; Townsend, Peter; Wedderburn, Dorothy; Friis, Hennig; Milhøj, Poul; & Stehouwer, Jan. 1968.   *Older People in Three Industrial Societies.* New York: Atherton Press.

Stack, Carol B. 1972.   Black Kindreds: Parenthood and Personal Kindreds Among Urban Blacks. *Journal of Comparative Studies, 3*, 194-206.

Stack, Carol B. 1974.   *All Our Kin: Strategies for Survival in a Black Community.* New York: Harper & Row.

Staples, Robert. 1976.   The Black American Family. In Charles H. Mindel & Robert W. Habenstein (Eds.), *Ethnic Families in America.* New York: Elsevier.

Staples, Robert. 1978.   Masculinity and Race: The Dual Dilemma of Black Men. *Journal of Social Issues, 34*(1), 169-183.

Starr, Joyce R., & Carns, Donald E. 1972.   Singles in the City. *Society, 9*(4), 43-48.

Stevens, D. J. H. 1975. Cohabitation Without Marriage. Unpublished doctoral dissertation. University of Texas at Austin.

Sussman, Marvin B. 1976. The Family Life of Old People. In Robert H. Binstock & Ethel Shanas (Eds.), *Handbook of Aging and the Social Sciences.* New York: Van Nostrand Reinhold.

Sussman, Marvin B., & Burchinal, Lee. 1962. Kin Family Network: Unheralded Structure in Current Conceptualizations of Family Functioning. *Marriage and Family Living, 24*(3), 231–240.

Townsend, Peter. 1966. The Emergence of the Four-Generation Family in Industrial Society. In Bernice L. Neugarten (Ed.), *Middle Age and Aging.* Chicago: University of Chicago Press, 1968. (Originally published in: *Proceedings of the 7th International Congress of Gerontology, Vienna, 8*, 555–558.)

U.S. Bureau of the Census. 1973. Age at First Marriage. *1970 Census of the Population,* PC(2)-40. Washington, D.C.: U.S. Government Printing Office.

U.S. Bureau of the Census. 1976a. A Statistical Portrait of Women in the U.S. *Current Population Reports,* Series P-23, No. 58. Washington, D.C.: U.S. Government Printing Office.

U.S. Bureau of the Census. 1976b. Number, Timing, and Duration of Marriage and Divorces in the United States: June 1975. *Current Population Reports,* Series P-20, No. 297. Washington, D.C.: U.S. Government Printing Office.

U.S. Bureau of the Census. 1977. Marriage, Divorce, Widowhood and Remarriage by Family Characteristics: June 1975. *Current Population Reports,* Series P-20, No. 312. Washington, D.C.: U.S. Government Printing Office.

U.S. Bureau of the Census. 1978. Marital Status and Living Arrangements: March 1977. *Current Population Reports,* Series P-20, No. 323. Washington, D.C.: U.S. Government Printing Office.

U.S. Bureau of the Census. 1979. Marital Status and Living Arrangements: March 1978. *Current Population Reports,* Series P-20, No. 338. Washington, D.C.: U.S. Government Printing Office.

van de Walle, Etienne. 1976. Household Dynamics in a Belgian Village, 1847–1866. *Family History, 1*(1), 80–94.

Willie, Charles V., & Greenblatt, Susan L. 1978. Four "Classic" Studies of Power Relationships in Black Families: A Review and Look to the Future. *Journal of Marriage and the Family, 40*(4), 691–694.

Wilson, Kenneth L.; Zurcher, Louis A.; McAdams, Diana Claire; & Curtis, Russell L. 1975. Stepfathers and Stepchildren: An Exploratory Analysis from Two National Surveys. *Journal of Marriage and the Family, 37*(3), 526–536.

Woehrer, Carol E. 1978. Cultural Pluralism in American Families: The Influence of Ethnicity on Social Aspects of Aging. *Family Coordinator, 27*(4), 329–339.

Wolf, Deborah Coleman. 1978. Close Friendship Patterns of Older Lesbians. Paper presented at the meeting of the Gerontological Society, Dallas, November, 1978.

Wood, Vivian, & Robertson, Joan F. 1976. The Significance of Grandparenthood. In Jaber F. Gubrium (Ed.), *Time, Roles and Self in Old Age.* New York: Human Sciences Press.

Interlude
Murray, Age 48

> *The serious problems in life . . . are never fully solved. If ever they should appear to be so it is a sure sign that something has been lost. The meaning and purpose of a problem seem to lie not in its solution but in our working at it incessantly [Jung, 1933, p. 11].*[1]

Murray was a 48-year-old successful vice-president in a large organization at the time of this interview. As he quickly points out, he has just published a book, teaches in a university, and lectures around the country. He is a man of many abilities and much energy; yet there is a sense in which he feels insecure and unfulfilled. Although George said it explicitly and Theresa implied it, Murray seems to be the person who is most clearly working at a problem that perhaps will never be fully solved. He has had serious problems with his marriage, problems with his son, and leaves the impression of having escaped into his work where he feels confident and secure, yet also strangely vulnerable.

Several intriguing questions are raised by this case example. How satisfied is he (actually) in his job? Why does the need for security remain so important? What is happening in his relationship with his son? Why did so many turning points occur when he was 28 (a major milestone for him)? How did his work life become so separate from the rest of his life? Are his future goals and plans for retirement realistic, or are they typical for a middle-aged person? Is he leaving his mark (in Erikson's sense of generativity)? Are his feelings about death realistic, or is the thought rather frightening to him; why?

What are some of the milestones in your life? As you look back over it, what are some of the events that stand out? Let me start from the present and go backwards. I wrote a book which came out last week. That probably is one of the most important things that's happened to me in my life. Going back from there, I was given an award this last year for outstanding contributions to literature in my field. That was an important milestone; one coming on top of the other. Over the last five years, I have been the president of _____. That was a milestone. One of the more important things that happened to me was finally getting the recognition in the company and becoming vice-president. That's a milestone for several reasons. I'll never forget that day, when the board passed on that. *Was it celebrated in some way, that event?* Yes, it was celebrated. My wife and I celebrated it. It was celebrated with friends as well; it was important. It really didn't change my role in the company, but it meant something to me. I can't really document what it meant, because it didn't change my salary; it didn't change the respect I receive from my peers; it didn't change my national reputation or my business reputation, but it had some effect on me. I considered it quite a moment. I suppose these are the most important things in my work career.

My social life, my life as a husband and a father, has had many milestones, some good and some bad. I'm going through a very important trying time now. My son left college after two years, settled in Europe for a while, and is trying to get himself out of Casablanca today. My son is my only child, so a great deal of

[1]See References for Chapter one.

my life has been affected by my son. My life with my wife has had many milestones, most of them not happy ones; so, that is another area. There are pockets. The third pocket of my life is my academic life, which I find probably the most rewarding of all my pockets. I'm an associate professor at _____ College in the Graduate Program. This has been the unique part of my life, because it's almost without any relationship to superiors. It's a very independent kind of existence. I find my life very free in the school. Another part of my life, which is really tied into my academic life, is the lectures I give around the country, and that's probably—with the lectures in the classroom—the most rewarding of all my endeavors.

Let me go back a minute and pick up on some of these. You mentioned the book that you've just published. I had published 50 articles before that, and I started together with a young member of the faculty to get this book out and we got it out in a year's time. It's being well received, and it's a damn good book. I think basically the real rewards I get out of life are tied in to the recognition I get outside in the field. Inside it's a real fight. It's a very, very complicated environment. . . . It's trying.

Probably the turning point of my life has been not to be an entrepreneur and work for a living. I love to live well, and I'm always tempted to parlay my success into something other than working for a living; but I do not do it. Probably because I'm a Depression child. And that's another part of my life, a milestone in my life, growing up as a young boy in the Depression years in more or less a limited-income family. I wouldn't say poverty, but a limited-income family. The second milestone in my life was the War, World War II, which was the first time I was away from home; and the constant knowledge that you might be killed. I got married when I was very young—21—right after I was discharged from the service. Another milestone was deciding that I didn't want to be an accountant after graduating as an accountant and starting a career in my present field. So these are the milestones; I never put them together.

What was it about the Depression that made that a milestone for you? Well, the struggle, to see my parents struggling, my father being out of work for almost two years; my mother having to work and be away. The whole era where . . . and it's very vivid . . . where small things were very important. Where certainly no one ever thought of luxuries. I think while I was living through it I didn't realize how my parents were sheltering me from it. The impact was later. It became more obvious as I got more affluent. We talked about it and reflected upon the little things that were so important then, that are so unimportant now. I never, never took a train or a trolley to school. I walked to school and that was several miles. One would never spend a nickel to do that. That was no sacrifice. Based upon that experience during the Depression, I find money to be very important as a base of security, and I'm not willing to gamble with it. That's what I came out of the Depression with. *That's what you meant earlier when instead of an entrepreneur, you don't risk?* That's right. No risk. I have to know what's going to be ahead for me in the next year, and that's why the relationship, employee to employer, is more satisfactory in that area. The more interesting facet of that is that it's probably the most unsatisfactory part of my life, inasmuch as I have a hard time accepting the superiors who are not really my superior intellectually or otherwise. And I find that in order to exist you must suppress that feeling, and in an organization such as ours you deal with many powerful people. And you walk a tightrope.

Let me tell you something that just, you know, popped in and out of my head. I never had this feeling of desire for security until in the midst of my career there was a milestone. I was 28 years old. I had a fairly nice job, and I lost the job because the place was in deep financial trouble. At the very moment my wife gave birth to our first and only child after six years of marriage where both of us worked and made comfortable salaries; we found ourselves—she not working—with the child; me not working with no savings, and I did not handle that situation well. I was out of work for eight weeks and it seemed like eight years. [I was] very frightened, extremely frightened. And that fear has really permeated the years subsequent to that. Up to that time I don't think I really thought about the Depression. I didn't think about security. I was happy-go-lucky. That changed my life, and that made me want to be in a very secure situation, and altered my later life. Now, 20 years later, where I have a national reputation, and I probably would have a job the day I was fired from this job or quit this job, that still gnaws at me. That has affected my ability to gamble, and yet I'm certainly not famous for my reserved attitude. I'm very outspoken, and that's a form of gambling. So, I don't know how you put it together. I haven't thought about it enough.

It sounds like there are some ways in which you are reserved in the sense of not taking financial risks, but other kinds of ways in which you really let it hang out. You're on an interesting point in this interview—many milestones all within the same week span—book coming out, my son on his way back from Europe, and I just decided to buy a country home. I've never been a homeowner. I've committed myself to a country home, an economic commitment I've never made in my life. I've been very cautious. For a man in my income level, as of this moment I have no, well, minor outstanding debt . . . minor. That's how cautious I am about that. And yet, I've taken that step. I thought that that's a major commitment, financial commitment. So, I don't know, that's certainly a milestone. What brought about that shift in terms of buying a country home? I suppose there are several things. One, I would like to have the comfort of a retreat like that. Two, I hope it will affect my son's desire to stay home, rather than float around the world; it might be this country home which is a little remoter than living in the city would help that. Third, economically I feel that it is feasible, and that I've been too cautious, and fourth, I think it's a good investment. [Telephone rings; call about son's arriving flight from Casablanca.]

I gather that was about your son. Yeah. That has dominated much of my life in the last 20 years. *You mentioned him earlier as a milestone.* Oh yeah. *In what sense? Can you say more about him?* Our whole relationship, my wife's and mine, is built around a deep concern about our son and investment in our son, emotionally an investment, probably far beyond what a psychiatrist would permit as normal. It's not unusual. It's not unusual in a Jewish family, okay. It's not unusual with an only son, an only child, and it's not unusual based upon my wife's background, which was abject poverty, an orphan at thirteen; and not unusual since we were both planning on not having a family when we had a family, although we were married six years without one. So we are . . . our son has a great deal to do with our moods, and with our satisfactions. We're highly protective . . . so when I consider it a milestone, it is a very important part of my life. I define milestones as important parts . . . negative, positive, or anything that changes your life. I consider my son as something that has had a deep effect on my life. *I gather both positive and negative?* Yeah. Yeah, both.

Have there been some crisis points in that relationship? Very, very many. And crisis points in my marriage as well. Crisis points, with anyone who has had a 20-year-old son, of the same type—directionless kind of existence, underachiever. I don't like the word, but basically what I'm saying is a lack of motivation . . . the drug scene . . . terrible crisis one time. We got a call from Canada that he was in jail; and going up there to get him out. *How did you feel about that?* I was . . . first of all, my wife almost cracked up. She's very . . . she gets very uptight. She's having a tough day today. She doesn't know . . . because he called us yesterday saying he couldn't get out of Casablanca and now we're hoping he's on one of these two planes. Ah, I felt the way I usually feel when there's a crisis with my son; I get very, very worried, but basically I attempt to handle it the same way I have success with handling my business life. I tend to get overpowering at that point with my wife, and that may be a mistake. I take charge, which I normally don't do. My wife is in charge in the house. My wife is in charge with my son. I quickly started the checklist and within hours I had a lawyer specializing in this, who I picked up at three in the morning; went down to the airport, had the tickets arranged, had several thousand dollars in cash in my pocket, got on the plane, got there; he got back on the plane with us within two hours. It's very interesting as I reflect back. I never was that kind of individual while my father was alive. And my relationship with my father was interesting. My father used to be an arranger. He was a bright guy but he wasn't an intelligent guy, and he was the arranger. And I did very well as a young man, everything was arranged. When I was in trouble, he would arrange things. I wasn't famous for being an arranger; in fact, most of my life 'til the last 10 years, I avoided problems. Now I've become an arranger. You asked me how I felt and I felt very troubled, deeply disturbed, but didn't get my mind off of what I had to do. I knew what I had to do. And nothing would stop me from doing it. Without a doubt, nothing would stop me, and it didn't stop me. *It sounds like a lot of the skills you use here on your job are relevant there.* Exactly. Exactly. That's the way I operate. It's successful in my job. I have not been successful in my marriage, so that . . . that's another area. At times I get too short-tempered about that kind of problem and I may operate too quickly, because basically I tend to want to do it myself. *I'm getting a sense that you would like a lot more out of this relationship with your son than you're getting.* Oh, sure I would. Sure. But I think every father would. My son's not going to follow in my footsteps and that's good. I didn't want him to. And he's not going to do what I want him to do. I have to come to accept that. Certainly I have disappointments, but I have a lot of satisfactions. He's a brilliant boy. He's starting to challenge my own sense of intelligence and that I like. I would like to see him less concerned with the occult and more concerned with day-to-day happenings. I am not a father who is interested in seeing him join the establishment as it's defined, but in some ways . . . yes, compromise. I don't think he has a sense of compromise yet, but he's only 20. I'm not sure I had it. At 20 I was dodging bullets. *You were doing what?* Dodging bullets. It was a favorite pastime of my generation.

You fought in the Second War? Yeah, I was in the Navy. It wasn't really that bad. *But you indicated that it was one of the milestones for you.* Oh, yes . . . it was a milestone, being away from the protected environment very young, naive, traveling around the world for better or worse. That's certainly a milestone. And, wondering if your ship is going to get hit or not by a submarine. That's a milestone. Getting by it was a milestone also.

I think I changed the direction of my life, and I did it rather than having it done for me. I decided that I didn't want to go on to accounting. I went on to evening school to do my graduate work in education, which I thought I wanted to do, and then got involved in industry and decided that the _____ field was a good field, and just by making the decision got into the field, which is very interesting. That I did myself. I had no preparation for it, and made a career out of it, and reached the point where I am considered the dean of my field; so that was an important turn in my life. Much has come from that decision. *It took you several years to reach that decision?* Oh, yeah, I didn't know what I wanted to do. I was just floating around, doing the best I could, like most people do, until I was 28. You do the best you can. *That was the time when you lost the job?* Right. *And your son was born?* Yeah. *And you made the decision to get into your present field?* Right. And I did it. I was in industry for many years and moved into my present specialty. That's another milestone. It afforded me an opportunity to make out of myself what I am now. It was a burgeoning industry, as far as my field of specialty. That was a little fortuitous also. After being with a firm for a long time, I took a job in Illinois because I had that feeling from the last time of being out of work, and I didn't want to go through it again, so I took the first job that was offered to me, and it was offered to me before my last check, and I made sure that I was set. And I moved to Chicago and my wife didn't want to move there. And we had a very difficult six months. She insisted that we come back to New York and, fortuitously, there was a job opening at this company. It changed my whole life. That was not planned. It was still in my same field that I planned on staying in, but not in the same industry, and that changed everything. *It was almost accidental that you wound up in this position?* Oh, very, very much so. But in reviewing it, it wasn't accidental that I made out of it what it turned out to be. That was me. No one could take that away from me. I had come to the company knowing that they had very little here, and it was not very difficult for me to look like a genius by rediscovering the wheel. I'll be very, very frank about it. Here I am with a bag of tricks . . . really a great magician . . . coming into a situation where all the tricks were perfect, useful. That was magnificent . . . unbelievable! I don't know how many men get that opportunity in their lifetime. That was unbelievable! Before I knew it, there was an industry-wide problem and I was an industry spokesman, and from there on in it was all very easy, to the point where anything I wrote would be published. It was just great! Not very many people find themselves.

That didn't make me happy, though. . . . Satisfaction with your job and overall happiness with your life are usually two different departments. One may have an effect on the other. I have an extreme satisfaction . . . I *had* extreme satisfaction from my job, tremendous recognition. I did not have that kind of satisfaction from my life, in the main. I've come to grips with that in the last two years. I think I have more of an understanding of the satisfaction I've had in the past, but during that time my life was work oriented. This was my total satisfaction. Certainly not satisfaction in my social life.

So your personal life was very different, very much less satisfying? Yes. *What was happening there?* Marital problems that are not untypical of affluent, middle-class people who have some satisfaction in their life and tremendous exposure to a different world. *Exposure to a different world?* Yeah, rather than the limited world of your home and your neighborhood. Yeah, my wife is in a terrible disadvantage. Women's lib . . . there's a lot of nonsense in it, but there's a lot of meat, and the whole business of being tied down to the home, although I think that's also a choice a person makes. Geographic exposure . . . a man's a successful executive like myself who travels around and is exposed to the academic world, is exposed to a work area that's large and interesting, has so many more contacts and so many more opportunities for satisfaction and for exploration, that it's definitely a threat when the woman is not exposed to anything other than the family and the home. And that caused a great deal of difficulty in my marriage. *What was some of that difficulty about?* Women. My exposure to many women, who happen to have the same drive I have. My feeling of lack of freedom, which has always been a pervasive feeling, that I was always tied down economically. You see that business from the Depression—although I didn't want to be tied down economically. I was frightened of economic responsibility. I always had it. So my hedge against it was a secure job, and yet innately what I wanted was freedom. I didn't want a secure job. I wanted to be able to not worry about economic pressures that most men do. When women's lib talks about exchanging roles with men, I wonder if they talk about or consider the economic pressures that are on most men in our society. Some real and some not real; but they are just as real if the person thinks the pressure is upon him. And most men do think that the economic pressure is upon them. *Were there other ways you felt tied down?* Oh, sure. I wanted to be a jet-setter. I always had that feeling of being able to enjoy, always wanting to enjoy. I suppose you kind of do that as a couple as well, so a lot of it is rationalization. An individual says he is tied down, but most people tie themselves down. I realized that a couple of years ago. It was not in my stars, but in myself that the problem lay. I'm coming to peace with myself on that.

Did you always feel this way in your marriage, or was there some point when it became a really definite feeling? When I was 28 and my son was born. That's probably the single most important milestone in my life. Because a lot turns on that. The feeling of the pressure of the responsibility of a child. My wife's own feeling about this. She was very, very hysterical about being a mother. Once it happened she became the ultra mother, the most mother. I suppose that was a guilt reaction, but all this happened then—the feeling of being tied in. That eight-week period of being unemployed had a tremendous . . . this is where . . . see, look at the economic responsibility that's on my shoulders, that I didn't want. My parents shielded me from the economic responsibility during the whole Depression. This is a direct relationship, my feeling about the need for freedom. How did I define that? Was I talking about girls? Yes I was talking about girls. Was I talking about traveling? Yes, I was talking about traveling. But when you got to the core of it I was talking about no need to provide for anybody but my-self. That's what I wanted when all this pressed in on me, and had an effect on me for a period of 10 years, 15 years. *What kind of an effect?* That I tended to run away from the responsibilities at home. And became more responsible on the job, but less responsbile at home. That business that happened with my son was atypical. The pressure was on me, and I had to deal with it. Usually I walked away from those problems. Those were my wife's problems . . . taking care of my son.

How did she feel about this? Terrible. We had a terrible relationship. It culmi-nated in our splitting up and going back together again. But it was all a function of my feeling of wanting less responsbility at home and more responsibilities at work. I never ran away from responsibilities at work. Figure that out. *So you did split up at one point.* Yeah. *How long ago was that?* Two years ago. *And you've recently gotten back together?* No, right away. It was a very short split. It was only two weeks that I was away, and we've restructured our lives since then. It's been satisfactory. *What do you mean you restructured your lives?* Well, there are a lot of things that bothered me in our relationship. We moved into the city. We started to do more things together. I made an investment, which I hadn't done in the past. Let me give you a mind picture. I'm like a bal-loon. I tend to fly with the air currents. That's been the opposite of my life in the business world. There I'm like a lead balloon—really anchored. And I tend to fly around from experience to experience and not make an investment; and you could be married a long time and never make an investment, you know. The fact that you see people celebrating their fiftieth anniversary together, their twenty-fifth anniversary together, doesn't tell you whether they've been together, really together. I find that many marriages are two separate lives that meet in the night. On the other hand, one of the problems I've had with marriage is that I find it didn't afford enough freedom, and I'm more and more enchanted with the writings on the open marriage concept . . . not that I practice it. I practiced a one-way open marriage for 15 years, 10 years, I should say. So we start to re-structure our lives. I did, it's never too late.

It sounds like you've decided to stay together. Yeah. Without a doubt. *Why is that?* Well, there are many factors. One is that I, for some reason, find divorce impossible to think of, and that deep-seated problem that I went through with a psychiatrist when we broke up for a period of time after that. It's my own feeling that I don't want to hurt people. That's interesting, because I'm in a business where you have to be real rough sometimes. But I don't see it the same way. I have a strong feeling of my responsibility for other people, and yet I don't. It's really a contradiction . . . that I really want to escape that. I've always felt I didn't want the responsibility . . . I always take on the responsibility. Being the arranger is part of that. I find this drive that I can't stop—to be the responsible person. That's the way we even manage the house. I take care of the complete finances. I pay all the bills. You know, it's the kind of thing . . . it's almost male chauvinism. But it's this . . . the two forces that are constantly at fight with each other. One is the force that gnaws at me . . . that I don't want responsibility. The other is constantly taking responsibility . . . feeling responsible. Therefore, divorce is something that I can advise other people about if I think it's appropriate, but I could never take it into my own life. *You could never take that step.* Yes, it's impossible. You can't kid yourself about it. You can pretend about it, but it's just not my makeup. I feel like I would be deserting my family, and you always, there's always a rationalization for it, but . . . there's always a good reason why you do it, but basically it's that sense of responsibility that I'm driven to. I always feel that I don't want to hurt anybody.

Have there been any crisis points in your relations with your parents? No. My parents were my children for a long time. Again I took the responsbility. My father always arranged things when I was younger, then, as soon as I got out and made something of myself in the business world, I became the arranger for my parents, and they depended on me. And I did it with great relish. When my father died I had my mother still alive, and I take care of her. I arrange everything for her. So, there have been no crisis points with my parents. My mother tends to be irresponsbile. When you're 75 you can be irresponsible, too. I don't mind it. I don't mind taking that responsibility. *Was it a crisis point at all when your father died?* No . . . a very sad point. It becomes sadder by the year because I reflect back more and more on it. It's funny about sons . . . although if my son treated me like I treated my father I would be ecstatic but, in reflecting back, I think I should have been closer to my father. *How long ago did he die?* Seven years now. Seven years.

Have your relations with your parents changed over the years? No! They were always childlike, whoever assumed the role of the child in the relationship. It was always me the child and then, finally, they became the child. No, it didn't change. I never discussed important matters with my parents . . . of intellectual or philosophical importance that my son discusses with me now . . . challenges me on. My father and mother thought that the sun rose on me, the sun set around me, and that I could do no wrong. They were very good to me. Whether it was because I never rocked the boat in exchange or not, I don't want to challenge. I closet that. It has been suggested to me that it was easier for them to be good to me than to face up to the problems. I can't deal with that. I had a good relationship with my parents.

Have there been any crisis points in your job? Oh, many. I have a terrible, terrible reaction to doing something wrong. And there's a depression that comes over me when I think I made a mistake. At my company I took on . . . or someone took me on, in a fight that I was unequal to. Now I'm the middle-weight champion, not the heavyweight champion, and the heavyweight champion took me on, and I didn't talk for two days . . . I couldn't speak. I ran away and didn't want to speak to anybody about it. That was a real crisis. *I take it you lost the battle.* No, I won the battle. *You won the battle?* Yeah, isn't that funny? I won the battle, but inside I had the feeling of having lost, of having been bested. In fact I not only won, I won the battle for the industry, inasmuch as what came out of it was very important for the industry. And that guy became a very close friend of mine, a very close backer. I won the battle, but it was very, very traumatic for me. *Traumatic in what sense?* I felt crushed that I was being singled out individually, and singled out for making an error. By the way, I didn't make an error then . . . you see, I started the story off by telling you that there are times I made errors. This was not an error, but it was considered as an error by some. I have a hard time when people criticize me. . . . It's strange. I would love to have the ability to be thick skinned. People think I am, but I'm very thin skinned, extremely thin skinned. That was the time where I needed a thick skin, and I was very thin skinned. He hit me hard and I thought he was unfair. I didn't do well emotionally. I've reached a level of acceptance and re-spect that when somebody doesn't give me acceptance and respect, I get child-ish about it. I sulk. I've got to be able to be like an actor who's got to be able to take a bad review. I haven't been able to take bad reviews too well, even when they were deserved.

In what ways have you changed on the job? What effect has the experience that you've had made? Well, let's first get out of the way the fact that I've be-come a true expert rather than a magician based upon a bag of tricks. After the years of dealing with the problems, I'm an expert in them. I have the confi-dence. I know my job. I am the best person I know in my job! So, that gives me a lot of confidence. That's how I've changed, and I've developed that over the years. Number two, I suppose the feeling of that whole thing about the outside of the organization. I've changed inasmuch as I expect less from the inside of the company and expect more and get more outside, again within the parameter of my business life. I'm talking about the respect of my peers outside. That's not a new change, but it's something that has developed over the years. I think I'm less defensive than I was. With all I told you, I think I do better at taking a bad review. I'm willing to say, "That's the way the cookie crumbles." I get a lot of comfort when I'm able to do that, because I know that that's a different person than the person I've been all my life. I think I churn up inside less—that's another thing—because I have so many outlets now. If I'm unhappy over what happened today at the job, tonight I'll be writing something; the next day I'm lecturing at _____. I've got that. So I have a lot of escape valves. And maybe they're not as haphazard as one may think. Maybe I put them there, because I'm worried about the repetition of that time when I had no escape valves. I've got lots of escape valves! The final escape valve for me is when I'll have enough money where I won't even need an escape valve. But I've never done anything about that. *In terms of building up money faster or something?* Yeah. We live extremely well! We live an upper-middle-class existence . . . within our means, but right up to the extent of our means. We never want for anything. We're opera goers, ballet goers, concert goers, Europe goers . . . we've done well by ourselves in that area.

How does your job future look to you? What do you see ahead for yourself? I see myself retiring in this job. Normal retiring age is 65 and I'm 48 now, so I see myself retiring in 17 years. I see myself continuing to teach during this period of time, continuing to write, and continuing to have outside activities. So, it's really a repetition of what I've had in the last few years, only with new challenges, variations on the challenge. I don't see myself outside of this job. *Does that mean after retirement?* Oh, after retirement? No. I want to get to retirement. I hope that within this period of time I'll be able to manage an early retirement. I would love to retire at age 55. I don't think it's realistic, but certainly no later than age 60. If I could manage a reduced retirement at age 55, I would certainly grab it. What do I see myself doing? Just what I told you . . . teaching, consulting, lecturing . . . that's my life . . . and writing more. *So it would be retirement from the job and not from all your other activities?* That's right. That would be the only retirement. The activities that I have outside the job are great, and I would love to be freed from the job with the same nice salary and be able to do the others. *Do you see yourself retiring from your other activities of teaching or writing?* Oh, yeah . . . I could . . . in fact I would see probably the first year that I retire, traveling around the world. I could do that. I would have no trouble, because I could keep myself busy; I would not be moping around. I would love the freedom. I would retire to my country home and retire on and off. When I say I would continue to do the other things, I would continue them, but not on a full-time basis. I want the freedom of retirement. I want the freedom of not having to work this week, you see. I look towards that. I don't look towards it to play golf or to settle in some retirement community . . . God I wouldn't . . . I would die . . . I look to it, towards the freedom it affords me to do whatever I want to do.

How do you see your personal life developing in the future? Do you think there will be more satisfaction there? Yeah, I think so. I'm optimistic. I think there is a . . . my friends would say a . . . good prognosis for my marriage. That's an area I've changed sharply in the last two years. Every problem doesn't make me say, "Let's fly away."

Has your outlook on life changed much over the years? Yeah, I think it has. I've been what might be considered a radical-liberal all my life and I think I am as close to being a conservative as possible now, so I would say that was a sharp change, and that's recently. *What brought that about?* I'm tired of violence. I'm tired of rationalizing the act on the basis of a cause. I think they're two separate things. I think the cause is important, and that causes, the root causes, should be remedied, but, on the other hand, that's where my former philosophy stopped, and my new philosophy incorporates dealing with the acts as well. A crime is a crime no matter what the cause. I'm tired of violence. So, that . . . and I suppose, now your getting to a more basic cause . . . my affluence is threatened by the radicalism, so I'm not going to kid myself about it. I've got it. I got it the hard way.

Would you say that you have a pretty firm sense of who you are? I've always had a firm sense of who I am. My problem was, was I happy with who I am? I'm getting a lot happier with it. But I knew who I was and what my limitations were, what my strong suit was for a long time. When I say a long time, I mean for ten years or so. That's a long time. *Before then you didn't have quite a . . .* No, I wasn't sure, I wasn't sure. I also think I have a firm understanding and realization of where I'm going, and where I'm not going. I've got a good thing going. I don't use the word "happiness." That's from my other life. Happiness equals good times equals excitement.

Do you sometimes look back over your life and kind of review it? Yes, I sometimes do that. I don't dwell on it. I like to review my life. I like to go back and think about things that happened to me, both pleasant and unpleasant. I do it every so often. I'm not afraid of doing it, but I don't dwell on it, and . . . I rarely have the feeling I would like to be seventeen or eighteen again.

I must say that I don't think of myself as destructible. I think I'm going to live forever. That's a nice feeling. I'm not worried. Maybe in about 10 years from now I'll start worrying about dying. I'm still not at the point where I'm worried about dying. Then, when you worry about that, you look back on your life more. No, I'm still looking ahead. I really think I have 20 productive years ahead of doing something and then maybe the kind of retirement where you sit around and contemplate your navel. I've got 20 years. I've got a lifetime ahead of me. *Do you sometimes think about death?* Death? Yeah, I think about it sometimes. In fact, recently I have prepared my will. I never had one. I think about it—not oppressively. When I say I think I'm indestructible, that's nonsense. I mean, I don't think about death as imminent. I think of it as a possibility, and it's not a . . . it's not within the context of my life right now. As I said before, it may be five years from now or ten years from now. On and off it appears. I was thinking of death a great deal two years ago when I had this great difficulty at home. *You mean in terms of possible suicide?* Just about death. Just about it being an easy way. Now I don't. I think of life more than I think about death. Much more. There's so much more of life right now. I'm very excited about what's ahead of me, you know, in the next year, with my country home, my son coming home, my book. There's a lot of exciting things ahead, so I've got a lot . . . it's not going to be a dull year. I say it's more of the same of what I'm doing, but it's always a variation on a theme. So it's a very exciting period ahead, very exciting.

Is sex as important to you now as it used to be? No. *In what way?* Well, it was very important to me. I don't know if you decide this or it happens to you, but it's just something that takes a back seat in my life now. It took a front seat for much of my life. *What do you mean that it takes a back seat now?* Oh, I'm not as hung up about the whole thing. Which I was in the past. Hung up inasmuch as I used to sleep around a great deal. I think I've come to some kind of understanding of that. Maybe it's accepting less. But in any case, it's an acceptance, and I'm not willing to rock the boat. I'm accepting it, and I'm not willing to go into the psychological roots of my acceptance. There's no question about it. It's a compromise. *What about sex with our wife?* That's what I'm talking about as well. It's a compromise. *A compromise in what sense?* I expect less. I give less too. I've always given less at home, but now every time I'm unhappy about my sex life, I don't run out and satisfy myself in a relationship. My relationships were always permanent relationships. When I say "sleep around," that's a very poor term. Always that sense of responsibility. They were long-term relationships—a strange phenomenon—my analyst enjoyed that. You see, I see a difference between a guy who sleeps around, and a guy who has a permanent mistress. Within the context of my stupid kind of morality, one is quite different from the other.

Would you say that you're having a close, intimate relationship now with someone? No. Other than my wife. *With your wife?* Yeah. I think we're close now. Closer than we've ever been. Extremely close now. More understanding on my part. *Was it very intimate earlier; for example, after your marriage?* No, we were children . . . absolute children . . . playing house. There should be a law. One big game. No responsibilities. *From the very beginning?* From the very beginning. Until my son was born. Then all of a sudden we found ourselves with responsibilities. It was a very free life. That's what it was. It was just an extension of our childhood. I came right out of the service . . . not even finished with college . . . and got married. My wife worked while I went to college. It was like being home with mama. The same thing, no difference. Just moved from one place to the other; in fact, we lived at home for a while, at my house for a while. No difference. Same kind of life. No responsibilities. My only responsibilities were getting good marks at school. That was very important. That had carried over from being at home with my mother and then later with my wife.

Would you say that you are different now than you were a few years ago? Oh, it's like day and night. Oh sure. *In what ways?* I tend, as I said before, and I'm very happy when it happens, to be reserved at times where I never was reserved, number one. Number two, I tend to accept more often than I have in the past, a bad review. Number three, I'm not looking for the excitement of the good life, the jet-set life, as I did in the past. And I could find happiness in a very comfortable relationship at home. That's very important. That's really the one thing that I needed to stabilize my life.

Do you have a sense now of leaving your mark: somehow being productive? Yeah. I think my obituary would interest me if I was reading it to someone else. Let me put it that dramatically. Yeah, my obituary would interest me now, if I read it in today's paper to somebody else. I think I will have left my mark. I will have left my mark with this book. This book will be around long after I expire, and with all I'm going to do after this. I set the standards. I've legitimized my profession in this industry. That's a deep mark. And in teaching I've left my . . . we didn't talk about it much, but of all the things I do, I teach with the best. I'm just alive in that classroom. I didn't even talk about it; that really is the thing that I do well. So, I've left my mark. I've left my mark now if I stop now. I'm not going to stop now. There's a lot more to do. Yeah, I'll leave my mark. They won't say, "He was a nice guy," like they did when my father died, with all of the accomplishments and say he was a nice guy. A lot of people will say I was a nice guy, but that won't be my accomplishment. I will have accomplished something.

Murray was interviewed again six years later; that interview is the next Interlude, following Chapter 6.

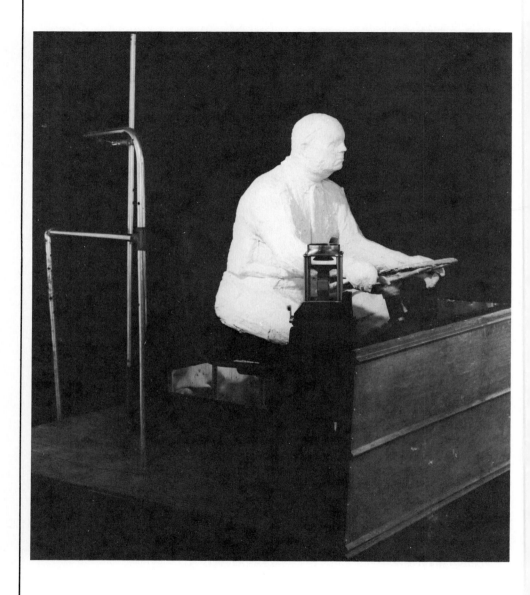

6
WORK, RETIREMENT, AND LEISURE

"Freud was once asked what he thought a normal person should be able to do well. The questioner probably expected a complicated, 'deep' answer. But Freud simply said, *'Lieben und arbeiten'* ('to love and to work')" (Erikson, 1968, p. 136).

Certainly these two aspects of human life are central during most of the years of adulthood; they encompass Erikson's stages of Intimacy versus Isolation and Generativity versus Stagnation; this lengthy period of generativity (that includes not only productivity and creativity in work but also the production and caring for offspring) extends from the resolution of the identity crisis to the beginnings of the final stage in Erikson's framework—Integrity versus Despair.

In the last chapter we discussed the first part of Freud's response, "to love"; here we turn our attention to the occupation, the job, or the career that occupies approximately 40 hours a week (but often up to twice that many hours) for 30 to 45 or more years of the life cycle. Perhaps such a large amount of time is a sufficient reason to take a careful look at the interaction between the occupation and the person during the middle years. But we are also interested in the interaction between the occupation and the family and in the role that the occupation plays in the final resolution of the identity crisis. We are interested in the occupational cycle, in the process of occupational choice, and in the process of socialization by which the individual is prepared for an occupation and comes to accept the roles and status that the occupation entails. We are also interested in the end point of the occupational cycle, retirement, and in the relation of nonworking time to leisure, since these issues are becoming more and more important in society today.

In regard to retirement, more people are living past 65 today than ever before and this trend will undoubtedly continue. Thus, more people are able to work up to the age of retirement and often beyond; consequently, more people are retiring and are living in retirement for a greater number of years or are entering a new career late in life. One effect of greater longevity has been to increase the significance of retirement as a developmental milestone; we will examine this milestone in detail in a later section of this chapter.

In regard to leisure, technological advances such as automation and computers have increased the amount of productivity for each hour a person works. The result of this change has been an evolving trend to reduce the effective size (number of person hours) of the work force. There are a number of ways this may be done, and most have been utilized to some degree: longer preemployment training keeps large numbers of young people off the labor market; longer vacations, shorter work weeks, and shorter work days reduce the number of hours a person works; earlier retirement shortens the total number of years of work, and, of course, increased unemployment is a temporary means of reducing the work force. This trend toward shortening the amount of time an individual spends working is likely to continue, resulting in an extension in the amount of time potentially devoted to leisure; we will discuss this relatively new phenomenon in the final section of this chapter. But first, let us look at work, the occupational cycle, and retirement.

WORK AND THE LIFE CYCLE

The proportion of women in the labor force has been increasing and is expected to continue growing, while the proportion of men has been decreasing in recent years because of earlier retirement and other factors (Figure 6.1). Black women have historically had higher employment rates than white women. Today, white women are rapidly reaching the same high levels. The rates for Hispanic men and women closely parallel the rates for white men and women. About 9 percent of the women in the labor force in 1976 were unemployed, representing 40 percent of all unemployed persons; the unemployment rate for men was 7 percent. As is also true for men, black and Hispanic women were much more likely to be unemployed and looking for work than white women (U.S. Bureau of Labor Statistics, 1977).

For women today, the trend is to enter the work force earlier and to work considerably longer than was true at the turn of the century. The opposite pattern is true for males; they tend to enter the work force later and to retire earlier today than in 1900 (Neugarten & Moore, 1968). However, because more people are living longer with better health today, the actual number of years that an average

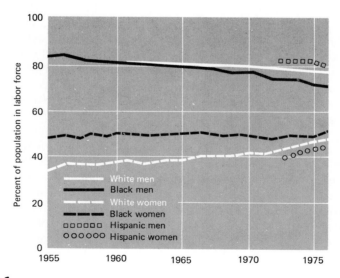

Figure 6.1

Labor force participation rates of women and men, annual averages, by race, 1955 to 1976, and Spanish origin, 1973 to 1976. (Source: U.S. Bureau of Labor Statistics, 1977, Chart 5.)

man spends working has lengthened about 8 years since the turn of the century (U.S. Bureau of Labor Statistics, 1977, Table 60).

Identity and Generativity

Particularly for men, but for growing numbers of women as well, the occupation involves a great investment of time, emotional energy, and commitment. Often the man is particularly engaged in his occupation during the middle years of the family cycle, while the woman is expected to be highly involved in the home and family—even if she is working too. These intense involvements mark the final phase of the identity issue for both men and women in Erikson's scheme of the eight ages of life. Success and satisfaction in the occupation and family reaffirm the individual's sense of identity and also provide social recognition for that identity. Clearly, the job is an important aspect of one's identity, ranking in importance along with one's name, sex, and citizenship. Although this close tie between one's identity and one's occupation may be more true for those in the professions ("I am a lawyer . . . doctor . . . teacher . . ."), we know that certain occupational characteristics (such as "blue collar" or "white collar") are reflected in attitudes, values, and politics; in addition, for most people the occupation reflects such factors as social class and amount of education.

Entry into the adult occupational and parenthood roles also marks the beginning of Erikson's stage of Generativity versus Stagnation. Thus, as these issues begin to become important, the central focus in the individual's developmental progression shifts to that issue in combination with the previous issue of Intimacy versus Isolation during the early years of the working life. Then, during the later years, the focus shifts to Generativity versus Stagnation and Integrity versus Despair, perhaps during the midlife transition. This suggests that the struggle over satisfaction versus frustration and success versus failure in one's job or in rearing one's children and managing a home not only brings the resolution of the identity issues, but also affects intimate relationships and may lead to a sense of leaving one's mark in the world in some way. This period might be termed, somewhat awkwardly, a "generativity crisis." Perhaps such a crisis would be an accurate description of the difficulties and frustrations experienced by some American housewives or businessmen who, as a result of the emotional discomfort of a sense of stagnation, become depressed or turn to alcohol or pills. It may also describe the experience of a man or a woman who makes a dramatic change in occupations at midlife. Thus, this emotional crisis may have some elements in common with the earlier identity crisis experienced by some adolescents; but it would follow from its occurrence later in life that the issue is less "who am I?" than "what am I doing with my life?"

Occupation and Family

The profound sense of satisfaction and accomplishment or of frustration and incompetence also influences other important aspects of an individual's life—

specifically, the other major theme during the middle years—the family. The interaction between the family and the occupation may be seen as a system of mutually interacting factors that can add to or compensate for dissatisfactions in either sphere. That is, a frustrating job, in depersonalizing surroundings, with no opportunity for a sense of pride or accomplishment often promotes the importance of the family (and of leisure time) as a source of satisfaction and feeling of competence. The strain that may result as the frustrations are transferred from the work place to the family is likely to counteract the person's needs, however, by adding to family tension and thus enlarging the degree of frustration felt not only by the worker but by the entire family. In addition, the requirement that the family provide satisfactions of such a degree as to compensate for the lack of satisfaction in the occupation is likely to overburden the family and may snowball into a family crisis reflecting, in this example, job frustration.

In the other direction, an unsatisfying family interaction and marital disharmony may shift the burden to the job as the primary source of satisfactions and rewards. Thus, the occupation may be used as an effective escape from the frustrations of family life, leading the person to acquire a second job, work longer hours, spend evenings entertaining clients, or be out of town as a substitute source of satisfactions. Sometimes, also, the family and the job are competing in their demands for the individual's time and loyalty. For example, the young executive or professional may be called upon to sacrifice a part of his or her family life in order to obtain advancement or to establish a career that may, of course, produce family tension. We will focus on this issue in the discussion of working women in the next section, since they are especially likely to feel conflict between their role as a parent and as a worker; also, we will discuss the special problems of dual-career families in which both spouses are working.

Women in the Work Force

Women have always worked in a variety of tasks that have differed only in terms of cultural norms and economic necessities. Nye (1974b) pointed out that women made substantial economic contributions in the work force during the Industrial Revolution and in Colonial America. It has been the exception in history for women to be confined to domestic responsibilities; in many cases, this was a privilege granted only to the wealthy who, in turn, employed female servants and bought goods manufactured by female workers. Even in recent American life, wives of farmers shared all of the work with their husbands and children, combining work in the fields with work in the home. Until recently, however, women have frequently not been paid for their work and few have directly competed with men for the same jobs at the same pay. Instead, middle-class women were given the opportunity to spend the time, made available by smaller families and time-saving housekeeping devices, in a variety of voluntary activities— much as was the case for upper-class women with servants a few decades earlier. However, today the labor force is swelling with substantially greater num-

bers of women seeking paid employment, while services that were built on feminine voluntarism are turning to public financing to hire paid workers and are
seeking to attract student and retired volunteers. At the same time, previously
all-male occupations are slowly allowing women to enter and are beginning to
face the complex set of issues that this involves.

In 1979, 38 million women over age 20 were in the labor force (either working or looking for work); this represented nearly half of all women over age 20
and about 41 percent of the nation's entire labor force (U.S. Bureau of Labor
Statistics, 1979,). Between 1950 and 1976, the number of married women increased nearly threefold to 21.6 million, or 57 percent of the total number of
women in the labor force. Overall, three out of four working women were employed full-time; even two out of every three employed married women with
children under three worked full-time (U.S. Bureau of Labor Statistics, 1977).

A number of interrelated changes have combined to produce the growing proportion of working women in this country. The most important change has been
the availability of birth control and family-planning information. This has given
women not only control over when they become pregnant, but also over the
number of children they have—and therefore how long they work before the
first child is born, as well as the age at which they are able to move from a child-
care career back into an occupational career. To a large extent, it has given them
control over their life-style and, ultimately, their own life course has come under
their own control. Perhaps the long and difficult struggles Margaret Sanger and
others had to fight to develop and publicize birth control early in the twentieth
century were fundamentally related to issues of economic power and a woman's
right to control her own destiny. Thus, it is not surprising that employed women
have fewer children than nonworking women (Hoffman, 1974b).

Other changes have also led to an increase in working women today. The
postwar "baby boom" has increased the number of young women, and many
are remaining unmarried longer today than in the past. Greater life expectancy
of the population has increased the need for workers in the general areas of
health care and human services; many of these job opportunities have been
taken by women. Our expanding economy, growing affluence, and desire for
expensive products and services during a period of economic inflation have also
prompted women to enter the labor force in order to increase family income. At
the same time, there is also a growing number of persons looking for work, and
a distressingly large number of younger persons, especially minorities, are unemployed. Thus, more jobs will be needed to accomodate the rising number of
women in the labor market and also to reduce unemployment.

Women in Various Occupations. Between 1950 and 1976, there has
been a significant increase in the proportion of women in some professional-
technical, managerial-administrative, and clerical jobs (Table 6.1). Women have
made substantial gains in fields such as accounting, law, finance, buyers-pur-
chasing agents, and sales management. However, women still make up the vast

Table 6.1   Employment of Women in Selected Occupations, 1950, 1970, and 1976

	Percent of All Workers in Occupation		
Occupation	1950	1970	1976
Professional-technical	40.1	40.0	42.0
Accountants	14.9	25.3	26.9
Engineers	1.2	1.6	1.8
Lawyers, judges	4.1	4.7	9.2
Physicians, osteopaths	6.5	8.9	12.8
Registered nurses	97.8	97.4	96.6
Teachers, except college and university	74.5	70.4	70.9
Teachers, college and university[a]	22.8	28.3	31.3
Technicians, excluding medical and dental	20.6	14.5	13.6
Writers, artists, entertainers	40.3	30.1	34.7
Managerial-administrative, except farm	13.8	16.6	20.8
Bank officials, financial managers	11.7	17.6	24.7
Buyers, purchasing agents	9.4	20.8	23.7
Food service workers	27.1	33.7	35.0
Sales managers, department heads; retail trade	24.6	24.1	35.4
Clerical	62.2	73.6	78.7
Bank tellers	45.2	86.1	91.1
Bookkeepers	77.7	82.1	90.0
Cashiers	81.3	84.0	87.7
Office machine operators	81.1	73.5	73.7
Secretaries, typists	94.6	96.6	98.5
Shipping-receiving clerks	6.6	14.3	17.3

Source: U.S. Bureau of Labor Statistics (1977), Table 8.
[a]Includes college and university presidents.

majority of secretary-typists, registered nurses, and noncollege teachers. Black women have made even more dramatic gains than white women among professional-technical and clerical workers between 1960 and 1976, although black women continue to be overrepresented in service occupations (including in private households) and low-status occupations; however, the proportion of black women working in private households dropped sharply during this period (U.S. Department of Labor, 1977).

Thus, while women have made significant gains in some occupations, one may be impressed either by these advances toward full participation in the male-dominated labor market, or by the continuing concentration of women in traditionally female-dominated jobs. For example, a recent study of women in the arts found that women occupy about half of all the jobs in arts councils, art centers, and nonprofit organizations in the arts; however, men had almost a two-to-one margin over women among chief executives while women were concentrated in the lower staff positions—where two-thirds of the directors of development/membership and over half of the business managers and assistants to the chief executive were women (Smith, 1978).

Earnings Gap between Women and Men. In general, women earn about 60 percent of the income men earn and this difference has been increasing (Figure 6.2). This difference is greater for white women (58% of white men's income) than for black women (74.5% of black men's income) or for women of Spanish origin (68%), primarily because white men earn more than either black men or men of Spanish origin; black women earned 96 percent of the income of white women, and women of Spanish origin earned 86 percent of white women's income in 1975 (U.S. Bureau of Labor Statistics, 1977, Table 39). There are two main reasons for this earnings gap between men and women. First, there is a preponderence of women in low-paying jobs that have been traditionally held by women and that offer little opportunity for advancement. Second, the dramatic increase in working women has meant that there are a large proportion of women who have entered their job recently and have not yet had time to advance to higher income levels (U.S. Department of Labor, 1976). In addition, women who leave the work force during child-rearing may also reduce their earning potential, and men are much more likely to work overtime than women. However, there is also evidence of discrimination against women, since they earn much less than men of equal educational backgrounds; in fact, in 1974,

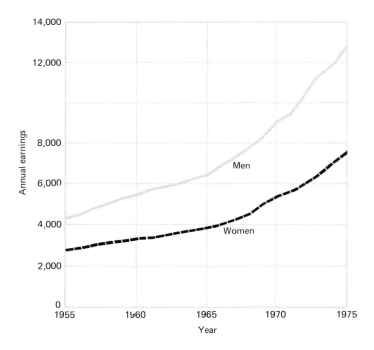

Figure 6.2
Median annual earnings of year-round full-time workers 14 years and over, by sex, 1955 to 1975. Data for 1955 to 1966 are for wage and salary workers only and exclude self-employed persons. (Source: U.S. Bureau of Labor Statistics, 1977, Table 37).

women who had four years of college earned less than men who had completed only eighth grade (ibid.). While never-married women do better than others, earning 85 percent of the income men earn, and women in professional-technical work earn 66 percent of the income of men in similar occupations, women who are widowed, divorced, or whose spouse is absent earned less than two-thirds of the income of men; married women with the spouse present earned only 56 percent, based on annual earnings of year-round full-time workers in 1975 (U.S. Bureau of Labor Statistics, 1977, Table 39).

Sexton (1977) examined this earnings gap in detail, finding considerable evidence of discrimination against women. For example, women start their career at almost the same level of income as men but, by the middle years, women earn only about half as much as middle-aged men earn. This suggests that women tend to be assigned to dead-end jobs and to be barred from career ladders that offer promotions to higher status jobs with higher earnings. Sexton found that some companies tended to assume that women did not want to be promoted; others raised the salary of good female secretaries instead of promoting them, while male clerical employees would be promoted; also women were often unaware of opportunities for promotions because these were not widely advertised and often were based on favoritism that could easily discriminate against women. In addition, women were usually not given training on the job for higher status positions because it was assumed they would not be long-term employees. Thus, there is evidence of a "dual labor market"—one for men and one for women:

> Discrimination, stereotyping, and traditional roles confine some women to a secondary labor market, some to the less desirable jobs in the primary market, and permit very few to enter the more desirable primary market jobs [Sexton, 1977, p. 1].

While the recent gains of women in some occupations may have begun the gradual erosion of this dual labor market, it probably continues to be an important means by which occupational discrimination against women is maintained in our society. It will be interesting to discover what changes in the pattern of women's employment will occur during the decade of the 1980s.

Maternal Employment. The proportion of mothers who are working has risen dramatically in recent years, especially among women with children under 6 years of age (Figure 6.3). By 1979, half of all women with children under 18 were in the labor force; in comparison, only 18 percent of those women were working in 1950. Black mothers were more likely to be in the labor market than white or Hispanic mothers; considering only married women living with their husbands who had children under 6, 58 percent of black mothers, 36 percent of white mothers, and 36 percent of mothers of Spanish origin were working in 1976 (U.S. Bureau of Labor Statistics, 1977, Table 47). Over half of all single

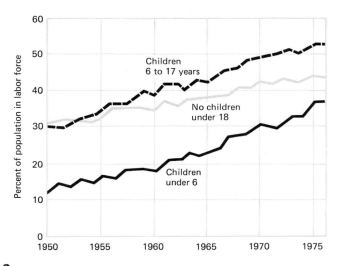

Figure 6.3
Labor force participation rates of married women, husband present, by presence and age of own children, 1950 to 1976. (Source: U.S. Bureau of Labor Statistics, 1977, Chart 4.)

mothers were also in the labor force; this was especially true for divorced women where the rate was 3 out of 4 (ibid., Table 19). As a result, over 40 percent of all children between 3 and 13 have mothers in the labor force. Usually a relative cares for the preschool-age children of working mothers; this was the case for 80 percent of black children and 72 percent of white children (U.S. Bureau of the Census, 1976). About 3 out of 5 of these are reported to be cared for by a parent, and black fathers are three times as likely to care for a 3-to-6-year-old child than white fathers when the mother is working. Relatively few children are cared for outside the home during the day; only 2 percent of all children between 3 and 6 were enrolled in day-care centers in 1975 (ibid.). Many working mothers are employed part-time—about 30 percent; this rate is slightly higher for mothers of young children—32 percent—and much lower for mothers who are divorced—about 14 percent (U.S. Bureau of Labor Statistics, 1977, Table 20).

What are the effects of maternal employment on the child? We would expect that cultural background, social class, whether the mother is living with a spouse or the sole support of the family, level of education, number and age of the children, patterns of relationships within the family, and the psychological needs of the husband and wife would be among the factors that influence the impact of maternal employment on the children and on the family. Hoffman (1974a) reviewed the studies on the effects of maternal employment on children. While adequate data are not available for all of the questions we might wish to answer, her review summarizes the conclusions about some of the important questions. She noted that if the mother works, the father is more likely to be involved in household and child-care duties, and the children are given more household responsibilities than if the mother does not work. Since this affects the relative influence of the mother and father on the children and also gives the children greater independence, the effects of maternal employment on the child are difficult to separate from other influences. However, there was evidence that daughters of working mothers saw women as more competent, had less traditional sex-role concepts, and had higher career aspirations (at least for college-educated women) than daughters of nonworking mothers; the data on related effects for males are less clear. The studies do not support the notion that school-aged children suffer from some kind of maternal deprivation, although there is not yet enough evidence one way or the other about preschool-age children. In some situations, maternal employment has clear positive effects—for example, if the children are adolescents, if the mother is highly educated, or if she is the sole economic support for the family. In general, however, the attitude of the mother seemed to be especially important.

The working mother who obtains satisfaction from her work, who has adequate arrangements so that her dual role does not involve undue strain, and who does not feel so guilty that she overcompensates is likely to do quite well and, under certain conditions, better than does the nonworking mother [Hoffman, 1974a, p. 213].

Dual-Career Families. Over 40 percent of all women living with their husband were in the labor force in 1976. They made a substantial financial contribution to the family income, although the lower earnings of women are clear (Table 6.2). Since the wife is earning money, her relative power in the marital relationship is likely to increase after she begins work, at least in financial deci-

Table 6.2   Median Family Income in 1975 by Type of Family, for White, Black and Spanish Origin Families, March 1976.

| | Median Family Income | | |
Type of Family	White	Black	Spanish Origin
All families[a]	$14,268	$ 8,779	$ 9,551
Husband-wife families:	15,125	11,526	10,950
Wife in paid labor force[b]	17,550	14,355	13,821
Wife not in paid labor force	13,042	8,543	9,191
Other families:			
Headed by women	7,651	4,898	4,785
Headed by men	13,793	8,955	10,415

Source: U.S. Bureau of Labor Statistics (1977), Table 54.

[a]Families as of March 1976.

[b]Persons 14 years and over are classified in the paid labor force if they were employed as wage and salary workers or self-employed workers during the survey week (in March 1976) or were looking for work at the time and had last worked as wage and salary or self-employed workers.

sions; however, it may decline in household areas as the husband takes greater responsibility in the home (Bahr, 1974). The effect on marital satisfaction appears not to be very large, especially in middle-class families, and particularly if the wife enjoys her work, her husband's attitude about her working is positive, only a small number of children are at home, and both husband and wife have advanced education (Nye, 1974a). The likelihood of the husband sharing household tasks is only slightly affected by the ratio of the wife's earnings to his, more influenced by the number of children, and most strongly affected by higher educational level (Farkas, 1976). Thus, couples with greater education—especially younger couples—are more likely to share housework; but younger husbands spent more time in both household chores and their occupations than older husbands.

However, even with the sharing of household responsibilities, there are complex issues that dual-career families often face. For example, advancing in one's career often requires geographic mobility, since promotions and higher status occupations often require moving to another part of the country. As long as one member of the couple (and this would include both heterosexual and homosexual couples) is willing to accept whatever employment is available, the couple can move together to maximize the career of the other partner. This has been one reason women have tended to hold low-status jobs; they exist wherever the couple happens to move, so women who hold these traditionally female occupations are seldom hampered by their need to move (if their husbands move) or by their immobility if the husband remains in one location (Van Dusen & Sheldon, 1976). In contrast, the task of maximizing the career development of two persons in high-status occupations is often difficult. Some couples may agree to remain in the same community, even if one or both limits his or her advancement by that decision. Other couples may strive to alternately maximize first one career and then the other. And some couples find it necessary to establish separate households in different cities, spending only weekends and vacations together for a brief, or more extended, period. Perhaps the difficulty of managing two separate high-status careers has been one reason women's work has traditionally been limited to managing the home or working in a secondary labor market.

Conclusion

We have examined some of the interrelationships between the occupation and the family in today's society. Many of these topics are receiving considerable attention as men and women search for ways to find greater equality between the sexes, higher financial security, and more opportunities for self-fulfillment. Since many of the issues raised by the growing employment of women depend on economic factors in the future that are impossible to predict, we will have to see what the eventual outcome of these issues will be during the next decade. For example, more women are receiving retirement benefits based on their own work history today; but because of women's lower income, these benefits tend to be less than men receive. Moreover, the trend toward smaller families and for young people to remain single longer than in the past is affecting work patterns of women who may be more established in a career before beginning a family than has been the case in the past. This may increase their demand for child-care facilities, and their greater income may also begin to reduce the difference in earnings between men and women.

In the next section, we will examine the occupational cycle for men and women, although it will be obvious that much more research attention has been given to the occupational development of men. Perhaps during the next decade, we will know a great deal more about the differences between the occupational cycles of men and women. Or it may be that women will move into the so-called primary labor market and begin moving up the same career ladders that have traditionally characterized the occupational cycle for men.

THE OCCUPATIONAL CYCLE

When we view occupations from a developmental perspective, we are sensitized to their progression over time and to potential turning points or crisis points in the occupational cycle. This cycle is more easily seen in careers that follow a relatively orderly sequence—the advancement up a "career ladder." However, many people do not experience a simple orderly progression in their occupation, either in one particular field or one particular company; often, there are shifts from one career ladder to another, or from one kind of work to another. Thus, there are many individual paths through the two clearly marked points on the occupational cycle—entry and retirement. Because of the importance of retirement as a major shift in the life cycle, we will discuss it in detail in a later section of this chapter. Here, we will focus on the point of entry into the occupation, as well as some of the factors involved in occupational choice. Also, we will look at variations in the patterns of occupational development and the concept of the career clock.

Occupational Choice

The process of entering an occupation is not a simple matter of choosing a job, but is a process by which a person becomes matched with an occupation. That is, the individual and the occupation are fitted together by the individual's selection of the occupation to meet his or her needs and also by the socialization process required by the new occupational roles and expectations. This usually involves a process of training or preparation (anticipatory socialization), and the role demands of the job itself also produce some degree of resocialization.

In addition, part of the earlier socialization process in childhood and adolescence serves to prepare the individual for eventual occupational requirements and roles. Although this "personnel office" model is an oversimplification of the socialization process, it calls attention to the ways in which schools and other socializing agents influence later occupational choice. For example, Cicourel and

Kitsuse (1968) point out the way in which high schools define "academic careers" and "delinquent careers" for their students and type the students according to "college preparatory" or "vocational" goals; this social typing defines many of the academic, cultural, and social experiences available and expected for each type of student. In many cases, racial or sexual discrimination in employment begins here, as well as in more subtle ways during childhood socialization that includes acceptable roles, selected activities, and dreams for boys, or girls, or "our kind of people."

Thus, the process of "occupational choice" in reality begins many years before an actual job is selected; and the factors that are involved in this "choice" do not usually include the (impossible) task of deciding among the thousands of possible occupations. Instead, background factors (reflecting the effects of early socialization), role models, experience, interests, personality, and the person's own research into occupations are some of the important factors that influence the selection of an occupation. We will discuss each factor here and later discuss the resocialization of the individual upon entry into the occupation, to complete the reciprocal view of the matching process.

Background Factors.   Socioeconomic status, ethnic origin, intelligence, sex, and race tend to operate in complex and often illegal ways to limit the range of occupations open to an individual. Many times a person may find a way to open the door to an occupation and be less bound by these background factors than others, but a simple survey of occupations indicates that some are disproportionately Jewish, white, male, black, or poor. Education, discrimination, and contacts in a particular occupation are some of the ways in which these characteristics operate for or against an individual's movement into an occupation. In general, they operate similar to the way that they do in the choice of a marital partner: by setting general boundaries within which one searches for an occupation (or a mate). In addition, since many occupations require specialized training or specific education, they are effectively unavailable to persons lacking those requirements. Thus, the occupational decision is usually between accepting a job at one's present level of preparation or getting more preparation that will allow entrance into a new range of possible occupations. The boundaries thus created are often unfair to particular groups of people (notably the poor, the black, and the Hispanic), particularly when individuals are unable to acquire the necessary skills at a later point because their prerequisites were denied in childhood and in adolescence by the socialization process and these background characteristics. However, there are at least two ways in which these boundaries may be overcome in childhood and adolescence: by selecting a role model in an occupation outside the usual range, or by having an experience different from the usual range for individuals of similar backgrounds that is related in some way to one's eventual occupation. Clearly, these solutions avoid the social problem involved in institutionalized racism in its subtle and overt forms, and that problem must be faced and dealt with; but our analysis here is intended to be general enough to also include persons who strive to move into an occupation out of the usual realm for their family and peers but who are not held back by racism.

Role Models.   Frequently one selects his occupation on the basis of an identification with someone in that occupation. Often this role model is a relative; and in more traditional societies one frequently followed in the footsteps of one's father or uncle. Some still do. However, the selection of and identification with a role model who does not share one's background is one powerful way to move into an occupation outside the common experience of one's peers. An example of this process is given by Brown (1965) in *Manchild in the Promised Land* in which one staff member in a school for boys had a lasting effect on him and his subsequent involvement in getting an education. Thus, a laborer's son or daughter may aspire to become a teacher or a doctor because of early role models and later find another role model who leads the person on to a career in biochemistry, for example.

Experience.   Similarly, an individual may choose a job on the basis of a particular experience. A man may become a policeman because he saw his older brother killed in a gang war; or a fireman chooses his occupation because his grandmother's house was destroyed by fire. Again, one may move out of the range of jobs common to one's peers because one was uniquely responsive to a particular experience; an example would be the decision to work with older people because of a chance opportunity to be a volunteer in a senior citizen's center when taking a course on adulthood and aging.

The influence of experience and role models on occupational choice was clearly shown in a study of psychiatrists, psychoanalysts, psychologists, and psychiatric social workers (Henry, Sims, & Spray, 1971).

Comparatively speaking, both psychiatrists and psychoanalysts, but especially analysts, were directed toward the general field of medicine primarily through "familial dynamics"—either by way of identification with a relative (most frequently a parent) who was a doctor, or through the setting of the goal of becoming a doctor by a parent (who was not in medicine). In short, the influences on psychiatrists and psychoanalysts operated early, consisted of persons rather than experiences, and were expressed through close relationships.

In contradistinction, clinical psychologists and psychiatric social workers were directed to their general fields at a later time and essentially equally by persons and experiences. For psychologists the most important person was the teacher, the most important experiences were training and reading, and the most important mode of influence was intellectual stimulation. For social workers the key figure was the nonrelated professional social worker, the crucial experience was the job, and the chief modes of influence were exposure to the field and the opportunity to recognize their ability and pleasure with the work [pp. 111-112].

It is interesting to note that, for these psychotherapists, a second specialized occupational choice was also made, usually at a later point. That is, after deciding on medicine, psychology, or social work, they later decided to specialize in psychoanalysis or psychiatry, clinical psychology, and psychiatric social work, respectively. The influences for this specialized decision were generally drawn from within the profession. The influence of the parent was largely replaced by the influence of peers, while teachers, supervisors, and experiences were also important influences.

Interests.   Of course, the individual's interests, preferences, and values play a large part in the choice of an occupation, at least insofar as there is an actual choice to make. In the case of psychotherapists, individuals in any of the professional disciplines would tend to be drawn to psychotherapy by similar interests (for example, understanding and helping people); but, conversely, these interests could be satisfied in several different occupations and professions. In general, a person's interests, values, and preferences partly reflect the effect of role models and individual experiences; they also reflect the unique range of past accomplishments, talents, and abilities, as well as the sense of "who I am" and "what I want to do with my life." Bolles (1972), in his best-selling manual for persons seeking jobs or thinking of changing jobs, points out the importance of taking an inventory of yourself in terms of your goals and skills. He suggests a number of practical ways to do this, including reflecting on memories of your past, your feelings about the present, and your visions of the future.

1. Your interests, wishes and happiness determine what you actually do well more than your intelligence, aptitudes, or skills do. . . . Maybe the word "feelings" or "wishes" sounds just too erratic, in your ears. OK, then borrowing a word from biology, let's speak instead of "tropisms"; things which living creatures instinctively go toward, or away from. Man is no exception, and in addition each one of us has his own personal, unique tropisms. You must know: what do you feel drawn toward, what do you instinctively go away from? Your own personal tropisms are determinative for your first, second (third, or fourth) career.

2. If you do work you really enjoy, and at the highest level that you can legitimately claim, you are bound to do an outstanding job, and be of genuine help to others. . . .

3. No tests or other instruments have been devised yet, that measure what you want so effectively as just *asking you* or having you *ask yourself* [Bolles, 1972, p. 85].

Personality.   In addition, occupational choice often reflects a "fit" in some sense between the person and the job. A number of studies have sought to identify the personality characteristics of adults in various types of occupations in order to specify the way in which personality factors correspond with the pattern of attributes and roles involved in different occupations. (Curiously, male psychologists tend to be the oldest child in the family and to have a younger sister; Conger, 1977, p. 441.) For example, Holland (1973) proposed six matching personality types and occupational environments; they are succinctly stated by Hall (1976):

1. *Realistic*—Involves aggressive behavior, physical activities requiring skill, strength, and coordination. (Examples: forestry, farming, agriculture.)
2. *Investigative*—Involves cognitive (thinking, organizing, understanding) rather than affective (feeling, acting, or interpersonal and emotional) activities. (Examples: biology, mathematics, oceanography.)
3. *Social*—Involves interpersonal rather than intellectual or physical activities. (Examples: clinical psychology, foreign service, social work.)
4. *Conventional*—Involves structural, rule-regulated activities and subordination of personal needs to an organization or person of power and status. (Examples: accounting, finance.)
5. *Enterprising*—Involves verbal activities to influence others, to attain power and status. (Examples: management, law, public relations.)
6. *Artistic*—Involves self-expression, artistic creation, expression of emotions, and individualistic activities. (Examples: art, music, education) [p. 13].

Of course, people do not fit neatly into any category of types, and both individuals and occupations may be thought to combine these types in a variety of ways. Thus, a clinical psychologist who conducts research might combine types 2 and 3; one who also teaches might combine types 2, 3, and 6; while one who works in a state hospital might combine types 3 and 4; and so on. In that sense, it is important to note that any occupation involves considerable variation within its general characteristics and often allows individuals to integrate their own personal style with the occupational role.

One interesting example of the correspondence between an occupation and certain personality characteristics is seen in a study by Henry (1965) of professional actors and actresses. He expected that this group would show many signs of "identity confusion" since their occupation consists of the portrayal of roles and, he reasoned, they may be attempting to compensate for a basic confusion about their own identity by taking on the roles of others. It was found that, indeed, this group of professional actors was lower on a measure of identity than comparison groups of nonactors; that the lower the identity score (that is, the more identity confusion), the more likely the person was to be successful as an actor; and that identity scores rose during the several weeks of play rehearsal preceding an opening performance. These findings suggest that, at least for actors, the occupation may serve as a source of satisfaction of (or compensation for) certain personality characteristics. It is also interesting that most of these persons chose acting as their career because the very first time they played a part in a play, they felt that they wanted to be actors; it is as if the choice was so good for them they could almost hear it "click" the very first time (similar to George's occupational choice of dancing in the first Interlude).

For persons who do not find this clear a response to an occupational field, vocational tests that compare one's response to a variety of questions with the typical responses of persons in various fields may be useful. However, the process of self-examination suggested by Bolles may be very helpful also because many successful persons are not necessarily typical personalities in that occupation. Some relevant dimensions include: do you like working with persons, or with ideas, or with things—or a mixture of two or three of these? Do you prefer working alone or with others? How much, and what kind of satisfactions do you need? How much frustration can you accept before it is balanced by satisfaction; and how long can you wait for the satisfaction? These dimensions, and other "personal tropisms" (Bolles, 1972) provide important cues to the characteristics you will want to pay attention to when you begin researching occupations.

Research about Occupations.   High schools and colleges teach students how to research all kinds of topics for class papers and projects. But they usually leave it up to the student to discover that these same research methods are useful for finding information about personally relevant topics such as occupations. Bolles (1972) provides a number of suggestions about ways to begin this research; it typically involves reading and interviewing a variety of sources and cross-checking the information to be sure it is accurate. One of the most helpful ways to discover an occupation is to talk with people in the occupation to find out what it is like and how they acquired the training and the job. If one has the opportunity, firsthand experience in the prospective occupation is very useful, for example, through fieldwork programs in high school or college, or as a volunteer. This can provide valuable information about how you respond to the job and will give you a chance to talk to people who are working in that field. It can also provide valuable experience that may be required to gain paid employment in that field.

Entry into the Occupation

In some cases one learns most of the skills required for the occupation on the job. But often one learns and practices many of the roles involved in the occupation during a period of anticipatory socialization before entering the job for the first time. Then, at the point of entry, the *real* demands of the job, the *real* expectations, and the *real* rewards are found. Probably, these will differ somewhat from what were expected; and there will be some conflict between the idealism of the earlier expectations and the actuality of the job. Consider, for example, a psychiatric social work student meeting her first patient in a mental hospital as a social work intern. She may not have been in a hospital ward before and certainly was never there as a staff social worker before; she needs to define the situation and to define her role in it; usually role models and resocialization by other staff members help her with these tasks during the first few weeks of the entry period. But during the first few months, she may begin to realize that her skills, the state of psychological knowledge, and the resources of the hospital are less than ideal, and that the needs of the patients are often greater than the resources available. She begins to feel that she may not be as helpful as she hoped she would be; perhaps she will not be able to solve the problems she sees around her because there is not enough time, enough staff, or enough money to provide effective treatment within the walls of the hospital, let alone to do preventive or afterdischarge work in the community. Thus, while her idealism may persist, she must readjust her expectations to the real demands of the actual situation. She may become frustrated and angry, she may become "radicalized" and begin working to change the situation, or she may decide to become the most effective social worker she can be and do her job with as much innovation and enthusiasm as possible.

In a similar way, a police officer, an accountant, and a factory worker are resocialized by the demands of their new jobs and go through a period of "adjustment" and potential emotional upset during the first weeks or months in their first full-time job. "Bootcamp" for army inductees would be a more extreme example of this resocialization process because, although the same process is involved, the situation is full-time, more intense, and less consistent with the inductee's previous roles and identity (Janowitz, 1965).

From a symbolic interaction perspective, the individual is developing a new *me* during this period of resocialization into the occupation. This involves taking the attitude of the others (employer, co-workers, and customers) toward oneself and learning the role behavior that is expected. At the same time, one sees oneself and reacts to oneself in this role. This process, which G. H. Mead called *self-consciousness*, allows one to analyze the correspondence between *I*'s inner feelings about the *me* in the occupation and the way one sees oneself behaving. For example, the social work intern we discussed above might feel some inconsistency between her behavior and her expectations about herself. Her *I* might experience this inconsistency, and she might attempt to find a *me* that fits her expectations and the demands of the situation. It is apparent that the greater the extent of this inconsistency, the greater the difficulty she will have in finding a *me* or set of *mes* that satisfies her *I*'s perception of both her *self* in that situation and the expectations from the point of view of the significant others in that situation. In addition, the greater the salience of that particular *me* to her *self*, the greater weight the inconsistency will have in *I*'s experiencing of her *self* in that situation.

In general, if one feels that the occupational *me* is relatively unimportant—one is just working to make money or having a *me* that is seen as a "nice person" is more important than the *me* as a "good worker"—then the inconsistency will be relatively trivial. On the other hand, if one's occupational *me* is a cornerstone of one's sense of identity—as a "doctor," a "psychologist," or an "artist"—then when *I* perceives the *me* as unsatisfying, or if *I* perceives others' attitudes toward the *me* as unfavorable, the crisis may be much more serious. An extreme example would be "malpractice" or "prostituting oneself as an artist in order to make money."

Even if there is no particular inconsistency that is upsetting, the shift in the self involves *I*'s integrating this new *me* into the array of other *me*s and attending to the expectations of a new group of significant other people. Thus, during this initial period of entry and socialization into the occupation, the individual may find it necessary to readjust aspects of the *self* because of the actual demands of the job and his or her ability to deal effectively with them.

The point of occupational entry, therefore, is a crucial point not only because it marks the transition into adult status and a shift in roles but also because it may involve a major shift in one's *self* and the emotional crisis that such a shift entails.

One Life—One Career?

Sometimes it is assumed that well-adjusted, normal people find their occupation, make it part of their identity, and remain in that same occupation as long as they live, or until retirement. This has been called "the one life—one career imperative" (Sarason, 1977). This notion may make the choosing of an occupation a very serious, almost fateful, matter. However, a longitudinal study of a representative sample of all civilian, noninstitutionalized men between the ages of 45 and 59 in the United States in 1966 found that three out of four had changed occupations since they began their first job after leaving school; over the five-year study (from 1966 to 1971) one out of four of these middle-aged men nearing retirement changed occupations (Kohen, 1975). Not surprisingly, professionals and technicians were least likely to change occupation, while clerical and sales workers were most likely to change. Those who moved from one firm to another were more likely to change occupations than those who remained working for the same company; and those who were dissatisfied with their job in 1966 were more likely to change occupations. For only three out of ten who changed firms, and one out of ten who remained with the same company, did this change in occupations result in downward mobility; upward mobility was also more likely for those who changed firms and for those with greater education. Surprisingly, men who were forced to seek another job were no less likely to move up in occupational status than men who left their job voluntarily; and neither local labor market characteristics nor race affected the likelihood that a middle-aged man would move up the occupational ladder. However, black men moved less far than the white men did, and it was estimated that "if middle-aged black men had had access to the same advancement opportunities as whites, the blacks would have moved nearly twice as far up the occupational hierarchy as they actually did" during this period from 1966 to 1971 (ibid., p. 149). Contrary to what might be thought, no evidence of age discrimination was found for this age group in terms of promotion, demotion, or hiring practices.

Finally, the results indicate that there are indeed economic and psychological payoffs to occupational change, even among middle-aged men. The psychological returns (in terms of increased job satisfaction) are evident and strong only among men who remained with the same firm over the five-year period. But the economic returns (in terms of relative improvement in hourly earnings) prevail both among those who changed employers and among those who did not. Moreover, the data provide support for the thesis that some mobile middle-aged workers trade off gains in some job characteristics (e.g., earnings) for losses in others (e.g., satisfaction) [ibid.].

These data clearly indicate that most working men change occupations at least once, that midlife occupational change is not uncommon, and that few men remain in one occupation all of their working lives—at least among the cohort of workers nearing retirement in 1971. Similar results were found from census data that included women as well as men (Table 6.3). One-third of all men and about

Table 6.3 Percent Distribution by 1970 Status of Persons 16 Years Old and Over Who Were Employed in 1965, by Major Occupation Group in 1965 and Sex

Major Occupation Group of Employment in 1965	Status in 1970					
	Transferred to Different Detailed Occupation			Employed in Same Detailed Occupation		
	Total	Male	Female	Total	Male	Female
All occupations	30.2	33.0	25.6	46.8	49.6	42.1
Professional, technical, and kindred workers	22.5	26.0	17.2	59.7	62.9	54.9
Managers and administrators	24.7	24.6	25.7	57.7	60.1	45.3
Salesworkers	27.5	29.7	24.0	49.3	55.0	40.6
Clerical workers	28.5	38.4	25.0	44.1	45.7	43.6
Craftworkers	23.4	23.3	24.0	59.4	60.0	47.8
Operatives, except transport	30.5	36.2	21.3	46.7	47.2	45.9
Transport operatives	28.9	29.0	26.7	54.5	54.6	51.5
Laborers, except farm	42.9	43.6	36.0	33.4	33.6	31.4
Farmers and farm managers	18.3	17.7	29.7	55.7	57.0	31.0
Farm laborers	34.5	36.7	23.3	34.9	37.3	22.5
Service workers	25.1	29.3	21.7	45.3	48.0	43.2
Private household workers	18.3	27.6	18.0	44.0	39.9	44.2
Occupation not reported	72.6	75.7	66.1	—	—	—

Source: Sommers and Eck (1977), Table 3.
Note: Dashes indicate no persons in category. Persons who were not employed in 1970 or who had died are not shown.

one-quarter of all women changed occupations between 1965 and 1970; conversely, about half of the men and four out of ten women were in the same occupation; the remainder had become unemployed or died by 1970 (Sommers & Eck, 1977). Although there are clear differences between occupations, even in the most stable occupations (professionals, craftworkers, managers), less than two-thirds were employed in the same occupation in 1970 as they were in 1965. Thus, there seems to be little evidence to support the belief in a one life—one career imperative.

Variations in the Occupational Cycle

As may by now be obvious, when we discuss the occupational cycle, we conjure up different ideas of the occupation itself. For example, when we think of a pattern of consistent socialization through a long training period, or a job whose demands for advancement may interfere with family life, we think of a career in which there are distinct steps in the pattern of advancement. The kind of occupation we imagine when we think of a frustrating, depersonalized job, however, tends to be that of a routine job on an assembly line.

Thus, it seems that there are vast differences between certain occupations and, indeed, between various patterns of occupations. First, consider the *career* in which there are well-defined steps of advancement, a hierarchical progression (or ladder) one follows if one is successful. This pattern is one of vertical movement—*up* the status ladder; it is a pattern of orderly progression, often within the same company over a period of years. Or, it may involve a horizontal progression of functionally related jobs with increased status (e.g., apprentice, journeyman, and foreman). As in the study of occupational mobility discussed earlier, a person's socioeconomic status can be inferred directly from their occupational classification (Duncan, 1961). Second, consider a *disorderly work history* in which there is no pattern to the sequence of jobs an individual holds; there is neither a vertical nor horizontal progression that provides increased status. Wilensky (1961) defines these criteria as one way of exploring the obvious differences in types of work histories. He found that, at most, one-third of the "middle mass" (persons who are economically secure but not upper-middle class) have work histories that may be characterized as orderly careers. Thus, the majority of those working are not involved in long-term career aspirations and in progressing up a status ladder but, instead, are likely to move up primarily on the basis of seniority with little increased responsibility or status on the job. In addition, Wilensky found that these two patterns were reflected in greater community involvement and in overlapping patterns of social participation on and off the job for the orderly group compared to the disorderly group.

Men who have predictable careers for at least a fifth of their worklives belong to more organizations, attend more meetings, and average more hours in organizational activitiy. Their attachments to the local community are also stronger—indicated by support of local schools and, to a lesser extent, by contributions to church and charity. . . .

. . . If we give a man some college, put him on a stable career ladder, and top it off with a nice family income, he will get into the community act. Give a man less than high school, a thoroughly unpredictable sequence of jobs, a family income of five to eight thousand and it is very likely that his ties to the community will be few and weak [Wilensky, 1961, p. 338].

Finally, Wilensky suggests that the pattern of the work history (orderly or disorderly) has more impact on a man's social life than any of the work positions that he may have picked up and dropped along the way.

These findings point to an important variable for understanding the role of the occupation, although there are several other factors that are also significant for the understanding of the interaction between the person and the occupation. These factors include motivation (money, sustenance, status, service, creativity, and so on) and sources of satisfaction (money, helping, status, skill, accomplishment, fame, and so on). Thus, potentially orderly careers such as physician, machinist, and engineer are characterized by a number of differing factors (such as motivations and satisfactions) that distinguish one from the other, despite the orderly progression common to all of them. Such differences between specific orderly careers may be as important as the similarities between them.

In addition, a third type of career progression may be suggested as an important variation of the orderly career; this type is a pattern in which the individual changes occupations in a relatively sudden and major way. Perhaps one does this out of frustration in an attempt to find a more satisfying career, or one does this from a position of success and accomplishment in an attempt to find new challenges. On one hand, this pattern differs from the disorderly pattern because there would be only one or two such shifts in an otherwise orderly career. On the other hand, the shift itself distinguishes this pattern from a strictly orderly career. Examples of this pattern include the business executive who switches to government service or the priest who enters a secular career. We expect that such individuals may have entered a career for which they were not suited; they also may be less willing to stick with an unsatisfying job (Wiener & Vaitenas, 1977). They may also be better able to take risks, to face insecurity, and to deal with challenges than the individual who remains in an unsatisfying career (Krantz, 1977).

The Career Clock

Frequently there is a crisis or turning point in the occupational cycle during the middle years. This experience contains elements similar to the issues at the entry point, in that it involves readjusting one's goals and idealistic hopes to what, at this stage, is perceived as one's realistic future possibilities in light of how much time is left in the occupation. An example might be a university professor, hoping to be famous in his field and to contribute great books, who decided, at the age of 50, that he had better begin on his first book if he is ever to write any! This crisis differs from the earlier occupational crisis, however, because it involves what may be called the *career clock*. This "clock" is similar to the "social clock" (Neugarten, 1968); it is the individual's subjective sense of being "on time" or "behind time" in career development. During the middle years (approximately 40 to 55), many people become aware of the number of years left before retirement and of the speed with which they are attaining their goals (recall the discussion of the midlife transition in Chapter 3). If they are markedly "behind time," or if their goals are unrealistic, they begin to adjust their goals to be more consistent with what is likely to be actually feasible; they may also decide to change jobs "before it is too late." Very little attention has been given to women's occupational cycle; while we might expect different patterns and issues for single, married, divorced and widowed women, so far research has focused on these issues only for males.

Men perceive a close relationship between life-line and career-line. Middle age is the time to take stock. Any disparity noted between career-expectations and career achievements—that is, whether one is "on time" or "late" in reaching career goals—adds to the heightened awareness of age. One 47-year-old lawyer said, "I moved at age forty-five from a large corporation to a law firm. I got out at the last possible moment, because after forty-five it is too difficult to find the job you want. If you haven't made it by then, you had better make it fast, or you are stuck" [Neugarten, 1967, p. 96].

In addition to the growing introspection involved in this period of taking stock and reassessment of career goals, Neugarten also found a sense of mastery, competence, and control in her sample of middle-aged male business executives. Often successful men at this point in their career report a highly developed decision-making ability, built from experience in similar situations over a period of years; a prevailing theme is a sense of "maximum capacity and ability to handle a highly complex environment and a highly differentiated self. Very few express a wish to be young again" (Neugarten, 1967, p. 97).

Once again, we see the changes in the self very much involved in these events of the middle years of the occupational cycle. There is the effect of experience very much in evidence, as we discussed in Chapter 2. And there is *I*'s ability to take the attitude of the generalized other involved in the career clock—noting when it is the "right time" to change jobs or obtain a promotion if one is to reach one's goals. But also, the process of selecting another job, or gaining the training and resocialization involved in a promotion such as from machinist to shop foreman, involves changes in the *me* and the active processes of *I* in selecting and integrating these changes in the self. In general, every step up a career ladder, or every job change that involves any resocialization, as well as every promotion that also involves moving to a new community, involves changes in the self. And *I* and *me* aspects of the self are always involved in these changes.

Of course, the career clock may also be involved in timing the milestones of career development (such as promotions and major advances); but it is less clear whether the career clock is a meaningful concept for understanding disorderly patterns of work history or whether its usefulness is limited to orderly careers. We might speculate that the awareness of age and of having little time left to work would increase for individuals with disorderly patterns during this middle-age period as well. The possibility of acquiring another job if one is laid off becomes more and more difficult as one approaches retirement age, since employers are hesitant to hire a person who may need to be retrained and who may receive a company pension but can only work for 10 or 15 years. Thus, the potential for an emotional crisis during this middle period of the occupation may be at least as great for the disorderly pattern as it is for the orderly career, especially if the change is "off time"—such as early forced retirement or being laid off and unable to find work at 55 or 60. Also, it is likely that a dramatic midcareer shift— such as giving up a job in management in an urban area and moving to a small city to become a farmer or construction worker—would also be a significant crisis, even if it was a chosen one; it also often involves marital disruption that probably increases the emotional crisis (Krantz, 1977).

In the next section, we will focus on the conclusion of the work cycle: the milestone of retirement.

RETIREMENT: A MAJOR MILESTONE

Retirement is a major turning point in adult development since it is the social milestone marking the shift from the middle years to old age. It may be seen as a transition point, similar to the transition point at puberty, but reflecting the increased importance of social factors in adulthood over the biological factors that are so important in the younger years. Retirement also marks the end of work and the beginning of a period of relative leisure. Thus, there are three relatively distinct aspects to the phenomenon of retirement: retirement as an event, the retired status, and the process of retiring (Carp, 1966). Each will be discussed, with the retirement process receiving the greatest attention.

Retirement as an Event

Retirement is partly an event that marks a transition point. Because of Social Security legislation in 1935, retirement has usually been placed at age 65. This age was apparently first selected by Otto Von Bismark who was the first chancellor of the German Empire and was instrumental in creating an Old Age and Survivors Pension Act in 1889 (House Committee on Aging, 1977). However, as a result of a variety of economic incentives for early retirement today, many people retire before age 65; and, in some occupations, workers become eligible to retire after 30 years of service. In 1976, the average age of retirement was 58.2 and, in 1974, almost three out of four retirees under Social Security retired before age 65 (ibid.). Considering only male retirees, nearly half accepted Social Security benefits between age 62 and 64 in 1975 (Burkhauser & Tolley, 1978). Economic incentives for retirement by age 65 are especially strong under the present structure of Social Security.

Consider a married worker, age 65, earning $12,000 per year who is entitled to average Social Security benefits of $4900 [1975 average, adjusted by legislated cost of living increases to 1978]. Monthly benefits are increased by only 1% (this will increase to 3% in 1981) for each year that acceptance is postponed after age 65, which is far below an accruably fair rate of return. Continuing to work for a year would mean that most of these benefits are lost. Acceptance while still working subjects him to the Social Security work test. By continuing to work, he loses $4500 in Social Security benefits. In addition, he must pay federal and state income tax on his earnings (Social Security benefits are tax free). Such a worker faces a true average tax rate of about 50%, and a marginal tax rate of almost 75% on each additional hour worked. This means that out of the last dollar earned by an older worker, he would take home only 25 cents. This rate of taxation is greater than that faced by even the upper end of younger wage and salary workers. If he is eligible for a private pension, which is now the case for nearly half the men age 65, any benefits from the private pension are lost. If his pension amounts to only 25% of current salary, he loses an additional $3000. It is not surprising that an older worker reacts to such powerful anti-work incentives by retiring [Burkhauser & Tolley, p. 450].

As a result of these economic factors, a disproportionate burden is placed on younger workers; not only does continued funding of the Social Security program require sharp increases in worker's payments into the system, but it has also been estimated that the average work week would be two to three hours shorter today if it was not for the transfer of work from the later years to the younger years (ibid.).

To partially offset these trends and to allow those older workers who wish to continue working to do so, the minimum legal age for mandatory retirement was raised to 70 for most, but not all, employees beginning in 1979. Social Security benefits still begin at age 65 (or at age 62 for reduced benefits), and all persons become entitled to Medicare coverage at age 65 (see Chapter 9). Thus, without restructuring the Social Security system, it does not seem likely that there will be much increase in the proportion of workers over the age of 65. In 1975, 22 percent of men and 8 percent of women over 65 were working (U.S. Bureau of Labor Statistics, 1977, Table 61); these rates have not declined since 1950 for women, but are about half of the 1950 rates for men (U.S. Bureau of the Census, 1973).

Because of rising life expectancy in the United States, most individuals now reach retirement age and move into a period of retirement that is also lasting longer today than in the past (Figure 6.4). Since the birth rate has declined and the post-World War II "baby boom" will reach age 65 at the turn of the century, our society will have to rethink the relation between work and retirement (Sheppard & Rix, 1977).

Retirement as a transition point, as a rite of passage from one social position to another, may be celebrated publicly with a banquet and a token of appreciation.

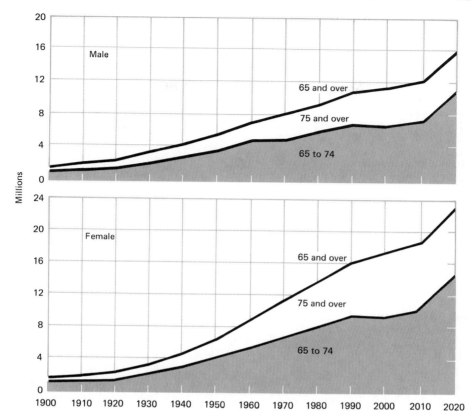

Figure 6.4

Growth of population 65 years and over, 1900 to 2020. (Source: U.S. Bureau of the Census, 1973, cover.)

The event may even be noted in the trade or union journal. But, more often than not, retirement occurs unceremoniously and is not noted as an item of public interest. Thus, retirement tends to be a social event without a precise social meaning; instead, its meaning must be understood within the social life-space of the individual (Maddox, 1966).

This social ambivalence about retirement was clear in the attitudes expressed in a nationwide study. Nearly half of the persons over 65 who were not working said they looked forward to retirement (48 percent); but almost as many did not look forward to it (45 percent); black persons and retirees who had lower incomes were less likely to look forward to it than white or middle-income persons (National Council on the Aging, 1975). Many reported they missed something about working, usually the income and their friends at work (Table 6.4). Eighty-six percent of all persons in the study (both those under and over 65) felt no one should be forced to retire (ibid.).

Table 6.4   Things Retired People 65 and Over Missed about Their Jobs

	Missed	Did Not Miss	Not Sure	One Thing Missed Most
The money it brings in	74%	24%	2%	28%
The people at work	73	25	2	28
The work itself	62	36	2	10
The feeling of being useful	59	38	3	11
Things happening around you	57	39	4	5
The respect of others	50	45	5	2
Having a fixed schedule every day	43	54	3	4

Source: National Council on the Aging (1975), p. 218. Copyright © 1975. Reprinted with permission.
Base: Sixty-nine percent of the public 65 and over who are "retired" or "unemployed."

Since an understanding of retirement involves not only the influence of the event itself but also characteristics of the individual and his or her situation, it is important to examine the biological, sociocultural, and psychological factors in retirement.

Biological Factors

Although the biological changes associated with aging will be discussed in detail in Chapter 7, the effects of physical health clearly affect the retirement process. The most obvious of these factors is whether poor health is the cause of retirement. Among those men who began receiving Social Security benefits in the latter half of 1969, 43 percent had health-related work limitations; for those who began receiving benefits at age 62, 61 percent had health-related limitations (Rubin, 1976). Health problems were also significant for women who retired—one-third reported that health was the reason for leaving their last job (Reno, 1976). In contrast, only 27 percent of the men and 45 percent of the women reported that they retired on their own initiative (Social Security Administration, 1976, Tables 4.7 and 7.11). An extreme example of retirement hindered by health would be persons so incapacitated by poor health that they could neither find a part-time job nor enjoy travel and recreation during retirement. More often, retirement for health reasons indicates an inability to continue the old kind of work full-time, but may allow a reasonably full participation in other activities at least during the early years of retirement.

Clearly, biological decline may be a major factor in a person's ability to find satisfaction in retirement; and disease is the major factor in biological decline associated with age (Birren, Butler, Greenhouse, Sokoloff, & Yarrow, 1963). If there is no disease, there are relatively few changes with age, although decrements in vision, hearing, and trust in one's body are frequently reported even in the absence of apparent disease. However, evidence on changes related to age and the way in which the changes affect productivity indicates little decline in the occupational performance of older workers. While there may be some decrease in problem-solving efficiency and in learning tasks, there is minimal loss in general intellectual ability (Baugher, 1978). Since those older persons who continue working are likely to be a select sample of older persons, there is no reason to assume that they will be less productive than younger workers and they may, in fact, be more productive.

In the future, medical progress will likely achieve a clearer separation between the time of onset of disease and retirement so that these events will not be interrelated. Only a generation ago, retirement was far less common because many persons died before reaching retirement age. So perhaps in another generation, retirement will seldom be influenced by disease and failing health in the way in which it often is today.

Sociocultural Factors

The meaning of retirement for the individual is also affected, to a large degree, by social variables and by the cultural definition of the meaning of retirement. For example, the individual's preretirement attitudes about retirement, willingness to retire, the effect of the decrease in income after retirement, and changes in the person's self-perception after retirement are some of the dimensions that are likely to affect the meaning and experience of retirement.

A major study of retirement—the Cornell Study of Occupational Retirement (Streib & Schneider, 1971)—explored these questions in a longitudinal study of persons nearing retirement age in the 1950s. They obtained a group of 1486 men and 483 women living in the 48 continental states; the respondents represented a wide variety of occupations and all social classes except the lowest. While the respondents were not entirely representative of all retiring persons in the country, the longitudinal design allowed them to explore important aspects of the process of retirement.

In general, Streib and Schneider found that both men and women with higher incomes, higher education, and higher status occupations continued working longer than others, and that persons who indicated they were "willing to retire" did, in fact, retire earlier than persons who were "reluctant to retire." Somewhat more surprising, however, they found that women tended to be less willing to retire than men, and that single or married women tended to retire earlier than widowed or divorced women. These complex patterns reinforce the idea that retirement can be understood only in terms of the life-space of the individual. Apparently, since the women generally had more education and a higher proportion in professional occupations than the men in the study, they were less eager to retire. Single or married women could plan for retirement better than divorced or widowed women, so they were more likely to retire earlier than divorced or widowed women.

Over half of the respondents reported a drop in income—about a 50 percent reduction from preretirement levels on the average for the entire group. Yet, the group reporting a decline in income was about twice as large as the group that reported that their postretirement income was "inadequate." Thus, a sizable ma-

jority found that their income was sufficient to meet their needs—however, most
did not have to face the economic drain of physical illness, which is likely to occur in later years of retirement. Perhaps a cohort-historical factor is also operating in their perception of having an adequate income, since they lived through
the Depression and may well be more economically secure than they were earlier in their lives.

Contrary to the notion that retirement is equated with "old age" in the minds
of retiring persons, there was no indication of any age-related change in the *self*
at the point of retirement beyond that which occurred in persons of the same age
who did not retire at that point. Although there was an increase in feelings of
"uselessness" at the point of retirement for some persons, over three-fourths did
not report feelings of uselessness. There was a tendency for persons who continued working to feel more useful than those who retired, but this may reflect part
of the reason they continued working. There was no difference between feelings
of "satisifcation with life" for persons who retired and persons who did not, nor
was there any consistent change in psychological health for persons who retired.

Those respondents who retired earlier tended to be more satisfied with retirement than the respondents who retired later, but the respondents' prior attitudes
about retirement ("willingness to retire") seemed more important for statisfaction
in retirement than whether the retirement was "voluntary" or "forced" by admin-
istrative regulations (and, as noted above, was associated with earlier retirement).

In sum, there was little evidence of a wide range of negative consequences
that are typically thought to be associated with retirement in the data provided by
these respondents.

> The cessation of the work role results in a sharp reduction in income, but
> there is no significant increase in "worry" about money in the impact year of
> retirement. There is no sharp decline in health, feelings of usefulness, or
> satisfaction in life after retirement. Neither do respondents suddenly think of
> themselves as "old" when they stop working [Streib & Schneider, 1971,
> p. 163].

These findings have been supported in more recent studies of retirement as
well. For example, in one study of 1486 retired persons (Kimmel, Price &
Walker, 1978), health was the major factor predicting retirement satisfaction;
preretirement attitude about retiring was the second most predictive characteristic of satisfaction in retirement. Whether the person retired voluntarily or not was
also important; voluntary retirees were likely to have higher income, higher
occupation, and higher health status, to have more positive feelings about retirement, and greater family support for retiring than nonvoluntary retirees. Voluntary retirees also had more positive attitudes about retirement and higher retirement satisfaction than those who did not retire voluntarily.

In general, retired persons seem to adapt to their change in roles and to tolerate
the negative aspects that may be associated with the retired status in our society

in much the same way that they probably adapted to the earlier changes they experienced. It may be that the changes associated with retirement are different from the changes associated with earlier milestones (such as puberty, entry into the occupation, or grandparenthood) but are not necessarily more devastating. After all, retired persons are "survivors" in an important sense—they have survived all kinds of social changes, milestones, crisis points, and personal difficulties earlier in their lives—so that retirement, like menopause, is only another of the transitions that survivors cope with. Also, persons who are willing to retire and look forward to it may find a number of positive satisfactions in it. One of Streib and Schneider's (1971) respondents said:

> I take it easy. But I keep busy—a man has to do something. I cut the grass, and pull the weeds. I monkey around—keep reading. I like to read the Reader's Digest. I take a walk—go one and a half miles. Then sometimes I go fishing with a couple of fishing partners—I went three times this year to an inland lake. I watch the ball games every night on TV. I walk over to my daughters' houses three or four times a week and see them and their families. We all go on picnics sometimes [p. 113].

Of course, there may be important changes in this retirement process that make it more traumatic for some individuals. For example, if retirement is the final step in a progressive, sequential career line in which the individual retires with a sense of completion, it may be more satisfying than if it occurs in a disorderly work pattern by the inability to find another job once the last one is lost. In the latter case, retirement may be an experience of great frustration, without a clear event or period of transition, without a sense of completion, and possibly at an early age.

The interaction of retirement and the family relationships is also important. For example, if the spouse is living, retirement will thrust the couple into a more intense, full-time relationship than they have probably experienced for many years. Although Deutscher (1964) and others have reported that these postparental years are very happy years for couples in general, it may also be a difficult period for some. In either case, C. S. Lewis in *The Screwtape Letters* is probably accurate in noting that "when two humans have lived together for many years, it usually happens that each has tones of voice and expressions of face which are almost unendurably irritating to the other" (Lewis, 1943). An additional family issue for the retiring man is that he is leaving his world of work and is entering and spending much of his time in what has been his wife's realm—at least in the tradition family pattern. Is she going to be willing to share her domestic roles and duties with him, and will he accept them as meaningful for himself? Alternatively, if the wife continues working after the husband retires (or retains a range of community activities), the shifts in family roles for both spouses may provide an added source of potential upset to this developmental turning point.

One of the most important implications of studies on retirement is the importance of preretirement planning—or anticipatory socialization—for the new set of roles that one will occupy when the work roles are no longer present. In our studies of retirement, we suggested that preretirement counseling focus particular emphasis on health monitoring and maintenance and on attitudes about retirement, since these were clearly related to later retirement satisfaction (Kimmel et al., 1978). This planning probably should also involve many aspects, such as planning for a reliable source of income after retirement, anticipating the kinds of roles and activities that would be desirable and are available in the family and community, developing a few interests that may deepen into satisfying leisure pursuits (and possibly provide a new circle of friends to help replace those one is leaving at the job), and generally raising one's level of consciousness about retirement. Since this process takes some time, it should begin a decade or two before retirement.

In sum, retirement is a major social shift for an individual, but it does not necessarily involve a major physchosocial crisis. It clearly involves a process of anticipation and adjustment but, in general, the meaning of retirement reflects a complex array of social and cultural factors that reflect one's unique life situation and also one's perception of the social meaning of retirement. Let us now turn our attention to the more personal perceptions of retirement and consider some of the psychological factors involved in the retirement process.

Psychological Factors

In the Erikson framework, retirement may frequently trigger the transition between Generativity versus Stagnation and Integrity versus Despair. Thus, the evaluation of one's contribution in the occupation and in the family gains importance as a crucial issue at the point of retirement. The sense of satisfaction, the sense of having produced meaningful products, and the sense of accomplishment in the occupation (as well as in the family) are therefore likely to become important sources of a sense of integrity during this stage of life. Conversely, a sense of stagnation and of frustration will increase the difficulty of this stage. But, of course, the possibility for generativity does not end at retirement, particularly with the current lengthening of the retirement period; nor is the issue of Integrity versus Despair suddenly important only after retirement. Instead, these two stages of the life cycle overlap; only the relative emphasis on generativity or integrity distinguishes one stage from the other. As other events occur during this period, the importance of the issues involved in Integrity versus Despair increases. These events include the growing awareness of death as something personally relevant; some friends may have died, one's spouse may be ill or deceased, and one's health may be failing. There may be extended periods of mourning over the loss of a friend or spouse, reawakening old memories that lead to a reevaluation of one's life. In addition, there may be a reduction in the variety of meaningful personal interactions after one no longer sees one's friends at work; the sphere of physical life-space may be shrinking; there may be a change in residence (to a smaller apartment or to a retirement community); and one may need to establish new social relationships and adjust to unfamiliar surrounding. Each of these would be likely to lead to increased introspection and reflection, shifting the developmental focus more and more to the issue of Integrity versus Despair. This introspective process may be called the life review (Butler, 1963) and will be discussed in detail in Chapter 10.

With retirement there is also a shift away from a complex world, in which one may have played an important, decision-making part, to a smaller, less complex life without the same kinds of tasks. However, there are considerable individual differences in the advantages and disadvantages of this change. For example, respondents in a nationwide study expressed very different views about retirement:

> Said a 69-year-old retired skilled craftsman in Glendale, California, with an income of under $3,000: "Younger retirement gives a person more of a chance to get around and see things he couldn't see when he was working, providing he has enough money."
>
> A 66-year-old retired craftsman in Duluth, Minnesota, explained: "Retirement lets you enjoy life, go fishing, continue the hobbies you don't have time for when you work. . . ."
>
> An 80-year-old retired skilled craftsman in Kirkwood, Missouri, felt this way: "I really feel a person should work longer if they can. It gives them something to do. They feel like they have something to live for."
>
> A 78-year-old Mexican-American woman in Goodyear, Arizona, explained why she is opposed to early retirement: "Well, for one thing, I have seen in my family when people retire too early they tend to become useless and unwanted, unproductive. An emotional metamorphosis occurs, where people feel life has now passed them by and they are declining" [National Council on the Aging, 1975, pp. 219–220].

An individual's personality appears to be an important factor in the smoothness of the shift at retirement. Reichard, Livson, and Peterson (1962) reported that three personality types were associated with good adjustment to retirement: (1) *Mature*: They moved easily into retirement and were relatively free of conflict, appeared to accept themselves realistically, and found considerable satisfaction in their activities and personal relationships. They took old age for granted, felt their lives had been rewarding, and made the best of it. (2) *Rocking-Chair Men*: They were generally passive, happy to be free of responsibility and to satisfy their need to be passive in old age. Old age for them brought satisfactions that made up for its disadvantages. (3) *Armored*: These men maintained a complex system of defenses against passivity and helplessness; they appeared to avoid their fear of physical decline and aging by keeping active. In that sense, their defenses served to protect them from their fear of growing old. Reichard et al. also found two types in their group of retired men who adjusted poorly: (1) *Angry Men*: They were bitter because they felt they had failed to achieve their goals, blamed others for their disappointments, and could not accept the fact they were growing old. (2) *Self-Haters*: These men felt their lives were disappointing and that they had failed, but they turned their anger inward and blamed themselves. They were likely to be depressed, especially since growing older increased their sense of worthlessness and inadequacy.

> With the exception of the mature group, many of whom had had difficulties in personal adjustment when they were younger, these personality types appeared to have been relatively stable throughout life. Poor adjustment to aging among the angry men and the self-haters seemed to stem from lifelong personality problems. Similarly, the histories of the armored and rocking-chair groups suggest that their personalities had changed very little throughout their lives [Reichard et al., 1962, p. 171].

These data suggest that an individual's style of personality is relatively enduring and that it affects one's ability to adjust to a developmental turning point such as retirement. The data also suggest that retirement may have different meanings for persons with differing personalities and that a satisfying retirement for some (e.g., the "rocking chair" group) may be quite unpleasant for others (the "armored" who seemed to have to keep active). We will discuss personality and the relationship between personality and life satisfaction among the aged in Chapter 8, but this study sensitizes us to the variety of ways in which individuals differ and to the importance these personality differences may have.

In general, it might be noted that retired persons differ from one another at least as much as younger persons differ from one another. Thus, the personal needs, goals, satisfactions, and coping abilities differ among retired persons just as they do among all persons. Persons involved in planning for the retired should therefore note that a satisfying life-style for one retired person is not necessarily satisfying for another. This implies that the individual's needs, interests, and personality should be considered, respected, and allowed to maximize the variety of roles and styles of retired persons. Ideally, retired persons are able to strive for their most fully human potentials in an environment that supports and encourages their independence and growth.

For many retired persons, their increased nonwork time is often an opportunity for leisure. In the next section, we will look at leisure and consider the question of the relationship between leisure and work, or nonwork time. In addition, as the amount of time spent in retirement, and away from work, during adulthood grows, the importance of an understanding of leisure becomes more and more significant for our society as a whole.

CHANGING LEISURE VALUES

One of the results of the increased productivity of the work force (resulting from automation and other technology) is that there is a greater amount of nonworking time becoming available in our society. For example, Kreps (1966) estimated that men born in 1960 will have nine more years of nonworking time than men born in 1900. She has projected several possible uses of nonworking time from 1965 to 1985 if the per capita gross national product were to remain constant (Table 6.5). In this extreme case, the amount of nonworking time would be sufficient to allow retirement at age 38, or a workweek of 22 hours, or 25 weeks of vacation time a year in 1985. If the nonworking time were invested in education and retraining of the labor force, nearly half of the labor force could be in training each year, or the average amount of lifetime education could be extended by 17.5 years! However, the most likely prospect would be increases in the per capita gross national product as well as some combination of these alternate uses of nonworking time. Thus, shorter workweeks, longer vacations, periodic "sabbatical leaves" for education and retraining, and earlier retirement may all occur together—and may characterize the future work-life of today's young people. Even today with a 40-hour workweek, some occupations are experimenting with four 10-hour work days. Consider for a minute: this is still a 40-hour week, but if it edges down to four 9-hour days, which are essentially three and a half 10-hour days, the amount of working time would *equal* the amount of nonworking time—three and a half days of each a week—in addition to the other 14 hours each day for sleeping, eating, and recreation that is not counted in the three and a half 10-hour days of nonworking time each week.

The obvious question is what will all of this nonworking time mean to individuals in our society? And what will it mean for society? Does it mean additional time to watch television, more time for travel, or increased time for socializing with friends? Will it mean more time spent in education, particpating in the arts, or in community service? As the amount of nonworking time increases, these decisions will be made as each person decides how he or she will spend this time. But society is also involved because it would seem that the socially defined

Table 6.5 Alternative Uses of Potential Nonworking Time

				Education and Training	
Year	Retirement Age	Length of Workweek (hours)	Vacation Time (weeks)	Labor Force Retrained[a] (percent)	Years of Extended Education
1965	65 or over	40	3	—	—
1966	65	39	4	2.9	1.2
1967	63	38	7	5.0	2.4
1968	61	36	7	8.7	3.4
1969	59	36	8	11.1	4.2
1970	57	34	10	13.8	5.1
1975	50	30	16	26.2	9.4
1980	44	25	21	37.2	13.8
1985	38	22	25	45.2	17.5

Source: Adapted from Kreps (1966), Table 1.

[a]Figures are in addition to the number of workers now trained in public and private programs.

meaning of nonworking time will be involved in the individual's decision. That is, will this nonworking time be a valuable blessing that allows individuals to spend their time in ways that, in the past, were only possible for a few upper-class persons who led a life of leisure? Or will it be a time that is irrelevant to social values so that "wasting time" will no longer have negative connotations? Or perhaps it may be seen as a negative, unproductive time that is best used by getting a part-time job or developing an interest in some hobby or activity to prevent idleness and boredom? At present, many persons are using this potential leisure time to get a second job in order to increase their standard of living, or to keep up with inflation.

Thus, it may be apparent that social values are intertwined with the meaning of nonworking time. For example, Pfeiffer and Davis (1971) concluded from a study of middle-class persons (age 46 to 71) that our society is a work-oriented, not a leisure-oriented, society. They found that about 90 percent of the men and 82 percent of the women in their sample would still work if they did not have to work for a living. The respondents also reported that they derived more satisfaction from work than from leisure activities (only 7 to 28 percent derived more satisfaction from leisure). Only a few wanted more free time (about 25 percent); and those men who were working said they had "more fun" recently than those who were not working. It is especially interesting that in the cohort that will soon have much more free time (those 61 to 65), 89 percent of the men and 79 percent of the women said they would still work if they did not have to work for a living. And only 20 percent of the men and 22 percent of the women in this cohort felt that leisure provided more satisfaction than work. It would seem that these respondents are approaching a period of increased leisure with little orientation to leisure as a positive activity in its own right.

The high degree of work orientation in our society is somewhat surprising since the actual amount of "free time" per week actually exceeds the amount of work time. Robinson and Converse (1972) surveyed the amount of time spent in various activities in eight European countries, the Soviet Union, and the United States in 1965–1966. The number of hours per day spent working ranged from 5.6 in Bulgaria to 3.7 in West Germany. The number of hours of free time per day ranged from 5.1 in Jackson, Michigan, and Kragujevac, Yugoslavia, to 3.2 in Gyor, Hungary. Time spent sleeping (about 8 hours in all countries) was the only activity that consumed more time than work or free time. In four countries (United States, Belgium, West Germany, and Yugoslavia) the amount of free time exceeded the amount of work time per day (averaged over the 7-day week, of course). In the United States there was about one more hour of free time than work time (Table 6.6).

What is the meaning of *leisure?* Is nonworking time the same as leisure time? Is *free time* the same as leisure time? The literature on leisure emphasizes that leisure is very difficult to define. Suppose a professor is reading a scientific book when she is at home and "not working." Or suppose a business executive goes out to play golf on Saturday morning because he knows a business contact will

Table 6.6   Number of Hours per Day Spent in Work and Free Time in 13 Survey Sites

Site	Work Hours/Day	Free Time Hours/Day[a]
United States (Cities 50,000)	3.8	5.0
United States (Jackson, Mich.)	4.1	5.1
France (6 Cities)	4.2	3.9
Belgium (425 Cities)	4.3	5.0
West Germany (100 Districts)	3.7	4.4
West Germany (Osnabruck)	3.7	4.9
Hungary (Gyor)	5.4	3.2
Poland (Torun)	4.9	4.4
Yugoslavia (Maribor)	4.3	3.6
Yugoslavia (Kragujevac)	4.0	5.1
Bulgaria (Kazanlik)	5.6	3.6
Russia (Pskov)	5.4	4.1
Czechoslovakia (Olomouc)	4.9	3.9

Source: Robinson and Converse (1972), Table 1, adapted. Reprinted with permission from *The Human Meaning of Social Change* by Angus Campbell and Philip E. Converse (Eds.), copyright © 1972 by Russell Sage Foundation.

[a]Includes time spent in resting, education, organizations, radio, television, reading, social life, conversation, walking, sports, various leisure, and amusements.

be there. And consider the salesman who "entertains" a customer with dinner and an evening in a night club. Are these examples of leisure—or of some other kind of job-related time? A worker in a plant may come home and watch TV because she is too exhausted from the job and the drive home to do anything else—is this leisure?

Two differing definitions of leisure have evolved in our society as we have become more of a technological society that has, on one hand, provided more time away from work and, on the other hand, caused us to pay more attention to the quality of our lives. One definition of leisure has emphasized the distinction between work and leisure (Kelly, 1972). In this view, pure leisure is a freely chosen activity that is not related to one's work. It reflects the long struggle of the past century to free people from long hours of work and to provide them with greater free time to use as they choose. However, it conflicts with the work-oriented values of our society in which free time is often seen as nonproductive time. In that sense, leisure has a somewhat negative connotation because it is similar to idleness and may in fact be a problem for people who have too much free time—such as retired or unemployed persons. As a result, this view tends to focus on how one "spends" this leisure time and the implicit assumption is that it should be spent in productive, but not work-related, ways. This perspective also does not allow the possibility that one might be able to merge leisure with work to enhance the quality of work time as well as leisure time.

An alternative perspective on leisure, proposed by Neulinger (1980), does not define leisure in terms of its relation to work or nonwork time. Instead of focusing on free time, Neulinger focuses on the quality of life that our technological society has made possible. Leisure, in this view, is a state of mind, defined by two interrelated dimensions. The first dimension is the perceived freedom, which is on a continuum from freedom to constraint in the activity he or she is engaged in at any given moment. The second is the motivation the person experiences that leads to engaging in that activity. The motivational dimension is also a continuum from intrinsic (activities engaged in for the satisfaction of the activity itself) to extrinsic (activities engaged in for the external rewards they provide, such as money, prestige, success, etc.). For simplicity, the model is presented in six cells reflecting each of the four possible extreme types and two types of mixed intrinsic and extrinsic motivation (Figure 6.5). Thus, pure leisure is the extreme type reflecting perceived freedom of choice about the activity and intrinsic motivation. Neulinger also uses two different words for the occupation: the *job* is an activity one performs because one has to do it, and it provides no reward in itself but only some extrinsic payoff; *work* is an activity one performs because one has

Perceived Freedom					
Freedom			Constraint		
M o t i v a t i o n			M o t i v a t i o n		
Intrinsic	Intrinsic and extrinsic	Extrinsic	Intrinsic	Intrinsic and extrinsic	Extrinsic
(1)	(2)	(3)	(4)	(5)	(6)
Pure leisure	Leisure work	Leisure job	Pure work	Work-job	Pure job

←————————————— State of Mind —————————————→

Figure 6.5
A psychological paradigm of leisure. (Source: Neulinger, 1976b, Table 2. Adapted and reprinted with permission.)

to do it, but it does provide a high degree of intrinsic motivation because the activity itself is personally satisfying to the individual. The other cells in the model are combinations of these three extreme types of activities and probably reflect the actual experience of most people most of the time; the extreme experiences of pure leisure, pure work, or pure job are probably fairly brief for most of us. The emphasis in the model is on the individual's state of mind, or experience of the activity. In that sense, Neulinger sees it as a psychological model of leisure in contrast to the sociological model proposed by Kelly that emphasizes classifying time periods rather than the individual's experience.

One of the most interesting aspects of Neulinger's model of leisure is that is not only allows, but encourages, the merger of one's leisure and occupaton.

> Since leisure is no longer defined in contrast to work, it is no longer the opposite of a positive value; there is no longer a struggle between leisure and work, but rather a coexistence [Neulinger, 1976b, p. 17].

Moreover, leisure in this model is not something one has or does not have, but, instead, it is something one *is*; it is a state of mind, an experience that one can achieve given the right conditions (*perceived freedom* and *intrinsic motivation*). In Neulinger's view, some of us, or perhaps all of us, may need to learn how to achieve this state, either through leisure counseling or through education.

> Education for leisure . . . means to promote the conditions, within the person and within the environment, that will bring about a certain state of mind. It is a state where one fulfills oneself and feels fulfilled; it is a state where one "works" with something one really likes to do; where things are done with enthusiasm, with joy, without haste or hurry, without undue pressure. . . . Leisure, conceived of in this way, takes on a high value, practical, moral, esthetic, and even religious. It is an ideal which we can never fully achieve, but which we can strive for [Neulinger, 1976a, p. 4].

The challenge of this view of leisure is to discover those activities that are intrinsically satisfying to the individual, that can be realistically chosen, and that enhance the quality of life for the individual and perhaps, in an ideal sense, the quality of life for others as well. It does not suggest irresponsible self-indulgence, but instead implies greater self-knowledge about the ways in which one may fill one's productive life with leisure. This is very different from filling one's free time.

The anticipated increase in nonworking time will interact with the family and with the occupation. That is, individuals now have the possibility of an additional source of satisfaction and meaning in their lives beyond that provided by the job or the family. A large part of this new leisure may initially involve families, community participation in athletics, social or cultural activities, and hobbies or recreation. However, not everyone may find satisfaction in these activities, particularly as the amount of free time continues to grow. Instead, the frustrations of an increasingly automated, routine job, poverty, or an unsatisfying family life may only be compounded by excessive free time. More optimistically, it may be that greater leisure will lead to new forms of community and new styles of community participation as well as greater integration of leisure with work that will improve the quality of life—including schools, natural resources, and the world of work. The essential question is whether the increase in free time will become a source of growth and fulfillment that allows individuals to actualize their human potentials to the fullest. The challenge implicit in that question is whether we will be able to develop the conditions necessary for leisure in our society, and whether these will be available to all persons or only to those who also have good jobs and good educations.

We will now turn to the second interview with Murray. Six years after the first interview, we find that the major concerns in his life have shifted from his family to his work. In the next chapter, we will discuss biological and intellectual processes of aging as we begin to shift our focus to the later years of adulthood.

CHAPTER SUMMARY

1. During the middle years, involvement in one's family and career is a major source of a sense of identity providing one a sense of being intimately involved with others as well as a sense of being productive.
2. Family responsibilities and the occupational role together may be seen as a system of mutually interacting sources of satisfaction and frustration that can add to or compensate for success or failure in either sphere. For example, a person who feels stuck in a nonrewarding job may put more energy into family life as a source of satisfaction and success, whereas a person with an unhappy family life may turn to the career for personal satisfaction.
3. Women currently comprise 41 percent of the nation's labor force. The increase in white working women over the past few decades has resulted from a number of reasons; the most important has been the availability of birth control and family planning that has given women more control over their lives.
4. During the last decade, there have been significant changes in the proportion of women in some occupations, but some remain limited primarily to women or to men.
5. Women earn only 60 percent of the income men earn. This earnings gap results in part from a dual labor market that tends to keep women in low-paying jobs that offer little opportunity for advancement.
6. The most dramatic change in women's employment has been the increase in the proportion of mothers entering the work force. High proportions of black mothers have worked in the past and still do, but

today more white and Hispanic mothers are also working. Today, half of all women with children under 18 are in the labor force.

7. Over 40 percent of all women living with their husbands are in the labor force. Working women in dual-career families are likely to have more power in the marital relationship, while their husbands have an increased responsibility for household duties.

8. The process by which an individual chooses a career involves a process of socialization that begins during childhood; many influences affect occupational choice, including one's background, role models, experience, interests, and personality.

9. Entering the job requires resocialization and is a crucial point in the life cycle, not only because it marks the transition into adult status and a shift in roles, but also because it may involve a major shift in one's *self*.

10. Most people change occupations at least once; midlife occupational change is not uncommon, and few people remain in one occupation all of their working lives.

11. We can recognize three patterns of the occupational cycle—the orderly career, the disorderly work history, and the sudden change in occupations.

12. The career clock, one's sense of being "on time" or "behind time" in career development, plays an important role in an individual's attainment of career goals.

13. Although the age of retirement has recently been raised from 65 to 70, in fact, most people retire before age 65 because of financial advantages in early retirement. Because of earlier retirement and greater longevity, the period of retirement is lasting longer today than in the past.

14. Biological factors such as poor health and physical decline affect one's level of satisfaction in retirement. Sociocultural factors—such as the individual's preretirement attitudes about retirement, whether one retires voluntarily or nonvoluntarily, and the interaction of retirement and family relations—may also influence one's satisfaction with retirement.

15. Three personality types have been associated with good adjustment to retirement: the mature, the rocking-chair, and the armored types; two personality types have been associated with poor adjustment to retirement: the angry men and the self-haters.

16. Advances in technology, resulting in the greater productivity of the work force, have increased the amount of nonworking time available; yet, our society remains work-oriented rather than leisure-oriented. Leisure may be defined as a freely chosen activity that is unrelated to work, or as a state of mind, defined by two interrelated dimensions of perceived freedom and intrinsic motivation.

REFERENCES

Bahr, Stephen J. 1974. Effects on Power and Division of Labor in the Family. In Lois Wladis Hoffman, F. Ivan Nye, & Associates (Eds.), *Working Mothers: An Evaluative Review of Consequences for Wife, Husband, and Child.* San Francisco: Jossey-Bass.

Baugher, Dan. 1978. Is the Older Worker Inherently Incompetent? *Aging and Work*, (Fall), 243–250.

Birren, James E.; Butler, Robert N.; Greenhouse, Samuel W.; Sokoloff, Louis; & Yarrow, Marian R. (Eds.). **1963.** *Human Aging: A Biological and Behavioral Study.* Publication No. (HSM) 71-9051. Washington, D.C.: U.S. Government Printing Office.

Bolles, Richard Nelson. 1972. *What Color Is Your Parachute: A Practical Manual for Job-Hunters & Career-Changers.* Berkeley, Calif.: Ten Speed Press.

Brown, Claude. 1965. *Manchild in the Promised Land.* New York: Macmillan.

Burkhauser, Richard V., & Tolley, G. S. 1978. Older Americans and Market Work. *The Gerontologist, 18*(5), 449–453.

Butler, Robert N. 1963. The Life Review: An Interpretation of Reminiscence in the Aged. *Psychiatry, 26*(1), 65–76.

Carp, Frances M. 1966. Background and Statement of Purpose. In Frances M. Carp (Ed.), *The Retirement Process.* U.S. Department of Health, Education and Welfare. PHS Publication No. 1778. Washington, D.C.: U.S. Government Printing Office.

Cicourel, Aaron V., & Kitsuse, John I. 1968. The Social Organization of the High School and Deviant Adolescent Careers. In Earl Rubington & Martin S. Weinberg (Eds.), *Deviance: The Interactionist Perspective.* New York: Macmillan.

Conger, John Janeway. 1977. *Adolescence and Youth* (2nd ed.). New York: Harper & Row.

Deutscher, Irwin. 1964. The Quality of Postparental Life. *Journal of Marriage and the Family, 26*(1), 263–268.

Duncan, Otis Dudley. 1961. A Socioeconomic Index for All Occupations. In Albert J. Reiss, Jr., et al. *Occupations and Social Status.* New York: Free Press.

Erikson, Erik H. 1968. *Identity: Youth and Crisis.* New York: W. W. Norton.

Farkas, George. 1976. Education, Wage Rates, and the Division of Labor Between Husband and Wife. *Journal of Marriage and the Family, 38*(3), 473–483.

Hall, Douglas T. 1976. *Careers in Organization.* Pacific Palisades, Calif.: Goodyear.

Henry, William E. 1965. Identity and Diffusion in Professional Actors. Paper presented at the meeting of the American Psychological Association, September, 1965.

Henry, William E.; Sims, John H.; & Spray, S. Lee. 1971. The Fifth Profession: Becoming a Psychotherapist. San Francisco: Jossey-Bass.

Hoffman, Lois Wladis. 1974a. Effects of Maternal Employment On the Child: A Review of the Research. *Developmental Psychology, 10*(2), 204–228.

Hoffman, Lois Wladis. 1974b. Employment of Women and Fertility. In Lois Wladis Hoffman, F. Ivan Nye, & Associates (Eds.), *Working Mothers: An Evaluative Review of Consequences for Wife, Husband, and Child.* San Francisco: Jossey-Bass.

Holland, John L. 1973. *Making Vocational Choices: A Theory of Careers.* Englewood Cliffs, N.J.: Prentice-Hall.

House Committee on Aging. 1977. *Mandatory Retirement: The Social and Human Cost of Enforced Idleness.* (U.S. House of Representatives, Select Committee on Aging.) Washington, D.C.: U.S. Government Printing Office.

Janowitz, Morris. 1965. *Sociology and the Military Establishment (Rev. ed.).* New York: Russell Sage Foundation.

Kelly, John R. 1972. Work and Leisure: A Simplified Paradigm. *Journal of Leisure Research,* 4(1), 50-62.

Kimmel, Douglas C.; Price, Karl F.; & Walker, James W. 1978. Retirement Choice and Retirement Satisfaction. *Journal of Gerontology, 33*(4), 575-585.

Kohen, Andrew I. 1975. Occupational Mobility Among Middle-Aged Men. In U.S. Department of Labor, Manpower R & D Monograph 15, *The Pre-Retirement Years, Volume 4: A Longitudinal Study of the Labor Market Experience of Men.* Washington, D.C.: U.S. Government Printing Office (Stock # 029-00237-1).

Krantz, David L. 1977. The Santa Fe Experience. In Search of a New Life: Radical Career Change in a Special Place. In Seymour B. Sarason, *Work, Aging, and Social Change: Professionals and the One Life — One Career Imperative.* New York: Free Press.

Kreps, Juanita M. 1966. The Allocation of Leisure to Retirement. In Frances M. Carp (Ed.), *The Retirement Process.* U.S. Department of Health, Education and Welfare. PHS Publication No. 1778. Washington, D.C.: U.S. Government Printing Office.

Lewis, C.S. 1943. *The Screwtape Letters.* New York: Macmillan.

Maddox, George L. 1966. Retirement as a Social Event in the United States. In John C. McKinney & Frank T. deVyver (Eds.), *Aging and Social Policy.* New York: Appleton-Century-Crofts.

National Council on the Aging. 1975. *The Myth and Reality of Aging in America.* (Conducted by Louis Harris & Associates, Inc.) Washington, D.C.: National Council on the Aging, Inc.

Neugarten, Bernice L. 1967. The Awareness of Middle Age. In Bernice L. Neugarten (Ed.), *Middle Age and Aging.* Chicago: University of Chicago Press, 1968. (Originally published in: *Middle Age.* Roger Owen, Ed. London: British Broadcasting Corporation.)

Neugarten, Bernice L. 1968. Adult Personality: Toward a Psychology of the Life Cycle. In Bernice L. Neugarten (Ed.), *Middle Age and Aging.* Chicago: University of Chicago Press.

Neugarten, Bernice L., & Moore, Joan W. 1968. The Changing Age-Status System. In Bernice L. Neugarten (Ed.), *Middle Age and Aging.* Chicago: University of Chicago Press.

Neulinger, John. 1976a. An Issue of Attitude Change. *Leisure Today,* (March), 4-5.

Neulinger, John. 1976b. The Need for and the Implications of a Psychological Conception of Leisure. *The Ontario Psychologist, 8*(2), 13-20.

Neulinger, John. 1980. To Leisure: An Introduction. Boston: Allyn & Bacon.

Nye, F. Ivan. 1974a. Husband-Wife Relationship. In Lois Wladis Hoffman, F. Ivan Nye, & Associates (Eds.), *Working Mothers: An Evaluative Review of Consequences for Wife, Husband, and Child.* San Francisco: Jossey-Bass.

Nye, F. Ivan. 1974b. Sociocultural Context. In Lois Wladis Hoffman, F. Ivan Nye, & Associates (Eds.), *Working Mothers: An Evaluative Review of Consequences for Wife, Husband, and Child.* San Francisco: Jossey-Bass.

Pfeiffer, Eric, & Davis, Glenn C. 1971. The Use of Leisure Time in Middle Life. *Gerontologist, 11*(3, Part 1), 187–195.

Reichard, Suzanne; Livson, Florine; & Peterson, Paul G. 1962. *Aging and Personality.* New York: Wiley.

Reno, Virginia. 1976. Retired Women Workers. In Social Security Administration, *Reaching Retirement Age: Findings from a Survey of Newly Entitled Workers 1968–70.* Washington, D.C.: U.S. Government Printing Office (Stock #017-070-00287-1).

Robinson, John P., & Converse, Philip E. 1972. Social Change Reflected in the Use of Time. In Angus Campbell & Philip E. Converse (Eds.), *The Human Meaning of Social Change.* New York: Russell Sage Foundation.

Rubin, Leonard. 1976. Disabling Health Conditions Among Men. In Social Security Administration, *Reaching Retirement Age: Findings from a Survey of Newly Entitled Workers 1968–70.* Washington, D.C.: U.S. Government Printing Office (Stock #017-070-00287-1).

Sarason, Seymour B. 1977. *Work, Aging, and Social Change: Professionals and the One Life—One Career Imperative.* New York: Free Press.

Sexton, Patricia Cayo. 1977. *Women and Work* (R & D Monograph 47, U.S. Department of Labor). Washington, D.C.: U.S. Government Printing Office (Stock #029-000-00285-1).

Sheppard, Harold L., & Rix, Sara E. 1977. *The Graying of Working America: The Coming Crisis of Retirement-Age Policy.* New York: Free Press.

Smith, Mitchell. 1978. Men Hold Top Arts Jobs 2-1. *ACA Reports,* (December), 16–17.

Social Security Administration. 1976. *Reaching Retirement Age: Findings From a Survey of Newly Entitled Workers 1968–70.* Washington, D.C.: U.S. Government Printing Office (Stock #017-070-00287-1).

Sommers, Dixie, & Eck, Alan. 1977. Occupational Mobility in the American Labor Force. *Monthly Labor Review,* (January), 3–19.

Streib, Gordon F., & Schneider, Clement J. 1971. *Retirement in American Society: Impact and Process.* Ithaca, N.Y.: Cornell University Press.

U.S. Bureau of Labor Statistics. 1977. *U.S. Working Women: A Databook.* Washington, D.C.: U.S. Government Printing Office (Stock #029-001-02112-7).

U.S. Bureau of Labor Statistics. 1979. *Employment and Earnings.* Washington, D.C.: U.S. Government Printing Office.

U.S. Bureau of the Census. 1973. Some Demographic Aspects of Aging in the United States. *Current Population Reports,* Series P-23, No. 43. Washington, D.C.: U.S. Government Printing Office.

U.S. Bureau of the Census. 1976. Daytime Care of Children: October 1975 and February 1975. *Current Population Reports,* Series P-20, No. 298. Washington, D.C.: U.S. Government Printing Office.

U.S. Department of Labor. 1976. *The Earnings Gap Between Women and Men.* Washington, D.C.: U.S. Government Printing Office.

U.S. Department of Labor. 1977. *Minority Women Workers: A Statistical Overview.* Washington, D.C.: U.S. Government Printing Office.

Van Dusen, Roxann A., & Sheldon, Eleanor Bernert. 1976. The Changing Status of American Women: A Life Cycle Perspective. *American Psychologist, 31*(2), 106-116.

Wiener, Yoash, & Vaitenas, Rimantas. 1977. Personality Correlates of Voluntary Midcareer Change in Enterprising Occupations. *Journal of Applied Psychology, 62*(6), 706-712.

Wilensky, Harold L. 1961. Orderly Careers and Social Participation: The Impact of Work History on Social Integration in the Middle Mass. *American Sociological Review, 26*(4), 521-539.

Interlude
Murray, Age 54

Murray responded quickly and eagerly to the request for a second interview in 1979. At the age of 54, family issues seem less troubling for him, and his son appears to have changed dramatically, at least from Murray's perspective. But he is still working on many of the issues he discussed in the earlier interview, with the added problem of feeling unhappy in his job. He appears to be facing a major decision about his career, although the idea of making a change is disturbing to him. Much of his life seems to him like it is following a "railroad track." He feels that he must have chosen to follow it but, at the same time, he thinks that there must be more to life than he is experiencing.

Viewing a person at two different points in life often reveals both change and continuity. Does Murray seem different in some ways than he did six years ago? How much of this change has been brought about by growing older. What else has affected it? Is there any evidence of a midlife transition (as discussed in Chapter 3)? What has remained fairly continuous in his outlook on life and his view of himself over these years? Has his attitude about death changed during this period? Why? How do you think things will work out for him in the future?

When we last talked in 1973, you had told me that you had just bought a house and that your son was at that moment expected to be arriving back from Casablanca. My oh my. So much has happened. That was a country house I bought; we had that for about three years. We sold it when my wife decided to go back to work; which she did. . . . My son has turned out to be a great joy. He came back from Casablanca after all the *Sturm und Drang* [Storm and Stress] that was involved around that incident and decided that he would go back to school and stay in the city. Moved away from the nebulous involvement he had in school before, which was actually majoring in nothing, and decided that he was interested in political science and graduated magna cum laude. An amazing turnabout. Not amazing from the point of his intelligence but rather his motivation. *What brought about the change?* It is very difficult to say, except maybe our apprehension was the misguided apprehension that parents have when their offsprings are not "straight" about the mores, that we accept—you know, the traditional mores—you have to be a professional, which is part of our own misconceptions about work and its place in a person's life. He was always interested in politics—less so from the direction that finally developed, which was an intense interest in political systems, but more from a humanistic point of view. He did so well, and of course the interesting thing is . . . if you are fortunate enough to find a professor who's interested, your whole direction can change. I've been on university faculties—I'm on three now, I cut back from five to three—for over twenty years and I know that the professor can really be instrumental in guiding, motivating the direction that some of the students that they have will take. In his case, he found a professor who related to him. He was extremely verbal, my son, and of course that's always a joy to a professor and he became very interested.

He did not come to live with us, which is very interesting. We took the house out in the country; we thought that way he might want to settle down because we had no hopes of his settling down, *per se*. But instead, he took a little apartment downtown and part-time jobs here and there and finished his baccalaureate and then finished his master's. He got married. He married an older woman; older than he . . . maybe seven or eight years older, I think, with two children. Real joys. I had my first grandchild—although I consider both of those my grandchild, both her children by her former marriage—about three years ago. Of course, my wife is ecstatic about it. My wife is the consummate mother, consummate grandmother. My wife's life is filled with concern and love for my son, as mine is, but with the grandchild it's a joy. I think if you go back over the six years, the highlights of our life has been the direction my son has gone. He's taken a job and has done very well. Not a job in an area he likes but of course, when you're a married man you have responsibilities. He's doing it because his wife's going on for her Ph.D. They made a decision—she's finishing her Ph.D. and then he'll go back. So that has turned out to be a real joy for me. . . . My son—amazing turnabout from the Casablanca days, if you will—great father, a wonderful son, a caring son, and a joy.

As far as my career is concerned, I published my fifth book about six months ago and it's a raging success, which is of course, great—because most of my success comes outside of my institution, and that's sad. The institution has changed as I approach my fifty-fifth birthday and I'm finishing my twentieth year at the end of this year. I have to start looking towards critical decisions—what I'm going to do, whether I'm going to stay here or do something else. A sixth book of mine will be out within about two months and I've just received a contract to edit a magnum opus, a collection of writings, which is an unusual undertaking because I like to write myself. I'm not so sure I'm going to enjoy editing other people's material. But that part of my life has been very successful; but that's outside the institution. In the institution itself there's been a revolutionary change in management style. I'm the oldest surviving senior person in the institution, in the administration, and it's a burden. Things have changed so dramatically in the last three years as far as my position in the institution that I have major problems dealing with it—personal problems dealing with it. I'm so used to being accepted that it's hard to fight my way through this new political and managerial environment and that brings me to a very difficult point in my life because I'm unhappy. It's hard [for others] to tell because I don't like to share discontent. It's a major problem I have. I think if I could share my discontent with my wife it would be a lot better, but I guard her from it—and that puts a burden on these days which are filled with thoughts of what else I should be doing with myself as far as my work is concerned. *But you can't discuss the problems . . .* I do, I do, but I temper my discontent which is basically a role I've played all my life. I've always been a pillar of strength, at least that's the role I play. Not that I've been a pillar of strength. So I've come to a critical point in my life; I'm 55, I'll be 55, I had an amazingly successful career, I'm extremely well paid, I have a national reputation, I'm a prolific writer, and I'm unhappy. Not unhappy about those things, but unhappy because I'm unhappy here on a day-to-day situation; that's more real than what's outside. I'm very proud about what I've accomplished, and it gets shot down now because there are new boys on the block. I never resent new boys, I can usually deal very well, but this is a completely different environment. What I'm talking about is a revisionist environment. I'm a historian. I know why things developed in my particular industry in twenty years, and it's just a burden to go back in each case and explain why we're where we are now and what happened then—that was quite different from what is now—and try to rationalize it. I find it very, very debilitating.

My life is very much, unfortunately, on a railroad track; nothing changes. I've given up on the part of my life that led to the crisis that I had many years ago—outside interests from my home. I've been very attentive at home. It's a very even plane and I'm wondering whether that isn't a source of my unhappiness. I doubt it. I *like* stability. . . .

This is a critical point in my life—a milestone if you will, that I put beside the milestones with my son, with my problems in my marriage, prior milestones—and that is to make this decision on where I'm going to go. It isn't easy. I thought it would be easy. It would be easier to do it at the point of my retiring, which I had always thought about possibly doing before the traditional date of 65, you know, somewhere between 60 and 62. But now I'm faced with it, I'm still young. By the way, I have no—it sounds defensive—no midlife crisis or whatever you call it about my age. I'm very comfortable about my age. I don't feel that the young people are inundating me and I never shrink from young people. I'm not deeply concerned about all the pretty young ladies who look at me—that I'm too old or that I have any desires that would make me feel that I want to be younger. I feel that if I have desires, I'm young enough. So, that's not a critical point. I've been trying to get to it, for now it's been a couple of years, because this thing has been coming for a couple of years in the institution. I think it's a matter of my great attention to stability; I live a certain life-style, I have a certain income, and everything is very comfortable. I take care of my son because he has a big family; I help him. I take care of my mother who's in her eighties now and I'm very comfortable about doing that. I don't want to give that up and the very lovely life-style we have. We live very well. My wife working and my working; we have freedom to move around. We don't move around a great deal, but we can if we want to. So I'm really grappling with this and I'm grappling with it alone, which has always been part of my problem—not being able to. . . . Discussing it with you is a relief, very interesting—I haven't been able to put it in place. . . . So, this is a crisis that, unfortunately fills every one of my free moments. I walk to the institution thinking about it. I walk home at the end of the day thinking about it. I go to sleep and I don't sleep as well as I used to sleep, which doesn't bother me, thinking about it. I think what bothers me is that I'm thinking about it so much. It's a crisis I think a lot of people in my situation face. You come to an age where in an institution you are older, 55 doesn't sound very old to me, but you're older, you have a reputation that's probably larger than you deserve and then you find yourself in less than a powerful position, that's that other end of it—power. I've always been enamored of power, even though the power that I've had was always very small power, it was very obvious, and maybe that's what bothers me. I'm not sure. I haven't really put the pieces together. I try to think about the positives; I've got so many positives in my life. I shouldn't be concerned about it. . . .

The rest of your life feels pretty comfortable, it's the work part of your life here in the institution that bothers you? The word comfortable bothers me. I use it a lot. Let me say that I'm at peace with the rest of my life. I don't know, if I weren't so concerned with the omnipresent grappling with what I'm going to do in the next year or so, I might be more concerned with the rest of my life. . . . I still think of myself as young and desirous of adventure and I live a nonadventuresome life. I've always thought that; it's nothing new. And I've always lived a nonadventuresome life. Other people might think it's adventuresome. I'm eclectic, I read a great deal, I'm very, very sensitive to world affairs. I dominate a lot of groups that I speak in, or I speak with, or socialize with, and you would probably get a misconception from the veneer, because I lead a very unadventuresome life. I come home every night; I read my books; I write. People might think that's adventuresome. Really I'm not an adventuresome person. I've got to accept it and I think I'm well on my way to accepting the fact that if I wanted to be adventuresome, really wanted to be, I'd be. I've had the opportunity to be. So it must be that I'm doing what I want to do. I then go back to the discontent in my career. I could remain the compromiser that I've always been in my lfe and stay out my years at this institution. That's a cardinal concern I have now. *Or you could be more adventuresome.* That's right. *I guess that's really the dilemma you're facing.* Always has been my dilemma. I've always opted towards stability. . . .

I've seen so many people who wind up, whatever that means, in their later years saying "I should have, I could have" and I don't know how to escape that. But, if I could have, then I would have done it; and I'm really coming to peace with that aspect of it. No one has stopped me; my wife never stopped me from leaving her. My wife never stopped me from doing anything, and yet there are so many times where you find yourself in a position, at least I do, where I said to myself "if it weren't for my wife," or "if it weren't for my responsibilities"— what does that mean? If it weren't for my being alive, that's what it means. I'm alive and I have options and I can't rationalize them. I very rarely have been in a Hopson's choice situation. I've always had choices. Life to me is constant choices. *By Hopson's choice you mean no choice?* No choice. Hopson's choice. Life to me is choices, it's always been; and I've always opted for the same choice. So there must be something that I'm telling myself and I can't sit back and cry about it. I could have had a more exciting social life, I could have had a more exciting sexual life, I could have had a very, very exciting work life. I could have been more adventuresome about money. But, I've always been very conservative. . . . Being poverty-stricken has always been one of my greatest fears. But I know why. I grew up in the Depression. *The* Depression.

I have that great fear and yet I'm a very opinionated person and I turn people off because I'm cocksure of too many things. And yet I really crave love. It's been the hallmark of my life, to be a good guy. My wife tells me I've succeeded and other people tell me that I've succeeded, but that is an underlying part of the fabric of stability. Stability to me is being accepted, being loved; and it's directed a lot of my decision making. It's a burden. *Your wife, your friends tell you you've succeeded in being a good guy?* Yeah. People think of me as basically a fair person, a caring person. I don't know whether that's good or not, strange to say at this late part of my life story. I think you tend to rationalize a lot of things. . . . I've tended to be maybe too accepting. Not with my wife. We've had constant arguments and debates. She thinks I'm aloof. And from my description you could probably see why that's possible. I'm bookish. I tend to—like at the end of the day—to sit in a chair and read my book or watch a good play or something like that, and less likely to get into idle conversation. Outside the house, social groups, I'm certainly the other extreme from being a wall flower; I'm gregarious. So, I can't think of myself as aloof. I think possibly in such a close relationship as a husband and wife there's a tendency to get into yourself too much and there is a threshold of boredom. There's a threshold of boredom with life, too. So, when I go back to the railroad track that I told you about, you really think, let me put it very, very sharp, maybe too dramatically— you get to a point, if you're a thinking person—not that it's good thinking—that some times you wonder, are you waiting to die. What do I mean by that? Not suicidal, but are you just living out whatever's left for you on the continuum. And that kind of thinking is a very destructive kind of thinking, but I often think of that. Am I letting things just roll down that track—there's a lot of track ahead of me, I don't think that I'm going to die in five years, ten years; I think I have a lot of track; I'm in very good physical condition—deeply concerned about "Should I be on that track or should I be really going over hills?" Shouldn't I be going into valleys and things like that? . . .

I really don't know. I see very little romance in life, in people my own age. Maybe romance is something that's limited to a period of time. *What do you mean by romance?* Oh, the joy of loving, the joy of. . . well, I suppose a lot of romance is sexual as well, but there's a nonsexual part of young romance which is less mature. See there's such a sense of maturity in every thing I do, such a sense of responsibility in everything I do. *It has to be kind of mature . . .* That's right. I think of romance as being immature, irresponsible, but joyful. But again, I always inject a degree of realism into all of this. I'm married over 30 years, give or take the liaisons that I've had in those 30 years. How could you kid yourself about romance in a marriage that's over 30 years old? You can't. And I suppose that that's what I'm talking about when I talk about romance. There it is again, the marriage is on a railroad track: very solid rails, very good locomotive, good motor man. A lot of people think that that's ideal. Interestingly enough, many of my wife's friends and mine are divorced. Amazing, you know, when we go to groups and we tell them we've been married over 30 years, they can't believe it. In today's world marriages don't last very long. A lot of what I'm referring to is not very unique. It's people who are in their fifties, or married a long time, who live typical middle-class lives, maybe with a little more money than some, see the mores of our society changing. They reflect upon their own life. . . . Well, I got married right after World War II and I got married when I was 21 years old. I've always been married! That's another interesting part of looking back and saying I really missed romance and excitement that's going on around us. I've always been married. I can't remember not being married to the same woman. I went to the war as a teenager. I came out of the war—where I was concerned with just living, getting through the war, and coming out alive—and got married right away. I had no five, six, seven years of adult life of nonresponsibility. I always assumed responsibility as quick as I could. Quick as I could. It almost sounds as if I'm saying that it's terrible—I'm really not saying that it's terrible, I'm saying that I have to come to grips, and I have, with the fact that that's my life. I made my life that way. It's something that I must need, that stability. At age 55 I want it to remain stable. I don't want to have to make these choices that I'm facing now. Even knowing intellectually that I'm going to succeed—that's never been the doubt in my mind. But it's the problem of coming from something that's planned—that railroad track that I told you before that I'm concerned about—it seems to be what I want. *But part of you, I guess, also feels that that's kind of unsettling, to think that everything is planned and stable.* I don't know whether it's unsettling; yeah, I think that would be good, unsettling—or maybe I should want more. *Maybe there should be more?* Maybe there should be more, that's better. You stop to think about it, you know; 55 years are behind you, you look forward to 20, so the major part of your years on earth are behind you. Is this the time to be thinking about exciting things or not? And that's the dilemma. I have discussed options with my wife; she would like me to take the burden off my back. She believes we can do anything we want to do. . . . *She's kind of supporting.* . . . Very supportive as far as my happiness is concerned. Extremely supporting. *So, she feels that even if you left your job, that if that made you happy, that would be fine?* Fine. No problem. Of course, she doesn't want to leave the city, she doesn't want to leave her son, my grandchild. So there are limits to my seeking out happiness, whatever that means. *You said she'd gone back to work.* Yes, she did. She works and she enjoys what she's doing. She says that she receives greater recognition at work than she does at home. Part of the problem is that problem of the housewife and the successful husband. I think it is a mistake for a woman not to work right from the beginning and not to have a career. I think one of the things that probably has a negative effect on marriage is the woman who wakes up and finds that the children are grown and maybe her work is unimportant. Now, I don't think the work is unimportant; the problem is that the women who find themselves in that situation find that they have nothing. They think they have nothing. I think managing a house is a very responsible job. Most women find that if they have a successful husband, the husband has another life and they may not have another life. We often discuss this—that I get a great deal of recognition. The business of being out in a successful career such as I had, being accepted, being known nationally, published books, teaching at universities, a lot of recognition and adulation—identity wherever you go. That's another life from the life at home. Very often, when a person who has that comes home you miss that, you don't have that at home; you have responsibilities at home. Now, that's that person's problem in that kind of situation. But the other person, the other mate who more often than not is the woman, who doesn't have a career, finds the comparison very destructive—the comparison meaning the recognition, the adulation the husband receives outside, the excitement as perceived by the mate—compares that to the responsibilites (in the home) as important as they are, and lack of recognition and lack of—purposeful work—that's very nonre-warding. Unfortunately, today being a housewife is not defined as being pur-poseful anymore. Now, I think that is one of the worst things that has happened with the whole movement towards equality. Somebody opts for that and really wants that and is not thrust into it without any choices. I see no reason to say it is not purposeful. Too many women were pushed into that rather than opting for it. In my wife's case she didn't have any career; she had very little outside work, if you will, outside interest, and she finds working very rewarding. Now, she comes home, she says she gets more recognition there than I give her. It's probably true because I want that stability. She comes home telling me all the stories of her day and I come home telling very few stories. That probably gets back to where I said I'm basically aloof. I don't like to share the burdens of my stories. I'll share some of the glories, if you will, but not the bad, the pressures, the pressures that every working person feels who is a breadwinner; breadwinner meaning providing for a family. Pressures of wanting to insure they'll be in that same position a year from now, five years from now. It's easy for her, at least in my eyes—she doesn't see it that way. It's easier for her because she doesn't need the job. She said that's not it; she does need the job. She doesn't need it financially; we don't need the money, but she needs it for her psychological well-being, for her soul. So, that has been a rather rewarding thing for her, the choice that she made. She went back to school for a while, went to college for a while, which she didn't have an opportunity to do before. I said I was married when I was 21, she was 18. We were both kids. There should be a law against it. There really should. Both children. I might have been a battle-scarred child, but I was a child—battle scar meaning from the war not from my parents. *What kind of work does she do?* She does the same kind of work that I do. Not in my industry. Same kind of work I do, which is interesting. So does my son. My son has a position in a major institution. He's just 26. Same position I have here. . . . I'm a vice-president, but that doesn't mean anything. I run the department, my son runs a [similar] department for a very large institution. He doesn't like it. It's very interesting; and it's fortuitous. Well my son, the first job he got when he got married and he needed a job, I got him in the field through an associate of mine. But he got [his present] job on his own. But he doesn't like it. He's doing very well as far as his finances are concerned at that job, but that's not his life's work. I'd hate to see him buried in something. You see, it's always been my life's work; I aspired to it, after doing something for many years before that, and I fought my way into it and I enjoyed it. So with me it was a choice that I made. With him it was not a choice, although it was a choice of earning—which is al-ways a bad reason to take a job. *Is he still in the field or.* . . . Yeah, he's still in the field. He has to 'til [his wife] finishes her Ph.D., and then she'll get a job very quickly. As you know, a woman today—it's easier for a woman to get a professorial job than it is for a man. So, to get back to my wife, it's been a good thing for her. I think it's been good also.

How have sexual relations been between you and your wife? For a period of, I would say about two years, there have been no sexual relations. They always have been very bumpy. It's always been a major problem. A problem that, I don't know, cause and effect. You know, I'm not as willing to say that she was the cause of it—of my philandering. By the way, my definition of philanderer is probably what the normal person does now in society—looking outside the marriage for sexual satisfaction. I'm not too sure how it all started, but it is not good. *You mentioned you haven't had any outside relationships in six years or so.* I've been, what the hell does that mean, a good husband. I don't know what that means. I haven't had the desire to. Although I don't say that I haven't thought about it. When I say outside relationships, given my situation of getting around the country and being out of town, I meet ladies and have relationships, but I'm talking about the kind of relationship I had, which was a decade, that relationship. Let me put it this way, I don't have a mistress. I get my sexual satisfaction on an ad hoc basis outside the house. It's almost as if it's an unspoken agreement. One never knows how that happens. I really don't know how [sex] stops. *An unspoken agreement between you and your wife?* That's right. How it stops. It's a difficult thing to discuss. It's very difficult. I don't know how it happens. I know that I have a view of sexuality that may be too youthful for my age. *In what way too youthful?* Talking about what an attractive woman should look like, *sexually* attractive; slim, young, etc. Now, that may be a rationalization for my lack of drive in the marriage but it's a mutual . . . none of these things happen on their own. Sexual problems in marriage very rarely happen because of one partner. So, I point no fingers; it is not a predominate concern of mine. *Do you share the same bedroom or . . .* Yes. Absolutely. We're loving. . . . *So there is a great deal of physical affection?* Well, there's physical affection, certainly. Yes. *So there hasn't been a point when separate beds . . .* No. No. That hasn't come up, although we have enough room. No. We don't talk about it. We've accepted it. Maybe we've rationalized it. It is not a bone of contention, as such. Again, I'm not sure whether it's because we both sublimated, or whether we're both on that track together, or we're comfortable on that track. *Do you think that she has outside relationships also?* I used to say no, never. Very possible. Very possible, now that she's in the working world. Knowing her own feeling about sex, it's not a predominate concern of hers. She's a very attractive woman, extremely attractive. She's a beautiful woman, so it's very possible. You always think that you're the only one who makes out on the outside. I think maybe I'm giving you the wrong impression; I have very few liaisons on the outside. It hasn't become, or it's not an obsession, I should say. At one time it was an obsession. *Having outside liaisons?* Oh, yes, very important. It's being loved. Besides the sexual gratification, a lot of it is being loved as well, being accepted. *Was that during the period that you had a mistress?* Oh, sure. *And liaisons as well?* Oh, sure. Absolutely. Which should have told me a little about the seriousness of my commitment to this other woman. That was a sad part of my life. Then, I was not a good guy. *You were not a good guy?* I should not have continued it. It was with a young woman who became old. Any man who has a relationship with a woman for a long time outside his marriage cannot be a good guy, because he knows what he's doing. If you know what you're doing, even if the woman says it's okay, you know that you are not available to that woman; and you're holding out the possibility of availability no matter how much you deny it. And that was a sad, sad conclusion that I have to come to in reviewing that part of my life. I used to absolutely condemn people who were philanderers and I didn't consider myself a philanderer, you see, because I had a permanent relationship outside the marriage. *That's* to be condemned. Not the guy who has one-night stands, or woman who has one-night stands, to satisfy some sexual needs—I'm not talking about bordellos—I'm talking about just meeting a woman—smiles at you, friendly with her—and then going to bed with her. That's not, within the context of my morality, to be condemned anymore. But having a long permanent relationship with a woman outside the marriage can't be rationalized. *That was a pretty painful ending for you?* The ending was probably the most painful thing that ever happened to me in my life. Not from having to end it, but from knowing what I had done. Leaving my wife. Holding out again, right there. Okay, now it's going to be something between this other woman and myself. And then, within a short time saying "I can't do it, I'm going back." It's funny, I think of myself as a good guy. No one can say they are a good guy who did that. No one. No one. There is no way to rationalize it. Even though I'd try to break off year after year and she always wanted me to stay in the other relationship. That has nothing to do with whether it is right or wrong. I wanted to break off. I still get back to my theory, you do what you want to do. And that was a horrible thing.

How has your health been? I am very, very commited towards being in good shape, and not by exercise; I will it. I have a feeling about obese people, a negative feeling, and about the need to stay slim and to be in good shape. I have a picture of myself which will not permit me to let my body to go to hell. I have the same body I had when I was a young man. Very good shape, and I'm not a golfer or a tennis player. I just keep in shape, I walk a lot. . . . I am not anxious to jog or to get into those kinds of things. But my health is good. *No health problems?* Nothing that would shorten my life. In fact, my numbers are such that I'll probably live to a ripe old age—not having high blood pressure; I'm very careful about my cholesterol; I see my doctor regularly; and if I have problems they take care of them right away. So, physically I'm in very good shape. And my sex life is not over in my marriage because I'm impotent, so that physically I'm in real good shape. Real good shape. . . . I don't think that I will have any physical problems, that I can forsee, that will debilitate me in my later life. The one that you have to think about is cancer, you can never know by the way you look now, and by the way you feel now, whether you're going to get cancer or not. I'm very sure I'm not going to have a heart attack. Given the model of . . . except for one thing, I am intense at my work. But, I seem to be able to moderate that intensity when it's necessary. So, the answer to your question is that I'm physically in good shape. I have no fears about dying. I have no concerns about being 60, and I never looked better. What the hell am I worried about? I told you what I worry about. *Right. Does death seem any more . . . real?* Yes. Yes, it seems more real. *In what way?* In that even though I will live, I imagine, more than the—what is it six score and ten, no, no, three score and ten in the Bible— I'm not going to live another 55 years. Okay? So you know you're more than halfway through. Right? If you are realistic about it, then you expect to live to 75-80; then I'm a good two-thirds through my life. So, death becomes real. Since I don't believe in an afterlife, nor do I believe in judgment day, I know that this is it. So death is real. The only concern I would have is dying of something like cancer or something where you're lingering and debilitating, which would be terrible; I see too many people in that situation. I see my mother debilitating, a very active woman, and that's why death is real to me. *Because of her?* Yeah. Because being so close to her. She was close and seeing her going downhill and knowing that she lives from year-to-year, I don't say day-to-day, but year-to-year, makes death real. It's not an obsession. *Her health is failing but she's not terminally ill yet?* No. It's just that the machine is breaking down. Which would bother me if my machine broke down. That would bother me. That's the only concern I have about death, that it's not [going to be] the kind of death I've seen too many people go through. *But there is kind of a different time perspective.* Oh, very much. I'm very realistic. I don't look as youthful as I feel and I'm not 25 any more. Therefore, death is real. · . . . You have to come to grips with death. I have a good handle on that. I don't have a fear of death. I have a fear of lots of things. Sometimes I have a fear of heights; but these are things that are not pervasive. But the fear of dying, no, that's not in the fabric right now. But the knowledge that I'm going to die is very, very much a part of my dealing with life. I am going to die. I'm not going to live forever and I'm getting closer to that, but not that close. I don't have to get my things in order. Although *every* so often I tell my wife where all the things are. *Have you written a will?* Yes, Yes. Oh, I'm a very responsbile person. I told you that. Everything is in order. I have to do everything right. I have to take care of those after me. I have written a will. I'm very careful about making sure my son is provided for, my grandchildren are provided for. My wife knows there's a drawer; she doesn't like to deal with that. But, there's a drawer where you go— everything is clear. *How long ago did you do that?* I've had a will for about, less than ten years, somewhere between five and ten years. My wife didn't want to hear about it at first; now she says it's very realistic. The thought of death doesn't bother me at all. It's the thought of dying a slow death that would bother me. So, I've got everything in order as far as that's concerned. I'm a very orderly person.

I guess the major question is where do you go from here to there. That's it! And how you do it. And how about doing it with a little less pressure on yourself. How about not being as . . . well known, as out front. How about relaxing? How about walking a nice pace toward there rather than jogging towards there? Or rather than running as I did for a long time towards bigger and better conquests. It almost sounds like I'm getting old (laughter). *Thank you very much.* It's a pleasure. You give me an opportunity I don't permit myself to take. And doing it *every* six years is cleansing. I just cannot relate—often when I have major problems, I thought of going to psychiatrists. . . . I can't do that because I find myself in a position very often of sounding too mature and saying to myself what the hell am I doing here. So you give me the opportunity of being on a couch once every six years, and I thank you for that opportunity.

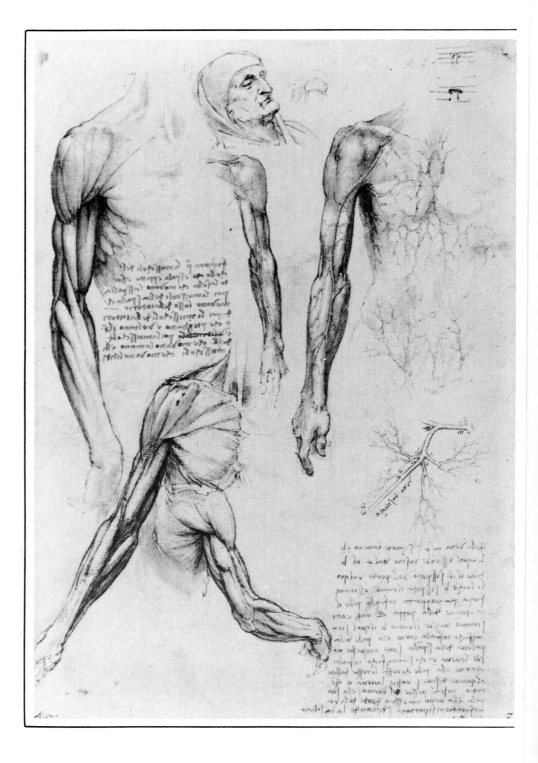

7
BIOLOGICAL AND INTELLECTUAL ASPECTS OF AGING

What does it mean to "grow old?" Why do humans and many domestic animals age and eventually die while other forms of life such as trees or single-celled organisms are able to live indefinitely? What causes human aging? And what changes occur in this period of biological aging and decline—that is, in the period of *senescence?*

Such questions are indeed puzzling, since we have not yet found satisfying answers to them. A great deal of research on aging today is delving into the nucleus of the cell in an attempt to find some of the basic causes of aging; other research is studying the process of age-related change in various organ systems of the human body; and much research is exploring aging in various animals. In addition, considerable research is focusing on the most prevalent causes of death—cancer, stroke, and heart disease. However, despite the medical progress of the last century, the life expectancy of individuals who survive to the age of 80 is no greater today than it was 100 years ago, and there is no evidence that the maximum length of human life is any longer today than it has ever been. Thus it seems clear that the length of human life is, in general, determined by biological factors that are related to the age of the organism. However, the nature of this relationship—that is, the actual cause of biological aging—is not yet clear; but we will discuss several theories of aging as well as some of the social implications of increased longevity that may eventually result from this intensive research into the nature of human aging.

In addition to considering the biological processes of aging, this chapter also shifts our focus to the later years of the life span, since with advancing age physiological aspects play an important role in the characteristics and changes in adulthood and interact with psychological and social factors in important ways. For example, with increased age, susceptibility to disease (especially chronic disease) increases dramatically; and even in the absence of disease, there is a general slowing down in many aspects of functioning involving the central nervous system (CNS). Thus, intellectual processes in particular, and all systems of the organism in general, are affected by the physiological changes of senescence. However, there is a crucial distinction between the physiological changes resulting from *aging* and changes resulting from *disease*. That is, while aging (if there is a process that is pure change with age) typically occurs along with disease in the ordinary population, disease itself has marked consequences for the total functioning of the organism. Thus, in order to understand the effects of aging per se, the effects of disease must be separated from those changes that occur with age in the absence of disease. Otherwise, the effects of aging are confounded with the effects of disease.

We begin with some of the major theories of aging, leaving the discussion of disease and its effects for the second section of the chapter. In the third section we will consider some of the important physiological changes with age (probably resulting from a combination of aging and disease) and will then discuss the changes in intellectual processes with advancing age.

THEORIES OF AGING AND MORTALITY

There are many different types of aging noted by biologists: bacteria are able to continue living indefinitely, limited only by the supply of food and physical space; annual plants complete their life cycle in one year of well-defined, genetically programmed stages; trees continue to grow until they can no longer transmit the sap to the upper branches or until the lower branches no longer receive adequate sunlight; and animals in the wild generally do not grow old but are killed by predators or starve when their physical strength declines. Also, the various mammals have characteristic life spans, many exceeding their reproductive life only slightly, if at all, in the wild; however, African elephants and perhaps Indian elephants live long enough after becoming infertile to rear their young (Sacher, personal communication; cf. Laws, 1971).

However, the human life span, while clearly characteristic of the species, lasts long beyond the end of reproductive capabilities (menopause) and involves a period of senescence atypical among animals in their natural habitat. In general, aging leads to a growing inability of the organism to adapt to the environment and thus to survive. We will discuss several aspects of this aging process, beginning with hereditary and external factors, and then we will consider physiological theories of aging. While none of these theories seems adequate to explain the process of aging at present, each makes a valuable contribution to our understanding of this elusive process.

Hereditary Factors

Clearly there is a hereditary component involved in the length of life characteristic of a particular species. However, the human life span exceeds the length that would be expected for a mammal of our size, and we are the longest-lived species of mammal. Comfort (1964) reports that Indian elephants are known to reach 60 years, and the horse, hippopotamus, and probably the ass are the only other mammals known to reach or exceed 50 years of age. Baboons, chimpanzees, and other primates (as well as large cats, bears, and the African elephant) may reach or exceed 30 years. The life span of whales and dolphins is probably between 30 and 50 years. In general, the length of life among various species of mammals is related to the size of the animal, with man as the marked exception. This is not the case for birds (some owls, cockatoos, eagles, parrots, condors, and pelicans have been found to live more than 50 years) or among reptiles (tortoises have been reported to live from 70 to over 152 years). Sacher (1959) has proposed that it is the ratio of brain weight to body weight that is best related to the longevity of mammals, including humans. That is, the much larger size of the human brain (largely because of the cerebrum) may be an important biological asset contributing to longevity (as body size alone contributes to the longevity of other mammals).

From these observations it appears that the life span of a species is relatively set by genetic or hereditary characteristics that, according to the theory of evolution, have evolved over countless years. Sacher's observations suggest that human thinking capacities may be a primary factor in the evolution of a long life span. However, it is not clear what evolutionary function is served by the long postreproductive life characteristic of the human species. Today the average woman lives about 25 years after menopause and about 45 years after the birth of her last child. What function could this postreproductive period have played for the survival of the human species? It would seem that the characteristics of this postreproductive period could not have been under evolutionary control since these old people are not passing their genes on to future generations. However, it has been argued, notably by Weissman (1891), that the aging process may have evolved as a means to promote the survival of children and grandchildren through social instead of biological mechanisms. That is, the aged would remember, for example, where food and water were found during the drought many years ago (Mead, 1972).

Others have argued that senescence results only from the "running out" of the genetic program and is not specifically developed through evolution. Instead, the greater mental ability of humans may simply have allowed them to live longer so that aging is a kind of "exhaustion of program." In that sense, our later years may be analogous to a rocket that was programmed to place a satellite in orbit and simply continues on for a time after accomplishing this programmed task until pulled back into the atmosphere by the earth's gravity (Comfort, 1964).

Another evolutionary model of aging is proposed by Birren (1960) in the *counterpart theory* of aging. This suggests that human senescence is affected by the later manifestation of negative characteristics that had their primary adaptive importance earlier (prior to the end of reproductive ability when they would directly enhance the species survival). Their negative effects in senescence would then be counterparts or by-products of those characteristics. For example, the nonreplacement of cells in the human nervous system may be highly adaptive for species survival (e.g., enhancing memory and learning abilities), but may also prevent indefinite functioning and life.

Thus, it is unclear whether the long life of the human species (and consequent period of aging) evolved directly because of its importance for survival of the species (perhaps because the elderly provided leadership and wisdom) or whether it results simply from the success of humans as an evolved species in coping with the environment and in surviving because of advanced cognitive powers.

Another type of evidence of a hereditary component in longevity is found in a study of identical twins (Kallmann & Jarvik, 1959). One-egg (identical) twins tend to have more similar lengths of life than two-egg (fraternal) twins; this indicates that even within the species, genetic factors play a role in an individual's length of life. This study also found striking physical similarities between identical twins well into old age, indicating the persistence of genetic influence even to changes in appearance during aging (Figures 7.1 and 7.2). In addition, many studies have found that offspring whose parents and grandparents were long lived are also likely to live longer. However, while such data indicate a genetic component in longevity, it may not be a directly transmitted genetic trait; for example, increased vigor and resistance to disease may be the genetically transmitted potentials that also lead to a longer life. Also, hybrids (rather than inbred animals), individuals with younger mothers (father's age does not seem to be relevant), and females generally live longer (Comfort, 1964).

External Factors

These hereditary factors are probably best seen as *potentials* that may only be realized to their greatest extent in a supportive environment. Obviously, an accident may terminate one's life regardless of genetic potentials, as may disease or starvation or lightning. For example, Jones (1959) estimates that external factors such as rural living or marriage increase the average length of life by five

Figure 7.1
Identical twins at the ages of 5, 20, 55, and 86 years. (Source: Kallmann & Jarvik, 1959, Figure 8. Copyright © 1959. Reprinted with permission.)

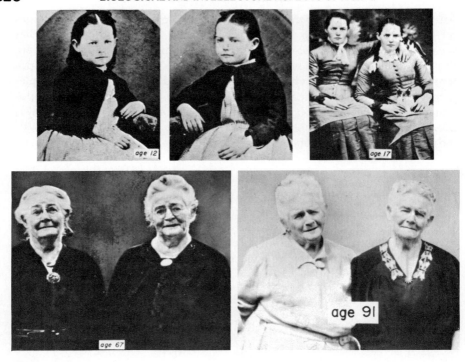

Figure 7.2

Identical twins before and after long separations (between the ages of 18 and 65). (Source: Kallmann & Jarvik, 1959, Figure 9. Copyright © 1959. Reprinted with permission.)

years while being overweight decreases the average life by 4 to 15 years (Table 7.1).

Radiation has received some attention as a possible cause of aging since everyone is exposed to a small amount of cosmic radiation daily. Although only much higher levels of radiation damage the nucleus of cells, Curtis (1966) reports that the amount of damage to cells (measured by the amount of chromosomal damage) is related to the amount of life shortening produced. This suggests that more rapid aging occurs because the chromosomes were destroyed. Numerous studies have reported a connection between radiation and decreased life span caused by an acceleration of all forms of disease in animals (Lindop & Rotblat, 1961). And a 15-year longitudinal study of residents of one of the Marshall Islands in the Pacific who were accidentally exposed to radiation from a nuclear test (compared with other residents who left the island during the test and returned) found evidence of increased chromosome loss among individuals exposed to the radiation; this suggests that radiation exposure "is related to and possibly accelerates the aging process" (Demoise & Conrad, 1972). However, there is evidence of a kind of spontaneous recovery process within the cell, so

Table 7.1 Effect of External and Physiological Factors on Length of Life

Reversible		Permanent	
Comparison	Years	Comparison	Years
Country versus city dwelling	+ 5	Female versus male sex	+ 3
Married status versus single,		Familial constitutions	
widowed, divorced	+ 5	2 grandparents lived to 80 years	+ 2
Overweight		4 grandparents lived to 80 years	+ 4
25 percent overweight group	− 3.6	Mother lived to age 90 years	+ 3
35 percent overweight group	− 4.3	Father lived to age 90 years	+ 4.4
45 percent overweight group	− 6.6	Both mother and father lived to	
55 percent overweight group	− 11.4	age 90 years	+ 7.4
67 percent overweight group	− 15.1	Mother lived to age 80 years	+ 1.5
Or: an average effect of 1 per-		Father lived to age 80 years	+ 2.2
cent overweight	− 0.17	Both mother and father lived to	
Smoking		age 80 years	+ 3.7
1 package cigarettes per day	− 7	Mother died at 60 years	− 0.7
2 packages cigarettes per day	− 12	Father died at 60 years	− 1.1
Atherosclerosis		Both mother and father died at	
Fat metabolism		age 60 years	− 1.8
In 25th percentile of popula-		Recession of childhood and in-	
tion having "ideal" lipo-		fectious disease over past century	
protein concentrations	+ 10	in Western countries	+ 15
Having average lipoprotein		Life Insurance *Impairment Study*	
concentrations	0	Rheumatic heart disease, evi-	
In 25th percentile of popula-		denced by:	
tion having elevated lipo-		Heart murmur	− 11
proteins	− 7	Heart murmur + tonsillitis	− 18
In 5th percentile of population		Heart murmur + strepto-	
having highest elevation of		coccal infection	− 13
lipoproteins	− 15		
Diabetes		Rapid pulse	− 3.5
Uncontrolled, before insulin,		Phlebitis	− 3.5
1900	− 35	Varicose veins	− 0.2
Controlled with insulin		Epilepsy	− 20.0
1920 Joslin Clinic record	− 20	Skull fracture	− 2.9
1940 Joslin Clinic record	− 15	Tuberculosis	− 1.8
1950 Joslin Clinic record	− 10	Nephrectomy	− 2.0
		Trace of albumin in urine	− 5.0
		Moderate albumin in urine	− 13.5

Source: Jones, Hardin B. A Special Consideration of the Aging Process. Disease and Life Expectancy. In J. H. Lawrence and C. A. Tobias (Eds.), *Advances in Biological and Medical Physics*, Vol. 4. New York: Academic Press, 1956. Reprinted with permission.

that the effects of radiation decrease with time (Curtis, Tilley, & Crowley, 1964). Thus, the effects of chromosomal mutations may reflect not only the amount of damage done but also the efficiency of the repair mechanism of the cell. Spiegel (1972), on the basis of an examination of the available experimental evidence, concludes that "radiation does not seem to play a major role in accelerating the celerating the aging process" (p. 570). Shock (1977) also finds it doubtful that radiation plays much of a part in cellular aging.

For the human as a species, however, the *force of mortality* (i.e., the risk of mortality) is clearly related to age. Gompertz (1825) is credited with giving a mathematical representation to the exponential increase in the probability of death with advancing age—a relationship that differs by constant parameters for different species (resulting from a differential length of life)—but that is relatively accurate for many different species. From his mathematical relationship one obtains an exponential increase in the risk of mortality with age; and it is on this basis that life insurance tables are devised. It may be seen that medical advances (for example in Sweden where the population has so benefited from medical technology) have markedly decreased the mortality for the younger age groups, while the older age groups have been little affected (Figure 7.3). That is, the increase in average life span has had little effect on the force of mortality in the later years. It has been estimated that if all cardiovascular and kidney diseases were eliminated, only about 7.5 years would be added to the average life span; and if all cancer were eliminated, only 1.5 years would be added to the average length of life (Dublin, Lotka, & Spiegelman, 1949; Kohn, 1963; Myers & Pitts, 1972).

Thus, it seems that while both hereditary and external factors (such as marital status, disease, and environmental factors) are related to longevity, these factors do not provide very satisfying answers to the puzzle of aging. What does aging mean? Why do people age? Indeed, so far we may have discovered some clues, but the questions remain unanswered. Let us search for some more clues (for there really are no answers . . . yet) by looking "inside" the organism.

Physiological Theories of Aging

Aging may be defined as "a decline in physiologic competence that inevitably increases the incidence and intensifies the effects of accidents, disease, and other forms of environmental stress" (Timiras, 1972, p. 465). Thus, with the passage of time, there is a greater probability of dying (the Gompertz curve); and an individual's death by "natural causes" means that enough important life-maintaining processes degenerate so that death results. Presently it is not clear whether there is a specific cause of aging, whether several potential causes operate together, or even if aging is simply an accumulation of physiologic deficits. The various physiological theories of aging we will present below may be equally valid, although some may be found to be more basic causes of aging than others. Actually, at this time we may be in a better position to apply our practical knowledge (gained from animal studies) to lengthen life by slowing the aging process than we are to understand the nature of the aging process itself (Comfort, 1972); it may be that we will develop the technology to extend life before we have an adequate theory of aging.

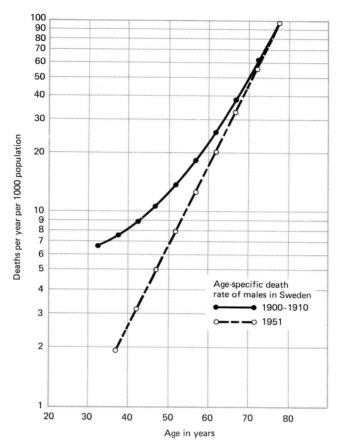

Figure 7.3

Log age-specific death rate versus age (Gompertz plot) for Swedish males before and after the advent of modern medicine. This shows the striking decrease in the death rate for young men, but the lack of change for old men. (Source: Curtis, 1966, p. 7. Reprinted with permission of Charles C Thomas, Publisher.)

Wear and Tear Theory. Perhaps the most commonsense theory of aging is that the organism simply wears out, similar to a machine. In this view, aging is the result of the gradual deterioration of the various organs necessary for life; this theory has currently given rise to an interest in the replacement of organs such as heart and kidney transplants. However, there is no conclusive evidence that either hard work or increased stress alone is responsible for shortening an individual's life span (Curtis, 1966). To a large extent, the effects of hard work and stress are removed by a period of rest, and even the effects of a severe chemical stress, once removed, leave the animal with as long a life expectancy as before as long as these stresses do not overwhelm the physiological capacity to adapt to the stress. Nonetheless, the total rate of metabolism seems to be a factor in aging; for example, underfed animals and cold-blooded animals living at lower than usual temperatures tend to live longer than usual. Thus, lower rates of metabolism may postpone some of the consequences of aging (Sacher, 1977). However, the interrelation of the various systems in the body is probably more implicated in aging than is the failure of any particular organ; thus, while transplants of organs may be particularly helpful when a single organ is diseased, it is not likely that "spare-parts replacement" will lengthen the human life span to an appreciable degree, since the declining efficiency of complex homeostatic mechanisms and the process of cellular aging (to be discussed below) would not be corrected by such transplants.

Homeostatic Imbalance. Comfort (1964) has proposed that the efficiency of crucial homeostatic mechanisms that maintain vital physiologic balances in the body (such as the pH and sugar levels of the blood) is central to the process of aging. Thus, in his view, "aging is characteristically an increase in homeostatic faults" (p. 178). Although there is little change in these mechanisms of self-regulating equilibrium between young and old persons under *resting conditions*, Shock (1960) has demonstrated that the rate of readjustment to normal equilibrium after stress is slower in old subjects than in young. For example, the capacity of the kidneys for maintaining homeostasis, the ability to maintain body temperature during exposure to heat or cold, and the efficiency of blood sugar regulation decrease with age[1] (cf. Timiras, 1972, pp. 558–561). Thus, the self-regulating feedback mechanisms decrease in efficiency with age (Shock, 1977). If they are no longer able to maintain the necessary equilibrium, the organism may die (Figure 7.4). Strains on the homeostatic mechanisms, easily tolerated in young persons, may threaten the survival of the aged. The stress that may disrupt these processes can be physical (such as exercise or glucose intake), or it may result from changes in the physical or social environment. Hence, the emotional stresses that accompany the aging process (loss of spouse, environmental changes, and so on) are more likely to increase the risk of death for the aged than for the young because of this homeostatic inefficiency (cf. Selye, 1950; Selye & Prioreschi, 1960). This lessened efficiency of the physiologic response to stress is perhaps the most general theory of aging and provides the clearest link between physiological, social, and psychological aspects of aging (cf., Eisdorfer & Wilkie, 1977). However, stress alone does not cause aging, as noted earlier. Instead, the impairment of the endocrine response to stress, the reduced sensitivity of detecting devices to homeostatic imbalance, and the lowered efficiency of the response mechanisms with age cause the greater sensitivity to

[1]Because of such changes, medication levels for the elderly are frequently different from the level tolerated by young adults. Also, older persons are more likely to die from cold (hypothermia) than younger people, because their body may not detect or respond to the lowering of body temperature as efficiently.

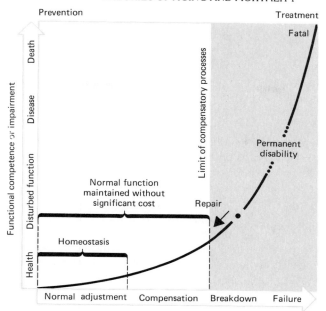

Figure 7.4

Progressive stages of homeostasis from adjustment (health) to failure (death). In the healthy adult, homeostatic processes ensure adequate adjustment in response to stress, and even for a period beyond this stage compensatory processes are capable of maintaining overall function without serious disability. When stress is exerted beyond compensatory capacities of the organism, disability ensues in rapidly increasing increments to severe illness, permanent disability, and death. When this model is viewed in terms of homeostatic responses to stress imposed on the aged and to aging itself, a period when the body can be regarded as at the point of "limit of compensatory processes," it is evident that even minor stresses are not tolerable, and the individual moves rapidly into stages of breakdown and failure. (Source: Timiras, 1972, Figure 28-1. Reprinted with permission of Macmillan Publishing Co., Inc. Copyright © 1972 by Paola S. Timiras.)

stress. Although the causes and effects of these age-related physiological changes are not yet fully understood, Shock (1977) concludes that those theories that focus on regulating and control mechanisms are very promising since they emphasize aging processes in the total organism.

Accumulation of Metabolic Waste and Cross-Linkage. Although it has been suggested for some time that organisms age because their cells are slowly poisoned or hampered in their function by the waste products of metabolism, Curtis (1966) argues that these waste products are more likely a symptom than a cause of aging. Yet, waste products clearly accumulate with age, may have an important role in the changes associated with aging, and have received a great deal of study. For example, *collagen*, a fibrous protein, is formed in some tissues at a rather slow rate and is eliminated only very slowly if at all. This connective tissue protein has also been found to change with age because of changes in the *cross-linkages* between the intertwined strands that comprise it. This buildup of collagen and its change with age are involved in the wrinkling of skin and the slowness of wound healing—both characteristic of old age. Shock (1977) suggests that the cross-linking theory of aging is a promising line of research, but it needs to be demonstrated that cross-linking affects intracellular proteins as well as the often-noted extracellular proteins such as collagen. Another group of substances, *lipofuscins*, build up in some nerve cells with age and give rise to pigments in these cells. Again, while they may be an important cause of a decline in function of those nerve cells, Curtis feels that they are primarily important as a symptom of aging rather than a cause. A third type of increase in waste material results from a defect in calcium metabolism that Selye and Prioreschi (1960) argue leads to a shift of calcium from bone to soft tissues (such as cataracts in the eye, calcification in the arteries, or wrinkled skin) with a consequent brittleness of bones. While such a shift in calcium deposits seems to occur for some aged persons, the calcification seen typically in old persons suggests that defects in calcium metabolism are not necessarily so severe as to be a dominant cause of aging (Strehler, 1962). Perhaps it is another aspect of a breakdown in homeostasis or one of the many interrelated consequences of cellular aging.

Autoimmunity.   The frequency with which the immune systems of animals reject their own tissues through the production of autoimmune antibodies increases with age and is involved in several diseases that increase with age, such as rheumatoid arthritis. Some leading causes of death (cancer, diabetes, vascular diseases, and hypertension) have also been linked to autoimmune reactions, and Blumenthal and Berns (1964) have postulated a link between this process and aging on the basis that those causes of death fit the Gompertz formula for the force of mortality. However, although the data presented by Walford (1969) supporting the concept that aging is a generalized, prolonged type of autoimmune reaction forms an attractive hypothesis of aging, these reactions may be related to other, more basic causes of aging and, like the other factors described in this section, may be more of a symptom rather than a general cause of aging. Nonetheless, recent data on the decreased ability of aging cells to reproduce suggest that this phenomenon may be related to an excessive immune reaction (Gelfant & Smith, 1972). Shock (1977) notes that, while the evidence for autoimmune reactions as a central cause of aging is sketchy, the hypothesis is an attractive one because it can be experimentally tested and may lead to methods that could modify the aging process. In addition, the thymus, a gland that plays an important role in normal immune processes, atrophies with age after sexual maturity and this may be related to the decline in certain immune responses with age, as well as to the increased susceptibility to autoimmune processes and cancer with age (Makinodan, 1977).

Cellular Aging.   A common misconception of aging is that cells of the body begin dying at a faster rate than they are produced some time in young adulthood, and that this decline continues until there are no longer enough cells to function and death results. The situation is hardly this simple. Although some cells seldom or never reproduce (notably cells in the brain, nervous system, and muscles), most cells continue to reproduce themselves and theoretically allow the organism to live indefinitely. However, cells may age in the sense that they reproduce only a finite number of times, or that they reproduce imperfectly because of age or a random accumulation of errors in replication (Medvedev, 1964). Hayflick (1965, 1966, 1970) has found that cells grown in cultures ("aging under glass") undergo a finite number of doublings (about 50), which suggests that a finite growth potential of cells might be a mechanism of aging. Whether this inability to reproduce occurs in the organism as well as "under glass" in the laboratory and whether it is a major factor in aging are unanswered questions. However, Gelfant and Smith (1972) report blockage of cell division in living animals that can be reversed by drugs that suppress the immune reaction. In addition, the doubling capacity of cells in cultures does decrease with the age of the organism from which they were taken (about 45 at birth to age 10; about 30 by 80 to 90 years of age).

Another line of evidence suggests that an impairment of RNA synthesis (Cristofalo, 1970) or faulty transcription of information from DNA leads to a "catastrophe of errors" (Orgel, 1963) that impairs or diverts cell function and cell division. Recent data (Johnson & Strehler, 1972) indicate a selective loss of DNA from the cells of aging animals that would impair the production of RNA by DNA and would impair the functioning of the cells. To be sure, the cell's ability to function would be affected by changes in this genetic material within the cell, since DNA (deoxyribonucleic acid) leads to the formation of RNA (ribonucleic acid) that produces the enzymes required for cellular functioning. Yet it is not clear whether these changes are genetically programmed in the sense that when the program is exhausted the cells break down, or whether these errors are essentially random events that accumulate with age until the cell becomes defective. All of these data suggest that the differentiation of cells, presumably evolved characteristics of the human species, may in some way interefere with the ability of those cells to reproduce indefinitely. More specifically, those highly differentiated cells that do not divide (such as in the CNS) may have developed that ability through evolution in order to provide continuity and regularity (of performance and experience) important for the survival of the younger individual. But, in old age, these same characteristics may be implicated in their greater susceptibility to the effects of mutations or cross-linkages or loss of DNA that brings about eventual cellular death. This may be an example of Birren's (1960) counterpart theory of aging in that evolutionary adaptations that grant positive survival value to young organisms bring about negative results in old animals. One of the important results of these changes may be an increase in the *chemical noise* within the cell, since it functions less effectively as an information system (Comfort, 1968). As we will discuss in the section on intellectual functioning, such an increase in chemical noise may account for a number of the age-related changes that occur.

Implications

As may be apparent from the preceding discussion, there is a great deal of complex research currently investigating the nature of aging and particularly the physiological changes that occur with advancing age. It appears that the secret of the "fountain of youth" may lie in the cellular processes of aging and perhaps equally in the other aspects we have discussed. Shock (1977) believes that there may not be any single cause of aging, but instead there may be different causes for the various organ systems. In any event, it apparently does not lie in the prevention of disease alone, as important as this factor clearly is, because there seems to be some kind of limit set by some unknown mechanism to the length of human life. However, as noted above, Comfort (1972), who describes himself as an "optimistic gerontologist," predicts that soon we will be able to extend life by 10 to 20 percent if the sort of techniques that work on laboratory animals can be made to work on humans. This may occur before we have gained a complete understanding of the causes of aging; and if we can modify the aging process, then we may come to understand it.

There are profound social issues raised by the possibility of a marked increase in life span. One is overpopulation, since more people would be living longer. A related issue would be the increased number of people who would be aged and living in retirement (or swelling the proportion unemployed). Although the problems of the aged in our society as well as the population problem will probably have to be solved regardless of an increased life span, serious problems remain. For example, will this "pill" (or whatever) be available to all, or will it be so expensive as to be used only by the rich? Who will support these aged persons? Will we have to choose between having children and living indefinitely? If so, who will decide who lives and who has how many children? And, most important of all, will this involve not only adding years to life but also adding life to years? Currently our medical technology has provided greater freedom from disease for more years. Probably attempts to lengthen life will increase this trend so that diseases that occur during the sixties now may occur during the seventies. This will be an important advance, but it must be matched by economic and social advances for the elderly also if these added years are to be fully beneficial.

DISEASE: A MOST IMPORTANT CONSIDERATION

In the preceding section we discussed the major theories of aging in an attempt to uncover some of the basic biological processes that change with age in the absence of disease. However, the effects of these two processes—aging and disease—are complexly intertwined, and it is difficult to disentangle them. That is, some of the age-related changes in biological processes may be involved in some diseases. For example, mutations in cells in the arterial wall may be involved in circulatory disease; and perhaps what now seem to be "normal age-changes" may eventually be found to be disease processes. Indeed, one additional theory of normal aging is that deficits such as disease accumulate over time so that disease itself is a cause of aging (Selye, 1970).

In general, it is very difficult to separate the physiological, social, and psychological effects of aging from the effects of disease since aging and disease are highly correlated. That is, as individuals age they generally become more troubled by chronic diseases (such as arthritis, heart conditions, or high blood pressure). And the effects of aging and disease compound one another. For example, aged persons tend to experience growing effects of disease, more social losses, and lessened hearing and visual acuity. As a result, accidents are more prevalent and bones break more easily and take longer to heal for the aged person.

Nonetheless, it is important to distinguish between the changes that result from aging per se, from disease, and from other social, psychological, and physiological factors. Otherwise, if these different variables are not disentangled, we are easily misled into equating aging with disease (for the aged very often are also chronically ill), as if sick old people are the only kind of old people there are. If we make that error, then we not only overlook the old people who are quite healthy, but we also do not know whether the characteristics of the sick old people result from their advanced age, their illness, or from the interaction of both. One example is that while religious feelings and beliefs do not decline with age, church attendance does decrease with advanced age (Moberg, 1965). In a sense, this change might be seen to reflect increased introspectiveness of older persons so that religion is more internal and less externally practiced in old age. However, a very important factor may be simply that the aged have more chronic illnesses that make attendance at such activities more and more difficult.

In this section we will describe the prevalence and effects of disease among the aged; and then we will discuss a study that attempted to separate the effects of aging from the effects of disease. In general, disease is a very potent factor in aging; in the absence of disease, the effects of aging are relatively minor; but when even a mild amount of chronic disease is present, a wide range of effects results. For our purposes, *disease* may be defined as a disorder of bodily functions that may occur within a broad age range. *Aging*, in contrast, involves changes that are caused solely by the passage of time. While there is a statistical relationship between aging and disease, this relationship varies in different environmental conditions. That is, the relationship between aging and disease is different today than it was in 1900, and it is different in the so-called underdeveloped and industrialized countries.

Prevalence of Disease among the Aged

Older persons are less often afflicted with *acute* diseases (such as infectious diseases) and are more often afflicted with *chronic* diseases (i.e., long-term diseases). They are also more likely to suffer disability restrictions because of their health than younger persons.

Acute Diseases. Temporary illnesses are much more common in childhood than at any other age, and their prevalence decreases with age for both men and women (Figure 7.5). Since acute conditions, by definition, only include those diseases that restrict one's activity or involve medical attention, the number of days of restricted activity because of acute conditions also decreases with age. Thus it is apparent that the control of acute illness with vaccines and antibiotics, and improved health conditions, have primarily affected young children and have had much less impact on either adults or the aged—on the average.

Chronic Diseases. In contrast, long-term diseases are much more common in adulthood and old age than among young people. Arthritis and rheumatism, heart conditions, and high blood pressure are the most prevalent chronic diseases afflicting persons over age 65, and they increase in prevalence with age. Other chronic conditions such as asthma, hayfever, and peptic ulcer show little consistent increase after age 45 (Figure 7.6). It is apparent that these chronic diseases may lead to restricted activity; and heart conditions, as well as high blood pressure, are associated with the leading causes of death. These diseases may also affect younger persons so they are correlated with, but not caused by, aging.

Chronic Impairments. Reduced hearing, blindness, or visual impairment, and reduced ability to get around because of arthritis, hypertension, and heart disease increase in prevalence with age during the adult years. For example, 29 percent of all persons over age 65, and about 75 percent of all persons between 75 and 79, have hearing impairments. Similarly, 20 percent of all persons over 65 have visual impairments; and for those between 75 and 79, only 15 percent have 20/20 vision even with glasses (National Council on the Aging, 1978). Various kinds of injuries, especially accidental falls, are an important cause of chronic impairment. In addition, loss of teeth is common; only one-half of all persons between 55 and 74 have any of their natural teeth (ibid.). When these

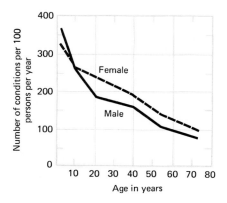

Figure 7.5
Incidence of acute conditions per 100 persons per year by sex and age, July 1974 to June 1975. (Source: National Center for Health Statistics. *Vital and Health Statistics*, Series 10, No. 114. Washington, D.C.: U.S. Government Printing Office, 1977, Figure 2.)

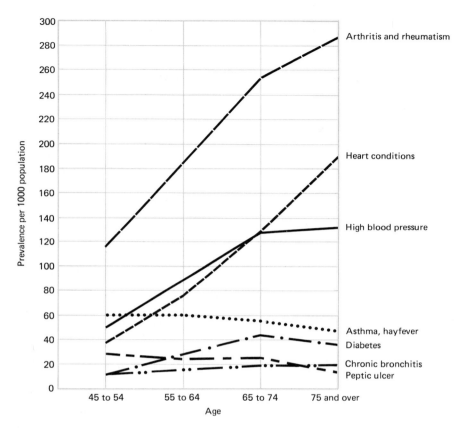

Figure 7.6
Prevalence of selected chronic illnesses among persons 45 and over in the United States, 1957 to 1959. (Source: United States Health Survey. *Health Statistics*, Series C, No. 4. Washington, D.C.: U.S. Government Printing Office, 1960, pp. 31, 35.)

impairments are combined with chronic disease, 86 percent of persons over age 65 are affected, compared with 72 percent of persons between 45 and 64 (ibid.). Since these impairments are caused at least in part by disease or by environmental factors, they are not necessarily caused by aging.

Restricted Activity.   As a result of this increase in chronic disease and chronic impairment with age, the prevalence of restricted activity increases with age for both men and women. That is, the greater incidence of chronic conditions offsets the decrease in acute conditions so that, overall, the proportion of persons with restricted activity increases with age. The degree of restricted activity also reflects family income, so that persons with higher income are less likely to be disabled (National Center for Health Statistics, 1972). At first glance it would appear that persons of lower income suffer more chronic conditons than persons of higher income; but chronic conditions might be a cause of the lower income as well as a consequence of it. Socioeconomic status was also found to be more related to the extent of physical disability than age or race among a sample of 256 volunteer (i.e., probably healthier than average), non-home-bound community residents over age 60 in the Duke Study of Aging (Dovenmuehle, Busse, & Newman, 1961). Persons in the higher socioeconomic group showed lower levels of disability than persons in the lower socioeconomic group. Several chronic conditions also occurred more often among the lower socioeconomic respondents: impairment of vision, arteriosclerosis, cardiovascular disease, high blood pressure, and lung disease. Arthritis was a prevalent condition reported by 35 percent of the respondents, but there was no significant social class difference in its prevalence. Dovenmuehle (1970) also found a significant increase in disability among the 180 surviving respondents 22 to 65 months later. Yet while 53 percent of the respondents suffered disability and there was a dramatic drop in respondents with no disability, 12 percent became *less* disabled over this period.

Taken together, these data indicate that, while physical disabilites are certainly more common among the aged than among the young or middle-aged adult, there is great individual variation; and socioeconomic factors probably both affect and result from these impairments. However, only a minority of aged persons suffer severe restrictions in their ability to get around in the community (Table 7.2); 83 percent had no impairment that limited their ability to function in their major activity, including 54 percent with no restricted activity at all. In

Table 7.2   Restricted Activity by Age and Sex, United States, 1974

Sex and Age	With No Limitation of Activity	With Limitation of Activity			
		Total	Limited but not in major activity[a]	Limited in amount or kind of major activity[a]	Unable to carry on major activity[a]
		Percent Distribution			
Both sexes					
All ages	85.9	14.1	3.5	7.3	3.3
65 years and over	54.1	45.9	6.6	22.1	17.1
Male					
All ages	85.7	14.3	3.6	5.6	5.1
65 years and over	50.3	49.7	4.8	15.0	29.8
Female					
All ages	86.0	14.0	3.5	8.8	1.7
65 years and over	56.9	43.1	7.8	27.2	8.2

Source: National Center for Health Statistics. Health Characteristics of Persons with Chronic Activity Limitations. *Vital and Health Statistics*, Series 10, No. 112. Washington, D.C.: U. S. Government Printing Office, 1976.
[a]Major activity refers to ability to work, keep house, or engage in school or preschool activities.

1970, only 5 percent were confined to their houses because of disability; 8 percent had difficulty but managed on their own; another 6 percent needed help to get around (Brotman, 1972). In 1974, only 5 percent of all persons over age 65, and only 25 percent of those over 85 years old, were in nursing homes (National Center for Health Statistics, 1977).

Causes of Death. About 80 percent of deaths after age 65 are attributed to cardiovascular disease (such as heart attacks and strokes), cancerous neoplams, or accidents. However, the proportion of deaths from these causes varies by age and sex (Figure 7.7). In 1973 the eight leading causes of death were: (1) dis-

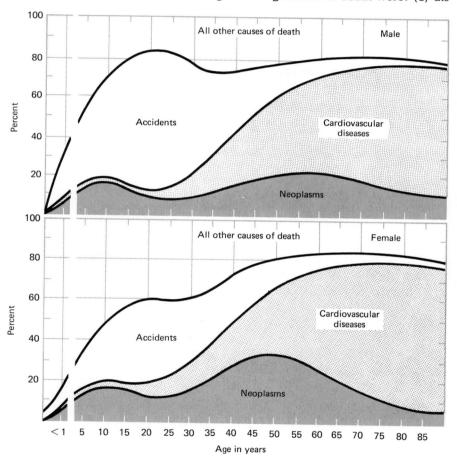

Figure 7.7

Mortality from malignant neoplasms (cancer), cardiovascular diseases (heart disease and cerebrovascular disease), and accidents in the United States, 1969. Expressed as a percentage of total mortality by age group and sex. (Source: Timiras, 1972. Figure 24-6. Reprinted with permission of Macmillan Publishing Co., Inc. Copyright © 1972 by Paola S. Timiras.)

eases of the heart; (2) malignant neoplasms (cancer); (3) cerebrovascular diseases (strokes); (4) influenza and pneumonia; (5) arteriosclerosis; (6) diabetes; (7) accidents; and (8) bronchitis, emphysema, and asthma. Each other cause accounted for less than one death per thousand population. Death rates for heart disease were nearly three times as great as the rate for any other cause (U.S. Bureau of the Census, 1979). Men had higher rates than women for nearly all causes of death. Their rates were much higher than women over age 65 for (in order) bronchitis, emphysema, and asthma; motor vehicle accidents; cirrhosis of the liver; malignant neoplasms; influenza and pneumonia; and heart disease. Racial differences in causes of death were also apparent. For persons 65 to 74, the ratio of black persons was about twice as high as for white persons for infections of the kidney, diabetes mellitus, cerebrovascular diseases, influenza and pneumonia, and arteriosclerosis (ibid.).

Health of Old Poor Persons. The interaction of aging, disease, social class, and leading causes of death can be vividly illustrated by a study of the health among welfare recipients over age 65 (Ostfeld, 1966). Although few of the respondents perceived themselves as sick, the health status as determined by physicians found only one out of five or six to be in "good" health. About half were rated to be in "fair" health; and about one-third were in "poor" health or were so gravely ill that death was felt to be imminent (Table 7.3). Black men were slightly more healthy in general, while white men and women were the least healthy (sex differences were slight). Perhaps since life expectancy is lower for black persons (especially men), the survivors over age 65 are more robust than their white counterparts. The most prevalent disease was hypertensive heart disease (high blood pressure); it was more common among black men and women (34.8 and 21.5 percent, respectively), while white women and men were lower (13.0 and 9.3 percent); an additional 10 percent of the respondents had some other heart disease, and 5 percent were so troubled by heart disease that they were not able to walk across the room without getting out of breath and had badly swollen ankles indicating poor circulation. Strokes, Parkinson's dis-

Table 7.3 Health Status of Old Age Assistance Recipients over 65 as Determined by Physicians

	Males		Females	
Categories	White	Black	White	Black
Good	16.0%	21.5%	16.3%	18.2%
Fair	45.6	49.7	46.7	48.2
Poor	33.5	24.7	31.9	30.0
Gravely ill	3.9	2.2	4.6	2.2
Unknown	1.0	1.9	.5	1.4
Total	100.0	100.0	100.0	100.0
Subjects	331	372	392	407

Source: Ostfeld (1966), p. 88.

ease, chronic bronchitis, and neurological gait disturbance (difficulty in walking, which may be an important cause of death or injury in accidental falls or pedestrian accidents) were other major illnesses in this sample. When standards applicable for younger subjects were used, one-half of the respondents had symptoms of diabetes (indicating that these standards may not be wholly appropriate for older persons). Many respondents had symptoms of thyroid problems and showed high cholesterol levels (leading the physicians to anticipate that 2.5 percent of the respondents would experience strokes in the future). One out of four subjects manifested a hearing loss (which may lead to withdrawal from social interaction); and 30 percent had cataracts, although 95 percent of the subjects had vision within correctable limits. As a group, three-fourths of these respondents should have been taking daily medication, according to Ostfeld, but most did not take any medication. Clearly, old people living in poverty are likely to be in poor health. This is frequently a result of inadequate nutrition (Barrows & Roeder, 1977).

Medical Care.   Recent advances in medical technology and its availability for all persons are likely to result in persons reaching old age with better health and fewer consequences of earlier acute disease than has been true in the past. However, it also allows persons with weaker health to survive to old age, which may lead to a less-healthy population of very old people (Riley, Foner, & Associates, 1968). Not surprisingly, in view of the data on the health of older persons, the number of visits to a physician increases with age as does the extent of hospital care. Women over 65 average one more physician visit a year than men of the same age, but women are less likely to be hospitalized than men. When hospitalized, the old person is likely to stay considerably longer than a younger person. And, on the average, persons over 65 spend almost three times as much for medical care as persons 19 to 65. In 1975, 30 percent of health expenses for medical care were for persons over 65; their average health bill was $1360; about two- thirds of this was paid by public funds such as Medicare or Medicaid (National Council on the Aging, 1978).

Implications.   One of the major concomitants of growing old is the growing susceptibility to chronic disease. While many old persons retain good health, many more may be expected to manifest the symptoms of one or more chronic impairments and possibly to be disabled to some degree as a result. And even when there is little apparent disability, decreased hearing, impaired vision, or the pain and reduced mobility resulting from arthritis can isolate the old person from social and psychological stimulation. These social and psychological isolations may enforce some disengagement from social activities and roles. Thus, aging, confounded as it typically is by disease and the consequences of disease, is often thought to bring about a wide range of changes that, in fact, probably result more from disease and its consequences than from aging per se. In the next section we will discuss one important study that attempted to separate the effects of aging from those of disease by studying very healthy old men. But before concluding here, let us call attention to the importance of good health care for the elderly—that is, health care that not only is adequate and economically available, but care that recognizes the differences between the elderly and the young. Robert Butler, Director of the National Institute on Aging, in his Pulitzer Prize-winning book on aging in America pointed out the problems of medical care for the older person.

> The majority of older people can't afford proper medical care; doctors and health personnel are not trained to deal with their unique problems; their medical conditions are not considered interesting to teaching institutions; and they are stereotyped as bothersome, cantankerous and complaining patients. Direct prejudices exist. Primitive health problems like malnutrition are widespread, partly because many older people are too poor to feed themselves properly, partly because loneliness, disability, depression or fear of crime may keep them from shopping for and cooking food. The close association between mental and physical health is largely ignored. The old are submitted to enormous emotional stresses and a low social position. Preventive medicine, and recognizing the complex interplay among physical, emotional and social factors, is set aside in favor of simplistic diagnoses of "senility" and prognoses of "chronic" or "irreversible" [Butler, 1975, p. 174].
>
> Drug metabolism is not as effective in old age. Blood flow in the liver, the organ of drug metabolism, may be reduced and thus the rate of drug detoxification slowed. Moreover, older people have a lower general bodily metabolism rate, and this prolongs drug action. Kidney impairments slow excretion of drugs and their metabolic products. Drug effects in the old may also be prolonged by the accumulation of drugs in body fat. It is wise to administer all drugs with caution, and to begin with low dosages. Patients must be under continuous laboratory and clinical surveillance [ibid., p. 200].

Since many older people suffer from several diseases and may visit more than one physician, especially if they are seen in hospital clinics, it is very possible for older persons to suffer from physician-induced problems that result from overmedication, or combinations of medications that interact to produce bad reactions. For that reason, it is important for the physician to be fully informed of all prescription and nonprescription medications that are being taken and for older persons to seek out physicians who are willing to provide nonprejudicial, high-quality medical care for older patients.

Another important aspect of geriatric medical care is that, unlike treating the young, many old persons cannot be restored to optimal health; while this may diminish the motivation of some physicians who seek to "cure" the patient, it does not diminish the importance of high-quality care, medical interest, and continuing research on ways of treating chronic disease. In addition, the extent of disease and its consequences are important to note in the design of nursing homes, retirement homes, or community housing for the aged. Simple architectural and environmental considerations such as a minimal number of stairs, adequate fire protection devices, handrails along the walls, signs printed larger than usual, amplification attachments for telephones, nonskid floors or carpets, special slow-crossing lights for busy streets, and handrails alongside toilets and bathtubs are some of the simple conveniences that make life easier for the elderly person. Transportation is typically a problem and, in particular, inexpensive transportation to allow frequent visits to a physician is of great importance. And, of course, maximum dignity, self-respect, and independence should be of paramount importance in designing housing for the elderly.

Aging and Disease among Healthy Elderly Subjects

While aging and disease typically occur together, the theories of biological aging presented earlier in this chapter suggest changes in cellular or homeostatic functioning that are a consequence of age alone and do not necessarily involve disease. Thus, in order to uncover the physiological changes that occur with age alone, it is necessary to separate out those changes that are primarily caused by disease. Put another way, what changes occur with aging in the absence of disease? The data we will present make two important points in this regard: (1) many of the changes usually attributed to aging are better seen as the result of disease; and (2) even in the absence of disease there are important changes in physiological functioning with age, although there is far less impairment than is commonly observed among the aged.

This classic study was carried out by Birren, Butler, Greenhouse, Sokoloff, and Yarrow (1963), and the subjects were restudied 11 years later (Granick & Patterson, 1971). Birren and his associates obtained a sample of 47 men between the ages of 65 and 91 who were extremely healthy on the basis of clinical examination. These subjects were given lengthy and extended examinations on a wide range of medical, physiological, psychological, and social variables. The first important (and serendipitous) finding was that this group of very healthy men actually consisted of two different groups: Group 1, whose subjects were in optimal health in every regard, and Group 2, whose subjects were without clinical symptoms of disease but who were found to have mild diseases that were discovered only through intensive medical examination. As will be clear from their data, this difference between those in optimum health ($N = 27$) and those with asymptomatic (subclinical) disease ($N = 20$) proved to be one of the most important differences in the study—on nearly all of the subsequent tests, the healthy group differed from the subclincial disease group in a positive direction. These findings make it abundantly clear that the presence of even a mild degree of chronic disease has major consequences for the aged on a wide variety of functions.

Medical Data. A considerable number of variables showed no difference between the optimally healthy aged men and standards for young men. For example, measures of cerebral blood flow and oxygen consumption during exercise did not differ, and the elderly subjects (mean age 71 years) were as vigorous and capable of exercise as young men (mean age 21 years). However, the important measure of cerebral blood flow differed between the young and the Group 2 subjects, suggesting that even their subclinical degree of disease may affect the efficiency of brain functioning.

Electroencephalogram. Even among the most healthy old people, the EEG was found to change with age, although all the patterns of electrical activity in the brain were within the normal range for younger persons. In general, the average frequency spectrum of these old subjects was approximately one cycle slower than the comparable young-adult rate. The EEG of the Group 2 subjects differed from Group 1 in the same direction as the general-age trend. Thus, there was some evidence of slowing down of the electrical activity of the brain with age, and disease seemed to increase this trend.

Psychometric Data. Scores obtained by the subjects in Group 2 were poorer than scores obtained by the optimally healthy group on 21 out of 23 tests of intellectual performance. Thus, one central finding is the negative effect of even mild disease on cognitive performance, particularly on the processes involved in the retrieval of stored information. However, the performance of the elderly subjects (both groups) was superior to the norms for young subjects on measures of verbal intelligence (such as vocabulary) and was also superior to previously studied aged samples (perhaps related to the superior health of both groups of subjects in this study). Nonetheless, both groups were significantly slower in psychomotor speed than young adults, and intelligence measures that involved fast responses were impaired for both groups. Thus, age was found to be most important in measures of the speed of response, such as reaction time, while health was more important than age on verbal measures that involved the retrieval of stored information. These data indicate that one effect of aging (in the absence of disease) is a *slowing down* of reaction time, regardless of the sensory modality (auditory or visual) and regardless of the muscle used for the response (foot, jaw, finger, speech, and so on). This change, since it occurred equally in both Group 1 and 2, seems to be related to aging rather than to disease (and it may be related to the slowing down of the EEG pattern noted above). This general slowing down was also found to be greater when there was a history of greater social and environmental losses, and it was more marked for respondents who were rated as "depressed" in psychiatric terms. Thus, this age-related change is apparently independent of mild disease but is modulated by social and psychological factors.

Personality and Psychosocial Data. The less-healthy group performed consistently less well on several personality tests than the optimally healthy group. That is, even this slight degree of illness affected the degree to which they terminated responses appropriately, adhered to the task goal, and showed an ordered sequence of thought. However, the optimally healthy respondents did not differ noticeably from young adequately functioning persons. The amount of loss suffered by the respondent in his personal environment was also related to psychological and psychiatric functioning. That is, men who had suffered marked losses, especially the loss of significant persons, tended to perform less adequately on the psychometric and personality tests and to be more likely to have been rated as depressed. In addition, slowing down (on psychometric tests) was related to less adequate daily functioning (i.e., the planful aspects of daily behavior and the nature of social interaction). Perhaps individuals who showed greater slowing down were, in a sense, physiologically "older." Finally, case analysis of personality styles suggested that some individuals adapted more easily to the crises that are associated with aging, while other personality styles (such as the "paranoid reaction") made the adjustment more difficult.

Implications. One of the major findings of this study is the integrated inter-relations of various systems (medical, cerebral, psychological, social-psychological, and psychiatric) in the aging person. That is, while no single factor of aging was found, the pattern is one of interacting factors reinforcing or canceling the effects of other factors in a complex interdependency. However, three aspects of the aging process (in the absence of disease) also were particularly striking: (1) the slowing down, or decrease in speed on psychological tests and on reaction time measures—perhaps related to depression and EEG frequencies through a general decline in cortical excitation; (2) the effect of personality style and the degree of social loss on psychosocial and cognitive performance, depression, self-perceptions, and adaptive responses to aging; and (3) the widespread effects of a mild degree of disease (especially the development of a kind of condition that may precede senility). Overall, the major finding was that, for the aged, the presence of even asymptomatic disease increases the statistical dependency of the psychological capacities on the physiological status of the organism; that is, moderate disease leads to a greater correlation between psychological capacities and physiological status, compared with relatively low correlation in the absence of disease. Perhaps, as the homeostatic imbalance theories of aging suggested, with advancing age the organism's ability to function becomes more marginal so that it is less able to adapt to stress; thus, even a small amount of disease may upset the balance, and many functions suffer.

Eleven-year Follow-up Study. These same subjects were retested after 11 years by a different team of investigators (Granick & Patterson, 1971)—one of the difficulties of longitudinal research. Two major findings stand out from this study of actual age changes. *First*, about half of the original sample had died; most (70 percent) of the Group 2 subjects did not survive, but most (63 percent) of the very healthy Group 1 subjects did survive. Clearly, the mild degree of disease that differentiated these two groups was important in terms of eventual mortality; and most of the differences initially found between the two groups were also related to survival (higher intelligence, faster reaction time, better personality adaptation, and lower social loss). In general, two measures—greater organization of daily behavior (organized, planned living and gratifying pursuits in the living pattern) and not smoking cigarettes—taken together, correctly predicted 80 percent of both the survivors and the nonsurvivors! While it is difficult to be certain whether both of these variables are related to physical health, they seem to indicate the harmful effects of cigarettes as well as the importance of psychosocial factors. Could this indicate a marked psychosomatic factor in mortality? *Second*, among the surviving subjects there was a "remarkably limited amount of change" (p. 132) with age; average age at that point was 81. However, the increased correlation between psychological and physiological functioning was even more marked than previously, and there was, in general, a gradual decline in "reserve capacities" of energy and of general physical status (such as a greater vulnerability to psychosocial stresses). Also, the decline in the speed of functioning was, again, found to be related to age. Thus, on the one hand, changes with aging alone seem to be relatively minor (in the absence of disease); but, on the other hand, these changes may have wide-reaching effects insofar as they involve increased vulnerability to stress and to disease.

PHYSICAL AND PHYSIOLOGICAL CHANGES WITH AGING

To be sure, some of the most obvious changes with aging are in such physical characteristics as graying or loss of hair, wrinkling of the skin, decrease in height, and loss of teeth; in such sensory modalities as decreased vision and hearing; and the slowing of CNS functioning. Some of these changes have major effects on the concept of self; others, especially decreased perceptual acuity and CNS slowing, have more widespread effects on psychosocial adjustment. There is much individual variation in the extent of these changes since they probably reflect the effects of both disease and aging combined. Also, nutrition, heredity, health care, and variations in wear and tear are each important factors related to the extent of these physical changes in any particular individual. Yet, in general, these changes are age related in the sense that they affect more and more individuals as they age.

Since these changes are typically associated with aging, they tend to be seen as negative changes in our society. However, it may be noted that smooth, unwrinkled, clear skin *could* be negatively valued since it may indicate inexperience, unfamiliarity with life's pain and pleasures, and irresponsibility. And it is fascinating to study an old face and to try to imagine what history might be written in those wrinkles and folds that are so uniquely individual to that face.

Physical Characteristics

The skeleton is fully formed by the early twenties and there is no change in individual bones after that time (Bromley, 1966). Yet there may be a slight loss in stature in old age because of changes in the discs between the spinal vertebrae caused by changes in collagen with age. This loss of stature may be exaggerated by stooping from muscular weakness; and it is also exaggerated by the population trend toward increased stature among younger persons (a cohort effect). Of course, the skeleton of old persons reflects previous damage or disease. Also, with advancing age, the chemical composition of the bones changes somewhat, perhaps because of changes in calcium metabolism and the decrease in estrogen among women, so that the risk of breakage increases in later life, especially among women (Strehler, 1977). Diseases of the joints (such as arthritis) may be the result of wear, the age-related changes in collagen, an immunological reaction, or the secondary effect of infection (ibid.).

Loss of teeth is a frequent mark of entry into old age and, undoubtedly, the surgery required and the adjustment to dentures may be a time of crisis or at least readjustment of the self-concept. Although advances in dentistry have been marked in the prevention and treatment of decay, which may decrease the proportion of elderly persons who have lost all or most of their teeth, these advances have often meant that adults lose fewer teeth to decay so that they will lose them later to the other major dental disease, *periodontal* (gum) *disease.* Unfortunately, little mass education is currently being devoted to informing young and middle-aged adults about the prevention and treatment of this major cause of tooth loss. When it begins, and it generally does to some degree in all adults, surgical treatment may be required to prevent tooth loss. Certainly, natural teeth are far more effective than dentures for chewing, but sound teeth in old age require lifetime care, proper diet, and occasional repair. Perhaps the failure of teeth is basically a result of their evolutionary selection under different dietary conditions when the average life span was much shorter. They may have evolved to last through the childbearing years, but now we want them to last twice as long!

One of the most apparent changes in old age is the increased paleness, change in texture, loss of elasticity, dryness, and appearance of spots of pigmentation on the skin; many of these changes are attributed to changes in collagen with age. As noted earlier in the chapter, these age changes in this fibrous protein are important symptoms of aging, but it is not clear to what degree they are a basic cause of aging; certainly, they are a cause of many of the signs of aging however. *Collagen* is one of the components of connective tissue and is found throughout the body; connective tissues function in many important ways, such as mechanical support of the body and in repair of injury. Collagen undergoes continuous change with age and has received much research attention; although its changes remain irreversible, the nature of those changes is slowly becoming understood. In addition to its effects on stature, joint diseases, and skin changes, collagen aging may also cause wounds to heal less quickly.

Compounding the loss of elasticity of the skin, the amount of subcutaneous fat and some of the muscle bulk built up during middle age (unless one cuts back the intake of food to match the reduced exercise and work of typical middle-age life) begins to decline, so that in old age the skin is left hanging in folds and wrinkles. Although older persons tend to need less food because of decreased exercise, adequate amounts of necessary nutritional requirements are important to prevent excessive weight loss, especially when the person is living in some degree of social isolation, as in widowhood. Much of the function of eating is social, and eating alone is not only likely to be lonely but also to be ignored or avoided. Thus, an important service to the aged person who lives alone are hot lunches at Senior Centers or programs such as "Meals on Wheels," which bring one hot meal a day and a bit of companionship.

These changes in body image certainly affect one's self-concept, confidence, and sense of value. In addition, changes in the voice, changes in hair color, or the loss of hair may affect one's self-image and mark oneself as "old." Bromley (1966) suggests that the gradual decline in secretion of the adrenal glands after the late twenties may be related to the loss of hair, although blood circulation in the scalp may also be involved. Gray hair results from the absence of pigment in the hair, presumably because the melanocytes that provide the pigment granules for the hair eventually run out of these granules. Genetic factors have long been recognized to determine hair pigmentation and loss of hair in men. Changes in the voice, which is often less powerful and more restricted in range in old age, seem to result from gradual bodily changes that may limit the capacity and control of expelled air, from upper respiratory congestion, or from atrophy of the muscles of the larynx (Timiras, 1972). Speech may also slow down somewhat, probably as a result of the general slowing down of the CNS.

The digestive system is the system least affected by ordinary aging (Bromley, 1966), although an age-related decline in sensitivity to smell or taste may decrease the appetite. In particular, there is no evidence of an increase in constipation with age, despite the impression (and stereotypes supported by TV commercials) that old people may complain more about it. These complaints may reflect cohort factors of rigid toilet habits stressed during their childhood rather than actual constipation, since there are marked individual differences in bowel function. Also, Bromley reports an increase in red blood cells and hemoglobin in later life, suggesting little general need for "iron" tonics for the aging.

Changes have been found in sleep patterns with age, although sleep time as well as the proportion of REM (rapid eye movement) and non-REM sleep is fairly constant to age 60. Spontaneous interruption of sleep, relatively infrequent through adolescence, increases with age and the amount of time spent awake in bed increases after the fourth decade; thus the aged often compensate by spending more time in bed. Also, Stage 4 sleep, the deepest, is virtually absent, and the amount of REM sleep begins to decline in old age (Timiras, 1972).

Circulatory System

Strehler (1977) points out that diseases of the heart and interference with blood flow to the brain are the leading causes of death. With age there is a decrease in pumping efficency of the heart, a change in the elasticity of arteries, and the deposit of fatty substances such as cholesterol in the arteries, leading to the deposit of calcium salts that reduce the efficiency of the circulatory system. An example of this condition, known as *atherosclerosis*, is shown in Figure 7.8. *Arteriosclerosis* results from decreased elasticity of the blood vessels. *Hypertension*, or high blood pressure, may result from either of these conditions, or from other factors; it is more common among black persons for reasons not fully understood. Diet is thought to be related to atherosclerosis since animal fats, egg yolks, and certain vegetable oils are particularly high in cholesterol; however, only one of two types of cholesterol seems to be harmful and the distinction between these different types of cholesterol is not clear. Blood clots in the veins, known as phlebitis, also increase with age and may break loose and block an artery in the lungs or heart, sometimes causing death.

Sense Organs

Older persons are more likely than younger persons to show decrements in at least four of the five senses as well as in the sense of balance. Although it is not clear how much of this decrement is from aging alone, the change is at least part-

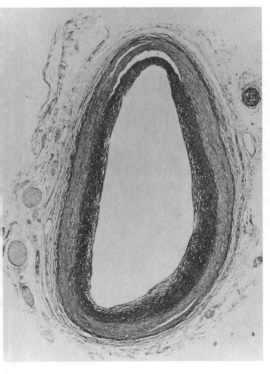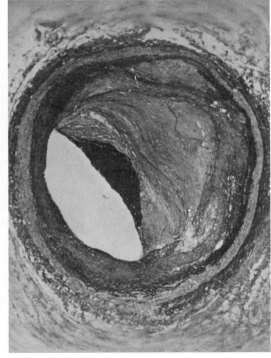

Figure 7.8
Cross sections of coronary arteries. Left, a near normal artery; right, an artery partially blocked by atherosclerotic plaques. (Source: National Heart, Lung, and Blood Institute.)

ly the result of higher thresholds of stimulation that are required for perception, suggesting that the sense receptors become less efficient with age. Thus, in general, the aged require higher levels of stimulation in vision, audition, taste, and smell for the sense receptors to perform as well as a young person's senses. These decrements, especially in vision and hearing, are important to note since they influence not only the individual's ability to function in the physical environment but also may create a kind of sensory deprivation and social isolation that may have important psychological and social effects. As a result, many older persons seem to move more cautiously than younger persons. Although this may result from decreased vision and hearing, the sense of balance may also be impaired by ear infections or decreased blood flow to the inner ear. Thus, falls and accidental injuries are more likely for older persons (Strehler, 1977). Also, the slowing of information processing by the central nervous system reduces the speed with which visual input is scanned and perceived, so that older persons may respond to sensory information less rapidly and efficiently than younger persons, further increasing the risk of accidents.

Vision.   Several aspects of vision decline with age (Fozard, Wolf, Bell, McFarland, & Podolsky, 1977). Visual *acuity* (the ability to see clearly at a distance) typically reaches its maximum in the late teens, remains fairly constant until 45–50, then declines gradually; less than 10 percent of persons under 45 have vision poorer than 20/70 while 40 percent of the men and 60 percent of the women over 65 have poorer vision than 20/70 (National Center for Health Statistics, 1964). In addition, the threshold for *adaptation to darkness* rises with age, indicating a decline in the ability to see clearly when illumination is low (as in night driving) and, in general, the ability of light to penetrate the lens, cornea, and vitreous humor of the eye declines with age (and is markedly affected by the presence of cataracts, a change in the lens making it opaque to light). Also, *accommodation* of the lens of the eye to focus on near objects decreases from age 5 to age 60 at a constant rate (Hofstetter, 1944); this is commonly noted in the growing necessity for bifocal glasses or reading glasses in middle age—as some individuals describe it, "My arms seemed to grow shorter so that I couldn't hold the newspaper far enough away to read it!"

Hearing.   Several studies report a marked loss of hearing among older persons (Corso, 1977). This decline is especially noted in the highest frequencies; also the auditory threshold declines regularly with age (Weiss, 1959). Long-term exposure to noise is probably a factor in addition to probable lowered sensitivity of the auditory receptors. It has also been found that the ability to understand speech decreases with age in a manner that implies some loss in auditory perception by the CNS, rather than just changes in auditory thresholds (Melrose, Welsh, & Luterman, 1963).

Taste and Smell.   Strehler (1977) reports that the number of taste buds decreases with age and there is an increase in the threshold for smell, similar to the threshold increase found for vision and hearing. Thus, higher levels of stimulation of taste and smell receptors are required for older persons than is the case for younger persons. This may be partly responsbile for the clinically noted increase in complaints about food among the elderly as well as the problem of malnutrition among older persons. However, Engen (1977) notes that other factors such as disease and smoking may be more important than an increased threshold, especially for the sense of smell.

Pain. The clinical impression is that sensitivity to pain may decrease with age, partly because many older persons experience more frequent pain from chronic disease (such as arthritis) than do younger persons and because the threshold for other kinds of stimulation increases with age. However, empirical studies have not validated this impression. Perhaps the (expected) higher threshold for pain sensitivity is offset by an actual lowered tolerance of pain—at least in the laboratory.

Central Nervous System (CNS)

Several neurophysiological changes are found with age. As we noted above, the speed of CNS functioning slows with age, and this change is one of the few age-related changes that seem to occur independently of (but are exaggerated by) disease. Also, since cells in the CNS do not reproduce themseves, it is widely accepted that when neurons are lost they are not replaced; thus, cell death, lack of oxygen, and changes within the cells could reduce the efficiency of the brain's functioning. There is evidence that the weight of the brain decreases with age (Himwich & Himwich, 1959) and that the number of cells in the cortical layers of the cerebral cortex decreases with age (Brody, 1955); however, adequate measurement from a representative sample is obviously difficult to obtain, and these observations remain open to question (Diamond, 1978).

The slowing of the CNS with age is most apparent in tests of *reaction time*. That is, the time between a signal and the subject's response has been consistently found by many investigators to increase slightly with age (Welford, 1959); we noted this earlier in the study by Birren et al. (1963). Clearly, reaction time involves a number of aspects of CNS functioning (e.g., perception, attention, short-term memory, and transmission of neural impulse), but it is not clear whether all of these processes slow with age or whether the slowing occurs only in some of the processes. For example, the *pupillary reflex* to light stimulation slows with age; Feinberg and Podolak (1965) report a slowing of .040 second between subjects aged 15 and 65. Such a slowing of an autonomic reflex indicates that at least some of this slowing may occur in the transmission of the neural impulse—perhaps caused by physical-chemical changes at the synapse (the juncture between two neurons), by reduced neural excitability, by fewer functioning neural cells, or by changes in subcortical centers (Birren, 1964).

A provocative hypothesis about the change in the CNS with age is that there is a disturbance of the signal resulting from interfering "noise" in the neural transmission; that is, a decrease in the ratio of signal-to-noise. This may be caused by a weakening of the signal strength (as suggested by the heightened threshold of sense receptors noted above) or by an increase in the amount of random background activity ("noise"). This decrease in signal-to-noise ratio might result from fewer functioning cells, from lower signal strength (decreasing the signal aspect of the ratio); and it might result from greater random activity, or from longer aftereffects of neural activity (increasing the noise in the system). Currently, the precise nature of the changes in neural activity is not known, but one day it might be possible to treat these changes by some sort of drugs to reduce the neurological effects of aging.

There are several additional factors that may affect the functioning of the CNS with advancing age, although they are too complex for discussion here (cf. Timiras, 1972). For example, changes in hormones that affect the level of brain excitability or changes with age in such cell components as nucleic acids (RNA and DNA), amino acids, proteins, and enzymes have been suggested as possible factors affecting the efficiency of the central nervous system. Another important factor is *oxygen deficiency* (hypoxia), resulting from impaired circulation of the blood (resulting from arteriosclerosis and the accumulation of collagen in the cerebral blood vessels). It has been suggested that the changes involved in adaptation to high altitudes resemble aging changes in some respects; and experimental administration of oxygen to senile subjects seems to improve their performance on several psychometric tests (Jacobs, Winter, Alvis, & Small, 1969).

Certainly, the effects of CNS changes are likely to be widespread and to influence a range of behaviors from intelligence test performance to driving skills. And, in general, regardless of the basic cause of CNS changes with age, all behavior mediated by the central nervous system can be expected to show the characteristic slowing with advancing age.

Sensorimotor Skills

Since only part of the increased reaction time has been explained by the slowing of CNS processing, an increase in *movement time* (the time required to physically respond) may also occur. And indeed, studies reviewed by Riley et al. (1968) indicate that, in general, there is a larger age-related increase in the time required for complex sensorimotor tasks (such as tracking a moving target or adjusting dials) than in reaction time alone. One important practical example of this increase in reaction and movement time may be automobile driving. Drivers over 65 are involved in a higher percentage of accidents and are in more accidents per miles driven than middle-aged drivers; they are also more likely to be found at fault (Figure 7.9); however, young drivers have the highest accident rate of all (McFarland, Tune, & Welford, 1964). Welford (1977) notes that the types of automobile and industrial accidents that increase with age result mainly from slowness in making decisions rather than from sensory or motor impairment. In terms of accidents on the job, Bromley (1966) suggests that the cause may often be inexperience for the younger worker but slowness to respond for

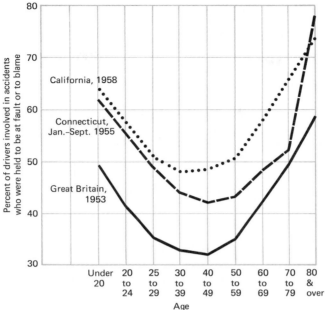

Figure 7.9

Drivers held to be at fault or to blame in accidents. (Source: McFarland et. al., 1964, p. 191. Reprinted with permission.)

the older person. And Birren (1964) points out that with age there are more accidents resulting from rapid evasive movements or falls and fewer resulting from poor judgment; however, he reports little change in occupational performance in general up to age 60 or 65. Of course, many successful workers are likely to move into jobs with less time-pressure and more emphasis on past experience or personal contacts so that slowness in reaction and movement time would be of little consequence to their job.

Other factors that might slow performance on sensorimotor tasks in the laboratory include cautiousness and avoidance of unnecessary risks; and it may be that these strategies tend to be adopted by the elderly as an effective means of coping with decrements of perceptual ability and response time in their daily environment. Thus, these coping strategies may hinder performance on laboratory tests while they allow the person to deal effectively with the real environment at the same time.

Summary and Implications

In sum, these data indicate that with advanced age the body becomes less efficient in perceiving, processing, and responding to external stimuli. While it is not clear to what degree these changes may be caused by aging per se or by the greater incidence of chronic disease among the aged, these findings clearly suggest important differences between the typical old person and the typical young or middle-aged person. Certainly it is important to note these changes in terms of the kind of physical environments that are better suited to the slightly slowed pace and heightened threshold for perceiving stiumuli than the fast-paced, stimulus-overload world of young adults. And perhaps as the pace of life continues to speed up, especially in urban areas, the elderly may find life more and more difficult because of the conflict between the rapid pace of change and the slowing of speed and behavior. However, because of a lack of experience, skill, and status, younger persons are likely to be working near the limit of their physiological capacities, while aged persons (with less reserve capacities and greater vulnerability to stress) are likely to have developed compensations to function effectively within the limits of their decreased physiological capabilities. Also, these capacities typically decline so gradually that the compensations are largely automatic, except when disease or injury brings a sudden and drastic change.

In the concluding section of this chapter we will consider the cognitive changes that occur with advancing age. Some of these changes will follow from the physiological changes we have discussed up to this point; others will shed some additional light on the nature of the changes that occur with aging in the human organism.

CHANGES IN INTELLECTUAL PROCESSES WITH AGING

We used an example of intellectual change in the first chapter to illustrate the difficulties involved in research in adulthood. Specifically, the example demonstrated the kind of error that may result from cross-sectional studies of age differences in intelligence (which confound age and cohort effects) and the kind of error involved in longitudinal studies (which confound age with selective dropout and other experimental factors). It may be recalled from that example that cross-sectional studies have found a decline in scores on intelligence tests with age after about age 30, but that differences in the amount of education received by subjects of different ages may largely explain this decline in intelligence test scores. Also, longitudinal studies have found little or no decline in intelligence test scores up to at least age 50; subjects who were initially above average tend to improve with age. However, selective dropout of less-able subjects and other factors appear to inflate the average scores in longitudinal studies. Thus, the data on age changes in intelligence are far from definitive; and, as we discussed in Chapter 1, they reveal a central difficulty in interpreting empirical data on age differences in adulthood.

We are now interested in a more detailed discussion of the specific nature of intellectual changes with age. That is, we are interested in the effects of the physiological changes we have discussed in this chapter on such intellectual processes as IQ test performance, memory, learning, thinking, and creativity. Do these processes change in predictable ways with advancing age? If so, what are some of the plausible explanations of the origin of these changes?

Individual differences in intellectual functioning are, of course, marked; and with age, these individual differences tend to become more pronounced as initially more-able subjects tend to improve slightly while less-able subjects tend to decline faster. In addition, the effects of disease and other noncognitive factors such as education, social class, personal losses, and even nearness to death act to add to the differences between individuals since persons close to death, persons suffering disease, or persons surviving psychosocial losses tend to decline in IQ performance while others remain higher. However, if senility occurs (and it is important to note that it is a chronic disease, not an inevitable sign of aging; see Chapter 8), individual differences tend to vanish; memory (especially recent memory) declines markedly, cognitive ability drops sharply, and creativity may be almost nonexistent. Thus, the findings we will discuss do not apply to persons who suffer from senility, since they are really a different population from the normal aged persons that are subjects in studies of intellectual functioning.

Simplifying considerably, there are two types of intelligence tests: one, typically used in the United States, measures the "quantity" of intelligence (IQ) and has been used to predict school performance, for example; we will discuss this measure in some detail. The other type of test measures the process of thinking, and Piaget has developed a series of tasks that children solve in differing ways as they grow older. Little attention has been given to possible changes in these processes of thinking with aging until recently; but the data so far are quite interesting. For example, Papalia, Salverson, and True (1973) report that aged persons tend to show less advanced thinking processes with age on these tasks (i.e., concrete operations, characteristic of school-age children). Piaget (1972) also reported that his laboratory has found a similar increase in concrete operational thinking and a decline in formal operational thinking among older persons. These findings are highly suggestive and deserve much further research; however, since these are cross-sectional studies, it is possible that cohort factors or a general lack of formal operational thinking among middle-aged and older adults in our society may be involved in these findings instead of age-related changes.

Age and Intelligence

The "classic aging pattern" of IQ test performance is a decline on tests that measure *performance* aspects of intelligence and little or no change with age on tests that measure *verbal* abilities. Botwinick (1977) points out that, although longitudinal studies show more stability and cross-sectional studies show more decline in intelligence with age, when cohort factors and selective dropout effects are considered, the classic aging pattern is found in both longitudinal and cross-sectional studies. However, the declines are often not found before the age of 50 or 60 and then are relatively small.

"Verbal" scores are based on tests that require the person to verbally answer questions such as defining a series of words, solving arithmetic story problems, or determining elements that two objects have in common. "Performance" scores are based on those tests in which the subject is asked to physically do something—such as to demonstrate psychomotor skill by filling in symbols that correspond to numbers or to perform perceptual integrative tasks such as putting pieces of a puzzle together. The performance subtests differ from the verbal ones in another important way than the verbal-performance distinction; the performance tests are scored on the basis of the amount of *time* required to perform the task so that a rapid performance is given a higher score than one with a slower time.

Thus, the general decline in intellectual functioning is largely a result of the declines in performance aspects of the standard intelligence tests, which may result from *slower* performances. That is, the slowing down of reaction time and other CNS functions with age may account for much of the decline in intellectual *performance* noted among elderly subjects. However, according to Botwinick (1977), even if time pressure is removed, age differences are not entirely eliminated, indicating that a decline in intellectual processes with age is responsible for some of the decline on performance tests among older people.

Verbal subtests generally do not show a marked decline with age and, for superior subjects, often increase with age. In particular, "vocabulary" functions are noted for their stability with age (in nonsenile samples). That is, stored information that is recalled with no direct time-pressure seems to be least affected with age. Other aspects of verbal intelligence are not quite as stable, however, and the pattern of age changes is rather complex. One important distinction, proposed by Reed and Reitan (1963) and supported by their data, is that *stored information* is relatively unaffected by advancing age, while *problem-solving ability* does show age changes. This suggests that there are changes in thinking processes to the point where finding solutions to new problems where past experience is no help becomes more difficult for older subjects—at least on IQ tests.

Individual differences in intelligence are as significant among older persons as they are among younger persons and may actually be exaggerated by the fact that some older persons show no decline while others show a marked decline with age. In addition, physical health and psychosocial stress may affect intellectual performance. Also, nearness to death has been found to bring a sharp decline in intellectual abilities. We will discuss this phenomenon of terminal drop in IQ in detail in Chapter 10, but it may be that CNS functions are highly sensitive to physiological changes leading to death. Thus, the aged population consists of persons who are quite healthy (often showing little or no intellectual decline) and persons who are suffering disease or nearing death (showing marked intellectual decline). The combination of these different aged populations may well account for much of the decline in intellectual performance found in studies of older persons (Riegel & Riegel, 1972).

In sum, age changes in intelligence have received considerable empirical study that has clarified the initial findings of general intellectual decline with age. Much of that decline is a result of a slowing down of performance speed, which seems to be a relatively pure age-related change; and much of the remaining decline is probably the result of changes in solving new and unfamiliar problems for which accumulated experience is little help. This implies that the typical elderly person is likely to be somewhat "slow" at intellectual tasks, somewhat impaired at mastering new problems in daily life (such as Medicare forms), but relatively unimpaired in many aspects of ordinary intellectual functioning. Certainly, these changes would be unlikely to affect a typical person's occupational functioning at least up to age 60 (Birren, 1964, p. 148). In general, the older person would be likely to select situations and tasks where accumulated experience and knowledge is important instead of tasks that involve time-pressures and the development of new approaches; thus his or her performance might be more effective than a young person's performance. Let us now turn to a discussion of memory and learning (and later to thinking and creativity) since these processes may also be affected not only by the slowing down of the CNS but also by the older person's lessened ability to solve new or unfamiliar problems.

Memory and Learning Changes with Age

As Botwinick (1970) points out, it is impossible to separate memory and learning skills since most tests of learning involve memory and memories nearly always involve learning. For example, memory may be thought of in three phases: acquisition, retention, and retrieval. Acquisition involves the stimulus registering on a sense receptor and registering in memory, which is essentially a learning process. Conversely, a learning test involves that memory being retained and retrieved upon command. Thus, changes in memory with age are likely to affect learning; and changes in learning with age are likely to affect recent memories (although not necessarily old memories). Further complicating studies in this area is the observation that a decline in performance ability (specifically a slowing down in movement time) may impair an old person's functioning on learning or memory experiments.

Memory.   Based on his review of the data, Botwinick (1967) points out that it is not correct to conclude that with advancing age there is a progressive loss of memory; instead, the data indicate that *memory decline describes more and more persons as they get older*, since many persons retain a sound memory regardless of their age. There are several theories about memory loss: that memories are lost through *disuse*; that memories are lost through the *interference* of other memories in the large store of memories that is accumulated with age; and that *neurochemical change* or loss of cells in the CNS is responsible for memory loss. Currently, the interference theory in combination with neurochemical factors seems to be favored; that is, the amount of stored information increases with age while the neural changes (loss of cells, increased chemical noise, and general slowing down) leads to slower and less-efficient processing of the stored information with age. However, we know almost nothing about the way in which memories are "stored" or "recalled" so that, at best, theories of either memory or forgetting are only plausible hypotheses. It seems that memory results from some kind of chemical changes in cells that may involve RNA and DNA molecules; and DNA molecules have been found to be selectively lost from brain cells of 10-year-old dogs; such a loss of genetic material would be likely to impair brain function (Johnson & Strehler, 1972). However, the mechanism behind the prevalence of memory loss with advancing age is unknown; certainly health factors are important and even a mild degree of vascular disease has been found to be related to a decline in memory ability (Klonoff & Kennedy, 1966; Spieth, 1964).

Acquisition and Retrieval of Memory.   There has been considerable debate about whether age-related decline in memory is caused by problems in the *acquisition* of the memory or the *retrieval* of the memory once it has been acquired. For example, it has been thought that older persons have very good long-term memory of events in the distant past, but may have difficulty learning new information. However, memory of past events declines with age and with the length of time that has passed since the event, so that younger persons do better than older persons in retrieving long-term memories (Craik, 1977). The fact that many older people remember events from the distant past may indicate that those events have been rehearsed over time and that memory continues to function fairly well for most older people. In terms of short-term memory of new information, several studies have suggested that interference with the acquisition process may be much of the cause of the decline in short-term memory with advancing age (Botwinick, 1970). That is, older persons may have more trouble remembering tasks in a psychology laboratory (or remembering what they went to the grocery store to buy) because they have more difficulty getting the memory into storage than a young person has. However, other studies have concluded that the age-related decline in short-term memory is a problem of retrieval rather than a problem of acquisition. For example, Johnson (1972) found that young subjects perform better than old subjects on "free recall," but there is no difference on "cued recall" or "recognition." Thus, remembering (retrieving) the words was easier for the young person than the old when no cues were given to aid in the recall, but both groups did equally well (and better) when cues were given. This indicates that the memory was equally well acquired but was harder to retrieve for the older subjects unless there was some cue to trigger the memory. It now seems that either acquisition or retrieval problems may interfere with memory for the older person and that the question is not whether the cause is acquisition *or* recall, but how the memory process functions (Craik, 1977). We might also note that at least some of the supposed memory loss among older people is probably related to the social expectation that it will occur. Thus, older persons may feel it is acceptable to complain about being forgetful and to attribute their forgetfulness to age.

Learning.   The decline in short-term memory seems rather clearly to indicate learning deficiencies with advancing age. However, pure learning deficits with old age are not particularly clear. Instead, performance factors seem to be of major importance in describing the declining ability of the aged in learning experiments. For example, many studies have found a decline in paired-associate learning with age. In such experiments the subject is to learn which response is associated with each stimulus as in the random pairing of nonsense syllables on a "memory drum"—the decline is in the speed with which a predetermined number of such pairings is learned. Other studies have found a similar slowness in acquiring a conditioned response among elderly subjects; and, once acquired, the conditioned response is readily extinguished. In both cases, the slowing with age would impair the performance of the elderly subject and thus the decline in learning ability may reflect a decline in performance ability instead of learning. In response to this critique of the early studies on learning among the elderly, more sophisticated methodology has been used (such as self-pacing, which allows subjects to select the speed at which they must respond in order for the answer to be correct). These studies have suggested that there may be some learning deficit, although the results place more emphasis on the performance deficit than on the learning deficit (Botwinick, 1970). It is also important to note that some 70-year-olds perform as well on learning tasks as younger persons (Arenberg & Robertson-Tchabo, 1977).

Implications. By this time it may be clear that the age-related decline in the speed of information processing by the CNS is a major change since its implications are widespread. Indeed, many of the social, psychological, and physiological changes with aging may be understood as reflecting this change, which probably has its origin in the physical-chemical functioning of neural cells. One practical implication of these findings is that health, education, and individual differences are more important than age alone in the ability (and interest) for continued learning. To be sure, comfortable, rehearsed skills may be more attractive than learning a new set of skills (e.g., on the job); but if retraining and continuing education occur during the early and middle-adult years (such as during leisure time or during sabbatical leaves from the job), there is little reason an elderly person could not learn as well as a young person. Certainly up to ages 60 to 65, there is little decline in learning or memory ability; factors of motivation, interest, and lack of recent educational experience are probably more important in learning complex knowledge than age per se. Learning may just take a bit longer for the elderly and occur more at the individual's own speed instead of at an external and fast pace. Of course, the presence of cerebral vascular disease, and especially senility, may bring marked changes in these abilities.

Thinking, Creativity, and Age

In this final section we will build on the previous discussions of general changes in intellectual functioning and of changes in learning and memory as they culminate in thinking processes and creativity. It is apparent that major impairment of either learning or memory would have consequences for the ability to think or to create; however, older persons would be likely to have developed ways to counteract the slight loss of memory or difficulty in learning new material so that their daily functioning would be impaired only slightly, if at all. In fact, some of these compensating strategies may be a partial explanation for the findings we have described; for instance, well-established approaches to problems may serve the individual quite well in daily life but interefere with finding novel solutions to the kind of laboratory tests devised by psychologists.

This introduction helps to provide the perspective for describing the experimental data on changes in thinking with age since these changes may be considerably more apparent inside the laboratory than outside it; yet they also help to understand the changes in intellectual processes with age. Thus, elderly subjects have been found to show decrements in *concept attainment* that are similar to those for nonverbal measures of intelligence. For example, Wetherick (1965) found that elderly subjects tended to take less advantage of negative information and were less likely to change concepts that were not adequate. Problem-solving ability, as noted earlier, has also been found to show declines among elderly subjects. Redundancy, difficulty in handling new concepts, and inability to make use of efficient strategies in problem-solving are other aspects of thinking processes that have been found to characterize elderly subjects (Botwinick, 1970).

Two other characteristics of thought processes of elderly persons that are commonly thought to be apparent from daily observations of aged individuals—rigidity and concreteness—are somewhat more difficult to observe in the laboratory, however. For example, elderly persons are sometimes described as being more rigid or more cautious in their thinking than young persons. One interpretation of these changes is that the old person sacrifices speed for accuracy ("rigidity"?) and sacrifices abstraction for functional conceptualizations ("concreteness"?). That is, when faced with various learning or memory experiments, the old person's adaptive strategies prove somewhat dysfunctional. However, it may even be incorrect to say that older persons become more cautious and avoid taking risks because the situation seems to be more complex. Botwinick (1969) found that old subjects will take a "no risk" option more frequently than young subjects on a questionnaire; but when there is no "no risk" option available, they will take the same extent of risk as younger subjects. This suggests that the "cautiousness" may be a tendency to avoid risky decisions (perhaps because of a fear of failure), but when a decision cannot be avoided, the elderly are as likely to take a "high risk" solution to a problem as young respondents.

Because of these changes in thinking processes with age, we would expect a similar decline in creativity. However, the definition of creativity, let alone the measurement of it, is a very difficult task. What is *creativity*? How can it be measured? If we were to give a lump of clay to an old person would he or she make less creative use of it than a young person? Are not some of the most brilliant creative works produced late in life; and are not some of the most brilliant minds a result of extensive experience, years of wrestling with ideas in search of an answer and a vast amount of slowly accumulated knowledge? For example, philosophers who had long lives reached their peak of creativity, on the average, between the ages of 60 and 64 (Lehman, 1953). However, other kinds of creativity, such as Einstein's, seem to be a result of discovering a new conceptualization and a new way of viewing an old problem—abilities that may benefit from relatively little experience with old ways of seeing the problem. And, of course, some creative individuals are more creative in their ordinary works than most of us will be in our greatest work. Can there then be a generalized description of changes in creativity with age; and, if so, how can creativity be measured?

Two divergent approaches to this problem have been formulated and, as might be expected, these different definitions have led to divergent findings about the age changes in creativity. The pioneering work in this area was done by Lehman (1953) who measured "creativity" by the percentage of *high-quality output* produced by great men during each year of their lives. He found that for most fields the greatest proportion of superior work was produced during the decade of the thirties (Figure 7.10). The percentage then declines with age so that about 80 percent of their superior work is completed by age 50—leaving 20 percent to be produced after age 50. The rate for worthy but less-superior work was found to peak somewhat later, and the decline through the later years of life was more gradual than for high-quality work. More recently, Lehman (1962) examined the creative rates for high-quality productions of a variety of scientists

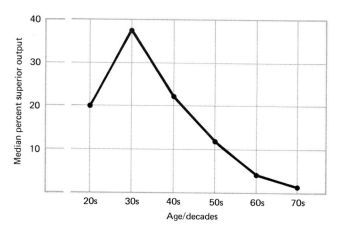

Figure 7.10

Percentage of superior output of creative persons as a function of age. This is a generalized curve representing a combination of various fields of endeavor and various estimates of quality. Data are from Lehman (1953), Table 34. (Source: Botwinick, 1967, Figure 20. Reprinted with permission from *Cognitive Processes in Maturity and Old Age*, copyright © 1967 by Springer Publishing Company, inc.)

(medicine, atomic energy, astronomy, mathematics, and botany)—and even psychologists (Lehman, 1966)—with similar results: a peak in the early years followed by a decline with age. He suggests that this decline with age is probably the result of a number of interacting factors, including

> a decrement in physical vigor and sensory capacity, more illness, glandular changes, more preoccupation with practical concerns, less favorable conditions for concentration, weakened intellectual curiosity, more mental disorders, and an accumulation of unfavorable habits. . . . Moreover, the individual who already has achieved prestige and recognition may try less hard thereafter to achieve further success [Lehman, 1962].

In contrast, Dennis (1966) studied the *total productivity* (not just the "high quality" works) of creative persons in the sciences, the arts, and other scholars. He found the decade of the forties was the most productive, or only slightly less than most productive, period of life. For scholars in the humanities, the decade of the seventies was as productive as the decade of the forties. Scientists showed a significant decline in the decade of the seventies, while the decade from 20 to 29 was the least productive. For artists, the decline was even sharper; and only for this group was the decade of the twenties more productive than the seventies (Figure 7.11). It would appear that a number of factors other than intellectual ability are involved in these trends. For example, the amount of time required to produce a creative work is probably much longer in a scholarly field than in the arts; also the amount of study required for scholarly or scientific fields may be

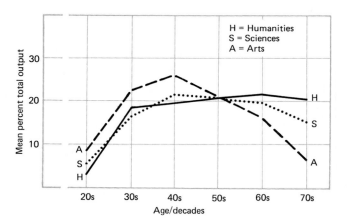

Figure 7.11

Percentage of total productivity of creative persons as a function of age. The humanities, sciences, and arts are represented by the means of several specific disciplines. Data are from Dennis (1966), Table 1. (Source: Botwinick, 1967, Figure 21. Reprinted with permission from *Cognitive Processes in Maturity and Old Age*, copyright © 1967 by Springer Publishing Company, Inc.)

considerably longer than for the arts; in addition, the contributions of assistants may greatly benefit the creative productivity of middle-aged scientists and scholars, but be of little importance to the creative production of artists.

Thus, depending on whether one defines creativity as a person's major and most superior works (Lehman), or as a person's total productivity (Dennis), the graphs for creativity differ considerably; also whether one examines creativity in one field or another, the peaks and changes in the graphs differ. For example, Manniche and Falk's (1957) study of the age during which Nobel prizewinners (1901-1950) did their work corresponds to Lehman's findings for physics and chemistry, but averages in the forties for medicine.

However, regardless of the way in which creativity is defined, the peaks and declines are, perhaps, more the result of noncognitive factors than intellectual changes. That is, following some major creative work, the scientist would be likely to be given greater responsibilities (department chairman or director of research, for instance), to become more involved in more scientific and governmental committees, and to find that there is less time and energy left over for creative productivity (Bjorksten, 1946). Nonetheless, there may also be some significant congitive factors involved that incline younger persons toward more unique or novel solutions to problems—not necessarily because their mind works differently (although that may be a factor also) but because they have a fresh perspective and have not learned to think about the field in conventional ways. At the same time, the older person might benefit from accumulated knowledge and perspective (as well as from research grants and assistants).

Undoubtedly, as with all of the changes we have detailed in this chapter on intellectual processes, health is perhaps a paramount consideration. For example, not only is one's potential creativity cut short by incapacitating disease or death before old age (that in itself tends to push the creativity graph toward the young ages when *all* creative persons are alive), but also failing health can reduce the time and energy, as well as the cognitive abilities, that may be devoted to creativity. In any event, these data on creativity reaching its peak in young adulthood (or the decade of the thirties) imply that if one began work at an earlier age, more creative production might result (assuming that sufficient knowledge could be accumulated to produce a creative work). However, the current trend in our society is toward an *increase* in the age of entry into careers, raising the probability that some of the potentially most creative years might be passed during the training preparatory to independent creative work. Perhaps this is inevitable in a rapidly advancing technological society, but many students wonder how creative they might be if they were not spending so much time in school learning the necessary skills for their profession.

The next Interlude will help to put these complex biological aspects of aging into a more personal perspective since it deals with the actual implications of chronic disease and specific concerns about health and diet within the context of an individual's life—in this case for an older person living in New York City.

CHAPTER SUMMARY

1. Each species of animal has a characteristic life span. In spite of medical advances, the maximum length of human life has not been increased, although more people are living into old age today than has been true in the past.

2. Heredity and external-environmental influences affect the life span of individuals. Children of long-lived parents have a longer potential life span, and factors such as urban living, marriage, exposure to radiation, and disease also affect an individual's longevity.

3. Aging is not simply the result of the organism wearing out, or the result of a loss of cells with age. Although there is no agreement about the cause of aging, there are a number of promising theories that attempt to explain the physiological processes involved in aging. There may be no single cause of aging, but different explanations for different organ systems.

4. Decreased efficiency of the processes that regulate the balance of the body's internal environment (homeostasis) is thought to reduce the body's ability to recover from stress. Accumulation of waste products in cells and changes in connective tissue protein (collagen) may reduce the efficiency of organ systems with advancing age. Changes in the immune processes by which the body protects itself from disease may be related to aging and to diseases that are more common among older people. Changes in cellular processes with aging may interfere with the replication and functioning of cells.

5. While older people are more susceptible to disease than younger people, disease processes are disorders of bodily functions that may occur at any age. Therefore, disease processes are distinct from aging processes.

6. Acute illnesses are more common in children; chronic illnesses are more common in older people. Chronic impairments, such as reduced hearing or vision, increase with age. The prevalence of restricted activity increases with age, but eight out of ten older people have no impairment that prevents them from carrying out their major activities.

7. Cardiovascular diseases are the major cause of death in older people. Men have higher rates than women for nearly all causes of death. Black persons have higher death rates than whites for diabetes and cerebrovascular diseases (such as strokes).

8. Although the medical expenses of older people average three times as much as those of younger people, serious problems exist in the medical care older people receive. Many specialized issues are involved in geriatric medicine. About two-thirds of the cost of medical care for older people is paid for by public funds.

9. In the absence of disease, the main change with advancing age is a slowing down in reaction time that suggests a decline in the speed of central nervous system functioning. A subclinical level of disease, however, has effects on a wide range of physiological capacities.

10. Changes in physical and physiological characteristics of aging persons reflect the interaction of age and disease. Most older people show changes in the skeleton and skin, circulatory system, sense organs, central nervous system, and sensorimotor skills. In general, the body becomes less efficient in perceiving, processing, and responding to stimuli; but most older people compensate for these changes and continue to function effectively into advanced age unless disease or injury brings a drastic impairment.

11. Individual differences in intelligence are as great among older people as they are among younger people. Most older people show some decline in intellectual functioning, especially in performance aspects of intelligence tests; however, they are often not found before age 50 or 60 and then tend to be relatively small.

12. Not all people experience memory impairment with advancing age, but it becomes more common among older people. It seems that memory loss may reflect problems either in acquisition of new material or in retrieval of the memory. Similarly, learning ability does not decline for some older people, when it does, it reflects memory impairment or the slowing of the speed of central nervous system processing.

13. Creativity appears to be higher in some fields at earlier ages, and higher in other fields during the later years. The way in which creativity is defined and measured also affects the ages at which it appears to rise or fall. Although health problems may affect creativity, older people continue to be a source of creativity in many fields.

REFERENCES

Arenberg, David, & Robertson-Tchabo, Elizabeth. 1977. Learning and Aging. In James E. Birren & K. Warner Schaie (Eds.), *Handbook of the Psychology of Aging.* New York: Van Nostrand Reinhold.

Barrows, Charles H., & Roeder, Lois M. 1977. Nutrition. In Caleb E. Finch & Leonard Hayflick (Eds.), *Handbook of the Biology of Aging.* New York: Van Nostrand Reinhold.

Birren, James E. 1960. Behavioral Theories of Aging. In Nathan W. Shock (Ed.), *Aging: Some Social and Biological Aspects.* Publication No. 65. Washington, D.C.: American Association for the Advancement of Science.

Birren, James E. 1964. *The Psychology of Aging.* Englewood Cliffs, N.J.: Prentice-Hall.

Birren, James E.; Butler, Robert N.; Greenhouse, Samuel W.; Sokoloff, Louis; & Yarrow, Marian R. (Eds.) **1963.** *Human Aging: A Biological and*

Behavioral Study. Publication No. (HSM) 71-9051. Washington, D.C.: U.S. Government Printing Office.

Bjorksten, J. 1946. The Limitation of Creative Years. *Scientific Monthly, 62,* 94.

Blumenthal, Herman T., & Berns, Aline W. 1964. Autoimmunity In Aging. In Bernard L. Strehler (Ed.), *Advances in Gerontological Research.* Vol. 1. New York: Academic Press.

Botwinick, Jack. 1967. *Cognitive Processes in Maturity and Old Age.* New York: Springer.

Botwinick, Jack. 1969. Disinclination to Venture Response versus Cautiousness in Responding: Age Differences. *Journal of Genetic Psychology, 115,* 55-62.

Botwinick, Jack. 1970. Geropsychology. *Annual Review of Psychology, 21,* 239-272.

Botwinick, Jack. 1977. Intellectual Abilities. In James E. Birren & K. Warner Schaie (Eds.), *Handbook of the Psychology of Aging.* New York: Van Nostrand Reinhold.

Brody, Harold. 1955. Organization of the Cerebral Cortex. III. A Study of Aging in the Human Cerebral Cortex. *Journal of Comparative Neurology, 102*(2), 511-556.

Bromley, D. B. 1966. *The Psychology of Human Ageing.* Baltimore: Penguin.

Brotman, Herman B. 1972. One in Ten: A Statistical Portrait. *Geriatrics/1972.* (Published by *Medical World News.*)

Butler, Robert N. 1975. *Why Survive?: Being Old in America.* New York: Harper & Row.

Comfort, Alex. 1964. *Ageing: The Biology of Senescence.* New York: Holt, Rinehart and Winston.

Comfort, Alex. 1968. Feasibility in Age Research. *Nature, 217,* 320-322.

Comfort, Alex. 1972. The Prospects of Longevity. Paper presented at the meeting of the Gerontological Society, San Juan, Puerto Rico, December, 1972.

Corso, John F. 1977. Auditory Perception and Communication. In James E. Birren & K. Warner Schaie (Eds.), *Handbook of the Psychology of Aging.* New York: Van Nostrand Reinhold.

Craik, Fergus I. M. 1977. Age Differences in Human Memory. In James E. Birren & K. Warner Schaie (Eds.), *Handbook of the Psychology of Aging.* New York: Van Nostrand Reinhold.

Cristofalo, V. J. 1970. Metabolic Aspects of Aging in Diploid Human Cells. In E. Holečková & V. J. Cristofalo (Eds.), *Aging in Cell and Tissue Culture.* New York: Plenum Press.

Curtis, Howard J. 1966. *Biological Mechanisms of Aging.* Springfield, Ill.: Charles C Thomas.

Curtis, Howard J.; Tilley, John; & Crowley, Cathryn. 1964. The Elimination of Chromosome Aberrations in Liver Cells by Cell Division. *Radiation Research, 22*(4), 730-734.

Demoise, Charles F., & Conrad, Robert A. 1972. Effects of Age and Radiation Exposure on Chromosomes in a Marshall Island Population. *Journal of Gerontology, 27*(2), 197-201.

Dennis, Wayne. 1966. Creative Productivity between the Ages of 20 and 80 Years. *Journal of Gerontology, 21*(1), 1-8.

Diamond, Marian C. 1978. Aging and Cell Loss: Calling for an Honest Count. *Psychology Today, 12*(4: September), 126.

Dovenmuehle, Robert H. 1970. Aging versus Illness. In Erdman Palmore (Ed.), *Normal Aging.* Durham, N.C.: Duke University Press.

Dovenmuehle, Robert H.; Busse, Ewald W.; & Newman, Gustave. 1961. Physical Problems of Older People. *Journal of the American Geriatrics Society, 9,* 208-217.

Dublin, Louis I.; Lotka, Alfred J.; & Spiegelman, Mortimer. 1949. *Length of Life: A Study of the Life Table.* New York: Ronald Press.

Eisdorfer, Carl, & Wilkie, Frances. 1977. Stress, Disease, Aging and Behavior. In James E. Birren & K. Warner Schaie (Eds.), *Handbook of the Psychology of Aging.* New York: Van Nostrand Reinhold.

Engen, Trygg. 1977. Taste and Smell. In James E. Birren & K. Warner Schaie (Eds.), *Handbook of the Psychology of Aging.* New York: Van Nostrand Reinhold.

Feinberg, Richard, & Podolak, Edward. 1965. Latency of Pupillary Reflex to Light Stimulation and its Relationship to Aging. In A. T. Welford & James E. Birren (Eds.), *Behavior, Aging, and the Nervous System.* Springfield, Ill.: Charles C Thomas.

Fozard, James L.; Wolf, Ernst; Bell, Benjamin; McFarland, Ross A.; & Podolsky, Stephen. 1977. Visual Perception and Communication. In James E. Birren & K. Warner Schaie (Eds.), *Handbook of the Psychology of Aging.* New York: Van Nostrand Reinhold.

Gelfant, Seymour, & Smith, J. Graham, Jr. 1972. Aging: Noncycling Cells— An Explanation. *Science, 178*(4059), 357-361.

Gompertz, B. 1825. On the Nature of the Function Expressive of the Law of Human Mortality on a New Mode of Determining Life Contingencies. *Philosophical Transactions of the Royal Society (London),* Series A, 115, 513-585.

Granick, Samuel, & Patterson, Robert D. (Eds.) **1971.** *Human Aging II: An Eleven-Year Followup Biomedical and Behavioral Study.* Publication No. (HSM) 71-9037. Washington, D.C.: U.S. Government Printing Office.

Hayflick, Leonard. 1965. The Limited *in vitro* Lifetime of Human Diploid Cell Strains. *Experimental Cell Research, 37*(3), 614-636.

Hayflick, Leonard. 1966. Senescence in Cultured Cells. In Nathan W. Shock (Ed.), *Perspectives in Experimental Gerontology.* Springfield, Ill.: Charles C Thomas.

Hayflick, Leonard. 1970. Aging Under Glass. *Experimental Gerontology, 5,* 291-303.

Himwich, Williamina A., & Himwich, Harold E. 1959. Neurochemistry of Aging. In James E. Birren (Ed.), *Handbook of Aging and the Individual.* Chicago: University of Chicago Press.

Hofstetter, H. W. 1944. A Comparison of Duane's and Donders' Tables of the Amplitude of Accommodation. *American Journal of Optometry and Archives of American Academy of Optometry, 21,* 345-363.

Jacobs, E. A.; Winter, P. M.; Alvis, H. J.; & Small, S. M. 1969. Hyperoxygenation Effect on Cognitive Functioning in the Aged. *New England Journal of Medicine, 281,* 753-757.

Johnson, L. K. 1972. Memory Loss With Age: A Storage or Retrieval Problem?

Paper presented at the meeting of the Gerontological Society, San Juan, Puerto Rico, December, 1972.

Johnson, Roger, & Strehler, Bernard L. 1972. Loss of Genes Coding for Ribosomal RNA in Ageing Brain Cells. *Nature, 240*(5381), 412-414.

Jones, Hardin B. 1959. The Relation of Human Health to Age, Place and Time. In James E. Birren (Ed.), *Handbook of Aging and the Individual.* Chicago: University of Chicago Press.

Kallmann, Franz, J., & Jarvik, Lissy F. 1959. Individual Differences in Constitution and Genetic Background. In James E. Birren (Ed.), *Handbook of Aging and the Individual.* Chicago: University of Chicago Press.

Klonoff, Harry, & Kennedy, Margaret. 1966. A Comparative Study of Cognitive Functioning in Old Age. *Journal of Gerontology, 21*(2), 239-243.

Kohn, R. R. 1963. Human Aging and Disease. *Journal of Chronic Disease, 16,* 5-21.

Laws, R. M. 1971. Patterns of Reproductive and Somatic Aging in Large Mammals. In George A. Sacher (Ed.), *Aging in Relation to Development and Reproduction.* Argonne, Ill.: Argonne National Laboratory.

Lehman, Harvey C. 1953. *Age and Achievement.* Princeton, N.J.: Princeton University Press.

Lehman, Harvey C. 1962. The Creative Production Rates of Present Versus Past Generations of Scientists. *Journal of Gerontology, 17*(4), 409-417.

Lehman, Harvey C. 1966. The Psychologist's Most Creative Years. *American Psychologist, 21*(4), 363-369.

Lindop, Patricia J., & Rotblat, J. 1961. Long-Term Effects of a Single Whole-Body Exposure of Mice to Ionizing Radiations. *Proceedings of the Royal Society (London),* Series B, *154*(956), 332-349.

Makinodan, Takashi. 1977. Immunity and Aging. In Caleb E. Finch & Leonard Hayflick (Eds.), *Handbook of the Biology of Aging.* New York: Van Nostrand Reinhold.

Manniche, E., & Falk, G. 1957. Age and the Nobel Prize. *Behavioral Science, 2,* 301-307.

McFarland, Ross A.; Tune, G. Sidney; & Welford, Alan T. 1964. On the Driving of Automobiles by Older People. *Journal of Gerontology, 19,* 190-197.

Mead, Margaret. 1972. Long Living in Cross-Cultural Perspective. Paper presented at the meeting of the Gerontological Society, San Juan, Puerto Rico, December, 1972.

Medvedev, Zh. A. 1964. The Nucleic Acids in Development and Aging. In B. L. Strehler (Ed.), *Advances in Gerontological Research.* Vol. 1. New York: Academic Press.

Melrose, Jay; Welsh, Oliver L.; & Luterman, David M. 1963. Auditory Responses in Selected Elderly Men. *Journal of Gerontology, 18*(3), 267-270.

Moberg, David O. 1965. Religiosity in Old Age. *Gerontologist, 5*(2), 78-87.

Myers, G. C., & Pitts, A. M. 1972. The Demographic Effects of Mortality Reduction on the Aged Population of the U.S.: Some Baseline Projections. Paper presented at the meeting of the Gerontological Society, San Juan, Puerto Rico, December, 1972.

National Center for Health Statistics. 1964. Binocular Visual Acuity of Adults, United States, 1960-1962. *Vital and Health Statistics,* Series 11, No. 3. Washington, D.C.: U.S. Government Printing Office.

National Center for Health Statistics. 1972. Disability Days, United States, 1968. *Vital and Health Statistics*, Series 10, No. 67. Washington, D.C.: U.S. Government Printing Office.

National Center for Health Statistics, 1977. Characteristics and Activities of Nursing Home Residents, United States. *Vital and Health Statistics*, Series 13, No. 27. Washington, D.C.: U.S. Government Printing Office.

National Council on the Aging. 1978. *Fact Book on Aging: A Profile of America's Older Population.* Washington, D.C.: The National Council on Aging, Inc.

Orgel, L. E. 1963. The Maintenance of the Accuracy of Protein Synthesis and its Relevance to Ageing. *Proceedings of the National Academy of Sciences, U.S.A.*, 49(4), 517-521.

Ostfeld, Adrian M. 1966. Frequency and Nature of Health Problems of Retired Persons. In Frances M. Carp (Ed.), *The Retirement Process.* PHS Publication No. 1778. Washington, D.C.: U.S. Government Printing Office.

Papalia, D. E.; Salverson, S. M.; & True, M. 1973. An Evaluation of Quantity Conservation Performance During Old Age. *International Journal of Aging and Human Developments;* 4(2), 103-109.

Piaget, Jean. 1972. Roundtable Discussion at the Graduate Center of the City University of New York, October, 1972.

Reed, Homer B. C., Jr., & Reitan, Ralph M. 1963. Changes in Psychological Test Performance Associated with the Normal Aging Process. *Journal of Gerontology*, 18(3), 271-274.

Riegel, Klaus F., & Riegel, Ruth M. 1972. Development, Drop, and Death. *Developmental Psychology*, 6(2), 306-319.

Riley, Matilda White; Foner, Anne; & Associates. 1968. *Aging and Society. Vol. 1. An Inventory of Research Findings.* New York: Russell Sage Foundation.

Sacher, George A. 1959. Relation of Lifespan to Brain Weight and Body Weight in Mammals. In E. W. Wolstenholme & Maeve O'Connor (Eds.), *Ciba Foundation Symposium on the Life Span of Animals.* London: Churchill.

Sacher, George A. 1977. Life Table Modification and Life Prolongation. In Caleb E. Finch & Leonard Hayflick (Eds.), *Handbook of the Biology of Aging.* New York: Van Nostrand Reinhold.

Selye, Hans. 1950. *The Physiology and Pathology of Exposure to Stress.* Montreal: Acta, Inc., Medical Publishers.

Selye, Hans. 1970. Stress and Aging. *Journal of the American Geriatrics Society*, 18(9), 669-680.

Selye, Hans, & Prioreschi, P. 1960. Stress Theory of Aging. In Nathan W. Shock (Ed.), *Aging: Some Social and Biological Aspects.* Washington, D.C.: American Association for the Advancement of Science.

Shock, Nathan W. 1960. Some of the Facts of Aging. In Nathan W. Shock (Ed.), *Aging: Some Social and Biological Aspects.* Washington, D.C.: American Association for the Advancement of Science.

Shock, Nathan W. 1977. Biological Theories of Aging. In James E. Birren & K. Warner Schaie (Eds.), *Handbook of the Psychology of Aging.* New York: Van Nostrand Reinhold.

Spiegel, Paul Martin. 1972. Theories of Aging. In P. S. Timiras, *Developmental Psysiology and Aging.* New York: Macmillan.

Spieth, Walter. 1964. Cardiovascular Health Status, Age, and Psychological Performance. *Journal of Gerontology*, 19, 277-284.

Strehler, Bernard L. 1962.   *Time, Cells, and Aging.* New York: Academic Press.

Strehler, Bernard L. 1977.   *Time, Cells, and Aging* (2nd ed.). New York: Academic Press.

Timiras, P. S. 1972.   *Developmental Physiology and Aging.* New York: Macmillan.

U.S. Bureau of the Census. 1979.   Prospective Trends in the Size and Structure of the Elderly Population, Impact of Mortality Trends, and Some Implications. *Current Population Reports*, Series P-23, No. 78. Washington, D.C.: U.S. Government Printing Office.

Walford, Roy L. 1969.   *The Immunologic Theory of Aging.* Baltimore: Williams & Wilkins.

Weiss, Alfred D. 1959.   Sensory Functions. In James E. Birren (Ed.), *Handbook of Aging and the Individual.* Chicago: University of Chicago Press.

Weissman, August. 1891.   *Essays on Heredity.* Oxford: Clarendon Press.

Welford, Alan T. 1959.   Psychomotor Performance. In James E. Birren (Ed.), *Handbook of Aging and the Individual.* Chicago: University of Chicago Press.

Welford, A. T. 1977.   Motor Performance. In James E. Birren & K. Warner Schaie (Eds.), *Handbook of the Psychology of Aging.* New York: Van Nostrand Reinhold.

Wetherick, N. E. 1965.   Changing an Established Concept: A Comparison of the Ability of Young, Middle-Aged, and Old Subjects. *Gerontologia, 11*, 82-95.

Interlude
Joan, Age 67

Joan is a 67-year-old black grandmother who lives in Harlem in New York City. She is one of 16 children; her mother was born during slavery in Georgia; she eventually moved to New York and brought Joan to the city as a young girl. Both Joan and her mother worked as "domestics" for a single family for 37 years, and Joan still works for them one day a week. Her mother died nearly 20 years ago at the grand age of 93, and Joan has five grandchildren; the oldest are in high school. Her proudest moment was the graduation of her two children from high school. She has some health problems now but works one day a week at a local Senior Center helping prepare the luncheon that is served daily.

Why did the milestones that she chose to discuss stand out in her memory? Does she choose different milestones from those a man might choose? What are some of the "timing events" in her life? In what sense are they "timing events"? What effect has her health had on her? Has she received adequate health care? How could it be improved? What are her feelings about death? How does living in Harlem affect her? In what ways has being black affected her developmental milestones and course of life? In what ways has poverty affected her? Are there any practical ways in which a Senior Center or the community might increase her opportunities for fulfillment? Do her many assets and strengths make her an atypical "senior citizen"?

As you look back over your life, what are some of the milestones that stand out? The education of my son and daughter; that's very hard if you're black. My son is 18 years in the Navy, and my daughter is 17 years with the telephone company, and I have five grandchildren. I'm 67 now. I was born January 1, 1906 in Georgia. I came to New York City as a young girl, attended school here, and then I started to work. And then I married and had my family. I never had any sickness until I reached my sixties. The doctor explained to me it comes with age—high blood pressure. He said high blood pressure gives me a blockage of the heart. When I feel so bad I go to the hospital and they give me treatments, you know; and he also discovered that I had sugar [diabetes] and I've been watching that. I have a diet that I don't really stick to, but I go in between—like if I eat bread one day, the next day I don't eat bread. He allows me three slices of bread a day, and no sodas, no beer, no alcoholic beverages, no jams and jellies. Plenty of fresh fruit, and so far I think that I'm in pretty good health excepting the high blood pressure. *Does that hinder you getting around at all?* No indeed. I can get out every day. He told me to walk 20 blocks a day, but walk slow. Don't walk against the wind. Stay in the bed two hours in the mornin' and one hour in the afternoon when I find myself getting dizzy. But other than that I get up, walk around the house, and do the shopping. Don't climb no subway stairs, no kind of stairs. And he says if I want to catch a bus, if I miss that one, just wait; no hurrying at all and no emotional upsets. And I find out it really pays off. I do an awful lot of reading, so that way it quiets my nerves.

What were some of the big events in your life? Well, the marriage of my two children; that was a very big event. And I had my son come home from Vietnam. He was in Vietnam for two years and when he came back I was very happy. And . . . I don't know. . . . *You have one son?* Yeah, and one daughter. They were born in the same year. I had two kids in one year; my son was born January 21, 1937, my daughter was born December 8, 1937. I had quite a time convincing the insurance company that I had two babies in the one year. That was quite an event in my life. With my first child I was in the hospital 21 days because I was in my thirties when he was born. The doctor explained to me that my pelvis didn't expand like a younger girl. But my daughter came in the ambulance. On December the eighth I went to the hospital and they said they didn't have a bed, so they put me in the ambulance and were taking me to _____ hospital and before we got there she was born; and I was ready to come home. They made me stay 10 days, but I was ready to come home. I came home and went right back to work and never had a sick day until I got in my sixties, you know the blood pressure and overweight.

What kind of work did you do? Domestic work; I cooked. You see, my mother came up before and she was a cook and then when I came up to public school, on the weekends I would go out to Long Island and cook there and then when the family moved back to New York City I continued to cook for them. Now I go in one day a week. But I just do ironing, or maybe they ask me to prepare a roast, a leg of lamb, you know, make something like that and leave it for them, 'cause all their kids are married now and it's just the two of them. So I run the wash through the machine and press his shirts, make a leg of lamb or something like that. I go one day a week, every Thursday. *You've worked with this same family for . . .* Over 37 years. My mother was in their family; so I go now. Sometime when they have somethin' special on the weekend I go and help them serve or cook. But they stopped entertainin' now because food is goin' up so high. They said no more entertainin' now (laughs). So I just take it easy; and I go to the [Senior] Center and I cook Wednesdays and Fridays there [the Center serves lunch daily]. We finish about 2:00 or 2:30 and I come home, look at my stories [on TV], and that's it.

I don't go out at night no more, because . . . well, you know the reason why that is. *Why don't you go out at night?* I'm afraid of being mugged; and don't have anyone to go out with me, so I stay home and do my entertainin' in the house; the neighbors come visit one another and that's it. We don't go out in the night, that's all. Because you can't get a cab half the time; and there's no shows that I would like to go to downtown and pay taxi fare all the way back here. So nighttime I'm in the house; definitely! There's no way I'm goin' out. Sometimes I have friends that have cars; they come and get me and they take me back. Then if I go to my daughter, I get a cab in front of my house, get out in front of her door, and then she and her friend bring me back. That's the way we have to travel—but never just to catch a bus or walk out at night. It took me a long time to get it through my head not to go out at night (she laughs). *Why is that; did something happen once?* Not only once. I've been very fortunate in that, you know. I went out one Saturday night and they told me to take a taxi home. So I stood on the corner and hollered "Taxi, taxi"; so I said I'll walk over to Eighth Avenue and get the bus. And I saw these two fellas and I got to the corner of Eighth Avenue and 23rd Street and one fellow asked me if I had a cigarette or somethin' and I said I don't smoke and he grabbed me and said, "Yes, you do," but when he went to grab at me I screamed and there's a hotel right across the street. There was a lady looking out the window and she started to scream; so when they turned around to see where the noise was comin' from—there's a restaurant right down there—and I ran into that. So I asked the cashier would he come out so I could get a cab. So he got a cab and I came home and that was all right. Then, another time, I was comin' home and got off the Eighth Avenue bus and a fellow ran up to me; I had a pocketbook. I don't know why I pulled back 'cause there was nothin' in it at all. My keys was in my coat pocket and I just had tissues and a compact and comb—stuff like that. So, when he grabbed at the pocketbook, I hauled off and hit at him. He was so young! It was unbelievable to think that a young kid like that could do somethin' like that. So when I saw him I said this is nothin' but a little kid. He was pullin' and I gave him a shove and he fell backwards. Naturally, I ran, screaming as usual, you know. Well, he didn't follow me; and I got to the corner; a couple of people was on the corner and they were laughin'. They said, "I don't think he'll snatch a pocketbook any more" (she laughs). I looked back and he was still layin' down. Another time too; so my daughter said, "That's it!" That's why I tell you I don't go out at night no more. You don't push your luck too far. That's why I said when you're comin', push my buzzer; if I didn't know you was comin' I wouldn't answer that buzzer.

Oh, then in 1960—that's another happy event—I was picked as a delegate to go to San Francisco, California, with my Eastern Star. So, my son and daughter tricked me into taking a flight; instead of taking an ordinary flight, I took a jet. I was in San Francisco before my daughter could get from Kennedy Airport to the Bronx. *Sounds like a big trip.* A wonderful trip! Six weeks. I was a delegate. From San Francisco we went to Tijuana. You see, we flew there, but I wouldn't get back on, so they made arrangements to come back through the country, which was beautiful. Anywhere I go now, I travel on a Greyhound bus; no plane. I haven't had a trip since 1960, besides ordinary ones to [New] Jersey and Atlantic City, like that.

Were there any other big moments in your life? The biggest one was when my son came home from Vietnam. When he was 17 years old he enlisted in the Marines; he was in high school and decided he wanted to be a pilot; when he graduated in June, he changed over to the Navy and when he was 18 years old he was in Capteown, Africa. Really, he had never been away from home and he wasn't 18 years old then when he was sent overseas. Then I started readin' about Formosa, those different little straits and islands. . . . So then I didn't hear from him in a long time and a letter came. He had came down with pneumonia; but he got well and everything and he went right back. He came home after a year. "I'm goin' back overseas," he said; he loved it. Well, he came back the third time and he got married. Then he was stationed in Rhode Island and New Jersey and his first kid was born in Rhode Island; his second kid was born in Florida; the third kid was born in California. From then on he left from San Diego for Vietnam. After he came back from Vietnam—he served two years—he was up for promotion; so now he has his office here in New York City. So it worked out beautifully.

How does it feel to become a grandmother? Well, it's a thrill! The first grandchild, I'm tellin' you. My birthday is January the first and he was born on December the thirty-first. So I had this big party to serve, and I said my daughter was goin' to the hospital, and I said if everything is all right then I'll serve the party. So I had her under the doctor's care and he said she will definitely deliver the latter part of December. She started her pains the thirtieth of December and I rushed her to the hospital, so the next morning at 3:28, she delivered. And they called me from the hospital. I was a nervous mother, believe it or not. I called the people who wanted me and said, "Go ahead, have the party; I'm a grandmother now." Oh, that was a happy evenin'. That was a happy time. Yessiree, that was a happy evenin'.

She was married one week, my son was married the next week. My first grandchild was born in December; my second grandchild was born that March. They married together, they started havin' their families together, so I started becomin' a grandmother in December and then in March. I went up to visit my daughter-in-law with my second grandchild; the third one was born in Florida and I went down there; and I said, "Look, the next grandchild you have, I'm not comin' out." *Why was it such a special event?* That was a very happy occasion. I thank God I had lived to be a grandmother and to see my kids married, grown, and have their own family. And believe me, you will never have a lonely moment. Never. I could never tell anyone I'm lonely, because they're here with their records and their rock 'n' roll, they keep me up to date on everything and I do an awful lot of readin' myself, you know. And then with their homework, believe it or not, I'm being reeducated. Because when I was goin' to school, we didn't have the things that they have. And now, I'm really reeducatin' myself on their homework, you know, which is very good. It keeps me very young and very happy, I can truthfully say. [Two of her grandchildren live with her during the week so they can live closer to their high school.]

How old were you when you came from Georgia? I was in my teens when I came. World War I ended in November, 1918, and I came here the very next year in September, 1919. And then I went to public school and after that I went to high school for two years, but I didn't graduate. I had to work with my mother, 'cause times was very hard then. Then I was supposed to go to school at night, and I went for a while, but it was gettin' me, you know, so my mother said, "No, I won't punish you like this." So we had to go to work to help support the family.

This is why I say a happy event is when my son graduated from high school and when my daughter graduated from high school; and then my son went to college on Uncle Sam [G. I. benefits]. My daughter went to _____ College, which I helped her pay for that. So, the education of my two kids is a really happy event in my life, 'cause that's what counts today, education. The work that I had to do, they don't have to do. Oh yes, that was a very happy event. He graduated one year and she graduated the next year. I don't know about other people, but that's a very happy thing; and they done it in three years.

What about some of the sadder points; have there been any crisis points in your life? The crisis points, well, when my mother had a stroke. She was in her nineties when she died. I had brought her to live with me then. She had her own apartment, but by workin' all day it was too hard for me to go to her apartment, cook, wash and iron, clean up, and ask the neighbor to look in on her, 'cause she didn't want to go in the hospital. So I brought her here to live with me, and she had her first stroke here. She was ninety in January, and in October she had her first stroke. Naturally, I had an ambulance come and take her to the hospital, and the doctor said that she was not able to be by herself any more, and I put her in a nursing home. She was out there, and she was able to get around a bit, not too much, in a wheelchair, and they worked on her. She was a wonderful musician; and she was born in slavery time too. So she was able to play for the Christmas carols and entertainment. The third year, she was 93, and in September she had her third stroke. It was on a Tuesday at 1:30, and on Wednesday at 2:30 she passed. That was sad because being close to your parents, you know, and my father went away when I was quite young. So, she was a mother and father to us.

And then I had a brother, who was in the service also; he was in Italy with World War II; and he had a murmur of the heart, and he came back and his hair had turned snow white. He always said, "I guess it was those bullets that frightened me." He had had pneumonia twice, and while he was up my mother passed, and he came down with lobar pneumonia the third time, and he went in the hospital on a Friday, and he passed the next Wednesday. It was so quick, you know, it was a shock to us, 'cause we thought he'd pull through that, but he didn't. So that was another sad time. So now it's only three girls left.

My mother had 16 children. *Sixteen children!* But see, my mother was born in slavery. She was married when she was 13, she said; you see, my grandmother was a "house slave," and my mother married what you called a "yard slave." You see, they had different kinds of slaves then. And she married at the age of 13; she had 14 children by him. After he died my grandmother brought her and some of her kids— 'cause some of them had died when they were quite young —to _____ Georgia. And she met my father, and she had two kids by my father, which is me and my brother. She raised us, and my sisters got married; one went to Chicago; one came to Baltimore; and then my mother used to go back and forth to Florida to work, go to Virginia to work. You know, she was a cook, so she worked seasonal, you know. So she finally decided she'd get us out of the South. *You went with her when she went to these different places?* No, you see, my older sister was takin' care of us. We had to go to school; and then somethin' happened—we had a lynchin' down there; it was frightening with the Klan and all. So my mother got me up here, then the next year she got my brother up here. Then my sisters got married and my brother got married up here. We had plots here in the cemetery and she said, "When I pass don't ever bring me back there; we got plots up here and bury me up here." So she never went back. But I went back. My brother wouldn't go back, but I went back (laughs), I certainly did. Yeah, my mother was 93 when she passed; and she had all her facilities 'til she was 90. She used to forget, but you know she never used a walkin' cane. *How old were you when she passed?* Oh, let's see now. She's been dead now about 19 years.

You said you did get back to Georgia once? Yeah, I went back in 1949 but I didn't know it. I wanted my kids to see my home and their father's home, so I carried them to Savannah and I went to _____, Georgia, but I didn't know my home. It was changed around. But my son, when we got on the buses, it said, "White to the front and Colored to the rear." My son was takin' a picture so he could bring it back to show and he said, "Momma, I'll never come back here any more" (she laughs). So I said, "Well Johnny honey, things will change in years to come." We went into a souvenir store 'cause I wanted to get some cards to send home. The girl refused to wait on me, a little white girl, you know. I went over to the manager and I said, "Mister, I would like to get some souvenir cards to send back to New York and the young lady won't give them to me." He goes over to her and says, "Look, if you don't want to work, you can go to the office and get your pay. This lady wants to buy some cards and you refused to wait on her." So the man waited on us.

Is you husband still alive? Yes. We separated over 20 years ago. *Twenty years ago?* When people try to stay together in New York, you know, I was considered to be very old-fashioned, bein' from the South. So we agreed to disagree. That's why I say when my son and daughter came out of high school I was very happy 'cause I worked very hard. I worked night and day; I used to cater parties at night and cook in the day. So when I saw them come up that aisle and get their diploma, believe me, my chest was out this big.

This question of welfare was. . . . I didn't go for that at all. *You didn't want any welfare?* No, no. Nobody in my family ever had any. Why should I have it? There's work here; there's work enough! If my heart wasn't bad now, I could probably do two or three hours work every day. But now Friday we serve 175 people every day for lunch. *At the Senior Center?* At the Center. Boy was I tired Friday afternoon. No, I could never work every day no more! 'Cause my breath is very short. I have my pills for my heart, you know, and I had an electrocardiogram not so long ago, and the doctor told me not to do strenuous . . . you know. He wanted to put me in the hospital and I said, "Oh, no. I'll take your advice." I come back here at 2:00 every afternoon and watch my stories on TV.

How long were you and your husband together? We were married in 1941. We married for the convenience of keeping him from going into the Army (she laughs); that's what I told him. We went together for three years and never got married; and when World War II broke out he said, "Oh, yes, we're goin' to get married," to my mother. They put him in 4E [classification for the draft] (laughs). *Was that a big day in your life when you got married, or not?* Yeah, we just went to City Hall. Got married and came back to my mother's house; we had presents and my mother baked a couple cakes and different friends came in. Now if you get married in a church you got to pay; I don't go in for things like that.

I don't like a whole lot of fancy things. This is why people say, "You're still staying in that dump [referring to the apartment]?" I say, "Look, the way they raise the rent, any apartment you move in now you're gonna pay over a hundred dollars." I've been here since February, 1933, so now why should I move? The landlord can't raise the rent, you know [some apartments in New York had their rent controlled by law so it could not be raised while the same tenant kept the apartment]. And I'm a Senior Citizen so I got [rent] exemption, 'cause my Social Security's only $103. So now I have to take my rent out of there and my telephone and gas and electric. *$103 a month?* Yeah. My daughter takes care of the kids [who stay with her during the week] and the food and all like that, but as I say, I'm not well enough to work every day, and when I go in on a Thursday, they give me $12, so that helps out. And I don't need a whole lot of clothes 'cause I don't go nowhere. My daughter says, "Now, Momma!" I say I don't need it. I don't need a pocketbook 'cause they're gonna snatch it from me, right? What do I need all those clothes to put in the closet? They're gonna come in here and rob me and take your things, you know. She's always sayin', "Momma, you need . . ." and I say, "You shut up! I know what I want." *So you have managed to stay off welfare so far?* Yeah, thank God. *You'd really hate to go on welfare if you had to?* At my age I wouldn't. None of my family ever been on it. And we're makin' out. My son is in the service; my daughter is workin'. I say I don't need clothes, and Social Security can pay my rent, and my telephone is for my comfort, for my health too. My daughter says, "Momma, come give me your gas and electric bill." When my son comes home he says, "Momma, give me your telephone bill." He says, "You got money to last you?" I say yeah, you know. So I budget myself. I got a Medicaid card; so I go to Harlem Hospital. For my eyeglasses I go to the eyeglass place; so now why should I go on welfare. I'm not goin' in and lay my life on the line for a few dollars.

Were there a lot of crisis points in your marriage? Was that a pretty difficult time? Yes it was. It was a problem trying to get him to come home with the salary; sittin' down and trying to budget ourselves, you know. I was workin' and meetin' the bills. Also, my mother used to help me too. And when his sister first got married, she and her husband were roomin' in the back room there. They was young and didn't have enough money, so they couldn't pay no rent. So we had to carry the rent, and feed them, you know. After five years, that's long enough. That was a terrible family problem, you know. *There were a lot of arguments about that?* Don't ever shack up with your in-laws! Take it from me. I'm tellin' you. That's what I went through; that's my problems! *That really destroyed your marriage?* That, and then after that, well you know, New York got a lot of glamour girls and he used to go to the bar. That was all right, but I couldn't go into the bar; but then they got a little too bold. I didn't want the kids to see that. Right now his son and daughter respects him, but they tell him, "Daddy, you know what you did to Momma." They don't like that, you know.

You said that you worked with this one family for 37 years; have there been any crisis points in your job there? No, a wonderful family! I am one of their family, and my mother was one of the family, and my children and grandchildren are part of the family. When the older girl got married I served at the party and my grandson helped me; my granddaughter helped me; my daughter helped. We were just one of his family. *It sounds like you're going to continue working there as long as you want.* I only work there one day a week now. I'm my own boss. I have my keys. When they first bought a house in Fire Island I used to go every weekend. So I've had a happy life. Poor, but happy. As I say, I don't go for welfare. I'm not against anybody gettin' it, especially some elderly people that we know. They really deserve it because some people they used to work for didn't pay Social Security for them and that's really unfair. I know I talked to one lady and she said that she worked 47 years for one family, and all the time they told her they were payin' Social Security, and they didn't pay. Now that's unfair to her. My people paid it. So when I got sick when I was 62 years old they said why don't you wait until you're 65 and you'll get more. I said there was no guarantee that I'm gonna live 'til I'm 65.

I was sick, really sick then. And two years ago I was takin' cancer tests. The doctor didn't tell me, but every test he would give me I would look it up, or ask my friends who are doctors or nurses and they told me what it was. I went and the last test I had was all the X rays. I was X-rayed a whole day; all different angles. And I came home; it was in July, I'll never forget it. I had a chill 'cause the hospital was air-conditioned and the metal tables that you lay on, you know. So I put on my clothes and got a cab and came home. Now I was in a terrible state for two weeks, waitin' for the hospital to send for me or get a letter. So I went back for a check-up, and they said my X ray hadn't come back, and the nurse told me not to worry. She said the X rays must have come back negative, otherwise they would have sent for you in a hurry. Well, that didn't satisfy me. In September I went back again. I said to the doctor, "Where's my X rays?" So he said, "Don't worry. How did you feel?" I said, "All right—Doctor, do I have cancer?" He said, "Get that out of your mind! Now go on home and enjoy yourself and if we need you we'll send for you." They never sent for me, so I go to the clinic for my weight and blood pressure now. *It must have been a pretty frightening time, though, waiting and not knowing. . . .* Yeah, this is the frightening part. In the meantime I had lost two friends that had cancer of the rectum.

Would you say that you've changed very much in the last few years? My reflexes—I could walk in the kitchen and forget what I go in there for, somethin' like that. I spoke to the doctor and he said, "Well, you realize. . . ." I said, "Don't you say that I'm gettin' old!" He said, "Do you want to stay like you were when you were 16?" So he said to stop worryin' about my reflexes. You know, I have to make a list to go to the supermarket. I have that list in my hand with the shoppin' cart, and I forget I have the list. But this comes with age.

Do you sometimes look back over your life and kind of review and think about the things that have happened? Well, I look back over the good times that I had, you know. I look back on my family life. You see, we was a big happy family. Every Thanksgiving my mother had us over to her house and she served everything from soup to nuts. And then Christmas we all would be together. And after my son went in the service and my daughter got married, well, I was here alone, and then my mother passed. So then after my daughter had children, it kind of gave me a second hold on life, you know. 'Cause I sat here by myself after the children got married; I couldn't expect them to stay here, you know. And then my mother was gone and my brother was gone. I used to get up 5:30 in the mornin' for work, but on the weekend I'd get lonesome, and I didn't want to go up to my daughter's house all the time. But after they had kids I always have a crowd here. You see, my Thanksgiving's gonna be here now. I carried on after my mother; and my sister have Christmas dinner; and then my daughter have me for New Year's. So, it's happy moments in my life. I can truthfully say I'm happy. *As you look back over your life, are you satisfied?* I'm very satisfied! I don't have no regrets. The one regret, I couldn't get the education that I wanted; but it was hard on my mother, so I had to come and start workin' with her. But I saw that my kids and my grandchildren are gettin' it. But I tell you one thing, a lot of peoples that know me they say, "Well, I don't know where you cut yourself short of education, 'cause you got a lot of mother wit." They say I think fast, you know. And if you keep your head above water in New York City, you're doin' pretty good, believe me.

Do you feel like you've left your mark here someplace? Yes, I have no regrets at all. I have a happy life. I have grandchildren. I have a son and daughter. So, you know, I'm happy.

Do you sometimes think about death? No. I had a pain in my chest last week. I was in the bed. I got up and said, "Oh, Lord, I'm not ready" (she laughs). It was pressin' down, you know. I said, "Oh, Lord, I'm not ready." So I called my sister. She burst out laughin'. She said, "What are you doing?" I said, "I'm sittin' up!" When I got up I took a small glass of 7-Up for the gas. The doctor told me don't let it worry me as long as I abide by his rules. *So you don't think about it very much at all?* No. That's why I stay in the house (laughs). No, I don't think about it. *You're not ready for it yet?* No, these are my golden years. I can truthfully say, I am happy, 'cause I can lay down in the bed, I have money to pay my rent, gas, and electric—things like that—when before it was a struggle. But it's not a struggle at all. It's just contentment. That's why I can sit in this house seven days a week and have no worries, no worries at all. When I was young I had them. I don't think about death.

How does the future look to you? It looks rosy for me, if Nixon don't cut off our Social Security. 'Cause if Nixon cut off mine, I would be right on his doorstep in Washington, D. C., 'cause I work very hard. A dollar's taken out of this and out of that. Now if you go back to work, your Social Security check is goin' to stop. I think that's very unfair! It's not like money that they have to give you. That's money that the people had to pay in! Now why take that from us? I think it's ridiculous, things like this. So these are my happy years. I'm 67, and I don't have to work hard. When I was younger I had to work very hard. Now if I wake up in the mornin' and it's rainin' or snowin' I don't have to go to the Center or to work. I can stay in the house all day, 'cause as I said, the rent will be paid and that means a lot. I can make it.

According to staff members at the Senior Center, Joan died in 1976. She had remained active in the Center until she was taken to the hospital after having a heart attack. She appeared to have been making a good recovery in the hospital and had a pacemaker installed to regulate the heart beat; she was in the hospital about a week and died of heart failure. She did live to see her grandson graduate from high school—she had raised him and her granddaughter since they were infants. The granddaughter also graduated from high school, and both now have good jobs. The grandson remained living in Joan's apartment until he married in 1978; he now has a child.

At a commonsense level we probably all assume that the human adult is a complex creature who possesses a unique and relatively stable *personality*. For example, some adults seem to be particularly daring, bold, and extroverted; others seem to be quiet, conservative, and introverted; and still others impress us with their enthusiasm, their gregariousness, or their dependability (and so on). Each of us, it would seem, has an individual style, a uniqueness, a characteristic set of attributes that distinguish us from others and also help to make us recognizably similar in different situations and at different times over the years. Such assumptions are clearly useful since most people are rather consistent from day to day (and those who are not tend to be labeled "mentally ill"). Moreover, the existence of relatively stable personalities is obviously a necessary assumption for human interaction to proceed smoothly. Consider the chaos that would result if we all woke up each morning with a new personality: one's cheerful, cooperative wife today might be a demanding tyrant tomorrow; the capable efficient boss of yesterday might be an indecisive guilt-ridden neurotic today and a dictator tomorrow; the calm, reliable newscaster last night might become a biased bigot the next morning; and one's trusted friends, the national leaders, and the corner druggist might all become totally unpredictable. In such a situation, human interaction as we know it would become, at least, unpredictable and immensely difficult; at worst, it would be totally impossible. If we could not rely on some kind of predictability of the personality characteristics of oneself and of others, we would be as unable to interact with each other in meaningful ways as would be the case (pointed out in Chapter 2) if we all stopped playing social roles; in either case, each interaction would have to begin anew without the great advantage of prior experience and a set of expectations. It would be an impossibly confusing world indeed!

But what is personality? Where does it come from? Why is it fairly consistent from day to day? And can it be changed, or does it change as one grows older? These questions will be the central focus of the first section of this chapter as we explore various perspectives on the nature of personality in adulthood. The second section will present a model of personality that is an attempt to integrate many of the different views of personality within an interactionist perspective. The third section explores the research on personality stability and change during middle and late adulthood. The final section of this chapter will be a brief overview of abnormal changes in personality, focusing in particular on the frequently misunderstood phenomenon of senility and the problem of severe depression during middle and late life that is associated with the sharp increase in deaths by suicide among white males, especially after age 65. Throughout this chapter, we will be picking up themes mentioned earlier in the book—the simultaneous processes of stability and change during adulthood, the interactionist conception of the self, the notion of transitions, the dialectical model of development, the effects of changes in the family and the occupation, the effects of physiological, biological, and intellectual changes, and many others. In that sense, this chapter pulls together many ideas we have discussed separately, and it also sets the stage for a discussion of the experience of growing old in our society that will be the topic of the next chapter. Let us then turn to an examination of the nature of personality in adulthood.

PERSONALITY PROCESSES IN ADULTHOOD

There are several different definitions of *personality*, but most of them emphasize three major characteristics. First, personality reflects an individual's *uniqueness* as a person. Whatever attributes are seen as making up an individual's personality, they set him or her apart from other individuals or groups of individuals and they describe that person or that "type" of person as someone different from other persons or other types of persons. Second, personality theories focus on those attributes of a person that are fairly *consistent* over long periods of time and across many different situations. Although we will argue later that personality is not actually as consistent as one might think, it seems that our Western culture is based on the assumption that an individual's personality is reasonably consistent under ordinary circumstances. Third, personality is seen as the *link between the human being and the social and physical environment*; in that sense, it reflects the person's pattern or style of adaptation to the environment from the time of conception to the present. This does not necessarily imply that the person is passively adapting to an all-powerful environment; instead, the individual may be seen as actively interpreting, creating, and modifying the environment while the environment also affects the individual.

Although each of the several differing approaches to personality tends to emphasize these three characteristics, most focus greater attention on only one or two of them. For example, anthropologists emphasize the link between the person and the social and physical environment—as in studies of differences between individuals in farming societies compared with hunting and gathering societies. Freudian psychoanalysts stress the consistency of personality, examining links between early childhood experiences and adult behavior. Personality psychologists are frequently interested in identifying those characteristics that make people different from one another, thus emphasizing those characteristics that are relatively unique to an individual or a group—as in studies of personality factors in occupational choice discussed in Chapter 6. Behavioral psychologists and sociologists tend to emphasize the role of the environment, sometimes almost to the exclusion of a focus on the uniqueness of the person or the consistency of personality across situations. And developmental psychologists tend to study the consistency (and change) of personality over time, often paying little attention to the uniqueness of specific individuals and sometimes ignoring the effects of the social and physical environment in which the person is developing. As may be apparent from the general perspective of this book, the view we will emphasize here includes all three of these characteristics of personality. That is, the Interludes in between the chapters emphasize the uniqueness of individuals; the interdisciplinary approach focuses on the link between the person and the environment; and the developmental framework calls attention to the issue of consistency and change in personality. Similarly, the model of personality we will present in the next section will include a focus on all three of these characteristics of personality.

In this section, we will begin with the question of why personality appears to be fairly consistent from day to day, even though we all recognize that people do change over time; then, we will explore four major models of personality and conclude with a discussion of personality as a process. This section will emphasize those concepts that will be integrated into the model of personality that we will study in the following section.

Continuity and Change in Personality

Throughout our discussions of transitions in adulthood and in the family and occupation, we have suggested numerous ways in which an individual's personality would be likely to change—in the resocialization of parenthood, in occupational socialization, in the midlife transition, and in widowhood, to mention a few. Yet, the concept of personality emphasizes the continuity of personality and would imply that individuals are not changed in important ways by such events. This raises several interesting questions: Does personality remain fairly consistent over 10 or 20 or more years? What aspects of personality are highly consistent? What are the processes that bring about this consistency? And, conversely, how much change is there in personality and in what aspects of it?

In Chapter 2, we discussed the process of stability and change in detail. We concluded that continuity and change are simultaneous processes, so that individuals change while they remain consistent in some way. We noted that change may be brought about by change in the external environment, by changes in social roles or by socialization and resocialization, or by changes within the self. Conversely, consistency results from the memory of past experiences and habitual patterns that work efficiently in social situations, the selection of fairly consistent social environments, the tendency to perceive situations as consistent even when they are not, and the tendency to pay more attention to situations that confirm what we expect while ignoring those that conflict with our expectations. In Chapter 1, we introduced the dialectical perspective that suggested that these processes of stability and change may be seen as a continuous dialectical interaction. That is, development consists of an ongoing struggle between stability and change. In this view, continuity is only a period when the various aspects of one's life are synchronized; discontinuity, or change, is much more frequent since all dimensions of one's life are seldom in total harmony. Most of this discontinuity is fairly mild; but during periods of transition the discontinuity is more dramatic, and significant changes sometimes result.

Taken together, these perspectives suggest that personality has two distinct facets—consistency and change. To a large extent, which aspect of personality one observes is determined by the lenses one uses. If one looks for continuity (as with Freudian lenses), it will be observed. If one seeks change (as with behaviorist lenses), it also can be found. In reality, both processes occur simultaneously, and the development of an individual's personality probably results from the dialectical struggle between change and continuity over time. Perhaps that dialectical process cannot be observed directly, so we are forced to choose between viewing it through consistency lenses or change lenses, or alternating from one to the other. Thus, it may be that there is always an element of uncertainty inherent in the unique ways humans link themselves to their social and physical environment. Similar to the uncertainty principle in physics, there may be an uncertainty principle in the study of personality.

An example of this uncertainty principle is seen in a study by Woodruff and Birren (1972) who found no statistically significant age changes in the scores of 85 respondents on a measure of self-adjustment over a 25-year age span; that is, there was no significant difference in the way in which the respondents described themselves in 1944 (at average age 19.5) and their self-descriptions in 1969 (at average age 44.5). However, they also found that their respondents' *retrospective* descriptions of themselves in 1969 (as they thought they had answered in 1944) were markedly different (lower in personal and social adjustment) from the *actual* score in 1944 (Figure 8.1). Apparently these respondents perceived that they had changed (and in positive ways) since young adulthood,

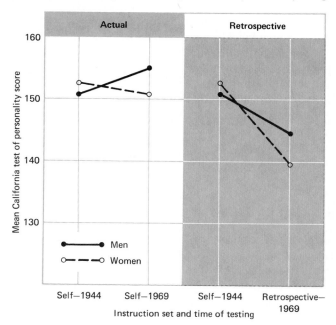

Figure 8.1

Level of personal and social adjustment as measured by the California test of personality scores in 1944 and 1969 for the 1924 cohort in the actual and retrospective condition. (Source: Adapted from Woodruff and Birren, 1972, p. 255. Reprinted with permission from *Developmental Psychology*, copyright © 1972 by the American Psychological Association.)

although this change was not present in their actual responses. Perhaps the test that was used and the statistical analysis employed reflected the consistency lenses, while the respondents were using change lenses when they looked back over the 25 years. Clearly the people felt they had changed, but the test did not show it. Clearly the people had been quite consistent, but they did not feel this was the case. We might conclude that people are more consistent in their self-perceptions than they believe themseves to be; or that objective tests of self-perceptions reveal more consistency than is actually experienced. Perhaps we cannot be certain because both conclusions are accurate, depending on which lenses we use to analyze the data.

In practical terms, this uncertainty principle implies that, while our society is based on the assumption that individuals are fairly consistent throughout their lives, we can never completely predict an individual's behavior in the future. Much of the consistency we see in ourselves and in others probably results from our socially encouraged and perhaps biologically based predisposition to use consistency lenses when we interact with others and with the social and physical world in which we live. Human evolution and social life as we know it would be impossible if we used change lenses continually, because we would never recognize similarities and patterns in the world. At the same time, there is more change and complexity in the world than we ordinarily pay attention to. Certainly, much of the excitement in human relationships results from the unpredictability, freshness, and new facets we experience with the other person; but a relationship would not be possible without trust in the consistency and stability of the person and the relationship over time.

Using four different perspectives on personality, let us explore the processes that are involved in personality consistency and change. The first two, cognitive and trait perspectives, tend to emphasize consistency; the last two, interactionist and behavioral perspectives, tend to emphasize change. However, each has important concepts to contribute to the model we will look at later in this chapter, combined in the model they describe personality as a system of interacting components.

Cognitive Perspective

Cognitive processes—such as thinking, perceiving, and conceptualizing—have been receiving more and more attention among psychologists, including those interested in personality, individuality, and psychotherapy (cf. Goldstein & Blackman, 1978; Raimy, 1975; Tyler, 1978). Since it is cognition that is involved in the mind's attempt to make sense out of the sensations, feelings, ideas, and experiences that it processes, it is logical to expect that cognition is deeply involved in the nature and meaning of personality.

Cognitive processes are involved in all three aspects of personality as we defined them earlier. First, cognition provides one of the most important links between the person and the environment, because the interpretation of the social and physical world requires the cognitive functions of perceiving and conceptualizing all the sensations the person receives from the environment. It is cognition that allows individuals to understand and think about their environment, to plan their responses, and to anticipate the future consequences of those responses. Piaget and others have demonstrated that these cognitive processes develop during childhood and adolescence, affecting children's understanding of the world and themselves (cf. Piaget & Inhelder, 1969). These processes may be affected by disease processes, such as senile brain disease, so that the person is less able to understand information from the environment and to plan adequate responses to it. There may also be developmental changes in cognition during the later years that lead to different styles of understanding and thinking about the world than those that characterize young adulthood; as we will discuss later in this chapter, Gutmann (1964) suggests that one dimension of this change may be a shift from "active mastery" to "passive and magical mastery" styles. Thus, cognitive processes in general are clearly involved in personality.

Second, cognition is involved in the perception of consistency and change — both in the world and in oneself. That is, the consistency lenses and the change lenses we discussed earlier reflect the cognitive processes of perceiving and conceptualizing the world. For that reason, it is likely that much of the consistency of personality results from selective perception of the environment so that more consistency is perceived than is acutally present, and from the selection of environments that are relatively consistent so that there is little external pressure for personality change. Thus, individuals may cling to misconceptions about themselves or about other people despite contradictory information; that information is often discarded because it contradicts one's beliefs about oneself or one's prejudices or stereotypes about others (cf. Raimy, 1975).

Third, individuals differ in the ways in which they typically perceive and conceptualize the world and themselves, so that cognition provides one basis for describing individual uniqueness. Specifically, individuals appear to differ in their characteristic cognitive style, as well as in the personal constructs they use in conceptualizing their experience.

Cognitive Style. Goldstein and Blackman (1978) define cognitive style as "the characteristic ways in which individuals conceptually organize the environment" (p. 2). This approach emphasizes the ways in which thought is structured, regardless of the content that is being structured. For example, rigidity, intolerance of ambiguity, and authoritarianism may be seen as cognitive styles that are related to anti-Semitism, ethnocentrism, and conservatism (Adorno, Frenkel-Brunswik, Levinson, & Sanford, 1950). Dogmatism may also be seen as a cognitive style that leads to a rejection of persons whose beliefs are at the opposite extreme — either left or right (Rokeach, 1960). One of the most content-free cognitive styles is field independence-field dependence (e.g., Witkin, Dyk, Faterson, Goodenough, & Karp, 1962). An example of the way in which this style is measured is the Rod-and-Frame Test (RFT):

> The subject taking the RFT is seated in complete darkness and views a luminous rod suspended within a luminous frame. Both the rod and frame can be tilted independently. Initially, the rod and frame are both tilted, and the subject is told to direct the experimenter to adjust the rod to a position that the subject believes is vertical. Some subjects are successful at this task and are termed *field independent*. Others orient the rod in relation to the tilted frame and are termed *field dependent*; that is, their perceptions are dependent on the surrounding environment [Goldstein & Blackman, 1978, p. 175].

Other procedures involve a tilting room and a tilting chair in which the subject's task is to orient the room to an upright position while seated in a tilting chair and then, while the room is tilted again, to orient the chair to an upright position. Although field independence increases with age among children, those children who were more field independent tended to remain so, relative to their peers at later ages. There is some evidence that field dependence increases late in life; however, these cross-sectional findings appear to reflect differences in health and education, so these age-differences are not necessarily valid. In addition, while women have been found to be more field dependent than men, these findings have been contradicted by recent research (ibid., pp. 186-189).

In general, cognitive style appears to be one of the most stable of all personality characteristics (Mischel, 1968). Since it tends to be highly correlated with measures of intelligence, the stability of cognitive style may result in part from the stability of intellectual processes.

Personal Constructs.   Kelly (1955) developed a concept closely related to cognitive style. He noted that individuals have characteristic ways of perceiving and organizing the world. He termed these "personal constructs."

> Man looks at his world through transparent patterns or templates which he creates and then attempts to fit over the realities of which the world is composed. The fit is not always very good. Yet without such patterns the world appears to be such an undifferentiated homogeneity that man is unable to make any sense out of it. Even a poor fit is more helpful to him than nothing at all [ibid., pp. 8-9].

These templates are the individual's constructs; each person's system of constructs is unique. Sometimes a person may apply one set of constructs and other times another set; thus, behavior may appear to be more consistent to the individual than it appears to an outside observer. In order to understand a person, one must share some of the constructs that person uses, or understand at least some of that person's construct system.

The Role Construct Repertory Test (REP) was developed to analyze the construct system people use in relations with other individuals. Several cards are filled out by the subject with the names of significant people in his or her life and then sorted into groups of people who are similar in some way. Then, the subject is asked to describe the way in which each group is similar. The construct system for an individual consists of several levels, with some contructs at a higher level of abstraction or generality than others. This approach to personality has provided information on individual uniqueness, information useful in psychotherapy, and even descriptions useful for understanding specific behaviors such as the utilization of birth control in terms of individual differences in the meaning of fertility (Tyler, 1978). Bonarius (1977) has developed a version of the REP that resembles a game that can be played by two persons who wish to understand each other better.

Although construct systems may change, and some constructs may be more open to change than others, Mischel (1969) pointed out that self-defined typologies of ourselves and of the world are highly stable across situations and over time.

> Studies of the self-concept, of impression formation in person perception and in clinical judgment, of cognitive sets guiding selective attention—all of these phenomena and many more document the consistency and tenacious continuity of many human construction systems [p. 37].

Certainly cognitive and intellectual processes are at the core of these construct systems, and together they may provide much of the continuity in personality. That is, much of the continuity may be in the eye of the beholder, and much of that perceived continuity results from the relatively stable construct systems and cognitive styles. Mischel (1969) refers to this selective perception of continuity as the mind functioning as "a reducing valve" decreasing the complexity of the real world through such mechanisms as construct systems (perhaps for the sake of stable social interactions).

Personality Trait Perspective

In the psychological view of personality, a number of relatively enduring characteristics, traits, or temperaments are seen as providing individual uniqueness and consistency. They link the individual with the world in two ways. First, they are thought to develop as a result of experience, usually during early childhood, often as a result of parental influence and child-rearing techniques. Second, they produce characteristic ways in which individuals respond to their environment throughout life.

Since this view of personality is widely known, it will not be discussed in detail. Examples of personality traits that have been proposed include introversion-extraversion described by Jung; oral, anal, and phallic types described by Freud; and a variety of characteristics such as aggressiveness, dependency, impulsivity, passivity, and sociability.

In general, research in which individuals are measured on the same traits over a period of time shows only moderate consistency. For example, data from the Fels Longitudinal Study indicate a fairly high degree of consistency from childhood into young adulthood on achievement, sex-typed activity, and spontaneity. However, while the childhood rating on these traits predicted the individual's rating on the same traits in young adulthood to a greater degree than would be expected by chance alone, there is still a great deal of variation in the young adult ratings that is not accounted for by the childhood ratings. To take another example, dependency of girls between ages 6 and 10 correlated only moderately with later dependence on family, and there was no correlation for boys (Kagan & Moss, 1962). Thus it appears that while personality is not random, it is not highly consistent either. Part of the difficulty is that these personality traits are measured by judges or raters rather than by the individual; thus, they do not tap the individual's cognitive constructs, but attempt to infer personality traits from behavior. It appears that personality traits are judged to be most similar for an individual when the situations in which he or she is judged are most similar (Mischel, 1968). Thus, one interpretation of these modest correlations (which sometimes reach as high as .60 to .70 for achievement orientation in the Fels study) is that both the individual and the situation are contributing to the behavior that is being rated.

Similar moderate correlations are found between personality characteristics of identical twins; this indicates that a genetic factor may be contributing to personality characteristics (Thompson, 1968). Moreover, the correlations between identical twins (Mz, or monozygotic) are generally somewhat higher than for fraternal twins (Dz, or dizygotic) and are about the same magnitude as the correlations for the stability of personality characteristics over 20 years in the Fels and other longitudinal studies (Table 8.1). Gottschaldt (1960) examined the consistency of a number of personality characteristics from adolescence to adulthood among twin pairs and found that age seemed to increase the importance of the genetic factor in these characteristics. So it appears that heredity plays a role in at least some personality characteristics (Tyler, 1978). These genetic factors may be partly responsible for the consistency of an individual's personality over time.

Interactionist Perspective

The interactionist perspective places greater emphasis on the link between the person and the environment and less emphasis on the consistency of personality than either the cognitive or trait perspectives. For example, Lewin (1935) argued that, "a person's behavior in any situation is jointly determined by the

Table 8.1 Similarities in Personality Traits between Monozygotic and Dizygotic Twin Pairs

	Mz	Dz	
		Like Sex	Unlike Sex
Neuroticism	.63	.32	.18
Self-sufficiency	.44	− .14	.12
Introversion	.50	.40	.18
Dominance	.71	.34	.18
Self-confidence	.58	.20	.07
Sociability	.57	.41	.39

Source: Carter, H. D. Twin Similarities in Emotional Traits. *Character and Personality*, 1935, 4, 61-78. Copyright©1935. Reprinted with permission of the Duke University Press.

characteristics of that situation, as he perceives them, and by the particular behavioral dispositions of which he is possessed at that time." He expressed this relationship by the equation $B = f(p, E)$—behavior is a function of the person and the environment. Sullivan (1953) emphasized a similar interactionist view: "Personality is the relatively enduring pattern of recurrent interpersonal situations which characterize a human life" (pp. 110-111).

This view incorporates cognitive processes, personality traits, and environmental influence in a reciprocal interaction so that the person, the person's behavior, and the environment each affect one another (Bandura, 1978). Thomas and Chess (1977) illustrate this reciprocal determinism in the report on their 20-year longitudinal study of personality development from infancy to adulthood:

> The interactionist view of behavior . . . demands that all behavioral attributes, including temperament, must at all times be considered simultaneously in their reciprocal relationship with other characteristics of the organism, and in their interaction with environmental opportunities, demands, and stresses. This process produces consequences which may modify or change behavior. The new behavior will then affect the influence of recurrent and new features of the environment. The latter may develop independently or as a consequence of the organism-environment interactive process. At the same time other characteristics of the organism, either talents and abilities, goals and motives, behavioral stylistic characteristics, or psychodynamic defenses, may be modified or altered as the result of this continually evolving reciprocal organism-environment influence [p. 193].
>
> The search for early behavioral determinants which fix the individual's psychological development in some permanent form has been a futile enterprise. This should hardly be a surprise. . . .
>
> At the same time, human personality structure does have stability and continuity. Flexibility does not mean that an individual's responsiveness to change or new demands is haphazard or capricious [p. 202].

One example of this approach is the social learning perspective described by Bandura (1978). He stresses the role of cognition in perceiving and interpreting the environment, the role of the person in affecting the environment, and the influence of the environment on the person. Thus, the person affects the environment and is affected by it; individuals produce behaviors that, in turn, affect them; and behaviors are affected by the environment and, reciprocally, are affected by the environment.

A second example is Carson's (1969) description of the intricate ways in which one plans, processes information, utilizes feedback mechanisms, and generates decisions as to future operations. He discusses an exchange view of interpersonal transactions in which the outcome is negotiated on the basis of costs and rewards that are involved in reaching the end result (cf. Kimmel, 1979; Thibaut & Kelley, 1959). He also suggests that individuals develop a *personal style* that, once it is established, tends to be maintained. Its stability results partly from reflected appraisals of others and partly from the relatively enduring characteristics of cognitive styles and personal constructs. These personal styles are interpersonal in nature, often developed through contractual arrangements with particular others and thus tend to be defined by the interaction rather than by the individual in isolation. We will use this concept of personal styles later in this chapter as a component of personality similar to personality traits; both tend to be moderately stable, but personal styles are seen as *inter*personal in nature, while personality traits are seen as *intra*personal characteristics of individuals.

Behavioral Perspective

The approach to personality that emphasizes the potential for change much more than consistency is social or psychological behaviorism. In both the frameworks the internal characteristics of the person, such as cognitive processes and personality traits, are seen as largely irrelevant, since the important influences on behavior are located in the environment. For example, in the sociological model, personality consists of an individual's unique collection of *social roles*. These roles are maintained by social sanctions and social expectations and are transmitted to the individual through the process of socialization (discussed in Chapter 2). Thus, in social behaviorism, an individual's roles and other social behaviors are maintained by the social and interpersonal consequences of one's behavior—if the behavior fits the expectations of others, it is reinforced; if it is not appropriate to the situation, then the behavior is eventually shaped to the expected or appropriate behavior. Clearly, change is easily explained, and consistency results from the stability of social expectations. Notably, in this perspective personality seems to vanish into a collection of roles (Heine, 1971). For example, one need not know a policeman's personality to know that he will, if necessary, risk his life to save you; or that a clinical psychologist will spend a great deal of time and effort attempting to help a patient whom she would ignore if she were to have first encountered that person on a bus quietly talking to himself. It seems that role theory is quite powerful in explaining behavior—particularly if other social variables such as age, sex, occupation, race, and religion are also considered.

Similarly, psychological behaviorism views behavior as maintained by the consequences of that behavior, so that (as in social behaviorism) behaviors that are reinforced in some way will be maintained. In order to change behavior, one need know nothing about the individual's personality except the technological question of what rewards are reinforcing to the individual; then the appropriate rewards (consequences) may be linked to the desired behavior. Thus, personality, insofar as it exists in this view, is seen as a collection of behaviors; in the social model, it would be a collection of *social behaviors*.

Personality as Process

Is it possible to integrate these differing views of personality? To do so we need to consider the interaction of genetic, physiological, cognitive, social, and environmental factors. We also need to focus on the simultaneous process of change and continuity as individuals progress through their lifespan. This approach requires an interactionist or dialectical perspective that views personality as a continuing process of transactions between the person and the environment over time.

Tyler (1978) described the process model of personality, tracing its philosophical origins to the work of Alfred North Whitehead ([1929] 1969) and Susanne Langer (1967, 1972). This perspective, similar to that of Mead (1934), sees humans as active beings that select their actions, instead of as machinelike beings that are programmed and that can behave only in predetermined ways. Thus, individuals select and organize their environment, there is an element of unpredictability or chance in behavior, and future behavior is a spontaneous creation.

Individuals create themselves. To understand a person completely, we would need to trace the road he or she has taken on one occasion after another. It is development we must study, but the development of the shaper rather than the shaped. Obviously such complete understanding of an individual, especially of oneself, is impossible, but it is not unrealistic to hope that an expanded theory and technology for studying individuality will enable us to assess more accurately what has been created in an individual so far through the endless process of becoming what one is, to appreciate more deeply the value of human diversity, and to utilize the unique contributions of individuals to enrich the pattern of our common social fabric [Tyler, 1978, pp. 233-234].

Her view incorporates the contributions of hereditary factors—seen as a process instead of as a compound of ingredients, cognitive processes that act as "mental screens" that individuals use to process input from the environment, and cognitive strategies that individuals employ to deal with different situations in their life. Combined with the effects of social interactions and individual experience, these factors suggest that personality is a process and that behavior of an individual cannot be assumed to be completely predictable, even in principle.

The dialectical view proposed by Riegel (1976), which we discussed in Chapter 1, suggests a similar perspective. In his approach, the individual is a "changing being in a changing world" (p. 696). Thus, personality would be seen as a continuing dialectical struggle between the various dimensions of personality: inner-biological, individual-psychological, cultural-sociological, and outer-physical. This process occurs over time, so that this approach is inherently developmental. We might see genetic and physiological processes as inner-biological; cognitive styles, personal constructs, personality traits, and personal styles as individual-psychological; social interactions and the social environment would be cultural-sociological; and the physical environment would be the outer-physical dimension. Personality would then be seen as the dialectical evolution of these dimensions over time.

Now let us build on the discussions in this section to develop a model of personality that begins to describe the complex nature of personality consistency and change during adulthood in an attempt to answer one of Neugarten's provocative questions:

> What terms shall we use to describe the strategies with which . . . [a business executive, age 50, who makes a thousand decisions in the course of a day] manages his time, buffers himself from certain stimuli, makes elaborate plans and schedules, sheds some of his "load" by delegating some tasks to other people over whom he has certain forms of control, accepts other tasks as being singularly appropriate to his own competencies and responsibilities, and, in the same 24-hour period, succeeds in satisfying his emotional and sexual and aesthetic needs [Neugarten, 1968, p. 140]?

TOWARD A CONCEPTUALIZATION OF PERSONALITY IN ADULTHOOD

If we view personality as a complex *system* that involves both the unique individual and his or her unique social environment, then personality may be seen as the dynamic interaction between the individual and the social environment. Consider as an example a living organism (such as a flower). Let us assume that "flowerness" is a characteristic of that organism that is its "personality." Now, obviously the flower exists only because it interacts with its environmental niche; otherwise it would die. And we can describe the "personality" of the flower either by its characteristic—"flowerness"—or by the dynamic processes that are involved in the flowering of the flower. The same is true with personality. We can look at the *contents* of the personality system—personality traits, personal styles, and even social roles—and we can describe them. Or we can look at the *processes* of the personality—the dynamic interaction between the person and the environment. Thus, the personality system consists of both content aspects and process aspects. These aspects exist and function simultaneously and, as noted earlier, what we see depends on the lenses with which we view the personality system.

The personality system, since it represents the interaction between the individual and his or her unique social niche, is both relatively stable and continuous as well as relatively flexible and changeable. That is, it can change while remaining fairly consistent at the same time. This ability of the personality system to change while it also remains continuous is an important ability since we feel that the personality is not fixed and stable during the adult years. Instead, like the self that we discussed in Chapter 2, the personality system is always open to change but is also relatively consistent over time.

As may be apparent, there are considerable similarities between our conception of the personality and our conception of the self. Both are dynamic, interacting systems that are made up of process and content aspects (in the self, these aspects are *I* and *me*, respectively). However, we mean something different by personality than we mean by the self. That is, the personality system is the interaction between the individual and the environment, while the self (system) is the interaction between the individual's experiencing (*I*) and the individual's self-perception (*me*). These two concepts fit together in our model in that we see the self as functioning at the core of the personality system. In other words, the personality system is the fit between the individual's *self* and the environment.

The model of the interacting personality system that we are proposing is diagrammed in Figure 8.2. Part of the personality system—the darkly shaded area—is "private" in the sense that it is internal, inaccessible to view by others, and able to be examined only by its external manifestations. For example, one cannot "see" heredity, but one can examine genes; one cannot "see" cognition, but cognitive style can be observed. Similarly, memory or physiological processes cannot be observed directly, even though memory tests or blood tests can show how well these respective processes are working.

In contrast, part of the personality system is "public" in the sense that these components are revealed to varying degrees in social interactions. Looking at Figure 8.2, the unshaded area outside the circle represents those public aspects of the personality system that are outside of the individual. That is, *social interactions* involve not only the individual, but also one or more other people; the interaction is defined by the characteristics of all of the individuals involved and by the nature of the interaction. *Social situations* may be defined as "the immediate social and physical environmental stimuli" with which the individual interacts (Feshbach, 1978, p. 447). The *social and physical environment* may be seen as "the broader social and physical context that provides situations their meaning and their continuity. Cultural ideologies, the economic system, social norms, and population density are examples" (ibid.). Thus, one's office, home, noise level, and cultural values may each affect the personality system; moreover, changes in any of these external factors may bring about a change in the personality as the personality system evolves toward a new fit with its changed environmental niche.

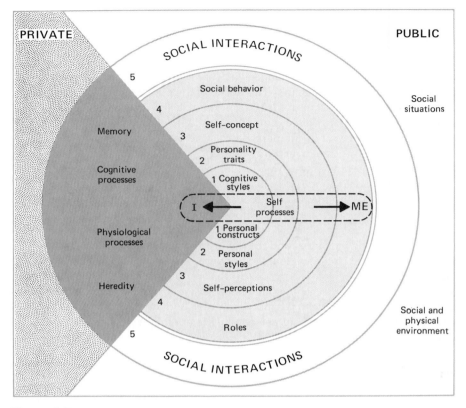

Figure 8.2
Interacting aspects of the personality system.

The aspects of the personality system that are diagrammed in the lightly shaded area between the private and the public extremes of the personality system are the various personality aspects that most clearly represent the dynamic interaction between the individual and the external environment; they include many of the concepts we discussed in the first section of this chapter. These aspects are diagrammed (somewhat arbitrarily) along the private-to-public continuum and also along the continuum from relatively stable to relatively changeable. Thus, social interactions (level 5) are highly public and changeable. Cognitive styles and personal constructs (level 1) are fairly private and relatively stable. Other aspects of the personality system between these two extremes include social behavior and roles (level 4), the individual's self-concept or self-perceptions (level 3), and personality traits and personal styles (level 2). These are a mixture of public and private characteristics often seen in daily interactions; but they may also be fairly private—that is, revealed on psychological tests or in intimate relationships but not necessarily revealed in ordinary interactions.

At the core of the model is the *self*: the interacting *I* and *me* aspects. It is apparent that *I* is private and *me* is public. In fact, as we pointed out in Chapter 2, the *me* includes social roles, or social behaviors. And certainly the self-concept and self-perception are *mes* (the way we see ourselves when we take the attitude of the other). Even personality traits and personal styles can be *mes* when they are aspects of ourselves that others see and react to in social interaction (and we may see them when we take the attitude of the other toward ourselves). Thus, while the self is at the core of our model, the *me* aspect of the self extends up to the physical boundary of the person and encompasses the first four levels of the public component of the personality system. We will discuss the implications of this when we examine the content and process aspects of personality in detail.

Let us conclude the description of the model by noting that some of these aspects of the personality system may not be fully recognized or "known" by the individual. That is, there may well be some social behaviors, roles, self-perceptions, personality traits, or cognitive styles (and so on) that the individual is only dimly aware or totally unaware of. Similarly, some of the internal aspects—such as memory or physiological processes (and so on)—may be unavailable to the individual's experiencing for some reason. This is not to say that they are necessarily "repressed" (in a psychoanalytic sense) but simply that they are unknown or unrecognized or unexperienced aspects of the personality system. However, we know that these unknown aspects may influence the personality system and daily behavior just as those aspects that are recognized may influence them.

Content and Process Aspects of the Personality System

Although this model may seem very complex, the phenomenon of a person interacting with a complicated social environment in adulthood is also quite complex. For example, adults have a wide range of internal and external experiences during their lives. They experience various feelings and moods; they experience their reactions to themselves and to others; and they experience a variety of social situations. The aspect of the personality system that is experiencing, reacting, feeling, and observing is one's *I*. *I* is at the core of the personality system and is a purely *process* aspect that provides the continuing possibility of innovative change—for the self (as we pointed out in Chapter 2) or for the personality system. In addition, the physiological processes and the cognitive processes in the personality system are process aspects that bring the continuing possibility of change to the personality system. And the dynamic, interacting nature of the personality system itself is a process conception of personality. Thus, our personality model conceptualizes the personality system as a processing, dynamic, changeable system that is continually fitting the changing individual and the changing social environment together. This is not to imply that the individual is "molded" to fit the environment; certainly individuals also mold the environment and perceive (or misperceive) the environment as they participate in this process of fitting themselves and their environment together.

We would also suggest that two of the motivating forces in the personality system are striving for *competence* (White, 1959) and striving for *self-actualization* (Maslow, 1950). This means that the personality system operates in its dynamic, processing manner of fitting the individual and the environment together to achieve a sense of competence in that environment. If one does not fit with one's environmental niche (which one has partially selected and created), then one is not likely to feel very competent and one's personality system will likely evolve toward a fit that provides greater feelings of competence. Similarly, we assume that one strives for self-actualization in the sense of realizing one's fullest human potentials. But if one does not fit in with one's niche (if the niche is too "small" or "dehumanizing," for example), the personality system ideally will evolve toward a new fit or find another niche that allows greater potential for self-actualization. Probably these idealistic goals of competence and self-actualization are not very fully realized in general. But it seems reasonable that the personality system represents the individual's best efforts to interact with the environmental niche in a competent, self-actualizing manner.

In addition to these process aspects of personality, the personality system also includes a number of *content* aspects. For example, roles, personality traits, the self-concept, self-perceptions, and personal styles all have an element of content to them. They are seen when individuals interact; we talk about them and measure them; and we see them in ourselves. They have a tendency to seem like "things" that we carry around inside—for example, "aggressiveness," "dependency," "inferiority," or all of the roles that we play. In this sense, personality traits, the self-concept, and social roles have an important common element— they are *me*s. These content aspects of the personality tend to be relatively stable because they tend to become habituated and reinforced by their success in fitting the individual with the environment in ways that are relatively competent.

In sum, we see personality as a complex, dynamic system that simultaneously consists of process aspects and content aspects. In a sense, whether we see the process of fitting or the content of that fit between the individual and the niche depends on what we are looking for. Similarly, this personality system allows both change and consistency simultaneously—and what we see depends, again, on the lenses we use when we look at the individual in interaction with the environment.

Consistency and Change in the Personality System

When personality is seen in terms of an interacting system, we note that a change in any aspect of that system will bring a change to the entire system. For example, changes in the external aspects of the system (social situations or the environment) tend to bring about changes in social interactions (level 5 in Figure 8.2) that lead to changes in social behavior and roles (level 4). These role changes tend to affect one's self-perception and self-concept (level 3) and may even have some effect on personality traits or personal styles (level 2). Cognitive styles and personal constructs (level 1), which show the least change with time, may also be affected—the degree probably depends on the extent of change in the social situation (which varies from a trivial change through ordinary changes such as marriage or a new job to a major change such as being placed in a concentration camp). This process is essentially the process of socialization (discussed in Chapter 2) cast in a different model. Similarly, changes in the entire system may result from changes in any other aspect. That is, changes in physiological processes—such as disease or more subtle changes—may bring a change to the entire system. In general, since the personality system is a dynamic process, any change in any of the aspects (roles, self-perceptions, cognitive processes, and so on) may bring about a dialectical process of change in the interaction between the individual and the environment. At the same time, there is considerable stability in the personality system. The private aspects of the personality system and the cognitive aspects of the system tend to change least, as we have noted. And even social roles (level 4) and external social situations tend to be fairly stable (or are perceived to be stable) through much of adulthood. These external consistencies tend to reinforce the consistency of the personality system over time. Thus, the personality system is characterized by simultaneous consistency and change throughout the life span. Let us consider some of the developmental changes we would expect in the personality system during adulthood.

Developmental Changes in the Personality System

We would suggest that during young adulthood the personality system is characterized by a *centrifugal* tendency that propels the individual from the self out into the external social world. This results from the necessity to master new roles and to develop new personal styles and new self-concepts to maximize the competence of individuals with their expanding social environment. In Chapter 1, we noted that Kuhlen (1964) described this period as one of "growth-expansion" in which strivings for achievement, power, self-actualization, and competence predominate. Social relationships are also expanding in addition to the number of roles and social responsibilities. There may be a tendency for young people to place more emphasis on the more external (i.e., social) aspects of behavior and to conform to the social norms of their associates. Also, they may tend to feel some tension between the inner aspects of the personality (nearest the self) and the more external aspects (such as roles) as if the centrifugal movement were denying the importance of the inner aspects (such as the experiencing of *I*).

During the middle years of adulthood there seems to be a balance of sorts in the personality system. On one hand, the individual's social world is no longer expanding rapidly, and patterns of dealing competently with it have been developed (through situation experience, as discussed in Chapter 2). On the other hand, the individual has also had greater self-experience and may have learned relatively comfortable ways of integrating the internal and external aspects of the personality system. In the ideal case, this leads to a smoothly functioning, competent interaction between the individual and the environment that also allows some striving for the goal of self-actualization. The potential for rigidity and a tendency to resist change to this balanced system may also occur during this period because it is well-established, competent, and familiar.

With advancing age there seems to be a kind of *centripetal* tendency in the personality system so that the importance of the external social situation becomes less salient and the internal processes become more salient. That is, as the number and variety of roles, social behavior, and social interaction (levels 4 and 5) decrease in frequency or in importance, the more internal aspects of the personality (such as personality traits) seem to be more clearly revealed. In addition, the feelings of competence that may have been experienced during the middle years, combined with the increased realization of a finite amount of time left to live, may shift the focus for self-actualization inward. The theories proposed by Bühler and Jung (discussed in Chapter 1) reached a similar conclusion about these changes during the life span. For example:

> Ageing people should know that their lives are not mounting and expanding, but that an inexorable inner process enforces the contraction of life. For a young person it is almost a sin, or at least a danger, to be too preoccupied with himself; but for the ageing person it is a duty and a necessity to devote serious attention to himself. After having lavished its light upon the world, the sun withdraws its rays in order to illuminate itself [Jung, 1933, p. 17].

In the next section we will discuss the empirical studies of personality change with advancing age. In general, they substantiate Jung's observations and are the basis for our own speculations on the developmental changes in the personality system presented above.

DATA ON PERSONALITY IN ADULTHOOD

Certainly, we would expect that there would be personality change with age for specific individuals; but the data presently available suggest that the general developmental change in personality is a shift toward a kind of contraction or centripetal development or increased internalization within the personality system for typical adults beginning, apparently, about age 50. For example, Riley, Foner, and Associates (1968) reviewed several studies of personality change in old age and reported that old people have been found to be more rigid than young people and less disposed to adapt to changing stimuli; their attitudes indicate a higher degree of dogmatism, a greater intolerance of ambiguity, and less susceptibility to social pressure. They are also reported to be more passive (i.e., conforming and accommodating), more preoccupied with their own emotions, physical functions, and inner-world orientation, and more introverted than young people. Although cohort factors may be important considerations in addition to age-related changes—such as in some data on increased "conservatism" or higher political interest and voting habits among the aged—these findings suggest a decrease in the salience of outer situational factors and an increase in the importance of inner processes in the personality system with advancing age.

Certainly, physiological factors such as a decline in vision, hearing, excitation levels of the central nervous system, and changes in intellectual processes with age may be important interrelated factors (in addition to a decline in social role participation and inner psychological changes) for explaining these age-related personality changes. Once again, the interaction of the various factors involved in the personality system is crucial; and each of the interrelated aspects plays an important role in changes of the personality system.

One of the major studies of personality change and continuity in adulthood was conducted by a group from the Committee on Human Development at the University of Chicago. We will discuss this study in detail because it attempted to investigate developmental change in personality structure; that is, instead of studying changes in specific personality characteristics (as did the studies mentioned in the preceding paragraph), the researchers sought to investigate age-related changes in the total personality system. While a major shortcoming of the study is the absence of data on physiological and health factors, in many ways this study is a classic because it is one of the few large-scale studies of "normal" community residents, and it contains both cross-sectional and longitudinal data on personality change in adults. Some of the major publications based on these data are Cumming and Henry (1961), Havighurst, Neugarten, and Tobin (1963), and Neugarten and Associates (1964). They obtained a sample of nearly 700 respondents between the ages of 40 and 90 who were in relatively good health and who were living in homes or apartments (not in institutions) in Kansas City in the mid-1950s. Respondents were selected on the basis of age, sex, and economic status and were interviewed repeatedly over a period of up to seven years. The studies found three age-related personality changes: a shift in sex-role perceptions, a personality shift toward "increased interiority," and a shift in the coping styles of personality. In addition, they found a number of personality aspects that did not change with age. Thus, there are data on both change and on consistency in personality; and many of these findings have been supported in other smaller studies of adult personality. Let us begin our discussion of these data with the findings of consistency; we will then deal with the specific age-related changes that were also found.

Consistency of Adaptive Personality Characteristics

Since *age* was a major variable in the Kansas City studies, one of the central findings was that some personality characteristics did not change with age of the respondent while other personality aspects did change. Those characteristics that did *not* change seemed to share a common theme—they dealt with "adaptive, goal directed, and purposive qualities of personality" that Neugarten (1964) described as "socioadaptational" characteristics of personality. That is, general adaptation (based on interview data), adaptive characteristics of the personality (such as integrity or adjustment or cognitive competence based on responses to projective tests), and general personality structure (based on personality tests) differed between individuals regardless of their chronological age. For example, they administered a personality test that, when the results were analyzed, yielded four general personality types: "integrated," "armored-defended," "passive-dependent," and "unintegrated." However, there were no consistent age differences among the respondents in each of these types. Similar data were obtained in another study on a different sample conducted by Reichard, Livson, and Peterson (1962) where they found no clear age differences among their five personality types (these were discussed in Chapter 6: "mature," "rocking-chair men," "armored," "angry men," and "self-haters"); instead, these personality patterns seemed to be consistent patterns of adaptation in the histories of the men in their sample. Other data on "adjustment" to aging found no age-related differences in a sample of healthy old men (Butler, 1963a). Indeed, in that study (discussed in Chapter 7), *disease* was identified as a far more important variable than chronological age. Another study, based on the Kansas City samples, found no relationship between age and a measure of "life satisfaction"—that is, again, a measure of adaptive adjustment to aging (Havighurst et al., 1963). However, personality types were related to life satisfaction (Table 8.2). That is, respondents who were high on the "integrated" style of personality had high life satisfaction regardless of whether they were active in a variety of social roles or not. At the other extreme, "unintegrated" types were low or medium in life satisfaction whether they were active or not. "Armored-defended" types who were high or medium in activity were high on life satisfaction. "Passive-dependent" types tended to be medium on life satisfaction regardless of their degree of activity. Thus, personality characteristics seem to be pivotal dimensions for whether successful aging is one of maintained activity or gradual disengagement from activity and social involvement (Neugarten, Havighurst, & Tobin, 1965).

Table 8.2 Personality Type in Relation to Activity and Life Satisfaction (N = 59)

Personality Type	Role Activity	Life Satisfaction		
		High	Medium	Low
Integrated	High	9	2	
	Medium	5		
	Low	3		
Armored-defended	High	5		
	Medium	6	1	
	Low	2	1	1
Passive-dependent	High		1	
	Medium	1	4	
	Low	2	3	2
Unintegrated	High		2	1
	Medium	1		
	Low		2	5
	Total	34	16	9

Source: Neugarten et al. (1965), Table 1. Reprinted with permission.

Thus, the data seem to indicate that there is little predictable change in these socioadaptational characteristcs of personality with advancing age. We interpret this finding as indicating that the *content* aspects of personality (i.e., personal styles, personality traits, and other *me* aspects) remain generally consistent during middle and old age; and that these objectifiable, relatively external aspects of personality are generally stable during adulthood. In addition, these data imply that the adaptive interaction between the person and the social environment remains fairly stable (that is, an old person seems to adapt and interact with the environment with as much satisfaction as a middle-aged person) so that—at least for generally healthy adults—there are a variety of ways in which a relatively stable personality (in terms of content) can adjust and adapt to changes in roles and status while remaining generally stable. Neugarten summarized this conclusion in the following way:

> In a sense, the self becomes institutionalized with the passage of time. Not only do certain personality processes become stabilized and provide continuity, but the individual builds around him a network of social relationships which he comes to depend on for emotional support and responsiveness and which maintain him in many subtle ways. . . .
>
> Behavior in a normal old person is more consistent and more predictable than in a younger one—. . . as individuals age, they become increasingly like themselves—and, on the other hand, . . . the personality structure stands more clearly revealed in an old than in a younger person [Neugarten, 1964, p. 198].

Thus, the content aspects of personality seem to be relatively stable over time. For example, a slightly hostile middle-aged person is likely to become more clearly hostile as an old person; and a passive or dependent person would be likely to remain passive into old age. In this sense, these personality "contents" remain relatively consistent, even when we might expect them to change due to situational changes such as role, status, and other changes associated with aging. However, the data from the Kansas City studies also found important age-related changes in personality that seem to involve changes in the *process* aspects of personality. Perhaps these changes in personality processes, in conjunction with stability in highly lmportant interpersonal and social commitments (despite role changes in the family and occupational cycles), allow the general stability of salient personality "contents" and general personal satisfaction and adaptation. Let us examine these changes in personality processes, and then we will examine the important role played by stability in social and interpersonal commitments for aging individuals.

Change in Personality Processes with Age

Three sets of data in the Kansas City studies indicate related changes in personality processes with age. In general, this change is one of "increased interiority of the personality" (Neugarten, 1968). It seems to begin in middle age in a tendency toward increased self-reflection and introspection (in the decade of the fifties for most persons). It becomes more marked in later life, perhaps leading to the reminiscence characteristic of many aged persons (Butler, 1963b; this reminiscence and the "life-review process" will be discussed in detail in Chapter 10). Two of these studies (each of which we will discuss) suggest this increased interiority; one study found a decrease in "ego energy" with age, and the second found a shift in "ego style" with age. A third study found a shift in sex-role perceptions and a growing responsiveness to inner impulses with age. Each of these studies was based on data from projective tests (in which pictures were presented to the respondents who were then asked to tell a story about the picture and to describe the characters) and each dealt with "intrapsychic" processes of personality in contrast with the "socioadaptational" and content aspects of personality discussed above.

Decrease in Ego Energy.   Rosen and Neugarten (1964) analyzed the responses of Kansas City respondents to five of the pictures in the Thematic Apperception Test (TAT) on four measures of "ego energy": introduction of non-pictured characters into the story told about the card, introduction of conflict into the story, extent of vigorous activity ascribed to the characters, and the intensity of emotion (affect) described for the characters. It was assumed that each of these four variables tapped the amount of psychic energy that the respondent devoted to the task of making up a story about the picture presented; hence, low ratings suggest that the respondent invested little energy in the task. Their data show a consistent decline with age on all four measures; differences between age groups were statistically reliable. Although these findings were obtained from a cross-sectional sample, since many of the respondents were interviewed subsequently it was also possible to obtain longitudinal data on these dimensions. Lubin (1964) administered the same TAT cards to 93 of the subjects five years later. He found a significant decline on a combined measure of ego energy over the five-year test-retest interval. Thus, these findings add considerable support to the notion that ego energy, which is available for tasks in the outer world, does decline with advancing age. "The implication is that the older person tends to respond to inner rather than to outer stimuli, to withdraw emotional investments, to give up self-assertiveness, and to avoid rather than to embrace challenge" (Rosen & Neugarten, 1964, p. 99).

Shift in Ego Style.   A change with age that is closely related to the decrease in available ego energy is a shift in ego style from active mastery to passive mastery and magical mastery styles. Gutmann (1964), again using TAT responses, rated the stories on these three ego mastery styles separately for males and females. The three mastery types were seen as points on a continuum of ego strength in which "active mastery represents the most vigorous, effective style of ego functioning and magical mastery represents stress-laden, maladaptive ego functioning" (Gutmann, 1964, p. 119). The data show a shift with age toward passive and magical mastery styles for both males and females (Figure 8.3). In subsequent studies of these same dimensions of ego style, Gutmann studied aging men in various different cultures including subsistence corn farmers in a remote Mexican province (Gutmann, 1967) and American Indians (Krohn & Gutmann, 1971). Similar shifts from active mastery to passive and magical mastery styles were found in these widely differing cultures; this suggests a developmental shift in personality processes with age that is not related to the culture in which the individual grows old. In a more recent report on many different cultures, Gutmann (1977) found added support for this change in men, but determined that the shift could occur in the opposite direction in women; thus, the cross-cultural evidence appears to contradict the shift in ego style found for

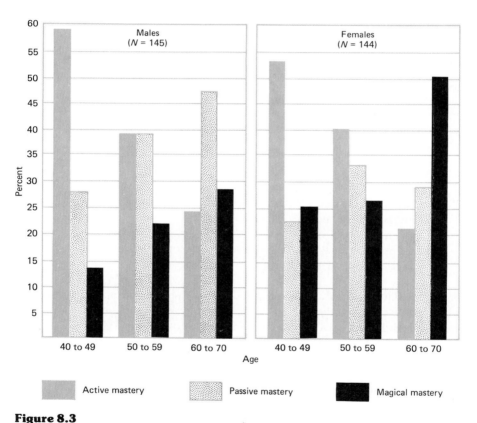

Figure 8.3

Percent of respondents exhibiting active, passive, and magical mastery styles by age and sex. By the chi-square test, the distribution of active, passive, and magical mastery totals by age groups is significantly different from chance at the .02 level. (Source: Adapted from Gutmann, 1964, Tables 6.1 and 6.2. Reprinted with permission of the Aldine Publishing Company.)

women in Kansas City. Clearly, additional research is required to determine the nature of changes in ego style among women.

Shift in Sex-Role Perceptions.   In a third study Neugarten and Gutmann (1958) asked respondents to describe each of four figures shown on a TAT card prepared especially for this study (Figure 8.4). The descriptions given by older respondents (age 55–70) differed significantly from descriptions given by younger respondents (age 40–54) when describing the old man and the old woman in the picture. The most striking differences were that the perception of the old man shifted in the direction of increasing submissiveness when seen by older respondents (both males and females) as compared with younger respondents; and the old woman's role shifted from a subordinate to an authoritative position when seen by older respondents as compared to younger ones. Essentially the same findings were obtained in a later study by Singer (1963) for a different sample of 47 old men. Although these projective data (in which respondents are describing figures in a picture instead of their own behavior) must be interpreted with caution in terms of actual changes in sex-role behavior among older persons, it was striking that the old man and old woman were consistently seen as playing reversed roles in regard to authority in the family by the older respondents as compared with younger respondents; the old woman was seen as dominant and the old man was seen as submissive, regardless of other qualities attributed to them. In addition to this role shift, these data also imply personality changes.

> For example, women, as they age, seem to become more tolerant of their own aggressive, egocentric impulses; while men, as they age, [seem to become more tolerant] of their own nurturant and affiliative impulses. To take another example, with increasing age in both men and women, ego qualities in the personality seem to become more constricted—more detached from the mastery of affairs and less in control of impulse life [Neugarten & Gutmann. 1958, p. 89].

Similar findings have also been reported in more recent research. For example, in interview and questionnaire studies of young and middle-aged adults who ranged from high-school seniors to pre-retirees, Lowenthal (1975, 1977) found that both men and women in the older age groups tended to move toward greater strength in those areas their sex role had restricted them from earlier— such as interpersonal relationships for men and self-assertion for women. Gutmann (1977) also found considerable cross-cultural evidence of a similar shift in sex-role behavior across a wide variety of differing cultures. While he studied cultures instead of individuals, these changes are closely related to his earlier work on ego style.

> We see traces of an autonomous current in human development that urges men in their younger and middle years towards competitiveness,

Figure 8.4
TAT picture designed for the Kansas City Study of Adult Life. (Source: Neugarten & Gutmann, 1958, Figure 1. Copyright by the Committee on Human Development, University of Chicago. Reprinted with permission.)

agency and independence, and in later life towards some reversal of these priorities: familism takes priority over agency; a receptive stance, particularly in regard to women, tends to replace independence; passive affiliation

with supernatural power tends to replace the control and deployment of individual strength. . . .

The available trans-cultural evidence suggests that women may reverse
the order of male aging: where adult men start from active mastery and
move towards passive mastery, women start from passive mastery—characterized by dependence on and deference to the husband—but move in
later life to active mastery. Across cultures and with age they seem to become more domineering, more agentic, and less willing to trade submission
for security [Gutman, 1977, pp. 308, 309].

He suggests that both men and women become androgynous as they grow
older, possibly related to the decreased importance of parental roles after their
children are grown, leading to "the normal unisex of later life" (p. 311).

These findings, based on a variety of research approaches, are especially striking because they substantiate Jung's clinical observations three decades before
the Kansas City Studies:

Man's values, and even his body, do tend to change into their opposites.

We might compare masculinity and femininity and their psychic components to a definite store of substances of which, in the first half of life, unequal use is made. A man consumes his large supply of masculine substance and has left over only the smaller amount of feminine substance,
which must now be put to use. Conversely, the woman allows her hitherto
unused supply of masculinity to become active.

This change is even more noticeable in the psychic realm than in the
physical. . . . Very often these changes are accompanied by all sorts of ca-
tastrophes in marriage, for it is not hard to imagine what will happen when
the husband discovers his tender feelings and the wife her sharpness of
mind [Jung, 1933, p. 16].

It might also be noted that their finding of increased interiority of the personality
with age also substantiates Jung's observations on the contraction of life noted
above.

Implications.   Although the shift in sex-role perceptions may be partly a reflection of the decreased authority of men in the home after retirement, or (alternatively) may reflect physiological changes in hormone levels (decreased levels
of sex hormones in both men and women at that age), these three areas of research seem to have a common theme of *increased interiority*. That is, in terms
of personality *processes*, there seems to be a shift with advancing age toward a
decreased concern with external social and environmental constraints toward an
increased focus upon internal interests and inner dynamics. Similarly, Neugarten (1977) notes that an increase in introversion has been the only personality
change consistently found in studies of aging. Such shifts in personality proc-

esses suggest a lessening concern with some kinds of external involvements, perhaps as a result of physiological changes (such as decreased vision, hearing, and a general slowing down—discussed in Chapter 7), perhaps as a result of physical illness and impaired ability to interact with a complex environment, and perhaps because of decreased participation in a wide range of social roles. This interiority may also reflect developmental processes. That is, as suggested earlier, the development of the personality system may progress from a period of maximal expansion (learning new roles, developing new *mes*, and attending to feedback from others about the "rules of the game") in young adulthood through a period of relative balance between internal processes and external demands in middle age to an increasing focus on internal processes in old age. This view, relating these data to our model of personality, is also consistent with the basic findings in the studies of midlife transitions discussed in Chapter 3.

However, while general developmental changes such as increased interiority and loss of some social roles may be typical for older individuals, their personality and their active *I* continues to reveal individuality and to influence their own interaction with the physical and social environment. That is, old persons, while they may show some similar developmental changes, remain (and perhaps become even more) like themselves. Thus they are no more like "older people" than young persons are like other members of their cohort. However, there may also be losses of significant persons who have supported an important aspect of the individual's self-esteem and personality organization with age. One of the most important of these losses (and one of the most important resources) for the aged is a close and trusted friend.

Importance of a "Confidant"

Lowenthal and Haven (1968) found that the presence of an intimate relationship—being able to confide in someone and to talk about yourself or about your problems—is highly important for older people (as it probably is for all of us). They found, in a study of 280 persons aged 60 and older who were living in the community, that the presence of such a *confidant* serves as a "buffer" against losses such as loss of role or a decline in social interaction. That is, those respondents who had a stable intimate relationship were less likely to be depressed (and more likely to be satisfied) than respondents without a confidant, even if their level of social interaction or their level of role status had decreased. This intimate relationship even seemed able to buffer these respondents against such significant losses as retirement and widowhood (Table 8.3). In fact, a slightly higher percentage of respondents were "satisfied" even though widowed if they had a confidant than if they were married but had no confidant. Similarly, a retired respondent with a confidant was as likely to be satisfied as a respondent who was still working but had no confidant. In addition, psychiatrists' ratings (for a subsample of 112) of the mental health of the respondents also showed the importance of a *stable* intimate relationship; that is, while the presence of a confidant

Table 8.3   Effect of Widowhood, Retirement, and Physical Illness on Morale in the Presence and Absence of a Confidant (Age 60 +)

	Morale	
	Satisfied	Depressed
	Percent	Percent
Widowed within 7 years:		
Has confidant	55	45
No confidant	(27)[a]	(73)
Married:		
Has confidant	65	35
No confidant	(47)	(53)
Retired within 7 years:		
Has confidant	50	50
No confidant	(36)	(64)
Not retired:		
Has confidant	70	30
No confidant	50	50
Serious physical illness within 2 years:		
Has confidant	(16)	(84)
No confidant	(13)	(87)
No serious illness:		
Has confidant	64	36
No confidant	42	58

Source: Lowenthal and Haven (1968), Table 5. Reprinted with permission.
[a]Percentages are placed in parentheses when the numbers on which they are based are under 20 ($N = 14$-19).

was only slightly related to psychiatric status, 80 percent of the respondents who maintained the *same* confidant during the past year were rated "unimpaired" (compared with 20 percent rated "impaired"). Thus, the maintenance of a stable intimate relationship seems to serve an important function in protecting the individual's morale and mental stability against the various social losses that are associated with aging and with social disengagement.

However, as shown in Table 8.3, a confidant does not seem to buffer the individual against the psychological effects of physical illness. It appears that physiological decline, and particularly the onset of disease, is a process of such significance to the total organism that even the apparently powerful buffer provided by a confidant is unable to prevent the loss of morale. The overpowering impact of disease was a central theme in Chapter 7, where it was noted that, more than any of the social and psychological changes associated with aging, *disease* seems to be the most important factor in a wide range of social and psychological changes. However, in the absence of disease (and, of course, even with illness a confidant would be important for the individual), a stable intimate relationship seems to be a profound asset for the aging person. Women were somewhat more likely to have such a confidant than men (69 percent and 57 percent, respectively); married persons were more likely to have one than widows, who were more likely to have a confidant than single persons; and the confidant was about equally likely to be a spouse, a child, or a friend, according to Lowenthal and Haven (1968). They suggest that this sex difference may be related to the greater longevity of women, the lower rate of suicide (which increases rapidly with age for white men), and the lower rate of mental illness following widowhood among women as compared with men.

Although the practical implications of these findings are apparent—that aged persons who have intimate relationships benefit from maintaining close ties and the loss of a confidant has a more negative effect on morale than any other social losses—there are three important related points. First, some persons have maintained adequate levels of functioning with relative isolation over a long period of time; they seem no more prone to mental illness than nonisolates (Lowenthal, 1964). These isolates may also have high morale, but the majority of those who had lost a confidant are depressed. Second, loss of a confidant may result from a general dislocation (such as moving into a smaller home or into a nursing home) that represents a double loss—a loss of social interactions and roles as well as loss of the confidant. Thus, when a confidant is needed most, he or she may be unavailable. Third, gaining a confidant may help some, but the importance of a stable relationship seems most significant.

Conclusion

Taken together, these data on personality continuity, change, and the importance of a confidant indicate that there is an important shift in the interaction of the personality and the social world as one moves from middle to old age. Neugarten (1964) has described this change as a "centripetal" movement, with an increasing focus on inner processes that begins in the middle years of life. Later, as social roles and social interaction begin to decrease, the personality structure comes to be laid bare, as it were, and individuals come to rely more heavily on the supports they have built up. For some, an important support seems to be a confidant. In general, however, life satisfaction does not decline markedly with age and ability to function, or general adaptation does not seem to be related to age. Disease, important social losses (such as a confidant), and long-standing personality characteristics seem to be more important than age per se in causing depression or, for some, mental illness. In the final section of this chapter we will discuss mental illness, especially in terms of the later years of adulthood.

PSYCHOPATHOLOGY IN ADULTHOOD

Up to this point, we have been focusing primarily on normal or typical processes of development during adulthood. *Psychopathology* is the study of abnormal personality functioning; it seeks to understand the nature and causes of psychological disorders or dysfunctions in emotional responses, thinking patterns, and ordinary daily functioning. It overlaps with the study of social deviance in sociology and with the study of psychiatry in medicine; thus, it is an interdisciplinary field and may be studied from a developmental perspective. However, because it is such a large field, we can only present a brief overview of some of the topics that are most relevant for understanding adulthood and aging. We begin with a discussion of the meaning of psychopathology, using the model of the personality system that we developed earlier in this chapter. Then, we will briefly discuss three of the manifestations of psychological dysfunction among older people— depression, suicide, and cerebral disease.

Dysfunctions of the Personality System

The model of the personality system presented earlier (Figure 8.2) provides a useful perspective for understanding the general nature of psychopathology. In that model, the person is seen as continually interacting with the environmental niche. This dynamic process involves the individual's memory, cognitive processes, physiological processes, and hereditary predispositions; it involves the social and physical environment; and it involves a number of characteristics of the individual and his or her social interactions. All of these processes, characteristics, and interactions change and evolve over time as the person strives to maintain a competent fit, or pattern of transactions, with the environment. A dysfunction in that system would represent a breakdown in the ability to maintain a reasonably competent pattern of transactions between the individual and the environmental niche. It could be brought about by a dysfunction in any of the processes within the person—such as a loss of memory, a breakdown in cognitive processes, or a physiological change that interferes with emotional responses. It could also be brought about by an overpowering environmental change that the personality system cannot adjust to or deal with competently—such as extremely stressful social pressures. Or, it could result from dysfunctional characteristics of one or more of the levels within the person—such as personality traits or the self-concept—that interfere with the competent interaction between the person and the environment. As a result, the personality system struggles to maintain effective functioning.

If the dysfunction is severe and involves the person distorting or losing contact with the external environment, it is called a *psychosis*. It may result from the drastic attempt of the personality system to maintain effective functioning by distorting or misinterpreting the environment; thus, individuals may have delusions about who they are, or where they are; or they may have hallucinations such as hearing voices or seeing visions. Sometimes the distortion or misinterpretation involves the meaning of social interactions; thus, some people believe they are being persecuted by others. Another form of psychosis involves extreme emotional reactions that are unrelated to external causes. In manic-depressive psychosis, a person's mood swings from a deep depression to an extreme feeling of elation for no apparent reason. While the causes of these major dysfunctions in the personality system are not fully understood, it seems likely that physiological processes, perhaps hereditary predispositions, experiences earlier in life, and overwhelming stress from the environment may be involved separately or in combination.

A less severe dysfunction is called a *neurosis*; it is characterized by intense *anxiety* that may be defined as an uncanny sense that something is very wrong, but one cannot identify what it is that is causing the feeling (Sullivan, 1953). Ordinarily, anxiety is a valuable reaction that serves as a kind of alarm within the personality system to call our attention to a problem in our interaction with the environment; it is a signal within our experiencing *I* that something is amiss. In our overmedicated society, many people take some kind of tranquilizer or drug to calm the anxious feeling, as if one should not feel that uncanny sensation; however, anxiety is often an important signal that can alert us to a problem in our interaction with the environment that needs attention. When the anxiety is severe, it can be paralyzing and may inhibit a person's ability to function in ordinary activities; in those cases, medication may be helpful in reducing the paralysis so that effective functioning of the personality system can be reestablished.

Psychological Dysfunctions and the Self.   The *self* is very much involved in dysfunctions of the personality system. The dysfunction may be seen as a breakdown of the *I-me* interaction that is central in the functioning of the self. When the dysfunction involves a neurosis, one's *I* may be experiencing anxiety because some part of the *me* is very upsetting. It may be that a part of the *me* is so unacceptable to the person that it has been severed off from the rest of the *me*s as a "not me" (Sullivan, 1953). Most of us probably experience this kind of a phenomenon—such as rejecting a part of oneself or one's feelings as not acceptable, or experiencing something in our *I* that is not able to be expressed as a *me*. Usually, we are able to continue processing our feelings and to work around the block and process it in part, returning to it now and then over a period of years. The anxiety may come back when that partially unprocessed aspect of the self reemerges, but we see that as a sign of incompleted processing, and we keep working at it. If too much processing is stopped, or if the anxiety is too high to allow fairly comfortable functioning in daily activities, we may seek counseling or psychotherapy to resolve the block and to reestablish the processing of the *I-me* interaction within the self. For example, in client-centered therapy, the therapist listens to the *me*s that are presented and reflects them back with their feeling component in an atmosphere of positive regard for the client and the feeling that is involved. This allows the client to examine the *me* that seems confusing and upsetting and to stimulate *I* experiencing of the variety of feelings that are involved. In general, listening, understanding, and accepting the person regardless of how unacceptable he or she may feel can be therapeutic—whether it is done by a therapist, a friendly person, or a confidant. Perhaps it is this process that makes the confidant relationship so important to the morale of many men and women in the study we discussed earlier in this chapter.

If the dysfunction in the *I-me* processing involves a near-total breakdown, so that the person is experiencing feelings that have little relation to the *me* that others perceive when they interact with that person, the dysfunction may result from psychosis. That is, one's *I* may experience something that is poles apart from the message given by the *me*—the classic catatonic schizophrenic may stand motionless for hours while internally being very aware of everything that is going on and fearing that any movement may bring world destruction. Or the *me* may be seen by others in one way, but not experienced the same way by one's *I*—the classic delusion that one is Napoleon, or that one hears voices. Similarly, the extreme variation in inner experience from deep depression to hyperexcitement that is unconnected with other's perceptions of oneself may reflect a breakdown of one's ability to take the attitude of others toward oneself and reflect an inability to engage in the *I-me* process that Mead called reflexive role taking.

Biological Changes and Psychopathology. Physiological factors—and particularly chronic disease—play an important part in mental illness, especially among the aged. A number of factors are involved. Decreasing hearing, sight, or physical mobility affect the kind of interactions one can have with others and also affect the inner experience of sensory stimulation. In addition, the general "slowing down" of reaction time, associated with aging itself rather than disease, makes it difficult to think and respond quite as fast as younger people. Sometimes these physiological changes make one less sure of oneself, more isolated from stimulation, and more likely to be confused and slow at daily cognitive tasks (such as counting out the change for purchases in a fast-moving supermarket). Taken together, and combined with feelings of decreased status, such changes can lead to some feelings of "persecution" that, in extreme form, could resemble psychopathology. One example of this perhaps common experience in old age is from a fictional story:

> They were all squabbles of one kind or another. The milkman had begun counting out the wrong change for me. The postman had held back my mail. The paper boy had delivered my newspaper or not, as the inclination struck him. And the clerks at the grocery store had amused themselves by playing petty tricks on me, breaking a few of my eggs as they packed the carton in a bag, or speaking so softly I could not hear them. The milkman wanted money, the postman and the newspaper boy convenience, the clerks amusement. To keep me from insisting on justice and courtesy, they relied on the precariousness of an old person's reputation, on the skepticism with which the word of the old is regarded, on my fear and feebleness. But I caught each of them up, and I did insist [Webber, 1963].

It is, of course, impossible to determine how much of these "persecutions" were actual (and related to the negative status of the aged) or were exaggerated because of some hearing loss, social isolation, and slower cognitive processes. However, more marked physical impairment can lead to a high degree of social isolation and also to mental illness. Lowenthal (1964) reported that a sample of aged respondents in a mental hospital were "considerably sicker physically" than a community sample of respondents of the same age (three-fourths reported "physical illness" as a major life-change since age 50). She also found that although lifelong extreme isolation did not seem to be conducive to mental illness in old age, late-developing isolation and physical illness seemed to be related to mental illness; this suggests that physical illness may precede and cause both relative isolation and mental illness in old age. Butler (1963a) reported significant interrelationships among "contemporaneous environmental deficits" (largely losses of significant persons), response time to psychomotor tasks, and depression as rated by psychiatrists. It seems that there is an important interaction among physiological, psychological, and social variables in the development of mental illness in the aged, even in the absence of cerebral disease.

Age and Psychopathology. First impressions of mental hospital wards and their outpatient services suggest that the aged comprise a relatively large proportion of persons with psychological problems. There are two factors involved: some persons have been hospitalized for many years and literally grow old in institutions or are maintained in the community through outpatient services or in nursing homes; and a large percentage of first admissions to mental hospitals are over age 60, largely because of cerebral arteriosclerosis or senile brain disease. Pfeiffer (1977) estimates that about one million persons over 65 (about one in 20) are in various kinds of institutions as a result of mental disorders. However, he estimates that a larger proportion, perhaps 15 percent, of persons over 65 suffers from some degree of psychopathology. Many of these older people do not receive necessary mental health services because they are thought to be too old to benefit from them; this is an incorrect assumption and a clear example of age discrimination (Butler, 1975). In addition, many hospitals are attempting to maintain patients in the community and to decrease the length of hospitalization through community facilities. With federal support provided by Medicare, many older persons have been discharged from mental hospitals into nursing homes where they often receive no treatment for their emotional problems except tranquilizers—which may do more to solve the problems of the staff than those of the patients.

In general, aged persons seem to be subject to the same range of psychopathology as young and middle-aged adults, and there does not seem to be much difference in the incidence of neuroses and psychoses with age. Although it is a bit difficult to conceive of childhood factors leading to a psychotic episode or the onset of major neuroses in old age, certainly physical illness and social trauma in the adult years would be relevant precipitating events for pathology in late life. Also, marital difficulties or identity problems can be important issues for young, middle-aged, and old adults. It is important, we feel, not only to try to understand what persons are "up against" regardless of their age, but also to be sensitized to particular crisis points from a developmental perspective as well. It may be true that different forms of therapy are useful for different types of issues and at different ages, but the general forms of psychopathology seem to be generally unrelated to age. However, there are three exceptions: depression, suicide, and cerebral disease.

Depression

Mild depression seems to be fairly common in old age; for example, Butler (1963a) reports that about one-fifth of his healthy elderly male respondents were rated "mild reactive depression" by psychiatrists, and this diagnosis was the largest single pathology. There are, of course, many physical and social losses that occur in old age that may lead to some degree of depression. Retirement may lead to a transitory depression, but severe depressions usually result from multiple stresses. Widowhood usually involves a period of depression also, and it seems to be more severe for men than women (Lowenthal, 1964). Busse (1959) suggests that depression in old age differs from young adult depression in that it results from a loss of self-esteem directly related to aging rather than from a turning inward of hostility. However, Butler and Lewis (1977) point out that old people are capable of guilt and actions that produce remorse, so that depression in late life may result from guilt, as is the case at any age. It may also be associated with physical disease; sometimes this is inappropriately seen as an excuse for not treating the depression.

Pfeiffer (1977) described the major symptoms of depression as: "abject and painful sadness, generalized withdrawal of interest and inhibition of activity, and a pervasive pessimism, manifesting itself as diminished self-esteem and by a gloomy evaluation of one's future and present situation" (p. 653). It may also be characterized by marked difficulty in making decisions, significant slowing of thinking and moving, and a number of physical symptoms including loss of appetite, fatigue, sleeplessness, loss of weight, and constipation (ibid.). Frequently depression may be the underlying cause of symptoms that are thought to be indications of "senility"; as a result it may not be treated at all.

While recent research has indicated that biochemical processes may be involved in many cases of depression, and while antidepressant medication or electroconvulsive therapy is often helpful, Jarvik (1976) noted that very little is known about the actual incidence of depression in various age groups, the causes of depression, or the reason that treatment is often effective. Clearly, there are many reasons that elderly persons would be depressed; nevertheless, most elderly people are not depressed; and many who suffer depression have also had episodes of depression earlier in life. Thus, continuing research on the nature and causes of this emotional disorder will be especially important for people of all ages.

Suicide

Although depression and suicide are not necessarily related, many suicides in old age result from severe depression, sometimes in association with other psychotic symptoms such as delusions. In some cases, suicide may seem to be a solution to an intolerable social situation or physical illness; that is, suicide is sometimes attempted when the depression seems intolerable and the person feels there is no chance for improvement, or because there is a decreased ability to function and compensate for the losses.

Suicide attempts are much more common than actual suicides among younger persons, but suicide attempts among older persons almost always reflect an intent to die (Pfeiffer, 1977). Suicide death rates increase steadily with age for white males (Figure 8.5). Although there is a marked difference between the rates for men and women among white persons, this difference is much less marked for black persons, and the increase with age is seen only for white men. Butler and Lewis (1977) speculate that "the explanation lies in the severe loss of status (ageism) that affects white men, who as a group had held the greatest

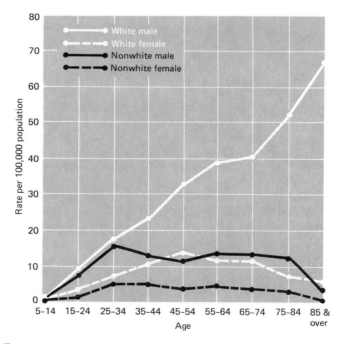

Figure 8.5

Suicide rates by age and color in the United States, 1964. (Source: Adapted from National Center for Health Statistics. *Vital and Health Statistics*, Series 20, No. 5. Washington, D.C.: U.S. Government Printing Office, 1967, p. 5.)

power and influence in society. Black men and most women have long been accustomed to a lesser status (through racism and sexism) and ironically do not have to suffer such a drastic fall in old age" (p. 68).

Marshall (1978) analyzed suicide rates for persons between 65 and 74 years old and found that there had been a dramatic decline in the rate for white males between 1948 and 1972 in the United States, although it was still much higher than for white women (data for black persons were not sufficiently reliable to be included in his analysis). He then compared the rising income status of the aged with the declining suicide rate and concluded that the change in the white male suicide rate was highly related to their income. Thus, improved economic well-being of older men appears to have substantially reduced their suicide rate. However, since social and political attitudes about aging, as well as general physical health, may have also improved during this period, we cannot conclude that greater income alone explains the decline in suicide—or that the loss of status with age in general is the cause of the high suicide rate for white men. For example, Miller (1978), in a study of white male suicides after age 60 in Arizona between 1970 and 1975, noted that the men who committed suicide were likely to have been widowed, to have lost a confidant or never have had one, and to have recently seen a physician; over half had given some clue of their suicidal intention. This suggests that the loss of a confidant, perhaps combined with physical complaints, an inability to discuss their problem with their physician, or lack of assistance from the physician were related to the suicide. Difficulty in coping with retirement also seemed to be a major problem for many of these men.

With regard to both depression and suicide, psychological factors (coping styles, personality integration, and past experiences), social factors (losses of roles, status, and significant others), and physical factors (disease, physiological changes that affect emotional reactions, and loss of hearing or sight or mobility) combine and interact to produce the reactions that may be so painful for the person that they may lead to a loss of desire to continue living.

Cerebral Disease and "Senility"

Senility is not a medical diagnosis, but it is often used as a "wastebasket" category for any old person with symptoms of confusion and disorientation. In contrast, *chronic brain syndrome* is a cerebral disease. While its causes are not well understood, it is usually differentiated into three types:

(1) *Senile Brain Disease.* A gradual and progressive decline in mental functioning may result from the gradual atrophy of the brain cells in the cerebral cortex. Senile plaques and neurofibrillary tangles are found in the neurons and brain tissue; also there is a loss of neurons, and an accumulation of lipofuscin (the "age pigment" mentioned in Chapter 7) in the brain tissue (Omenn, 1977). It has been suggested that these changes result from an autoimmune disease, from genetic factors, or from environmental and personality factors (Butler &

Lewis, 1977). In many respects it is very similar to Alzheimer's disease and quite different from cerebrovascular disease.

(2) *Alzheimer's Disease.* "Presenile dementia" caused by Alzheimer's disease is characterized by a decline in intellectual functioning in the forties or fifties compared with an average onset of senile brain disease at age 75 (ibid.). The progressive decline is more rapid than senile brain disease; in both, the deterioration sometimes halts, but the causes of either the deterioration or the factors that halt it are not known (Pfeiffer, 1977). A different form of presenile dementia, Jakob-Creutzfeldt disease, appears to be caused by a "slow" virus, so it is possible that the cause of Alzheimer's disease may eventually be discovered; in turn, this may provide a key to senile brain disease at all ages (ibid.).

(3) *Cerebrovascular Disease.* The interruption of blood flow to a part of the brain may also result in the death of brain cells because the supply of oxygen has been disrupted. In the typical case, the intellectual impairment begins abruptly and is accompanied by some neurological deficit such as paralysis or decreased sensation on one side of the body. In many cases, this is diagnosed as a cerebral vascular accident, or "stroke," and there may be gradual improvement of both intellectual and neurological impairments. However, repeated episodes may lead to a cumulative impairment that parallels senile brain disease. Frequently it turns out that the stroke is only the latest symptom in the progressive development of cerebral arteriosclerosis. That is, patients often have noted some loss of memory earlier; and they may have suffered headaches, blackouts, and palpitations of the heart before the onset of the stroke. Gradually the effects of the disease affect habitual behaviors, memory loss becomes more marked, and the person becomes unable to grasp the meaning of social situations. The abrupt onset of marked symptoms disrupting the person's compensations for a gradual loss of memory and the fluctuating nature of the subsequent deterioration of memory are generally seen as indicators of cerebral arteriosclerosis. Butler and Lewis (1977) report that it is more common in men than in women and that female sex hormones may play some preventative role; senile brain disease is more common in women than in men, perhaps because women live longer.

In general, the symptoms associated with cerebral disease are an impairment of both short- and long-term memory, disorientation or inability to remain oriented to one's environment, impairment of comprehension such as learning spatial arrangements or assimilating new information, impairment of judgment such as choice of appropriate behavior or clothing, shallow or unpredictable emotionality, and inability to carry out sequential tasks (Butler & Lewis, 1977; Pfeiffer, 1977). Cerebral disease is one of the major causes of death in old age; senile brain disease is eventually fatal, and cerebrovascular disease often results in death caused by additional cerebrovascular accidents, arteriosclerotic heart disease, or pneumonia. However, physical and emotional support, as well as group and individual therapy, can help the person cope as effectively as possible with the intellectual impairment. Butler and Lewis (1977) note that "many persons would be able to remain in their own homes throughout most of the course of illness if adequate services and assistance were available" (p. 86).

Another organic disease of the central nervous system is *Parkinson's disease*. Butler and Lewis (1977) report that it is more common in men than women, usually begins between age 40 and 65, and often can be treated by medication such as L-dopa. It is characterized by a tremor that is most visible when the person is at rest, diminishing when the person moves or sleeps. It may affect language, head and arm movements, and eyelids. A "pill-rolling" movement of the fingers, shaking head, and shuffling gait are characteristic and often cause embarassment. Therapy can help the person deal with the embarassment and depression that are frequently associated with the disease. While the cause of most cases is not known, extended use of some tranquilizers (phenothiazines) may be responsible; and there may be a relationship between the emergence of this disease late in life and the 1919 influenza epidemic (ibid.).

While these and other diseases are fairly common among nursing home residents, largely because they may be the reason the person needs nursing care, it is important to remember the significant distinction between aging and disease discussed in Chapter 7. One does not develop any of these organic diseases simply by growing old; and since they do not necessarily occur only in old age, they cannot be assumed to be either a cause or a result of aging.

Unfortunately, it is widely assumed that everyone becomes senile if they live long enough; too often health-care professionals, family members, and even older people themselves are inclined to dismiss physical and emotional problems of the elderly as "senility." As a result, the so-called diagnosis of senility is used as an excuse for not treating the underlying problem, and the person may be institutionalized or termed incurable when, in fact, the problem might be reversible. Robert Butler notes:

> The failure to diagnose and treat *reversible brain syndromes* is so unnecessary and yet so widespread that I would caution families of older persons to question doctors involved in care about this. Reversible brain syndromes are characterized by fluctuating levels of awareness which may vary from mild confusion to stupor or active delirium. . . .
>
> The causes can be malnutrition and anemia, congestive heart failure, infection, drugs, head trauma, alcohol, cerebrovascular accidents, dehydration, reactions to surgery and many others. If the patient does not immediately die (from accompanying physical diseases or exhaustion) and if treatment of the cause is quickly given, the chances for recovery are high, especially if there is no serious underlying physical problem. If reversible brain syndromes are not swiftly diagnosed and treated, however, they can become chronic and irreversible. Thus they represent a true medical emergency. Unfortunately many doctors dismiss the symptoms, assuming that the person is demonstrating typical confusion from chronic brain syndromes

caused by hardening of the arteries or senile brain disease, and fail to treat the patient.

Chronic brain disorder is, of course, a reality for numbers of older people, but it has become a wastebasket diagnosis applied whenever anyone starts "acting senile." Not only are reversible brain disorders misdiagnosed, but depression and anxiety can also cause the same symptoms and also will respond to treatment. Serious physical diseases such as heart attacks or diabetic comas may be undetected and thereby go untreated because they first present themselves as mental confusion and are diagnosed as chronic brain disorders [Butler, 1975, pp. 175-176].

Even in institutions such as nursing homes, "acting senile" can result from depression, overmedication, lack of emotional stimulation, or be a withdrawal from an unpleasant environment. Butler and Lewis (1977) note that physician-induced reversible and irreversible brain disorders can result from certain drugs such as cortisone and extended use of tranquilizers; and even small amounts of medications may have marked negative reactions in older people.

Although this overview of psychopathology in adulthood has been quite brief, it is important to consider psychopathology as a dysfunction of the personality system—involving the interaction of psychological, physiological, and social factors. With advancing age, the environmental niche in which the individual lives typically changes; this brings a shift in the fit between the individual and the environment. At the same time, physiological changes often occur that may place additional stress on the personality system as it seeks to maintain patterns of competent interaction with the environment. Sometimes these internal and external stresses overwhelm the system, and a dysfunction occurs. Thus, at all ages, psychotherapy may be useful to help the person cope with this dysfunction.

In the next chapter we will focus on the social and environmental problems that older men and women face in our country. But, first, we will pause for another Interlude—a 75-year-old man who has to continue working because he does not qualify for a pension.

CHAPTER SUMMARY

1. Definitions of personality involve three characteristics: the uniqueness of a person, attributes that are consistent over time and across different situations, and the interaction between the human being and the social and physical environment.
2. Personality has two distinct facets—consistency and change; both processes occur simultaneously. Depending on the lenses used to view personality, one will emphasize either consistency or change.
3. The cognitive perspective of personality emphasizes the individual's interpretation and selective perception of oneself and others. Cogni-

tive styles and personal constructs are among the most stable of all personality characteristics.

4. The study of personality traits or temperaments emphasizes individual uniqueness and stability. However, personality traits are not found to be highly consistent within individuals over long periods of time.

5. The interactionist perspective of personality views personality as jointly determined by the characteristics of the environment and the behavioral dispositions of the individual. This perspective incorporates cognitive processes, personality traits, and environmental influences that reciprocally affect one another.

6. The behavioral perspective of personality emphasizes the potential for change in personality as a result of environmental factors that influence behavior.

7. The model proposed in this chapter conceptualizes personality as a system that is continually fitting the changing individual and the changing environment together. A change in any aspect of this system will bring a change in the entire system, while at the same time there is considerable stability in some aspects of the personality system.

8. The Kansas City studies of personality during middle and late life indicated that socioadaptational characteristics that deal with adaptive, goal-directed, and purposive qualities of personality remain generally stable. Change with age was found in three areas of personality: ego energy that is available for tasks in the outer world declines; ego style shifts from active mastery toward passive and magical mastery styles for men, but the pattern for women is not clear; and older women appear to have a greater tolerance of their own aggressive impulses, while older men seem to be more tolerant of their own nurturant and affiliative impulses.

9. The presence of an intimate relationship—a confidant—is important for the morale of many older people; it serves as a buffer against the loss of roles, the decline in social interaction, and widowhood. However, a confidant does not protect an individual against the psychological effects of physical illness.

10. Psychopathology is the study of abnormal personality. Dysfunctions in the personality system involve a breakdown in the ability to maintain competent patterns of transactions between the individual and the environment. Psychopathology may also be seen as a breakdown in the *I-me* functioning that is central to the functioning of the self.

11. Physical disease, social isolation, and losses of significant persons increase the risk of mental illness in old age. While about 15 percent of older persons suffer some form of psychopathology, they often do not receive mental health services.

12. The number of changes and losses that occurs during the later years may cause depression; but it may also be caused by guilt, hostility,

and a loss of self-esteem related to aging. However, most older persons are not depressed, and the incidence of depression in various age groups is not known.

13. Suicide rates increase dramatically with age for white males. Loss of social status, reduced income, loss of a confidant, and increased health problems are among the factors that may lead to suicide.
14. "Senility" is not a medical diagnosis, but often is used as an excuse for not treating the physical, psychological, or social problems of old people.
15. Three types of cerebral disease are senile brain disease, Alzheimer's disease, and cerebrovascular disease; each may cause impairment of memory, comprehension, and judgment.
16. Reversible brain syndromes may be caused by malnutrition, dehydration, and many other conditions; if they are not diagnosed and treated, they may lead to chronic brain impairment.

REFERENCES

Adorno, T. W.; Frenkel-Brunswik, Else; Levinson, Daniel J.; & Sanford, R. Nevitt. 1950. *The Authoritarian Personality.* New York: Harper & Row.

Bandura, Albert. 1978. The Self System in Reciprocal Determinism. *American Psychologist, 33*(4), 344-358.

Bonarius, Hans. 1977. The Interaction Model of Communication: Through Experimental Research Toward Existential Relevance. In A. W. Landfield (Ed.), *1976 Nebraska Symposium on Motivation: Personal Construct Psychology.* Lincoln: University of Nebraska Press.

Busse, Ewald W. 1959. Psychopathology. In James E. Birren (Ed.), *Handbook of Aging and the Individual.* Chicago: University of Chicago Press.

Butler, Robert N. 1963a. The Facade of Chronological Age: An Interpretive Summary. *American Journal of Psychiatry, 119*(8), 721-728.

Butler, Robert N. 1963b. The Life Review: An Interpretation of Reminiscence in the Aged. *Psychiatry, 26*(1), 65-76.

Butler, Robert N. 1975. *Why Survive: Being Old in America.* New York: Harper & Row.

Butler, Robert N., & Lewis, Myrna I. 1977. *Aging and Mental Health: Positive Psychosocial Approaches* (2nd ed.). St. Louis: Mosby.

Carson, Robert C. 1969. *Interaction Concepts of Personality.* Chicago: Aldine.

Cumming, Elaine, & Henry, William E. 1961. *Growing Old: The Process of Disengagement.* New York: Basic Books.

Feshbach, Seymour. 1978. The Environment of Personality. *American Psychologist, 33*(5), 447-455.

Goldstein, Kenneth M., & Blackman, Sheldon. 1978. *Cognitive Style: Five Approaches and Relevant Research.* New York: Wiley-Interscience.

Gottschaldt, K. 1960. Das Problem der Phanogenetick der Personlichkeit. In P. Lersh & H. Thomas (Eds.), *Personlichkeits Forschung und Personlichkeits Theorie,*

Handbuch der Psychologie. Vol. 4. Göttingen: Hofgrefie. (Cited in Thompson, 1968.)

Gutmann, David L. 1964. An Exploration of Ego Configurations in Middle and Late Life. In Bernice L. Neugarten & Associates (Eds.), *Personality in Middle and Late Life.* New York: Atherton Press.

Gutmann, David L. 1967. Aging Among the Highland Maya: A Comparative Study. *Journal of Personality and Social Psychology, 7*(1), 28-35.

Gutmann, David. 1977. The Cross-Cultural Perspective: Notes Toward a Comparative Psychology of Aging. In James E. Birren & K. Warner Schaie (Eds.), *Handbook of the Psychology of Aging.* New York: Van Nostrand Reinhold.

Havighurst, Robert J.; Neugarten, Bernice L.; & Tobin, Sheldon S. 1963. Disengagement and Patterns of Aging. In Bernice L. Neugarten (Ed.), *Middle Age and Aging.* Chicago: University of Chicago Press, 1968. (Paper presented at the meeting of the International Association of Gerontology, Copenhagen, August, 1963.)

Heine, Patricke Johns. 1971. *Personality in Social Theory.* Chicago: Aldine.

Jarvik, Lissy F. 1976. Aging and Depression: Some Unanswered Questions. *Journal of Gerontology, 31*(3), 324-326.

Jung, Carl G. 1933. The Stages of Life. (Translated by R.F.C. Hull.) In Joseph Campbell (Ed.), *The Portable Jung.* New York: Viking, 1971.

Kagan, Jerome, & Moss, Howard A. 1962. *Birth to Maturity: A Study in Psychological Development.* New York: Wiley.

Kelly, E. Lowell. 1955. Consistency of the Adult Personality. *American Psychologist, 10*(9), 659-681.

Kimmel, Douglas C. 1979. Relationship Initiation and Development: A Life-Span Developmental Approach. In Robert L. Burgess & Ted L. Huston (Eds.), *Social Exchange in Developing Relationships.* New York: Academic Press.

Krohn, Alan, & Gutmann, David. 1971. Changes in Mastery Styles with Age: A Study of Navajo Dreams. *Psychiatry, 34*(3), 289-300.

Kuhlen, Raymond G. 1964. Developmental Changes in Motivation During the Adult Years. In James E. Birren (Ed.), *Relations of Development and Aging.* Springfield, Ill.: Charles C Thomas.

Langer, Susanne K. 1967. *Mind: An Essay on Human Feeling.* Vol. 1. Baltimore: Johns Hopkins University Press.

Langer, Susanne K. 1972. *Mind: An Essay on Human Feeling.* Vol. 2. Baltimore: Johns Hopkins University Press.

Lewin, Kurt. 1935. *A Dynamic Theory of Personality.* New York: McGraw-Hill.

Lowenthal, Marjorie Fiske. 1964. Social Isolation and Mental Illness in Old Age. *American Sociological Review, 29*(1), 54-70.

Lowenthal, Marjorie Fiske. 1975. Psychosocial Variation Across the Adult Life Course: Frontiers for Research and Policy. *The Gerontologist, 15*(1), 6-12.

Lowenthal, Marjorie Fiske. 1977. Toward a Sociopsychological Theory of Change in Adulthood and Old Age. In James E. Birren & K. Warner Schaie (Eds.), *Handbook of the Psychology of Aging.* New York: Van Nostrand Reinhold.

Lowenthal, Marjorie Fiske, & Haven, Clayton. 1968. Interaction and Adaptation: Intimacy as a Critical Variable. *American Sociological Review, 33*(1), 20-30.

Lubin, Marc. 1964. Addendum to Chapter 4. In Bernice L. Neugarten & Associates (Eds.), *Personality in Middle and Late Life*. New York: Atherton Press.

Marshall, James R. 1978. Changes in Aged White Male Suicide: 1948-1972. *Journal of Gerontology*, *33*(5), 763-768.

Maslow, Abraham H. 1950. Self-Actualizing People: A Study of Psychological Health. In W. Wolff (Ed.), *Personality Symposium*. No. 1. New York: Grune & Stratton.

Mead, George Herbert. 1934. Mind, Self, and Society. In Anselm Strauss (Ed.), *George Herbert Mead: On Social Psychology*. Chicago: University of Chicago Press, 1965. (Originally published in: *Mind, Self, and Society*. Charles W. Morris, Ed.)

Miller, Marv. 1978. Geriatric Suicide: The Arizona Study. *The Gerontologist*, *18*(5), 488-495.

Mischel, Walter. 1968. *Personality and Assessment*. New York: Wiley.

Mischel, Walter. 1969. Continuity and Change in Personality. *American Psychologist*, *24*(11), 1012-1018.

Neugarten, Bernice L. 1964. Summary and Implications. In Bernice L. Neugarten & Associates (Eds.), *Personality in Middle and Late Life*. New York: Atherton Press.

Neugarten, Bernice L. 1968. Adult Personality: Toward a Psychology of the Life Cycle. In Bernice L. Neugarten (Ed.), *Middle Age and Aging*. Chicago: University of Chicago Press.

Neugarten, Bernice L. 1977. Personality and Aging. In James E. Birren & K. Warner Schaie (Eds.), *Handbook of the Psychology of Aging*. New York: Van Nostrand Reinhold.

Neugarten, Bernice L., & Associates. 1964. *Personality in Middle and Late Life*. New York: Atherton Press.

Neugarten, Bernice L., & Gutmann, David L. 1958. Age-Sex Roles and Personality in Middle Age: A Thematic Apperception Study. *Psychological Monographs*, *72*(17, Whole No. 470).

Neugarten, Bernice L.; Havighurst, Robert J.; & Tobin, Sheldon S. 1965. Personality and Patterns of Aging. In Bernice L. Neugarten (Ed.), *Middle Age and Aging*. Chicago: University of Chicago Press, 1968. (Originally published in: *Gawein: Tijdschrift van de Psychologische Kring aan de Nijmessgse Universitiet*, Jrg. 13, Afl., May, 1965, 249-256.)

Omenn, Gilbert S. 1977. Behavior Genetics. In James E. Birren & K. Warner Schaie (Eds.), *Handbook of the Psychology of Aging*. New York: Van Nostrand Reinhold.

Pfeiffer, Eric. 1977. Psychopathology and Social Pathology. In James E. Birren & K. Warner Schaie (Eds.), *Handbook of the Psychology of Aging*. New York: Van Nostrand Reinhold.

Piaget, Jean, & Inhelder, Bärbel. 1969. *The Psychology of the Child*. New York: Basic Books.

Raimy, Victor. 1975. *Misunderstandings of the Self: Cognitive Psychotherapy and the Misconception Hypothesis*. San Francisco: Jossey-Bass.

Reichard, Suzanne; Livson, Florine; & Peterson, Paul G. 1962. *Aging and Personality*. New York: Wiley.

Riegel, Klaus F. 1976.   The Dialectics of Human Development. *American Psychologist, 31*(10), 689–700.

Riley, Matilda White; Foner, Anne; & Associates. 1968.   *Aging and Society. Vol. 1. An Inventory of Research Findings.* New York: Russell Sage Foundation.

Rokeach, Milton. 1960.   *The Open and Closed Mind.* New York: Basic Books.

Rosen, Jacqueline L., & Neugarten, Bernice L. 1964.   Ego Functions in the Middle and Late Years: A Thematic Apperception Study. In Bernice L. Neugarten & Associates (Eds.), *Personality in Middle and Late Life.* New York: Atherton Press.

Singer, Margaret T. 1963.   Personality Measurements in the Aged. In James E. Birren, Robert N. Butler, Samuel W. Greenhouse, Louis Sokoloff, & Marian R. Yarrow (Eds.), *Human Aging: A Biological and Behavioral Study.* Publication No. (HSM) 71-9051. Washington, D.C.: U.S. Government Printing Office.

Sullivan, Harry Stack. 1953.   *The Interpersonal Theory of Psychiatry.* New York: W. W. Norton.

Thibaut, John W., & Kelley, Harold H. 1959.   *The Social Psychology of Groups.* New York: Wiley.

Thomas, Alexander, & Chess, Stella. 1977.   *Temperament and Development.* New York: Brunner/Mazel.

Thompson, William R. 1968.   Genetics and Personality. In Edward Norbeck, Douglass Price-Williams, & William M. McCord (Eds.), *The Study of Personality: An Interdisciplinary Appraisal.* New York: Holt, Rinehart and Winston.

Tyler, Leona E. 1978.   *Individuality: Human Possibilities and Personal Choice in the Psychological Development of Men and Women.* San Francisco: Jossey-Bass.

Webber, Howard. 1963.   Games. *The New Yorker*, March 30, 1963, 42–46.

White, Robert. 1959.   Motivation Reconsidered: The Concept of Competence. *Psychological Review, 66*, 297–333.

Whitehead, Alfred North. 1969.   *Process and Reality.* New York: Free Press. (Originally published in 1929.)

Witkin, H. A.; Dyk, R. B.; Faterson, H. F.; Goodenough, D. R.; & Karp, S. A. 1962.   *Psychological Differentiation.* New York: Wiley.

Woodruff, Diana S., & Birren, James E. 1972.   Age Changes and Cohort Differences in Personality. *Developmental Psychology, 6*(2), 252–259.

Interlude
Henry, Age 75

Henry is a 75-year-old man who recently suffered the death of his wife of 52 years. He has continued to work because he could not manage on Social Security alone and because he will soon be eligible for a small pension from his union; he would have received a pension earlier, but he was unable to work for a time and lost the pension payments that he had built up; now he must work two more months in order to fulfill 15 continuous years work and receive his pension. He works as a waiter in a small restaurant, but when he was interviewed his feet were "burning" with arthritis after finishing his day's work, so our interview was ended prematurely. He is also suffering an increasing loss of hearing, which may reflect a general decline in health. He does not see how he will be able to continue working. And, with the death of his wife, he has suffered a severe emotional upset.

What will the future hold for him; what resources might he have to offset the loss of his wife and confidant? In what ways does he seem typical of old people in this country today? In what ways is he atypical? Why did he choose to talk about the milestones he picked—is there a sex difference in the milestones that men and women seem to choose to discuss? Is his difficulty in getting a pension a frequent problem for old people today? If he is no longer able to work, what do you think he will do? What could a social worker or a friend do to help?

What are some of the milestones that stand out in your life as you look back? What do you mean by "milestones"? *Some of the important events?* Was very important when I was married and had a nice son, a school teacher, a very nice man. And I was very happy 'til 1972 when my wife passed away; I lived with her 52 years. *She just passed away?* Yeah, in November the 21st. *That must have been a very sad time for you.* That was very sad, a very sad time for me. And now life is not so much interested where it used to be. *How is your life different now?* Well, for a senior citizen, it's a very great difference when you lose your wife and you lose your companion; it is not so easy. When you're young you don't mind so much, but when you get old, it's pretty tough. *In what way is it so tough for you?* Tough in every way. In general, in life and everything. You've got no companionship; in everything. When I go home now I'm all by myself. Just coming into the house . . . making a little dinner for myself, and straighten out the house; see everything should be in order; and watch television, read a book. Don't sleep so good no more. *You were married 53 years ago now?* It's going on 53. I was married in 1920, October the 24th, 1920. *Was that a big event in your life?* Oh yeah. I had a beautiful wife, good looking, smart woman in every way; and I enjoyed life even though I wasn't a rich man. I was a poor man, but I enjoyed my life.

Were you born in this country? No, no. I was born in Russia. *How old were you when you came to this country?* I was about 18 years. *Was that a big event for you?* It was very surprising for me. I was studying, I don't know how they call it in English, not a rabbi, [the man] who kills the cattle—kosher, and all that. That's what I was supposed to be, but they drag me to the army because my brother and me was twins. One remain home, the other go because my father needed him for work, and I went to the army. I was in the army six months and I came to this country. Oh, it wasn't so easy. *Tell me about it.* When I came to the Russian Army, I was there six months, and then after six months when you take the second oath, they let you go in the city. Before I went to the city I wrote a letter home to my sister that I hate to be in the army. It's very tough to be in the Russian Army. So she said, "All right, I'll try to get together a few dollars and get an agent and we'll take you out of there." But it's very dangerous, because God forbid if you get caught—no court-martial, nothing; they shoot you right there on the spot. But finally I take the chance. I took that chance and came to the city. She wrote me where, and the agent was waiting for me, and he took me over and took off my uniform and everything, and he sent me away to a different city. Even if they should catch me without the clothes they would shoot me right away. Yes, martial law. *And then you came to America?* Yes, then I came here. It took me a long time. I came here with the boat. I was sailing about 26 days and nights and I lost . . . I weighed 160 pounds when I left; when I came here I weighted 120 pounds. I lost on the boat, because I couldn't eat and I couldn't drink nothing. I was vomiting. I couldn't take the sea. Seasick.

And what did you do when you came here? So when I came here I got a little job, you know, in the grocery store, because I couldn't speak. I got sick after that. I got a tumor and I lost my speech. That's why I became the counterman in the waiter business; my buddy who was singing in the Hebrew College, I learned with him, he was the sexton in the temple. I couldn't make it [as a cantor] on account of my voice. Finally I had an operation. At that time years ago they did not know so much about cancer, and Dr. B. operated on me and took out that growth; and it took me three years to get back my voice and my speech, and then I was off my track. It was too late already to go again.

Then I worked as a grocer for three-and-a-half dollars a week, but 12 hours a day or more, six-and-a-half days a week; no, no, too many hours. It was very tough, very tough. And then I bought myself a suit for two dollars. An old one, secondhand; you could put two like me in there [it was so big]. I went to the man and I paid him a quarter a week; eight quarters; in eight weeks I paid him off for the suit and then I bought myself a pair of secondhand shoes. You shouldn't wear no secondhand shoes. I didn't have the money. What can I do? I slept by a shoemaker on the floor for a dollar a week. *Could you speak English?* No, I went to night school to learn a little; but I was so tired. As soon as I came into school I fell asleep right away. So the teacher say it's no good for you; you come to school, you sleep, you don't learn. So I says to her I try to learn by myself, and I did. I used to get books and learn by myself little by little; it takes me a long time, but I learned. Well, of course, I speak a little bit an accent, you know.

Then my brother came along from Russia too, so after a few years we work together. He was a carpenter, and I went with him to help him bring the lumber. So we saved a little money and then we opened up a candy store. And I was in the candy store and he was working as a carpenter. So I was making a little money. I was making that time about nine, ten dollars in the candy store and it was a tough life. Used to get up five o'clock in the morning and work 'til two o'clock in the morning. Oh, it was very tough.

When did you get married? I got married about eight years later. I met the girl in the candy store. She was a nice girl; she came to buy a piece of candy so I got acquainted with her and she brought another friend. So the friend my brother took . . . he should rest in peace, he's dead already . . . and I took this one here. So that's how it is. *Was it a big moment when your children were born?* I have only son. Of course I was very surprised. It was a boy. And my wife said, "Well, once you sell the candy store you buy another candy store, you fix up the candy store, you can't have too many children because you're moving around; one is enough." So we had one child.

Were there any other big moments in your life? Yes, I remember some. Three . . . (he counts on his fingers) . . . three years and eight months [ago] I went to Russia to see my brother, the youngest one. I had a very nice time. I was in Moscow, in Kiev, and Leningrad. And I met my brother and I enjoyed myself very nicely because I haven't seen him close to 60 years. And he remained alive. All the other family, my sisters and brothers, Hitler killed them. There was about 220 people from the family; everybody was killed. But this trip I enjoyed very very much. That was a great surprise in my life.

Do you have any grandchildren? Yes, one grandson. He goes to college. Oh, a beautiful boy; he was on the hockey team; a powerful kid, very nice boy. And I got my daughter-in-law; she is a manager in a department store; very nice person.

How about crisis points; were there any very difficult points for you? Difficult? Oh, yeah; was plenty of problems. When my son was drafted I felt very very bad. He was drafted and he was sent away on the other side and I didn't hear from him about six months. And I felt very bad and I got from loneliness—I figured that maybe I lose my son—I got like a paralytic stroke on my right side. Oh, was terrible! It took me about a year to get better. One day I was downstairs with a cane and I see under the door there's a telegram laying for me. I was so upset I couldn't take out the telegram, so I had the next door neighbor come over. So she took out the telegram, she says okay, your son is in the hospital. Thank God, you know, my son was in the hospital, he isn't killed. But he was very sick; he was there with malaria, very bad sickness.

What happened with your paralysis? I went to a chiropractor. And he takes my leg and brings it over here to my head in the back and I fainted. He went over and got a pitcher of cold water and washed me down and I came to and he said, "Don't worry, you wouldn't die." And he take the same leg and bring it here. Finally he gave me about 25 adjustments. Every day I supposed to come there and I couldn't ride a taxi because I couldn't take the shaking; that was terrible. *Did he cure you?* He did! *You weren't able to work then, were you?* No, I couldn't bend! I couldn't walk! No, I didn't work. Was no financial money; my brother-in-law helped me a little, but that time was no union, nothing to help you. So [one day] when I came home my wife wasn't home so she prepared me something to eat and I walked into the house; instead of eating the sleep went on me. I couldn't keep my eyes open. So I crept into the bed with my clothes and I laid down and I fell asleep and I slept maybe five, six hours. And then when I get up, I get off the bed like a new man. I got off the bed and I started walking. I could walk! *And that was it?* So, I called the doctor and he said, "Go to work! And come to me once a week and then I'll massage you." And then I went to work.

What kind of job did you go to then? I worked in a restaurant. I worked there quite a number of years. Then the restaurant went under, and I went to work for a man on Broadway, and I'm working for him 28 years already. And to him it's just like I came today. He don't give a damn! No pension, no nothing.

No pension? No pension, because I'm in the union not even 15 years. I worked without a union. And I can't work; I got to retire. I can't work. Impossible for my legs. Don't forget, I'm 75 years old. I can't work, and I've got no pension. *Why don't you have a pension at 75?* I'm trying to finish up yet; another couple weeks maybe, to pay into the union, to the pension. It's got to be paid in $160 and I haven't got the money to pay. *How long do you have to work before you get a pension?* You got to work at least 15 years in the union. *How much longer do you have to go?* The union says another couple months. And I can't do it. Here I'm sitting now. My feet are really burning like fire. *So you're just living on Social Security now?* Yeah, I get $165.20 a month. *Is that enough?* No. I need what I make here. I make here a couple dollars. But if I wouldn't work, then it would be tough for me. And from the union I could get, if I do get a pension, I get $52.75 a month. *That's not much.* Sure not. Especial the way, oh years ago—about 30 years ago—it would be fine, because the rent is very high. My rent is $150 a month. *So that's almost all your Social Security right there for rent.* Yeah, and then you got electric, telephone! And lodge money, insurance. Big expense! *What do you think is going to happen?* I have to go on welfare. They wouldn't take me. They wouldn't give me welfare. *Have you applied for welfare?* Yeah, they wouldn't give me. *How would you feel about going on welfare if you have to?* I don't want to; I don't want to; I hate that. Maybe Medicare would better for me—the medicines and doctor bills, because it's a lot of medications. It costs a lot of money. I'm trying this (he stands up)—maybe this way it should be better circulation; oh, it [his feet] feels burning. Okay Professor, we're going to go!

I talked with Henry about six months after this interview and learned that he had received his pension after working only a couple of additional weeks; his employer paid the necessary amount to the union pension fund and did not require Henry to work the remaining time. He seemed to be feeling well, and his health had improved after he no longer had to work everyday. However, I was unable to contact him in 1979; although the union had no record that he had died, he did not respond to my letter requesting an interview and his telephone had been disconnected.

9

GROWING OLD IN A CHANGING WORLD

It is striking: more and more people are growing old today, but they appear to be taking a longer time to do it. Improved health care, better nutrition, and the large reduction in mortality earlier in life are allowing greater numbers of people to live into old age today. These changes have also slowed the disease processes often associated with aging so that a decade or more of active life has been added to the life span of many people in our society, effectively pushing the beginning of old age from the sixties up to the seventies or eighties. At the same time, attitudes about aging are changing so that older people are being seen more positively now than they were earlier in this century—in part because they are more numerous today, and in part because they are more active and in better health than they were 50 or 75 years ago. As we look toward the next century, aging is likely to be very different than it is today, or than it was in the past. At the beginning of this century, only 5 persons out of every 100 in the United States were over age 65, and only 1 out of every 3 of those lived to age 80. Now about 11 persons out of every 100 are over 65, and half of those will live to age 80. By the year 2020, perhaps as many as 15 out of every 100 persons will be over age 65 (U.S. Bureau of the Census, 1976). In addition, older people in the future will have had more education and better health care throughout their lives than older people today.

This chapter will examine aging within the perspective of cultural and social influences. Our changing world affects the experience of aging; and the growth of the older population is bringing about some of the important social changes around the world. We begin this chapter with a discussion of aging in cultures that differ from our own. Then, we will examine the link between aging and society in our own culture. Next, we will focus on some of the most important issues faced by older people today—including income, health, and the more general issue of the quality of life, which necessarily involves housing, transportation, and fear of crime. The final section will describe some of the educational and occupational opportunities for work with older persons.

CROSS-CULTURAL PERSPECTIVES ON AGING

It is frequently assumed that aging is a more positive experience in other cultures—especially in nonindustrial societies such as those that are based on agriculture, rearing animals, or hunting and gathering for food. Similarly, it is often assumed that industrialization has led to a breakdown of traditional social supports so that older persons are especially vulnerable in modern, highly developed societies, while older people were protected within a close-knit community in simpler times and simpler societies. However, the situation is actually far more complex than these assumptions suggest and, on balance, the elderly in today's modern societies are probably about as well cared for as old people have ever been. Of course, there are some cultures where it is better to grow old than others, and persons of higher socioeconomic status generally are treated better than persons of lower socioeconomic status in all societies. In this section, we will focus on aging in different cultures, the effects of industrialization on the status of older people, and groups of long-living people.

Aging in Other Cultures

Two central conclusions may be drawn from the cross-cultural studies on aging. First, the meaning, status, and experience of aging differs greatly among cultures. Some cultures honor their elderly; others honor only those older persons who are wealthy or powerful; still others leave the aged to die when they cannot care for themselves; and in a few societies the elderly live very much like younger people (Beauvoir, 1972; Simmons, 1945). Second, the nature of aging is intertwined with the other cultural patterns of each society, so that the status and treatment of older persons depends on the nature and structure of the society. For example, in some cultures prestige is based on the number of wives a man has; this results in a delay in age of marriage for young men (because all available women are already married), and an accumulation of wives among older men. In some of these societies, older persons arrange marriages for the younger men, and the oldest man in the household may also count the wives of his sons as if they were his wives. All of this would seem to provide older men with greater power and prestige. However, wives may be lost to other men, return to their kin after menopause, or die and not be replaced. Thus, the aging man in these cultures may lose his prestige sometime after middle age, or he may remain head of a household consisting of many wives while his son takes over much of the actual power and responsibility of the household (Goody, 1976). Moreover, as this example implies, the status of aged men may differ from and be based on different characteristics than those that determine the status of aged women; this also depends on the nature of the cultural patterns within the particular society.

Several cultures have extremely harsh or extremely reverent attitudes toward the aging. Beauvoir (1972) described some of the cultures in which old people were killed or allowed to die when they were no longer productive; these events usually involved a ceremony of some kind, were sometimes seen as a way to enhance the old person's life after death, or sometimes were viewed as a sacrifice for the well-being of the community.

> Among the Chukchee, a Siberian tribe that was in contact with white traders, those who lived on their fishing found it extremely hard to get enough to eat. They used to kill deformed children at birth, as well as those who looked as though they might be difficult to rear. Some few elders managed to carry on trade and to amass a little capital: they were respected. The others were a burden, and they were led such a life that it was easy to persuade them to prefer death. A great feast was given in their honour, a feast in which they took part: the assembly ate seal-meat, drank whisky,

sang and beat upon a drum. The condemned man's son or his younger brother slipped behind him and strangled him with a seal-bone.

Among the Hopi, the Creek and the Crow Indians, and the Bushmen of South Africa, it was customary to lead the aged person to a hut specially built for the purpose away from the village and there to abandon him, leaving a little food and water. The Eskimo, whose resources are meagre and most uncertain, persuade the old to go and lie in the snow and wait for death; or they forget them on an ice-floe when the tribe is out fishing; or they shut them into an igloo, where they die of cold [Beauvoir, 1972, p. 51].

Simmons (1945) examined the records that had been compiled on 71 different tribal societies, finding that violent killing of older people was fairly common in 11 tribes and neglect or abandonment of the elderly was common in 18 of them. He noted that abandonment was more common among nomadic peoples and hunters, while violent killing was more likely in tribes living in a severe climate, with impermanent residence and an irregular food supply. These practices were less common among tribes that cultivated grain or relied on other agricultural food supplies, which were fairly constant so that they did not have to move frequently, and among those that had developed a concept of property rights, centralized authority, and codified laws. Thus, harshness of the environment and necessity appeared to be the main factors that inclined some tribes to treat their aged harshly. Also, a few societies where the aged were especially powerful, because of magic or secret ceremonies, sometimes treated the aged harshly after their magic power had gone. Beauvoir (1972) noted that, in some cases, societies with no cultural tradition for the elderly to pass on to younger persons also killed or abandoned the aged who were unable to care for themselves. An example of this pattern is the Ik tribe in Uganda described by Turnbull (1973). After their hunting territory was made part of a national park, the Ik tribe were forced to resettle and to become dependent on government welfare. This led to the deterioration of their cultural traditions and to the development of a society based on a "mere survival system" where old people were allowed to starve when there was not enough food.

At the other extreme, a number of cultures treat the elderly with great respect. The reasons for this are as varied as the reasons for the harsh treatment in other cultures. In some cases, the old people play an important part in ceremonies and rituals; in other cultures it is part of the religious tradition to honor the elders; and in still others they gain respect because of their memory of ancient myths or cultural history.

Old people often acquire a high, privileged status because of their memories. This is the case among the Miao, who live in the high forest and bush country in China and Thailand. At one time the Miao began to evolve a high degree of civilization, but their development was checked, no doubt by wars. The family is patriarchal, and the son does not leave his father's roof until he is thirty. Theoretically the head of the house has the right of life and death over all its members, but in fact the relationship between father and son is very good, each taking the other's advice. The Miao run to large families, and the grandparents look after the grandchildren. Women, children and old people are very well treated. If, having outlived his descendants, an old person is quite by himself, he will seek the protection of the head of an important family; he is always accepted, even though he is a burden. The Miao think that the souls of the dead live in the house and guard it, and that they are reincarnated in the new-born. It is the old who hand on the traditions, and the respect in which they are held is chiefly based upon the ability to do so; their memory of the ancient myths can provide them with a very high standing. They are the community's guides and counsellors [Beauvoir, 1972, p. 71].

Beauvoir noted several other societies where high status was granted to the elderly—the Navajo in North America, the Jivaro in South America, the Lile and Tiv in Africa, and the Mende in Sierra Leone. Of course, the traditional Japanese and Chinese cultures provide high status to the elderly, and this has been maintained, at least in Japan, in spite of the dramatic industrialization of that country in this century (Palmore, 1975).

Between these two extremes, there is wide diversity in the status and treatment of the elderly. In fact, even within the cultures that have been described as extremely harsh or extremely respectful, it is likely that there are subtle exceptions and distinctions that were not recorded in the anthropological reports on which these analyses have often relied. A good example of the sometimes subtle cultural factors that affect aging is Harlan's (1964) report on the status of the aged in three different villages in India. In one village, the oldest male had great authority, but only until about age 65; he lost his status if his wife died because she played the key role in his control over the household; however, when that role was taken over by the wife of the eldest son, he then gained the authority once held by his father. Thus, age alone did not provide status, for it depended also on marital status and the nature of intergenerational relations. In community matters, prestige was based largely on economic status and education; age was not particularly relevant.

In a second village, the oldest man had great authority in only two-thirds of the families; here the status of the old woman was highly dependent on her husband being alive—as long as he lived, no one dared to mistreat her. After her husband died, a woman would retain her prestige as long as she was able to aid the family (perhaps through a hidden cache of jewelry or gold that would be given to family members after her death) and behaved well toward other family members.

In the third village, respect was given to older people only on formal occasions, but in day-to-day life they were not shown particular respect; the son often ran the house even though the father was regarded as the head of the family. Thus, Harlan concluded that the status of older people depends on a wide variety of factors, even within nonindustrialized societies. He noted that special attention should be given to the level of prestige granted old persons based on their socioeconomic status, that actual family and community power or authority may differ from the reported norms of the culture, and that many factors other than the degree of urbanization or industrialization may contribute to the difference in status of the elderly between urban industrialized countries and rural nonindustrial societies.

Effects of Industrialization

A number of studies have suggested that the status of older persons is lower in "modern" industrialized societies than it is in "traditional" agricultural societies (Cowgill & Holmes, 1972). The assumption is that aging is less prestigious in modern societies for a number of reasons: the knowledge older people have is out of date when social change is rapid; their memory is no longer needed when cultural traditions are written down; increased education and training makes their skills easily replaceable; and the sheer growth of their numbers makes aging itself less unique and revered (Hauser, 1976).

One refinement in this debate is to differentiate modernization of the society from the individual's contact with modernity. For example, a recent study focused on attitudes of young people toward the aged in six "developing" nations—three were relatively industrialized and three were more traditional (Bengtson, Dowd, Smith, & Inkeles, 1975). The young people in each country were from three different occupational groups: (1) rural farmers who had little contact with modern industrialization; (2) factory workers who had direct contact with modern industrialization; and (3) urban nonindustrial workers. It was found that attitudes about aging did not differ between these three occupational groups. If anything, the data tended to show that those individuals who had more contact with modern life had more positive attitudes about aging and the aged than those who had less contact. However, on the general cultural level, those persons in the more industrialized countries were found to have less positive attitudes about aging than those young people in the less industrialized countries. Thus, industrialization appeared to affect general cultural attitudes about aging, lowering the prestige and status of the aged; but, individual contact with modern industrialization within a culture did not appear to lead to less positive attitudes about aging on an individual basis. This question requires continued research because it may be that industrialization only initially brings greater cultural disorganization and devaluation of the elderly; eventually, the higher productivity and standard of living may improve the quality of life for everyone in the society.

In general, it is important to be cautious about romanticizing "the good old days" within any culture, including our own. Laslett (1976), reviewing the data on societal development and aging, concluded: "Then, as now, a place of your own, with help in the house, with access to your children, within reach of support, was what the elderly and the aged most wanted for themselves in the preindustrial world. This was difficult to secure in traditional England for any but fairly substantial people. It must have been almost impossible in many other cultural areas of the world" (pp. 115-116). In contrast, some industrialized countries have made this goal potentially available to every elderly person in the society.

Long-Living Peoples

Cross-cultural research on aging has also focused on the various pockets of long-living people around the world. The most frequently reported example is the Abkhasians in the Caucasus region of the Soviet Union, but similar groups of long-living people have also been discovered in other areas of the world: in the harsh regions of Siberia, in the foothills of the Himalayan mountains—the Hunzukuts, and in the Highlands of Ecuador—the Villacambans (Gutmann, 1977). Although these relatively isolated communities of people have attracted attention because they have unusually large numbers of people who claim to be very old, this claim is often not supported by written birth records, so the determination of their actual age is questionable (Medvedev, 1974). Usually, researchers can rely only on the old persons' memory of recorded past events they claim to have witnessed; but there is always the possibility that the person is reporting events that had been relayed by others and not directly experienced, so it is often not possible to be certain that the people are as old as they claim to be.

Leaf (1973) reported that these long-living people were generally held in high status in their communities because of their wisdom; they worked hard, enjoyed sex, and had very moderate diets. Benet (1974) reported that the Abkhasians remained active as long as possible and that retirement was unknown to them; old people were given increased status, avoided overeating, and experienced a high degree of integration in their lives within the society. Their diet was low in calories and they ate little meat; large amounts of garlic were used; tobacco and coffee or tea were seldom used; and a buttermilk-like drink, fresh fruit, pickled vegetables, and wine were consumed regularly. Perhaps this diet, combined with continuing productive work and a high status within a well-integrated culture, contributes to the general longevity in this society. Benet also emphasized the importance of cultural factors that provide a sense of certainty to life, as well as the continuity of activities among the Abkhasians. However, it is also possible that genetic factors in this relatively isolated community, or the rigorous life over many generations, may have contributed to the longevity. Of course, these people may be simply exaggerating their age because old age is given high status in their culture.

Conclusion

There is great diversity around the world in the patterns of aging, and there is no convincing evidence that aging was better for the typical old person in historical times or in preindustrial societies. In some societies, aging appears to be a very good life experience, especially if one has power, money, or some kind of magic, and the society values these things—even if one is infirm or widowed. In other societies, the aged are treated harshly, usually when they are no longer productive or protected by a powerful spouse or family. There is considerable debate and no clear consensus about the factors that differentiate cultures to make them positive toward aging or negative toward it; but even these terms are too simplistic when the great diversity of cultures and the complexity within a culture are recognized.

Much further work needs to be done on the difficult questions raised by this cross-cultural perspective on aging. Additional anthropological research will be important, not only because it can provide a perspective in which we can see aging in our own society more clearly, but also because it will help us to understand the complex interaction of aging processes and culture. In addition, it will help us to appreciate more fully the cultural background of aging persons within our own society. In the next section, we return to our own culture and begin a detailed examination of aging in the United States.

AGING AND THE SOCIAL CONTEXT

Clearly, there is a complex relationship between aging and society. In general, the social status of older persons within a particular society reflects the political and economic structure of that society, as well as the cultural values, traditions, and beliefs of the society. Changes in economic and political conditions, or changes in cultural values, can affect the status and characteristics of the aged. Conversely, changes in the relative proportion of older persons within a society, or changes in the characteristics of older persons—such as better health, can affect the economic and political structure of society. All of these factors are closely intertwined in a complex system of interacting forces. A single invention, such as the automobile or the transistor, can radically alter social and cultural patterns that, in turn, may affect the relationship between generations within a society. For example, the automobile not only encouraged families to move apart, but also allowed them to remain in contact. Similarly, the transistor has played a major role in low-cost long-distance telephone service, jet travel, and medical advances; each in its own way has helped to maintain relationships between generations, even as each has helped to transform relationships. Thus, to understand aging, we need to examine the changing social context in which it occurs. We begin with a brief historical overview of aging in the United States since 1900. Next, we will focus on the growth of the older population and its impact on society. Then, we will examine the ways in which the social structure of our society affects the aging process of persons with different socioeconomic status, ethnic-group membership, and sex.

Historical Overview: 1900 to 1980

Earlier in this century, older persons were looked upon as worn out, useless, a drain on the nation's productivity, and a hindrance to advancing technology. Many were in poor health and relatively few survived to ages that we now consider to be old. There were no Social Security or welfare programs, so being retired meant being out of work and living on savings, depending on one's family, or taking charity. This was a period of rapid change, and older persons had to cope with the revolutionary impact of the automobile, electricity, and industrialization.

Gruman (1978) traced the historical patterns in attitudes about older people and concluded that the origins of present-day negative views of aging date back to the close of the Western frontier in the 1890s. At that time, the American emphasis was on becoming a strong aggressive nation and on conquering new territories; the young were seen as a vital resource, while the old were weak and inadequate. He noted that it was "standard practice for industry to shut out workers over the age of 40" and that immigration quotas restricted the entry of older persons to the United States (ibid.). These were also the days of "sweat shops," child labor, and union organization. Life in urban areas often meant living in a tenement with only cold running water on the ground floor and an "outhouse" in the backyard. Tuberculosis and pneumonia were very serious diseases and often fatal; millions of persons died in the flu epidemic in 1918. Old people were especially vulnerable to many of these social conditions.

After World War I, a period of rapid social change affected a large range of traditional values as women received the right to vote, young people began a dramatic sexual revolution, and the migration from farms into the cities began in earnest. The Great Depression of the 1930s, combined with a serious drought in the Midwestern farmlands, wiped out the savings of a lifetime for many and brought about dislocation and poverty. In comparison to other historical periods, this period probably exhibited the lowest point in the status of older persons. They still made up only 5 percent of the population—unchanged from the turn of the century—but often poverty was extreme, savings were gone, and younger men needed to work. Retirement was established to move old workers "out to pasture," and Franklin Roosevelt attacked the "nine old men" on the Supreme Court as blocking the country's progress. Many older people lived with their children's families because they had no choice; they could not afford to live alone. Partly to remain active, and partly to repay this charity, they often helped out with chores and odd jobs around the house. However, others were less fortunate and wound up living in poor farms or in state mental institutions—nearly the only facilities available in those days. Thus, during the first four decades of this century, the aged were seen as a social problem: What should be done with those few old people who have outlived their usefulness, need care, but do not have families to take them in?

From the 1940s to the 1970s, the number of older people has grown rapidly, largely because of medical advances such as the discovery of penicillin in 1928 and streptomycin for treating tuberculosis in 1943. As the "problem of the aged" became more acute, social resources began to be organized to meet their needs; this led to a dramatic growth in federal and community programs to relieve these problems. At the same time, during the 1960s and 1970s, there has been a great increase in research on the characteristics of older people, the nature of aging processes, as well as on the problems of the elderly. Tibbitts (1979), reviewing these historical changes, argued that there has been a gradual improvement in the status of older people since World War II.

> My thesis is that over the past 30 to 40 years American society has been transforming itself from one in which older people were held in increasingly low esteem and characterized by a multiplicity of derogative stereotypes to one in which the roles and styles of life of older adults will be viewed as positive and contributive to the quality of life for themselves, for their communities, and for the total society [Tibbitts, 1979, p. 10].

Today, it seems we are evolving a new perspective that sees the problems of older people as symptoms of the problems of our society as a whole. For example, health care for older persons is now being seen as a symptom of the greater social problem of health care for all persons. Thus, Medicare, created to help older persons cope with one of the major problems of aging, may eventually be replaced by a system of comprehensive national health insurance for all persons. Similarly, inflation has long been a major problem for older persons living on a fixed income, but it is now being recognized as a serious problem for all persons. Perhaps the perspective is shifting to an analysis of the problems of our total society in which older persons are harbingers of future issues that are now only on the horizon for most of us. In that sense, we will not only face the problems of aging ourselves if we live long enough, but we also will recognize that the problems of older persons no longer seem to be unique to older persons. We are slowly discovering that the elderly are as diverse a group as young or middle- aged persons and therefore not all that different from other people. But they may be more vulnerable to problems that seem less serious to younger people— problems such as broken sidewalks, poor transportation, inadequate housing, fear of crime, and so on. Although much remains to be accomplished and negative attitudes about older people persist, the growing proportion of healthy, well-functioning older persons is beginning to call public attention to the inaccuracy of past stereotypes that all older people are sick, impaired, dependent, or troubled.

Growth of the Older Population

One of the primary reasons for the changes in social attitudes toward older persons in our society since the 1940s has been the rapid growth of the older population. We have already noted the rising proportion of older persons earlier in this chapter, the increased life expectancy in our country (see Figure 1.5), and the growing number of older persons (see Figure 6.4). Thus, it may come as a surprise that the proportion of person over 65 in the United States is relatively low in comparison with other industrialized countries; Austria, Belgium, France, Great Britain, Norway, and Sweden have higher proportions—some as high as 14 percent. In Africa, Asia, and Latin America the proportion is much lower—as few as 3 percent in some countries. Generally, those countries with high birth rates have lower proportions of older persons, and those with low birth rates have greater proportions of older persons. Immigration can contribute to the *number* of older persons, and many of the older people in the United States to-day came to this country during the period of high immigration around the turn of the century; but they also have children and grandchildren, so immigration does not increase the *proportion* of older persons very much. Similarly, de-creased mortality does not necessarily increase the proportion of older persons, contrary to what one might expect, unless the decrease in mortality affects the older age groups much more than other age groups. Thus, the future age struc-ture of the population is determined primarily by fertility (birth rate). As a result, those born during the "baby boom" (after World War II) will swell the ranks of older age groups during the years 2010 to 2030, when this cohort reaches age 65 (U.S. Bureau of the Census, 1976).

The dramatic increase in the older population is a worldwide phenomenon, with different impacts in different cultures. Hauser (1976) notes that the growth of the older population will be especially dramatic in less developed countries.

> While older persons in the more developed countries will increase by 58 percent between 1970 and 2000, those in the less developed countries will almost triple. In consequence, whereas the less developed countries had only 45 percent of the world's aged in 1970, they would have 58 percent by the century's end [p. 74].

Thus, the *number* of older persons is increasing more rapidly in those societies with high birth rates whose population is growing rapidly; these societies also tend to be less economically developed, so the growth of the aged population is more likely to be an economic burden. The *proportion* of older persons is in-creasing more rapidly in those societies with a declining birth rate—for example, in Europe and North America. In the United States, the oldest segments of the population are growing most rapidly; the population over age 75 will increase by 60 percent between 1975 and 2000, while the population between 65 and 74 will increase by 23 percent (Brotman, 1977b).

In the United States, one of the most dramatic changes in the older population has been the growing proportion of women over age 65 (Figure 9.1). As recent-ly as 1930, there were about as many men as women over 65 but, in 1975, there were only 69 men for every 100 women over age 65; by the year 2000

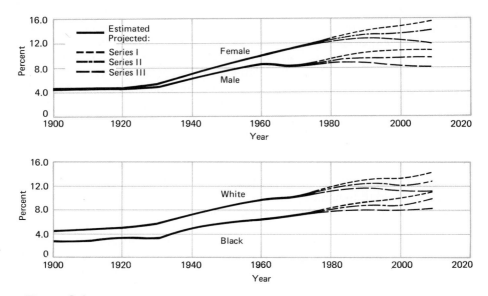

Figure 9.1
Percent of the total United States population 65 years old and over, by sex and race: 1900 to 2010. The differing projections reflect different assumptions about the fertility rate; series I assumes a birth rate of 2.7 children per woman, series II a total fertility rate of 2.1 (replacement level), and series III a rate of 1.7. (Source: U.S. Bureau of the Census, 1976, Figure 3-2).

this ratio is expected to decline to 65:100. In 1975 this meant that there were 4.1 million more women than men over age 65; by the year 2000 there will be 6.5 million more women than men (U.S. Bureau of the Census, 1976). As noted in Chapter 4, males have higher death rates than females at all ages, so the ratio of males to females declines steadily with age (see Figure 4.1). At the same time, life expectancy has been increasing more rapidly for women than for men, so the greater growth of the older female population probably reflects various health-related sex differences (such as greater cigarette smoking among men until recently). However, greater life expectancy among women has not been a recent development as suggested by Figure 9.1. The relative balance between men and women over 65 earlier in this century resulted from the heavy, predominately male immigration before World War I. This inflated the number of adult men and temporarily offset the sex difference that would have been a much more gradual increase if it had not been for the abnormal immigration patterns around the turn of the century.

A smaller proportion of the black population is over 65, compared to the white population, although this difference may decrease in the future depending on fertility rates (see Figure 9.1). At present, much of this difference reflects the greater birth rate in the black population, so that the proportion of older people is lower in comparison to the total population than is true for the white population with a lower birth rate. By the year 2010, if the black fertility rate drops below the "replacement level" (of 2.1 children per couple) and the white fertility rate rises above this level, the proportion of persons over 65 in each population will be similar. Only 3.6 percent of the Hispanic population in the United States is over age 65; this does not necessarily reflect lower longevity, however. A high birth rate combined with immigration patterns that have been predominately younger and male have produced not only the low proportion of older Hispanics, but also the relatively high ratio of males to females (87:100; ibid.).

Another significant characteristic of the older population in the United States today is the relatively low level of formal education. In 1975, only about one-third of all persons over 65 were high-school graduates, compared with about 60 percent of all persons over 25. However, this difference will change dramatically in the future, since those younger people today will be the older people of the future. In addition, a sizable number of older people today are foreign-born, and they tend to have higher illiteracy rates and lower educational levels than native-born older persons; because of reduced immigration, the proportion of foreign-born older persons will decrease in the future. Thus, it is expected that nearly half of all persons over age 65 in 1990 will have graduated from high school (ibid.). Looked at another way, 70 percent of those persons entering old age in the year 2000 (i.e., those between 60 and 64) will have graduated from high school, including over 25 percent who will have had some college education (Uhlenberg, 1977). Clearly, this increased level of education among older people will affect many aspects of aging, including political attitudes, use of free time, and ability to cope with bureaucratic institutions.

Finally, let us look at one measure of the effect of the growth of the older population on the rest of the population. The *dependency ratio* reflects the relative burden of older "dependents" on those persons who are economically "productive." Of course, not all persons over 65 are dependent, nor are all persons between 18 and 64 economically productive, but if we compare the relative size of these groups, the dependency ratio has risen steadily from 1900 to 1975. It is expected to level off at about 0.19 between now and the turn of the century (i.e., 19 persons over 65 for every 100 persons between 18 and 64); however, it will increase sharply to 0.29 in 2030 when the postwar "baby boom" reaches age 65. This suggests that a considerable economic burden may fall on the shoulders of working men and women in the future as a result of the growth of the older population. This would occur only if older persons had no earned income or no income from previous earnings. Thus, one way of preventing this burden is to develop effective pension and savings plans that will "transfer" income from one's earlier work-life to one's retirement years.

Aging and the Social Structure

The social meaning of aging reflects the individual's location within the social structure of society. In our society, an individual's socioeconomic status, ethnic-group membership, sex, and age may be seen as indices of that person's position in the social structure. In turn, the individual's location in the social structure influences his or her "*life chances*"; that is, "the probability that an individual will be born healthy, or live to age 75, or get married, or have children, or have a comfortable income. . . . Stratum location also influences certain *life-style* experiences reflected in an individual's interpersonal and broader social relationships" (Bengtson, Kasschau, & Ragan, 1977, p. 331). Growing older does not remove the importance of these social status characteristics; it may, in fact, add the additional dimension of "retired" or "senior citizen" to the indices that determine the person's social status. As a result, older people are not a homogeneous population, but in many ways are more varied than younger people. That is, older people typically retain much of the diversity in social status that they experienced in middle age, but have added to this the considerable diversity that has resulted from their individual variability in health, family relationships, income, and so on. For example, in the United States, there are disproportionate numbers of old people at both extremes of the economic scale—among the very poor and the very rich (Streib, 1976). Thus, we cannot describe the aged as a single homogenous social group but, instead, must examine the variations among older people in terms of those social characteristics that influence their status in society. In this section, we will examine the ways in which three indices of social status—sex, socioeconomic status, and ethnic-group membership—affect aging in our society.

Sex Differences in Aging.   As noted in earlier chapters, women generally live longer than men and are more likely to be widowed. Bengtson et al. (1977) reviewed the studies of sex differences in patterns of aging and noted that older women are more likely than men to be living on their own, less likely to be living with a spouse, and likely to have suffered a greater decrease in income. Perhaps as a result, older women have more negative self-images and more negative views of aging and of other old people than is true for older men. However, older women seem to be more involved than older men in social activities, religious organizations, and community groups. Women also tend to have more friends and to be more involved in family relationships than is the case for men.

The two major events related to aging—retirement and widowhood—also differ considerably for men and women. Since a woman's status often reflects her husband's social position, her husband's retirement or her widowhood may affect the woman's social status more than the wife's retirement or death would affect the man's status. If the woman's retirement involves the end of child-rearing rather than the end of an occupational career, it would occur several years before a man retires from his job and would involve different changes at a different time in her life than is the case for men. Widowhood might mean that the woman must take over the economic and financial responsibilities once managed by her husband—for example, half of all millionaires are women, and it is likely that many of these women are managing the estate accumulated by their husband (Streib, 1976). Also, when a woman is widowed late in life, she is likely to find a group of similar widowed women who can provide support and a network of friendships. When a man is widowed, he is likely to find that most men his age are married and that he is greatly outnumbered by widowed women in social and community activities.

Thus, many aspects of aging differ between men and women in our society. While some of these differences seem to favor men, others appear to favor women; that is, older men are less likely to lose as much social status and income in old age and have more opportunity for heterosexual social and sexual partnerships, but women have more extensive friendship networks and are more likely to be involved in community activities—frequently with other widowed women.

Socioeconomic Differences in Aging. Socioeconomic status (SES)— reflecting income, education, and occupation—has dramatic effects on patterns of aging in our society; it also has an important influence on an individual's "life chances" in terms of longevity, health, housing, and marriage. In general, the negative changes with aging typically occur later in life among persons of higher SES levels, compared with earlier aging decrements among persons of lower SES levels (Bengtson et al., 1977). Whether the measure is health status, life expectancy, days of disability per year, or limitation of activity, individuals with higher income have an advantage over persons with lower income—at least to age 75 when many of these differences are equalized. Lifetime patterns of nutrition, health care, living conditions, and occupational hazards are some of the factors that cause these differences. Since many of these factors continue in old age, problems of inadequate nutrition, health care, and housing often characterize the aging experience for persons of lower SES—as well as for persons whose level of income has dropped sharply in old age. Since the difficulties of this disadvantaged segment of the older population are so serious, this group has received considerable research attention; we will discuss these problems later in this chapter. However, much less is known about the characteristics of blue-collar and white-collar middle-class patterns of aging. Many older people in the white-collar group own their own homes and have accumulated a small amount of savings by retirement age. When their income drops after retirement, property taxes, inflation, and medical expenses may be major concerns. This group is neither affluent enough to be free of financial worries, nor poor enough to be eligible for public assistance. Moreover, older people often hope to leave an inheritance to their children; Chen (1973) reported that 72 percent of a sample of homeowners in Los Angeles desired to do so, but with a median income of only $3600 in the early 1970s, many of the 65-to-75-year-old respondents were sacrificing their own expenditures in the hope of leaving money to their heirs.

In many ways, higher levels of lifetime income increase an individual's range of choices and available options for aging. The very affluent can live wherever they please, afford the best health care, and lead a life-style that buffers them against many of the problems of aging. Less affluent middle-class people may choose to live in a retirement community, remain in a home that may be paid for by that time, sell the home and move to an apartment, or buy a mobile home and live in a mobile-home retirement community. In contrast, low-income older persons may be trapped in a home or apartment in a deteriorating part of a city or rural area and not be able to afford to move.

Bengtson et al. (1977) point out that lower SES persons have more negative views of aging, are more likely to view themselves as "old" (rather than "middle-aged") if they are elderly, and see "old age" beginning earlier, compared with higher SES persons. Lower SES persons also report lower life satisfaction than higher SES persons, largely because of the differences in income (Edwards & Klemmack, 1973). Persons in lower SES levels have less frequent and less extensive contacts with friends, family, and neighbors, but are more likely to live with their children, compared with higher SES persons. Middle-class older persons are more likely to provide monetary help to their kin, while lower-class older persons are more likely to give various kinds of service assistance. In addition, older people are less likely to be involved in community activities if they have lower socioeconomic status; but there is no difference between higher and lower SES groups in participation in religious activities (Bengtson et al., 1977).

Ethnic Differences and Aging. Differences between ethnic groups frequently reflect SES characteristics in our society; thus, those groups that have experienced greater discrimination because of their racial or cultural heritage are also likely to have shorter life expectancy at birth, poorer health, more physical impairment, and an earlier onset of diseases associated with aging as a result of lower income, less education, and lower-status occupations that have led to inadequate nutrition, housing, and health care. However, as we noted in Chapter 1, life expectancy for black men and women at age 65 is about equal to life expectancy for whites; the survivors who live long enough to reach old age are a select group of unusually fit individuals, especially among disadvantaged minorities. Other ethnic differences do not equalize among older age groups. While a number of white persons, especially white women, experience poverty for the first time in old age, 36 percent of all black persons over age 65—but only 14 percent of all white persons over 65—were receiving incomes lower than the officially defined poverty level in 1974 (U.S. Bureau of the Census, 1976). Similarly, among people over 65 in 1974, about three times as many whites as blacks had completed a high-school education (Bengtson et al., 1977); this difference is likely to increase for several years until the recent gains in education among younger generations of blacks reduces this difference as they grow into old age.

In a major study of aging among 1269 black, Mexican-American, and Anglo (white) persons between the ages of 45 and 74, Bengtson et al. (1977) found that health problems, feelings of being old, and negative views of aging were more common among the minority groups. For example, Anglos were much less likely to report poor health in all age groups, and the contrast was greater among the older respondents (Table 9.1). Older blacks were more likely to have difficulty walking up three flights of stairs than Anglos. About half of the blacks

Table 9.1 Percent of Black, Mexican-American, and Anglo Respondents Who Consider Their Health to be Poor or Very Poor, by Ethnicity and Age

| | Ethnicity | | |
| | Black (N = 413) | Mexican-American (N = 449) | Anglo (N = 407) |
Age			
45–54	13.8%	16.9%	1.7%
55–64	15.2	20.8	9.1
65–75	27.0	23.2	4.0

Source: Bengtson et al. (1977), Table 1. Copyright©1977 by Litton Educational Publishing, Inc. Adapted and reprinted with permission.

and Mexican-Americans reported that they retired because of poor health, compared with 27 percent among the Anglos. The Mexican-American respondents were likely to consider themselves "old" or "elderly" (rather than "middle-aged" or "young") at earlier ages than black or Anglo respondents (Figure 9.2). Both blacks and Mexican-Americans had less positive perceptions of aging than Anglos. The older Mexican-Americans had the most negative evaluations of the quality of their own lives—greater sadness and worry, feelings that life is not worth living, and a belief that things get worse as one gets older; this was also related to feelings of being "old" among Mexican-Americans, but not among blacks or Anglos. Other differences between these groups—in community par-

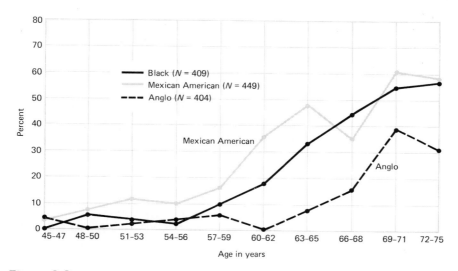

Figure 9.2
Percent of black, Anglo, and Mexican-American respondents considering themselves "old" or "elderly." (Source: Bengtson et al., 1977, Figure 1. Copyright©1977 by Litton Educational Publishing, Inc. Reprinted with permission.)

ticipation, interaction with family, and friendship patterns—parallel the ethnic differences discussed in Chapter 5.

Implications.   The three major indices of an individual's location in the social structure—socioeconomic status, ethnic-group membership, and sex—provide important tools for analyzing the variation in patterns of aging in our society. In our discussion we have focused on the characteristics of older people in the 1970s. Since many of these social-structural characteristics are changing as sex roles are being challenged and as discrimination among nonwhite minority groups is being reduced in at least some areas of our society, it is likely that future generations of older people will be somewhat different from older people today. Even now, those people over age 65 are a very diverse group; in some ways, they may be even more diverse in the future, but it is possible that the vast differences between white and minority groups of older people will be reduced in the future. No one can predict whether sex differences and socioeconomic variation will be reduced in our society, although improved Social Security and national health insurance might reduce these variations among future generations of older Americans.

BEING OLD IN AMERICA

What does it mean to be an older person in the United States today? Does it mean that one is over age 65? Does it mean having poor health? Is it a period of economic hardship? Does it mean being a member of a group with special problems, or a group with special interests and special benefits? Certainly, much public attention is being given to the dramatic problems of many older people—nearly every day newspapers or television reports remind us of the vulnerability of older people to crime, loneliness, malnutrition, inadequate housing, and poverty. These problems are very real and afflict too many people, not all of whom are old; but they represent only part of the complex picture of what it means to be old in America.

We cannot view older persons as if they were a single group with similar characteristics. For example, Neugarten (1974) has argued that it is important to distinguish between the group of "young-old" persons and "old-old" persons. Assuming that retirement marks the beginning of the young-old years, and noting that the retirement age has been lowered to about age 55 for many people, she sees the young-old period lasting from age 55 to 75. Many of these people think of themselves as middle-aged, not old; only about one-quarter of them have health limitations; most of the men and over half of the women are married and they see their children frequently; a large proportion have a living parent, which in itself gives a sense of youthfulness to this group; they are highly active and influential politically, although there is no evidence of the formation of age-related political voting blocks; they are vigorous and fairly well educated. Thus, they are likely to want a variety of options for self-enhancement, community participation, employment, and style of life. At present, this segment of the population represents 15 percent of all persons in the United States, compared with 4 percent in the old-old group; the 55-to-75-year-old group is likely to remain about that size, while the over-75 group will grow in the future. For the old-old group, health status is, in many ways, more important than age alone in determining the characteristics of aging; while a growing minority are remaining active, many need supportive services and special physical environments to function adequately in the community. As the likelihood of illness increases, the need for nursing home care or in-home health services increases; therefore, the growth of the old-old segment of the population will result in greater costs for these services (ibid.).

As noted earlier in this chapter, many of the problems faced by older people may be seen as manifestations of social problems that exist for all people; they are seen in sharp focus for the elderly, because older people—as a group—are especially vulnerable. While we cannot discuss all of the problems and issues faced by older people in the United States today, we will briefly focus on three of the most important concerns of older people: income, health care, and quality of life.

Income

Very high proportions of older persons feel that their income is satisfactory—only 15 percent in one national survey reported that not having enough money was a serious problem (National Council on the Aging, 1975). However, these persons may be comparing their financial situation with the economic hardship they experienced during the Depression of the 1930s, or with the stories they have heard about other older people living in extreme poverty; also, they may have anticipated the drop in income at retirement and have reduced their standard of living in order to get by. Nonetheless, the loss of income at retirement is compensated for, to some degree by lower expenses after the children are grown and by special benefits for the elderly. Social Security payments are not taxable; older persons receive a second personal exemption for income tax purposes; and many communities reduce property taxes for persons over age 65. In addition, older persons receive various nonmonetary benefits, such as health insurance through Medicare, and many smaller benefits, such as reduced transit fares or senior citizen discounts in private stores. Many older people have accumulated sizable assets, but usually these are not available for day-to-day living expenses; they may be in savings accounts to cover unexpected expenses such as an illness or to leave as a legacy, or they may be equity in a home. About three-quarters of all older people own their own home or have equity in it; although this represents a considerable financial asset, there is seldom any way to use this equity for improving one's present standard of living unless one is willing to sell the home (Schulz, 1976, p. 44). Havighurst (1978) estimated that, at most, three out of four older persons "have incomes adequate enough to maintain the material standard of living to which they have been accustomed" (p. 21); for them the major economic problem is inflation. For the remaining 25 percent, economic problems are serious, and government assistance programs do not raise the income of the poorest of the elderly above the officially defined poverty level.

Inflation has often been cited as *the* major problem for older persons who, it is assumed, are living on fixed incomes. To be sure, inflation erodes savings, so that money put aside in 1960 buys less in 1980. However, the major source of retirement income is the Social Security program, and since 1972 it automatically adjusts benefits to take inflation into account. Similarly, the Supplemental Security Income (SSI) program automatically increases its benefits with inflation (although supplemental state payments under SSI are not automatically adjusted for inflation). Even private pension payments reflect inflation prior to retirement since there has been a growing trend toward basing payments on income just before retirement; however, pensions are frequently not adjusted for inflation *after* retirement. Thus, inflation is a major problem for those older persons who have substantial savings, a fixed pension, or an unmortgaged home they do not wish to sell; but persons whose income is based primarily on Social Security are somewhat insulated from the effects of inflation. However, in 1979, the average Social Security income for a couple was just $5684 (*New York Times*, 1979).

Although families in which the head of the family is over 65 have, on the average, substantially lower incomes than younger families, when the size of the family is considered, the ratio of per-person income is more nearly equal. In 1974, families headed by persons over 65 had incomes just 18 percent below the income of all families when total family income was divided by the number of persons in the family. However, black elderly families had only one-half of the per-person income of older families of all races; and families headed by elderly black women had an income only 45 percent as high as the per-person income of all elderly families (U.S. Bureau of the Census, 1976).

A sizable proportion of all older persons have incomes below the officially defined poverty level. In 1974, 15.7 percent of all persons over age 65 were living in poverty, including 8.5 percent of those older persons living in families and 31.8 percent of those persons not living in families (ibid.). Put somewhat differently, in 1975 one-tenth of the population was over age 65, but 13 percent of the poor were over age 65 (Brotman, 1977a). Clearly, a major problem for many older persons is basic economic survival.

There are three sources of income that have been established especially for older people: Social Security retirement benefits, Supplemental Security Income (SSI), and private or public pensions. In addition, there are a variety of sources of income that may apply to older people as well as to younger people; these include employment, income from investments, and nonmonetary benefits such as food stamps, public medical care (Medicaid), and veterans benefits. We will briefly describe the first three sources of income.

Social Security.   Supported by payments from employers and employees, this federal program provides retirement benefits, disability protection, and medical insurance programs (Medicare). Disability protection is provided for: disabled insured workers, many of their dependents, certain disabled surviving spouses of insured workers, and unmarried, dependent adult children of insured workers who were disabled before age 22. Medicare covers nearly all persons aged 65 and over as well as some younger persons eligible for disability benefits; we will discuss Medicare in detail later in this chapter.

Retirement benefits are based on a legislated formula that considers the age at which the benefits begin (between ages 62 and 65) and the average income up to a maximum ceiling during a specified number of years. Persons who delay receiving benefits until after age 65 receive an additional 1 percent for each year up to age 72 that they do not receive benefits (3 percent after 1981). Benefits rise automatically with an increase in the Consumer Price Index each July. In 1979, this increase brought the minimum monthly benefit for eligible retirees to $133.90; the maximum benefit for a person retiring at age 65 was $553.30; the average benefits for individuals living alone were $283, and $482 for an elderly couple (*New York Times*, 1979).

Retirement benefits equaling one-half of the basic benefit may be paid for children under age 18 (age 22, if full-time students) and to the spouse of the retired person if he or she is over age 62, not earning over a specified amount and not eligible for higher Social Security benefits on the basis of his or her own work record. Widowed persons may receive 100 percent of the deceased spouse's basic benefits if they are over age 60, or disabled and over age 50. If the widowed person remarries, he or she continues to collect either the survivor's benefit or the spouse's benefit, whichever is higher. In addition, a payment of $255 is made to the person responsible for burial expenses when a person covered by Social Security dies. Unmarried dependent children may be entitled to a pension equal to 75 percent of the deceased parent's pension. In 1975, about 40 percent of Social Security pensions were paid to survivors and to disabled workers and their dependents (Schulz, 1976).

In 1979, retired persons eligible for Social Security benefits may earn up to $3480 if they are under 65 and $4500 if they are between 65 and 72 without losing benefits; benefits are reduced 50 cents for each $1 earned over those amounts. Persons over age 72 may earn any amount without losing benefits.

Supplemental Security Income (SSI). Persons who are legally blind, over age 65, unable to work for 12 months or longer, or suffering from a deteriorating medical condition that will result in death may be eligible to receive SSI. This program is administered by the Social Security Administration, but its funds come from general tax revenues; many states supplement the federal benefits. To qualify for SSI, an individual must have less than $1500 in resources such as savings ($2250 for a couple); an individual may earn as much as $65 a month without losing benefits. Unearned income (in most cases over $20 a month), such as Social Security payments, is deducted from the SSI payment. Thus, older persons with low Social Security benefits may also be eligible for SSI payments if they have less than $1500 in resources and earn not more than $65 a month. As with Social Security, federal SSI benefits are adjusted each July to reflect changes in the Consumer Price Index; thus, they are adjusted for inflation automatically. After the 1979 increases, the maximum federal SSI benefits were $208.20 for an individual and $312.30 for a couple (*New York Times*, 1979); each state may supplement these benefits, and those supplements may also be raised to reflect inflationary changes.

Persons eligible for SSI also are eligible for Medicaid and may receive food stamps, although other persons may also be eligible according to each state's regulations. Thus, as of August 1979, in New York State (which has one of the highest SSI supplements in the nation) an individual living alone with no other income would receive $271.41 each month, perhaps $28 in food stamps, and (in theory, at least) receive all medical care without charge. With housing costs increasing, rising utility bills, telephone, clothing, and food expenses, it is obvious that it is difficult to manage on this income; spiraling energy costs are likely to increase the hardship.

Pensions.   Until the Pension Reform Act was passed by Congress in 1974, many workers did not receive the pension they thought they were entitled to because of various loopholes, conditions, or inadequate funding of the pension plan (this was the case with Henry in the Interlude preceding this chapter). The 1974 law established several controls over private pensions and also allowed individuals to set up individual retirement accounts (IRAs) if they are not covered by a qualified pension plan; that is, an individual can set aside up to 15 percent of earned income (up to $1500 a year) in some sort of savings plan and does not pay taxes on that income until it is paid out. For example, a worker without a pension plan could put $1500 in an IRA account and pay no tax until after retirement when the money is withdrawn in installments; this would provide retirement income as well as a lower tax on the income, since taxable income is usually lower after retirement. Also, the 1974 law increased the amounts self-employed persons may contribute to retirement plans (Keogh or HR 10 plans); under these plans, the person may set aside up to 15 percent of earned income (up to $7500) in a program similar to the IRA accounts (Schulz, 1976).

The pension reform legislation established insurance for persons whose retirement plans are terminated with inadequate funds, provided mechanisms to regulate pension plans, required disclosure statement to participants, and required reports to Social Security that, in turn, notifies employees of their pension rights when they apply for Social Security benefits. In addition, the legislation provided minimal standards for vesting (ibid.). *Vesting* refers to the individual gaining rights to part or all of the pension benefits so that, if workers leave the job for any reason, their pension rights are protected. However, they may have to put in five or ten years service before vesting is achieved and then may be eligible for only 25 to 50 percent of the accrued benefits. Even then, their pension rights are not necessarily *portable* in the sense that they can be transferred to another pension fund, or invested in an IRA account, unless the pension plan approves. This may mean that no interest benefits accumulate after the person leaves the employer, although the pension fund retains the money until the person's retirement age.

Other problems with current pension programs are that over half of the private work force is not covered by a pension; few private pensions adjust benefits for inflation after retirement; state and local government pension plans are not covered by the 1974 pension reform legislation; the individual may be penalized if the pension lacks portability; few plans offer survivor benefits and these benefits are often low; and private pensions discourage hiring of older workers who are near to retirement because of the high cost of the worker's pension (ibid.).

Implications. Although significant improvements have been made in the programs that provide income for older persons—such as automatic inflation-related increases in Social Security, the creation of SSI that replaced the widely unacceptable old age assistance programs, and the pension reform legislation—it is apparent that the problem of income for older persons is at the core of the problems that confront them. Inadequate income affects the availability and maintenance of adequate housing, health, transportation, and a generally satisfying lifestyle. Consumer fraud, exposure to crime, and availability of legal services are all less-serious problems if one is able to retire with a comfortable income from some source. Indeed, the promise of a "golden age" in retirement has too often been a cruel hoax. But the dream of a secure retirement income is probably the aim of most Americans. While the economic considerations that are involved in providing that goal are complex, the goal should not be beyond the means of our affluent society. Robert Butler (1975) proposed an ideal, but perhaps attainable, plan to meet the income needs of all persons as they grow old.

So that the American people do not grow poor as they grow old in our affluent society a universal pension system should be established. It should incorporate under one umbrella all private and public pension plans, including Social Security. Benefit levels should depend on the length and level of lifetime work-related earnings—that is, "contributions"—in turn a function of a graduated income tax. There should be immediate 100 percent vesting and mandatory portability. Funds should be fully insured to afford total protection. There should be survivor benefits. There should be two escalators: one related to the cost of living, the other reflecting a share in the nation's productivity. Retirement income would then conform to the current standard of living. The costs would be great but not beyond our capacity, with two-thirds of the financing coming from general federal tax revenues and one-third from trust funds.

All this is, of course, an ideal program. In reality, however, Americans may choose or be forced by the present economic system to continue to chance growing poor as they grow old [p. 63].

Health Care

Until the fairly recent enactment of Medicare in 1965, older persons had only the protection of their savings, private insurance, and charity to buffer them against their increasing susceptibility to disease. But there has also been an enormous increase in the cost of medical, hospital, and nursing home care for older persons since 1966 (Table 9.2). This has placed an extraordinary burden on the financial resources of older persons, as well as on programs such as Medicare and Medicaid, which provide public funding for the medical expenses of older persons. In 1973, about two-thirds of the total expenditure for health services to older persons was provided by public funding; however, the older person covered by Medicare received, on the average, only 40 percent reimbursement and paid a total of $311 "out of pocket" for medical expenses (Shanas & Maddox, 1976). Thus, there is considerable doubt whether Medicare provides adequate protection, and several important items are omitted from its coverage (such as prescription drugs; care of eyes, ears, teeth, and feet; and eyeglasses, hearing aids, and dentures).

Briefly, *Medicare*, Title XVII, *Part A* of the Social Security Act, provides hospital insurance for any person over age 65 who is entitled to Social Security or railroad retirement benefits; various provisions also exist for some persons under age 65, and surviving spouses or dependent spouses may also be covered. Generally, protection is provided for hospital inpatient care, posthospital extended care, and home health visits by nurses or other health workers; doctors' services or drugs are not covered. Funding is from federal Social Security funds. However, as of 1979, $160 of the hospital bill is deductible (paid by the individual; up from $68 in 1972 and $40 in 1966); when the hospital stay exceeds 60 days, the individual pays $40 a day up to the ninetieth day and then $80 a day after 90 days. All of these "out of the pocket" costs have gone up since Medicare was enacted in 1966 and have more than doubled between 1972 and 1979.

Table 9.2 Estimated per Capita Personal Health Care Expenditures for Population 65 and Over, 1966-1974

Year	Hospital Care	Physicians' Services	Nursing-home Care	Total
1966	$177.84	$ 89.57	$ 68.39	$ 445.25
1967	223.58	108.97	84.94	535.03
1968	282.89	122.40	113.56	646.65
1969	335.76	127.49	133.18	735.19
1970	375.13	141.60	162.76	828.31
1971	418.55	154.37	202.39	925.98
1972	468.61	172.58	237.79	1033.51
1973	508.93	180.74	265.11	1119.78
1974	573.18	182.14	289.10	1217.84

Source: U.S. Department of Health, Education and Welfare, *Compendium of National Health Expenditure Data*. Washington, D.C.: U.S. Government Printing Office, 1976.

Medicare, Part B, helps to pay for doctors' bills, outpatient hospital services, medical supplies and services, home health services, outpatient physical therapy, and other health care services. This insurance is voluntary and in 1979 cost $8.70 a month (up from $3 in 1966). Usually this is subtracted from the Social Security check each month if the person elects this optional coverage. However, the first $60 of the individual's annual expenses are not covered by this program, and only 80 percent of the "approved" charge is reimbursed to the individual; if the physician charges more than the approved charge, the patient pays the difference. For these reasons, persons over 65 who do not qualify for Medicaid often purchase private medical insurance to defray part of the expenses that are not paid by Medicare; but even the private insurance does not usually pay all of the remaining cost—for example, charges above the "approved" amounts are not generally paid.

Medicaid is funded jointly by the federal and state governments from general tax revenues and is available to all recipients of public assistance and to the "medically needy" as defined by each state—such as persons who have resources for daily living, but not for needed medical care, and all children under 21 whose parents cannot afford medical care. In New York State, individuals with incomes under $275 per month ($3300 a year) and less than $2100 in resources (including life insurance) are eligible for Medicaid. It covers costs for physicians, dentists, other professionals, hospitals, nursing homes, outpatient or clinic services, home care, drugs, eyeglasses, and so on. Payment is directly to the medical person or service, and there is no "out of the pocket" expense to the individual (unless the person earns more than the maximum allowed; in that case the difference must be spent on medical expenses before Medicaid will cover the balance). Other states have more stringent financial requirements to qualify for Medicaid, and not all health professionals accept Medicaid reimbursement. Nonetheless, a substantial proportion of public health care expenditures for older persons is paid through the Medicaid programs; for example, many persons in nursing homes are supported by Medicaid, often because the cost of nursing home care has depleted their savings.

It is apparent that total physical and mental health care involves more than financial resources, whatever their source. Health education is of primary importance, and the related task of health assessment is crucial to increase the extent of good health among the aged—for example, hypertension (high blood pressure) is easily diagnosed and generally treatable, but individuals need to learn that it is important to have their blood pressure checked periodically. Such goals imply greatly expanded preventive and outreach services, such as mobile clinics that could visit rural as well as urban and suburban areas for education, assessment, and preventive medicine. Health care also involves rehabilitation, including occupational rehabilitation that too often is emphasized only for younger persons. And it involves not only maintenance or restoration of health but also long-term care if disability occurs. In addition, health care for older persons may require specialized training of physicians and a broader range of services than those that are generally available in our country today (Butler, 1975).

Three important areas of health care of older persons, in addition to those discussed in Chapters 7 and 8, include nutrition, drug use, and nursing homes. Here we can only briefly discuss these complex issues, but each is receiving more and more research attention and each involves a growing amount of public expenditure through nutrition programs for the elderly, medical prescriptions, and spiraling costs for private and public nursing home care.

Nutrition.   Several studies of the diets reported by persons over age 60 have indicated a general pattern of deficiencies. Calcium is noted as deficient in many studies; iron and vitamins A and C are also frequently reported as inadequate; and a nationwide survey found that calories were consumed at only 82 percent of the recommended dietary allowance (Rawson, Weinberg, Herold, & Holtz, 1978). In one study of a representative sample of rural elderly, 75 percent of whom were below the "poverty" level, deficiencies were noted in calcium, calories, and vitamin A; the inadequacy was higher for calcium in women and higher in the other two nutrients for men (ibid.). Weg (1978) reviewed the research on nutrition among older persons and concluded that a large number of questions remain to be answered; for example, it is not known whether the recommended dietary allowance of essential nutrients adequately reflects the requirements of elderly persons, especially those who may be experiencing stress caused by life changes such as retirement or widowhood. In addition, more research is required on a number of specialized topics, including the effects of vegetarian diets, the effect of high-meat or high-protein diets, and the interaction between various nutrients such as calcium, phosphorus, and magnesium that may be related to the disease of osteoporosis in which bones become thinner, lighter, and more porous. Age-related changes in the metabolism of nutrients and the decreased efficiency in some organ systems that are involved in maintaining the proper balance of chemicals in the body are other topics that need further study. A set of dietary guidelines for older persons is given in Box 9.1; it shows some of the alternate sources of various nutritional elements. Meals need not occur only three times a day, so the total food intake may include snacks or be divided into five or six smaller meals; this may help to reduce boredom as well as to aid digestion (Bailey, 1978).

Nutrition involves more than food, however. It involves "motivation towards eating, customary and cultural attitudes and practices, general mental and physical health, isolation, availability of food, geography, transportation, economics, and education in the use of food" (Weg, 1978, p. 133). To take only one example, Rawson et al. (1978) noted that the low intake of calcium found in their study may have resulted from low consumption of milk, because the respondents often depended on family and neighbors for shopping and so did not purchase perishable items frequently enough to have fresh milk available; in addition, they seemed to be unaware of alternate sources of necessary nutrients.

In general, nutritional requirements of older persons are not necessarily the same as those for younger people, and the dietary needs of the well older person are often not appropriate for chronically ill older persons (Weg, 1978).

Thus, there is a need for greater education about the nutritional needs of individuals throughout the life cycle.

Drug Use.   Older people consume a disproportionate share of prescription medication, including both psychotropic drugs (such as antidepressants and tranquilizers) and nonpsychotropic drugs (such as medication for hypertension or pain relief). For example, in a study of the California Medicaid (Medi-Cal) population in 1975–1976, persons over age 60 represented 18 percent of the

Box 9.1   Guidelines and Meal Patterns for Older Persons

Try, each day, for *at least:*

- 1 serving each meal of whole grain cereal, bread, or macaroni product.
- 2 glasses of milk or its equivalent, such as yogurt, eggnog, milk shake, puddings, custard, ice cream, cheese, or soups.
- 2 servings of meat or meat substitutes of high quality protein such as beef, pork, lamb, fish, eggs, poultry, peas, beans, legumes, nuts, and seeds.
- 2 servings of fruit, including at least one which is rich in vitamin C.
- 2 servings of vegetables, one of which should be a leafy, dark green type.
- 8 glasses of liquids, including water. Tea, coffee, milk, consomme, soups, fruit juices, and watery fruits and vegetables can all contribute to this total.

Note: An average serving of bread is one slice.
      An average serving of cereal is 1/2 to 3/4 cup.
      An average serving of fruits or vegetables is at least 1/2 cup.
      An average serving of cooked meat is three ounces.

Meal patterns can be used as checklists for nutritional adequacy. Here are some examples:

BREAKFAST	LUNCH
Fruit	Main dish from meat group
Egg or cereal or both	Vegetable
Toast or hotbread and butter	Bread and butter
MIlk	Fruit

DINNER

Main dish from meat group	Potato
Other vegetable	Bread or hotbread with butter
Milk	Dessert

Source: Bailey (1978), p. 154. Reprinted with permission.

recipients of assistance, but consumed 35 percent of prescription drug expenses (Zawadski, Glazer, & Lurie, 1978). On the average, these older persons received a total of $132 in prescription drugs per person per year—including $17 in psychotropics and $115 in nonpsychotropic medication—compared with $54 for younger Medi-Cal recipients (Figure 9.3). Older persons in institutions, that is, the 60,000 aged in long-term care facilities such as nursing homes, received almost half again as much nonpsychotropic medication but 17 times as much psychotropic medication as noninstitutionalized elderly Medi-Cal recipients. While the explanation of the much greater use of psychotropic medication among the institutionalized elderly is not clear, it is possible that it results at least in part from institutionalization. That is, when a small sample of older persons who qualified for long-term care were maintained in the community through a day health program and were compared to institutionalized and noninstitutionalized older persons, their drug usage was similar to that of noninstitutionalized older persons. Thus, older persons in institutions may have been admitted in part for psychiatric disorders, developed psychiatric disorders as a result of being institutionalized, or were given psychotropic medication for the benefit of the institution (ibid.).

Another study of a representative sample of persons over age 60 in Washington, D.C., in 1976 found that 62 percent of these community residents used prescription medication (Guttmann, 1977). The most frequently used drugs were cardiovascular (39 percent), sedatives and tranquilizers (14 percent), and

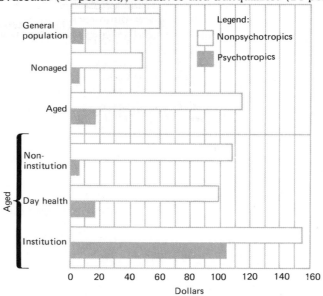

Figure 9.3
Psychotropic versus nonpsychotropic prescription drug expenditures per eligible person for Medicaid reimbursement per year, by group. (Source: Zawadski, Glazer, & Lurie, 1978, Figure 3.)

antiarthritic drugs (9 percent). Persons who reported higher use of prescription drugs also "tended to be less satisfied with their lives, tended to use more over-the-counter drugs as well, and tended to have a lower perception of themselves in terms of intelligence and capability" (ibid., p. 4). Sixty-nine percent indicated that they used over-the-counter drugs; over half of these were for the relief of pain. Fifty-six percent reported little or no alcohol use; one-quarter said they used alcohol no more than a few times a week; and 19 percent used it daily. Twenty-one percent reported using psychotropic drugs, and almost all said that they obtained the drugs through physicians' prescriptions. While noting that the great majority of respondents in this study indicated that they used these medications appropriately, Guttmann pointed out the danger that may result from using these drugs in combination with each other or with alcohol. Petersen and Whittington (1977), in a review of drug use among the elderly, summarized the problems posed by the high rate of drug use by older persons.

Although, as with the young drug abuser, many problems are the result of excessive self-medication or other inappropriate use, a considerable amount of attention has recently been directed to the effect of the aging process on pharmacological efficacy and safety. Specifically, interest has centered on drug interactions, side effects, and long-term management for the elderly. . . . For example, in elderly patients with multiple chronic conditions for which different drugs are being ingested concurrently, drug interactions are extremely likely occurrences. . . . Older patients metabolize drugs more slowly than younger persons, and when two are taken simultaneously each can have a potentiating effect on the other, thus heightening the risk of drug intoxification. Moreover, many drugs produce side effects— physical, emotional or both—which must be anticipated, and for many reasons, such side effects are more common and often more severe in elderly patients. . . . Thus, health care professionals concerned with problems of the aged have become increasingly aware that the elderly may experience drug-related problems that are not attributable to misuse on their part [Petersen & Whittington, 1977, p. 34].

Nursing Homes.   Although slightly fewer than 5 percent of persons over age 65 lived in institutions such as nursing homes in 1975, the proportion of older persons in institutions has grown from 3.7 percent in 1960, reflecting in part the increase in the proportion of very old persons in our society. There has also been a shift away from institutionalizing older persons in mental hospitals, as was the case for most of the institutionalized older population in 1960; today, most live in nursing homes, extended-care facilities, or homes for the aged (U.S. Bureau of the Census, 1976). However, these figures represent only those persons who are living in these institutions at the time of the census. Kastenbaum and Candy (1973) found that 24 percent of all deaths of people 65 and over during one year in Detroit occurred in some kind of extended-care facility. Palmore (1976) found that 26 percent of a longitudinal sample of 207 persons over age 60 who died within 20 years (between 1955 and 1975) had been institutionalized at least once before death; another 64 persons in the study had not died. This suggests that the risk of institutionalization before death is about one in four, although the eventual fate of the survivors clouds this interpretation somewhat. The age of the person affects both the likelihood of death and the chance they will be institutionalized if they die within a specified period of time. For example, a study of a representative sample of residents in one county in California found that the risk of being institutionalized before death within a ten-year period was only one in six for persons between the ages of 55 and 64, but was two out of three for persons over age 85 (Vicente, Wiley, & Carrington, 1979). Thus, we do not know what the risk of institutionalization for an average person of a specified age would be, since *all* persons of that age in a representative sample would have to be followed until they died to determine how many were institutionalized along the way. Until better data are available, Palmore's estimate of one in four may be the most reasonable prediction of the risk that an individual will eventually live in a nursing home or facility for the aged. Persons living alone, those without living children, women, and white persons have been found to be those groups with the highest risk of institutionalization (Palmore, 1976; Riley, Foner, & Associates, 1968; Vicente et al., 1979). Therefore, it is not uncommon to find nursing home residents who are very old and who have outlived their spouse, children, and other family members.

Although all nursing homes are institutions that inevitably exert some degree of institutionalization on the residents (such as restricting privacy, structuring the person's day, reducing independence, and enforcing requirements of group living), some nursing homes provide better care than others, and some are very bad. Kosberg and Tobin (1972) surveyed all of the nursing homes serving older persons in the Chicago area and found marked variation in a wide range of characteristics among the homes. For example, only 37 percent of the homes had physical therapy equipment. Two out of five homes did not employ physical therapists at all; three out of five did not have an occupational therapist; 85 percent did not employ a social worker at all.

From these findings, it is apparent that the nursing home field, *in toto*, is composed of institutions varying considerably in their ability to provide restorative care and treatment—as indicated by the extent of treatment resources. On one end of the continuum are nursing homes which have high proportions of nursing personnel . . . , contain medical and therapeutic equipment, and frequently have a variety of professionals available for the residents. On the other end of the resource continuum are those nursing homes which have few professionals available, low proportions of nurses to total staff and residents, and little equipment to meet the medical and therapeutic needs of the residents. This latter group of nursing homes can offer little more than custodial care to the elderly population [Kosberg & Tobin, 1972, p. 216].

Kosberg and Tobin conclude that upgrading nursing home standards, which are often taken to represent maximum extent of care, is an important means to improve the conditions of these homes, combined with efficient formal and informal surveillance (e.g., by family, friends, and the physician). But the worst homes were those that cared for the poor, indicating a "cycle of indifference" that reflects not only the inadequacy of national policy and social welfare but also wider social values and attitudes about the aged and the poor.

However, upgrading nursing homes is only one aspect of a possible solution. Much additional emphasis needs to be centered on alternatives to institutional care. One particular service, available in many communities, is a homemaker or home health aid. Such a person—carefully trained, screened, and supervised—may visit several times a week as needed to cook hot meals and to provide or to coordinate shopping assistance, services, and information, as well as to provide companionship. These homemakers may be young, middle-aged, or older persons, perhaps providing a double benefit of added jobs for persons previously unable to support themselves. Other programs such as "Meals on Wheels" or other community meal programs can also help to prevent institutionalization, especially if they are part of a comprehensive program of community services that are designed to meet the individual needs of each older person who needs assistance to remain living independently. Home health services, outpatient occupational and physical therapy, transportation to physicians and other services, and day centers are some of the resources that may be required. Public funds may provide payment for these services for eligible persons. The goal is to allow older people the choice of remaining in their own homes instead of moving into a nursing home or other institution. Frequently the family—if there is one—wishes to care for the older person, but lacks the ability to do so; providing additional services and financial resources to families who maintain an older person at home may be another alternative to institutionalization. In addition, a variety of sheltered housing arrangements need to be developed so that older persons would be able to live as independently as possible, but would have appropriate services such as meals, health care, and assistance in emergencies if and when they were needed. Thus, perhaps the ideal would be a range of alternatives—from totally independent living with a variety of supports available if they are needed, to sheltered housing that provides as much or as little independence as the person desires or needs, to nursing home care. This would allow the older individual the choice among a variety of options and would reduce the risk of unnecessary institutionalization.

Quality of Life

It is apparent that old age is often a negative social position in our country. One way of seeing this position is to consider the combination of negative social statuses that may characterize an older person. First, there is clearly the negative status of being old—bad enough in our youth-oriented society, characterized by what Butler (1969) termed *ageism*. Add to this the other negative statuses that may be present: not working, poor, black (or Hispanic, Native-American, Orien-tal, etc.), and female (probably widowed). The result is a compounding of nega-tive social positions that is frequently intensified by chronic illness and loneliness. In large cities, there may be the advantages of activities, programs, and services that result from the concentration of older persons in urban areas; but there are also disadvantages such as the fear of crime, decaying neighborhoods, and indif-ferent landlords and neighbors. In rural areas, although the physical situation is quite different, the problems are no less severe—transportation, lack of nearby medical care, absence of senior citizen centers, and physical as well as social iso-lation. In short, there is a great deal about aging in our country that can reduce the quality of life for older people.

However, the problems faced by some older people are only part of the total experience of aging in America. At the other extreme are those older persons for whom aging appears to bring extraordinary benefits. Because these examples contrast so sharply with stereotypes about aging, they are often reported in the news media; this one is from the *New York Times.*

> A year and a half ago, Alberta Hunter, an obscure, retired nurse, set out to resume her previous career as a jazz and blues singer, a career she aban-doned more than 20 years ago in order to study and practice nursing. Miss Hunter's remarkable comeback at 82 was officially launched in October of 1977 at Barney Josephson's Cookery when she began a limited engage-ment that has become an indefinite run. Moreover, Miss Hunter's new ca-reer is running at full throttle with television appearances ("60 Minutes," "The Mike Douglas Show," "Camera Three" and the recent Kennedy Cen-ter gala), and a new Columbia soundtrack recording of the film "Remember My Name.". . .
>
> Her 83-year-old voice remains a strong, flexible instrument, and she pro-jects an authoritative, hard-hitting approach to the blues that eclipses the work of many contemporary performers decades her junior [Lissner, 1979, p. D-23].

To be sure, Miss Hunter is a remarkable woman; but there are similar, if much less dramatic, examples of older men and women in all racial and ethnic groups who find that aging is an exciting, challenging, and fulfilling time of life.

Thus, as we focus on the quality of life for older persons, we need to consider both the positive and negative extremes, as well as the majority in between who are aging, despite the obstacles, with a sense of satisfaction and meaning. In an anthropological study of a community of elderly Jews in California, Myerhoff (1979) points out that younger people often see aging only from the outside, so that it appears to be a tragic series of losses; but the anthropological perspective provides a view of aging from the older person's own frame of reference as a challenging career that has meaning in itself.

The women were describing some of the strategies they had cultivated for coping with their circumstances—growing old, living alone and with little money. Each in a different way, with a different specialization, had improvised techniques for growing old with originality and dedication. For these women, aging was a career, . . . a serious commitment to surviving, complete with standards of excellence, clear, public, long-term goals whose attainment yielded community recognition and inner satisfaction [ibid., pp. 250-251].

She also found that the older persons' own behavior often contrasted sharply with the stereotypes about aging, including those that they expressed themselves.

Even those who stated flatly that old age was a curse, with no redeeming features, could be seen living engaged lives, passionate and original. Nearly every person in the Center community—men and women—had devised some career, some activity or purpose to which he/she was committed. They had provided themselves with new possibilities to replace those that had been lost, regularly set new standards for themselves in terms of which to measure growth and achievement, sought and found meaning in their lives, in the short run and the long [ibid., p. 251].

In addition to the multiple factors that have been discussed in earlier chapters such as the family network, leisure, and health, three issues are especially important to the quality of life for older persons: housing, transportation, and the fear of crime.

Housing.   Just as there is no substitute for an adequate income if individuals are to be able to exercise free choice about the style of their lives, there is no substitute for a variety of alternate housing arrangements for older people to exercise their freedom of choice. The poor, minority, disabled, and rural aged are particularly in need of adequate and well-maintained housing and neighborhoods (cf. Struyk, 1977). But it also needs to be the kind of housing that meets their personal, health, and economic needs, as well as housing that is located where they want to live and where they can readily visit places of interest.

Ethnic elderly often have neighborhood and housing preferences that are important. How available are the preferred foods? Can family ties be maintained? Are there other persons who speak their language? For these reasons, many old persons prefer to remain in their deteriorating family homes or apartments; others stay for sentimental reasons or because the neighborhood is familiar. It may also be cheaper to stay. But in urban areas, this too often means that the neighborhood is decaying around them, fear of crime makes them a prisoner in their home, and friends and family have often moved away. Many rural elderly live in a community that is migrating to the cities; the doctor and dentist may have died or left, as many as one out of five residents may also be old, and their housing often lacks basic necessities. Many urban elderly live in apartments sometimes paying moderate rents, or benefiting from rent subsidies, but receive less than adequate services, or they are forced to move because the apartment is in an "urban renewal" area or is turned into a condominium and they cannot afford to purchase their apartment. Some public housing projects reserve apartments for the elderly, but often the location and fear of crime keep older persons from moving in. In 1977, about 600,000 older persons were living in housing that was constructed for the elderly; this can provide important benefits, including better health and lower death rates compared with similar persons who did not move into the housing (Carp, 1977). However, even in well-designed housing there may be subtle physical barriers that make shopping trips, visits to neighbors, and travel to places of interest very difficult for those older persons with physical handicaps. Stairs, unguarded streets or intersections without crosswalks, and high curbs or broken sidewalks can be significant barriers. In the design of housing for the elderly, it is also important to consider the availability of stores and their pricing policies, the access to public transportation, and physical characteristics of the building that increase security (Blank, 1979).

However, more than adequate housing is necessary to enhance the quality of life of older persons. Often the tasks of shopping, cooking, caring for household duties, laundry, and short errands become difficult, painful, and (if living alone) not particularly meaningful duties that may be avoided. If there is chronic disease, physical impairment, stairs to climb or cold to endure, and a sense of uselessness or depression, older persons may become trapped in their homes. Combined with more general social isolation and poverty, these difficulties compound one another—for example, food delivered to the home costs more; not going out increases social isolation; isolation and lack of adequate foods makes eating less enjoyable, and eating becomes more infrequent. A lonely period of wasting away or being moved to an institution may follow. Community programs of friendly visitors—volunteers who visit one or two older persons or provide telephone reassurance more frequently—and senior centers can often reduce these problems to some degree. However, these programs and other resources described earlier in this chapter are not always available. Greater attention is now being given to the problems of these "frail elderly" and considerable progress has been made to provide supports for the most vulnerable older persons; but continued emphasis must be on those older persons who are no longer able to maintain the successful struggle in their aging career.

Transportation.   There are three obvious facets to the problems of transportation for older persons. First, whether it is available near their residence and is economical so that it is truly available; second, whether it is safe, convenient, and designed with the special needs of physically impaired elderly in mind; and third, whether there is any place worth going on it. Certainly, the elderly, like all of us, depend on transportation to participate in spiritual, cultural, social, and recreational activities; and lack of transportation implicitly denies full participation in the community. For example, a study conducted in Philadelphia found that 30 percent of older persons who were participating in senior centers or other programs for the elderly reported that they needed more transportation than was available; one out of five of these older persons needed transportation to attend church on Sunday (Stirner, 1978).

As with other problems, income issues are paramount, since with limited income older people frequently live in areas that are not well served by mass transit, and they often do not have resources for taxi fares or for private automobiles. For some, even transit fares may be a large expense. Also, there are several physical and psychological barriers to most forms of mass transit: steps to climb, closing doors to dodge, jerking trains or buses, waiting in the rain or cold, the painfully high step into many buses, infrequent service, slow travel, long walks, and fear of crime. Adequate transportation is an especially severe problem in rural areas, and distance may be a major barrier to health care, social interaction, and community participation.

Programs are being developed in many communities to help meet the transportation needs of older people and persons who are handicapped. Some of these include specially designed vans or "Medicabs" for persons confined to wheelchairs, "dial-a-ride" programs in which older persons can arrange a reduced-fare taxi ride by reservation, reduced transit fares for persons over 65, and high-school driver education classes that provide rides to older persons who request them in advance.

Fear of Crime. Nationwide surveys in 1973 and 1974 indicated that about half of all older persons fear crime, compared with 41 percent of those under age 65; 69 percent of older women and 34 percent of older men said they were afraid (Clemente & Kleiman, 1976). This study also found that fear of crime is higher among blacks than whites—47 percent of white elderly and 69 percent of black elderly said they were afraid to walk around their neighborhood at night; and urban elderly were more fearful than older persons in smaller cities and towns, suburbs, or rural areas (ibid.). Thus, there are major differences among different groups of older persons in their fear of crime; but it is a very serious fear among older women living in large cities, especially for black women.

However, a national survey that asked representative samples of persons about their experiences with crime indicated that in fact persons over 65 were less likely to be victimized than other age groups, were less likely to be subject to violent crimes, and were no more likely than other groups to be robbed on the street. Nonetheless, they were more likely to experience "predatory incidents" such as robbery or mugging in or near their home and were more likely to be victims of unplanned attacks by young, inexperienced criminals who were unarmed, acting alone, and unknown to the victim, as compared to other age groups (Antunes, Cook, Cook, & Skogan, 1977; Cook, Skogan, Cook, & Antunes, 1978). Although older persons are not found to suffer larger financial losses or greater physical harm than other age groups, their *relative* financial losses compared with monthly income are larger than for middle-aged persons but lower than for younger persons (age 33-39). While they are less likely to be attacked than other age groups, if they are attacked, older persons are more likely to be injured, to suffer internal injuries, and to lose consciousness, but are less likely to suffer wounds and broken bones or teeth than other age groups (Cook et al., 1978). The cost of medical care as a result of crime is no higher for older persons, but it is a larger proportion of their income than that of other age groups. Thus, to the degree that crime affects the elderly more than other age groups, it is largely a consequence of the lower income of older persons, so that losses resulting from crime have a greater relative impact on older persons than middle-aged persons (ibid.).

Nonetheless, the fear of crime remains high, despite the actual lower risk among older persons; perhaps this results in part from the dramatic nature of occasional crimes against older people. Valerie Levy, Director of Minority Affairs in the New York City Department for the Aging, has pointed out the complexity of the problem since it reflects not only the many factors involved in urban crime, but also reflects the attitudes of some young people toward the elderly. Perhaps, she suggested, if the country can mount a yearly public relations campaign to protect school children, there might be a similar public campaign to protect the elderly. One slogan that comes to mind is: "Was *Your* Grandmother Ripped Off Today?—Protect Our Elderly!" At some senior centers, police volunteer to escort older persons to the bank on days when Social Security checks are received; some high-school and college students have also volunteered as escorts for older persons. But much more is needed to reduce the fear of crime that too often makes older people prisoners in their own homes.

Conclusion

Older people in the United States today are such a diverse group of individuals that it is important to avoid both positive and negative stereotypes about the elderly. Large differences exist in terms of income and health status, and these differences interact with the individual's social and psychological resources, bringing still greater heterogeneity. In turn, this interaction of strengths, resources, and problems is intertwined with the changing patterns of life in America. Thus, the problems of urban elderly reflect, often in intensified ways, the problems of life in American cities—such as crime, housing, and transportation. The economic problems of older persons also reflect nationwide problems of inflation, the energy shortage, and lack of adequate jobs. Similarly, the need for comprehensive health care for older people may lead eventually to national health insurance for all persons. Significant efforts and progress have been made by the federal government and by state, local, and community groups to aid the most vulnerable elderly—but too often this has taken the form of making older persons more dependent rather than more independent. We need to move toward providing greater freedom of choice among constructive alternatives for older persons so that the diverse needs of this varied group of people can be met according to their own desires, abilities, and resources.

In our rapidly changing world, future generations of older persons are likely to be better educated, in better health, and even more diverse than older people today. They will be more numerous, more will be in the "old-old" age group, and their life-styles will reflect the varied life-styles of younger people today. They will, after all, be ourselves grown old. How can we play a role in improving the quality of life for older persons—and for ourselves if we are fortunate enough to grow old? This will be the focus of the brief final section of this chapter.

EDUCATION AND OCCUPATIONS IN GERONTOLOGY

There is scarcely a profession that is not directly or indirectly connected with the needs of aging persons. In the fields of psychology, sociology, social work, medicine, nursing, and psychiatry there are specialities in gerontology or geriatrics that train persons to provide direct service to the aged. In biology and physiology there is a great need for research on the basic mechanisms of aging. In anthropology there is a need for research on the effects of cultural variations on the aging process—both in different cultures and in different subcultures within a society. In fields such as architecture and engineering there are great challenges for designing barrier-free environments, housing, and transportation for the elderly. In political science, history, literature, drama, and the arts (to mention some less obvious examples) there are fascinating studies or applications waiting to be made concerning aging—one example may suffice: how have films portrayed aging and how is it portrayed presently; what symbols are used and what is its symbolism?

The past decade has seen the emergence of a number of training programs in adult development and aging, or human development, or gerontology. They have been established in a number of universities across the nation and have emerged in a variety of settings—both in established academic disciplines such as sociology, psychology, and social work as well as in interdisciplinary programs that draw faculty and students from a range of specialities. It is obvious that these training and research programs are important for advancing our understanding of the aging process and for equipping professionals to work with the aged. However, since the federal government has been the only governmental agency in the past that has been effective in advancing research and innovative programs for the elderly, these training programs—as well as a range of direct services for the aged—are largely dependent on federal funding. Hence, the political power of the aged and the political question of national spending priorities directly affect research, training, and services concerning the elderly.

The past decade has also seen an increase in the membership of professional organizations concerned with the aged such as the Gerontological Society. This organization is made up of persons in a wide range of professions concerned with research in the natural and social sciences and with planning and services concerning the aged. It has been deeply involved in training programs and serves as an important forum for the exchange of research and ideas about the field of gerontology. It also serves as a major clearinghouse and center for information about this rapidly growing field.

Thus, the field of adulthood and aging is one that offers a range of professional training opportunities; and since the field is relatively new, it offers one the possibility of playing an important part in its growth.

However, there are also a number of occupations that serve the aged directly in various contexts, but do not specifically involve gerontology. For example, administration, accounting, clerical work, and computer science are all fields that are important in hospital or nursing home management, in city and state and federal offices for the aging, and in organizations for the aged (such as the American Association of Retired Persons). And lawyers, accountants (especially for taxes), dentists, podiatrists, chiropractors, optometrists, and clergymen all serve the aged professionally and might even specialize in the aged or volunteer their services for the elderly. In addition, several occupations are involved with the aged in hospitals and nursing homes. These occupations include, in addition to the ones already mentioned, physical therapists, occupational therapists, recreational therapists, music or dance therapists, and speech therapists. Dietitians, pharmacists, laboratory technicians, radiologists and, indeed, the entire health services field are represented in some of the best hospitals and homes for the aged. In many of these fields there are excellent opportunities for employment and advancement as well as for personal satisfaction.

Thus, there are countless ways in which students may be trained to work with the elderly (or with adults generally). There are also countless paraprofessional jobs and roles being developed for persons with less than a bachelor's degree. Some of these include work in the community to improve the quality of community life and to maximize the independence of older persons. Nearly every senior citizen center and home or hospital for the aged or chronically ill appreciates volunteers for a variety of roles. Actually, there is little better way to gain an understanding of an area such as adulthood and aging than by directly experiencing it; and volunteer roles provide this opportunity as well as an important additional benefit—they allow a young person to test out some of the jobs that are interesting and to talk with persons who are actually doing that kind of work.

Since one of the keys to aiding the minority aged person is having trained minority persons (often bilingual) who can provide direct services to the aged and can serve as resource persons on ways to improve the condition of the aged they know best, it is clear that minority students need to be attracted into these fields. A heterogeneous group of aged persons demands a heterogeneous supply of trained professionals and paraprofessionals.

But education of young persons is only one aspect of the educational needs in this area. Middle-aged and older persons can also benefit from greatly expanded educational opportunities—in reality, throughout one's life—not only to fulfill themselves, but also to acquire new skills to aid others. Certainly, the aged themselves represent a rich resource for services and programs for the elderly; and the range of skills needed to serve as representative members of groups on governmental boards setting priorities, establishing policies, and providing funding—or to provide direct services to the aged themselves—may require new education in a variety of fields. Many colleges have recently opened their doors to persons over 65, and the impact of this concept might revolutionize thinking about the place and function of education in life and in our society.

As we look toward the future and imagine what kind of lives we want to have for ourselves in a diversified society that is faced with serious social problems and the fast pace of technological change, the opportunities and challenges are truly astounding. As years are added to life, will life be added to years? How quickly will the inequities faced by the aged and all of the other minority groups be adjusted? What will we do with these opportunities and challenges? Perhaps the place to begin is with that lonely old person who reminds us of what might happen to us if nothing changes but ourselves as we grow old.

CHAPTER SUMMARY

1. The meaning, status, and experience of aging differs greatly among various cultures around the world. Anthropologists have studied variations in the treatment and prestige given older people, the effect of industrialization on the status of the aged, and various groups of long-living people.

2. Industrialization, while possibly lowering the relative status of older people compared to younger people, often brings improved living conditions for all age groups. Thus, it is not necessarily true that older people in modern societies are generally disadvantaged in comparison to those in less industrialized societies.

3. The growing number and proportion of older people in the United States has brought greater social attention to their problems and, in many respects, the situation of the elderly appears to have improved in recent years. Today, the problems of older people are perhaps best seen as manifestations of problems faced by all age groups in our country.

4. Improved health care, better nutrition, and medical advances that have reduced mortality earlier in life have increased the number of people who live into late life. Future generations of older people in the United States are likely to have better health and more education than is the case today. In the less-developed countries, the growth of the older population will be especially dramatic and may create significant economic problems.

5. In our society, socioeconomic status, sex, and ethnic background affect the characteristics of aging as well as the living conditions that in-

fluence an individual's chances of having a long life. These differences also produce much of the diversity that exists among older people today.

6. Persons who may be described as "young-old" (ages 55 to 75) differ in many respects from persons who are "old-old" (over 75). The more numerous younger group is likely to have a significant impact on our society and our attitudes about aging because they tend to be healthy, active, and well-educated. The rapidly growing older group will increase the need for publicly financed health care, community services, and a variety of appropriate housing arrangements.

7. While most older people feel that their income is adequate, a disproportionate number of older persons are living in poverty. Social Security, tax benefits, Medicare, and other government programs have eased the economic problems of many older persons. However, for the vast majority of Americans, there is no guarantee that one will not become poor in old age.

8. Rising costs of health care are a problem for everyone, but especially for the elderly. In addition, adequate and appropriate nutrition, as well as the use of medication, over-the-counter drugs, and the combination of medications, are important issues for older persons.

9. Although only one in twenty persons over 65 are in institutions on any given day, the chances of entering an institution such as a nursing home before dying appear to be about one in four. Greater attention needs to be given to the creation of a system of community supports and sheltered living arrangements so that older people have a greater range of housing alternatives—from living independently in the community (or with one's family) to living in a nursing home. Continued emphasis must also be given to providing high-quality care in nursing homes and other housing for old people.

10. While the quality of life for some old people is very poor, other older people find significant opportunities for fulfillment and lead highly satisfying lives. For many older people, aging is a kind of career that provides meaning through a commitment to survive with originality and the support of friends in spite of the obstacles that may be present.

11. Problems of housing and transportation and fear of crime (especially for persons living in cities, women, and black persons) often impair the quality of life for older persons. Housing and transportation problems are especially acute for the rural elderly.

12. Greater social attention to older persons has created a wide range of opportunities for education and occupations related to aging. While nearly every field of study can be relevant to working with older persons, new programs in the field of gerontology offer a variety of resources for both older and younger students.

REFERENCES

Antunes, George E.; Cook, Fay Lomax; Cook, Thomas D.; & Skogan, Wesley G. 1977. Patterns of Personal Crime Against the Elderly: Findings from a National Survey. *The Gerontologist, 17*(4), 321-327.

Bailey, Anne. 1978. The 7 Day Diet: A Computer-Analyzed Diet for Older Americans. In Ruth B. Weg, *Nutrition in the Later Years*. Los Angeles: University of Southern California Press.

Beauvoir, Simone de. 1972. *The Coming of Age*. (Translated by Patrick O'Brian.) New York: G. P. Putnam's Sons.

Benet, Sula. 1974. *Abkhasians: The Long-Living People of the Caucasus*. New York: Holt, Rinehart and Winston.

Bengtson, Vern L.; Dowd, James J.; Smith, David H.; & Inkeles, Alex. 1975. Modernization, Modernity, and Perceptions of Aging: A Cross-Cultural Study. *Journal of Gerontology, 30*(6), 688-695.

Bengtson, Vern L.; Kasschau, Patricia L.; & Ragan, Pauline K. 1977. The Impact of Social Structure on Aging Individuals. In James E. Birren & K. Warner Schaie (Eds.), *Handbook of the Psychology of Aging*. New York: Van Nostrand Reinhold.

Blank, Thomas O. 1979. Older People Doing Their Shopping. Paper presented at the meeting of the American Psychological Association, New York City, September, 1979.

Brotman, Herman B. 1977a. Income and Poverty in the Older Population in 1975. *The Gerontologist, 17*(1), 23-26.

Brotman, Herman B. 1977b. Population Projections: Part 1. Tomorrow's Older Population (to 2000). *The Gerontologist, 17*(3), 203-209.

Butler, Robert N. 1969. Age-Ism: Another Form of Bigotry. *The Gerontologist, 9*(4, Part 1), 243-246.

Butler, Robert N. 1975. *Why Survive? Being Old in America*. New York: Harper & Row.

Carp, Frances M. 1977. Impact of Improved Living Environment on Health and Life Expectancy. *The Gerontologist, 17*(3), 242-249.

Chen, Y. P. 1973. A Pilot Survey Study of the Housing-Annuity Plan. Offset. Los Angeles: University of California, Graduate School of Management. (Cited in Streib, 1976.)

Clemente, Frank, & Kleiman, Michael B. 1976. Fear of Crime Among the Aged. *The Gerontologist, 16*(3), 207-210.

Cook, Fay Lomax; Skogan, Wesley G.; Cook, Thomas D.; & Antunes, George E. 1978. Criminal Victimization of the Elderly: The Physical and Economic Consequences. *The Gerontologist, 18*(4), 338-349.

Cowgill, Donald O., & Holmes, Lowell D. (Eds.). **1972.** *Aging and Modernization*. New York: Appleton-Century-Crofts.

Edwards, John N., & Klemmack, David L. 1973. Correlates of Life Satisfaction: A Re-examination. *Journal of Gerontology, 28*(4), 497-502.

Goody, Jack. 1976. Aging in Nonindustrial Societies. In Robert H. Binstock & Ethel Shanas (Eds.), *Handbook of Aging and the Social Sciences*. New York: Van Nostrand Reinhold.

Gruman, Gerald J. 1978. Cultural Origins of Present-Day "Age-ism": The Modernization of the Life Cycle. In S. F. Spicker, K. M. Woodward, & D. D. Van Tassel (Eds.), *Aging and the Elderly: Human Perspectives in Gerontology.* Atlantic Highlands, N.J.: Humanities Press.

Gutmann, David. 1977. The Cross-Cultural Perspective: Notes Toward a Comparative Psychology of Aging. In James E. Birren & K. Warner Schaie (Eds.), *Handbook of the Psychology of Aging.* New York: Van Nostrand Reinhold.

Guttmann, David. 1977. *A Study of Legal Drug Use by Older Americans* (NIDA Services Research Report). Washington, D.C.: U.S. Government Printing Office.

Harlan, William H. 1964. Social Status of the Aged in Three Indian Villages. *Vita Humana, 7,* 239–252.

Hauser, Philip M. 1976. Aging and World-Wide Population Change. In Robert H. Binstock & Ethel Shanas (Eds.), *Handbook of Aging and the Social Sciences.* New York: Van Nostrand Reinhold.

Havighurst, Robert J. 1978. Social Change: The Status, Needs, and Wants of the Future Elderly. In Barbara R. Herzog (Ed.), *Aging and Income.* New York: Human Sciences Press.

Kastenbaum, Robert, & Candy, Sandra E. 1973. The 4% Fallacy: A Methodological and Empirical Critique of Extended Care Facility Population Statistics. *International Journal of Aging and Human Development, 4*(1), 15–22.

Kosberg, Jordan I., & Tobin, Sheldon S. 1972. Variability Among Nursing Homes. *The Gerontologist, 12* (3, Part 1), 214–219.

Laslett, Peter. 1976. Societal Development and Aging. In Robert H. Binstock & Ethel Shanas (Eds.), *Handbook of Aging and the Social Sciences.* New York: Van Nostrand Reinhold.

Leaf, Alexander. 1973. Everyday Is a Gift When You Are Over 100. *National Geographic, 143*(1), 93–119.

Lissner, John. 1979. The Robust Artistry of Alberta Hunter. *New York Times,* June 3, D-23.

Medvedev, Zhores A. 1974. Caucasus and Altay Longevity: A Biological or Social Problem? *The Gerontologist, 14*(5), 381–387.

Myerhoff, Barbara. 1979. *Number Our Days.* New York: Dutton.

National Council on the Aging. 1975. *The Myth and Reality of Aging in America* (Conducted by Louis Harris & Associates, Inc.). Washington, D.C.: National Council on the Aging, Inc.

Neugarten, Bernice L. 1974. Age Groups in American Society and the Rise of the Young-Old. *The Annals of the American Academy of Political and Social Sciences.* 1974 (Sept.), 187–198.

***New York Times.* 1979.** Benefits Raised 9.9% Under Social Security; Average Increase $25. April 27, A-16.

Palmore, Erdman. 1975. *The Honorable Elders: A Cross-Cultural Analysis of Aging in Japan.* Durham, N.C.: Duke University Press.

Palmore, Erdman. 1976. Total Chance of Institutionalization Among the Aged. *The Gerontologist, 16*(6), 504–507.

Petersen, David M., & Whittington, Frank J. 1977. Drug Use Among the Elderly: A Review. *Journal of Psychedelic Drugs, 9*(1), 25–37.

Rawson, Ian G.; Weinberg, Edward I.; Herold, Jo Ann; & Holtz, Judy.

1978. Nutrition of Rural Elderly in Southwestern Pennsylvania. *The Gerontologist, 18*(1), 24-29.

Riley, Matilda White; Foner, Anne; & Associates. 1968. *Aging and Society. Vol. 1. An Inventory of Research Findings.* New York: Russell Sage Foundation.

Schulz, James H. 1976. *The Economics of Aging.* Belmont, Calif.: Wadsworth.

Shanas, Ethel, & Maddox, George L. 1976. Aging, Health, and the Organization of Health Resources. In Robert H. Binstock & Ethel Shanas (Eds.), *Handbook of Aging and the Social Sciences.* New York: Van Nostrand Reinhold.

Simmons, Leo W. 1945. *The Role of the Aged in Primitive Society.* New Haven, Conn.: Yale University Press.

Stirner, Fritz W. 1978. The Transportation Needs of the Elderly in a Large Urban Environment. *The Gerontologist, 18*(2), 207-211.

Streib, Gordon F. 1976. Social Stratification and Aging. In Robert H. Binstock & Ethel Shanas (Eds.), *Handbook of Aging and the Social Sciences.* New York: Van Nostrand Reinhold.

Struyk, Raymond J. 1977. The Housing Situation of Elderly Americans. *The Gerontologist, 17*(2), 130-139.

Tibbitts, Clark. 1979. Can We Invalidate Negative Stereotypes of Aging? *The Gerontologist, 19*(1), 10-20.

Turnbull, Colin M. 1973. The Mountain People. *Intellectual Digest, 3*(8:April), 49-56.

Uhlenberg, Peter. 1977. Changing Structure of the Older Population of the USA During the Twentieth Century. *The Gerontologist, 17*(3), 197-202.

U. S. Bureau of the Census. 1976. Demographic Aspects of Aging and the Older Population in the United States. *Current Population Reports,* Series P-23, No. 59. Washington, D.C.: U.S. Government Printing Office.

Vicente, Leticia; Wiley, James A.; & Carrington, R. Allen. 1979. The Risk of Institutionalization Before Death. *The Gerontologist, 19*(4), 361-367.

Weg, Ruth B. 1978. *Nutrition and the Later Years.* Los Angeles: University of Southern California Press.

Zawadski, Rick T.; Glazer, Gerald B.; & Lurie, Elinore. 1978. Psychotropic Drug Use Among Institutionalized and Noninstitutionalized Medicaid Aged in California. *Journal of Gerontology, 33*(6), 825-834.

Interlude
Mrs. K., Age 89

Mrs. K. is an 89-year-old woman who lives in a nursing home; she has been in the home 11 years and is remarkably vigorous and independent. Her bed was covered with handcrafts she had made and she apparently works in her own private room. She is one of the longest residents in her home, living first in the small building next door (which she calls her "white house") until the new modern building was built a few years ago. The home seems close to an ideal nursing home; but like most of the patients in this private (proprietary) nursing home, she depends on Medicare and Medicaid to pay her expenses. Mrs. K. (no one called her by her first name) came to the United States 43 years ago and learned English on her own. She seems to have been quite independent and on her own for most of her life, although some of this independence may reflect the personality shift in the later years described in Chapter 8. She has outlived her husband by many years and has no children. After working until the age of 70 she had to "retire" and give up her apartment a few years later when her health failed.

This example raises important questions not only about her life but also about the problems of the aged in our society. If she were not living in a nursing home, where would she live? How could she pay the expensive rates for such excellent care without government help? Turning to her life, we wonder whether she married "late" for her time and, if so, why? Why did she and her husband (Karl) not have children? Was their marriage satisfying for her? Might her strong personality be related to her ability to cope with the several traumatic events in her later years (the death of her husband, her illness, giving up her apartment, and moving from the old nursing home to the new building)—and possibly with her longevity? Has she worked through her feelings about death? Does she have a sense of meaningfulness in her life?

As you look back over your life, what milestones stand out? What milestones; let me think. I think there are many things where I am really interested and was always interested since a child. I was a child more reserved. I don't know why. That time when I was young I didn't know what's what. But later when I knew more, then I knew I was—I can say—a special girl, special child. I always wanted to learn something. We lived that time in the country for several years because father was transferred from the city to the country; then after [that] we came to the city again. . . .

What things stand out in your memory of your life? What should I say? What kind of things stand out? . . . Having a job; of course this took most of my time; and then getting married is something different too; and then, the biggest moment was when we came to America. *That was really a big moment for you?* This was. This was an unexpected big moment, because my husband knew a gentleman from the German-American Consulate. And he asked my husband, "What do you do for a living? Would you like to go to America?" "No," my husband said, "this is not for us," because we made out good, you know. But then was the war [World War I]. We lost everything, so we couldn't make out anymore; and through that gentleman my husband came here in three weeks. Because my husband was in agriculture, diplomas he has, you know, he can work in big estates and everything. He comes himself from a big estate in Germany. He was always interested in horses; he raised horses and trained them. He was here in three weeks; I came here 10 months later, because I had to sell my household, you know. And this took me a little time. And then [I] came right away over too, and then I was working because I could not fulfill that job what I used [to] be, so I was sitting in the workroom and make dresses, and then after that . . . the worsest part was we couldn't speak English. That was the hindrance for me. Then, when I knew a little bit [of] English and I came higher up, and then I started as a fitter, you know . . . ladies' body dresses. I pinned them up . . . and all of them had girls sitting in the workroom and then I was all right. This I did until I was 70 years [old]. *You did that until you were 70 years old!* I'm older now. Naturally (she laughs). I'm 89. *Are you really! I never would have guessed.*

The last few years I grew older very much on account of my sickness, you know . . . swollen . . . (gestures to her legs) and it goes down and gets all flabby. Anyway . . . once we have to take something and I know this very well, so that's that. They leave me all alone; I can do just as I want. Of course, I don't do wrong things. I am very satisfied here and have a few nice, nice friends; and this makes me happy too. And I think I make them happy too, because they all look for me to talk with me. This makes me proud. Yesterday I received a card from a lady again. I met her in the hospital. She went to another residence; and through her I met her sister. Ever since then the sister comes and visits me and send me always money. She's good off. So I have two other wonderful friends I met here and this makes me happy. You know, they come always once in a while and [it] is happy. So, I can say I'm never lonesome. I'm always occupied and happy so-called, you know. And that's the main thing, you know. And when I can have people I always try my best. This is not much, but. . . .

You've lived here for 15 years? No, 11; I'm here in this room 11 years. Only, I'm here 43 years in the United States. So, now I keep on as long as I can.

Do you have any children? No, I have no children. My husband is dead 26 years already. *I see.*

Then, I was still working, working, working, 'til I got sick and then I came here. I was very much crying when [I was] told in the hospital I come to the home. I had my apartment, but I couldn't go. So, they couldn't let me go home and I cried. And the social worker said to me, "You are a citizen. You must receive everything that other people get. It's coming to you." I said, "No, I cannot do it; I had so much saved I could live to 90 years old with my Social Security." And now came all different, took sick. Was laying down and they brought me to hospital. You see, unexpected comes, you know. *It was a very sad time for you when you had to leave your apartment.* Yah, I didn't see it any more. They brought me back here from the hospital and I never saw my apartment again. *You just went to the hospital and then came here.* Yah, it was two months. I was two months in hospital and then they sent me here [to the old building]. I call it my "white house." *Your "white house."* And then I make always about [it] little poems or little essays, you know. It's nothing much but I do the best. . . . And it comes here in the paper—we have a monthly paper here, we write everything. So I put it in there for Christmas and for holidays and so on . . . little poems. So I always occupy myself. I must have something which, you know, I must create this myself (she laughs).

Your husband, did he live on some kind of an agricultural farm? No, my husband was in the academy when he came . . . in the riding academy in _____ [town in Germany]. He taught ladies and children riding. And then after . . . there was not enough money . . . then I came over and my husband was there with his horses. We rode out with the lady here, there, and everywhere on the big estate and all that kind of things. Then he took off; it was not enough money. When I came over I made some myself, but it was very little because we couldn't speak English. And then my husband met a man; he was a painter . . . inside; he was German. He said, "Why don't you take [up] painting? You can make money." He learned my husband painting and my husband liked it very much and he made the nicest color, made everything nice and fine and even. We lived on _____ Street for 25 years until I took sick. We were always in New York.

Was getting married a big event for you? I married very late. I didn't want to get married at all because I had a wonderful position in Germany since 1910 and I could support myself. And I didn't want to take from a man money. I had plenty of opportunities to marry, but I said to my mother, "Nothing doing. I want to learn something. I want to make my own money. I don't want to take from a man. I just take what I want and do what I want, and that's good." So I did. I was 39 years old already. And I would have shoved him over also, but he was persistent. And I thank God for this, because through him I came to America; otherwise I would be destroyed in the Second World War. We came here in '29. See, when Hitler came, then we would have finished, you know. We didn't know him. But I have relatives over there and these [we] supported very much. I supported many many. I've never been [back] in Germany because, I say this cost a few thousand dollars and I'd rather give it to them because people need that more than. . . .

What kind of a profession were you in? I was in dressmaking. I was a directress in the best places in _____ [large German city] since 1910. And had girls sitting, eight girls apart more or less, in the workroom. I cut the dresses; I made the patterns; I fitted the dresses; and the girls would finish the dresses after that. It was a very good life. We had a few countesses; we had a few baronesses; we had one princess even, from Germany; this one I didn't fit because I was not a fitter. "Directress" we called it. I had a wonderful position for money. I didn't need to marry for money. Then when my husband was dead I was still working, always. Sure, I miss this, but as I say, I got sick and couldn't come [fit] in shoes; I get swollen. That was the hindrance.

So you had to stop working at 70? Yah, then I was sitting home. Seven years I was constantly in doctor's care; then he said, "I cannot help you anymore Mrs. K. You must go into hospital; they have facilities which I am not allowed to use." So, then I was sitting seven years in my house not going . . . I didn't want to go in hospital. Then I fall together several times; then they picked me up and brought me to hospital and that was that. So this was the end and then I came here. Since then I was always happy here and worked, worked, worked.

Do you sometimes look back over your life and think about the things that happened? I think back and look back constantly, from a little child on . . . how it happened, why it happened. Yes, I do, but I do not regret. I'm alone, have nobody. Even if I would have children I wouldn't live with them. I would leave them alone. They should be happy. I wanted that too when I was young. I would leave them too. I would go in a home. *Do you wish that you did have children sometimes?* No, on account of the war [World War I], you know. We losed every penny; then, how can you get children? I had to work. And at least you want your children raised like you are raised, you know. And especial you would want a little decent, and this we couldn't do. Then was the big moment when we came here, you know. That was the biggest moment for me in the later years. I was glad to be here, and still am, you know.

Why was that such a big moment for you? You know, I never thought we could come to America! Imagine! We had a nice income and a flat [apartment], but through the war we lose everything; no work, no nothing. We had debts by my parents and this couldn't go on anymore. So, finally my husband met this man and through him he came here; and then, of course he sent the fare back to my mother. Then, months later I came, and I made my own money too. We saved a little. This was the biggest, the nicest moment. That's what I must say. I loved here when we came how cheap everything was. In Germany, it cost a pound of butter, two dollars—marks, we say; and here, we bought four pounds of butter from dollar. I say, "You bring it right back." He said, "You are a funny woman. Why don't you taste?" It can't be good; you know how much cream you need for a pound of butter." He was an agricultural man, you know. Then he was stunned and thought it over. He said, "Taste it," and I tasted; it was the good butter. So, everything was so cheap here. Food! Oh, I love food. I always ate food, food, food. Every Saturday we bought food. Everything for the whole week. I like food still, all my life. *You still like food.* Oh, crazy about it! I cannot do without food.

How was your marriage? My marriage was fairly good. You know, there's always a little smoke in every kitchen; but this was overcome, you know. You must give in. My husband had his own mind and I had my own mind; but I always helped him. When something happened I always told him in advance what can happen and he didn't believe me. "Can't do nothing with that woman! Can't do nothing with that woman! Can't do nothing with that woman!" he always said. When sometimes trouble came, for instance, he wanted to participate with a partner. He wanted to make a little business. We had a little money saved. Not much, but a little. I say, "Karl, you do not do that. We are strange in this country. We don't have the language exactly right and we don't know the rules and everything. We leave our hands off! You lose the money." Twice we lose and I say, "No; now I keep my money and you keep yours. You can do with it what you want, and I keep my money." And that's why sometimes we get trouble. We had a few troubles and I balled him out in the right place in the right way. That's why he always said, "You're a smart woman!" But I said, "You don't listen when I tell you in advance, 'don't do it!'" That was really the idea, because I had the feeling in me, you know . . . I have the house of Cancer ruling me, you know. I made all the horoscopes. We learned to make all the horoscopes—a hell of a work. You need charts of the stars, where they are at this and that moment, and all the tables and all that. This I wouldn't want anymore, but that's why I said I feel. There are people who see, not directly, but they see. I feel; I feel in advance something is wrong, not coming right. And that's really true. I advised people and helped people. You think they did it? They didn't do it, see! You must always work, work and improve more and more and more; but they have not that ambition in them. That's what I believe . . . in the stars and how they stand in nature of the almighty universe. That is my special, how you say, work. If I could write very good as a writer I would make a nice book, but I'm not so intelligent so I can write. I make little things.

I get up in the morning [at] quarter to five. Bathe myself down every morning; nobody is up then. Then I'm finished; make my bed; pick everything up and then I sit here 'til seven and then get breakfast; and then we start working (she laughs). That's my life. *You work down in the craft shop?* No, I do not, because I'm on my own. *You work up here [in her private room]?* Yah, I'm all my own, because I could be the instructor of everything. I don't want to be under. They wanted me under them to show the others. But, I must say, I'm never—how should you say—high-headed. But this is what I worked out for myself, and this I keep. I didn't work under other people. I'm a creator in everything. What I do is all my own. *I get the feeling you've always been that way.* When I was a child already. But then I didn't know what's what. I had to learn first how to go, what is what. And then I figured out how, why, and so. Then I was able. So, no, I worked for things, but all on my own. I made recently for Mrs. D. a suit—crocheted suit with skirt and jacket, and she wears it once or two times, three times, four times. She's very pleased. I made very, very many things for Mrs. D., for her daughter, for her daughter-in-law; all sorts of dresses and outfits. Everything I make, everything. Other people cannot do that, you know. There are a few now [who can make] a little something, yes sure, but when they want really something now, then they ask me. And I gladly advise when I can help, sure.

Were you and your husband very close to one another? Oh yah. I loved my husband very much. And he loved me too. Because, what should I say, he was an educated man, came from a good family; he was also in the war and he had nice position there and he kept this. Yah, I loved my husband; we were happy, but as I said, sometimes was smoke in the kitchen (she laughs). *You had your arguments too?* Oh sure, sure. For instance, I tell you what was the biggest argument we had. When that damn, excuse me, Hitler was . . . and he heard from other German men on 86th Street . . . Saturdays he usually went there, or Sundays. And then he talked about everything, and he listened and listened. Now my husband was from a big estate, and he was the oldest son. He would have inherited it if he stayed. I said, "Karl, you leave the hands from it. We have no children; we are both alone. We have good work. We are satisfied and we want peace now." "No, no" he said. "I understand you stay in your house or you lose it, but imagine what you have to pay. You pay the trip over and you have to pay the man to look out for it. What is left for you—only work," I said. "Don't do it." No, he didn't want it [her advice]. And there was that Bund [club or association] from Hitler, and he would like to join that too, those meet- ings. [The German-American Volksbund, or Bund, was a pro-Nazi organization in the United States during the 1930s and 40s.] I said, "You leave the hands from this," I said. "We are new in America. We do not participate in anything." "He promised you get back what you lost." I said, "Karl, don't you believe that!" "Yah, yah, yah, yah," he said. "I go over to Germany," he said. I said, "You go over from here to Germany? No!" And I talked with him over that often, very often. He insisted that he wanted to get his estate back. I told him everything as it comes and how it is away. I never believed in Hitler. I know. He said, "Yes, yes, yes." And I said, "No, Karl, let's make it here. You go over to Germany. I don't keep you. You know, I don't need you. I make my own money. I never needed no husband for making money. You go over. I don't keep you away. But once I tell you now in advance. I know you wouldn't like it. It won't come out as you think. You will be glad to come back here, but I don't give you a penny to come back. Stay there!" That was the biggest moment in all. Otherwise was nothing. *That was a big fight?* Oh yah, always fighting. And then finally when it came out what Hitler was and that Bund was, then he said, "I know you are a smart woman." I said, "Don't say that. You don't do when I tell you in advance." That was . . . oh . . . we had many fights. I would have let him go if he really wanted to go, but then find out a little bit before; so he stood here. Oh, yah, we had big fights. Now, how could we [have gone back to Germany?] . . . I was glad to be here, you know. Oh, I never liked that man [Hitler]. I didn't know him personally. . . . We were here already in '29 and he was there I think '33, you know, he started. No, I said, "Nothing doing." Other- wise, I said this was a very big moment—coming to America and having this event with him; he wanted to go.

Were sexual relations very important between the two of you? Oh, we were both [on] in years, you know, and—how should I say . . . I said to my husband before we were married, "One thing, think it over; when we marry don't go with other woman. If you cannot do this, we don't get married then." We never talked about this later . . . I don't think so. No, that's all right. That was not my main thing, you know. My main thing was working and learning. *Sexual rela- tions weren't very important in your relationship then?* No, not so, not so. I could not say that. He was a very nice man with manners and so, and that's all.

Was his death quite a shock for you? Yes, very, yah, sure; because I was all alone here, and I just came from work and he was before me in the house, and we always had little dogs and they were always with him. They sat outside in the street and waited for me. So I came home and I wanted to go to the doctor because I get injection for my sickness. And I had the feeling that I don't like to go today. I'd rather go home. I went home, you know. Then I came, he was sitting in the sofa in the front, and sick. I said, "What's the matter, Karl?" He said, "Now I am finished." I said, "What's the matter?" "I have all here these things. It hurts me here, here, here. I have double pneumonia," he said. But I said, "It is not pneumonia." I said, "Come in the kitchen just the same," and I made him a wet pack and I knew this was not pneumonia; but I didn't know either what it was. So I did this and bedded him on the couch, and then he said, "Give me a little drink," and I gave him ginger ale. He drank that and I turned my back and wanted to set it on the table and then there was (she makes gasping, choking sounds) and I look back and I say, "Karl! You are not dying!" And then . . . he was finished. He had the heart, how you say, blood clot on the heart. That was quite a . . . that was, of course, big moment. This was very . . . I was all alone then, but I was used to things. I could manage. I was courage person, you know. Of course, was a long time 'til you get over that, but I worked and a lady called me from the shop and said, "Mrs. K. you better come and work; you'll overcome the things better." I had everything regulated so far in advance back in my shop. Then after . . . little by little. You know how it is. Yes, this was hard moment. Since then I am all alone. Nothing was too much for me. Day and night I would work and everything. So now we sit here . . . and we see how long (she laughs). *We see how long we stay here.* Oh, here we stay; but when the death comes, you know.

Do you sometimes think about death? I often think and I pray always. There is nothing what I do without praying. Nothing. When I take something and do something, I always pray, pray, pray, pray. So, of course, I think often on the death; and . . . I always think about this; I always say, "If I die, I would wish to die nicely, quietly, without pain." That is my only wish, my last wish, nothing else. But this we don't know. *Right; but we can pray.* I hope, I hope. Yah, we hope the best. I do nothing without praying to God . . . nothing. People don't know. I say when the minister comes, you know. Those things I know, of course, I should do it and did it Sunday morning [go to services in the home], but usually not, because I know how I act, what I do, and that's enough. I think so at least. Maybe I'm wrong. I could be wrong, but that's all right.

Do you feel you left your mark here somewhere; that your life has been meaningful and productive? I think, if I understood right, I think . . . I was from child on already dedicated to help people. Now in my age I still do. I always helped, I always did, and nothing was too much for me. And still I'm this way; and I think I was a person who was so-called dedicated to do those things, otherwise you couldn't do. *So helping people has been very important for you; and you've done that?* Yes, I did plenty. Not with money so much, because I had to make my own living, but whatever I could help . . . helping them . . . doing things for them. I never took money from anybody, not a penny, not a penny. As long as I had what I needed. I'm not crazy for money. So I need a little—a certain amount to have this and this and that and many things that you do too, but not overdoing. It's not necessary. But give a poor old man something, a little bit; help poor people.

According to nursing home records, Mrs. K. died about a year after this interview in her room at 5:30 A.M. She had been suffering from diabetes and arteriosclerotic vascular disease, but her health had been generally deteriorating for some time before she died. Unfortunately, she did experience considerable pain before her death; it was described as "generalized body pain" that probably resulted from arthritis—she had complained of it for about a year. She chose not to go to a hospital to determine the cause of the pain, but wished to remain in her room at the nursing home. Her death was attributed to pulmonary edema—fluid in the lungs.

10

DYING AND BEREAVEMENT

In many ways, death is a subject that may be both frightening and of deep interest at the same time. Perhaps the topic of death is an even more sensitive and avoided topic than sexuality is today; in that sense, death may have replaced sex as the taboo topic in our culture. So it is probably realistic to begin our discussion somewhat slowly and to recognize from the outset that until recently death has been a topic not readily discussed in free and relaxed conversation in our society. At the deepest levels of our being, denial of death is probably necessary to function in a world where accidents, illnesses, wars, and killings are present. We may need to feel that these events will happen to others, not to us, or we would be unable to take risks, drive cars, or even leave the house. However, a pervasive denial of death that prevents any consideration of our own mortality and fears of death may affect our attitudes about living as well as our reactions toward older people (who tend to be seen as closer to death than younger people).

Perhaps most of us typically avoid thinking about death, the dying, and hence the aged or terminally ill person. Sometimes the avoidance of older persons, the tendency to push them out of sight—psychologically and socially—suggests that they are treated as if they were reminders of our common fate as mortal human beings. It is as if one might "catch" aging and death by touching or becoming too close to an older person. Thus, as we become more aware of our own mortality and our fears of death, we may become more comfortable in relations with older people and with terminally ill people of any age. In our own lives also, we may find that the uniqueness of each day may be more appreciated than if the finiteness of life is ignored and each day is seen as just one more of an endless flow of days.

We probably (and perhaps necessarily, at least in our "unconscious") feel that *we* shall surely never die—accidents, heart attacks, and fatal illnesses happen to others, but not to me. Yet death is obviously inevitable for every person, and we will probably experience the death of persons close to us during the course of our lives. Perhaps, then, this discussion of death will lead us to a more humane perspective toward the dying while only partially lifting the denial of our own mortality and death. The mystery and the fear of death are very real, but we can work toward understanding death and dealing with our own denial and fears of death. One result of the denial of death and avoidance of the topic is to avoid and sometimes to dehumanize those who are dying otherwise very human deaths.

He may cry for rest, peace, and dignity, but he will get infusions, transfusions, a heart machine, or tracheostomy if necessary. He may want one single person to stop for one single minute so that he can ask one single question—but he will get a dozen people around the clock, all busily preoccupied with his heart rate, pulse, electrocardiogram or pulmonary functions, his secretions or excretions but not with him as a human being. He may wish to fight it all but it is going to be a useless fight since all this is done in the fight for his life, and if they can save his life they can consider the person afterwards. Those who consider the person first may lose precious time to save his life! At least this seems to be the rationale or justification behind all this—or is it? Is the reason for this increasingly mechanical, depersonalized approach our own defensiveness? Is this approach our own way to cope with and repress the anxieties that a terminally or critically ill patient evokes in us? Is our concentration on equipment, on blood pressure our desperate attempt to deny the impending death which is so frightening and discomforting to us that we displace all our knowledge onto machines, since they are less close to us than the suffering face of another human being which would remind us once more of our lack of omnipotence, our own limits and failures, and last but not least perhaps our own mortality? [Kübler-Ross, 1969, p. 9].[1]

This view of the critically ill patient in modern hospitals and the provocative questions that it raises was written by Elisabeth Kübler-Ross in the introduction to her report on a seminar she conducted on death and dying with terminally ill patients, students from a theological seminary, and hospital staff. Her concern was to learn from the dying patients themselves about the process of dying and simultaneously to learn ways of helping persons with terminal illnesses resolve this very significant milestone of adult life in the most positive and human way possible. We will discuss her work in considerable detail in the middle section of this chapter, for it has increased our awareness and understanding of the dying process and has shaken and opened to discussion a wide range of assumptions about dying in our culture; by implication it has also called attention to the assumptions and values about life in our society.

In reality, is the dying process any less important or meaningful an aspect of life than the birth process? Have we turned away from the actual process of birth in much the same way as we turn away from the process of dying? Do we favor birth in a hospital with anesthetics, with the husband separated from the wife, and with the actual birth behind closed doors? Perhaps there may be a parallel between the growing popularity of "natural childbirth"—still in a hospital, but with the parents jointly sharing this important event and hearing the first cries of the child—and the perspective Kübler-Ross might call "natural dying"—possibly in a hospital, but with the humanness of patients not obliterated by the machines and tubes and technology that seem almost to turn them into an extension of the machine. She does not, of course, advocate a denial of medical technology but, instead, affirms the dignity and humanness of dying persons who may need psychological, religious, and family support and the chance to resolve the issues involved in this final important event in their own meaningful ways.

Indeed, if we come to humanize the dying process and to deal somewhat with our own fears of death (at least at a conscious level), perhaps we may also come to more fully humanize living. From the existential point of view, the reality of

[1]All quotations from Kübler-Ross (1969) are reprinted with permission of Macmillan Publishing Co., Inc., and Tavistock Publications, Ltd., from *On Death and Dying*, copyright © 1969 by Elisabeth Kübler-Ross.

death is necessary for life to be meaningful; if death is denied, life is also denied. Yet we are inundated by statistics of death—on the highways, in disasters, and in the cities—and are exposed to countless TV deaths. If death has lost its sting, where is the value of living? In one particularly provocative section, Kübler-Ross suggests, "Is war perhaps nothing else but a need to face death, to conquer and master it, to come out of it alive—a peculiar form of denial of our own mortality?" (ibid., p. 13). As she suggests, perhaps an understanding of death in all its reality, rather than its denial, may bring with it "a chance for peace" and "perhaps there could be less destructiveness around us" (ibid.). In the decade since her book was first published, there has been considerable interest and research on death, dying, and bereavement. However, her book appears to retain its popular appeal and has remained on the best-selling list of paperback books for over ten years.

In this chapter we will discuss three aspects of the stage of life that precedes death. We will begin with the psychological issues and changes that appear to precede the actual dying process and that seem best understood as developmental changes timed by the approach of death. Next we will present Kübler-Ross's insights and understanding of the dying process itself, which she sees as consisting of five characteristic reactions that both dying and bereaved persons may experience. In the last section we will discuss the process of mourning and the issues faced by the survivors and conclude with a brief discussion of the social view of death as a status passage for the dying person and also for the survivors. From time to time we will quote from the classic short story by Leo Tolstoy (1828-1910), *The Death of Ivan Ilych*, an exceptional example of the parallel between the insight of the artist and the insight of the social scientist.

DEVELOPMENTAL CHANGES PRECEDING DEATH

Up to this point we have been discussing developmental changes, milestones, and sequential issues of adulthood with reference to the length of time the person has been alive—that is, *timed by the years since birth* (age). However, the data available so far suggest that the changes or developmental progression in the late years of life may not be timed entirely by chronological age, but rather they may be set in motion or *timed by the nearness of the individual to death*. For example, the Erikson stage of Integrity versus Despair, the last of his eight ages of life, would be the developmental issue faced by persons who are nearing death and in the later years of their lives, although they might be as young as 40 or as old as 90. His theory states that the beginning of this final stage is triggered by the realization of one's approaching death and by the recognition that it is too late to change one's life in major ways for the time is too short to start over. Cues such as illness, advanced age itself, the death of one's cohorts, and perhaps inner cues of the approaching end of life would be likely to be involved in triggering this final turning point. In addition, some psychological processes have been found to change as death approaches, suggesting that nearness to death itself brings developmental change. Moreover, some of Neugarten's (1967) data on middle-aged persons also point to a shift in time perspective during the middle years from "time lived" to "time left to live" as an important marker for timing and for regulating one's internal social clock.

> Both sexes, although men more than women, talked of the new difference in the way time is perceived. Life is restructured in terms of time-left-to-live rather than time-since-birth. Not only the reversal in directionality but the awareness that time is finite is a particularly conspicuous feature of middle age. . . .
>
> The recognition that there is "only so much time left" was a frequent theme in the interviews. In referring to the death of a contemporary, one man said, "There is now the realization that death is very real. Those things don't quite penetrate when you're in your twenties and you think that life is all ahead of you. Now you know that death will come to you, too" [Neugarten, 1967, p. 97].

Thus, in the later years a *future event* (death) may be a marker replacing, to some degree, the importance of the number of years since birth, which was a timing factor in earlier years.

Erikson's Eighth Stage: Integrity versus Despair

The last stage in Erikson's theory is described as the fruition of the previous seven stages. It involves "the acceptance of one's one and only life cycle and of the people who have become significant to it as something that had to be and that, by necessity, permitted of no substitutions" (Erikson, 1968, p. 139). In this framework, one would look back over one's life and deal with the question of the meaningfulness of one's life, the intersection of one's life with history, and the degree to which one's life was a worthwhile venture. One pole of the struggle is a sense of integrity; the other pole is a sense of despair: "Time is short, too short for the attempt to start another life and to try out alternate roads to integrity" (ibid., p. 140). Erikson sees old age as providing the link between past heritage and future generations and thus giving perspective to the life cycle. The resolution of this stage involves *wisdom*: "ripened 'wits' . . . accumulated knowledge, mature judgment, and inclusive understanding" (ibid.). The essence of wisdom is often provided by *tradition* and consideration of *ultimate concerns* about transcending the limitations of one's identity.

In Tolstoy's short story, *The Death of Ivan Ilych*, Ivan Ilych is slowly dying from the effects of an injury. In his career he was (as a fictional character) a judge in Russia in the late nineteenth century; thus there are political and religious themes written into the story, but Erikson's concept of a struggle between integrity and despair is clearly portrayed.

Ivan Ilych saw that he was dying, and he was in continual despair.

In the depth of his heart he knew he was dying, but not only was he not accustomed to the thought, he simply did not and could not grasp it [Tolstoy, 1886, p. 131].

It occurred to him that what had appeared perfectly impossible before, namely that he had not spent his life as he should have done, might after all be true.. It occurred to him that his scarcely perceptible attempts to struggle against what was considered good by the most highly placed people, those scarcely noticeable impulses which he had immediately suppressed, might have been the real thing, and all the rest false. And his professional duties and the whole arrangement of his life and of his family, and all his social and official interests, might all have been false. He tried to defend all those things to himself and suddenly felt the weakness of what he was defending. There was nothing to defend.

"But if that is so," he said to himself, "and I am leaving this life with the consciousness that I have lost all that was given to me and it is impossible to rectify it—what then?" [ibid., p. 152].

Existential Anxiety and Death.

This view of the final struggle to resolve the meaning of life (in terms of Integrity versus Despair) seems similar to the existential argument that people strive to find meaning in their great or mundane lives, and that the absence of a sense of meaning leads to despair. However, in the existential view, death is an ever possible choice that provides ultimate freedom—one is always walking along the edge of the abyss and is free to jump or to continue walking—and this ultimate freedom is at the core of the meaning of existence. Put another way, "one finds meaning in life when one is committed to something for which one is willing to accept death" (Barnes, 1959, p. 81). Similarly, "the confronting of death gives the most positive reality to life itself. It makes the individual existence real, absolute, and concrete" (May, 1958, p. 49). But death also represents the threat of nonbeing and thus brings existenial anxiety as an essential characteristic of humans who, after all, are perhaps the only animals that can be aware of their own impending death. May defines this anxiety as: "the subjective state of the individual's becoming aware that his existence can become destroyed, that he can lose himself and his world, that he can become 'nothing'" (ibid., p. 50).

As profound as these insights into the basic nature of the human condition may be, we wonder if they do not pertain to the contemplation of death by those for whom death is not acutally imminent; that is, how could existential anxiety about death have the same impact on an aged, suffering, cancer patient as it would have on a healthy young person or a powerful middle-aged person who is not facing death? Do these views imply that patients in hospitals for the chronically ill (where nearly all of the patients do not leave until they die) are actively contemplating the meaning of their lives and attempting to resolve their anxiety about becoming no-thing? Beauvoir (1972), a noted existentialist, in her treatise on old age, points out that death for the aged may not be feared because it is an acceptable alternative to a life that has become meaningless.

> Even if the old person is struck by no particular misfortune [physical suffering, outliving all those he loves], he has usually either lost his reasons for living or he has discovered their absence. The reason why death fills us with anxiety is that it is the inescapable reverse of our projects: when a man is no longer active in any way, when he has ceased all undertakings, all plans, then there remains nothing that death can destroy. It is usual to put forward wearing-out and fatigue as an explanation for the way some old people resign themselves to death; but if all a man needed was to vegetate he could put up with this life in slow motion. But for man living means self-transcendence. A consequence of biological decay is the impossibility of surpassing oneself and of becoming passionately concerned with anything; it kills all projects, and it is by this expedient that it renders death acceptable [Beauvoir, 1972, p. 443].

Thus, it may be that anxiety about nonbeing, introspection about the meaning of one's life, and concern with the issue of Integrity versus Despair—in sum, resolution of the "death issue"—may not be highly significant *immediately* before death in old age (although it may occur when death seems imminent among younger persons). Instead, these issues may be more salient when death is not at the doorstep (so to speak), and our interest in life is high—for example, in late middle age when the imminence of death is not upon us, but its inevitability becomes apparent as parents, friends, and loved ones begin to die one by one. So while the Integrity versus Despair issue may be triggered by the reailization of one's eventual death, we need not assume that the final days of a person's life (especially in old age) are spent in coming to a resolution of that crisis—it may occur a decade or two earlier. Let us examine some data on this question.

Studies on the Acceptance of Death

On the basis of their research, Lieberman and Coplan (1970) speculated that the acceptance of death is a more significant issue for middle-aged persons than it is for older people. Many of their aged respondents living in a nursing home or in the community had "worked out the meaning of death for themselves and most have developed a personal viewpoint toward their own death" (p. 83). These respondents were willing to talk openly about death; and most anxiety or disruption about death was related to change in their socioenvironmental conditions. That is, those respondents who (as it later turned out) were near to death and were living in the home or in stable environments in the community seemed to be dealing with the task of facing death without storminess or disruption; "it was as if they were dealing with a developmental task that they were coping with adequately" (p. 82). In contrast, persons who were waiting to enter the home or had only recently entered felt much more anxiety and disruption, and many appeared to lack a personal philosophy about death. It was as if these changes in living arrangements had forced them to readjust once more and had perhaps disrupted their previous resolution of the death issue. Thus, although older persons are often willing to talk about death, it does not appear to be a major psychological issue dominating the last decade or two of life.

Bengtson, Cuellar, and Ragan (1977) studied fear of death among black, Mexican-American, and white persons selected to be representative of each group in terms of age (from 45 to 74) and socioeconomic status (low, medium, and high). Only about a quarter of the older respondents expressed fear of death, as compared with about half of the middle-aged respondents (young adults were not included in the study); sex, racial/ethnic group, and socioeconomic status had relatively little effect in comparison with age (Figure 10.1). There was no clear relationship between age and the frequency of thinking about death. Less than one in five respondents in any of these age-ethnic subgroups reported that they often thought about death; among whites, less than one in twelve. Clearly, these data support the notion that neither fear of death, nor thoughts about death, dominate the later years of life; instead, they seem to be more significant in middle age. However, there may be ethnic and racial differences reflecting cultural factors in attitudes and a denial of death. One example of these differences that may reflect denial of death is the respondents' expectation of the number of years they will live (Figure 10.2). Although life expectancy is lower for nonwhites, the black respondents in this study had much greater expectations than did the white respondents; statistically, life expectancy for whites at age 50 is 26.4 years and at 70 it is 12.2 years, for nonwhites it is

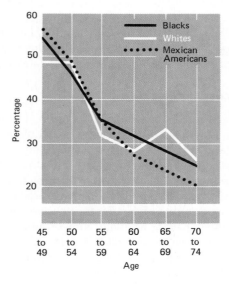

Figure 10.1
Percentage responding "very afraid" or "somewhat afraid" of death, by age and ethnicity. (Source: Bengtson et al., 1977, Figure 1. Reprinted with permission of the *Journal of Gerontology*.)

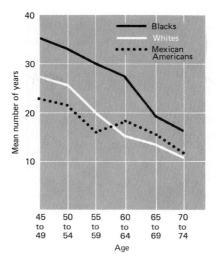

Figure 10.2

Mean number of years that respondents report they expect to live, by age and ethnicity. (Source: Bengtson et al., 1977, Figure 3. Reprinted with permission of the *Journal of Gerontology*.)

23.8 and 12.0, respectively (ibid.). Thus, while whites tended not to report that they thought about death very often, they predicted their future life expectancy fairly accurately. Mexican Americans tended to think about death more frequently than whites, but also predicted their life expectancy fairly accurately. Blacks thought about death about as much as the Mexican-American respondents, but were much more optimistic (and statistically unrealistic) in the prediction of the number of years they expected to live.

These findings suggest that research on the acceptance of death is very complex and that any simple conclusions are likely to be misleading. In the Bengtson study, one of the respondents, whom they called Mrs. Garcia, suggested that the meaning of death, and of the acceptance of death, depends on one's life events and personal definition of dying.

> It's interesting you should ask me if I fear death. I don't want to die any more than you do, but I'm not afraid of death. Why? Because I'm a woman. I have lived with a man who drank too much and was always running around, and I've sent two sons to war. Every time the phone rang or there was a knock at the door I would die. I've died a thousand times. Why should I be afraid of death? But, I still don't *want* to die [Bengtson et al., 1977, p. 85].

In addition, these data are cross-sectional, so that the smaller proportion of respondents reporting fear of death may reflect less fear of death among people born around the turn of the century compared with those born in the 1920s. However, the interview data suggest that the difference does reflect developmental change. Although other studies have found that greater education is related to less frequent thoughts of death, especially among younger people, and to more positive attitudes about death (Riley, 1963), this tricultural study did not find education or other socioeconomic variables to be important (Bengtson et al., 1977). Thus, the only clear conclusion we can draw is that older adults are less likely than the middle-aged adults to report that they are afraid of death; most other studies also support this finding (Kalish, 1976).

Fear of death does not seem to be a major fear for most people. Kalish (1976) notes that only one out of four respondents in his multiethnic study reported a fear of death. Riley (1963), in a nationwide sample of 1500 adults, found that, at all ages, the attitude was more one of acceptance ("death is sometimes a blessing" or "death is not tragic for the person who dies, only for the survivors") than of fear ("death always comes too soon" or "to die is to suffer"). Over 60 percent of his respondents described death as "a long sleep." Generally, more religious people tend to have lower fear of death than less religious persons, although some studies have found that moderately religious persons, such as irregular churchgoers who possibly have uncertain religious beliefs, are more fearful of death than either devoutly religious or irreligious persons (Kalish, 1976). There is also some evidence that preparation for death increases with age, especially for persons with higher education (Riley, 1963); these data from a nationwide survey suggest that persons with at least a high-school education began making specific plans—such as making a will and funeral arrangements—during the decade of their forties or fifties; for persons with less than high-school education, this planning did not begin until the decade of their sixties (Table 10.1).

Table 10.1 Percent with High Degree of Preparation for Death[a] by Age and Education (N = 1500)

Age	Junior High School or Less	High School	College	"Effect" of Higher Education
30 and under	0	1	3	+ 3
31 to 40	2	4	8	+ 6
41 to 50	8	14	22	+ 14
51 to 60	8	25	40	+ 32
61 +	20	30	44	+ 24
"Effect" of older age	+ 20	+ 29	+ 41	

Source: Riley (1963). Exhibit 14.20 reprinted with permission from *Aging and Society*, Vol. I, by Matilda White Riley, Anne Foner, and Associates, copyright © 1968 by Russell Sage Foundation.
[a]Based on positive answers to questions about whether it is best in general to make any plans about death, and whether specific actions have been taken (discussing with those closest, making funeral or cemetery arrangements, making a will).
Note: The smallest base for any percentage is 45.

However, relatively few people prepare for death; Phalon (1978) reports that seven out of ten people die without leaving a will.

One interesting study of attitudes about death among college students found that those respondents most fearful of death were also afraid of aging (Salter & Salter, 1976). However, anxiety about death was not associated with a rejection of the elderly, as might be expected—at least for the sample as a whole. Instead, it was related to agreement with the need for a "national awareness campaign" about the needs of the elderly, a willingness to visit older people, and to take them to religious services. This suggests that one effect of the fear of death may be to help older persons as a means of reducing one's own fears of aging and death. While this optimistic conclusion is appealing, it may apply to only one group of the respondents; another smaller group may deal with their fear of death by rejecting the elderly, but this cannot be determined from the correlational analyses reported.

In summary, Erikson's concept of Integrity versus Despair is often seen as emerging only at the conclusion of life, but the available data indicate that the growing awareness of death and the reduction in the fear of death appear to begin during middle age. Although much more research is needed on the acceptance of death, it appears that this issue is gradually resolved over several decades and that fear of death during the last months or years of life may result from a crisis in the social environment, disrupting one's previous resolution of the issues involved in accepting death. Thus, while it may be that the resolution of questions about the existential meaning of life and the acceptance of death is a typical task one undertakes as one begins to see the end of one's life on the horizon, apparently it does not dominate the last decade or two of life. The first emergence of the Integrity versus Despair issues may well be during middle age, perhaps as a part of the midlife transition (discussed in Chapter 3.).

The Life Review Process

Another concept of the psychological tasks preceding death and triggered by one's closeness to death is the process of the life review, suggested by Butler (1963). The life review is defined as a "naturally occurring, universal mental process . . . prompted by the realization of approaching dissolution and death, and the inability to maintain one's sense of personal invulnerability." It potentially proceeds toward personality reorganization, including the achievement of such characteristics as wisdom and serenity in the aged; thus it is a potential force toward increased self-awareness. However, it may also lead to some pathological manifestations as well, such as depression, guilt, or obsessional ruminations about past events. The process consists of reminiscence, thinking about oneself, reconsideration of previous experiences and their meanings, and "mirror gazing" (this may serve as one of the best indications that the process is taking place). One example of mirror gazing (i.e., pausing to look into a mirror, perhaps for several moments and perhaps with some verbal comments intended for one's self) is given by Butler: "I was passing by my mirror. I noticed how old I was. My appearance, well, it prompted me to think of death—and of my past—what I hadn't done, what I had done wrong" (ibid.). A similar episode is described in the Tolstoy story of Ivan Ilych:

> Ivan Ilych locked the door and began to examine himself in the glass, first full face, then in profile. He took up a portrait of himself taken with his wife, and compared it with what he saw in the glass. The change in him was immense. Then he bared his arms to the elbow, looked at them, drew the sleeves down again, sat down on an ottoman, and grew blacker than night [Tolstoy, 1886, p. 127].

The symbolic interaction interpretation of this process would be that the person is actively working to integrate the new (physical) *me* into the relatively continuous sense of self and is, in a sense, attempting to gain mastery and integration of the changed physical *me* and the internal experiencings. The *I* is striving for a new integration based on this different *me*, memory of past *mes*, and current bodily experiencings. Possibly, the body *me* is changing as rapidly as it ever did (for example, at adolescence), and these changes may require a reintegration of rather massive proportions. Thus, the past is reviewed as one attempts to sense the consistency between past *mes*, present *mes*, and future *mes* in the light of current reality and future potential. Perhaps the feedback from others (such as a "confidant," discussed in Chapter 8) would be important in this process. That is, just as when one's sense of identity is the crucial issue during adolescence and young adulthood and feedback from others is signficant, so also it may be that such feedback is important for this later, potentially massive reorganization of the self in preparation for death.

However, Butler's concept of the life review emphasizes not only the potential reorganization of the self but also the adaptive aspects of reminiscence among the aged. Often this reminiscence might be seen as beyond the older person's control, or as an escape from the present, or as simply filling up empty time; but he sees the life review as an important and characteristic step for those, whether old or young, who expect death (and it may be a general response to other types of crises as well). Although Butler does not draw the parallel between this life review process and Erikson's stage of Integrity versus Despair, it seems clear that a central aspect of this stage involves looking back over one's life. This psychological reorganization, which might involve ignoring or selectively recalling old memories in the search for meaning, would be deeply involved in the eventual resolution of the Integrity versus Despair crisis. Tolstoy (1886) also illustrates the life review quite explicitly; and it is one major source of Ivan Ilych's despair.

> He lay on his back and began to pass his life in review . . . [p. 152].
> And in imagination he began to recall the best moments of his pleasant life. But strange to say none of those best moments of his pleasant life now seemed at all what they had then seemed—none of them except the first

recollections of childhood. There, in childhood, there had been something really pleasant with which it would be possible to live if it could return. But the child who had experienced that happiness existed no longer, it was like a reminiscence of somebody else.

As soon as the period began which had produced the present Ivan Ilych, all that had then seemed joys now melted before his sight and turned into something trivial and often nasty.

And the further he departed from childhood and the nearer he came to the present the more worthless and doubtful were the joys [p. 147].

Although the concept of the life review is associated with reminiscence among older persons and may be seen as a part of the Integrity versus Despair issues during the second half of life, reminiscence clearly occurs among people of all ages. For example, Cameron (1972) interviewed respondents by interrupting them and asking them what they were just thinking about, the topic of their thoughts, and whether they were thinking about the past, present, or future. He interviewed three different groups varying in age from 18 to 65 + at their home, at work, or on a beach. At all ages the most frequent orientation was present, followed by the future, and then the past. Thus, he found no evidence that old people think about the past more than the present or the future, or that they think about the past more than young people do. Similarly, Giambra (1977) interviewed about 1100 men and women between the ages of 17 and 92 about their daydreams and whether the daydreams were oriented toward the present, past, or future; he also found no correlation between age and the number of past-oriented daydreams. However, he found differences among age groups in the *proportions* of daydreams that dealt with the past as compared with the present or future. When he compared the ratio of daydreams concerned with the past to those concerned with the present, he found that both his youngest (ages 17-23) and his oldest (60 +) respondents tended to be equally concerned with past and present, while those in between were much more likely to daydream about the present than the past (Figure 10.3). When he compared past with future, he found that his youngest respondents were much more likely to daydream about the future than about the past, whereas his older respondents—especially females—were more likely to daydream about the past than about the future (Figure 10.4). Thus, the relative proportion of daydreams about the past appears to increase with age, especially in comparison with daydreams about the future. However, as in Cameron's study, thoughts about the past do not dominate the daydreams of older persons; they appear to increase to the point of approximately equalling daydreams about the present (and younger people also daydream about the past as much as the present).

Studies have also explored the relationship between reminiscence and the resolution of the Integrity versus Despair issues. Havighurst and Glasser (1972) found that there was an association among positive feelings about reminiscence, frequent reminiscence, and "good personal-social adjustment" in various rela-

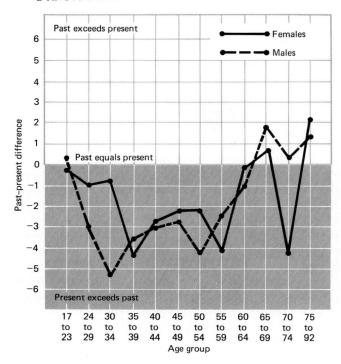

Figure 10.3
Differences between past and present orientation in daydreams for individual respondents, by age and sex. (Source: Giambra, 1977, Figure 1. Reprinted with permission.)

tively elite samples of older persons; however, it was not clear whether frequent reminiscence caused good adjustment, or vice versa. Another study focused explicitly on Erikson's concept of integrity in terms of reminiscence (Boylin, Gordon, & Nehrke, 1976). Their respondents were elderly men living in a Veterans Administration hospital. They found that about two-thirds of their respondents reminisced occasionally but, unlike the Havighurst and Glasser study, their respondents reported negative feelings about the content of their memories, especially about those memories from their fifties and sixties. However, frequency of reminiscing was significantly related to their measure of integrity (e.g., "life has been good," "would not change my life if I lived it over," "accept myself the way I am"). Thus, they speculate that these men were reviewing and evaluating their life in both its positive and negative aspects and were achieving, or at least working toward, a sense of integrity through reminiscence. Perhaps the physical reasons for their hospitalizations played a part in their negative feelings about their memories, but even this negative aspect of reminiscing was related to integrity. We cannot conclude that these data support Butler's concept of the life review as a process of reminiscence that leads to greater personality reorganization, but

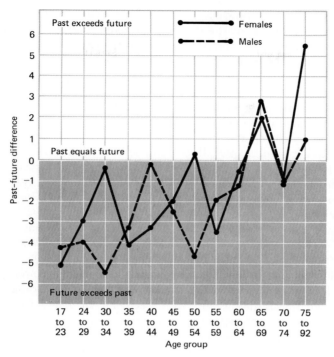

Figure 10.4

Differences between past and future orientation in daydreams for individual respondents, by age and sex. (Source: Giambra, 1977, Figure 2. Reprinted with permission.)

this study suggests that this concept may be a productive hypothesis that can be empirically tested.

Psychological Changes Predicting Nearness to Death

Although the study of psychosocial aspects of the dying process is fairly new, there is a growing body of data indicating that there are important changes associated with nearness to death—that is, changes that are brought on not by age alone, but by the closeness to death. These data are particularly interesting since they suggest that developmental changes occur in the last few years of life and are apparently timed by impending natural death. In addition, these data indicate that in many cases psychological changes may serve as better predictors of the nearness to death than medical or physical factors alone. The studies are conducted by giving a series of psychological tests, usually over a period of several months or years, and comparing those persons who later are found to die within a specified period of time with those who remain alive.

Lieberman (1965) conducted some early research in this area. He reported developing an interest in possible psychological changes preceding death when one of the nurses in a nursing home where he was working displayed a "remarkable accuracy" in predicting the death of residents several months in advance and before there were any pronounced physical changes. She was unable to identify what led to her predictions except that a person approaching death "just seemed to act differently."

To explore this phenomenon, he administered several psychological tests to a group of 25 elderly volunteers. The data suggested a decline in energy, complexity, and organization in drawings made by persons who died less than three months after completing at least five drawings three or four weeks apart (ibid.). Two subsequent studies using larger numbers of aged persons (Lieberman, 1966; Lieberman & Coplan, 1970) failed to replicate the earlier findings but, they did find related differences in a range of psychological realms between those who were a year or less away from death and those who were at least three years away from death. In both studies respondents were "matched" so that all comparisons could be made between similar respondents in the death-near and death-far groups. They found a decline in various measures of cognitive functioning, in emotional complexity, in introspection, and in several aspects of self-image among the death-near respondents, compared to their matched death-far "control" (Lieberman & Coplan, 1970). These results supported the hypothesis that distance from death, rather than chronological age, appeared to be the most useful time dimension for organizing changes in psychological functioning in the aged.

This hypothesis must be examined very closely, however, because many other studies have not considered the chronological age of the respondents (Lieberman and Coplan did consider age in matching the death-near and death-far groups). That is, if the changes occur normally with advancing age and the persons near death are also older, then this decline could be caused by either age, nearness to death, or both. For example, several studies have reported various terminal declines in intelligence between those who died within a few months, or a few years, compared with those who remained alive. These data have been inconsistent—one finding that the decline affected only those who died within one year (Reimanis & Green, 1971), another finding that it affected only those who died after one year (Wilkie & Eisdorfer, 1974), and another finding it was much more marked for those under age 70 (Riegel & Riegel, 1972). Palmore and Cleveland (1976) point out that aging changes must be distinguished from terminal changes; they found that intelligence shows "a large aging decline and a small but significant terminal decline" (p. 81)—similar to the data, but not the conclusion, reported by Riegel and Riegel (1972). Thus, sophisticated research and analyses will be required to clarify these death-related psychological changes.

In a preliminary, but carefully designed, study that included age of the respondent, Botwinick, West, and Storandt (1978) attempted to determine which psychological tests and questionnaires would allow prediction of those respondents near to death. Using a group of 732 persons who had applied for housing in a senior citizens' apartment complex, they found that thirteen psychological measures and two medical health ratings differentiated those respondents who died within five years and those who were still living after five years. However, none of these measures alone predicted survivorship as well as all of them together. A combination of eight of the psychological test and questionnaire items together was able to correctly classify 71 percent of the living respondents and 64 percent of those who had died, even though they varied in age. There was no evidence of a decline over time on any of these measures, so that the first administration of the tests and questionnaires was used as the basis for the classification of the living and the deceased respondents five years later. Administration of all eight procedures requires about 30 minutes; three involve speed of response, two involve learning and memory, one measures depression, one asks "what degree of control do you feel you have over things," and one asks the respondent's self-rated health (from poor to excellent). They found that physicians' ratings were not as predictive of survival as the respondent's own self-rating; a clinically assessed health measure and age did predict survival, but not as accurately as the eight other procedures combined. They conclude that these measures can serve as a "medical alert" for older persons, calling the physician's attention to possible health problems that may have been overlooked; this may be particularly important since the physicians' ratings were not accurate predictors of survivorship. However, further validation of these findings is necessary, in part because it is not clear why these particular measures predict survival. Nonetheless, they clearly suggest a *psychosomatic* interaction in which bodily decline and progression toward death affect psychological processes. The earlier findings of Lieberman and Coplan (1970) also deserve further study since they make a similar point and may provide additional measures that could be combined with these measures to further increase the accuracy of prediction.

THE DYING PROCESS

Elisabeth Kübler-Ross, who described herself as "a country doctor," was a psychiatrist at the University of Chicago (which operates a teaching-research hospital) when she was approached by some graduate students in theology for help on a paper on terminally ill patients. Her approach was: "If you really wish to share and experience what it is like to have a very limited time to live, sit with your dying patients and listen" (Kübler-Ross, 1970). A seminar on death and dying developed from this idea, as dying patients were invited to talk with her or other participants, sometimes observed through a viewing window by various members of the "helping professions" (doctors, nurses, chaplains, rabbis, priests, social workers, and so on). If necessary, patients were interviewed in their beds with whatever medical attention was needed (transfusions, infusions, and so on).

Initially the project met with a great deal of resistance since it seems to be generally assumed, as another pioneer in studying death was asked, "Isn't it cruel, sadistic, and traumatic to discuss death with seriously ill and terminally ill people?" (Feifel, 1963, p. 9). Kübler-Ross reported initially insurmountable difficulties and hostility:

> Suddenly, this big teaching hospital did not have a single dying patient!
>
> During the first year of this undertaking it required an average of ten hours per week to search for a patient—and to get permission from a physician. . . .
>
> In general, the very young physicians or the very old ones were more amenable to our requests, the nurses and nurses' aides the most interested, and the patients themselves the most enthusiastic. With few exceptions, the patients were surprised, amazed, and grateful. Some were plain curious and others expressed their disbelief that "a young, healthy doctor would sit with a dying old woman and really care to know what it is like." In the majority of cases the initial outcome was similar to opening floodgates. It was hard to stop them once the conversation was initiated and the patients responded with great relief to sharing some of their last concerns, expressing their feelings without fear of repercussions [Kübler-Ross, 1970, pp. 157-158].

Much of Kübler-Ross's work can be seen as an attempt to humanize the dying process, to counteract the tendency in America of depersonalizing the dying person, and to reinstate the process of dying back into the full course of human life. Part of the difficulty, she argues, is that death is feared and denied in our unconscious: "In simple terms, in our unconscious mind we can only be killed; it is inconceivable to die of a natural cause or of old age. Therefore death in itself is associated with a bad act, a frightening happening, something that in itself calls for retribution and punishment" (Kübler-Ross, 1969, p. 2). But also, this anxiety about death is aided by our highly developed technology that attempts to find a "solution" for every "problem"—so that, too often while attempting to preserve life, we tend to turn the patient into a "thing" in which something has "gone wrong" and that needs to be "fixed." Often someone else makes the decision that individuals require hospitalization; they are then rushed to the hospital, endure the siren and hectic rush in an ambulance, and are subjected to busy hospital staff, tests, X rays, cardiograms, and so forth. They may overhear discussions of their "case" but have no real chance to participate in the discussion; they are the "case," the "object." And once in the hospital, they must learn the rules and regulations of that institution and, in short, become resocialized into the role of patients—especially in chronic or geriatric hospitals.

She reports (1969) one extreme and memorable case of a woman who seemingly had to resort to a "psychotic break" in order to prevent one last operation that might prolong her life although she was prepared to die and wanted only to die in peace. Questions of "mercy killing," relations between physician and patient, between nurse and patient, and between family and patient all come to be provocative and unanswered issues. Perhaps medical schools might do more to train physicians to deal with the incurably ill and dying patient; currently, the emphasis is often—understandably—on preserving life and on maintaining health; in a sense, death is a medical failure. Perhaps nurses, clergy, aides, and orderlies should be given some opportunity to work through their own feelings about dying patients so that they might be more helpful. Perhaps psychologists, psychiatrists, and hospital staffs might be better able to facilitate the final communication between the patient and the family. And Kübler-Ross argues that, while hope of recovery needs to be maintained, patients often would be aided by being told that the illness is very serious (they usually know it anyway) in a manner that respects their dignity yet allows them to complete their life without being forced into deceptions and lies. Tolstoy has Ivan Ilych making this point quite eloquently.

> What tormented Ivan Ilych most was the deception, the lie, which for some reason they all accepted, that he was not dying but was simply ill, and that he only need keep quiet and undergo a treatment and then something very good would result. He however knew that do what they would nothing would come of it, only still more agonizing suffering and death. This deception tortured him—their not wishing to admit what they all knew and what he knew, but wanting to lie to him concerning his terrible condition, and wishing and forcing him to participate in that lie. Those lies—lies enacted over him on the eve of his death and destined to degrade this awful, solemn act to the level of their visitings, their curtains, their sturgeon for dinner— were a terrible agony for Ivan Ilych. . . . He saw that no one felt for him, because no one even wished to grasp his position. Only Gerasim recognized it and pitied him. And so Ivan Ilych felt at ease only with him. . . . Once when Ivan Ilych was sending him away he even said straight out: "We shall all of us die, so why should I grudge a little trouble?"—expressing the fact that he did not think his work burdensome, because he was doing it for a dying man and hoped someone would do the same for him when his time came [Tolstoy, 1886, pp. 137–138].

Kübler-Ross reminds me considerably of Gerasim (Ivan's servant) in the story; but this aspect of her work is only a part of her contribution to our understanding of death and dying. She also described five "stages" of the dying process that help us to understand the process of dying as she discovered it from her interviews with dying patients.

Reactions during the Dying Process

From her interviews with over 200 dying patients, Kübler-Ross (1969) distilled five characteristic reactions to terminal illness. Although she called these reactions "stages," it is not clear why they would necessarily occur in a regular sequence or why one person might not alternately express some or all of the reactions within a few hours. In a later book she clarifies this point: "Most of my patients have exhibited two or three stages simultaneously and these do not always occur in the same order" (Kübler-Ross, 1974, pp. 25-26). Thus, these reactions may best be seen as characteristic responses in dealing with the reality of a terminal illness and as crucial issues that increase our understanding of the experience of the dying person. They should not be seen as developmental stages that dying persons should go through. This is important to note because some well-intentioned people may misinterpret this aspect of her work and try to push the person through the "stages"; another misinterpretation is to use these reactions to label and dismiss the response of the person (e.g., "patient in bed 12 is in anger stage"). Ideally, these five characteristic responses provide a few clues to help us begin to understand individuals as they cope with all that is involved in having a very serious, probably terminal, illness. These responses are *denial and isolation, anger, bargaining, depression*, and *acceptance*; through all of the period of the final illness, she sees *hope* as a central theme. We will present each of these characteristic responses in summary form and will use brief quotations from *The Death of Ivan Ilych* to illustrate the issues. Then we will discuss some of the criticisms of her approach by other persons who have studied death and dying.

Denial and Isolation. The first response made by most of the patients she interviewed was: "No, not me, it cannot be true." Some felt a mistake had been made (the X ray or lab tests had been confused with someone else—and we know of one case where this did occur); others would find another physician or go to many doctors or to faith healers in an attempt to obtain a more positive diagnosis (of course, seeking a second opinion would be a realistic response but a manifestation of denial nonetheless). Denial is seen as a healthy manner of coping with shocking, unpleasant news; it functions as a buffer in the short term, allowing the patient to develop less-radical defenses to cope with long-term suffering and the reality of impending death. Only 3 of her 200 respondents maintained denial to the very end; most replaced it with "partial acceptance" after the central buffering function of denial had served its purpose. Clearly, when a patient is heavily invested in denial of the seriousness of the illness, attempting to discuss feelings about death would be threatening; hence, the patient's willingness to discuss dying may be the best indicator of readiness to begin dealing with the issue. Other patients may not be terminally ill, but may wish to deal with the possibility of death before it becomes an immediate reality. Also, the sensitive listener will note the times when the patient occasionally needs to deny the reality of impending death and to psychologically *isolate* that reality from awareness; but after the initial shock gives way to partial acceptance, the periods of denial are usually transient. Examples of this type of denial are prevalent in the story of Ivan Ilych; for example:

> The progress of his disease was so gradual that he could deceive himself when comparing one day with another—the difference was so slight. But

when he consulted the doctors it seemed to him that he was getting worse, and even very rapidly. Yet despite this he was continually consulting them.

That month he went to see another celebrity, who told him almost the same as the first had done but put his questions rather differently. . . . A friend of a friend of his, a very good doctor, diagnosed his illness again quite differently from the others. . . . A homoeopathist diagnosed the disease in yet another way, and prescribed medicine which Ivan Ilych took secretly for a week. . . . One day a lady acquaintance mentioned a cure effected by a wonder-working icon. Ivan Ilych caught himself listening attentively and beginning to believe that it had occurred [Tolstoy, 1886, p. 124].

The syllogism he had learnt from Kiezewetter's Logic: "Caius is a man, men are mortal, therefore Caius is mortal," had always seemed to him correct as applied to Caius, but certainly not as applied to himself [ibid., p. 131].

Anger. As the fact that the illness is fatal begins to register, and the patient has some beginning acceptance of that fact—that is, when denial is less complete—the response is often "Why me?" The central feeling is one of anger, envy (at those who are healthy), and resentment. This anger is often very difficult to cope with for the family or the staff, yet from the patient's point of view it is quite understandable. It tends to be anger directed at anyone who happens to be available—doctors, nurses, staff, family, and visitors. And perhaps, as Kübler-Ross states, all of us might well be angry if our lives were interrupted prematurely, we were confined to a hospital bed, and others rushed around doing things to and for us that indicated our helplessness and dependency. Perhaps part of the message of anger is: "I am alive, don't forget that. You can hear my voice, I am not dead yet!" (Kübler-Ross, 1969, p. 52). Her suggestion to deal with this difficult situation is to provide respect and understanding to the patient instead of taking the anger as a personal message (which it frequently is not) or avoiding patients. Instead, they need to feel cared for and to feel that they will be visited not because they ring the bell or are angry but because they are valued and it is a pleasure to drop in for a short visit—especially when the result of such attention and visits is a reduction in their anger. Ivan Ilych shows considerable anger and rage when he begins to accept the reality of his dying and, as noted above, his servant Gerasim comforts him and relieves the anger and bitterness because he values Ivan as a human being.

"Death. Yes, death. And none of them know or wish to know it, and they have no pity for me. Now they are playing." (He heard through the door the distant sound of a song and its accompaniment.) "It's all the same to them, but they will die too! Fools! I first, and they later, but it will be the same for them. And now they are merry . . . the beasts!"

Anger choked him and he was agonizingly, unbearably miserable. "It is impossible that all men have been doomed to suffer this awful horror!" [Tolstoy, 1886, p. 130].

After that Ivan Ilych would sometimes call Gerasim and get him to hold his legs on his shoulders, and he liked talking to him. Gerasim did it all easily, willingly, simply and with a good nature that touched Ivan Ilych. Health, strength, and vitality in other people were offensive to him, but Gerasim's strength and vitality did not mortify but soothed him [ibid., p. 137].

Bargaining. Kübler-Ross suggests that this response is helpful to the patient for brief periods of time. It is as if knowing that one cannot get what one wants by demanding (in anger), one turns to "asking nicely," hoping to strike a bargain— with God, or the staff, or with the illness itself. The notion is akin to "time off for good behavior"—but is successful for only short periods of time since the illness tends quickly to invalidate the "bargain." She gives a poignant example of a patient who wished to live long enough to attend the marriage of her oldest and favorite son. By efforts from several staff, she was taught self-hypnosis and could control the pain for several hours and left the hospital to attend the wedding "an elegant lady." "I will never forget the moment when she returned to the hospital. She looked tired and somewhat exhausted and—before I could say hello—said, 'Now don't forget I have another son!'" (Kübler-Ross, 1969, p. 83). Examples of bargaining do not seem to be as obvious as the other stages; and possibly not all patients attempt to cope with dying in this way or, if they do, their bargains are relatively subtle. Yet, such attempts, although rather short-term, may be seen as positive attempts to cope with death and, insofar as they are appropriate, need not be discouraged. One possible instance of bargaining in Ivan Ilych indicates some of the forms it may take and also the subtlety of this stage.

He would say to himself: "I will take up my duties again—after all I used to live by them." And banishing all doubts he would go to the law courts, enter into conversation with his colleagues, and sit carelessly as was his wont, scanning the crowd with a thoughtful look and leaning both his emaciated arms on the arms of his oak chair. . . . But suddenly in the midst of those proceedings the pain in his side, regardless of the stage the proceedings had reached, would begin its own gnawing work. . . . He would shake himself, try to pull himself together, manage somehow to bring the sitting to a close, and return home with the sorrowful consciousness that his judicial labours could not as formerly hide from him what he wanted them to hide, and could not deliver him from *It* [Tolstoy, 1886, pp. 132-133].

Depression. Another characteristic response is a great sense of loss that Kübler-Ross differentiates into two different reactions. *Reactive depression* results from past losses and may be accompanied by guilt or shame at the loss— such as a woman who has her breast removed due to cancer, or whose teeth have been removed, or whose body is disfigured by the illness. *Preparatory depression* involves the "preparatory grief" that is involved in giving up the things of the world and in preparing oneself for the final separation from the world.

"The patient is in the process of losing everything and everybody he loves. If he is allowed to express his sorrow he will find a final acceptance much easier, and he will be grateful to those who can sit with him during this stage of depression without constantly telling him not to be sad" (Kübler-Ross, 1969, p. 87). This type of depression is often "a silent one" and frequently silent gestures and mutual expression of feelings and tenderness can be quite helpful. In contrast, the reactive depression may require some intervention, some "cheering up" and some support for the patient's self-esteem. Thus, it seems useful to distinguish between these types of depression. Kübler-Ross suggests that members of the helping professions and patients' family members should realize that this preparatory type of depression "is necessary and beneficial if the patient is to die in a stage of acceptance and peace" [ibid., p. 88].

Although most of Ivan Ilych's depression was more typically seen as despair (the negative pole of Erikson's Integrity versus Despair crisis) resulting from his meaningless life and his inability to find any semblance of integrity until the very end, there are also some examples of preparatory depression.

> No one pitied him as he wished to be pitied. At certain moments after prolonged suffering he wished most of all (though he would have been ashamed to confess it) for someone to pity him as a sick child is pitied. He longed to be petted and comforted. . . . Ivan Ilych wanted to weep, wanted to be petted and cried over [Tolstoy, 1886, p. 138].

But Ivan remained in continual despair, and made little progress in working through this preparatory grief. Finally, near the end, "the screaming began that continued for three days, and was so terrible that one could not hear it through two closed doors without horror" (ibid., p. 154).

Acceptance.   This experience in the Kübler-Ross scheme is a quiet culmination of the previous trials and preceding reactions. Here the patient, if he or she is able to work through the denial, anger, depression, and general fear/anxiety about death, comes to "contemplate his coming end with a certain degree of quiet expectation. He will be tired and, in most cases, quite weak" (Kübler-Ross, 1969, p. 112). This period is described as "almost void of feelings" and, as one of her respondents phrased it, of "the final rest before the long journey" (ibid., p. 113). This is the time, she suggests, when short visits, often in silence, sometimes holding the patient's hand, are the most helpful. She preferred to visit such patients at the end of the day when she too was tired and enjoyed a few minutes of peaceful silence. Visits with such patients may be meaningful for the visitor also, "as it will show him that dying is not such a frightening, horrible thing that so many want to avoid" (ibid., p. 114). It is also a time when the wishes and feelings of the patient may be more accepting of death than is true for the family. She cites one case we noted above in which the husband wished one last operation to save his wife, who had accepted death and wished to be left in peace; her only recourse was to develop a psychotic episode in the operating room that effectively prevented the operation. The next day she told Dr. Kübler-Ross in reference to her husband, "Talk to this man and make him understand" (ibid., p. 117).

Despite Ivan's three days of agonized screaming, there is some indication of his acceptance of death:

> This occurred at the end of the third day, two hours before his death. Just then his schoolboy son had crept softly in and gone up to the bedside. The dying man was still screaming desperately and waving his arms. His hand fell on the boy's head, and the boy caught it, pressed it to his lips, and began to cry.
>
> At that very moment Ivan Ilych fell through and caught sight of the light, and it was revealed to him that though his life had not been what it should have been, this could still be rectified. . . .
>
> And suddenly it grew clear to him that what had been oppressing him and would not leave him was all dropping away at once from two sides, from ten sides, and from all sides. He was sorry for them, he must act so as to not hurt them: release them and free himself from these sufferings. "How good and how simple!" he thought. "And the pain?" he asked himself. "What has become of it? Where are you, pain?". . .
>
> He sought his former accustomed fear of death and did not find it. "Where is it? What death?" There was no fear because there was no death.
>
> In place of death there was light.
>
> "So that's what it is!" he suddenly exclaimed aloud. "What joy!" [Tolstoy, 1886, pp. 155-156].

Hope.   Through all of the five reactions that, as indicated before, do not necessarily follow one another in sequence but instead may come and go as successively more complete acceptance of death is achieved, Kübler-Ross sees hope as an important, continuing factor. She suggests that it is the hope of eventual recovery (a new drug, a last-minute success in a research project, or some kind of cure—which, of course, *has* occurred; for example, in the discovery of insulin or penicillin) that maintains the patient through the weeks and months of suffering. She notes that patients showed greatest confidence in doctors who allowed some hope to remain; and also a majority of her respondents made a "comeback" in some way or another—often from talking about the seriousness of their illness and from regaining that glimpse of hope that they are not forgotten or rejected. And certainly this hope is not only for a recovery, but also the hope that one may die without pain and with the important issues worked through with family and loved ones. If the last bit of life can be valued and meaningfully comprehended by those left behind, and if there can be some real communication between the dying and the bereaved while there is still time for it to occur, she argues very persuasively that both the dying and the bereavement are made both more humane and more meaningful.

If this book serves no other purpose but to sensitize family members of terminally ill patients and hospital personnel to the implicit communications of dying patients, then it has fulfilled its task. If we, as members of the help- ing professions, can help the patient and his family to get "in tune" to each other's needs and come to an acceptance of an unavoidable reality to- gether, we can help to avoid much unnecessary agony and suffering on the part of the dying and even more so on the part of the family that is left be- hind [Kübler-Ross, 1969, p. 142].

Critique of the Kübler-Ross Approach

As suggested earlier, the most frequent criticism of the Kübler-Ross approach to death and dying has been that the responses she described are not "stages" that occur in sequence; she now agrees that these reactions do not occur in any par- ticular order. Perhaps they were first presented as a series of stages because there appears to be a kind of logical order to the reactions—denial would appear to be a typical first reaction; as denial subsides, anger is felt, and so on; thus ac- ceptance seems to be a logical final stage. However, death, and the process of dying, is not logical. It is quite likely that the first reaction may be anger, or de- pression. Some persons may die shaking their fist at death, fighting to the end; this need not be wholly incompatible with acceptance, since acceptance of death does not mean wishing to die (Kalish, 1976). Therefore, the Kübler-Ross ap- proach should not be seen as a kind of prescription for a successful death. Indi- viduals die in individual ways and this should be respected to the greatest extent possible if we wish to humanize the dying process. This implies that individuals should not be fit into some predetermined mold, especially with regard to such a significant experience in their lives.

After describing the Kübler-Ross approach and noting that she does not pro- vide any information about the proportion of respondents who experienced any or all of her "stages," Shneidman (1973), a therapist who works with dying per- sons, pointed out that his experience has revealed a much wider range of emo- tional reactions with no particular order to them at all.

Rather than the five definite stages discussed above, my experience leads me to posit a hive of affect, in which there is a constant coming and going. The emotional stages seem to include a constant interplay between disbelief and hope and, against these as background, a waxing and waning of an- guish, terror, acquiescence and surrender, rage and envy, disinterest and ennui, pretense, taunting and daring and even yearning for death—all these in the context of bewilderment and pain.

One does not find a unidirectional movement through progressive stages so much as an alternation between acceptance and denial. Denial is a most interesting psychodynamic phenomenon. For a few consecutive days a dy- ing person is capable of shocking a listener with the breathtaking candor of his profound acceptance of imminent death and the next day shock that listener with unrealistic talk of leaving the hospital and going on a trip. This interplay between acceptance and denial, between understanding what is happening and magically disbelieving its reality, may reflect a deeper dialogue of the total mind, involving different layers of conscious awareness of "knowing" and of needing not to know [Shneidman, 1973, p. 7].

This critique suggests that the Kübler-Ross approach tends to be both too simple and too sanitized.

Kastenbaum (1975) points out that there are several important questions raised by the Kübler-Ross perspective that should be explored in future research. For example, what effect does the nature of the terminal disease have on the person's reactions? Are there differences between men and women in their reactions to dying? What is the effect of racial and ethnic background? How does personality or cognitive style affect coping with death? What are the effects of age or developmental level? How does the sociophysical milieu in which the person is hospitalized or living affect reactions to dying? For each of these questions, Kastenbaum suggests a number of factors and interesting bits of data that make these topics significant for further study. To take only one example, some preliminary findings in one of his studies indicated that women are disturbed more by the effect of their terminal illness on others, and men are concerned more with dependency, pain, and the effect of the illness on their occupational role. Thus, he is especially critical of the image of one single process of dying, with universal stages that are assumed to apply to all persons.

It is always a specific person dying in a specific environment that has its own social and physical dynamics, and the person approaches death through one or more specific disease modalities, responding in terms of the idiosyncratic integration of personality, ethnic, sex-role, and developmental resources. Viewed in this light, each death is individual. The five stages, if they do exist, are found within the context of the situation but do not necessarily dominate it [Kastenbaum, 1975, p. 44].

Previous research has clearly suggested that all individuals do not die in the same manner. For example, Hinton (1967) reported that about one-quarter of the persons dying in a general hospital showed a high degree of acceptance and composure; but circumstances surrounding the illness and hospitalization played an important role. He suggested that about half of the patients eventually come to acknowledge openly and to accept the end of their life (and it was more common among the elderly); a quarter expressed distress; and another quarter said little about it. Weisman and Kastenbaum (1968) reviewed the data on fear of death and offered a few tentative conclusions: "Only a few elderly subjects express fear of death . . . fear of death is more likely to be found among elderly people who are suffering from acute emotional or psychiatric disturbances . . . elderly people manifest a variety of orientations toward death, not a uniform pattern" (p. 35). They suggested two distinct patterns of dying among their chronic patients in a geriatric hospital—the ones who seemed to be aware of and to accept impending death and who slipped into withdrawal and inactivity until the final illness, and the ones who remained actively engaged in hospital activities until they were interrupted by death.

Moreover, it is obvious that many people die from accidents or experience sudden deaths that do not allow time for the Kübler-Ross "stages" to occur, except possibly in the most fleeting manner. In these situations, the reactions are more likely to be felt by the bereaved persons who are left to deal with the death; we will discuss these bereavement reactions later in this chapter.

In sum, these critiques of the perspective proposed by Kübler-Ross call attention to the need to expand her model in order to take into account the variety of individual styles of dying and the complex reactions that this experience involves. One approach that might be helpful in this goal is the *psychological autopsy* described by Weisman and Kastenbaum (1968). They suggested that the persons involved in the care of a deceased person analyze the psychosocial aspects of the person's death with the aim of improving the psychosocial support that they might have provided. The psychological autopsy has five principal objectives: adequate medical care, encouragement of competent behavior, preservation of rewarding relationships, maintenance of a dignified self-image, and attainment of an acceptable and, if possible, appropriate death. They suggest that little attention has been paid to dying patients in the past, especially during the "preterminal" period, largely because little attention is given to the aged in general. Since the person in the hospital is likely to become "a patient" (a social role), attention needs to be given to the other roles the person maintains (parent, spouse, and so on) and to the social situation within the hospital so that the person's identity is not diminished to that of only "patient in bed number 14" or, worse, that the person becomes a "thing." They point out, "Many aged people suffer from devaluation, not disease" (ibid., p. 37).

Clearly, the work of Kübler-Ross and many others has brought a great increase in attention to death and dying and has begun to bring greater awareness to the issues involved in this final stage of life. But we need to move beyond her work if we are to reach her goal of humanizing the dying process.

The Hospice Concept

In the Middle Ages throughout Europe, in large cities, at major river crossings and mountain passes, at monasteries, and along the route of pilgrimage to the Holy Land, one could find refuge at a *hospice*. Weary travelers, the sick, the poor, the orphaned, women in labor, and the dying were offered hospitality. They may have received some medical care, but primarily they were given protection, fellowship, and refreshment. The words hospice, hospitality, hospital, hostel are from the original root *hospes*—"the mutual caring of people for one another" (Stoddard, 1978). In this century the term has been revived and is being used as a concept of caring for persons who are terminally ill. First in England, then in Canada and the United States, a number of hospices have been created as community-based systems of care for dying persons, especially those in pain who cannot be aided by modern medical technology and are expected to live at least several more days or weeks. In keeping with their ancient tradition, the modern hospice provides relief from the pain, a refreshing physical environment (or continuous support for the person at home), and the kind of fellowship and hospitality that a weary traveler longs to receive.

St. Christopher's Hospice in London and its founder Cicely Saunders are perhaps the best known representatives of this concept. However, St. Christopher's is less than a decade old (construction began in 1971); its pioneering re-creation of this concept of care grew out of St. Joseph's Hospice that had been welcoming dying patients for over 70 years; it was there that Saunders, a physician, developed effective techniques for pain control (ibid.). In the United States, hospices have been established in New Haven, Connecticut, and in Marin County, California—each directly influenced by the work of Cicely Saunders and Elizabeth Kübler-Ross. Other hospices and similar programs are developing rapidly across the United States and Canada; some are affiliated with hospitals and others are community-organized programs of care in the person's own home. The National Cancer Institute and the Administration on Aging have indicated a willingness to support experimental hospices with federal funds. Thus, it is clear that the hospice movement is rapidly emerging as a new resource for those terminally ill persons who desire and would benefit from this type of care.

Stoddard (1978), in an engaging description of the hospice movement written for the general public, described the general characteristics of the hospice model of care.

> First and foremost, a hospice is a caring community. . . . A group of people who are growing (or have grown) into a community by means of their shared dedication to a particular task: promoting the physical, emotional, and spiritual well-being of the dying and their families. . . .
>
> Second, a hospice is a community of people who are highly trained in their various skills, particularly in the art and craft of medicine. The medical staff must be expert not only in conventional disciplines, but in the newer methods of pain control and symptom control taught at St. Christopher's. . . . A hospice must provide 24-hour-a-day, 7-days-a-week availability of medical and nursing staff for any patient and family it accepts. . . .
>
> Third, the hospice offers its services and its fellowship, not only to the patient, but to the entire family unit. . . . Close attention to the spiritual well-being of patient and family is an integral part of hospice care. . . . The hospice community embraces patient, family, and close friends, not only during the final days and weeks of the patient's life, but long after death, offering consolation and support during the time of bereavement.

Fourth, the hospice cares for as many patient-family units as staff and volunteer support will allow, without distinction between any on the basis of race, color, creed, or ability to pay. . . .

Fifth, the hospice is a community operating on its own principles, which are not the principles of a hospital or nursing home; therefore, the hospice must be autonomous in terms of its professional procedure. . . .

Finally, a hospice is a community in need of a home, if it does not already have one. English hospices have usually begun their work in an inpatient facility, and have then reached out to the surrounding neighborhood with domiciliary care services. In America . . . the majority of hospices now springing up consist of interdisciplinary teams committed to caring for people at home, and some include visits to nursing homes, hospitals, or wherever the patient may be at the time. . . .

The hospice inpatient unit must function, not as a fortress removed from the rest of society, but as a house of life, a place where dying is seen as a natural part of our human pilgrimage, and where death receives consecration and celebration appropriate to this view. It must offer true welcome, not only to the patient but to his family and friends, to young children, to beloved pets, personal possessions, and whatever amenities belong to the life style of the person who is dying [pp. 219-223].

Holden (1976) reports that St. Christopher's accepts patients who live within six miles, with those in severe chronic pain receiving preference. There are 70 beds, with the average length of stay only 12 days. Pain control is the first priority. The person is made free of pain, and of the memory of pain; this is usually achieved through a variety of pain-killing medications administered so that they effectively relieve the pain and are given frequently enough so that the patient need not fear that the pain will occur again. For the most severe chronic pain, a "Brompton mix" was originally used that contained heroin, cocaine, and gin (ibid.). Continuing research on the most effective pain medication has found that a morphine solution is as effective and more widely available; thus, morphine is now used in many hospices. Once the pain has been removed, the dosage can often be reduced and patients generally manage their own medication, maintaining a "comfort chart." Because they no longer have to fear spending the rest of their days in physical torment, there is little problem with addiction since there is no longer a need to crave relief from pain. In contrast, conventional pain control can be inadequate, attributed in part to "pharmacological ignorance on the part of doctors, and partly to the belief that analgesics should be administered sparingly to prevent the patient from becoming addicted and to avoid damaging side effects. But such considerations are irrelevant to the dying" (Holden, 1976, p. 390). In addition to this effective pain control that also provides the patient with a sense of control over one of the most disturbing aspects of dying, the patient receives continual attention from the staff and volunteers in a pleasant environment where the person need never be alone or have to hide the seriousness of the illness from others. "There is sun and fresh flowers, and patients are surrounded by photographs and other personal belongings. Visiting hours are 8 A.M. to 8 P.M., and relatives are all over the place" (ibid.). Of course, privacy is available for couples when they desire it (Stoddard, 1978). Thus, the care is physical, psychological, and social—with the reality of death clearly acknowledged and accepted as a familiar reaility instead of as something to be prevented or postponed at any cost. The person's own physician ordinarily continues to provide medical care and, of course, the patient is free to enter a hospital for aggressive medical treatment. However, the hospice concept emphasizes the person's physical and psychological comfort instead of futile attacks on the disease.

Most of the patients return to their homes after the pain is under control and frequently they regain much of their ability to function on their own with whatever support is needed arranged by the hospice. Assistance, if it is needed, is always available. In this way, many more patients can be cared for than are able to be accommodated in the facility; and some hospices operate, at least temporarily, on an entirely home-care basis. Volunteers are especially important, often outnumbering staff by 12 to 1. Thus, the hospice functions as a community of volunteers, staff, patients, and families working together very much as equals in the task of providing a place of rest and hospitality on the road toward death.

Since many of the medical and social concepts of the hospice movement are somewhat foreign to the conventional attitudes about death in our society, it will be very interesting to watch the future development of this movement in our country. Some may criticize it, as they have Kübler-Ross's concepts of dying, as a romanticized approach that ignores the diversity of styles of dying and the horror and ugliness of death. But others will argue that the horror of death results from the inadequate care given to dying persons and that death in a hospice is neither horrible nor frightening. Certainly, the application of effective pain control will do a great deal to reduce the fear and terror of dying. Although empirical studies of the hospice concept will be important to evaluate the benefits of the care and the kinds of patients or diseases that benefit more from hospice than from conventional care, it seems clear that the hospice provides one important way in which the dying process may be brought back into the life of the community. As a result, fears and denial of death may be reduced, and dying made more fully human and humane.

BEREAVEMENT AND GRIEF

Much of Kübler-Ross's work on dying and the hospice concept of care are aimed at helping the dying person to resolve the last issues and weeks of life with dignity and psychological integrity. However, these approaches clearly involve the family. A central theme is the importance of relatively open and honest communication between the hospital staff, the patient, and the family (at least to the extent that the patient is open and responsive to such honesty). Such communication aids the patient and also aids the family in saying good-bye to one another for the last time. Such a farewell involves many deep, complex, and sometimes conflicting emotions within each person; and the interaction of these deep feelings between the dying and the bereaved is even more complex. For example, as patients experience the reactions Kübler-Ross describes, they may confuse, confound, and conflict with those of the family. They may express denial, anger, depression, and acceptance intermittently over a few days, while the family may be seeking acknowledgement that they are not being rejected and have behaved properly toward the person. Also the patient may experience such phases as preparatory depression and acceptance while the closest relatives may still be denying the imminence of death. Perhaps the bereaved also have reactions similar to those of the dying person, and it would be helpful if the family and patient could assist one another through these reactions. Yet, often the anger (aimed in reality at the disease or at death) is misinterpreted as directed at the patient or at the family; or it may be choked back by feelings of guilt at being angry. Such guilt—at this anger, at the inability to prolong the life, at the inability to pay for some famous specialist, or at some real or imagined "wrong" that may have been done—can be a particularly heavy burden for the bereaved, and it would often be helpful for this kind of feeling to be worked through while the patient can still participate. Thus, one therapeutic task might be to facilitate the discussion of such dysfunctional, conflicted, and uncompleted feelings between the family and the patient while there is still time. If that is possible, the burden may be less for both the patient and for the family. Somehow, helping the bereaved and the dying say farewell to one another—even though that farewell may involve some anger or resentment as well as sadness, grief, and loneliness—would seem to be a primary goal from a psychological point of view for the sake of both the dying and the bereaved. Also important would be the family's understanding of the dying process; for example, anger may be expressed by the patient and may be felt by the family, or the dying person may need to say good-bye to some persons earlier than others so that the fading energy may be focused on saying farewell to those very few that have been saved until last. But even these persons may erroneously feel rejected when the patient focuses nearly all energy inward in coping with oncoming death or has so little energy left he or she can not even squeeze the hand or acknowledge the kiss. The bereaved are often overly sensitive to clues about their value to the dying person and may leave the hospital feeling rejected, guilty, or depressed because their need for acceptance was not met; in reality, the dying person clearly has important internal issues to deal with and often little energy left.

A similarly important task during this period of final farewell is to begin the expression of grief before death actually occurs. That is, once some of the guilt, anger, and resentment have been resolved by the patient and by the family, they may then share together some of the preparatory grief, supporting one another in that process, and sharing this deep emotion with the one whose absence will be so keenly felt. We all know, for example, that pretense and facade that cover up honest feelings frequently block communication, require a great deal of effort, and make a close relationship more difficult. Perhaps then, during the last few days and weeks when a relationship with the dying person is possible, these facades (which the patient can probably see through anyway) may interfere with that relationship and might best give way to the genuine sadness and preparatory grief.

Psychological Reactions to Bereavement

We would expect that the reactions to bereavement would be related to a large number of variables. Was the deceased old, or "cut down before their time" (the social clock, again)? Was the dying sudden, of a few weeks duration, or a prolonged illness? What was the relationship of the bereaved and the deceased person? Is the bereaved a man or woman? What age? How is his/her physical health? Was death discussed? Were plans made? What is the ethnic or racial or cultural heritage of the bereaved and relevant family members? Each of these deceptively simple questions conceals a wealth of possible factors that might affect the nature of bereavement. For example, the relationship between the bereaved and the deceased could be examined in terms of closeness, dependency, involvement, duration, storminess, openness, and so on. Or it could be explored in terms of relationship categories: parent whose child dies, child whose parent dies, spouse of deceased, grandchild of deceased, and so forth. At once we expect that age would also be important, for example in terms of the death of a parent. Ethnic differences in the meaning of death and the social supports for bereavement would also be involved.

Few of these questions have been explored in a systematic way; instead, studies have tended to find a sample of bereaved persons and to determine the characteristics they have in common, or those that differ between bereaved and nonbereaved persons. The bereavement reactions that have been found are sometimes of almost pathological intensity. Gorer (1965) reported that many of his respondents were unable to adjust to their loss and characterized the grieving of one-third of his respondents as "unlimited." Similarly, Lopata (1973) found that one-fifth of her widowed respondents felt that the grief lasts "always; never get over it." An early study by Lindemann (1944) of persons bereaved by an accidental fire at the Cocoanut Grove nightclub in Boston found that somatic distress, preoccupation with the image of the deceased, a sense of unreality, guilt, hostile reactions, loss of patterns of conduct, and irritability were characteristic of the bereaved. It may be that these relatively extreme symptoms resulted in part from the accidental crisis that caused the deaths since other studies have found that these symptoms may be present but are not the most common ones. For example, a study by Clayton, Halikes, and Maurice (1971) based on interviews with 109 widowed persons during the first month of bereavement found that the most common symptoms were crying, depressed feelings, and difficulty in sleeping; difficulty in concentrating or poor memory, lack of appetite or weight loss, and reliance on sleeping pills or tranquilizers were also noted in more than half of the randomly selected subjects in the study. However more pathological reactions were relatively infrequent (Figure 10.5). About one-third of the respondents complained about the physician or hospital—often that the physician did not indicate the severity of the illness, especially if it was short and unexpected; and 21

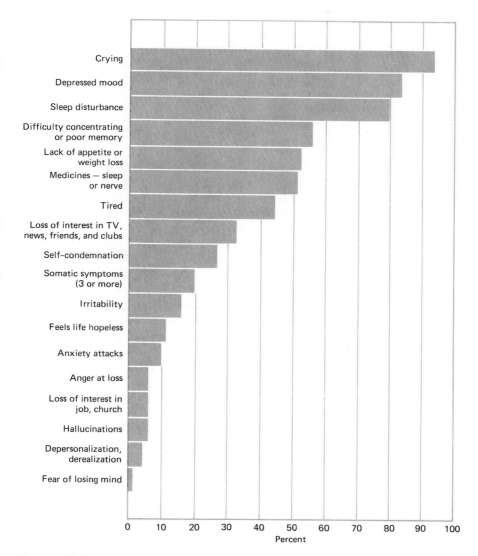

Figure 10.5
Percentage of randomly selected recently widowed persons reporting various symptoms of bereavement ($N = 109$). Somatic symptoms include headaches, blurred vision, dyspnea, abdominal pain, constipation, urinary frequency, dysmenorrhea, and other body pains. (Source: Adapted from Clayton et al., 1971, Table 1. Reprinted with permission.)

percent reported guilt feelings. They report that the bereaved indicated a benefit from reviewing the terminal illness during the study and suggest that reviewing the illness (perhaps with the physician) aids the bereaved by allowing them to express pent-up emotion and to confirm the reality of the death. Perhaps the funeral service provides a similar institutionalized setting for this process to occur. The respondents also reported that their children were the most helpful persons in their environment after the death, while the undertaker and the lawyer were also often viewed as helpful—perhaps because they aid the widowed person in the important task of making immediate decisions. Clayton et al. (1971) suggest that helping with immediate plans may be the most beneficial aid that can be given to the bereaved and that decisions about the future should be avoided, at least during the first month.

Bereavement and Health

While many studies have found a relatively low incidence of suicidal thoughts among the bereaved in the first month, other studies have reported that the incidence of natural death among the recently widowed is higher than among married persons of the same age (Hinton, 1967; Rees & Lutkins, 1967). Schulz (1978) reported that several studies have confirmed these findings, both in the United States and in England. He concluded that the hopelessness, loss of will to live, and the "broken heart syndrome" probably are largely responsible for lowered resistance to disease or changes in behavior that may lead to death. Perhaps also the lack of attention to one's own physical health during a lengthy terminal illness of a relative or spouse aggravates one's own health problems. Clayton (1971) reported that surviving relatives have been found to have a higher death rate than expected during the first year. In general, surviving spouses are more vulnerable than other relatives; the risk is greater for men than for women; and higher for younger than older spouses. However, the increased risk seems to be most pronounced in the first six months after bereavement. Similarly, suicide rates are higher for the widowed (both male and female) especially in the first year after the death of the spouse and especially for older men. Rees and Lutkins (1967) found a higher risk of close relatives dying during the first year of bereavement if the death causing the bereavement occurred in a hospital compared with at home, perhaps because of the added stress of hospitalization.

Several studies have reported an increase in physical complaints and visits to physicians following bereavement. For example, Parkes (1972) found that three out of four widows had seen their physician within the first six months of bereavement—often for psychological difficulties associated with grief, but also for physical complaints—in all, there was a 63 percent increase in physician visits during the six months after bereavement, compared with the six months before. However, it may be that these physical symptoms had been ignored during the period before bereavement if the husband was sick. It may also be that the ordeal of a prolonged illness has a pronounced effect on the health of the surviving spouse. One study that examined the relative effects of short-term acute illness, short-term chronic illness (lasting less than six months), and long-term chronic illness (lasting more than six months) found that those persons with the long-term chronic illness prior to the bereavement reported more physician visits and greater incidents of illness without seeking medical help than either of the short-term groups; men were even more affected than women by an extended death-watch (Gerber, Rusalem, Hannon, Battin, & Arkin, 1975). The authors point out that these findings indicate that the presumed impact of sudden death may in fact be no more pronounced in terms of the health of the survivor than the impact of death caused by chronic illness. Thus, practitioners should pay close attention to both groups, especially widowed men and those who experienced long-term chronic illness. In addition, they concluded that the period of "preparatory grief" made possible by a long-term chronic illness did not appear to have a positive effect as the work of Kübler–Ross might predict; in fact, it had a negative effect. However, a deathwatch does not necessarily involve preparatory grief or any discussion of dying, bereavement, or plans for the future; since they did not measure the extent of mutual grieving in preparation for the death, this interpretation remains speculative. Also, since the age of the survivor was not considered (average age was 67 years), it is possible that those bereaved by a sudden death were younger than those who experienced the long-term chronic illness and that this might be related to the health problems experienced by the latter group. Additional research will be needed to clarify these points.

The Process of Mourning

Bowlby (1960) distinguished five phases of grief and mourning: (1) thought and behavior directed toward the lost love object; (2) hostility toward the lost object or others; (3) appeals for help and support from others; (4) despair, withdrawal, regression, and disorganization; and (5) reorganization of behavior directed toward a new love object. He emphasized the importance of mourning (the psychological process set in motion by the loss of the loved object) and grief (subjective states that follow the loss and accompany the mourning) for the full resolution of the loss that leads to a reorganization of behavior. However, he maintained that a person may become stopped at any stage of the process. For younger adults, he noted that the reorganization directed toward a new love object may involve a period of promiscuity for both men and women. While this may be true for younger persons, social pressures undoubtedly restrict promiscuity and the search for a new love object for the older person and may inhibit the process of reorganization following bereavement.

More recent research by Parkes (Glick, Weiss, & Parkes, 1974, Parkes, 1972) has suggested three phases of bereavement, lasting about one year. Interestingly, some of these reactions are similar in humans and other animals. According to Schulz (1978), the *initial response* lasts a few weeks; it is characterized by shock and disbelief, followed by great sorrow with crying and weeping. Fears of "not making it" or having a breakdown are common. Some use alcohol or tranquilizers to control this anxiety; others try to keep busy. Sometimes social pressure to control one's emotions can inhibit grief behaviors with no negative effects, but it may also exaggerate the fears of not being able to overcome the grief. In general, however, allowing or encouraging the expression of grief is beneficial. The *intermediate phase* begins after several weeks and lasts during most of the first year of bereavement. It typically involves a repetitious reviewing of the death and events leading up to it and a search for the meaning of the death. There is also an uncanny kind of searching for the person who has died and often a comforting feeling that the person is still present.

> People who attempt to avoid painful reminders of the dead person by moving away usually come back, and the bereaved person who avoids reminders is aware of a sense of being pulled in two directions. One widow, for instance, moved into the back bedroom of her house to get away from her memories but found that she missed her husband so much that she moved back into the front bedroom 'to be near him.' Two widows felt drawn towards the hospital where their husband had passed his final illness and one found herself walking into the hospital ward before she realized that he was not there. Another thought of her husband as being upstairs in the bed in which he had remained for many months before his death. She found herself listening out for him and sometimes thought she heard him calling for her [Parkes, 1972, p. 52].

The *recovery phase* begins about one year after bereavement. Often there is a conscious decision to proceed with life, an increase in social involvement, and renewed feelings of strength and competence. Not infrequently, however, widowed persons may be treated as stigmatized persons. It is likely that this results in part from the fear others have that a similar fate may be in their future. It may also be that an "available" single person in a social world predominately filled with couples is inherently threatening. This also probably depends on the age of the widowed persons, whether they are male or female, and other ethnic and personal characteristics.

In sum, the psychological response to bereavement involves a period, often a year or two, of grief and mourning during which the person's ability to function is somewhat impaired, but it does not generally involve overt pathological symptoms (unless previous symptoms were present). There seems to be an increase in health problems and in the risk of a fatal illness, accident, or suicide among spouses of the deceased, perhaps resulting from physical exhaustion, loneliness, and grief itself. Reworking the events leading up to the death of the spouse may often be helpful, especially with someone (such as the physician) who knew the deceased up to the end. Perhaps one of the most traumatic aspects of the loss would be the loss of a confidant, as discussed in Chapter 8; such a confidant generally seems to buffer the aged against losses and even against bereavement as well as the general difficulties of aging. When such a confidant is lost it is often a severe loss indeed for there is no longer anyone to provide a buffer for the loss. Kübler-Ross (1969) suggests that the worst time for the bereaved may come when the funeral is over and the relatives have left, and one is all alone for the first time. It would seem that visits by family and friends during this long period of mourning might aid as much, if not more, than immediate aid and company after death. Yet the lonely hours of evening and night, the quiet home, and the empty bed are often reported to be the worst of all.

Social Aspects of Bereavement

In concluding this chapter, we will briefly consider some of the social aspects of the dying process and of bereavement. Glaser and Strauss (1965) point out that death can be seen as a *status passage* that, like other institutionalized changes in status, involves a shift in social roles and presents some difficulties for the maintenance of the social system; for this reason, many aspects of the status passage are structured by society. For example, the complex legal process of inheritance and wills is institutionalized to insure the continuance of a stable social structure and to provide for an acceptable distribution of the deceased's economic assets. Similarly, the funeral is a socially structured event to commemorate this status passage and to provide a means for public expression of grief. Mandelbaum (1959) lists three social functions of the funeral: disposal of the body, aiding the bereaved in reorienting themselves (i.e., beginning the resocialization process into their new roles), and publicly acknowledging the death of the person and the viability of the social group. In addition, he suggests several latent functions beside these manifest functions of the funeral: to reaffirm the stability of the social order, to demonstrate family cohesion, to affirm extended family ties, and to reaffirm the social character of human experience. Kalish (1976) notes that funeral rites and related ceremonies are apparently in a state of transition; the sending of flowers is sometimes replaced by charitable donations, and cremation with the ashes sprinkled over land or water instead of burial has become more frequent. He feels these changes may represent the development of new sacred rituals and are not a secularization of death.

Socially, recently bereaved persons are often treated as if they were sick themselves—they are given time off from work, visited by relatives, and others take over decision making (Parkes, 1972). There are also social norms about proper behavior of the bereaved. Kalish and Reynolds (1976) interviewed 434 residents of Los Angeles about preferred mourning practices and found general agreement that one should wait at least one year before remarrying, and at least six months before dating; about one-third felt a few days off from work was preferred.

In general, the death of a friend or relative leads to some degree of resocialization; that is, it leads to some adjustment in one's *self*. There is a new relationship with the deceased now, one located primarily in the memory of past experiences. There is a new social identity if one becomes widowed; there are some *mes* that, in a sense, are stored away—for the other to whom they were significant is no longer present. There are new feelings of grief and shock and loss that are slowly integrated into the self by one's *I*. Some of these changes were discussed in Chapter 5; but these social and psychological shifts, changes, and reorientations are important to note again. Perhaps these "adjustments" (far too mechanistic a term for this process) begin with the death, perhaps during the period of preparatory grief with the dying person, perhaps with the funeral. They may be aided by the support of family and friends, and a confidant may be an important resource for those fortunate enough to maintain a close relationship. But these supports cannot satisfy the loneliness, and the bereaved have to do their grief work alone, often with the increased realization of their own impending death. Clearly there is a place for persons whom Strauss and Glaser (1970) term "Grief-Workers," who are sympathetic listeners or comforters helping the bereaved to work through their long mourning process. The Widow-to-Widow program (Silverman, 1970) is one example of this type of service. In some cases short-term psychotherapy is also helpful. Also, recent popular books (e.g., Caine, 1975; Kohn & Kohn, 1978) can provide helpful advice and reassurance that one's bewildering array of reactions to bereavement is not that unique after all.

Epilogue

When a relationship ends, it is important to spend a little time reviewing the meaning of the relationship with the other person, to affirm that it has been a worthwhile experience, and to say good-bye. This is true in psychotherapy relationships and in professional relationships in human services of all kinds. It may also be important in personal relationships, especially when they have been significant. Much of human development involves endings and beginnings. Perhaps, in a sense, the same is true with books. Some are like friends, and we pick them up again and again over the years. Others may have been worthwhile experiences that stay with us only in memory. Hopefully this has been one of those kinds of books.

We have covered much ground on our tour of adulthood and aging. We have explored some new perspectives, and perhaps some useful concepts have been discovered. Perhaps too, we have gained a deeper appreciation of older persons, and as a result have developed a greater awareness of our own life course. Our goal has been to raise the level of consciousness about the diversity, beauty, and potential of human development through all of the adult years—to add life to years at the same time that years are being added to life.

Knowing that one day we shall all surely die, let us smell the flowers, hear the birds, appreciate our relationships, and pay attention to those aspects of our lives that we cherish. This seems to be one important lesson dying persons can teach us about living. So, may your lives be long, and your years full of life!

CHAPTER SUMMARY

1. Some developmental processes during the second half of life appear to be affected by the individual's nearness to death, as well as by chronological age.

2. Erikson's eighth stage of development defines the issues of the last years of life as a struggle between a sense of integrity—experienced as an acceptance of one's life and a belief that it had meaning—and despair—the feeling that one's life was lived in vain and that it is too late to seek meaning because there is so little time left to live.

3. From an existential perspective, the possiblity of death provides meaning to life. Existential anxiety about nonbeing, introspection about the meaning of one's life, and concerns with the issues involved in dying are important throughout life.

4. Fear of death does not seem to be a major concern for most people; in general, the attitude of adults is more one of acceptance than of fear. Older persons express less fear of death than middle-aged persons; but few persons in middle or old age report that they think about death frequently. Thoughts of death do not ordinarily dominate the later years of life.

5. The life review process, identified by Butler, consists of reminiscence, "mirror gazing," and a reinterpretation of one's past life. It is thought to be a naturally occurring mental process for individuals nearing death. Daydreams about the past relative to the present increase with age, but thoughts and daydreams about the past do not dominate the lives of most older people. Reminiscence appears to be associated with feelings of integrity about one's past life, but for some older people it may involve negative feelings about the events or actions that are recalled.

6. Nearness to death brings about a number of psychological changes. A combination of psychological tests may be able to predict many of those older persons who would survive over five years compared with those who would die within five years. Various measures of cognitive functioning, emotional complexity, introspection, and self-image have been found to decline among persons who were a year or less away from death, compared to respondents who were at least three years away from death.

7. Kübler-Ross proposed five characteristic responses that are evident among terminally ill persons. Although the responses do not necessarily follow a particular sequence, they provide helpful clues to understand the reactions of individuals who are facing death. These re-

sponses are: denial and isolation, anger, bargaining, depression, and acceptance; hope is also important throughout the dying process.

8. The Kübler–Ross model should not be seen as a prescription for successful dying. Emotional reactions to death are frequently very complex; the nature of the terminal disease and a variety of psychosocial factors may affect the reactions of the dying person.

9. A hospice is a system of care for dying persons, especially those who are in great pain and who cannot be aided by aggressive medical treatment. The atmosphere of the hospice is one where dying is seen as a natural process and where both patient and family may find comfort and support during the dying process.

10. Bereavement brings a number of reactions that parallel the responses of dying persons. Crying, depressed mood, and sleep disturbance are common symptoms of bereavement. Increased health problems and a greater incidence of death after bereavement have been reported in several studies. A prolonged terminal illness may have as significant an impact on the bereaved spouse as a sudden death.

11. The process of mourning lasts about one year. The expression of grief and reviewing the events leading up to the death are often helpful. Frequently there is a searching for the deceased and often a comforting feeling that the person is still present. The worst time is after the funeral, when one is left alone; frequently there are fears of not being able to cope.

12. Many of the events surrounding death are structured by society, such as the funeral and the process of inheritance. These social aspects of death reaffirm the social character of human experience and demonstrate the cohesion and continuity of the family and society. Bereavement also brings a shifts in roles, resocialization, and some adjustment in the *self*.

REFERENCES

Barnes, Hazel E. 1959. *Humanistic Existentialism: The Literature of Possibility.* Lincoln: University of Nebraska Press.

Beauvoir, Simone de. 1972. *The Coming of Age.* (Translated by Patrick O'Brian.) New York: G. P. Putnam's Sons.

Bengtson, Vern L.; Cuellar, José B.; & Ragan, Pauline K. 1977. Stratum Contrasts and Similarities in Attitudes Toward Death. *Journal of Gerontology, 32*(1), 76-88.

Bowlby, John. 1960. Grief and Mourning in Infancy and Early Childhood. *Psychoanalytic Study of the Child, 15,* 9-52.

Botwinick, Jack; West, Robin; & Storandt, Martha. 1978. Predicting Death from Behavioral Test Performance. *Journal of Gerontology, 33*(5), 755-762.

Boylin, William; Gordon, Susan K.; & Nehrke, Milton F. 1976. Reminiscing and Ego Integrity in Institutionalized Edlerly Males. *The Gerontologist, 16*(2), 118-124.

Butler, Robert N. 1963. The Life Review: An Interpretation of Reminiscence in the Aged. *Psychiatry, 26*(1), 65-76.

Caine, Lynn. 1975. *Widow.* New York: Bantam.

Cameron, Paul. 1972. The Generation Gap: Time Orientation. *The Gerontologist, 12*(2), 117-119.

Clayton, Paula J. 1971. Bereavement: Concepts of Management. *Psychiatry/ 1971,* 59, 63. (Published by *Medical World News.*)

Clayton, Paula J.; Halikes, James A.; & Maurice, William L. 1971. The Bereavement of the Widowed. *Diseases of the Nervous System, 32*(9), 597-604.

Erikson, Erik H. 1968. *Identity: Youth and Crisis.* New York: W. W. Norton.

Feifel, Herman. 1963. Death. In Norman L. Farberow (Ed.), *Taboo Topics.* New York: Atherton Press.

Gerber, Irwin; Rusalem, Roslyn; Hannon, Natalie; Battin, Delia; & Arkin, Arthur. 1975. Anticipatory Grief and Aged Widows and Widowers. *Journal of Gerontology, 30*(2), 225-229.

Giambra, Leonard M. 1977. Daydreaming About the Past: The Time Setting of Spontaneous Thought Intrusions. *The Gerontologist, 17*(1), 35-38.

Glaser, Barney G., & Strauss, Anselm L. 1965. Temporal Aspects of Dying as a Non-Scheduled Status Passage. *American Journal of Sociology, 71*(1), 48-59.

Glick, Ira O.; Weiss, Robert S.; & Parkes, C. Murray. 1974. *The First Year of Bereavement.* New York: Wiley.

Gorer, Geoffrey. 1965. *Death, Grief and Mourning in Contemporary Britain.* London: Cresset.

Havighurst, Robert J., & Glasser, Richard. 1972. An Exploratory Study of Reminiscence. *Journal of Gerontology, 27*(2), 245-253.

Hinton, John. 1967. *Dying.* Baltimore: Penguin Books.

Holden, Constance. 1976. Hospices: For the Dying, Relief from Pain and Fear. *Science, 193*(4251), 389-391.

Kalish, Richard A. 1976. Death and Dying in a Social Context. In Robert H. Binstock & Ethel Shanas (Eds.), *Handbook of Aging and the Social Sciences.* New York: Van Nostrand Reinhold.

Kalish, Richard A., & Reynolds, David K. 1976. *Death and Ethnicity: A Psychocultural Study.* Los Angeles: University of Southern California Press.

Kastenbaum, Robert. 1975. Is Death a Life Crisis? On the Confrontation with Death in Theory and Practice. In Nancy Datan & Leon H. Ginsberg (Eds.), *Life-Span Developmental Psychology: Normative Life Crises.* New York: Academic Press.

Kohn, Jane, & Kohn, Willard. 1978. *The Widower.* New York: Beacon Press.

Kübler-Ross, Elisabeth. 1969. *On Death and Dying.* New York: Macmillan.

Kübler-Ross, Elisabeth. 1970. The Dying Patient's Point of View. In Orville G. Brim, Jr., Howard E. Freeman, Sol Levine, & Norman A. Scotch (Eds.), *The Dying Patient.* New York: Russell Sage Foundation.

Kübler-Ross, Elisabeth. 1974. *Questions and Answers on Death and Dying.* New York: Macmillan.

Lieberman, Morton A. 1965. Psychological Correlates of Impending Death: Some Preliminary Observations. *Journal of Gerontology, 20*(2), 181-190.

Lieberman, Morton A. 1966. Observations on Death and Dying. *The Gerontologist, 6,* 70-73.

Lieberman, Morton A., & Coplan, Annie Siranne. 1970. Distance from Death as a Variable in the Study of Aging. *Developmental Psychology, 2*(1), 71-84.

Lindemann, Erich. 1944. Symptomatology and Management of Acute Grief. *American Journal of Psychiatry 101*(2), 141-148.

Lopata, Helena Znaniecki. 1973. *Widowhood in an American City.* Cambridge, Mass.: Schenkman.

Mandelbaum, D. G. 1959. Social Uses of Funeral Rites. In Herman Feifel (Ed.), *The Meaning of Death.* New York: McGraw-Hill.

May, Rollo. 1958. Contributions of Existential Psychotherapy. In Rollo May, Ernest Angel, & Henri F. Ellenberger (Eds.), *Existence: A New Dimension in Psychiatry and Psychology.* New York: Basic Books.

Neugarten, Bernice L. 1967. The Awareness of Middle Age. In Bernice L. Neugarten (Ed.), *Middle Age and Aging.* Chicago: University of Chicago Press, 1968. (Originally published in: *Middle Age.* Roger Owen, Ed. London: British Broadcasting Corporation.)

Palmore, Erdman, & Cleveland, William. 1976. Aging, Terminal Decline, and Terminal Drop. *Journal of Gerontology,* 31(1), 76-81.

Parkes, Colin Murray. 1972. *Bereavement: Studies of Grief in Adult Life.* New York: International Universities Press.

Phalon, Richard. 1978. Family Money. *New York Times,* March 30, 1978, C-9.

Rees, W. D., & Lutkins, S. G. 1967. Mortality of Bereavement. *British Medical Journal,* 4, 13-16.

Reimanis, Gunars, & Green, Russel F. 1971. Imminence of Death and Intellectual Decrement in the Aging. *Developmental Psychology,* 5(2), 270-272.

Riegel, Klaus F., & Riegel, Ruth M. 1972. Development, Drop, and Death. *Developmental Psychology,* 6(2), 306-319.

Riley, John W., Jr. 1963. Attitudes Toward Death. Unpublished. (Cited in Matilda White Riley, Anne Foner, & Associates. *Aging and Society. Vol. 1. An Inventory of Research Findings.* New York: Russell Sage Foundation, 1968.)

Salter, Charles A., & Salter, Carlota deLerma. 1976. Attitudes Toward Aging and Behaviors Toward the Elderly Among Young People as a Function of Death Anxiety. *The Gerontologist,* 16(3), 232-236.

Schulz, Richard. 1978. *The Psychology of Death, Dying, and Bereavement.* Reading, Mass.: Addison-Wesley.

Shneidman, Edwin S. 1973. *Deaths of Man.* New York: Quadrangle.

Silverman, Phyllis Rolfe. 1970. The Widow as a Caregiver in a Program of Preventive Intervention with Other Widows. *Mental Hygiene,* 54(4), 540-547.

Stoddard, Sandol. 1978. *The Hospice Movement: A Better Way of Caring for the Dying.* New York: Vintage Books.

Strauss, Anselm L., & Glaser, Barney G. 1970. Patterns of Dying. In Orville G. Brim, Jr., Howard E. Freeman, Sol Levine, & Norman A. Scotch (Eds.), *The Dying Patient.* New York: Russell Sage Foundation.

Tolstoy, Leo. 1886.   The Death of Ivan Ilych. In Leo Tolstoy, *The Death of Ivan Il-ych and Other Stories.* New York: New American Library (Signet), 1960.

Weisman, Avery D., & Kastenbaum, Robert. 1968.   *The Psychological Autopsy: A Study of the Terminal Phase of Life.* Community Mental Health Journal Monograph No. 4. New York: Behavioral Publications, Inc.

Wilkie, Frances, & Eisdorfer, Carl. 1974.   Terminal Changes in Intelligence. In Erdman Palmore (Ed.), *Normal Aging II.* Durham, N.C.: Duke University Press.

REVIEW QUESTIONS

These questions are intended to aid readers who are studying the material in this book for examinations and to call attention to the important concepts presented in each of the chapters. As in any book, it is useful to read the chapter outline first, to skim through the chapter noting especially the figures and tables, and to read the summary before beginning the detailed reading of the chapter. After carefully reading the chapter and making notes of the important points you wish to remember, these review questions will help you to check your understanding of the material and to call your attention to sections of the chapter that need to be read once more. It may also be helpful to discuss these questions with others who have read the chapters in order to be certain that the major concepts in each chapter are correctly understood. These questions can also be used for class discussion.

The assistance of Steven H. Zarit and Willis R. King III in the preparation of these review questions is gratefully acknowledged.

Chapter 1   Adulthood: Developmental Theory and Research

Concept of the Life Cycle

1. What is a milestone?
2. Draw a lifeline for your own life up to the present, marking the milestones you have passed (refer to Figure 1.1). Then extend that lifeline into the future, imagining the milestones that may occur in your life.
3. What years are usually seen by most people as "the prime of life"?

Theories of the Life Cycle

4. What characteristics do the theories developed by Bühler, Jung, and Erikson have in common?
5. What are the major themes of the Bühler and Kuhlen models?
6. What is the essence of Jung's view of adult development?
7. Define the four crucial turning points (or stages) during adulthood in Erikson's theory.
8. Name the four dimensions of development proposed by Riegel and describe his system of dialectical analysis.
9. Cite some criticisms of the general developmental theories of adulthood.

Individual Life Cycles and Historical Time

10. Place yourself, your parents, and your grandparents on separate individual lifelines (similar to Figure 1.3) and compare the historical events that each generation directly experienced.
11. How does living during these different historical periods affect your grandparents, your parents, and you?
12. What is a cohort? What are cohort effects in developmental research?

13. Why has life expectancy at birth increased more than life expectancy at age 65 since 1900 (refer to Figure 1.5)?
14. Does either the developmental or the cultural discontinuity explanation of the so-called generation gap adequately account for the differences that exist between generations?

Developmental Research Methodology

15. What is the meaning of age in developmental research?
16. Give an example of each of the following: biological, psychological, social, and perceived age.
17. Define cross-sectional and longitudinal research. What are two advantages and two disadvantages of each method?
18. What does the example of change in intelligence with age demonstrate about the importance of cohort effects? Can you think of other examples that also demonstrate this point?

Chapter 2 Psychosocial Processes of Development: Stability and Change over Time

Symbolic Interaction Approach to Adulthood

1. What are the two aspects of the self that Mead described? Define them.
2. Mead's concept of the *me* is also called the "social self." Why do you think it is called that?
3. Describe how *I* and *me* interact to produce the self.
4. What is the role of significant symbols, significant others, and the generalized other in the development and functioning of the self?
5. Give an example of "taking the role of the other." How does this process affect the self?
6. What is "self-consciousness" as defined by Mead? Give an example.
7. What does the idea that the self is *process* mean?
8. What do you feel is the major shortcoming in Mead's approach?

Social Timing Factors: Norms, Status, and Roles

9. Define and give some examples of age norms in our society (refer to Table 2.1). Describe age norms you have experienced.
10. How are age norms internalized, according to the symbolic interaction framework?
11. Define the concepts of age-status and age-sex roles and give some examples.
12. What is the "social clock"; how does it act as a "prod" or a "brake" in an individual's development?

Socialization: Learning Norms and Roles

13. How does the process of socialization differ from socializing at a party?
14. Give some examples of anticipatory socialization and resocialization that you have experienced.

15. Which of the typical adult socialization situations suggested by Brim have you and your parents experienced?

Adult Development: A Social Interaction Perspective

16. Define "timing events" and give examples of timing events that are: *(a)* caused by a change in roles; *(b)* brought about by a moment of self-consciousness, in Mead's sense; and *(c)* triggered by the social clock.
17. Define the three types of experience suggested by the symbolic interaction perspective. Give examples.
18. What factors tend to bring about consistency in the behavior and personality of an individual over several years? What factors tend to bring about change?

Chapter 3   Transitions in Adult Development: Early to Middle Adulthood

Transitions in the Life Cycle

1. How do normative and idiosyncratic transitions differ? Give an example of each type.
2. Describe and contrast internal and external causes of transitions.
3. What are your conclusions about the link between transitions and crises in adult development?

Developmental Periods of Early Adulthood

4. Describe the strengths and weaknesses in the studies by Levinson, Gould, Vaillant, and Sheehy.
5. According to Levinson, what are the major issues in each of the following developmental periods: *(a)* Early Adult Transition; *(b)* Entering the Adult World; *(c)* Age 30 Transition; and *(d)* Settling Down?
6. What issues did Vaillant's study find during the period corresponding to Levinson's Early Adult Era (age 17 to 40)?
7. What does Levinson mean by his concepts of the "mentor," the "special woman," and the "Dream"? Do you think these concepts apply to both men and women, and to persons in all socioeconomic levels?
8. In your opinion, why do these transitions seem to be so closely linked to chronological age?

The Midlife Transition

9. Describe the major issues that appear to be involved in the midlife transition. Is this a period of emotional crisis?
10. What do the studies of Livson add to the other studies of the midlife period?
11. What role does the family play in the midlife transition?
12. Which of Erikson's stages of development are involved in the Early Adult Era and the Midlife Transition?
13. What considerations would you be sure to include if you were designing a study to explore development during early and middle adulthood?

Chapter 4   Male and Female in Adulthood

Physiological Differences between Men and Women

1.   Summarize the process by which typical male and female babies are produced during the prenatal period.
2.   How do Money and Tucker view the role of prenatal hormones and later social experience as influences on sex-role behavior?
3.   Describe Figure 4.1 in your own words. Using this figure, what are the chances for remarriage of a widowed man or woman over age 65? Compare it with Figure 1.5 for life expectancy at birth.
4.   What are the hormonal changes during the monthly female sex cycle and how do they relate to mood changes?
5.   When does menopause occur and what changes does it involve?
6.   What are the characteristics of the four stages of sexual excitation in men and in women?

Interaction of Physiological, Psychological, and Social Sex Differences

7.   What does Margaret Mead's description of sex differences in various cultures suggest about the interaction of physiology and the social environment in the process of becoming a man or a woman?
8.   How does a person's gender influence *I* and *me* aspects of the self?
9.   What conclusions do you draw from the studies of sex differences in personality characteristics?
10.   How do sources of self-esteem and patterns of achievement and affiliation motivation differ for men and women?
11.   Define androgyny and explain what is meant by the statement that this is a dualistic model rather than a bipolar model of sex differences.

Sex Differences Through the Life Cycle

12.   In what ways have the female role and the male role, as defined by society, affected the patterns of adult development for men and women?
13.   Why are male and female roles changing today? What effects do you think this will have on adult development in the future?

Chapter 5   Families and Singles

The American Family

1.   Describe the various family patterns in the United States today (refer to Table 5.2).
2.   Define each of the following types of families: extended, nuclear, and modified extended. Which type of family is most prevalent in America?
3.   Give some examples of differences in patterns of family relations among various ethnic groups.
4.   What are some of the characteristics of black American families that reflect their cultural heritage?

The Family Cycle

5. Define the concept of the family cycle. In what ways has the family cycle changed since the 1880s (refer to Figure 5.1)?
6. What are the major tasks of the Establishment phase of the family cycle?
7. Describe the transitions that occur during the New Parents phase of the family cycle. What are some of the reasons that the birth of the first child may bring a period of crisis for some couples?
8. What special difficulties are encountered in a family with a stepparent? What have studies found about children raised by stepparents?
9. Cite several of the issues faced by single mothers and by single fathers.
10. Describe the transitions that occur during the Postparental period. Why is this period in the family cycle receiving more attention today than earlier in this century?
11. How does menopause affect the sexual functioning and emotional health of women? Is menopause one of the problems that women worry most about during middle age (refer to Table 5.4)?
12. What are the five styles of grandparenthood identified by Neugarten and Weinstein? Does the meaning and satisfaction of grandparenthood differ among various ethnic groups?
13. What did Masters and Johnson conclude about sexuality and aging? List several factors that affect sexual functioning in older men and in older women.

Singles: The Unmarried and the Previously Married

14. List several of the causes of divorce. What social factors influence the rate of divorce?
15. What are some of the issues dealt with during the period of resocialization after divorce?
16. Describe the five homosexual life-styles identified in the study by Bell and Weinberg. What special problems are faced by older gay men and women?
17. What are some of the reasons that younger and older heterosexual couples live together without being married?
18. How are the transition periods (change in status and resocialization) similar and different for widowed and divorced persons? What issues do the widowed face that are not encountered by the divorced?

Chapter 6   Work, Retirement, and Leisure

Work and the Life Cycle

1. Which of Erikson's stages is/are related to the work experience? How?
2. In which fields has the proportion of women increased considerably since 1950? In which fields has there been relatively little change (refer to Table 6.1)?
3. What changes have combined to produce the growing proportion of working women in this country?

4. Is the earnings gap between men and women growing larger or smaller (refer to Figure 6.2)? What factors contribute to this difference in earned income?
5. Describe Figure 6.3 in your own words. What are the major changes shown?
6. According to Hoffman, what are the effects of maternal employment on the child?
7. What is a dual-career family? What are the advantages and disadvantages of this kind of family?

The Occupational Cycle

8. Describe five major influences that affect occupational choice. Give one example of each.
9. From a social interaction perspective, how does one's *self* change upon entering an occupational career?
10. Do most people have only one occupational career during their lifetime? Explain.
11. Contrast the concepts of a "career" and a "disorderly work history." What is one consequence of having an orderly or predictable career?
12. Define the career clock. Give some examples of how it functions.

Retirement: A Major Milestone

13. Why do many people choose to retire before or at age 65? Do you think this will change in the future?
14. Describe some of the biological, sociocultural, and psychological factors that affect retirement.
15. In the Cornell Study of Occupational Retirement, what were the changes with retirement in: *(a)* income; *(b)* feeling useful; *(c)* health?
16. Describe the three personality types found by Reichard et al. that were associated with good adjustment to retirement. Describe the two personality types they found to be associated with poor adjustment to retirement.

Changing Leisure Values

17. Give two different definitions of leisure. How does "leisure" differ from "free time"?
18. Neulinger defines leisure as a state of mind. What does this mean? Define the terms in Figure 6.5 in your own words. Do you agree with this view of leisure?

Chapter 7   Biological and Intellectual Aspects of Aging

Theories of Aging and Mortality

1. Give an example of how aging and mortality may be affected by: *(a)* hereditary factors; *(b)* external factors.
2. Identify the five theories of physiological aging and discuss two of them.

3. What would be some social consequences of a lengthened life span?

Disease: A Most Important Consideration

4. How prevalent are each of the following among older persons: (a) acute diseases (refer to Figure 7.5); (b) chronic diseases (refer to Figure 7.6); (c) chronic impairments?
5. To what extent do these impairments affect the ability of persons over age 65 to get around in the community? How many are unable to carry out their "major activity" (refer to Table 7.2)? How many are confined to their homes? How many are confined to nursing homes?
6. Describe Figure 7.7 in your own words. What is the leading cause of death for older persons?
7. What are some of the special issues involved in medical care for older persons?
8. In the study by Birren et al. of healthy elderly men:
   (a) What was the difference in health between Group 1 and Group 2?
   (b) How did both groups compare to younger persons in intelligence and speed of response?
   (c) How did the two groups compare to each other on personality measures?
   (d) What did the study conclude about the effects of aging in the absence of disease?
9. Why is it important to distinguish between the effects of aging and the effects of disease when most older persons show the combined effects of age and chronic disease?

Physical and Physiological Changes with Aging

10. How are physical characteristics affected by the combination of aging and disease-related changes that are common among older people?
11. What are the effects on the circulatory system?
12. How are the sense organs affected?
13. As shown through studies of reaction time, how does the functioning of the CNS change with age? What effect does this have on sensorimotor skills?

Changes in Intellectual Processes with Aging

14. Summarize the findings on the relationship of intelligence to age (refer to Chapter 1, Figures 1.8 and 1.9).
15. Define the performance and verbal aspects of intelligence. What is the "classic aging pattern" of changes on these different measures of intellectual functioning?
16. Discuss the statement: "There is no progressive decline in memory with age. Instead, memory decline describes more and more persons as they get older."
17. How do the studies of Lehman and Dennis differ in their findings on creativity during the life span? What do you conclude about creativity and age?

Chapter 8 Personality Processes and Psychopathology

Personality Processes in Adulthood

1. Define personality in three different ways.
2. How can there by continuity and change in the personality at the same time?
3. Define two aspects of personality that are based on cognitive processes.
4. What are personality traits? How stable are they over long periods of time? What is one of the major problems in studying these traits?
5. Describe an interactionist approach to personality.
6. Which approach to personality emphasizes the potential for change much more than consistency? Explain this approach.

Toward a Conceptualization of Personality in Adulthood

7. What are some of the "content aspects" of personality? Define the "process aspect" of personality.
8. According to Figure 8.2, what part of the personality system is public? Which is private? Give an example of each of these from your own personality. What is represented by the area outside the boundary of the person (the unshaded area in Figure 8.2)?
9. How do each of the levels of the personality system interact and affect each other? Which parts of the personality system are likely to show change over time and which are likely to be relatively stable?

Data on Personality in Adulthood

10. According to the Kansas City studies, what is the common theme in those personality characteristics that do not change with age? Define this characteristic.
11. In studies of adjustment to aging and degree of life satisfaction, which variables have been found to be the most influential: aging or disease; personality style or level of activity?
12. Describe the changes in ego energy and ego style with age.
13. How are the sex roles of older men and women described by middle-aged respondents and by older respondents? What are the implications of these differences?
14. Define a confidant. What is the effect of having a confidant in later life if one (a) experiences a social loss; (b) has a major illness?

Psychopathology in Adulthood

15. Give some examples of dysfunctions in the personality system that might be considered to be psychopathological. Define psychopathology.
16. List several causes of depression among the elderly. What are the symptoms of depression?
17. In your opinion, what accounts for the dramatic differences in suicide rates shown in Figure 8.5?

18. Contrast "senility" with the three types of cerebral disease. Why should the label "senile" be avoided?
19. What are some of the causes of reversible brain syndrome? Why is it important to diagnose it promptly?

Chapter 9   Growing Old in a Changing World

Cross-Cultural Perspectives on Aging

1. What conclusions may be drawn from the studies of aging in different cultures? Give some examples of cultural variations in the treatment of older people.
2. Give three reasons why some cultures honor their elders.
3. What reasons are given for the idea that aging is less prestigious in modern societies?
4. List some of the characteristics that are thought to promote longevity in groups of long-living people. What is the major problem in studying this phenomenon?

Aging and the Social Context

5. Where did the negative attitude toward the elderly in America originate? Why do you think this happened? Is it changing today?
6. What accounts for differences in the proportion of persons over 65 in different countries? What factor determines the future age structure of the population?
7. Why is a relatively low level of formal education a characteristic of the older population today? Name some aspects of aging that will be affected by an increase in the level of education among the elderly in the future.
8. What is the "dependency ratio"? How does the growing proportion of older persons affect the working individual? How can the economic burden of older persons be reduced in the future?
9. In what ways are the elderly not a homogeneous group? What role do social strata play in making this a heterogeneous group?
10. Describe some of the differences between older men and older women.
11. Give some examples of the ways ethnic background affects characteristics of aging. Describe Figure 9.2 in your own words.

Being Old in America

12. What three sources of income have been established for older persons? Explain each and give their limitations. Approximately how many older persons have serious economic problems? How many are living in poverty?
13. Describe Medicare, Parts A and B. What is Medicaid and who is eligible to receive it?
14. What dietary deficiencies have generally been found among the elderly? Cite some of the reasons older people may not receive adequate nutrition.

15. Why is drug use high among the elderly? What problems may result from a pattern of multiple medication? In your opinion, why is psychotropic medication more widely used for institutionalized than noninstitutionalized older persons?

16. Describe some of the alternatives to institutionalized care for the elderly that exist or should be created.

17. Which factors contribute to a poorer quality of life for older persons?

18. What does Myerhoff mean by "aging as a career"?

19. What considerations should be taken into account when designing housing, transportation, and crime protection for the elderly?

Education and Occupations in Gerontology

20. Name a few of the ways students may be trained to work with older persons and some of the occupations where knowledge about older persons would be useful.

Chapter 10   Death and Bereavement

1. According to Kübler-Ross, why do we tend to dehumanize those who are dying?

Developmental Changes Preceding Death

2. Describe Erikson's eighth stage of development.

3. Summarize the findings of studies on the acceptance of death (refer to Figures 10.1 and 10.2).

4. What is the process of "life review" as proposed by Butler? What are some functions of this process?

5. What have studies on reminiscence shown about the prevalence of past versus present and future-oriented thought among young, middle-aged, and older individuals (refer to Figures 10.3 and 10.4)?

6. Describe the method used in studying psychological changes that are associated with nearness to death. Why must the age of the respondents in the study be considered in addition to nearness to death?

The Dying Process

7. Describe the five characteristic reactions of terminally ill persons that Kübler-Ross identified. Why is it important that these reactions not be seen as *stages* of dying?

8. How might the behavior of a person who is dying be misinterpreted by family members or the hospital staff?

9. What are some of the limitations and criticisms of the Kübler-Ross approach?

10. What is a hospice? How does it aid dying individuals and their families? What is your reaction to the hospice concept?

Bereavement and Grief

11. What are some common feelings and reactions of the bereaved person (refer to Figure 10.5)?
12. How are health and bereavement related? How does one affect the other?
13. Describe the process of mourning proposed by Bowlby. What are some of the characteristic reactions during the initial, intermediate, and recovery phases of bereavement?
14. Give some examples of how a "grief worker" might be helpful during this period.

Chapter 1   Gustav Vigeland. Oslo Kommunes Kunstsamlinger, Oslo, Norway.

Chapter 2   Alice Brickner. Reprinted from "American Way", inflight magazine of American Airlines.

Chapter 3   *Relativity* 1953, by M.C. Escher. M.C. Escher Foundations, Haags Gemeente-museum, The Hague, Netherlands.

Chapter 4   *Fiesta Tehuana* by Diego Rivera. Collection of the IBM Corporation.

Chapter 5   *Nathan Hawley and Family* 1801 by William Wilkie. Collection Albany Institute of History and Art.

Chapter 6   *The Bus Driver* 1962 by George Segal. Collection, The Museum of Modern Art, New York. Philip Johnson Fund. Photo by Eric Pollitzer.

Chapter 7   Leonardo da Vinci. Royal Library, Windsor Castle. Copyright reserved.

Chapter 8   *Malle Babbe* by Frans Hals. Metropolitan Museum of Art, purchase 1871.

Chapter 9   Congress of Senior Citizens of Greater New York.

Chapter 10   *Burial of Stef Halatschek* by Ivan Generalić. Museum of Modern Art, Zagreb.

AUTHOR/CITATION INDEX

Pages in *italics* refer to citations in figures footnotes and tables. Pages in **boldface** refer to references.

Bem, Sandra L.
  Bem (1974), 161, **173**
  Bem (1975), 161, 162, **173**
  Bem (1977), 161, 162, *163,* **173**
  Bem & Lenney (1976), 161, **173**
Benedek, Therese F.
  Benedek (1952), 206, **241**
  Benedek (1959), 141, **173**
Benet, Sula (1974), 445, **479**
Bengtson, Vern L.
  Bengtson, Cuellar, & Ragan (1977), 500–502,
    532
  Bengtson & Cutler (1976), 27, **39**
  Bengtson, Dowd, Smith, & Inkeles (1975),
    444, **479**
  Bengtson, Kasschau, & Ragan (1977), 452,
    453, 454–456, **479**
Bernard, Jessie (1975), 225, 229, **242**
Berns, Aline W.
  Blumenthal & Berns (1964), 332, **366**
Birren, James E.
  Birren (1960), 324, 333, **365**
  Birren (1964), 351, 353, 357, **365**
  Birren, Butler, Greenhouse, Sokoloff, &
    Yarrow (1963), 6, **39**, 290, **304**, 343–
    345, 351, **365–366**
  Birren & Renner (1977), 30, 32, **39**
  Woodruff & Birren (1972), 115, **119**, 389, **430**
Bjorksten, J. (1946), 363, **366**
Blackman, Sheldon
  Goldstein & Blackman (1978), 390, 391, 392,
    427
Blank, Thomas O. (1979), 472, **479**
Block, Jeanne H.
  Block (1973), *151,* 161, **173**
  Block (1976a), 154, *155,* **173**
  Block (1976b), 154, **173**
Blumenthal, Herman T.
  Blumenthal & Berns (1964), 332, **366**
Bohannan, Paul
  Bohannan & Erickson (1978), 209, **242**
Bolles, Richard Nelson (1972), 278, 280, **304**
Bonarius, Hans (1977), 393, **427**
Botwinick, Jack
  Botwinick (1967), 357, *361, 362,* **366**
  Botwinick (1969), 360, **366**
  Botwinick (1970), 357, 358, 359, 360, **366**
  Botwinick (1977), 34, **39**, 355, 356, **366**
  Botwinick, West, & Storandt (1978), 508, **532**
Bower, Donald W.
  Bower & Christopherson (1977), 235, **242**
Bowlby, John (1960), 527, **532**
Boylin, William
  Boylin, Gordon, & Nehrke (1976), 506, **533**

Bradway, Katherine
  Kangas & Bradway (1971), 35, **40**
Brannon, Robert
  David & Brannon (1976), 167, **173**
Brim, Orville G., Jr.
  Brim (1968), 63, **75**
  Brim (1977), 102, 114–115, **118**
Brodie, H. Keith
  Doering, Kraemer, Brodie, & Hamburg
    (1975), 141, **173**
Brody, Elaine (1977), 218, **242**
Brody, Harold (1955), 351, **366**
Bromley, D. B. (1966), 346, 348, 352, **366**
Bronfenbrenner, Urie (1975), 199, **242**
Brotman, Herman B.
  Brotman (1972), 339, **366**
  Brotman (1977a), 458, **479**
  Brotman (1977b), 449, **479**
Broverman, Donald M.
  Broverman, Vogel, Broverman, Clarkson, &
    Rosenkrantz (1972), 156, *157,* 158, **173**
  Rosenkrantz, Vogel, Bee, Broverman, &
    Broverman (1968), 156, **175**
Broverman, Inge K.
  Broverman, Vogel, Broverman, Clarkson, &
    Rosenkrantz (1972), 156, *157,* 158, **173**
  Rosenkrantz, Vogel, Bee, Broverman, &
    Broverman (1968), 156, **175**
Brown, Claude (1965), 277, **304**
Brown, Terry
  Orthner, Brown, & Ferguson (1976), 211,
    245
Bühler, Charlotte (1968), 8, 10, **39**
Burchinal, Lee
  Sussman & Burchinal (1962), 193–194, **246**
Burkhauser, Richard V.
  Burkhauser & Tolley (1978), 287–288, **304**
Busse, Ewald W.
  Busse (1959), 420, **427**
  Dovenmuehle, Busse, & Newman (1961),
    338, **367**
Butler, Robert N.
  Butler (1963), 295, **304**, 503–504, **533**
  Butler (1963a), 406, 419, 420, **427**
  Butler (1963b), 408, **427**
  Butler (1969), 469, **479**
  Butler (1975), 342, **366**, 419, 424–425, **427**,
    461, 463, **479**
  Birren, Butler, Greenhouse, Sokoloff, &
    Yarrow (1963), 6, **39**, 290, **304**, 343–
    345, 351, **365–366**
  Butler & Lewis (1976), 219–220, **242**
  Butler & Lewis (1977), 420, 421–422, 422–
    423, 423–424, 425, **427**

Caine, Lynn (1975), 530, **533**
Cameron, Paul (1972), 505, **533**
Candy, Sandra E.
  Kastenbaum & Candy (1973), 467, **480**
Carns, Donald E.
  Starr & Carns (1972), 234, **245**
Carp, Frances M.
  Carp (1966), 287, **304**
  Carp (1977), 472, **479**
Carrington, R. Allen
  Vincente, Wiley, & Carrington (1979), 468,
    481
Carson, Robert C. (1969), 396, **427**
Carter, H. D. (1935), *395*
Carter, Hugh
  Carter & Glick (1970), 225, **242**
Chavez, Linda (1979), 208, **242**
Chen, Y. P. (1973), 453, **479**
Chess, Stella
  Thomas & Chess (1977), 395, **430**
Chiriboga, David A.
  Chiriboga (1978), 81, **118,** 226, 227, **242**
  Chiriboga & Cutler (1977), 226, **242**
  Chiriboga, Roberts, & Stein (1978), 226, **242**
  Lowenthal, Thurnher, Chiriboga, & Associates
    (1975), 81, 87, **119**
Christopherson, Victor A.
  Bower & Christopherson (1977), 235, **242**
Cicourel, Aaron V.
  Cicourel & Kitsuse (1968), 275–276, **304**
Clark, R. A.
  McClelland, Atkinson, Clark, & Lowell (1953),
    159, **175**
Clarkson, Frank E.
  Broverman, Vogel, Broverman, Clarkson, &
    Rosenkrantz (1972), 156, *157,* 158, **173**
Clayton, Paula J.
  Clayton (1971), 526, **533**
  Clayton, Halikes, & Maurice (1971), 524–526,
    533
Clayton, Richard R.
  Clayton & Voss (1977), 235, **242**
Clemente, Frank
  Clemente & Kleiman (1976), 473, **479**
Cleveland, William
  Palmore & Cleveland (1976), 508, **534**
Cole, Sue P.
  Hobbs & Cole (1976), 205, *206,* **243**
Coleman, Richard P.
  Coleman & Neugarten (1971), 58, **75**
Comfort, Alex
  Comfort (1964), 323, 324, 325, 330, **366**
  Comfort (1968), 333, **366**
  Comfort (1972), 328, 334, **366**

Comfort (1974), 222, **242**
Comfort (1976), 145, **173,** 220, **242**
Conger, John Janeway
  Conger (1971), 27, **39**
  Conger (1975), 232, **242**
  Conger (1977), 87, **118,** 279, **304**
Conrad, Robert A.
  Demoise & Conrad (1972), 326, **366**
Converse, Philip E.
  Robinson & Converse (1972), 298, *299,* **306**
Cook, Fay Lomax
  Autunes, Cook, Cook, & Skogan (1977), 473,
    479
  Cook, Skogan, Cook, & Autunes (1978),
    473–474, **479**
Cook, Thomas D.
  Autunes, Cook, Cook, & Skogan (1977), 473,
    479
  Cook, Skogan, Cook, & Autunes (1978),
    473–474, **479**
Cooley, Charles H. (1911), 50, **75**
Coplan, Annie Siranne
  Lieberman & Coplan (1970), 499, 508, 509,
    534
Coppen, Alec
  Coppen & Kessel (1963), 141, **173**
Corker, C. S.
  Exley & Corker (1966), 141, **173**
Corso, John F. (1977), 350, **366**
Cowgill, Donald O.
  Cowgill & Holmes (1972), 444, **479**
Craik, Fergus I. M. (1977), 358, **366**
Cristofalo, V. J. (1970), 333, **366**
Cromwell, Ronald E.
  Cromwell & Cromwell (1978), 200, **242**
Cromwell, Vicky L.
  Cromwell & Cromwell (1978), 200, **242**
Crowley, Cathryn
  Curtis, Tilley, & Crowley (1964), 327, **366**
Cuellar, José B.
  Bengtson, Cuellar, & Ragan (1977), 500–502,
    532
Cumming, Elaine
  Cumming & Henry (1961), 405, **427**
Curtis, Howard J.
  Curtis (1966), 326, 329, 331–332, **366**
  Curtis, Tilley, & Crowley (1964), 327, **366**
Curtis, Russell L.
  Wilson, Zurcher, McAdams, & Curtis (1975),
    209, **246**
Cutler, Loraine
  Chiriboga & Cutler (1977), 226, **242**
Cutler, Neal E.
  Bengtson & Cutler (1976), 27, **39**

Datan, Nancy
Datan & Reese (1977), 19, **40**
David, Deborah S.
David & Brannon (1976), 167, **173**
Davis, Glenn C.
Pfeiffer & Davis (1971), 298, **306**
Pfeiffer & Davis (1974), 221–222, **245**
Pfeiffer, Verwoerdt, & Davis (1974), 221, **245**
Dean, Gillian
Dean & Gurak (1978), 227, **242**
Demoise, Charles F.
Demoise & Conrad (1972), 326, **366**
Dennis, Wayne (1966), 362, **366**
Deutscher, Irwin (1964), 212, **242**, 293, **304**
Diamond, Marian C. (1978), 351, **367**
Doering, Charles H.
Doering, Kraemer, Brodie, & Hamburg (1975), 141, **173**
Dovenmuehle, Robert H.
Dovenmuehle (1970), 338, **367**
Dovenmuehle, Busse, & Newman (1961), 338, **367**
Dowd, James J.
Bengtson, Dowd, Smith, & Inkeles (1975), 444, **479**
Dublin, Louis I.
Dublin, Lotka, & Spiegelman (1949), 328, **367**
Duncan, Otis Dudley (1961), 284, **304**
Duvall, Evelyn Millis (1971), 223, **242**
Dyk, R. B.
Witkin, Dyk, Faterson, Goodenough, & Karp (1962), 391–392, **430**

Eck, Alan
Sommers & Eck (1977), *283*, 284, **306**
Edwards, John N.
Edwards & Klemmack (1973), 454, **479**
Ehrhardt, Anke A.
Money & Ehrhardt (1972), 139–140, **175**
Eisdorfer, Carl
Eisdorfer & Wilkie (1977), 330, **367**
Wilkie & Eisdorfer (1974), 508, **535**
Engen, Trygg (1977), 351, **367**
Erickson, Rosemary
Bohannan & Erickson (1978), 209, **242**
Erikson, Erik H.
Erikson (1963), 13, *14*, **40**
Erikson (1968), 13, 15–16, 26, **40**, 264, **304**, 497, **533**
Erikson (1976), 13, 14–15, 16, **40**
Exley, D.
Exley & Corker (1966), 141, **173**

Falk, G.
Manniche & Falk (1957), 363, **368**
Farkas, George (1976), 274, **304**
Faterson, H. F.
Witkin, Dyk, Faterson, Goodenough, & Karp (1962), 391–392, **430**
Feifel, Herman (1963), 510, **533**
Fein, Robert A. (1978), 168, **173**, 207, **242**
Feinberg, Richard
Feinberg & Podolak (1965), 351, **367**
Feldman, Harold
Rollins & Feldman (1970), 109, **119**
Fendrich, James M. (1974), 28–29, **40**
Ferguson, Dennis
Orthner, Brown, & Ferguson (1976), 211, **245**
Feshbach, Seymour (1978), 399, **427**
Fiske, Marjorie (1978), 81, 87, **118**
(*see also* Lowenthal, Marjorie Fiske)
Flacks, Richard (1967), 29, **40**
Foner, Anne
Riley, Foner, & Associates (1968), 341, 352, **369**, 404, **429**, 468, **481**
Fozard, James L.
Fozard, Wolf, Bell, McFarland, & Podolsky (1977), 350, **367**
Frank, R. T. (1931), 141, **173**
Frenkel, Else (1936), 9, **40**
Frenkel-Brunswik, Else
Adorno, Frenkel-Brunswik, Levinson, & Sanford (1950), 391, **427**
Friedman, Meyer
Friedman & Rosenman (1974), 167, **173**
Friis, Hennig
Shanas, Townsend, Wedderburn, Friis, Milhøj, & Stehouwer (1968), *195*, 203, **245**
Fromm, Erich (1941), 108, **118**

Gallion, Teresa E.
Rogers & Gallion (1978), 194, **245**
Gebhard, Paul H.
Kinsey, Pomeroy, Martin, Gebhard, & Associates (1953), 149, **174**
Gelfant, Seymour
Gelfant & Smith (1972), 332, 333, **367**
Gendlin, Eugene T. (1964), 52, **75**
Gerber, Irwin
Gerber, Rusalem, Hannon, Battin, & Arkin (1975), 527, **533**
Giambra, Leonard M. (1977), 505, *506*, *507*, **533**
Gilbert, Fred, Jr.
Goodman, Grove, & Gilbert (1978), 144–145, **179**
Goodman, Stewart, & Gilbert (1977), 212, **243**

Glaser, Barney G.
   Glaser & Strauss (1965), 529, **533**
   Strauss & Glaser (1970), 530, **534**
Glasser, Richard
   Havighurst & Glasser (1972), 505, **533**
Glazer, Gerald B.
   Zawadski, Glazer, & Lurie (1978), 466, **481**
Glenn, Norval D.
   Glenn & Weaver (1977), 227, **242**
Gleser, G. D.
   Gottschalk, Kaplan, Gleser, & Winget (1962), 142, **174**
Glick, Ira O.
   Glick, Weiss, & Parkes (1974), 527, **533**
Glick, Paul C.
   Glick (1975), 228, **243**
   Glick (1977), 192–193, *202*, **245**
   Glick (1979), 208, **243**
   Carter & Glick (1970), 225, **242**
Godow, Annette
   Pocs, Godow, Tolone, & Walsh (1977), 222, **245**
Goldberg, Philip A.
   Pheterson, Kielser, & Goldberg (1971), 159, **427**
Goldstein, Kenneth M.
   Goldstein & Blackman (1978), 390, 391, 392, **427**
Gompertz, B. (1825), 328, **367**
Goodenough, D. R.
   Witkin, Dyk, Faterson, Goodenough, & Karp (1962), 391–392, **430**
Goodman, Madeleine J.
   Goodman, Grove, & Gilbert (1978), 144–145, **174**
   Goodman, Stewart, & Gilbert (1977), 212, **243**
Goody, Jack (1976), 441, **479**
Gordon, Susan K.
   Boylin, Gordon, & Nehrke (1976), 506, **533**
Gorer, Geoffrey (1965), 524, **533**
Gottschaldt, K. (1960), 394, **427–428**
Gottschalk, L. A.
   Gottschalk, Kaplan, Gleser, & Winget (1962), 142, **174**
Gould, Roger L.
   Gould (1972), 87, *88*, **118**
   Gould (1978), 87, *89*, 92, 94, 98–99, 100, 103, 109, 114, **118**
Goulet, L. R.
   Baltes & Goulet (1971), 31, **39**
Goy, R. W.
   Young, Goy, & Phoenix (1964), 139, **176**

Granick, Samuel
   Granick & Patterson (1971), 343, 345–346, **367**
Greeley, Andrew (1971), 198, **243**
Green, Russel
   Reimanis & Green (1971), 508, **534**
Greenblatt, Robert B.
   Greenblatt & Stoddard (1978), 213, **243**
Greenblatt, Susan L.
   Willie & Greenblatt (1978), 199, **246**
Greenhouse, Samuel W.
   Birren, Butler, Greenhouse, Sokoloff, & Yarrow (1963), 6, **39,** 290, **304,** 343–345, 351, **365–366**
Group for the Advancement of Psychiatry (1973), 207, 209, 210, **243**
Grove, John S.
   Goodman, Grove, & Gilbert (1978), 144–145, **174**
Gruen, Walter (1964), 14, **40**
Gruman, Gerald J. (1978), 477, **479–480**
Gubrium, Jaber F. (1976), 235, **243**
Gump, Janice Porter (1972), 164, **174**
Gurak, Douglas T.
   Dean & Gurak (1978), 227, **242**
Gutman, Herbert G. (1976), 200, **243**
Gutmann, David L.
   Gutmann (1964), 391, 408–409, **428**
   Gutmann (1967), 409, **428**
   Gutmann (1977), 85, **118**, 409, 410–412, **428**, 445, **480**
   Krohn & Gutmann (1971), 409, **428**
   Neugarten & Gutmann (1958), 410, 411, **429**
Guttmann, David (1977), 466–467, **480**

Habenstein, Robert W.
   Mindel & Habenstein (1976), 197, **244**
Hagestad, Gunhild O.
   Neugarten & Hagestad (1976), 60, *61*, **76**, 81, 84, **119**
Haley, Alex (1976), 200, **243**
Halikes, James A.
   Clayton, Halikes, & Maurice (1971), 524–526, **533**
Hall, Douglas T. (1976), 279, **304**
Hamburg, David A.
   Doering, Kraemer, Brodie, & Hamburg (1975), 141, **173**
Hampson, J. G.
   Hampson & Hampson (1961), 138, **174**
Hampson, J. S.
   Hampson & Hampson (1961), 138, **174**
Hannon, Natalie
   Gerber, Rusalem, Hannon, Battin, & Arkin (1975), 527, **533**

Melrose, Jay
  Melrose, Welsh, & Luterman (1963), 350,
    368
Mendes, Helen A. (1976), 210, **244**
Milhøj, Poul
  Shanas, Townsend, Wedderburn, Friis, Milhøj,
    & Stehouwer (1968), *195,* 203, **245**
Miller, Marv (1978), 422, **429**
Mindel, Charles H.
  Hayes & Mindel (1973), 201, **243**
  Mindel & Habenstein (1976), 197, **244**
Mischel, Walter
  Mischel (1968), 392, 394, **429**
  Mischel (1969), 393, **429**
Moberg, David O. (1965), 335, **368**
Money, John
  Money (1977), 139, **175**
  Money & Ehrhardt (1972), 139–140, **175**
  Money & Tucker (1975), 139, 140, **175**
Moore, Joan W.
  Neugarten & Moore (1968), 265, **305**
  Neugarten, Moore, & Lowe (1965), 6, **40,**
    55–56, *57,* **76,** 113, **119**
Morgan, Leslie A. (1976), 238, **244**
Morin, Stephen F.
  Morin (1977), 233, **244**
  Riddle & Morin (1977), 232–233, **245**
Moss, Howard A.
  Kagan & Moss (1962), 394, **428**
Moos, Rudolf H. (1968), 144, **175**
Murdock, Steve H.
  Murdock & Schwartz (1978), 194, **244**
Myerhoff, Barbara (1979), 470–471, **480**
Myers, G. C.
  Myers & Pitts (1972), 328, **368**

National Center for Education Statistics (1978),
    170, **175,** 228, **244**
National Center for Health Statistics, *336,* 337,
    338, 339, 350, **368, 369,** 421
National Council on the Aging
    (1975), 289, *290,* 295, **305,** 457, **480**
    (1978), 336–337, 341, **369**
Nehrke, Milton F.
  Boylin, Gordon, & Nehrke (1976), 506, **533**
Neugarten, Bernice L.
  Coleman & Neugarten (1971), 58, **75**
  Havighurst, Neugarten, & Tobin (1963), 405,
    406, **428**
  Neugarten (1964), 405, 407, 415, **429**
  Neugarten (1967a), 110, **119,** 213, 214, **244**
  Neugarten (1967 or 1967b), 7, **40,** 50, 54, 60,
    67, 68, 70, 72–73, **76,** 108, **119,** 165, **175,**
    238, **244,** 286, **305,** 497, **534**

Neugarten (1968), 59, 67, **76,** 81, **119,** 286,
    305, 398, 408, **429**
Neugarten (1974), 7, **40,** 456–457, **480**
Neugarten (1977), 82, 84, 85–86, **119,** 412,
    429
Neugarten & Associates (1964), 405, **429**
Neugarten & Gutmann (1958), 410, *411,* **429**
Neugarten & Hagestad (1976), 60, *61,* **76,**
    81, 84, **119**
Neugarten, Havighurst, & Tobin (1965), 406,
    429
Neugarten & Moore (1968), 265, **305**
Neugarten, Moore, & Lowe (1965), 6, **40,**
    55–56, *57,* **76,** 113, **119**
Neugarten & Weinstein (1964), 215–216, **244**
Neugarten, Wood, Kraines, & Loomis (1963),
    110, **119,** 213, **244–245**
Rosen & Neugarten (1964), 408, **430**
Neulinger, John
  Neulinger (1976a), 301, **305**
  Neulinger (1976b), *300,* 301, **305**
  Neulinger (1980), 300, **305**
New York Times (1979), 458, 459, 460, **480**
Newman, Gustave
  Dovenmuehle, Busse, & Newman (1961),
    338, **367**
  Newman & Nichols (1960), 221, **245**
Nichols, Claude R.
  Newman & Nichols (1960), 221, **245**
Nobles, Wade W. (1978), 199, **245**
Nydegger, Corinne N. (1973), 60, **76**
Nye, F. Ivan
  Nye (1974a), 274, **305**
  Nye (1974b), 267, **306**

Oetzel, R. (1966), 159, **175**
Offer, Daniel
  Offer & Offer (1975), 87, **119**
Offer, Judith B.
  Offer & Offer (1975), 87, **119**
Olsen, Kenneth M. (1969), 60, *61,* **76**
Omenn, Gilbert S. (1977), 422, **429**
Orgel, L. E. (1963), 333, **369**
Orthner, Dennis K.
  Orthner, Brown, & Ferguson (1976), 211,
    245
Ostfeld, Adrian M. (1966), 340–341, **369**
Owens, W. A. (1966), 35, 37, **40**

Paige, Karen E. (1971), 143, **175**
Palmore, Erdman
  Palmore (1975), 194, *195,* **245,** 443, **480**
  Palmore (1976), 467–468, **480**
  Palmore & Cleveland (1976), 508, **534**

Papalia, D. E.
Papalia, Salverson, & True (1973), 355, **369**
Parkes, Colin Murray
Parkes (1972), 526, 527, 528, 529, **534**
Glick, Weiss, & Parkes (1974), 527, **533**
Parlee, Mary Brown (1978), 144, **175**
Patterson, Robert D.
Granick & Patterson (1971), 343, 345–346,
367
Peck, Robert C. (1955), 16–17, **40**
Peters, Marie F. (1978), 199, **245**
Petersen, David M.
Petersen & Whittington (1977), 467, **480**
Peterson, Paul G.
Reichard, Livson, & Peterson (1962), 295–
296, **306,** 406, **429**
Pfeiffer, Eric
Pfeiffer (1977), 419, 420, 421, 423, **429**
Pfeiffer & Davis (1971), 298, **306**
Pfeiffer & Davis (1974), 221–222, **245**
Pfeiffer, Verwoerdt, & Davis (1974), 221,
245
Phalon, Richard (1978), 503, **534**
Pheterson, Gail L.
Pheterson, Kiesler, & Goldberg (1971), 159,
175
Phoenix, C. H.
Young, Goy, & Phoenix (1964), 139, **176**
Piaget, Jean
Piaget (1972), 355, **369**
Piaget & Inhelder (1969), 391, **429**
Pitts, A. M.
Myers & Pitts (1972), 328, **368**
Pleck, Joseph H.
Pleck & Sawyer (1974), 166, 168, **175**
Pocs, Ollie
Pocs, Godow, Tolone, & Walsh (1977), 222,
245
Podolak, Edward
Feinberg & Podolak (1965), 351, **367**
Podolsky, Stephen
Fozard, Wolf, Bell, McFarland, & Podolsky
(1977), 350, **367**
Pomeroy, Wardell B.
Kinsey, Pomeroy, Martin, Gebhard &
Associates (1953), 149, **174**
Price, Karl F.
Kimmel, Price, & Walker (1978), 292, 294,
305
Prioreschi, P.
Selye & Prioreschi (1960), 330, 332, **369**

Ragan, Pauline K.
Bengtson, Cuellar, & Ragan (1977), 500–502,
532

Bengtson, Kasschau, & Ragan (1977), 452,
453, **479**
Raimy, Victor (1975), 390, 391, **429**
Rallings, E. M. (1976), 209, **245**
Ramey, Estelle (1972), 144, **175**
Rawson, Ian G.
Rawson, Weinberg, Herold, & Holtz (1978),
464, **480**
Reed, Homer B. C., Jr.
Reed & Reitan (1963), 356, **369**
Rees, W. D.
Rees & Lutkins (1967), 526, **534**
Reese, H. W.
Datan & Reese (1977), 19, **40**
Reichard, Suzanne
Reichard, Livson, & Peterson (1962),
295–296, **306,** 406, **429**
Reimanis, Gunars
Reimanis & Green (1971), 508, **534**
Reitan, Ralph M.
Reed & Reitan (1963), 356, **369**
Renner, V. Jayne
Birren & Renner (1977), 30, 32, **39**
Reno, Virginia (1976), 290, **306**
Retherford, Robert D. (1972), 167, **175**
Reynolds, David K.
Kalish & Reynolds (1976), 529, **533**
Rice, F. Philip (1978), 209, **245**
Riddle, Dorothy
Riddle & Morin (1977), 232–233, **245**
Riegel, Klaus F.
Riegel (1976), 17–19, **41,** 398, **429**
Riegel (1977), 18, **41**
Riegel & Riegel (1972), 356, **369,** 508, **534**
Riegel, Ruth M.
Riegel & Riegel (1972), 356, **369,** 508, **534**
Riley, John W., Jr. (1963), 502, **534**
Riley, Matilda White
Riley, Foner, & Associates (1968), 341, 352,
369, 404, **429,** 468, **481**
Rix, Sara E.
Sheppard & Rix (1977), 288, **306**
Roberts, John
Chiriboga, Roberts, & Stein (1978), 226, **242**
Robertson, Joan F.
Wood & Robertson (1976), 216, **246**
Robertson-Tchabo, Elizabeth
Arenberg & Robertson-Tchabo (1977), 359,
365
Robinson, John P.
Robinson & Converse (1972), 298, *299,* **306**
Roeder, Lois M.
Barrows & Roeder (1977), 341, **365**
Rogers, C. Jean
Rogers & Gallion (1978), 194, **245**

Rogers, Carl R. (1972), 203–204, **245**
Rokeach, Milton (1960), 391, **430**
Rollins, Boyd C.
　Rollins & Feldman (1970), 109, **119**
Rosen, Jacqueline L.
　Rosen & Neugarten (1964), 408, **430**
Rosenkrantz, Paul S.
　Broverman, Vogel, Broverman, Clarkson, &
　　Rosenkrantz (1972), 156, *157*, 158, **173**
　Rosenkrantz, Vogel, Bee, Broverman &
　　Broverman (1968), 156, **175**
Rosenman, Ray H.
　Friedman & Rosenman (1974), 167, **173**
Rosenthal, Kristine M.
　Rosenthal & Keshet (1978), 211, **245**
Rotblat, J.
　Lindop & Rotblat (1961), 326, **368**
Rubin, Leonard (1976), 290, **306**
Rusalem, Roslyn
　Gerber, Rusalem, Hannon, Battin, & Arkin
　　(1975), 527, **533**

Sacher, George A.
　Sacher (1959), 323, **369**
　Sacher (1977), 330, **369**
Salter, Carlota deLerma
　Salter & Salter (1976), 503, **534**
Salter, Charles A.
　Salter & Salter (1976), 503, **534**
Salverson, S. M.
　Papalia, Salverson, & True (1973), 355, **369**
Sanford, R. Nevitt
　Adorno, Frenkel-Brunswik, Levinson, &
　　Sanford (1950), 391, **427**
Sarason, Seymour B. (1977), 282, **306**
Sawyer, Jack
　Pleck & Sawyer (1974), 166, 168, **175**
Schaie, K. Warner (1977), 34, **41,** 115, **119**
Schneider, Clement J.
　Streib & Schneider (1971), 291–292, 293,
　　306
Schulz, James H. (1976), 457, 459, 460–461, **481**
Schulz, Richard (1978), 526, 527, **534**
Schwartz, Donald F.
　Murdock & Schwartz (1978), 194, **244**
Selye, Hans
　Selye (1950), 330, **369**
　Selye (1970), 334, **369**
　Selye & Prioreschi (1960), 330, 332, **369**
Sexton, Patricia Cayo (1977), 271, **306**
Shanas, Ethel
　Shanas (1979), 193, 217–218, **245**
　Shanas & Maddox (1976), 462, **481**
　Shanas, Townsend, Wedderburn, Friis, Milhøj,
　　& Stehouwer (1968), *195,* 203, **245**

Sheehy, Gail (1976), 85, 88, *90,* 92, 95, 97,
　99–100, 101, 109–110, 114, **119**
Sheldon, Eleanor Bernert
　Van Dusen & Sheldon (1976), 170, **176,** 274,
　　307
Sheppard, Harold L.
　Sheppard & Rix (1977), 288, **306**
Sherfey, Mary Jane (1972), 146, 148–149, **175**
Shneidman, Edwin S. (1973), 517–518, **534**
Shock, Nathan W.
　Shock (1960), 330, **369**
　Shock (1977), 328, 330, 331, 332, 334, **369**
Silverman, Phyllis Rolfe (1970), 530, **534**
Simmons, Leo W. (1945), 441, 442, **481**
Sims, John H.
　Henry, Sims, & Spray (1971), 277–278, **304**
Singer, Margaret T. (1963), 410, **430**
Skogan, Wesley G.
　Autunes, Cook, Cook, & Skogan (1977), 473,
　　479
　Cook, Skogan, Cook, & Autunes (1978),
　　473–474, **479**
Small, S. M.
　Jacobs, Winter, Alvin, & Small (1969), 352,
　　367
Smith, David H.
　Bengtson, Dowd, Smith, & Inkeles (1975),
　　444, **479**
Smith, J. Graham, Jr.
　Gelfant & Smith (1972), 332, 333, **367**
Smith, Mitchell (1978), 269, **306**
Social Security Administration (1976), 290, **306**
Sokoloff, Louis
　Birren, Butler, Greenhouse, Sokoloff, &
　　Yarrow (1963), 6, **39,** 290, **304,** 343–
　　345, 351, **365–366**
Sommers, Dixie
　Sommers & Eck (1977), *283,* 284, **306**
Sontag, Susan (1972), 166, **176**
Spence, Janet T.
　Spence & Helmreich (1978), 161, **176**
　Spence, Helmreich, & Stapp (1975), 161,
　　162, *163,* **176**
Spiegel, Paul Martin (1972), 327–328, **369**
Spiegelman, Mortimer
　Dublin, Lotka, & Spiegelman (1949), 328,
　　367
Spieth, Walter (1964), 358, **369**
Spray, S. Lee
　Henry, Sims, & Spray (1971), 277–278,
　　304
Stack, Carol B. (1972, 1974), 201, **245**
Staples, Robert
　Staples (1976), 194, 199, 200, **245**
　Staples (1978), 169, **176,** 199, **245**

Stapp, Joy
  Spence, Helmreich, & Stapp (1975), 161, 162, *163,* **176**
Starr, Joyce R.
  Starr & Carns (1972), 234, **245**
Stein, Judith A.
  Chiriboga, Roberts, & Stein (1978), 226, **242**
Stehouwer, Jan
  Shanas, Townsend, Wedderburn, Friis, Milhøj, & Stehouwer (1968), *195,* 203, **245**
Stevens, D. J. H. (1975), 235, **246**
Stewart, Cynthia J.
  Goodman, Stewart, & Gilbert (1977), 212, **243**
Stewart, Vivien (1976), 155, **176**
Stirner, Fritz W. (1978), 473, **481**
Stoddard, Leland D.
  Greenblatt & Stoddard (1978), 213, **243**
Stoddard, Sandol (1978), 519, 520–521, 522, **534**
Storandt, Martha
  Botwinick, West, & Storandt (1978), 508, **532**
Strauss, Anselm
  Strauss (1964), 45, **76**
  Glaser & Strauss (1965), 529, **533**
  Strauss & Glaser (1970), 530, **534**
Strehler, Bernard L.
  Strehler (1962), 332, **370**
  Strehler (1977), 347, 348, 350, **370**
  Johnson & Strehler (1972), 333, 358, **367**
Streib, Gordon F.
  Streib (1976), 452, **481**
  Streib & Schneider (1971), 291–292, 293, **306**
Struyk, Raymond J. (1977), 471, **481**
Sullivan, Harry Stack (1953), 395, 417, **430**
Sussman, Marvin B.
  Sussman (1976), 195, *196,* 197, **246**
  Sussman & Burchinal (1962), 193–194, **246**

Talbert, George B. (1977), 144, **176**
Tanner, J. M.
  Harrison, Weiner, Tanner, & Barnicot (1964), 138, 139, **174**
Thibaut, John W.
  Thibaut & Kelley (1959), 396, **430**
Thomas, Alexander
  Thomas & Chess (1977), 395, **430**
Thompson, William R. (1968), 394, **430**
Thurnher, Majda
  Lowenthal, Thurnher, Chiriboga, & Associates (1975), 81, 87, **119**
Tibbitts, Clark (1979), 448, **481**
Tilley, John
  Curtis, Tilley, & Crowley (1964), 327, **366**

Timiras, P. S. (1972), 328, 330, *331, 339,* 348, 352, **370**
Tobin, Sheldon S.
  Havighurst, Neugarten, & Tobin (1963), 405, 406, **428**
  Kosberg & Tobin (1972), 468–469, **480**
  Neugarten, Havighurst, & Tobin (1965), 406, **429**
Tolley, G. S.
  Burkhauser & Tolley (1978), 287–288, **304**
Tolone, William L.
  Pocs, Godow, Tolone, & Walsh (1977), 222, **245**
Tolstoy, Leo (1886), 498, 504–505, 511, 512–516, **535**
Townsend, Peter
  Townsend (1966), 203, **246**
  Shanas, Townsend, Wedderburn, Friis, Milhøj, & Stehouwer (1968), *195,* 203, **245**
True, M.
  Papalia, Salverson, & True (1973), 355, **369**
Tucker, Patricia
  Money & Tucker (1975), 139, 140, **175**
Tune, G. Sidney
  McFarland, Tune, & Welford (1964), 352, *353,* **368**
Turnbull, Colin M. (1973), 442, **481**
Tyler, Leona E. (1978), 390, 393, 394, **430**

Uhlenberg, Peter (1977), 451, **481**
U.S. Bureau of Labor Statistics, 265, 268, *269,* 270, 271–272, *273,* 288, **306**
U.S. Bureau of the Census, *23, 24,* 25, *26,* 41, 139, 199, 210, 222, 224, 225, 227, 228, 229, *236,* 237, **246,** 272, 288, 289, **306,** 340, **370,** 440, 449, 450–451, 454, 458, 467, **481**
U.S. Department of Health, Education, & Welfare (1976), *462*
U.S. Department of Labor, 269, 270–271, **306**
United States Health Survey (1960), *337*

Vaillant, George E. (1977), 87, *90–91,* 94, *95,* 97–98, 103–105, 109, 114, 115, **119**
Vaitenas, Rimantas
  Wiener & Vaitenas (1977), 285, **307**
van De Walle, Etienne (1976), 194, **246**
Van Dusen, Roxann A.
  Van Dusen & Sheldon (1976), 170, **176,** 274, **307**
Veroff, J. (1969), 160, **176**
Verwoerdt, Adriaan
  Pfeiffer, Verwoerdt, & Davis (1974), 221, **245**
Vicente, Leticia
  Vicente, Wiley, & Carrington (1979), 468, **481**

SUBJECT INDEX

Aging in other cultures, 440–446
  effects of industrialization, 444–445
  and harsh treatment of the elderly, 441–442
  long-living peoples, 445
  number of older persons in various countries,
    449
  and privileged status of the elderly, 442–443
Aging in United States, 446–475
  ethnic differences in, 197–197–198, 216–217,
    454–456
  growth of the older population, 289, 440,
    448–451
  health care, 462–469
  historical overview, 447–448
  housing, 471–472
  income, 457–461
  nursing homes, 467–469
  nutrition, 464–465
  pensions, 460–461
  poverty, 454, 458
  quality of life, 469–475
  Social Security, 458–459
  socioeconomic differences, 453–454
  and the young-old, 456–457
Alzheimer's disease, 423
Androgyny, 160–163
  and aging, 412
Anger and dying process, 513–514
Arteriosclerosis, 338, 340, 349, 352
Arthritis, 336, 338, 347
Atherosclerosis, 349
Autoimmunity theory of aging, 332

Bereavement, 522–530
  death rates during, 526
  and health, 526–527
  phases of, 527–529
  and process of mourning, 527–529
  psychological reactions to, 524–526
  social aspects of, 529–530
  symptoms of, 524–526
Biological age, 30
Black persons:
  causes of death, 340
  divorced or separated (percentage by age and
    sex), 224
  earnings gap between women and men, 270
  employment rate, 265
  family structure of, 198–201
  and fear of death, 500–502
  and grandparenthood, 217
  growth of the older population, 450–451
  health of, by age, 454–455
  health of elderly poor, 340

income of elderly families, 458
life expectancy of, 24–26
and maternal employment, 271–272
median family income (by type of family), 273
and perceptions of aging, 455
and sex-roles, 168–169
suicide rates of, 421
widowed, 237

Calcium metabolism and aging, 332
  and osteoporosis, 464
Cancer, 339–340
Career, 284–285
Career clock, 285–287
Career consolidation and early adult develop-
    ment, 97–98
Causes of death, 339–340
  cerebral disease and, 423
Cellular aging, 332–333
Central nervous system (CNS) and aging,
    351–352
  slowing of functioning, 344, 345, 346, 351,
    356
Cerebral disease, 352, 422–425
  reversible brain syndrome, 424–425
  and "senility", 422, 424–425
  symptoms of, 423
Cerebrovascular disease (stroke), 339, 340, 423
Chronic brain syndrome, 422–425
  symptoms of, 423
Chronic impairments and age, 336–337
Chronological age, 30–32
  and transitions, 81–83, 92, 93, 113–116
Circulatory system, change with age, 348–349
Climacterium, 145
  see also Menopause
Cognitive development and aging, 356
Cognitive perspective of personality, 390–393
Cognitive style, 391–392, 400
Cohabitation, 234, 235–236
Cohort effects, 22–24, 33–34
  definition of, 22
  in intelligence, 35–36
  and midlife transition, 111–113, 115
Collagen, 331–332, 347
Communal family, 196, 197
Confidant, 413–415
Contraception (family planning), effect on
    women's life cycle, 169–170, 268
Cornell Study of Occupational Retirement,
    291–292
Counterpart theory of aging, 324, 333
Creativity and age, 360–363
Crime, fear of, and elderly, 473–474

Ego style, age differences in, 408–410
Electroencephalogram (EEG) and aging, 344
Empty nest (launching center family), 211–212
Entering the adult world, 95–99
Environmental factors and aging, 325–328
Estrogen, 141–143
  and menopause, 145
  and mood, 141–144
  and pregnancy, 148–149
Ethnic differences:
  and aging, 197–198, 216–217, 454–456
  and crisis at parenthood, 205–206
  in families, 197–201
  in fear of death, 500–502
  and grandparenthood, 216–217
  and launching center family, 211–212
Evolution and aging, 324
Existential anxiety and death, 498–499
Experience, 68–71
  interaction, 69–70
  and occupational choice, 277–278
  self, 70
  situation, 69

Family, 192–222
  and aging, 211–222
  in America, 192–201
    prevalence of types of, 195–197
  and care of older persons, 218
  communal, 196, 197
  cycle, 202–222
  dual-career families, 273–275
  ethnic diversity and, 197–201
  extended, 193–195, 196
  and kinship networks, 193–198, 200–201, 217–218
  maternal employment and, 271–273
  midlife transition and, 105, 108–111
  modified extended, 193–194
  multigenerational, 194–195, 196
  nuclear, 193–196
  occupation and, 266–267
  retirement and, 293
  see also Family cycle
Family cycle, the, 202–222
  age at milestones of, 202–203
  crisis points in, 204–206, 211–212, 225–227, 237–238
  and sexuality, 218–222
  stages of, 202–222
    child-rearing, 206–211
    establishment, 203–204
    launching center (empty nest), 211–212

new parents, 204–206
postparental, 211–222
Family income (by type of family and race), 273
Fathers and children, 207–208
  single fathers, 210–211
Fathers and maternal employment, 274
Field independence/dependence, 391–392
Follicle stimulating hormone (FSH), 141, 142
  and menopause, 145
Free time, cross-national comparisons of, 298, 299
  see also Leisure
Friendship and the male role, 168
  see also Confidant

Gay persons, 230–233
  and aging, 231
  life styles of, 230–231
  milestones in the life of, 233
  sexual interaction among homosexual and heterosexual couples, 232
Generalized other, 48–49
Generation gap, 26–29
Generational stake, 27
Generativity versus Stagnation (Self-Absorption), 16
  occupation and, 266
  retirement and, 294
Gerontology, education and occupations in, 475–477
Goal setting and life cycle, 8–12
Grandparenthood, 203, 213–217
  ethnic variation in, 216–217
  styles of, 215–217
Great-grand-parenthood, 203
Growth of older population, 289, 440, 448–451

Hair, change with age, 348
Health and bereavement, 526–527
Health care of older persons, 341, 342–343, 462–469
  cost of, 341, 462
  Medicaid, 463
  Medicare, 462–463
Health of older persons, 340–341, 454–455
Healthy older persons, study of, 343–346
Hearing and aging, 350
  prevalence of impairment, 336, 341
Heart disease (cardiovascular disease), 336, 337, 338, 339, 340
Heredity and aging, 323–325, 327
Heredity and personality characteristics, 394, 395

Lipofuscins, 332, 422
Longitudinal research methods, 32–33
    and selective drop-out, 33, 36–37
    in studies of early and middle adulthood, 87,
        90–91, 105–108
    in studies of intelligence, 35–36
    and time of measurement effects, 34
Long-living peoples, 445
Luteinizing hormone (LH), 141

Male role in adulthood, 166–169
Marriage, 203–204
    and divorce, 192–193, 223–228
    and early adult development, 97, 105
    and remarriage, 193, 227–228, 237
    sex differences in, 164–165
    socialization in, 203
Maternal employment, 271–273
    and child care, 272
    effect on children, 272–273
Me, 47
    and social roles, 58
    see also, Self, the
Mead, George Herbert, 45–46
Medicaid, 462–463
Medical care of older persons, 341, 342–343,
        462–469
    cost of, 341, 462
Medicare, 462–463
Medications and older persons, 330, 341, 342,
        465–467
    nonprescription drug use, 467
    psychotropic drug use, 466
Memory and aging, 357–358
Menopause, 144–145, 212–213, 214
    estrogen replacement after, 213
    and midlife transition, 110
    prevalence of symptoms, 212–213, 214
    sex hormones and, 145
Menstrual cycle, the, 141, 142
    and menopause, 144–145
    and moods, 141–144
    and sexual arousal, 149
Mental illness and aging, 418–425
    see also Psychopathology
Mentor, 96–97, 98
Mexican-American persons:
    fear of death, 500–502
    health of, by age, 454–455
    and perceptions of aging, 455
    see also Hispanic persons
Middle age, 6–7, 101–116
    and career clock, 286–287
    challenges of, 16–17

and family as launching center, 211–212
and fear of death, 497, 500–502
and grandparenthood, 203, 213–217
and menopause, 110, 212–213, 214
the midlife transition, 101–116
and retirement planning, 293–294
sex differences in, 165–166
and sexuality, 219–220, 221–222
studies of, 87–89, 105–108
see also Midlife transition
Midlife transition, 101–116, 266
    and age norms, 113
    age of, 102
    and aging parents, 111
    cohort effects and, 111–113, 115
    and death, 102, 103, 104
    and the family, 105, 108–111
    historical influences in, 111–114
    issues of, 102–108
    midcareer occupational change, 282–284,
        287
    studies of, 87–91, 105–108
    see also Middle age
Milestones, 5–7
    definition of, 5
    and family cycle, 164–166, 202–203
    of gay persons, 233
    of single adults, 223
    as timing events, 68
Mood and sex hormones, 141–144
Morale and presence of confidant,
        413–415
Motivation and personality system, 402
Motivation, sex differences in, 159–160
Mourning, process of, 527–529
Movement time, 352–353

Norms (social), 55
    age, 55–57
Nuclear family, 193–196
Nursing homes, 467–469
    alternatives to, 469
    characteristics of, 468
    and families, 218
    proportion of elderly in, 467–468
Nutrition, 464–465
    guidelines for older people, 465
    and health among elderly poor, 341
    malnutrition, 342

Occupational change, 282–284, 287
    and socialization in adulthood, 64
Occupational choice, 275–280
    background factors and, 276–277

in suicide rates, 421–422
in terminal illness, reaction to, 518
Sex ratio, by age, 138, 139
Sex-role behavior and prenatal differentiation, 138–140
Sex-roles and aging, 410–412
Sexual behavior, 218–222
    and age, 221–222
    and aging, 218–222
    among homosexual and heterosexual couples, 232
    and heart attacks, 219–220
    and impotence, 219
    after menopause, 213, 214, 219
    of single parents, 211
Sexuality and midlife transition, 109–111
Sexual response, 145–150
    and aging, 218–222
    and menstrual cycle, 149
    phases of, 146–148
    and pregnancy effect, 148–149
    sex differences in, 147–149
    sex similarities in, 146–147
Significant others, 48
    and socialization, 62
Significant symbols, 48
Single adults, 222–239
    and aging, 231, 234–235
    and cohabitation, 234, 235–236
    divorced persons, 223–228
    gay persons, 230–233
    single parents, 196, 199, 209–211
    unmarried heterosexuals, 233–236
    unmarried persons, 228–236
        living arrangements of, 228–229
        percentage of (by age and sex), 229
    widowed persons, 237–239
Single parents, 196, 199, 209–211
    number of, 209–210
Skin, change with age, 347
Sleep patterns, change with age, 348
Smell (sense of), change with age, 350–351
Social age, 30
Social clock, 59–60
    as career clock, 286
    death and, 497
    and family cycle, 222
    and midlife transition, 113
    off-time events and crises, 85–86
    and timing of development, 67
    and transitions, 81–85
Socialization, 60–66
    anticipatory (concept of), 63
    bereavement and, 530

changes in family and, 64–65
of children in family, 207
divorce and, 225–227
downward mobility and, 65–66
entry into the occupation and, 280–282
and female role, 164–166, 169–171
geographic mobility and, 65
and male role, 166–169, 170–171
marriage and, 203
occupational change and, 64
and occupational choice, 275
process of, 61–62
resocialization (concept of), 63
retirement and, 293–294
role change and, 64
and sex differences, 153
status change and, 64
widowhood and, 237–238
Social Security, 287–288, 458–459
Social timing, 66–68
    see also Social clock
Special woman, 96–97
Stature, change with age, 346–347
Stepparenting, 208–209
    effect on stepchildren, 209
Stress and aging, 329, 330–331
Stroke, 339, 340
Student activists, 28–29
Suicide, and age, 421–422
Supplemental Security Income (SSI), 459–460
Symbolic interaction theory, 45–54
    analysis of change and consistency, 71–74
    analysis of experience, 68–71
    and self, (I and me), 46–47
    and timing of development, 66–68
    see also Self

Taste (sense of), change with age, 350–351
Teeth, loss of, and age, 336, 347
Testosterone, 141, 144, 145
Thymus and aging, 332
Timing (of development), 66–68
    age norms and, 55–57
    age-sex roles and, 58–59
    age-status systems and, 57–59
    career clock and, 285–287
    and family cycle, 202–203, 222
    and midlife transition, 111–115
    by nearness to death, 496–497, 507–509
    social clock and, 59–60
    timetable of expected events and, 66–67
    of transitions, 81–85, 92
Timing events, 67–68